Merry Christ~
Home [from the]
Christmas 2000
Love
Gretchen

A COMPANION TO CALIFORNIA WINE

A Companion to
CALIFORNIA
WINE

AN ENCYCLOPEDIA OF WINE AND WINEMAKING FROM THE MISSION PERIOD TO THE PRESENT

CHARLES L. SULLIVAN

with a foreword by HUGH JOHNSON

University of California Press
Berkeley and Los Angeles, California

University of California Press, Ltd.
London, England

Sullivan, Charles L. (Charles Lewis), 1932–
      A companion to California wine : an encyclo-
pedia of wine and winemaking from the mission
period to the present / Charles L. Sullivan.
            p.   cm.
      Includes bibliographical references and index.
      ISBN 0-520-21351-3 (alk. paper)
      1. Wine and wine making—California—
Encylopedias.   I. Title.
TP557.S768   1998
641.2'2'0979403—DC21   97-32186
                                                           CIP

Printed in the United States of America
9 8 7 6 5 4 3 2 1

For my father—
Who thought of it
and then made me do it.

Del Norte
Siskiyou
Modoc
Humboldt Trinity
Shasta
Lassen
Tehama
Plumas
Mendocino
Glenn Butte
Yuba Sierra
Lake Colusa Nevada
Sutter Placer
Sonoma Yolo
Napa Sacra- El Dorado
mento
Marin Amador Alpine
Contra Solano Calaveras
Costa San
San Joaquin
Francisco Alameda Tuolumne
San Mateo Stanislaus Mariposa Mono
Santa
Santa Cruz Clara Merced
San Madera
Benito Fresno
Monterey Inyo
Kings Tulare
San
Luis
Obispo Kern
Santa
Barbara
Ventura Los
Angeles San Bernardino
Orange
Riverside
San Diego
Imperial

Historic wine county
Major wine county today
Historic and still major

0 20 40 60 80 100 miles

CONTENTS

FOREWORD

It is completely appropriate that Charles Sullivan's monumental *Companion to California Wine* should be, in the main, history based. Since my first own visit to the California wine country, and that was forty years ago, its extraordinary patina of history has always given me goose bumps. I can't even say the names of Calistoga, or the Silverado Trail, or Russian River Road, or even Oakville Grade, without their romantic swagger tipping me off balance.

It doesn't happen when someone says Pessac-Léognan, or Clos de Vougeot (though I admit Romanée-Conti has a certain ring). It can't just be the savour of the wine. Perhaps it is simply the closeness of even ancient history—by California standards—that makes the past so palpable and the present so richly textured. In northern California history is just two biblical lifetimes long—and none of the bravura of the first of those lives has been forgotten, or allowed to die.

For modern purposes it is easy to divide the story of California wine into two. Pre-Prohibition we can call Pioneer. That's what it looks like from here—although such monumental establishments as Greystone or Inglenook or the vast Kohler & Froehling wine warehouse that was destroyed in the San Francisco earthquake and fire certainly didn't feel that way to the armies of cellarmen and clerks who manned them. A century ago they were already working in a mature and hugely successful industry.

Post-Prohibition sounds, on the face of it, like the steady buildup to what is now called state-of-the-art modernity. Again, that is not at all how it felt to be a struggling vintner in the 1950s, when the whole industry boasted only a score of wineries and the highest price was $3 a bottle. To their generation the legacy of the past was largely an embarrassment: big buildings dwarfing the present. True the oenological scholarship that started with Eugene Waldemar Hilgard was a cornerstone. But they were pioneers all over again: Lee Stewart at Souverain, Fred McCrea at Stony Hill, James Zellerbach at Hanzell, the Taylors at Mayacamas, and above all André Tchelistcheff at Beaulieu Vineyard, doing the frontier work that prepared the ground for modern times. I suppose the Gallos had just about reached the Thunderbird stage then. So when did modern times start? Some say with Joe Heitz in the early 1960s; others with the Robert Mondavi winery in 1966. Let's say thirty-five years ago.

This is pretty much where I came in, as a curious observer, first introduced to the roster of B.V., Martini, Inglenook, Charles Krug, the Christian Brothers, Italian Swiss Colony, Paul Masson—that was about it—as a Cambridge student with pickier taste buds than most. It seems to me that modernists are often inclined to be patronizing about the wine California was making before the drums started to roll in the sixties. Of course it is very hard to remember just how good a wine was that you drank so long ago. But with the help of friends' collections, above all of Bob Thompson's astonishingly vertical St. Helena cellar, and a few treasured relics of my own, I have tried to keep a realistic view. And what the old bottles, or some of them, say is that methods have changed far more than long-term results have done.

The great old B.Vs, Martinis, and Inglenooks have simply revealed over time the essence of their vineyards; the true *terroir* of Napa. It is a fair bet, then, that those of their successors that survive forty-odd years will be telling the same story. (And should anyone think it is only red wines that can have this sort of span, a 1962 Chardonnay from Joe Hertz was a sumptuous bottle in its thirty-fifth year.)

The revelation of *terroir* takes time, both in the bottle and in the vineyard. (If you find you have planted grapes in the wrong place it will be a good while before you admit it, even to yourself.) The dramatis personae of California wine have not, in the main, been exceptionally patient people. Hence, I believe, the stubborn reluctance to discuss the elements of *terroir,* microclimate apart, that has characterized California winegrowing. It is only in the past ten years that soil has had more than a passing mention. Still today, as Charles Sullivan attests, very little is said or known about it, beyond how well it drains.

Perhaps it will be in the evolution of Viticultural Areas (eighty-odd are outlined in this *Companion*) that the characters and qualities of California's finest wines will find definition. At this stage AVAs are still entities looking for a purpose—beyond mere geographical reference. But it is in the nature of good vintners to hone their sensibilities, and it seems improbable, to say the least, that *terroir* with all its implications will remain for long a concept without a recognized place in the vocabulary, maybe even in the legislation, of California.

One can speculate. One can reminisce. (A good bottle of wine is a great provoker of both.) But it is always better to have the facts available. Charles Sullivan's *Companion* will provide the grist for debate, speculation, and reminiscence from now on. With admirable dispassion he sets before us just what has happened in the plot so far.

Hugh Johnson

PREFACE

This handbook is intended for anyone interested in California wine today and in its past. Although there are many guides for wine buyers and tourists, until now there has been no general reference work on the California wine industry and its history. This book thus serves a wide range of readers, among them consumers, wine writers, winemakers, and scholars. It has a strong historical component—of history as events and situations that might be reported in this morning's news.

The dramatic, almost turbulent course of the California wine industry during the past thirty years has necessitated a system of selection for the entries that may not satisfy every reader's immediate needs. I have taken into account the healthy condition of the current literature of California wine. For the consumer there is an abundance of good handbooks that evaluate wineries and their current offerings, and the periodical literature in this area has become a welcome flood. For that reason many fairly new wineries are not included here, unless there is some aspect of their operations or history that deserves special notice. Nevertheless, most California wineries are represented. The same cannot be said for brands. Today large wine operations may have dozens of brands—the total for California wine since World War II is almost ten thousand—and, for some, the labels suggest, possibly misleadingly, that the brand is that of a specific winery. Therefore, although a few brands do have entries, most are included under the producer's entry.

I have attempted to include all producers of historic importance, along with biographical data on the principal individuals involved. The industry itself is treated in the same manner, with special emphasis on institutions and personalities that have helped to give California wine a tradition of continuity.

Geography is another aspect of California wine that I have emphasized, with a particular concern for historical geography. If a county, town, valley, or mountain in California has a wine-growing tradition, there is an entry for it. I have also given attention to a new aspect of the geography of wine—the American Viticultural Area. Since 1980 the U.S. Treasury Department has established a series of viticultural areas. Some, such as Napa Valley and Monterey, are well known to wine drinkers; others have boundaries that are confusing and do not coincide with the historical development of the area. Each of those in California has an entry.

Wine lovers often want to know how wines happen. I have, therefore, included many entries on the technology of the vineyard and cellar and attempted to include such matters in a historical context so that current practices may be viewed with an eye to techniques of bygone days; in some technical areas things haven't changed much. I have taken the same approach with grape varieties, tracing the history of all of the important varietals, and some not as important any more, from their arrival in the Golden State up to the 1996 vintage and planting season.

From *A* to *Z* I have written and interrelated the entries with the clear understanding of the need for and the current lack of a comprehensive history of California wine and the acknowledgment that a reference work such as this *Companion* cannot supply the interpretative content or narrative continuity to be found in a well-wrought history. I do, however, believe that here the reader can pursue broad topics in the world of California wine and acquire a sound understanding of them. The existence of cross-references has been indicated by the typographical device of small capitals and, for some, the addition of an asterisk, by which I mean to prod the reader to go to the entry indicated for information that will expand on or give depth to the entry in which the asterisk is encountered. There are as well many explicit *see* and *see also* references. Still, many useful terms would be buried in numerous entries were there no index.

This book, three years in the writing, is the result of thirty years of research. The idea that I should write it came from my father, about twenty years ago, when he asked me for the title of an encyclopedic handbook, one that he might use as a reference much as he used Hart's *Companion to California* and Schoonmaker's *Encyclopedia of Wine.* Surprised to hear that there was no such book available, he has been encouraging me ever since to produce one. Another important stimulus in the book's production has come from Thomas Pinney of Pomona College, the author of *A History of Wine in America,* also published by the University of California Press. When Professor Pinney discovered what I was planning, he agreed to read the manuscript and to make suggestions where he could. The result is a text improved immeasurably by his advice, encouragement, and didactic power. How could I hope to have had a better adviser than an English professor who is also an expert on wine history?

I did not follow all of Professor Pinney's suggestions; the selection of the entries, their length, and content has been mine. In the hope that they will draw to my attention the shortcomings of this book, I would like to extend an invitation to my readers to let me know about errors and omissions they come across in these pages. It is my hope that this handbook may continue with subsequent editions, updated to reflect the vitality of the California wine industry at all levels.

Los Gatos, California
March 1998

ABBREVIATIONS AND A NOTE ON ORGANIZATION

Entries run in alphabetical order, letter-by-letter. Names beginning with MC are treated as if they were spelled Mac; St. is treated as if it were spelled Saint. Wineries with the word Chateau in their names are listed under that word; wineries named after people are listed according to the alphabetical order of the last name, even when the business name is preceded by a first name or initial, e. g., S. Anderson Vineyard will be found among the As.

Cross-references to other entries are indicated by SMALL CAPS. Particularly useful cross-references are embellished with asterisks as well. Bibliographic references at the end of individual entries indicate further sources of information; a select bibliography of general literature is supplied at the end of the book.

The following abbreviations have been used extensively:

AVA = American Viticultural Area
BATF = Bureau of Alcohol, Tobacco, and Firearms
BW = Bonded Winery, followed by the number of the bond certificate
BW CA = Bonded Winery, California
BWC = Bonded Winery Cellar
DSP = Distilled Spirits Producer

ACACIA WINERY (BW 5067). A winery in the Carneros district, Napa County, founded in 1979 by Michael Richmond and several partners. Concentrating on Pinot noir and Chardonnay, Acacia emphasized single-vineyard wines for both varietals, but reduced yields forced them to modify this approach. After a try at wines in a red Bordeaux style in 1984, the partnership dissolved and the winery was sold to CHALONE* in 1986. In the 1990s Acacia raised its total annual production to about 55,000 cases, mostly of Chardonnay, and about 1,000 cases of sparkling wine. The second label is Caviste. The winery buildings are surrounded by the 42-acre Marina Vineyard.

ACETALDEHYDE. Wines too heavily endowed with acetaldehyde are often described as *oxidized*, a reference to a particular flavor that is a virtue in good SHERRY but a fault in young table wines. Before the 1950s high aldehyde levels were often a serious problem in white table wines in California; see OXIDATION.

ACETIC ACID, the chief flavor constituent in VINEGAR and almost always detrimental to good wine if the concentration is detectable. The most common volatile acid, it usually develops when wine is exposed to oxygen. Acetification was the chief quality problem in California wine production before World War II.

ACID. Acids give wine its tartness. Good wine demands a flavor balance between alcohol and acid. There are several acids in the grape before fermentation, chiefly tartaric, malic, and citric. Other acids, chiefly acetic, lactic, and succinic, develop during fermentation.

A standard gauge of the acidity of wine is its pH* number. Distilled water has a pH of 7.0. Lower numbers indicate an acid, higher an alkaline solution. Most California wine runs from a pH of 3.0 to 3.5. In early years before Prohibition, winegrowers in California often let grapes ripen so long that sugars were too high and acids, which diminish during ripening, were far too low, particularly in the white wines. At that time, wines overly high in acid were corrected by adding deacidification agents, such as calcium carbonate. This is rarely done today. In recent years producers have paid close attention to acid levels, which may legally be corrected today in the cellar. TARTARIC ACID is usually added if the winemaker wants to lower the pH.

A constant problem in California wineries, today and in early years, is the formation of ACETIC ACID and its volatile ester, ethyl acetate, which gives wine a taste and smell of vinegar. The use of SULFUR DIOXIDE in California wineries, beginning in the 1890s, has made such acescence, or volatile acidity, far less common. In recent years attention to cleanliness in the winery has made it possible to reduce the use of sulfur dioxide.

Adamson bought his spread in 1870 and had 140 acres in vines when this drawing was made in 1878. His name became a tragic footnote in California history: His first wife died in 1883 after an abortion, an event that led to a strict state antiabortion law.

There is often a tendency during and after primary FERMENTATION for the MALIC ACID in wine to be converted to lactic acid and carbon dioxide, the so-called malolactic or secondary fermentation. This process was not well understood by California winemakers until the 1960s, resulting in spoiled wine when the process took place after bottling. California winemakers today use maolactic fermentation in the production of many red wines because it raises the pH, softening the acid. Where tartness is a goal, such as wine in a Beaujolais style, the conversion is inhibited. For white wines today, particularly Chardonnay, some wineries promote malolactic fermentation for the special flavors that result. Other wineries inhibit the process to promote a tarter wine with a fresher flavor. See also LACTIC ACID.

> Jancis Robinson, ed., *The Oxford Companion to Wine* (Oxford: Oxford University Press, 1994) 4.

ADAMS, LEON D. (1905–95), a journalist, publicist, historian, and cofounder of the WINE INSTITUTE. His *Commonsense Book of Wine,* published in 1958, helped sweep away some of the meaningless rituals and taboos that had hindered the American public's accep-

tance of table wine as a part of everyday life. His *Wines of America* has gone through many editions since it was published in 1973, and is still the most thorough work on the subject, particularly on the California wine industry. The first two editions included a comprehensive treatment of the history of wine in California, a topic subsequently abbreviated.

> Leon Adams, *California Wine Industry Affairs* (Regional Oral History Office, Bancroft Library, 1990).
>
> L. Morton, "On the Road with Leon Adams," *Wines & Vines,* November 1995, 20–25.

ADAMSON, CHRISTIAN P. (1830–18). A native of Denmark, Adamson was a pioneer settler in the Rutherford area of Napa Valley. His winery, which dates from 1884, has been restored and can be seen just west of the Silverado Trail on Highway 128 in Napa Valley. See also FROG'S LEAP.

ADELAIDA CELLARS (BW 5162), a small winery in the Paso Robles area of San Luis Obispo County, it was founded by John Munch in 1981. At first Munch concentrated on producing SPARKLING WINE under the Tonio Conti label. In 1990, with new partners, Munch built a new winery east of Paso Robles. Specializing in Cabernet Sauvignon, Zinfandel, and Chardonnay, the winery produces about 7,500 cases of still wine annually.

ADLER FELS (BW 5024). Before David Coleman and his wife, Ayn Ryan, started this winery in the hills above Sonoma Valley in 1980, he designed wine labels and she was a sales representative for CHATEAU ST. JEAN. Annual production is about 15,000 cases, principally of white wines. They occasionally make a sparkling Gewürztraminer/White Riesling labeled Mélange à Deux.

AETNA SPRINGS WINE RANCH (BW 5352), a small winery in Napa's Pope Valley, founded by Paul and Sally Kimsey in 1986. Their total production of about 1,000 cases consists mainly of Cabernet Sauvignon, Merlot, and Chardonnay.

AGING WINES. Originally in California wines were not aged lest they spoil. By the 1860s aged California wine was considered that which had rested in cask or tank for at least a year. The problem of bottling a wine that was not yet chemically stable induced premium producers to keep their wines for at least two, perhaps three, years in cask, barrel, or tank, before shipping or bottling them. Charles LEFRANC, the founder of New Almédan Vineyards, was often cited, particularly by his son-in-law, Paul MASSON, for having said, "I shall sell no wine before its time."

The idea of bottle aging wines, particularly red Bordeaux and vintage Ports, for long periods of time gradually caught on with European connoisseurs in the last half of the nineteenth century and was adopted by some Americans. Californians started talking about the effects of bottle aging for such wine in the 1890s. Some producers and consumers of California wines from red Bordeaux grapes, particularly Cabernet Sauvignon and Malbec, pointed with pride to their cellared 1886s and 1890s in later years. It was also found that Zinfandels made in the style of long-lasting red Bordeaux also improved for many years. Sweet wines and ANGELICA were also commonly held in the barrel for extended periods.

Since the 1950s a growing element of American winelovers has focused its attention on bottle aging table wines, both red and white. California producers, particularly in the coastal valleys north of Santa Barbara, often aim at styles that cater to this interest. In the 1970s some producers made "monster" red wines that may never be ready to drink, so powerful were their TANNINS.

Styles today in California red table wines tend to favor earlier drinkability, but with enough acid and tannin to encourage some bottle aging. This is still particularly true for wines from red Bordeaux and Rhône varieties of grapes and, of course, from Zinfandel. Some consumers and producers believe that certain Chardonnays and Sauvignon blancs will improve in the bottle for a decade or more. Late-harvest white wines, particularly those from grapes infected by BOTRYTIS CINEREA, are also considered candidates for the cellar. Even so-called Vintage Ports from California appear to improve with age.

AGUARDIENTE, from the Latin, *aqua ardens,* fiery water, was, during the mission and rancho period of California history, the name used for distilled spirits made from the wine of the Mission grape. This was the hard liquor most commonly available to Americans here during the Gold Rush period. The term is Spanish and may refer to any form of distilled spirits.

AHERN, ALBERT. See FREEMARK ABBEY WINERY

AHLGREN VINEYARD (BW 4764). Dexter and Valerie Ahlgren founded this small winery in the Santa Cruz Mountain in 1976. Producing about 3,000 cases from grapes grown in the California coastal valleys, they have developed a good reputation for their Cabernet Sauvignon.

ALAMBIC. See BRANDY

ALAMBIC, INC. See GERMAIN-ROBIN

ALAMEDA COUNTY. Two important wine-growing areas developed here on the east side of San Francisco Bay in the nineteenth century. The first was in the foothills facing the Bay, around the old MISSION SAN JOSE* in Washington Township. The other was the LIVERMORE VALLEY,* a few miles to the east.

TABLE I. WINE GRAPES IN ALAMEDA COUNTY, SELECTED VARIETIES

| YEAR | PERCENT OF TOTAL | | CABERNET SAUVIGNON | CHAR-DONNAY | (ACRES) GREY RIESLING | SAUVIGNON BLANC | SÉMILLON | TOTAL |
	RED	WHITE						
1920								2,625
1930								3,600
1940								3,829
1950								3,313
1960								2,910
1970	27	73	16	153	170	117	361	1,868
1976	28	72	25	130	285	101	322	1,936
1982	22	78	57	191	444	125	183	1,748
1988	27	73	243	700	114	264	103	1,795
1997	37	63	199	635	29	93	74	1,433

NOTE: Until 1961 statistics for acreage under various varieties of grapes were not published.
SOURCE: California Agricultural Statistics Service, Sacramento, Calif.

The older area, mostly in today's city of Fremont, dates from the founding of the mission in 1797. It became one of California's most famous premium wine districts in the 1880s. But, with the expansion of the East Bay suburbs since the 1950s, winegrowing has almost come to an end here. The Livermore winegrowing area dates from the 1880s and developed quickly into a premium district now best known for its white wines. This area too has seen suburban pressures on its vineyard acreage since World War II. Wine grapes have been grown in other areas in the county, particularly the Suñol area between Livermore and Mission San Jose. In the East Bay before World War II there were commercial vineyards among the orchards around Hayward, San Leandro, and Castro Valley.

Wine grape growing in Alameda County peaked in the 1890s at close to 7,000 acres. Of those, about 2,100 acres were in the East Bay, the rest in the Livermore Valley. In the 1930s, after Repeal, there were about 3,000 acres of grapes in the county and 32 wineries, six of them in the East Bay. The decline continues; between 1986 and 1994, the wine grape crop in the county had been reduced by half.

Since the 1960s the proliferation of the urban winery has been noticeable in Alameda County. In 1995 five of the county's fifteen bonded wineries were small operations in the East Bay producing premium wines from numerous Northern California grape sources.

In 1994, the wine grape crop in the county was 56 percent of the crop in 1989.

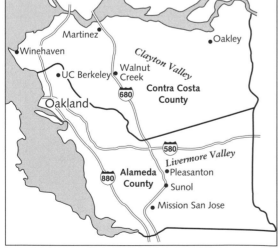

Alameda County

ALCOHOL. When grapes ferment, the enzymes created by yeast cells convert grape SUGAR into alcohol and carbon dioxide. In a wine fermented "dry," there is virtually no sugar left. Wines can be fermented until the alcohol content is about 16.5%, at which point the fermentation process is cut off by the action of the alcohol. Some residual sugar may remain in the wine.

Normally California table wines have an alcohol level between 10% and 14%. The fermentation of sweet wines can be cut short by the addition of alcohol, leaving residual sugars, as are found in ports and sweet sherries. These are often termed FORTIFIED wines.

Modern production techniques enable winemakers to make what are called "light, sweet wines." The fermentation is stopped in order to retain a small quantity of residual sugar and still have a low level of alcohol.

During the 1930s, table wine in California was required to have an alcohol content of at least 10 percent. This was higher than federal requirements and was supported by producers in California to help insure biological stability in wine that was shipped long distances. Scientific and technical developments since World War II made it possible to lower the alcohol levels. Since 1979 it has been legal to produce so-called soft or light wines with alcohol levels as low as 7 percent. This change has made it possible to produce white wines, particularly White Rieslings, in a low-alcohol German style. In the early 1980s wines made in this style were a short-lived fad.

The alcohol level of wine affects the federal tax rate on producers. Wine with alcohol levels above 14 percent are taxed at a significantly higher rate, a rate that is applied to all fortified wines. Some wines meant to be consumed as table wines occasionally exceed 14 percent and so, legally, may not be labeled as table wines although that is what they are. Most of these wines are made from Zinfandel, a few from other varieties.

Recent inventions have also made it possible to lower the alcoholic content of a wine to improve its flavor. The machines are very expensive but have caused quite a stir in the wine industry for the high quality of their products.

Processes have also been developed to produce wine from which all alcohol has been removed. With a rising awareness of health and the social consequences of excessive alcohol consumption, such "wines," and unfermented wine grape juice, have become more popular in America. See ARIEL.

ALDERBROOK WINERY (BW 5112) in the Dry Creek area of Sonoma was founded in 1982 and for years concentrated on white wine. Total annual production is now up to 30,000 cases. In 1992 the original partners sold the 63-acre ranch to G. W. Gillemot, a partner in SCHRAMS-BERG. Since then Zinfandel and Merlot have become a larger part of the production mix.

ALEATICO, a rare Italian variety of grape noted for its sweet wines. It was imported to California before Prohibition but never caught on. It was grown here and there in southern California and the Central Valley after Repeal, mostly to give a little muscat flavor to inexpensive port. This is a variety that shows some promise in California. In 1990 MONTEVIÑA WINERY planted two acres and in 1992 began producing a medium-sweet Aleatico.

ALEXANDER VALLEY is a major winegrowing area in Sonoma County and received APPELLATION status in 1984. The district runs south from the Mendocino County line, along the Russian River, to Healdsburg, and extends east to Knight's Valley. It includes about 7,000 acres of wine grapes.

The valley itself, which is much smaller than the official viticultural area, was part of the Sotoyome Mexican land grant made to Henry Fitch in 1841. Cyrus Alexander (1805–72) received a large part of that grant in 1847 and he planted the first vines here. He is buried in the family cemetery, today part of the ALEXANDER VALLEY VINEYARDS, land purchased from his heirs in 1962.

Winegrowing began here in earnest in the 1880s as wheat and sheep-grazing land between Healdsburg and Cloverdale was converted into a gigantic vineyard. Until recent years the Alexander Valley designation was reserved for the land southeast of Geyserville, out to Knight's Valley. Thus, the ITALIAN SWISS COLONY and all the winegrowing operations to the north were considered to be in Geyserville or Cloverdale. In the old days the wineries of Horace Chase (of STAG'S LEAP fame), S. L. Osborn (Lone Pine Ranch), and O. H. Michelson (Alexander Valley Winery) were dominant. In 1896 400,000 gallons of wine were produced in this area. Following Prohibition, the area supported a complex mixed agriculture of fruit, grazing, and fodder crops until the 1970s, when viticulture became prominent. By the 1980s the area was an established part of Sonoma's production of premium wine, noted particularly for Cabernet Sauvignon and Chardonnay.

Gerald Asher, "Alexander Valley," *Gourmet*,
November 1994, 74–86.

ALEXANDER VALLEY FRUIT & TRAD-ING COMPANY (BW 5379), a small winery whose name and colorful, old-fashioned label express the diversity of this family operation. Steve and Candy Sommer started in 1983, making up gift packs from local products. They received their winery bond in 1987. The tiny emporium is on Highway 128 just west of Jim Town. Annual wine production is about 7,500 cases.

ALEXANDER VALLEY VINEYARDS (BW 4685). Harry Wetzel bought this 140-acre estate in 1962 from heirs of the family of Cyrus Alexander, the pioneer white settler of the valley. Wetzel and his family renovated the his-

toric buildings on the property and began planting vines, mostly Chardonnay and Cabernet Sauvignon, in 1964. They sold their grapes until 1975 when their winery had its first vintage. Since then production has risen to over 55,000 cases a year.

ALICANTE BOUSCHET, a French hybrid grape (Petit Bouschet × Grenache) developed in 1886 by Henri Bouschet. Its purpose was to supply dark color to poorly colored red wines, but it adds little to their flavor. The French term for such dark-juice grapes is TEINTURIER, or dyer.

Henri's father, Louis Bouschet, had developed one of this vine's parents, the Petit Bouschet, in 1824. This vine entered northern California vineyards in the early 1880s, probably first imported by Charles MCIVER of Mission San Jose. The Alicante Bouschet was introduced in the 1890s and became the most popular dyer grape planted in the years before Prohibition. By 1919 there were about 18,000 acres in California, mostly in the Central Valley. When PROHIBITION* came in 1920, the popularity of the Alicante Bouschet as a shipping grape for eastern home winemakers soared. By 1932 there were 39,000 acres, still concentrated in the Central Valley. But their high prices during the dry years also promoted much planting of the variety in the coastal valleys. The total acreage gradually dropped to 19,000 acres in 1949. Between 1960 and 1997 acreage in California dropped from 10,000 to 1,600 acres, more than 90% of which was in the Central Valley. Since the 1970s a few premium producers have brought out a varietal Alicante Bouschet as a table wine.

ALLHOFF, MARTIN (?–1867), a native of the Rhineland, was a pioneering winegrower in El Dorado County who had his first vintage in 1858, five barrels of CATAWBA. He had previously worked at Nicholas Longworth's cellars in Cincinnati. After he committed suicide, his widow married Robert CHALMERS, who operated the winery in Coloma until the 1880s. Alhoff's grave is across the road from the winery's impressive ruins.

ALLIED GRAPE GROWERS, a huge winegrowers' cooperative organized by Louis PETRI in 1951. Petri also controlled several large wineries organized into UNITED VINTNERS, which was purchased by HEUBLEIN in 1969.

ALMADEN VINEYARDS. According to tradition Almaden's first vineyard was planted by Etienne Thée, a Frenchman from Bordeaux who came to California seeking gold. In 1852 he acquired a large tract of land south of San Jose at the northern end of the Almaden Valley and planted some Mission vines. In 1858 his son-in-law, Charles LEFRANC (1824–87), imported cuttings of first-class French wine grapes and began the first successful large-scale commercial wine venture in the Santa Clara Valley. He called the place NEW ALMADÉN VINEYARDS, after the great quicksilver mine nearby.

By the 1860s Lefranc was in full control of the operation and had expanded the vineyard

to 75 acres of the 350-acre estate. In 1876 he built a large stone winery. Two years later Paul MASSON,* a student from Burgundy, went to work at New Almadén. When Lefranc died in 1887, the young man married his daughter, Louise, and formed a partnership with Henry Lefranc, Charles's son. Its purpose was to produce first-class, bottle-fermented sparkling wine. The wine was a great success, drawing critical acclaim when released in 1892. The partnership ended but Masson continued to produce sparklers from Henry's grapes. In 1896 Masson bought property in Saratoga, where he would later build his mountain winery.

Henry Lefranc (1861–1909) ran Almaden until 1902 when Louise and her sister, Marie, gained full control of the estate. In fact, Paul Masson ran the winery, although he never owned it outright. In 1930 the family traded the winery estate for cattle land in San Benito County. In 1932 the winery was acquired by a partnership that began winemaking in 1933. The Almaden wine was good but the management was not and in 1938 the bank took over the bankrupt property, closing the winery but still operating the 700-acre vineyard

The Almaden estate in 1894. Today, only the original winery, built in 1859, right foreground, survives. (William A. Wulf Collection, Los Gatos, Calif.)

In 1941 Louis Benoist (1900–75), a financier in San Francisco, acquired Almaden and, with the wine expert Frank SCHOONMAKER, and the winemaker, Oliver Goulet, fashioned one of the most successful wine operations in modern American history. At first they concentrated on bottle-fermented sparkling wine and then medium-priced varietal table wines. In the 1950s Benoist, feeling the pressure of suburban expansion, began acquiring vineyard and winery property in San Benito County, the most important being the historic VALLIANT-PALMTAG Winery and vineyards in the CIENEGA VALLEY. In 1956 Benoist bought a 2,200-acre ranch in nearby Paicines and began planting what would eventually be the largest premium vineyard in the world. More vineyards were also planted in nearby Monterey County.

Augmented by the production of jug wines in the Central Valley, Almaden's sales soared. But Benoist's financial problems outside Almaden and his lavish lifestyle forced him to sell the entire operation to National Distillers in 1967. For the next fifteen years National continued the expansion, taking advantage of a rising demand for inexpensive white jug wine in the 1970s. In the process, the parent company allowed the Almaden label to lose its premium luster. An attempt to revive an image of quality with a line of premium varietals under the label of Charles Lefranc and a series of aggressive ad campaigns did not halt the decline.

In 1987 HEUBLEIN bought Almaden and began selling off its assets, mostly thousands of acres of vineyards in the Central Coast and Central Valley. Production was concentrated at a facility in Madera, where jug wines and inexpensive varietals are produced under the Almaden and Blossom Hill labels. Blossom Hill refers to the historic Lefranc Almaden Winery, which was on Blossom Hill Road, and was probably the oldest commercial wine operation in California. It was sold to developers in 1988 and the next year the great 1876 winery was destroyed in a mysterious fire. But the original winery dating from 1859 survives. The land is now covered with houses. In 1994 Heublein sold the Almaden brand name to CANANDAIGUA. Annual sales are about 8 million cases, mostly inexpensive Central Valley wines.

William A. Dieppe, *Almaden Is My Life* (Regional Oral History Office, Bancroft Library, 1985).

ALPEN CELLARS (BW 5208). A tiny winery in Trinity County whose vineyards are just over 2,500 feet in altitude. Mark and Keith Graves started planting their 7-acre vineyard in 1984 and bonded their winery in 1988. They specialize in White Riesling, Chardonnay, and Gewürztraminer. Annual production is about 1,500 cases.

ALTIMIRA, JOSÉ (1787–1860?), a Franciscan priest who led an expedition in 1823 that explored the Sonoma and Napa regions and later that year founded the Sonoma MISSION, which he ran for a while. He also supervised the planting of the historic vineyard there.

ALTA VINEYARD CELLAR (BW 4921). C. T. McEachran was a neighbor of Jacob SCHRAM in the hills west of Napa Valley. In 1878 he built a little winery and had a "patch of vines" when Robert Louis STEVENSON dropped by in 1880 on his way up to Schramsberg and "exchanged one or two words of Scots with Mr. M'Eckron," who, he thought, "had the look of a man who succeeds." (Later he did succeed as the superintendent of the Weinberger Winery in St. Helena.) In 1978 Benjamin Falk bonded the winery building. Today it is part of the modern SCHRAMSBERG estate, even though Falk retains the bond and uses the winery name elsewhere in Calistoga.

ALTA VINEYARDS (BW 30), a bulk winery in Fresno, dates from 1883. It was a 4-million-gallon operation when it became part of GUILD WINERIES in 1962.

ALTAMURA VINEYARDS AND WINERY (BW 5891). The Altamura family's 55-acre vineyard on Napa's Silverado Trail produces several grape varieties. Starting in 1985, a small portion of these grapes began going into wine under the Altamura label. Frank Altamura makes about 3,000 cases per year, with an emphasis on Cabernet Sauvignon, Chardonnay, and Sangiovese wines. Since 1994 the winery itself has been in Wooden Valley.

ALTAR WINE. Wine produced for the clergy and used by them often, but not always, in performance of religious rituals; also referred to as sacramental wine. They are often dry table wines, not necessarily sweet dessert wines. During Prohibition wineries in California produced about 20 million gallons of altar wine, and a number of wineries, among them Beaulieu and Concannon, were able to stay afloat at least partially as a result. Today altar wine is a very small part of the sales of a few California wineries.

AMADOR COUNTY, a Mother Lode county located east of Sacramento in the Sierra foothills. By the time of the Gold Rush and soon thereafter, the area was dotted with vineyards and small wineries producing wine mostly for local consumption. By 1885 a panel of distinguished wine experts stated that an 1883 Amador Zinfandel "merited approval for its taste and its true fruit expression." But by the 1890s only fourteen commercial vineyards and one winery had survived. During Prohibition there were about 500 acres of vines in the county, a number that grew to about 900 shortly after Repeal. In 1936 there were three small wineries: Bianchetti, Esola, and D'AGOSTINI.

The revival of Amador County as a fine wine area began in the 1960s when home winemakers discovered the old Zinfandel vineyards here, concentrated in the SHENANDOAH VALLEY near Plymouth. Soon established wineries,

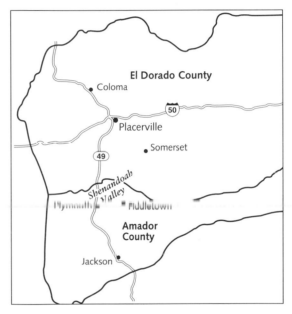

Amador County

TABLE 2. WINE GRAPES IN AMADOR COUNTY, SELECTED VARIETIES

YEAR	PERCENT OF TOTAL		BARBERA	CABERNET SAUVIGNON	(ACRES) SAUVIGNON BLANC	ZINFANDEL	TOTAL
	RED	WHITE					
1974	97	3	5	56	2	681	861
1981	78	22	10	62	258	1,097	1,606
1987	77	23	16	50	247	1,097	1,626
1997	90	10	146	54	50	1,602	2,271

SOURCE: California Agricultural Statistics Service, Sacramento, Calif.

led by SUTTER HOME (see the label on page 408), were seeking out those vineyards and planting new vines. By 1995 there were eighteen bonded wineries here.

The tonnage of wine grapes grown in Amador County in 1995 was 213 percent higher than the tonnage grown in 1990.

> Eric J. Costa, *Old Vines: A History of Winegrowing in Amador County* (Jackson, Calif.: Cenotha, 1994).
>
> J. Hutchinson, "The Action Is Intense in Amador," *Wines & Vines*, September 1981, 39–44.

AMADOR FOOTHILL WINERY (BW 4963), a small winery in the Shenandoah Valley in Amador County, bonded in 1980. The owner, Ben Zeitman, has used Zinfandel grapes from such old local vineyards as Eschen, Esola, Grandpère, and Ferrero. For many years, a good part of his 10,000-case annual production was of White Zinfandel. Recently he has been making more Barbera and Sauvignon blanc wines. The winery's labels include beautiful drawings of flowers and culinary herbs.

AMERICAN SOCIETY FOR ENOLOGY AND VITICULTURE, founded in 1950, and centered at the University of California at Davis, to promote scientific work in enology and viticulture. The society publishes the *American Journal of Enology and Viticulture* to disseminate information about the work of scientists and field practitioners in the improvement of grape growing and winemaking.

AMERICAN VITICULTURAL AREA (AVA), a geographic region, distinguished from surrounding areas by a particular climate, soil, and historical tradition of grape growing.

AVA status is granted by the BUREAU OF ALCOHOL, TOBACCO, AND FIREARMS (BATF) as the result of a petition or petitions made by growers and/or wine producers in an area. The petition must show that the area within the proposed boundaries meets the BATF's requirements. The BATF began granting AVA status to winegrowing districts in 1980; the first in California was to Napa Valley, 31 March 1981. Today AVAs are often loosely referred to as appellations, but the U.S. system does not address, let alone assess, the quality of the area's wines, nor, unlike the French system of *appellation d'origine contrôlée,* does it require any particular varieties to be grown.

Several petitions from California have led to lively controversy, usually as a result of certain areas being left out of the original proposed district (see NORTH COAST; STAGS LEAP). The Bureau has tended to be inclusive when there is controversy. By the mid-1990s California has about eighty individual AVAs, although some overlap. The requirements notwithstanding, some areas, relatively few in California, that have virtually no history as winegrowing regions have been granted AVA status.

The chief value of an AVA is the distinction gained from having certain areas identified on a producer's label. In the minds of many consumers, wines from certain areas, such as the ALEXANDER VALLEY, HOWELL MOUNTAIN, and PASO ROBLES, have particular merit. But many AVA petitions have been granted for areas that few consumers have ever heard of. See also APPELLATION.

AMERINE, MAYNARD, Professor Emeritus of Enology and Viticulture at the University of California at Davis. As a young scholar in the 1930s he toured California with Professor A. J. WINKLER assessing the condition of the state's vineyards. In doing so they developed a classification of CLIMATES useful to grape growers. In 1957 he succeeded Winkler as department chairman. Over the years he has written several important textbooks and well over 200 scholarly articles on winemaking and viticulture. With Vernon Singleton, he wrote *Wine, An Introduction for Americans* (1965). This book and scores of articles in popular periodicals have brought the ordinary wine lover a readable, authoritative, and dependable picture of California wine.

Maynard A. Amerine, *The University of California and the State's Wine Industry* (Regional Oral History Office, Bancroft Library, 1971).

———, *Wine Bibliographies and Taste Perception Studies* (Regional Oral History Office, Bancroft Library, 1988).

J. Hutchinson, "Maynard Amerine," *Wines & Vines,* March 1989, 18-21.

AMIZETTA VINEYARDS (BW 5221). Spencer and Amizetta Clark bought bare land above Conn Valley to the east of the Napa Valley in 1979. They planted vines and in 1984 bonded their 10,000-gallon-capacity winery, concentrating on the production of Cabernet Sauvignon wines.

AMPELOGRAPHY. From *ampelos,* the Greek word for vine, the science of identifying vines through observation and description. It is by no means a perfect science. In California there has been confusion and controversy over the identification of several varietals. The development of isozyme and DNA FINGERPRINTING has helped to bring some order to the confusion. (For examples of varieties for which ampelographic identification has caused some confusion, see PINOT BLANC, PETITE SIRAH, and SYRAH.)

ANAHEIM, a city in Orange County in Southern California with German origins. In 1857 a joint stock company headed by Charles KOHLER, and including several entrepreneurs from northern California, was formed to promote a large winegrowing cooperative. Named the Los Angeles Vineyard Society, it is usually called the Anaheim Colony after the Santa Ana River. By 1859, fifty families of German settlers had planted almost 1,000 acres of vines. Wine production grew from 70,000 gallons in 1861 to 600,000 in 1868. The settlers owned and managed their own vineyards, and several individual wineries were established, most notably those of Otto Rust and T. J. F. Boege.

Producing mostly ordinary bulk wine, the agricultural community was fairly prosperous until the 1880s. In 1884 a strange malady struck the Anaheim vineyards and spread. By 1893 viticulture in Orange County was almost dead. The disease was first called the Anaheim disease, but today is referred to as PIERCE'S DISEASE. Prosperity returned to the area later in the 1890s with the planting of orange and walnut orchards. Since the 1950s these have gradually given way to suburban sprawl.

Vincent P. Carosso, *The California Wine Industry, 1830–1895: A Study of the Formative Years* (Berkeley: University of California Press, 1951), 60-73.

Thomas Pinney, *A History of Wine in America, from Beginnings to Prohibition* (Berkeley, University of California Press, 1989), 285–94.

ANAHEIM DISEASE. See PIERCE'S DISEASE

S. ANDERSON VINEYARD (BW 4917). Stanley Anderson (1927–1994) and his family bought this vineyard land in Napa Valley's Stags Leap District in 1971 and bonded their winery in 1979. The Chardonnay grapes planted near the Yountville Crossroad go into their still wine and MÉTHODE CHAMPENOISE sparkling wine, which is aged in cellars dug deep into the knoll behind the winery. The Anderson vineyards now total about 120 acres, which include 70 in the Carneros. In 1989 their first Stags Leap Cabernet Sauvignon was produced from the nearby Richard Chambers Vineyard. Total annual production is about 12,000 cases.

ANDERSON'S CONN VALLEY VINEYARDS (BW 5406). A winery on Rossi Road above Conn Valley in Napa; bonded in 1987 and specializing in Cabernet Sauvignon wines. The vineyard was established in 1983. The annual production from the 26-acre estate is about 5,000 cases, and now includes small quantities of Pinot noir wine.

ANDERSON VALLEY, in MENDOCINO COUNTY, west of Ukiah, drained by the Navarro River and running northwest about thirty miles to the sea. The valley was granted appellation status in 1983, and, by the 1990s, had thirteen wineries and about 1,000 acres of wine grapes. It was settled in the 1850s. Small vineyards were planted then but they had little commercial importance. In 1893 one vineyard with five acres of MUSCAT was mentioned in the statewide survey. It was near the village of Boonville, the commercial center and world famous among linguistic scholars for Boontling, the homegrown language developed thereabout after the Civil War. After the turn of the century Italian settlers planted vineyards above the valley around Greenwood Ridge. Several of the Zinfandel vineyards survive today.

Weather in the valley and its environs limits viticulture. Toward the sea the breezes and fog make a very cool, Region I climate (See HEAT SUMMATION). Inland, the valley has a Region II climate, but is still fairly cool. Thus such varieties as GEWÜRZTRAMINER, PINOT NOIR, and CHARDONNAY thrive here. The cool climate suggests sparkling wine production, but when ITALIAN SWISS COLONY tried planting 200 acres here for that purpose in the late 1940s, the company chose the wrong white varieties.

The wine revolution reached here in 1963 when Donald Edmeades began planting his vineyard. HUSCH VINEYARDS became the first bonded winery in 1971. In the 1980s the valley's potential for sparkling wine production was proved by John SCHARFFENBERGER and the French Champagne house of Louis ROEDERER.

"Exploring the Climates of Anderson Valley," *Wines & Vines,* September 1991, 42-43.

ANGELICA, a wine-cordial that was invented in California during the mission era, although other places in the winemaking world produce a beverage by similar methods. It was made usually from common Mission grapes, and the fermentation was stopped by the addition of AGUARDIENTE, leaving a very sweet, high-alcohol product that, if given at least eight years barrel aging, became a luscious, nutty dessert drink. Often the grapes had not begun fermenting before aguardiente was added. Of the wines described by early travelers in pastoral California, usually only Angelica was praised. It was perhaps named for Los Angeles. According to the historian, H. H. BANCROFT, that made by Father Narciso Duran at Mission San José de Guadalupe was the best. The logevity of Angelica is almost unbelievable. In 1979 Harvey Steiman, the editor of *Wine Spectator,* proclaimed an 1875 Angelica "the most magnificent" California sweet wine he had ever tasted.

In recent years a few small producers in California, such as TRENTADUE, JOSEPH HEITZ, and J. W. MORRIS, have made Angelica. The EAST-SIDE WINERY'S Royal Host Angelica was praised by connoisseurs, but was discontinued in 1990. Nevertheless, in 1993 that winery had two barrels aging in its cellar, to be released in the twenty-first century.

B. McGinty, "Angelica," *Vintage,* October 1975, 33–37.

ANHEUSER BUSCH. See HECK CELLARS; KORBEL CHAMPAGNE CELLARS

ANNAPOLIS WINERY (BW 5355). This most westerly winery in Sonoma was founded in 1986 and is located on Soda Springs Road, about six miles from the Pacific Ocean and the same distance from the Mendocino County line. There are 15 acres in vines. The annual production of Gewürztraminer, Sauvignon blanc, and Cabernet Sauvignon wines comes to about 1,500 cases.

APÉRITIF, a French word, from the Latin, *aperire,* to open, for a small alcoholic drink taken before a meal as an appetizer. Before Prohibition the most popular apéritifs in California were sweet wines and dry SHERRY. In recent years dry table wines have become more popular. The European tradition of flavored wines as apéritifs has not caught on in California, except among Italian-Americans who often favor dry or sweet VERMOUTH.

APPELLATION. In the U.S., a synonym generally used loosely for the legal term AMERICAN VITICULTURAL AREA (AVA). Many California wine writers began using the term in the 1970s when referring to winegrowing areas in the state, adopting the usage from the French national system of *appellation d'origine contrôlée,* which since 1935 has strictly regulated the use of place names in France in connection with the production and sale of wine there. By the 1980s, when the BATF began granting official designations to winegrowing districts in America, the word had become ensconced in California's wine vocabulary. As a synonym for AVA it is not a legally defined term, even though the BATF itself occasionally uses it in that context, and certainly carries no connotation of quality. The word is, however, part of the legal term prescribed by the BATF for winegrowing areas whose borders are essentially political. Such areas, states and counties for example, may not carry the AVA designation, but are to be described as "appellations of origin." See also AMERICAN VITICULTURAL AREA.

ARAUJO ESTATE WINERY. See EISELE VINEYARD

ARCIERO WINERY (BW 5223). Planting for the 750-acre Arciero Vineyards began in 1983, six miles east of Paso Robles, in San Luis Obispo County. The imposing 78,000-square-foot winery was bonded in 1984 and

has a capacity of 500,000 cases per year. This large-scale operation also markets wine under the Monte Verde label. Annual production passed 100,000 cases in the mid-1990s. There is a strong emphasis on white wines and White Zinfandel.

ARIEL, a nonalcoholic "wine" developed by the J. LOHR WINERY in 1985. Since its introduction, sales of Ariel have risen to almost 150,000 cases per year. Chardonnay and White Zinfandel are the leading varietals. There are several methods for producing such beverages; all include a means of maintaining or recapturing the aromatic components that might be lost in the process of removing the alcohol.

ARMIDA WINERY (BW 5519) is a small winery at the southern end of Dry Creek Valley in Sonoma. The owner, Robert Frugali, a long-time grower, named the winery after his grandmother. He was bonded in 1990 and his first wines, Chardonnay, Merlot and Pinot noir, came from that vintage. Annual production is about 8,000 cases from about 70 acres of vines.

ARMSTRONG RIDGE. See KORBEL CHAMPAGNE CELLARS

AROMA. Purists contend that the term *aroma* is reserved for the smells of a young wine, particularly the fruity odors, and should be distinguished from BOUQUET, the smell of an aged wine. The aroma of a wine is said to be like the taste of the grape. Wines made in California from muscats, White Riesling, Gewürztraminer, and Sauvignon blanc have pronounced aromas that do remind one of the grape itself.

ARROWOOD, RICHARD. The winemaker who built the reputation of CHATEAU ST. JEAN,* in 1990 Arrowood resigned his posts there as vice president and winemaster and concentrated his efforts on his own winery a few miles down the road. He began **Arrowood Vineyards & Winery** (BW 5388) in 1985. His first wines, a Chardonnay and a Cabernet Sauvignon, were released in 1988. By the 1990s his production was up to 20,000 cases annually, the wine made mostly from purchased grapes, although he does have 19 acres of vineyard at the winery planted mostly to red Bordeaux varieties.

ARROYO GRANDE is the southernmost official viticultural area in San Luis Obispo County, granted AVA status in 1990. Chardonnay and Pinot noir dominate the area's 425 acres of vineyards. About 45 percent of the acreage belongs to MAISON DEUTZ, and there are two other wineries there, Saucelito Canyon and TALLEY VINEYARDS.

ARROYO SECO. Officially recognized as an AVA in 1983, Arroyo Seco is a triangular area in Monterey County adjacent to Arroyo Seco Creek, which flows into the Salinas River south of Soledad. The area consists of sloping bench land above the river. WENTE, J. LOHR, and VENTANA are important growers here. Chardonnay is the variety most commonly grown in the area, which has a total of about 2,200 acres of wine grapes.

ARROYO SECO VINEYARDS (BW 5603). In 1991 the owners of ASV WINES bought the old SAN MARTIN WINERY and converted it to a custom-crushing operation under this new name.

VINCENT ARROYO WINERY (BW 5206) is a small winery located just north of Calistoga in Napa Valley. It was bonded in 1984 and produces about 4,500 cases per year, specializing in Cabernet Sauvignon, Petite Sirah, and Chardonnay.

ASSOCIATED VINTAGE GROUP (AVG) (BW 4765, 4831, 5436, 5726). In 1993, Allan Hemphill, an executive in the wine industry, together with his associates, bought the MCDOWELL VALLEY VINEYARDS facility as the base of production operations for AVG. This CUSTOM CRUSHING business, which

The MAISON DEUTZ winery is the most important production facility in the Arroyo Grande viticultural area.

was incorporated in 1993, had previously acquired the premises of other wineries, MARK WEST, near Healdsburg, GRAND CRU, in Glen Ellen, and a sparkling wine facility belonging to CHATEAU ST. JEAN in Graton. (The organization of AVG before the early 1990s is obscure and several players moved in and out.) The group also has a working agreement with MARTINI & PRATI. In 1996 AVG produced 900,000 cases of wine, and production continues to increase. By 1997, the crushing capacity in Sonoma County had reached 4 million gallons. A typical customer is RAVENSWOOD, whose lower-priced Zinfandel is made at AVG under the supervision of the Ravenswood winemaker.

ASSUMPTION ABBEY. See BROOKSIDE VINEYARD

ASTI. See ITALIAN SWISS COLONY

ASTRINGENCY. A puckery tactile sensation noticeable in many young California red wines. It is often associated with the bitter taste of TANNIN.

ASV WINES (BW 5087). A 5 million-gallon bulk winery in Delano, founded in 1981. In 1991 the owners bought the SAN MARTIN WINERY and began a custom-crushing operation there in 1993. See also ARROYO SECO VINEYARDS.

ATKINSON, JOSEPH BURR (1830–?). A clothier in San Francisco who in 1881 bought 126 acres in Rutherford, planted 105 acres of vines, and built a winery there in 1885. He formed a partnership with the state senator Seneca Ewer (see EWER & ATKINSON) that lasted until 1896. In 1899 Atkinson went bankrupt and lost his vineyards. Today his restored home is the centerpiece of the modern ST. SUPÉRY winery, named for Edward St. Supéry, who bought the Atkinson property in 1899.

ATLAS PEAK, a winegrowing area located in the hills to the east of the Napa Valley and named for the nearby mountain, which is the highest point in the Vaca Range. The American Viticultural Area now covers 11,400 acres; when it was officially recognized by the BATF in 1992, it included only 565 acres of vines, almost all of which were in Foss Valley.

ATLAS PEAK VINEYARDS (BW 5410). In 1986 a combination of foreign interests bought from William Hill 1,110 acres in Foss Valley, east of Napa Valley. The partners were Whitbread (United Kingdom; brewing), J. Bollinger (France; Champagne), and L & P Antinori (Italy; Chianti). By 1990, 460 acres of vines had been planted and 36,000 square feet of caves dug. To oversee the operation, the owners hired Richard PETERSON. But in 1990 he resigned after Allied-Lyons (Hiram Walker in the United States) had acquired a controlling interest from Whitbread and decided not to build a large winery then. For a while the scaled-down operation sold most of its grapes. In 1993 Antinori acquired ownership of the vineyards, but the WINE ALLIANCE (Hiram Walker) maintains the brand and manages the vineyards and winery.

Atlas Peak still sells a large portion of its grapes. About one-third of the vines are Sangiovese, which is the company's leading variety. Consenso is its Cabernet Sauvignon/Sangiovese blend. Annual sales are about 30,000 cases.

AU BON CLIMAT (BW 5107). This winery's name suggests a good place to raise grapes. James Clendenen founded the winery in Santa Barbara County in 1982. He concentrates on Pinot noir and Chardonnay, many with vineyard designations, in the Santa Maria Valley. He also sells wines, including a Nebbiolo and a Barbera, under the Il Podere dell'Olivos label. Other proprietary wines sold under this label are white blends, such as Bricco della Moano (Sauvignon blanc and

Chardonnay). Clendenen also markets wines under the VITA NOVA label with Robert Lindquist, who also sells wine under the QUPÉ label. Annual production at Au Bon Climat is about 10,000 cases.

AUDUBON CELLARS (BW 4562) began business in San Leandro in 1977. In 1984 it was moved to Berkeley and a new partnership took over in 1986. This group began marketing wines with labels based on Audubon's paintings of birds. The winery purchases grapes from a wide range of sources for its own label and for several of its custom-crush customers. The 200,000-gallon facility, with annual production of about 30,000 cases, is near Aquatic Park in Berkeley.

AUSTIN CELLARS. See LOS OLIVOS VINTNERS

AVA. See AMERICAN VITICULTURAL AREA

AVG. See ASSOCIATED VINTAGE GROUP

AXR#1. See ROOTSTOCK, RESISTANT

BABCOCK VINEYARDS (BW 5194), a winery in the Santa Ynez Valley west of Buellton in Santa Barbara County, founded in 1984. The Babcock family produces about 13,000 cases per year from 50 acres of vines, mostly planted to white varieties.

BACCALA, WILLIAM. See ZELLERBACH WINERY

BAG-IN-BOX-WINE: Introduced in the United States in 1980 from Australia, a method of delivering wine to the consumer in a large container, usually 3 liters or more, without spoilage. The wine is removed glass by glass from a plastic or foil bag that is in a heavy-duty carton; the bag gradually collapses without oxygen entering. FRANZIA pioneered the concept, but it took several years to catch on. Gallo, Canandaigua, and Golden State are now solidly in the field. The system is also used by restaurants and bars that sell inexpensive wine by the glass. In 1995 about 30 million units were sold in the United States.

BAILY VINEYARD & WINERY (BW 5347), founded in 1986 in the Temecula District of Riverside County. Baily produces about 4,000 cases of white wine per year.

BAJA (LOWER) CALIFORNIA, the lower portion of old California and today a part of Mexico, from Tijuana to Cape San Lucas. The first MISSION in Alta (upper) California was established at San Diego in 1769. The first vinifera grape cuttings that survived there were brought from Baja California a few years later. Only five of the fifteen missions in Baja California had vineyards and produced wine. Chief among these was Mission San Francisco Xavier under Father Juan UGARTE, who might be regarded as the first winemaker of any note in the Californias.

BALDINELLI VINEYARDS (BW 4913), a winery in Amador County near Plymouth, in the Sierra Foothills. Edward L. Baldinelli (1923–96) acquired the Dickson Vineyard there in 1972. Its Zinfandel vines were planted during Prohibition. In 1979 he and his partner John Miller bonded their 60,000-gallon winery and expanded the vineyard to include Cabernet Sauvignon and Sauvignon blanc. After Baldinelli's death the winery ceased to operate under this name. The bond was acquired by William Easton and now the winery is known as DOMAINE DE LA TERRE ROUGE.

BALDWIN, CHARLES A. (1861–1934), a wealthy San Franciscan who planted a 70-acre vineyard in Cupertino and built his winery there in 1895. He also built a fancy country estate around a replica of the Petit Trianon at Versailles. Phylloxera killed the vines and the earthquake in 1906 destroyed much of the Baldwin fortune. The buildings survive today

Las Flores Vineyard Claret
Vintage of 1890
Cupertino Sta. Clara Co. California.

Charles A. Baldwin marketed his wine under the Las Flores and Beaulieu Vineyard labels. His mansion on the estate is today the California History Center at De Anza College. (California History Center, De Anza College)

as part of De Anza College, the old winery serving as the college bookstore.

BALDWIN, ELIAS JACKSON (1828–1909). "Lucky" Baldwin made his fortune in the Comstock silver mines and in 1875 purchased 8,500 acres of land in southern California, in what is now Arcadia. This, his Santa Anita Ranch, is the site of a huge racetrack park today. By 1890 he had 1,200 acres in vines and, by the turn of the century, had earned a solid reputation for his sweet wines and brandy. His aged ANGELICA once fooled a panel of English connoisseurs who identified it as a "delicate and rich Madeira," and there were still bottles of Baldwin brandy to be found in private cellars after Prohibition. A. R. MORROW thought it excellent. He leased out the rancho and wine operation in 1901. The ruins of the old distillery can be visited on the grounds of the racetrack.

Frona E. Wait, *Wines and Vines of California*, (1889; reprint; Berkeley, Calif.: Howell-North, 1973) 179–83.

BALLENTINE. After Prohibition **John J. Ballentine** had owned and operated the DEER PARK WINERY on lower Howell Mountain. In

1992 another generation of Ballentines resurrected the family label. The family owns 110 acres of vineyard above St. Helena. When they opened their little **Ballentine Winery** in 1995, they were granted their grandfather's old bond number (BW 3595). Production of about 4,000 cases emphasizes Merlot and Zinfandel.

BALVERNE VINEYARDS (BW 4884). The 200-acre vineyard near Windsor in Sonoma was planted in 1974. The winery was bonded in 1980 and eventually had a capacity of 230,000 gallons. In 1992 the winery went out of business and the vineyard was acquired by SONOMA-CUTRER.

BALZER, ROBERT LAURENCE. His book *California's Best Wines* (1948) drew early attention to the state's few premium wine producers. Since then he has written several popular books about wine in California.

BANCROFT, HUBERT HOWE (1832–1918). After arriving in San Francisco from Ohio in 1852, Bancroft opened a book and stationery store that grew into an important publishing house. By the 1860s he had also amassed a huge collection of books and other materials relating to the history of the New World, and particularly to California. His seven-volume *History of California* (1886–90), with more than 150 references to wine and viticulture, is a useful resource on the state's early wine industry. He and his staff also interviewed and created short biographies of several pioneers of the state's wine industry, among them Charles KOHLER and Arpad HARASZTHY. In 1905 he sold his great collection to the University of California as the nucleus of the Bancroft Library on the Berkeley campus. It is the most important repository of primary materials on the history of wine in California before Prohibition.

BANCROFT VINEYARDS. James Bancroft began buying land on Howell Mountain in

1969 and planted vines in the early 1980s. The Cabernet Sauvignon and Merlot grapes from his 90-acre vineyard have become important elements in BERINGER'S private reserve wines. Some Chardonnay is produced under the Bancroft label at a local winery.

BANDIERA WINERY (BW 3998) was founded in 1937 in Cloverdale, Sonoma County, by Emilio Bandiera. For years a small-scale bulk producer, the winery was taken over in 1957 by Emilio's son, Rolo, who produced some varietals, but on a small scale. In 1975 new owners sold wine briefly under the Arroyo Sonoma, Potter Valley, and Sage Creek labels. Today's owners acquired the winery in 1980 and concentrate on moderately priced Cabernet Sauvignon, Chardonnay, and White Zinfandel, with annual production of about 100,000 cases. Bandiera is currently owned by the California Wine Co., a group of British investors that, in 1996, bought STONEGATE WINERY in Napa.

BARBERA. A variety of red wine grape from northwestern Italy first imported to northern California by John DOYLE. His first Barbera vintage was in 1884 from vines grown in Cupertino. In the 1890s the ITALIAN SWISS COLONY used the variety for several of its successful red table wines. Its deep color, brilliant tartness, and sharp tannins and astringency, coupled with a luscious grapiness contributed to the Colony's success before Prohibition. But the Barbera did not regain its popularity after Repeal. In recent years a few producers, particularly Louis MARTINI since 1954, have brought out good examples. But in 1997 only 277 acres were planted in all the coastal valleys and the Sierra Foothills, slightly more than half in Amador County, where a small Barbera revival is taking place; In 1994 MONTEVIÑA WINERY made 7,500 cases of Barbera. There were, however, almost 10,000 acres planted in the Central Valley, where the Barbera's color and acid are used to raise the quality of inexpensive red table wines. In 1996, 99,303 tons of Barbera were crushed, 109 percent of the tonnage crushed in 1990. Barbera is now California's number five red-wine variety.

BAREFOOT CELLARS (BW 5626). In 1988 Davis BYNUM* sold his popular Barefoot label to investors who have been producing medium priced varietals at their 300,000-gallon facility in Geyserville. They have also brought out a

TABLE 3. BARBERA GRAPES, SELECTED COUNTIES

YEAR	AMADOR	STANISLAUS	MERCED	(ACRES) MADERA	FRESNO	KERN	TOTAL
1968	*	52	773	0	83	0	1,214
1971	2	1,324	1,026	414	1,822	1,674	7,529
1974	5	1,729	1,363	3,751	5,694	4,313	20,576
1978	5	1,872	1,216	3,784	5,891	3,702	21,085
1982	10	1,636	1,173	3,789	4,891	3,326	17,422
1986	16	1,116	1,131	2,779	4,427	2,202	13,417
1990	34	1,199	1,109	2,608	4,168	1,027	10,666
1994	102	902	911	2,418	5,326	905	11,283
1997	146	837	690	1,914	5,756	904	11,133

* Nothing is recorded in the official statistics, but it is believed that some Barbera was being grown in Amador County in 1968.
SOURCE: California Agricultural Statistics Service, Sacramento, Calif.

low-alcohol line under the California Beau label. Total annual production is about 200,000 cases. In 1993 they were forced to change the label of their Chateau La Feet line to Chateau La Foot by *the* Château Lafite in Bordeaux.

BARENGO CELLARS (BW 3877). The 2 million-gallon Acampo Winery near Lodi was founded in 1934, although the winery structure dates from 1868. Dino Barengo bought the operation in 1944, changed the name, and ran it until 1976. During those years, he produced lots of bulk wine and made many good varietals, some of which, such as Muscadelle du Bordelais and Muscat of Pantelleria, are rarely seen anywhere.

Since 1976, the facility has had four different owners and was closed after the 1994 season.

BARGETTO'S SANTA CRUZ WINERY (BW 3859). No other producer has been making Santa Cruz Mountain wine as long as Bargetto has, and yet the winery is outside the official viticultural area, on the main street of Soquel. It was founded by the Bargetto family, Philip (1874–1936) and John (1885–1964), and for years produced sturdy rustic wines from grapes grown in the Santa Cruz Mountains and in the Santa Clara Valley. In the 1960s, under John's son, Lawrence (1922–82), the

winery began emphasizing a wide range of varietals and fruit wines. Since the seventies the line has been narrowed with more emphasis placed on the premium end, where Bargetto Chardonnay has been particularly successful. By the early 1990s annual sales had passed the 35,000-case mark. In 1992 the Bargetto family began planting Chardonnay, Pinot noir, and Merlot in their 40-acre vineyard near Corralitos, in the Santa Cruz Mountains, east of the winery.

BARON HERZOG, a premium kosher table wine made by the Royal Kedem Wine Company in New York. Annually, the company produces about 650,000 cases of kosher wine, of which about 150,000 cases sold under the Baron Herzog and WEINSTOCK labels are produced from California grapes.

BARON WINERY (BW 5373), in the Paso Robles District, was founded in 1985 by James Kolb and Thomas Baron. Along with several varietals, chiefly Cabernet Sauvignon, they produce a Firehouse Red and Firehouse White. Annual production is about 3,000 cases.

BARREL, a wine container, usually made of staves of white oak bound with metal hoops, and holding between 50 and 60 gallons, but

The finishing touches are given to a wine barrel being constructed in the Napa Valley from oak staves imported from France.

sometimes less. Before World War II, the barrel had a very different function in the California wine industry. Until the 1940s, almost all wine in California left wineries in barrels, casks or tank cars to be bottled in urban centers throughout the country. Most of the wine sold at retail in California was bottled in San Francisco. Only a few premium wineries, such as INGLENOOK, which was the first, bottled wine on the premises. Much wine was sold at retail from barrels in grocery stores, wine shops, and saloons.

In the late 1950s the function of the barrel began to change radically, as a few California producers began employing traditional French methods of aging wine in small barrels. Today many of the best wines are barrel aged and pick up flavors from the new barrels that enhance their appeal. Both American and French oak barrels are used. Some French oak barrels are now assembled in California. Some wineries prescribe certain specifics when ordering barrels. One such is the amount of charred "toast" developed on the inside of the staves when they are heated for assembly. Cabernet Sauvignon, Pinot noir, Zinfandel, Chardonnay, and Sauvignon blanc are the wines considered to be the best candidates for small-barrel aging. Some producers put the two white varieties through their primary fermentation in new oak barrels for the special flavors the wines derive from the process.

With the rising cost of barrels, several techniques have been developed to extend the life of a container's oakiness. Sometimes the inside of the barrel is shaved to expose a new wood surface; sometimes interstaves of new oak are inserted. Some producers of less-expensive wine use oak chips for flavor. In 1995 a French oak barrel cost about $700, approximately double the cost of one made from American oak; a pound of oak chips costs about $4.00. See also OAK.

BARRETT. James L. Barrett has been in charge at Chateau Montelena since 1969. His son, **James P. (Bo) Barrett**, who has been the winemaker there since 1982, married Heidi Peterson, Richard PETERSON's daughter. **Heidi Barrett** is today one of Napa's leading winemakers and enological consultants. She also makes a small amount of Sangiovese under her own label. She is devoted to aquatics; and her label is La Sirena, Italian for siren, or mermaid.

BARTHOLOMEW, FRANK. See BUENA VISTA WINERY

BARTHOLOMEW PARK WINERY (BW 64). On land that was once part of Agoston HARASZTHY's BUENA VISTA, the Sonoma Valley Hospital was built in the 1920s. Frank Bartholomew bought the Buena Vista estate in 1941 and later established HACIENDA CELLARS* in 1973 after he sold the Buena Vista Winery, but not all of its land. The old hospital became the Hacienda winery. After the Hacienda brand was sold in 1992, the old building became the Sonoma Valley Wine Museum and the Bartholomew Park Winery, where production began in 1994, with about 4,500 cases per year, mostly of Cabernet Sauvignon and Merlot.

BARTOLUCCI, an important winegrowing family in Napa; they acquired vineyard land in 1922 and in 1933 opened their winery in Oakville. By 1970 the winery had a capacity of 600,000 gallons. In 1971 the facility was sold to the ill-fated OAKVILLE VINEYARDS. In 1979 Louis and Andrea Bartolucci founded MONT ST. JOHN CELLARS in the Carneros district.

BARTON, ROBERT (1840–91), made his money as a businessman and engineer in San Francisco. In 1881 he founded the largest of several wine estates that were established in Fresno in the 1880s. By 1884 Barton's 525-acre vineyard was producing 225,000 gallons of mostly fortified wine, and by 1885, his wine shipments to the East Coast were totaling over 200 carloads per year. He sold the operation to a Scottish syndicate in 1887 and managed it until his death. The huge wine factory was destroyed by fire in 1915.

BATF. See BUREAU OF ALCOHOL, TOBACCO, AND FIREARMS

BAZIN, JEAN-FRANÇOIS, a Burgundian author and publicist whose book *Le vin de Californie,* published in 1984, was the first French book on California wine.

BEAR CREEK VINEYARD ASSOCIATION (BW 3865). In 1934 grape growers in the Lodi area formed Bear Creek as a cooperative winery in response to low grape prices. By 1953 its capacity had grown to 5 million gallons. It was one of the original members of GUILD WINERIES.

BEARD, JOHN LYMAN (1845–1903), an important winegrower in the Mission San Jose area. His father, E. L. Beard, was one of the original American settlers there in the 1840s, acquiring vineyard and orchard land from the old mission. Beard's Marciana Vineyard produced about 50,000 gallons in the 1880s.

BEAR MOUNTAIN WINERY (BW 4389), a huge bulk winery founded as a cooperative in 1966 by a group of grape growers in Kern County. It is on part of the Di Giorgio Ranch, which was founded in 1919. In the 1950s, 5,600 acres of grapes, mostly table and raisin varieties, were being grown on the ranch but, by the 1960s, most of the land had been sold off to independent growers because water from federal irrigation projects was not available to owners of more than 160 acres of land.

In June 1978 John Labatt, Ltd., a Canadian brewing company, bought the facility, called it Lamont Winery, and in 1982 began making bulk table wines for Anheuser-Busch. These wines were sold, under the Master Cellars label, mostly to restaurants and bars. In 1986 Anheuser-Busch acquired the winery and later, in 1991, renamed it Heck Cellars after acquiring KORBEL CHAMPAGNE CELLARS from the HECK family.

Today the 28 million-gallon complex produces table and fortified wines, coolers, concentrate, and brandy.

BEAUCANON (BW 5391), a winery in the Rutherford area of Napa Valley owned by the deConinck family of Bordeaux. It began operations in 1987. The winemaker Louis deConinck grew up at Château Canon in Fronsac and has been making wine since he was fifteen years old. He makes a wide range of varietal wines with annual production of about 25,000 cases.

BEAUJOLAIS. See GAMAY

BEAULIEU VINEYARD (BV) (BW 71). Georges de Latour (1858–1940) came to California from Périgord in 1883 with an academic background in chemistry that drew him to the cream of tartar business, first in San Jose and then in Healdsburg, buying the tartar crystal from local wineries (see also TARTARIC ACID). He went into the wine business, first as a distiller in Sonoma and then as a winegrower in Rutherford, in the Napa Valley, where he set up a tartar plant in 1900.

The grape planting boom after 1900 and the rising profits from wine encouraged his entrepreneurial zeal. Over the next decade he acquired several choice vineyard properties and centered his winemaking in the old EWER AND ATKINSON plant in Rutherford. In 1906 he began using the Beaulieu brand name and by 1913 had a production capacity of 300,000 gallons. In 1915 he owned 240 acres of vines, half of which were planted to Cabernet Sauvignon, Sauvignon blanc and Sémillon, making him the largest grower of premium varietals in the Napa Valley.

When Prohibition arrived he continued to prosper by producing altar wines for the Archdiocese of San Francisco, whose custom he acquired in 1908. This business was expanded throughout the country by the early twenties. At Repeal, de Latour had a good collection of aged wines, a national sales network, and an excellent reputation for high quality. In 1938, after an expansion of the national program had led to concern over the quality of Beaulieu Vineyard wines shipped east, de Latour hired André TCHELISTCH-EFF* to modernize the winery's production facilities and techniques. Specifically, his first task was to improve the chemical stability of Beaulieu Vineyard's nationally distributed wines. He brought more fame to Beaulieu, particularly for its Cabernet Sauvignon, and under his leadership the winery consistently won awards.

In 1969 the de Latour family sold Beaulieu to HEUBLEIN, which greatly expanded production but did not debase the old label, as it had at INGLENOOK. In the nineties, BV's production has been focused on Cabernet Sauvignon, Pinot noir, Chardonnay and Sauvignon blanc. The Private Reserve Cabernet Sauvignon, a jewel in the crown of Napa Valley winegrowing since 1936, still has an excellent reputation. The winery's 300 acres of land in Carneros have added to the quality of its Chardonnay and Pinot noir. Total acreage is now about 1,100. Annual production is about 700,000 cases and rising.

In 1994 Beaulieu expanded its moderately priced Beautour line with wines from grapes grown in Napa and the Central Coast. These were priced a bit higher than FIGHTING VARIETALS. The new Signet line includes trendy varietals such as Mourvèdre and Sangiovese, and, a first in the winery's history, a Zinfandel (1994).

Leigh Knowles, *Beaulieu Vineyards, from Family to Corporate Ownership* (Regional Oral History Office, Bancroft Library, 1990).

James T. Lapsley, *Bottled Poetry: Napa Winemaking from Prohibition to the Modern Era* (Berkeley, Calif.: University of California Press, 1996).

BECKSTOFFER, W. ANDREW, with more than 2,100 acres of vines in Napa and Mendocino counties, including over 400 in the Carneros region, the largest independent vineyard owner in northern California. In recent years he has acquired the famous Vineyards no. 3 and 4 from BEAULIEU VINEYARD. Today he sells grapes to between thirty and forty of northern California's best wineries.

He came to Napa in 1969 as an executive with HEUBLEIN and helped negotiate the company's purchase of Beaulieu. Then he set up a subsidiary to farm and manage vineyards for the conglomerate, an operation he eventually acquired. During those years he introduced drip irrigation to Napa. From 1988 to 1991 some of his grapes went into wine sold under his own Fremont Creek label. When the brand was discontinued in 1993, production had reached about 25,000 cases per year.

L. Walker, "Andy Beckstoffer," *Wines & Vines*, October 1996, 16–19.

BÉCLAN. A variety of red-wine grape from the French Jura introduced to California before Prohibition. It may be a relative of the Peloursin (from the Isère River region in France), which is also known as the Gros Béclan and is the variety from which the DURIF was developed as a seedling. All those varieties may be related to what Californians call PETITE SIRAH.

In the 1960s, there were about 100 acres of Béclan in California, some in Sonoma but most in the Central Valley. In 1981 the variety disappeared from state statistics.

BEL ARBORS. See FETZER VINEYARDS

BELLA LUNA. See CHARLES F. SHAW WINERY

BELLA NAPOLI WINERY (BW 4126) was founded in 1934. The 100,000-gallon winery in Manteca sells its products under the Vine Flow and Family Vineyard labels.

BELLEROSE VINEYARD (BW 4955). In the Dry Creek area of Sonoma, the winery, founded in 1978, is on the property that was once the home of a winery belonging to Everett and Marion Wise, which dated from the 1880s. Annual production is about 10,000 cases and the principal varietals are Zinfandel and Cabernet Sauvignon.

BELL, THEODORE (1872–1922), the son of a vineyard owner in St. Helena and a gun-toting district attorney, famous for shooting it out with the notorious desperado Buck English. But he was more famous in the California wine community for his leadership of the industry. He was elected to Congress in 1902 where he led the fight for a pure wine bill and against prohibition. He was the unsuccessful Democratic candidate for governor in 1912. From then until his death he led the legal fight against state and national prohibition as counsel for the California Grape Protective Association, the wine industry's chief organization weapon in the fight against prohibition. He died in an automobile accident in 1922.

BELVEDERE WINERY (BW 5051). Peter Friedman founded the Belvedere Wine Company in 1979 and designated his varietal wines by vineyard. He also had a line of medium-priced wines, the Discovery Series. Since 1989 William R. Hambrecht has had a controlling interest in the operation, which now includes production under the Peterson Winery label. He also controls more than 500 acres of vineyard land in Sonoma and Mendocino counties that supplies a large portion of the grapes for the operation. He now owns the winery, which has a capacity of 400,000 gallons and produces about 75,000 cases annually. The second label

is Grove Street. The entire operation now does business as the Hambrecht Wine Group.

BENESSERE VINEYARDS. See CHARLES F. SHAW WINERY

BEN LOMOND. In 1988 a petition by James Beauregard, a vineyard owner in the Bonny Doon area, to have Ben Lomond Mountain recognized as a VITICULTURAL AREA was approved by the BATF. His view was historical, in that, before Prohibition, one of the most important wineries in the Santa Cruz Mountains had been located here in the highlands north of Felton. The Ben Lomond Wine Co. was founded in 1885 and became the center of commercial wine production in the Santa Cruz area. Annual production reached 100,000 gallons before a fire and Prohibition closed down the huge operation in 1918.

BENMORE VALLEY, a viticultural area in Lake County that received appellation status in 1991. Its 170 acres of grapes are mostly Chardonnay, planted by the GEYSER PEAK WINERY.

BENNION, DAVID R. See RIDGE VINEYARDS

BENZIGER FAMILY WINERY (BW 4911). In 1980 Bruno Benziger (1925–89) and his family founded their GLEN ELLEN WINERY* on the lower slopes of Sonoma Mountain. (The property had been the winery estate of Julius Wegner before Prohibition.) Benziger's goal was to make affordable wine of good quality. His first Proprietor's Reserve, 12,000 cases of Chardonnay and Sauvignon Blanc, was released in 1982. Soon the Benzigers were buying and blending bulk wines. Other wines were made in rented space at MARTINI & PRATI and DELICATO. By 1987 Benziger was selling more than 1,500,000 cases a year. His marketing background in wine and spirits had prepared him to be the master of the FIGHTING VARIETAL category. His timing was perfect, as there was a surplus in California of such varietals as Chardonnay and Cabernet Sauvignon in these years. In 1986 the Benzigers brought out their lower-priced M. G. Vallejo brand. By 1988 total sales were up to 3,250,000 cases. In that year they brought out their premium line of varietals, using the family name on the label. When Bruno died in 1989, his son Michael was already general manager of the operation, having been directly involved in running the business since the very first days. In 1993 the family sold the Glen Ellen and M. G. Vallejo brands to HEUBLEIN, but kept the premium Benziger line, which amounts to about 165,000 cases per year, principally of Cabernet Sauvignon, Chardonnay, and Merlot.

BERGFELD WINERY (BW 3565). When the NAPA VALLEY COOPERATIVE WINERY began producing a premium line of varietal table wine in 1987, the facility at which it was made was called Bergfeld. An old winery dating from 1885, on the property near St. Helena had once borne this name. When GOLDEN STATE VINTNERS* bought the winery in 1994, the new owners continued to use the Bergfeld brand. But their Napa operation is now listed in the wine industry directory as Golden State Vintners Napa.

BERG, HAROLD W. (1910–84). After years of work in the California wine industry, Berg became a member of the faculty of the University of California at Davis in 1949. A specialist in the chemical stability of wine, he was chairman of the Department of Viticulture and Enology from 1966 until 1973.

BERINGER VINEYARDS (BW 46). Jacob Beringer (1844–1915) and his brother, Frederick (1840–1901), were born in the German city of Mainz and knew winegrowing and coopering before they came to New York in the 1860s. In 1869 Jacob came to Napa and went to work for Charles Krug, whom he served as foreman until 1878; Frederick stayed in New York. The

brothers pooled their resources and in 1875 bought the 97-acre ranch across the road from the Krug place. Chinese laborers built a cellar and dug tunnels into the mountainside. By 1878 Jacob was producing 100,000 gallons of wine a year. In 1884 Frederick eventually came west and had his impressive Rhine House built on the property. It is still a tourist attraction. The Beringer vineyards were named Los Hermanos for the two brothers. The winery played an important part in winegrowing in Napa right through Prohibition. By 1936 its production was back up to 200,000 gallons and it was still in family hands. But the Beringers could not generate the capital to maintain the quality of their wine in the period after World War II. In 1970 Beringer Vineyards was sold to the Swiss Nestlé Corporation, and run by Nestlé's Wine World subsidiary, which also acquired many other wine properties in California. In 1995 Wine World was sold to a group of investors for about $300 million; see BERINGER WINE ESTATES.

In the 1970s the quality of the Beringer wines was revived by Nestlé's patient flow of capital and the winemaking and organizational skills of Myron NIGHTINGALE,* who was in charge of production until 1983. Nestlé expanded Beringer's vineyard holdings in Napa and Sonoma to almost 2,000 acres, and produced well over 2 million cases per year.

Beringer's Cabernet Sauvignon, particularly the private reserve, has gained world-class stature. But far more profit is generated by sales of White Zinfandel, which amounted to about a million cases in 1996, almost one-third of Beringer's production. Since 1985 the Napa Ridge label has been used for very successful, moderately priced varietals, but the company's management has not allowed this label to be associated with the Beringer brand.

E. Michael Moone, *Management and Marketing at Beringer Vineyards and Wine World, Inc.* (Regional Oral History Office, Bancroft Library, 1990).

The Rhine House on the Beringer estate has become one of the chief tourist attractions in the Napa Valley. It dates from 1884.

BERINGER WINE ESTATES. In 1970 the Nestlé Corporation of Switzerland acquired Beringer Vineyards. Later several other important brands and properties were added: MERIDIAN (producing 475,000 cases a year), CHATEAU SOUVERAIN (125,000 cases), NAPA RIDGE (750,000 cases), and CHATEAU ST. JEAN (200,000 cases). These and Beringer Vineyards were controlled by Nestlé's American corporate subsidiary, Wine World, Inc., which also owned about 6,000 acres of vineyard land in California.

In 1995, Nestlé sold the entire operation to a group of investors. The name was changed to Beringer Wine Estates (BWE). Since then, the organization has acquired STAGS' LEAP WINERY, and the combined capacity of BWE is now about 16 million gallons.

BERNARDUS VINEYARDS AND WINERY (BW 5568). When Robert TALBOTT moved his winery operation to the Salinas Valley from the Carmel Valley in 1989, the Dutch business man Bernardus Pon bought Talbott's Carmel place and a 220-acre piece of land nearby in the rugged Cachagua area of the valley. He planted 60 acres of vines, mostly red Bordeaux varieties and Sauvignon blanc. In 1992 he bought grapes and produced his first estate wine the next year. In 1994 he bought the nearby Domaine de Clarck winery (BW 5516) which had specialized in Pinot noir. Pon produced 7,500 cases in 1993, but production increased to almost 40,000 cases by the mid-1990s.

BIALE VINEYARDS (BW 5872). Just north of Napa City the Biale family owns a 17-acre vineyard most of which was planted to Zinfandel in the 1930s. In 1991 they brought out a small quantity of highly praised Zinfandel under their own label and have since raised production to about 3,000 cases a year. In 1995 they made Zinfandel from vines on the historic G. B. CRANE* ranch, where Napa's reputation for fine wine began in the 1860s.

BIANCHI VINEYARDS (BW 4662). A winery in Kerman in Fresno County, founded in 1974. The 1,500,000-gallon plant produces about 250,000 cases of moderately priced generic and varietal wines under the Bianchi and Vista Verde labels.

BIANE, PHILO B. Long a leader of the wine industry in southern California, Biane revived the BROOKSIDE VINEYARD COMPANY in the 1950s. Earlier he had worked for Paul GARRETT and A. R. MORROW. Since 1975 Biane has produced cream sherry at his **Ranch de Philo** (BWC 4689) in Alta Loma, near Cucamonga, where he has a small vineyard of Mission variety grapes.

> Philo Biane, *Wine Making in Southern California and Recollections of Fruit Industries* (Regional Oral History Office, Bancroft Library, 1972).

BIEN NACIDO VINEYARDS, a vineyard complex covering almost 900 acres in the Santa Maria Valley. It is chiefly planted to Chardonnay and Pinot noir, but there are also 45 acres of Syrah. Bien Nacido's 256-acre propagation nursery is the largest in California. The owners' intent is to make its product live up to the vineyard's name, which means well born in Spanish. The nursery supplies huge amounts of budwood for the propagation of young vineyards throughout the state. In 1995 the owners opened a CUSTOM-CRUSHING plant.

BIOLETTI, FREDERIC T. (1865–1939). Little is known about Bioletti as a young man. His mother, an Englishwoman, married J. H. DRUMMOND, whose will contained a spiteful attack on Bioletti. He worked in the Viticulture Department of the University of California at Berkeley in the 1890s and between 1901 and 1904 taught in the Cape Colony, South

Africa. He returned to Berkeley and then taught viticulture at the University of California at Davis, retiring in 1935. His scholarship covered most aspects of viticulture and enology, but perhaps his most important contributions were to the education of such students as WILLIAM V. CRUESS and A. J. WINKLER. Ever concerned about practical questions needing scientific answers in the vineyard and cellar, he was a frequent and useful visitor to all of the state's wine districts. Bioletti's years are a link between Eugene HILGARD's tenure at the university and those later leaders whose research since Repeal has helped raise the quality of California wine to its present level. See also VINA.

BIRDS, in some areas of California a scourge in the vineyards. Techniques to discourage their depredations are an important aspect of the scientific work done in recent years to raise production. Where huge tracts of vineyard cover the land, growers can afford to feed the birds. But in small vineyards, particularly those in mountainous areas or surrounded by forested land, carbide sound guns, recorded distress calls, plastic covers, chemical repellents, and shotguns are often used. The chief culprits in California are starlings and linnets.

BISCEGLIA BROTHERS WINE COMPANY. The Bisceglia family began making wine near San Jose in 1880 and later owned several large bulk facilities in the Central Valley. For a short time after Repeal they owned Napa's historic GREYSTONE WINERY. Their last facility, the 2 million-gallon Yosemite Cooperative Winery in Madera, was sold in 1974 to the huge CANANDAIGUA WINE COMPANY, which now markets a line of inexpensive wines under the Bisceglia label.

BLACK, HOLLIS (?–1965). In 1934 Black revived his family winery (BW 328), which had been founded in 1905, and was located east of the Russian River south of Cloverdale. He was an industry leader and one of the founders of the WINE INSTITUTE. In 1945 he rebuilt the old winery and added to its capacity, bringing it to 330,000 gallons by 1952. For years he supplied wine to the ITALIAN SWISS COLONY and was particularly noted for his Petite Sirah. A few months after he closed the winery and retired in 1965 he was killed in an automobile accident. In 1979 the winery was opened again briefly as Cordtz Brothers Cellars.

BLACK MALVOISIE. The name used in California until recently for what is now known to be the Cinsaut (often spelled Cinsault) grape of southern France. There it is considered a good grape for blending, adding substance to ordinary bulk wines in the Hérault and Gard, and complexity to some Châteauneuf-du-Pape. It was imported into California in the 1860s, but its early history here is obscure. In the 1870s it became popular as a CLARET grape and was often used to blend with Zinfandel. But growers tended to let it hang too long, producing a dull, flabby wine. By the 1890s it was in general disrepute. During Prohibition some old vineyards survived and the grape gained some stature among a few Italian winegrowers here, some of whom sold it as a varietal up to the 1960s, sometimes labeled Malvasia Nera. In 1971 there were still 810 acres in the state, mostly in the Central Valley. When interest in Rhône varieties for California blossomed in the 1980s, the variety was rediscovered and appeared here and there as the varietal, Cinsaut. But in 1997 only 92 acres remained in the state. These produced about 450 tons of grapes.

BLACK MOUNTAIN VINEYARD See J. W. MORRIS WINERY

BLACK MUSCAT. There are many muscat-flavored grapes with dark skins, but most are for the table rather than the wine cellar. In California the Muscat Hamburg (or Black Ham-

bourg) was an exception. It was used here before and after Prohibition in dessert wines. The NOVITIATE OF LOS GATOS produced a very popular Black Muscat wine from this grape after World War II. After 1991 the variety disappeared from the state's official statistics. For many years previously there had been fewer than 100 acres listed, mostly in the Central Valley.

BLACK SHEEP VINTNERS (BW 4705). Founded in 1976 as Chispa Cellars, the winery in Calaveras County was acquired in 1989 by David Olson, who produces about 2,000 cases a year, mainly Zinfandel and Sauvignon blanc.

BLANC DE BLANCS, sparkling wines made solely from white grapes. In California the implication is that a large portion of the wine is Chardonnay, but there is no legal requirement.

BLANC DE NOIRS, sparkling, or still wine made from red wine grapes in a style that extracts little color from the dark skins and usually leaves a wine with a hint of pink. It is possible with some varieties, such as Pinot noir, to produce a white wine. White Zinfandel is almost always pink, but with time may turn to a yellowish orange. Some still blancs de noirs are so rosily pink that they might more properly be termed ROSÉ; see also BLUSH.

In California the first successful sparkling wine was Arpad Haraszthy's ECLIPSE, whose CUVÉE from the late 1860s to the 1880s was predominantly Zinfandel made as a blanc de noirs. In 1905 Paul MASSON began marketing the first Californian blanc de noirs sparkling wine made from Pinot noir, which he named Oeil de Perdrix (Eye of the Partridge). Today many of California's top sparkling wine producers make their blancs de noirs from Pinot noir grapes.

BLENDING. Today winemakers in California blend wines to enhance the complexity of flavor. In premium wines much of the blending follows the tradition of European producers, particularly those of Bordeaux, where Cabernet Sauvignon is regularly combined with Merlot, and Sauvignon blanc with Sémillon. The blending traditions of Champagne have also caught on. There, not only varieties but also wines of different vintages and vineyards are blended to raise the perceived quality.

The blending of JUG WINES grown in hot climates is common in California. In the Central Valley, varieties such as Barbera and Chenin blanc are selected for their acidity and flavor and used to improve those varieties widely grown in this region for their heavy yields, such as French Colombard and Grenache. Throughout the state, until the 1960s, this was almost the only reason for blending sound wines. It was also common then to improve poor-quality or chemically flawed wines by blending, a practice not unknown today.

As early as the 1860s winemakers knew that the ubiquitous Mission grape would not make a satisfactory table wine. Blending with darker colored varieties was the answer, unless chemicals and dark fruit juices were used. In the 1880s many premium producers worked on blends in the style of Bordeaux, the Rhône, and Champagne. German-style wines were sometimes pure varietals, but most were blends of the better White Riesling and Sylvaner with "stretchers" such as Burger and Palomino. For such concoctions, it was also common to blend in a small quantity of white MUSCAT wine to give the final product a brighter, more fruity flavor. Jacob SCHRAM called the wines he blended in this way *verbessert,* or rectified. The production of VARIETAL wines, labeled as such, was quite rare. Most Californian wines were blends traveling under GENERIC names such as burgundy, claret, rhine wine, and chablis. This propensity for blending changed after Repeal as more and more producers brought out varietals in which a specific grape variety was dominant, but these, too, were

mostly blends, as the dominant grape need constitute no more than 51 percent of the wine in the bottle. Today the requirement is 75 percent. This higher standard has caused problems, because some producers are interested in blends in which no variety dominates to that extent. The result has often been interesting proprietary names on labels, such as JOSEPH PHELPS's Insignia. For example, the 1983 Insignia blend was 60 percent Cabernet Sauvignon, 20 percent Merlot, and 20 percent Cabernet franc. The creation of a special industry term, MERITAGE, was intended to solve this problem. Some producers simply use a description such as Red Wine on their labels and then carefully spell out the particular blend.

BLUSH. The rise in popularity of pink California wines in the 1980s, particularly of White Zinfandel, caused the need for a quasi-generic term other than ROSÉ, particularly when a varietal was not indicated on the label. "Blush" was that term, invented by MILL CREEK VINEYARDS IN Sonoma in 1977. In 1988 a survey of the industry revealed that 28 percent of wine produced in California the previous year fell into the Blush category.

BOARD OF STATE VITICULTURAL COMMISSIONERS. See STATE VITICULTURAL COMMISSION

BODY, an almost tactile descriptor used of wines with a high alcohol and/or sugar content.

BOEGER WINERY (BW 4652). Located just east of Placerville in El Dorado County, Greg Boeger's winery, founded in 1973, was the first in the county since Prohibition (see photo on page 101). It is on the site of an old winery, but those vineyards were converted to pear and apple orchards years ago. Boeger produces a wide range of varietals, mostly Cabernet Sauvignon and Chardonnay, totaling about 15,000 cases per year. He also makes a lower-priced Hangtown Red and Hangtown Gold. Boeger, a grandson of Anton Nichelini, is also the winemaker at NICHELINI WINERY in Napa.

BOGLE VINEYARDS (BW 4937). Grapes and wine are but two of the products of the huge Bogle family estate in the Clarksburg area of the delta region. Much of the production from the 650-acre vineyard is sold, but since 1979 the estate has been producing wine as well, about 95,000 cases a year of mostly moderately priced varietals, principally Chardonnay and Merlot.

BOISSET, JEAN-CLAUDE (BW 5678), a large-scale Burgundian wine producer who also markets California wines under his Christophe and Juliesse labels. In 1992 he acquired the WILLIAM WHEELER and LYETH Winery brands. Sales of these wines are about 290,000 cases per year. This expanding company operates under the name Boisset Wines USA. See also NÉGOCIANT.

BON, CHARLES A. See CHAUCHÉ & BON

BONDED WINERY (BW). Before Prohibition wineries were required to post bond as surety that taxes would be paid to the federal government for wine produced. Numbers were assigned to the wineries, but during Prohibition the records of these bonds were destroyed. At Repeal wineries that could prove their origin were allowed to claim their old numbers. But neither historical records nor anyone's memory at the BATF can explain how some wineries acquired certain very low numbers. Since Repeal each new winery has been given a number that has some relationship to when the winery went into business, actually producing wine by fermenting grapes.

There were about 600 bonded wineries in California at Prohibition. In the 1930s there were about 300, but the number had dropped to 227 by 1965. Since then, the number in California has been rising steadily, up to more than 700 in the 1990s.

It is often difficult to tell exactly how old a winery is from its BW number; but there is something of a correlation:

Up to 3499:	Wineries that, usually, predate Prohibition
3500–3999:	1933 to 1936
4000–4299:	1937 to 1940
4300–4449:	1941 to 1950
4450–4499:	1951 to 1965
4500–4599:	1966 to 1972
4600–4799:	1973 to 1977
4800–5199:	1978 to 1983
5200–5499:	1984 to 1988
From 5500:	Since 1988

A **bonded wine cellar** (BWC) is a facility in which some wine production steps may take place, such as blending or bottling, but the primary fermentation does not. Some wineries in California add the letters CA to their BW number, but this addition has no special significance.

Many wine labels indicate a brand name that includes the word "winery" or "cellars" when neither, in fact, physically exists. Something labeled Blue Ridge Cellars could be one of a dozen brands produced at a huge wine factory in the Central Valley. The BATF does not require the BW number on a wine label, so it is often difficult to figure out where a wine was actually produced. Also, CUSTOM-CRUSH* wineries supply facilities for small-scale winemakers who do not have the capital resources to put up their own facilities. This is another way that several really unrelated brands may come from one bonded winery. In 1990 the BATF began issuing an alternate-premises license, which allows more than one producer to operate in one location under the same BW number. It is particularly confusing for many consumers to see brands such as Napa Ridge and Rutherford Vineyard on wines with a California AVA, indicating that the wine was probably produced by a large industrial winery from grapes grown in places other than those indicated by the brand name.

BONESIO WINERY (BW 2908), a country winery in the Hecker Pass area of Santa Clara County, founded in 1916. It was noted for its good varietal wines particularly its vintage-dated Grignolino, as early as the 1940s. In 1976 the winery was purchased by Nikola Chargin, who has since operated it as **Kirigin Cellars**.

BONFORT'S WINE AND SPIRIT CIRCULAR, a prestigious trade publication much interested in the California wine industry, published in New York City from 1871 to 1919. It is an important source for the history of California wine.

BONNY DOON. Since the 1870s a winegrowing area of the Santa Cruz Mountains above Felton. After Prohibition its surviving vineyards moved professors at the University of California to name it a winegrowing area with great potential. Since the 1960s, several new vineyards and a few small wineries have been established there. In recent years PIERCE'S DISEASE has devastated several vineyards in the area.

BONNY DOON VINEYARD (BW 5167). Alan Grahm is the proprietor but his son, Randall, has been running Bonny Doon in the Santa Cruz Mountains since it was bonded in 1983. The Grahms produce delicious wines in attractive and often unique styles, from varietals often almost unheard of in California, or in ill repute, and market them with flair and a certain panache that cannot help but attract the consumer's attention. Randall Grahm's clever, erudite writing and adept marketing skills are best illustrated by his Clos de Gilroy, a fruity and powerful Grenache, whose label bears the likeness of Marcel Proust and the

Randall Grahm of Bonny Doon Vineyards talks viticulture with the author in 1986. (Photo Ray Kaleda)

legend, "Le Gil de Rois, Le Roi de Gils" (cf. the label of Château Gruaud-Larose).

Grahm began with a keen interest in Pinot noir and Chardonnay. He then shifted to a light-hearted focus on RHÔNE VARIETIES,* including whites such as Marsanne and Roussanne. Considered the spiritual father of the rebirth of interest in Rhône varieties in California, he rides the white horse for the RHONE RANGERS. He has virtually resurrected the old MATARO under its French name, Mourvèdre. PIERCE'S DISEASE in the Bonny Doon area had destroyed Grahm's home vineyard by 1995. In 1996 he acquired control of the RUBY HILL winery in the Livermore Valley as a center of operations. (The tasting room and distilling facility remain in Bonny Doon.)

Grahm also makes fruit infusions (juice and spirits) and, since 1989, distilled spirits such as eau-de-vie and grappa. He has a growing interest in Italian varieties such as Sangiovese and Nebbiolo, using them for Italian-style wines marketed under the Ca' del Solo brand. Total production is about 35,000 cases per year.

Dennis Schaeffer, *Vintage Talk* (Santa Barbara, Calif.: Capra, 1994).

BORDEAUX VARIETIES. See CABERNET FRANC, CABERNET SAUVIGNON, MALBEC, MERLOT, PETIT VERDOT, SAUVIGNON BLANC, and SÉMILLON

BORDONI VINEYARDS (BW 5502), the only winery in the city of Vallejo. For years James Bordoni's father kept the 2-acre vineyard here. Recently it has been replanted to Cabernet Sauvignon and Chardonnay. The little winery was bonded in 1989. Annual production is about 1,500 cases.

BOTRYTIS CINEREA. Often called gray mold, a fungus that can damage grapes and ruin a harvest. In the fall, however, when conditions are just right, this fungus is known as noble rot, because it helps produce delicious sweet wines, such as those of Sauternes and the Rhine and Mosel. Humid conditions are important for botrytis to do its work, shriveling the grapes, concentrating their sugar, and imparting a certain honeyed flavor. Because harvest time in California is usually dry, botrytised late-harvest wines have not been common. Nevertheless, since the 1970s some wineries have brought out such wines successfully. In the 1950s K. E. Nelson and Maynard AMERINE, two professors at the University of California at Davis, developed a technique for artificially infecting harvested grapes with *B. cinerea*. Myron NIGHTINGALE successfully produced a botrytised wine in 1959 at CRESTA BLANCA. Within a few years, other wineries were producing wines, mostly White Riesling, from naturally infected grapes. Today vineyardists in California are always ready to guard against *B. cinerea* in the spring and, if the varieties and the situation are right, to promote it in the fall. See also LATE-HARVEST WINE.

D. Kelly, "Botrytis," *Vintage*, January 1985, 4-15.

Jancis Robinson, *The Oxford Companion to Wine* (Oxford, Oxford University Press, 1994), 134-37.

BOTTLE. Before San Francisco had its first bottle factory in 1861, any size or shape sufficed for wine in California. Gradually the shapes and sizes we recognize today became standard, although quarts, rather than "fifths," (one-fifth of a U.S. gallon; about 1½ pints), were standard until the 1940s. In the 1970s the metric .75 liter bottle, which holds about 25½ ounces or a bit less than a fifth, became standard.

For well over a hundred years, Californian wine has usually been sold in bottles with shapes similar to those used in the wine regions of western Europe. Cabernet Sauvignon and Zinfandel come in the claret bottle we associate with Bordeaux wine. Long-necked Rhine wine bottles hold White Riesling and Gewürztraminer. Occasionally, but rarely, a producer will cross the line, perhaps bottling a Zinfandel in a burgundy bottle. A few producers have developed distinctive proprietary shapes. In the 1970s the so-called California bottle was created, something of a cross between the bordeaux and burgundy shapes. It has not caught on, but several producers use it for the half bottle (.375 liter). A few large-scale producers have brought out single-serving bottles (.1875 liter) for airlines.

The oversize bottle, or jug (1 gallon), common in pre-Prohibition California, was often the customer's own, filled at the local barrel shop or grocery store. These 3- and 4-liter jugs are still used for low-priced generic wines. In recent years some premium producers have put up a small portion of special vintages in magnums (1.5 liters). This size has also become popular for JUG WINES,* varietal and generic, which still account for a large percentage of California wine production. Extremely large bottles, often etched and colorfully decorated, have also become popular for superpremium wines or special bottlings. These are often offered at wine auctions.

BOTTLES & BINS, a pioneer consumer newsletter first issued by the Charles Krug Winery in 1949. It was edited by Francis Lewis GOULD* and "uncorked and poured from time to time" until his death in 1979 at age ninety-five. Today the winery newsletter is a normal part of many marketing schemes. Such early and successful efforts have acted as examples for the modern publications.

BOTTLING. Today most wine in California is bottled at the winery. Before World War II this was not the case. In the early years of the industry, most producers sold their wine in bulk to wine dealers and merchants, who bottled and blended some for local consumption and sent the rest off by ship or railroad car to the East Coast, New Orleans, Chicago, and other cities. There it was sold by the local bottler under his own label, or by the California merchant, who often had agencies in large cities throughout the country. Some California producers established their own brands, and their own agencies in other parts of the country. A very few bottled their wine at the winery for sale elsewhere. The first to do so, for a short time, was Gustav Niebaum at INGLENOOK.

The technology of sterile bottling was perfected in the 1920s by the burgeoning soda-pop industry. This know-how and the shortage of tanker cars in World War II led to the "bottled at-the-winery" movement, which has since become the industry standard. Very small wineries, for which a sterile bottling line is not always cost-efficient, take advantage of the traveling bottling line. Itinerant bottlers pull up to the little winery on a set date and put to work a compact line of bottling machinery that does the job, often in a carnival spirit and usually in one day. Then they move on.

BOUCHAINE VINEYARDS (BW 4263). The facility on Buchli Station Road in the Carneros district of Napa Valley was originally the site of the Garetto Winery, which was founded in 1934, and later part of the Beringer operation. Bouchaine began independent operations in 1980 with a special emphasis on custom crushing. The tenure of the winemaker Jerry Luper (1982–85) brought atten-

tion to the label for his Pinot noirs and Chardonnays. The winery produces 250,000 gallons of wine annually and estate wines are especially emphasized. In 1992 a line of wines, named for Q. C. Fly, a pioneer vineyardist in the area, was added.

BOULDER CREEK, a small community in the Santa Cruz Mountains between Saratoga and Felton. Wine grape growing filled many of the empty spaces here in the 1880s, but the two wineries nearby burned down in the great forest fire of 1898. Since the 1960s several new vineyards have been planted in the area.

BOUQUET. The odors of wine that develop as the result of fermentation and later bottle aging. Bouquet in an old wine may be a delight to the nose. See also AROMA.

BOURN, WILLIAM BOWERS (1857–1936), and his mother, Sarah, were longtime vineyardists in the St. Helena and Rutherford areas of the Napa Valley. He put together a group of investors and financed the building of Napa Valley's great GREYSTONE WINERY in 1888.

BRADY, ROY, a wine writer and wine historian. Since 1968 his great collection of wine books has resided at Fresno State University. For the Sonoma County Wine Library he produced a fascinating oral history on his life with wine.

BRANDBORG CELLARS (BW 5340). Terry Brandborg began as a home winemaker in Marin County in 1975. He received his bond in 1986 and moved his tiny urban operation to Richmond in 1991. There, producing about 3,000 cases of wine per year from purchased grapes, he specializes in Pinot noir, Zinfandel, and Charbono.

BRANDER VINEYARD (BW 4947) in the Los Olivos area of Santa Barbara County was bonded in 1980. C. F. Brander planted his 40-acre vineyard in 1975 while he was the winemaker at the SANTA YNEZ WINERY. Today the 8,000-case winery specializes in Sauvignon blanc and Chardonnay.

BRANDS. See BONDED WINERY; LABEL

BRANDY. Distilled wine. When the term brandy stands alone, always the product of the grape; brandies from other fruits must be labeled explicitly, e.g., pear brandy.

Brandy has been made in California since the mission days when AGUARDIENTE,* as it was called, was a staple commodity. After the first great influx of gold seekers in 1848 and 1849, brandy was produced in large quantities, particularly in southern California. As the state's wine industry grew, California brandy was often the distilled product of a winery's mistakes or of rain and bunch rot in the vineyard. By the 1870s most wine from Mission grapes was going into brandy, a development that did much to improve the table wines.

By the 1880s, however, several producers were making California brandy from better varieties and gained a reputation for high quality. The best were those of Henry NAGLEE (San Jose), Elias BALDWIN (Santa Anita), Leland Stanford (VINA, in Tehama County), George WEST (Stockton), and KORBEL Bros. (Sonoma). Brandy was also used to fortify sweet wines and sherry. When the federal government decided to tax fortifying brandy at a lower rate than beverage brandy, sweet wine production soared, particularly between 1895 and 1915. But World War I and Prohibition knocked out the legal brandy industry in California, although illegal "jackass" brandy stills abounded everywhere grapes were grown.

When Repeal allowed the stills to start up again after 1933, the result was a flood of fortifying brandy for the inexpensive sweet wines that were the dominant product of the California wine industry until the 1960s. Beverage brandy tended to be rather heavy and was not popular. But in 1938, to cut the oversupply of California grapes, the federal government instituted a prorate program, by which half a million tons of grapes were made into beverage brandy. During World War II, emigré European brandy experts examined these huge stocks and blended a lighter brandy that became popular and has grown in the years since. The CHRISTIAN BROTHERS' brandy business was the most successful of those early efforts. After the war, brandy consumption declined as the whiskey distillers went back into business. But it soon began rising steadily and then took off. American consumption of California brandy doubled from 1955 to 1965. California was the best market for its own brandy, followed by Wisconsin, New York, Illinois, and Minnesota. In 1980 California produced 77 percent of the brandy consumed in the United States. Between 1968 and 1979, the state's production rose by 58 percent. All this time the gallonage going to sweet wine dropped sharply as sales of that product plummeted.

In the 1980s the leading producers were E. & J. GALLO, Christian Brothers, and Korbel. A special development in the 1980s was the growth of superpremium brandies whose producers hoped to challenge the likes of Cognac and Armagnac. Several producers (see CARNEROS ALAMBEC DISTILLERY; GERMAIN-ROBIN) have brought out expensive brandies, sometimes described as alambic (or alembic) brandies, named for the traditional copper pot stills, called *al-anbiq* in Arabic, in which they are made. These elegant contraptions stand in vivid contrast to the large continuous stills used by most brandy producers in California.

Maynard Amerine and V. Singleton, *Wine: An Introduction for Americans* (Berkeley, Calif.: University of California Press, 1977), 171–86.

G. Barnwell, "The Potstill Revolution," *Wines & Vines*, April 1987, 21-25.

A model of an alambic still is located in the visitors' center at CARNEROS ALAMBIC DISTILLERY.

BRANNAN, SAMUEL (1819-89), a famous Mormon apostate who had his hand in almost every aspect of California's early state history. He is important to California winegrowing for his work in developing wine and brandy production in the upper Napa Valley. He concentrated his efforts at the head of the valley, whose "urban" center he dubbed CALISTOGA in 1859, hoping his investment there would make this place the California counterpart of New York's resort spa at Saratoga. In 1860 he went to France and sent home twenty thousand cuttings of French grape varieties. In 1868 he set up a distillery and later shipped his Calistoga Cognac around the Horn to New York. In the 1870s Brannan's economic world fell apart and his Calistoga estate was foreclosed in 1875. He lived out his years in obscurity in Escondido in southern California.

BRAREN PAULI WINERY (BW 5150). The winery is located in Petaluma but the owners, Larry Braren and Bill Pauli, own 102 acres of vines in Mendocino County. Their 10,000-case winery was bonded in 1979 and emphasizes Cabernet Sauvignon, Merlot, and Chardonnay. In 1995 they bought the WEIBEL winery near Ukiah, and changed the name to REDWOOD VALLEY CELLARS. Custom crushing will be the facility's primary business.

BRENDEL, LEON (1884-1963). A native of Alsace and a professional enologist, Brendel came to southern California at Repeal and worked at several wineries there. In 1949 he retired to Napa where he bought land just south of St. Helena and planted 9 acres to Grignolino vines. He made wine and marketed it under his Only One label (BW 4454) until he sold the place to Joseph Heitz in 1961. The vineyard is still there but the Grignolino vines are gone; it is now the site of the Heitz Cellars tasting room.

BRETTANOMYCES, often found in wine, a genus of yeast that includes seven species with many separate strains. Its sexual, or sporulating, counterpart is called Dekkera. The effects of these substances in wine have been confusing and controversial. Although usually considered to spoil the wine, different strains in the several species have various sensory effects. Brett, as it is often termed in California, may cause wines to taste mousy (bad) or clovelike (good). It subdues the flavor of fruit esters and gives some wines an aged taste, an effect that has been reported by some members of consumer tasting panels as quite appealing when the brett level is low.

Brett appears now to be almost ubiquitous in California wineries and is seen mostly as a management problem, although some winemakers have actually promoted it at low levels for its beneficial effects on flavor. Research on this yeast continues, centered in California at Fresno State University.

S. Hock, "Coping with Brettanomyces," *Practical Winery & Vineyard,* January 1990, 26–30.

BRICELAND VINEYARDS (BW 5284). Founded in 1985 with an acre of vines near Redway in Humboldt County, on the Briceland–Shelter Cove Road. The chief varietals are Sauvignon blanc and Pinot noir. Annual production is about 1,250 cases.

BRIX. One of many scales used to measure sugar content in grapes before fermentation. This scale is the standard among California winemakers today. One can get a good forecast of the eventual alcohol content of a wine by multiplying the Brix level by .56. Most table wines are harvested at between 19° and 25° Brix. Sparkling wines and blush wines may come from sugars below 19°. Until the 1960s, California winemaking texts usually used the almost identical **Balling** scale.

JFJ BRONCO WINERY (BW 4666). After the FRANZIA family sold its huge winery east of Manteca in the Central Valley in 1971, three of the brothers built the Bronco winery complex south of Ceres. Today the 44-million-gallon operation produces large quantities of inexpensive table wines and Charmat-process sparkling wines. Starting in 1991 the principals, operating as **Classic Wine Co.,** began acquiring

When David Bruce brought out his Côte de Shandon wine, the reference was to a winegrowing area east of Paso Robles, the source of the wine's Petite Sirah grapes. Domaine Chandon objected to the term and Dr. Bruce responded with his David & Goliath label.

established brands from wineries often in financial trouble. Bronco now owns the GRAND CRU, HACIENDA, LAURIER, J. W. MORRIS, Napa Creek (see KENT RASSMUSSEN WINERY), and RUTHERFORD VINTNERS brands. (The Rutherford Vintners Merlot was produced from grapes grown in Stanislaus County.) Other brands Bronco has developed are Cedar Brook, Forest Glen, ForestVille, Foxhollow, MONTPELLIER, and Silver Ridge.

BROOKSIDE VINEYARD CO., one of the brightest stars of the California wine revolution of the 1960s, was organized by Philo BIANE in 1952 and moved to the old GUASTI estate in Cucamonga in 1957. The operation expanded and based its growth on a huge string of tasting rooms all over California, even in Nevada and Arizona. In 1973 the company was acquired by Beatrice Foods, a large conglomerate headquartered in Chicago. Sales declined in the 1980s and by 1985 Brookside was out of business. The company adopted the name Brookside after Emil VACHÉ's winery near Redlands, which had been founded in 1881. The Biane and Vaché families were related by marriage.

DAVID BRUCE WINERY (BW 4495). A 100,000-gallon winery, averaging about 30,000 cases per year, started from scratch by David Bruce in 1964. It is perched atop the Santa Cruz Mountains above Los Gatos. The founder practiced dermatology until 1985 and made his first wine from Concord grapes at medical school in Oregon. His passion for wine was aroused by drinking some of the concentrated masterpieces of Martin RAY in the 1950s. Diversity and experimentation have been the hallmark of David Bruce's wines, but his primary interest has been to make great Pinot noirs and Chardonnays from Santa Cruz Mountain grapes.

A decade before the RHONE RANGER movement caught on, he was producing wines from varieties originally grown in southern France. His 1964 White Zinfandel was the first

made in California since before Prohibition, and in the sixties his LATE-HARVEST Zinfandels were both loved and loathed. In recent years his estate Pinot noirs have won remarkable critical acclaim.

BRUCK, BISMARK (1870-1926). Charles Krug's nephew; he took over the management of the KRUG* estate from its new owners in 1894 and ran it until his death. He was acknowledged as one of the most powerful leaders of the California wine industry between 1905 and 1920. His experimental work in the 1890s led to the acceptance of the RUPESTRIS St. George rootstock in replanting California vineyards after 1900. As a member of the state legislature he led the antiprohibition forces there.

BRUN & CHAIX WINERY. Originally A. Brun & Co., founded in 1877 by the French wine merchant Jean Adolph Brun (1845–94). In the 1880s he teamed up with Jean V. Chaix (1851–1902) to develop one of Napa Valley's leading wineries. They called their Oakville winery Nouveau Medoc and specialized in claret and a blend of Sauvignon blanc and Sémillon. Their vineyards on HOWELL MOUNTAIN helped pioneer winegrowing in that district. Their production averaged about 100,000 gallons per year. Just before Chaix's death, the winery was sold to the giant CALIFORNIA WINE ASSOCIATION, which pushed up production to 500,000 gallons before Prohibition. Portions of the old winery survived as part of the NAPA WINE COMPANY, later owned by Heublein.

BRUT. French, meaning crude or raw. For reasons that are obscure, it is used of fairly dry Californian or French SPARKLING WINE. There is no legal limitation on the term.

BRUTOCAO CELLARS (BW 5580, 5713). The Brutocao family has been growing grapes near Hopland in Mendocino County since the 1940s. Having begun to make small quantities of commercial wine in 1980, the family now has about 200 acres of vines and a new winery built in 1995. Annual production is about 12,000 cases with emphasis on Merlot, Zinfandel, and Chardonnay.

BUCKLEY, CHRISTOPHER (1845–1922), often referred to as the "blind boss" of the city, was a power in San Francisco politics in the 1880s. In 1889 he purchased Henry Wagoner's winery in Livermore, named it Ravenswood, and made it a valley showplace. (The estate should not be confused with the modern winery of that name in Sonoma.) Under Buckley the winery never did establish any continuity of quality. In the years before Prohibition, the facility was leased out to several local winemakers. The Buckley home has been preserved and the vineyard replanted as part of a historical restoration project in the Livermore Valley and a historical wine museum is being planned there.

W. A. Bullough, *The Blind Boss & His City* (Berkeley, Calif.: University of California Press, 1979).

BUEHLER VINEYARDS (BW 4841). The Buehler family bought land in Napa above Conn Valley in 1972 and planted a 60-acre vineyard, Vista del Lago, which looks down on Lake Hennessey. Concentration has been on Cabernet Sauvignon and Zinfandel since the winery was bonded in 1978. Including the lower-priced Bon Marché line, total annual production is about 60,000 cases.

BUENA VISTA VINICULTURAL SOCIETY. After settling in the Sonoma Valley in 1857, Agoston HARASZTHY established a great wine estate and called it Buena Vista. But the expense sapped his resources and in 1863 he was approached by capitalists in San Francisco who wanted to take part in the future expansion of the infant California wine industry.

The consortium, calling itself the Buena Vista Vinicultural Society, was primarily underwritten by William Ralston, the mercurial San Francisco banker. Within ten years, wrote the promoters then, the corporation would be producing 2 million gallons per year. After a promising start, the venture began to unravel as wine prices dropped and expenses rose. In 1866 Haraszthy was forced to resign his position of superintendent. In the 1870s production averaged about 100,000 gallons per year from about 500 acres of vines. Buena Vista's wines, particularly the company's line of sparkling wine, were well received (A bottling session during the 1870s is shown on page 213.) But the 1873–77 national depression forced the Society to liquidate its assets and eventually to go into bankruptcy. In the 1880s, the old estate became the home of Robert C. Johnson, a businessman in San Francisco.

Thomas Pinney, *A History of Wine in America from the Beginnings to Prohibition* (Berkeley, Calif.: University of California Press, 1989), 269–84.

BUENA VISTA WINERY (BW 4428, 4702): Although the winery's production facilities are now concentrated in the Carneros District of Sonoma County, Buena Vista was established by Agoston HARASZTHY* in 1857 and taken over by the BUENA VISTA VINICULTURAL SOCIETY in 1863. The original cellars just east of the old town of Sonoma have been handsomely restored and are today a visitors center.

After phylloxera had destroyed the last of the Buena Vista vineyards before World War I, the old estate saw virtually no winegrowing until it was resuscitated by a newsman, Frank Bartholomew (1899–1985), in 1941. He bought the 435-acre tract at auction and replanted some of the old vineyards. In 1943 he bonded the old winery and became one of the early entrepreneurial enthusiasts to produce premium Californian wine after Prohibition. His varietal wines won scores of awards over the next 25 years.

Harvest time at Buena Vista, ca. 1875. The famous photographer, Eadweard Muybridge, took a series of photographs at the estate soon after he was acquitted of murder after shooting and killing his wife's lover in 1874 at a resort in the Napa Valley. (Wine Appreciation Guild)

In 1968 Bartholomew sold the winery to Vernon Underwood of Young's Market Company, a seasoned wine wholesaler in southern California. Bartholomew kept most of the original vineyards when he sold the winery and, after 1973, used the grapes for his HACIENDA WINE CELLARS,* which he founded that year. In 1979 Buena Vista again changed hands, sold this time to the German beverage firm of A. Racke & Co. Since then operations have moved to the Carneros, where the company has planted more than 900 acres of vines. Production has gradually risen to almost 200,000 cases per year. Buena Vista produces a wide range of varietals, with special emphasis on Chardonnay, Pinot noir, Sauvignon blanc, and Cabernet Sauvignon, the latter a rarity in Carneros vineyards, but quite successful at Buena Vista. The line of brands has been expanded by the purchase of the Robert STEMMLER label in 1989 and the HAYWOOD label in 1991.

BUGBY, BENJAMIN N. (1827–1914). A pioneer winegrower in El Dorado County; his Natoma Vineyard was probably started in 1858. He built his winery in 1861. He was also a pioneer in raisin production. Bankrupted in 1879, he lost his winery and went into politics.

BULK PROCESS. See CHARMAT PROCESS

BUNDSCHU. One of the great family names in California wine history. Charles (1842–1910) came to California in 1868 and, after he had married Jacob GUNDLACH's daughter, helped develop Sonoma's Rhine Farm. His son **Carl** (1878–1947) managed the family estate before Prohibition and, following Repeal in 1933, managed the INGLENOOK WINERY for six years. He was one of the leaders in the California wine industry's post-Repeal work to establish high quality standards for the state's wines. In 1973 the firm of GUNDLACH-BUNDSCHU was revived by **James Bundschu**, Carl's grandson. This winery again controls a portion of Sonoma's historic Rhine Farm, which dates from 1857. See also GUNDLACH-BUNDSCHU.

THE BUREAU OF ALCOHOL, TOBACCO, AND FIREARMS (BATF) of the U. S. Treasury Department regulates the labeling, distribution, and advertising of wine. Many production practices are also regulated by the Bureau under authority derived from the Internal Revenue Code. The BATF also supervises the establishment of official viticultural districts; see AMERICAN VITICULTURAL AREAS.

BURGER. A highly productive variety of white wine grape. Some contend it is the Elbling of Germany, others that it is the rarely seen Monbadon of southern France. It was very popular in northern California before Prohibition, used for stretching better varieties in the production of inexpensive hock or Rhine wine. After Repeal it was used in southern California in the production of Charmat-process sparkling wines. In 1939 there were about 3,000 acres in the state, in 1975 about 1,700, about half in the Central Valley. By the 1990s there were about 2,000 acres left (98 percent in the Central Valley) yielding 25,000 tons of grapes in 1996 .

BURGESS CELLARS (BW 945). When J. Leland Stewart sold his renowned SOUVERAIN CELLARS* in 1970, the buildings—the old Rossini Winery, established in 1884—were purchased by Thomas Burgess. Since Burgess brought out his first wines in 1973, his winery on the lower slope of Howell Mountain in Napa Valley has been a major factor in premium wine production there. He buys most of his grapes, but has owned the Trière Vineyard in Yountville since 1979. Its Chardonnays have received superior evaluations. Burgess counts Chardonnay, Cabernet Sauvignon, and Zinfandel as his top varietals in a total production of about 30,000 cases per year.

BURGUNDY. The name of the wine region in France (Bourgogne) has been used as a generic name on bottles of California wine since the 1860s. The wines marketed under this name were rich and fruity, almost always red, and the darker the color the better. For years winemakers searched for dependable varieties for such wines. By the turn of the century, PETITE SIRAH, GRENACHE, BÉCLAN, CARIGNANE, and MATARO (Mourvèdre) were those favored. When true Burgundian PINOT NOIR was the variety employed, the few producers using it tended to call these wines Chambertin. Attempts to stretch Pinot noir through blending were never satisfactory.

After Prohibition, a large percentage of red table wine from California traveled under the burgundy designation. Red sparkling wine with a good dose of residual sugar was usually labeled Sparkling Burgundy. Some few wines were white. Since the 1960s, the intense concentration on varietal designation has meant that the designation is now little used except for inexpensive jug wines. Nonetheless, a few premium wineries such as BEAULIEU and CONCANNON, used to produce superior red wines marketed as burgundy.

BUTTE COUNTY. In the northern part of the Sacramento Valley, with an almost desert climate that is not a happy environment for fine wine grapes. In the 1860s the pioneer John Bidwell produced several thousand gallons of wine per year at his Chico Ranch, until his wife became a prohibitionist. The few hundreds of acres that survived into the 1920s had all but disappeared by the 1960s. Then the wine boom encouraged the planting of about 600 acres, but these had declined to about 100 acres by the 1990s.

BUTTERFLY CREEK WINERY (BW 5385), one of the few wineries in Mariposa County, was founded in 1987. The 19-acre vineyard is planted to Pinot blanc, Merlot, and Chardonnay. Annual production is about 4,000 cases.

BUTTONWOOD FARM WINERY (BW 5473). Located near Solvang in Santa Barbara County, Buttonwood Farm was bonded in 1989.

It produces about 5,000 cases a year, mainly Sauvignon blanc, Merlot, and Cabernet franc.

BV: See BEAULIEU VINEYARD

BW. See BONDED WINERY

BWC. See BONDED WINERY, **bonded winery cellar**

BYINGTON WINERY (BW 5522). One of the newest in the Santa Cruz Mountains, it is an imposing chateau above Boulder Creek. Bonded in 1990, its first wines were made from purchased grapes from several areas, but there are 8 acres planted on the property. Production in the mid-1990s is about 12,000 cases. Top varietals are Chardonnay, Cabernet Sauvignon, and Pinot noir.

DAVIS BYNUM WINERY (BW 4634). The son of Lindley Bynum, one of the pioneer California wine writers after Prohibition, Davis Bynum left a career in journalism in 1964 to establish his urban winery in an old plumbing warehouse in Albany next door to Berkeley. In 1971 he bought land in Napa Valley, but local opposition to his building a winery there sent him to Sonoma, where he bought 82 acres outside Healdsburg. He built

his winery in 1973 from a hop kiln on the property. Bynum concentrated on top varietals, helped early by a "cellar rat" named Gary FARRELL, who became his winemaker in 1978. In 1991 the *Los Angeles Times* named Farrell California winemaker of the year. Bynum continued to make his generic Barefoot Bynum wines, a label from the Albany days, until he sold the brand in 1988. Since then he has concentrated on increasing his varietals, Pinot noir, Sauvignon blanc, and Chardonnay, from the Russian River District. His production holds at about 17,000 cases per year.

BYRON VINEYARD & WINERY (BW 5234). Byron Brown was the first winemaker at ZACA MESA WINERY. In 1984 he established his own operation in the Santa Maria Valley. In 1990 MONDAVI bought his winery to act as its center of operations in the Central Coast area. At the time Brown owned about 120 acres there. Since then Mondavi has expanded its holdings in the region to more than 600 acres. The winery concentrates on the production of Pinot noir, Chardonnay, and Sauvignon blanc. Brown has remained winemaker and general manager. Production in the 1990s is about 45,000 cases a year and rising. In 1996 Mondavi built a new 32,000-square-foot winery on the property.

CABERNET. For many years after Repeal California wines that contained legal amounts of any variety of grape that had the word Cabernet in its name could be described as Cabernet wines. Most often it was used in the 1950s and 1960s for wines made from RUBY CABERNET, sometimes blended with CABERNET SAUVIGNON. Gradually that usage almost disappeared from California wine labels. In 1996 the BATF ruled that the term alone might not be used on labels after 1999.

CABERNET FRANC. An important red wine grape of the Loire Valley and Bordeaux, particularly in Pomerol and in St-Émilion, where it is called Bouchet. Today it is a major variety in Napa and Sonoma Counties, where about 70 percent of California's production is found. In 1996 4,400 tons in those counties were crushed, but this is a recent development.

TABLE 4. CABERNET FRANC GRAPES,
SELECTED COUNTIES

		(ACRES)		
YEAR	NAPA	SONOMA	MONTEREY	TOTAL
1980	125	11	N.A.	156
1983	224	89	55	413
1987	430	220	121	975
1992	714	634	222	1,894
1997	756	508	192	1,986

SOURCE: California Agricultural Statistics Service, Sacramento, Calif.

The variety was first imported to California in 1872 by J.-B. J. PORTAL of Cupertino and was later recommended by Professor Eugene HILGARD. To Kalon and INGLENOOK had the variety in the 1880s. It was also grown in San Benito County and around Mission San Jose. Virtually all of those vines eventually succumbed to phylloxera and were not replanted. (A small vineyard did survive Prohibition on the Pourroy estate, later CONGRESS SPRINGS, in the hills behind Saratoga.)

A few acres were planted in the Napa Valley in the 1960s, enough for Robert MONDAVI to use 40 percent of the variety in his 1971 Reserve Cabernet Sauvignon. By 1976 the entire state had 77 acres and varietal wines had been produced by the MOUNT VEEDER and SPRING MOUNTAIN wineries. As the acreage grew in the 1980s, most of the grapes went into Cabernet Sauvignon and MERITAGE blends. Producers tend to think that Cabernet franc is a bright flavor complement to Cabernet Sauvignon. There are now about 25 wineries that market a varietal, most using a small percentage of Cabernet Sauvignon and/or Merlot as well.

Between 1990 and 1996, the tonnage of Cabernet Franc grapes grown in California had grown by 99 percent.

CABERNET PFEFFER. A variety of grape named for William PFEFFER, who bred grapes in Santa Clara County in the nineteenth century. It was planted here and there in northern

California but disappeared after the phylloxera epidemic of the 1890s. Pfeffer had by then bred a better variation as a seedling and grafted it onto resistant rootstock. In 1908 he gave cuttings to Harold Ohrwall and Frederic BIOLETTI, who planted them in the Cienega Valley of San Benito County. The few vines that survive today there and in Monterey County are the progeny of these Pfeffer seedlings. The only historic hint concerning its origin came from H. W. CRABB in the 1890s; he thought it was the French Robin noir.

The wine from this variety has a peppery flavor and was thought by Hilgard to be a relative of true Cabernets. In 1897, in a case involving the proper price per ton, a judge in Santa Clara County declared this to be true. In the 1980s ALMADEN produced a varietal. Others have recently experimented with the variety in blends and as a varietal. No statistics on the acreage are available.

CABERNET SAUVIGNON. In 1992 Cabernet Sauvignon became the leading red-wine grape variety in California, nosing out Zinfandel for but one year. For many wine lovers, the world-class position of California wines is owed primarily to this variety, but this is a controversial proposition. In 1997 the historic origins of the Cabernet Sauvignon were suggested by a discovery made by Professor Carole Meredith of the University of California at Davis. Working with DNA, she found that two of the parent grapes of the variety, which probably crossed by chance centuries ago, are the Cabernet franc and the Sauvignon blanc.

The grape's renown is based on its success in Bordeaux, particularly in the Haut Médoc where it is the leading variety. It first came to California in 1852, imported by a nurseryman in San Jose, Antoine DELMAS, in whose catalogue it was listed as both Cabrunet and Medoc. Charles LEFRANC of ALMADEN marketed the first commercial wine from this variety. He called it Cabernet-Malbec, but we do not know the proportions of this blend he sold beginning in the 1860s. The variety's potential in the North Coast was first demonstrated in Sonoma by J. H. DRUMMOND in 1882. By the end of the 1880s, numerous producers had experimented with Cabernet Sauvignon, often in blends in the style of Bordeaux. Some even copied the precise percentages of the varieties used in first-growth

PRODUCERS OF SUPERIOR CABERNET SAUVIGNON BEFORE PROHIBITION

PROPRIETOR	WINERY OR VINEYARD	AREA	COUNTY
Chauché & Bon	Mont Rouge	Livermore	Alameda
Isaac De Turk	De Turk Winery	Santa Rosa	Sonoma
John T. Doyle	Las Palmas	Cupertino	Santa Clara
Morris Estee	Hedgeside	Napa City	Napa
Grau & Werner	Los Amigos	Irvington	Alameda
Gundlach-Bundschu	Rhine Farm	Sonoma Valley	Sonoma
W. S. Keyes	Liparita	Howell Mountain	Napa
Pierre Klein	Mira Valle	Monte Bello	Santa Clara
C. C. McIver	Linda Vista	Mission San Jose	Alameda
Tiburcio Parrott	Miravalle	Spring Mountain	Napa
Felix Salmina	Larkmead	Larkmead	Napa
John Stewart	Etta Hill	Scotts Valley	Santa Cruz

châteaux of the Haut Médoc. But only the most idealistic persisted, because yields were low and economic conditions in the 1890s were terrible.

GENERIC TERMS were standard for designating California wines before Prohibition, but the term *claret,* which would have been understandable for Cabernet Sauvignon, would not do, as it implied blends of lesser varieties. The generic term that producers and merchants hit on was Medoc, but there was no fixed standard for its meaning. The term Cabernet was also seen on some labels.

Very little Cabernet Sauvignon survived Prohibition. Georges de Latour at BEAULIEU in the Napa Valley probably had the largest holding in the state. With Repeal came a small surge in planting: The acreage increased from about 200 to 450 acres between 1932 and 1940. By then the name of the variety was usually mentioned on the label, but only 51 percent of what was in the bottle had to be the varietal listed. If gold medals at the State Fair were the best criterion for picking the best Cabernets through the 1950s, INGLENOOK, Beaulieu, and CHARLES KRUG would take the palm. Louis MARTINI was late to enter the field, LARKMEAD left early, and some small producers such as Lee Stewart at SOUVERAIN, Robert Mayock at Los Amigos, and Martin Ray at PAUL MASSON rarely entered early competitions.

The wine revolution of the 1960s and after was fueled to a great extent by a growing passion for California Cabernet. In 1960 there were 600 acres in the state; by 1976 there were 26,742. Hundreds of wineries came on line in those years and most felt that good Cabernet Sauvignon was necessary to establish a brand. But the variety was overplanted and often planted where it was inappropriate, particularly in the southern Central Valley. Acreage declined. Then in the 1990s, planting took off again, a large percentage of the increase occurring in the Central Valley, in San Joaquin County. Between 1988 and 1992, the number of acreas planted to Cabernet Sauvignon increased by 199 percent.

The rise of modern California Cabernet Sauvignon wines began long before the symbolic event in 1976 that made the process newsworthy and historic—a blind tasting held in PARIS and attended by many of the elite in the French wine world. The winner in a pairing of California Cabernets and Bordeaux wines was a 1973 STAG'S LEAP WINE CELLARS Cabernet, preferred over wines with the stature of, for example, a 1970 Château Mouton-Rothschild. Since then the critical acclaim for the top-end California Cabernets has soared, as have their prices. The average price of Cabernet Sauvignon grapes has risen from about $400 to $1,100 per ton since 1980; Napa Valley Cabernet commands about $1,800, Central

TABLE 5. CABERNET SAUVIGNON GRAPES, SELECTED COUNTIES AND AREAS

				(ACRES)			
YEAR	NAPA COUNTY	SONOMA COUNTY	OTHER NORTH COAST	CENTRAL COAST	CENTRAL VALLEY	SIERRA FOOTHILLS	TOTAL
1961	387	74	3	123	0	3	606
1971	2,684	1,628	656	2,091	306	10	7,616
1976	5,562	4,607	2,610	9,843	3,099	106	26,742
1982	5,988	4,522	1,882	6,152	2,341	107	22,042
1988	7,910	5,641	2,253	6,005	3,007	205	26,404
1992	10,234	6,441	2,705	7,799	6,033	297	34,667
1997	10,335	7,011	2,642	8,242	11,622	407	40,457

SOURCE: California Agricultural Statistics Service, Sacramento, Calif.

Valley about $750. Today the best California Cabernets come from the North Coast area, particularly from Napa and Sonoma counties. Other excellent wines have been made in the Santa Cruz Mountains, in the Paso Robles area of San Luis Obispo County, and in El Dorado County.

The best VINTAGES in recent years have been: 1996, 1995, 1994, 1992, 1991, 1990, 1987, 1986, 1985, 1984, 1978, 1974, 1970, 1968, 1966, 1964, 1958, and 1951.

Great historic vintages: 1946, 1940, 1933, 1916, 1910, 1900, 1890, and 1885.

In 1997 the Cabernet Sauvignon crush in California was 234,132 tons; in 1990 it was 101,853 tons.

James Laube, *California's Great Cabernets* (San Francisco; Wine Spectator Press, 1989).

CADENASSO WINERY (BW 3823). Founded in 1907, the original winery stood on the Vallejo-Sacramento highway outside the town of Fairfield in Solano County. In the 1950s it was a 300,000-gallon bulk winery with 60 acres of vineyards. The Cadenasso family also sold jug wine to neighbors and travelers. Urban development and the new interstate highway forced the family to relocate the winery in nearby Suisun in 1986.

CAFARO CELLARS. Joseph Cafaro is a well-known consulting enologist in Napa. In 1986 he began making commercial wine on a small scale, about 2,000 cases of Cabernet Sauvignon and Merlot annually. Many of these wines have had excellent critical success. In 1997 he planted 14 acres of red Bordeaux varieties on slopes above the Silverado Trail.

CAIN CELLARS (BW 5135), a remarkable château built atop Spring Mountain in 1982 on the old 542-acre McCormick cattle ranch. By the 1990s the estate had 100 acres of vines and the winery was producing about 20,000 cases per year. The original owner, Jerry Cain, pro-duced red wine in the style of Bordeaux, as has the new owner, James Meadlock, since 1991. Cain Five is the wine at the top of the line here, a blend of the five principal red varieties of Bordeaux, first produced from the 1985 vintage. Cain Cuvée, a less expensive blend, began with the 1988 vintage.

CAIRE, JUSTINIAN. See SANTA CRUZ ISLAND

CAKEBREAD CELLARS (BW 4732). In 1971 Jack Cakebread, taking a break from running his garage in Oakland went to the Napa Valley on a photographic assignment. There he caught the winegrower's bug and bought a piece of land in the Oakville area. Today his winery, bonded in 1973, produces about 65,000 cases per year from his own 77 acres of vines and from purchased grapes, the wines mainly Chardonnay, Sauvignon blanc, and Cabernet Sauvignon. His son Bruce has been the wine-maker since 1977. The winery, an understated, barnlike structure, has won awards from the American Institute of Architects. An expansion project began in 1995.

CALAVERAS COUNTY in the Sierra foot-hills had a few vineyards planted in Gold Rush days and by the 1880s had two wineries. Until the 1960s the wines were made for local con-sumption; there were then about 120 acres of vines. In the 1990s there were about 230 acres, half red and half white, and six wineries

CALERA WINE CO. (BW 4826), one of the top Pinot noir producers in California, was established by Josh Jensen in 1976 in the Gav-ilan Mountains above Hollister in San Benito County. The land has large outcroppings of limestone, one of the characteristics of some of the best red-wine districts of Burgundy. *Calera* is Spanish for limekiln.

Jensen has planted 38 acres of Pinot noir in four separate vineyards: Reed, Jensen, Mills, and Selleck, and the wines are designated by vineyard. Since his first releases in 1978, Calera Pinot noirs have won critical acclaim. At the San Francisco Vintners Club tasteoff of Pinot noirs in 1985, Jensen's wines from the 1982 vintage took three of the top four places, against the very best in California.

Calera is on Mount Harlan, which was designated a specific viticultural area in 1990. Jensen has six acres of Chardonnay, which he labels Mt. Harlan Vineyard. There are also 2 acres of Viognier. The total production of Calera was approaching 25,000 cases in the 1990s.

CALIFORNIA. The nation's great vineyard, California supplies grapes for more than 80 percent of all the wine produced in the United States. The state has almost 350,000 acres of wine grape vines, whose average crop is well over 2 million tons per year. In addition about 1 million tons of raisin and table grapes go into California fermenters. About 60 percent of California's wine grapes are white. In the 1990s the average price per ton has been about $325, making a typical crush worth about $1 billion. In 1996 the average value of a ton jumped to $452. The yearly shipment of California wine into all markets has more than tripled since the late 1950s. That figure equaled 424 million gallons in 1987, but slid to 353 million in 1996. Revenue from sales that year was about $5,200,000,000. If California were an independent state, her production would place her fifth in the world. As consumers, Californians annually drink almost three gallons of wine per capita per year: the national average is about 1.8 gallons.

The coastal regions of California, having an almost classic Mediterranean climate, are a natural home for the grape. The native *Vitis californica* thrives here but makes poor wine. It was in these coastal areas that a string of MISSIONS* was established by the first Europeans to settle here, Franciscan padres, Spanish soldiers and officials, and Mexican settlers. The missions extended from San Diego (built in 1769) to Sonoma (built in 1823) and all, except for one, had vineyards. The first to have a wine vintage, in 1783, was Mission San Juan Capistrano. Wine and brandy were important products in the old province, most of it for local consumption; there was little real commerce.

The American Conquest (1846) and the subsequent Gold Rush (1848–54) brought many Americans and Europeans to California, some of whom knew, or thought they knew, the essentials of viticulture and winemaking. When good European varieties of grapes began arriving from France, Germany, and New England in the 1850s, a few good commercial wines were produced. By the 1860s there was a real wine industry, centered in southern California, where most of the old vineyards were located. But the seeds of an industry based on better varieties and better climate were planted in the San Francisco Bay Area and the lower Sacramento Valley. Because the markets were in the northern part of the state and production was concentrated in the south, a real commerce was established, with large quantities of the wine produced in the Los Angeles area and shipped to San Francisco to merchants who built large cellars for blending and aging. The most important pioneer in this young industry was Charles KOHLER.*

In the 1870s the center of production shifted to northern California, specifically to Sonoma, Napa, and Santa Clara counties. Here, wines of good commercial quality were possible. But the national economy during much of the 1870s was dominated by a great industrial depression. When that cloud passed, demand for California wine sky-rocketed, particularly among immigrants who flocked to American shores in the 1880s. Demand was also stimulated by the decline of the French wine industry, battered by the infestation of PHYLLOXERA.* The resulting explosion of planting and capital investment made the California wine industry a multimillion-dollar institution.

TABLE 6. THE CALIFORNIA WINE INDUSTRY, SELECTED MEASURES, 1880–1996

YEAR[1]	WINE GRAPES (ACRES)	(TONS)	RAISIN & TABLE GRAPES (TONS CRUSHED)	WINE (GALLONS)[2]
1880	36,000			4,800,000
1885	65,779			13,000,000
1890	90,228			19,900,000
1900	86,000			23,400,000
1910	145,000			45,000,000
1920	118,384	338,000		
1925	172,569	442,000		
1930	200,823	486,000		
1935	184,026	569,000		
1945	193,935	619,000		
1955	138,856	524,068	985,451	
1965	139,160	693,794	1,949,119	
1969	147,400	711,004	1,273,980	
1972	232,431	594,754	859,514	
1975	322,650	1,122,650*	941,959	
1980	336,841	1,601,400*	973,732	
1985	343,056	1,897,200*	773,211	
1990	330,356	2,067,400*	361,716	
1996	378,603	2,206,830*	613,731*	

NOTES:

1. Statistics for years 1880–1910 are best guesses taken from industry publications and the press. Thereafter, official statistics have been used.

2. No official statistics for gallons of wine produced were collected after 1919. Instead, production was measured in tons of grapes crushed. See Table 7 for statistics on gallonage.

* Averages for year indicated and immediately preceding unlisted years; e.g., tonnage of wine grapes given for 1975 is the averaged tonnage for years 1973 through 1975.

SOURCE: California Agricultural Statistics Service, Sacramento, Calif.

Wine grape acreage increased from about 35,000 to over 100,000 acres. Large-scale irrigation made it possible to plant thousands of acres in the Central Valley, mostly to varieties for fortified wine and brandy.

The next decade was marked by hard times for the young wine industry. Vineyards had been overplanted in the 1880s and a national depression in the 1890s also helped to dry up demand. Part of the potential overproduction was forestalled by the spread of phylloxera. When good times returned in 1898, a large part of the industry was now controlled by a giant monopoly, the CALIFORNIA WINE ASSOCIA-TION, founded in 1894 to bring order out of the chaos occasioned by the depression. This wine trust did stabilize the industry and regulate the planting boom that took place at the turn of the century, when huge tracts of land were opened to viticulture, specifically in the Lodi-Stockton area, in the southern Santa Clara Valley, and in the Cucamonga area of San Bernardino County.

The period from 1880 to 1915 was one in which scientific improvement in wine quality was an important factor in the industry's growth. Much of that improvement came from the work of scientists and practical agronomists at the University of California. A series of agricultural EXPERIMENTAL STATIONS brought the findings of scientists to the vineyard and cellar. But, although the quality of the average bottle of California wine in 1915 was much higher than it had been in 1895, fewer world-class quality wines were produced here. Most of the enthusiastic entrepreneurs who had established so many of the small premium wineries in the 1880s had, by 1915, died, retired, or had been bought out by the Wine Association.

The rise of the national prohibition movement after 1900 also made a career in wine-growing less appealing. Aimed as an attack on the saloon and the liquor trade, the movement was propelled to a startling victory during the patriotic fervor of World War I. The result was PROHIBITION, which lasted from 1920 to 1933, and outlawed the commercial production and sale of beverage wine. But home winemaking was not illegal and vineyards in California were actually expanded in the 1920s by the upsurge of demand, mostly in the urban centers east of the Rockies, for wine grapes. It was not until the planting boom of the 1970s that California grape acreage surpassed the record of 1926. Most wineries closed their doors during the dry years, but a few continued to operate, producing medicinal and altar wines.

Because the country was in another deep economic depression, repeal in 1933 did not bring prosperity to the industry. Vineyards were planted mostly to common shipper varieties, but there was little demand for premium wine anyway. What profits were to be made came mostly from FORTIFIED WINES, now a cheap substitute for hard liquor.

After World War II, the industry struggled to survive and grow. The University of California continued to work for better standard wine quality, and industry advertising campaigns worked to picture table wine with meals in a better light. Gradually consumption grew in the 1950s and the ratio of table to fortified wine also grew. Then in the 1960s another

great wine boom occurred. The previous boom in the 1880s had been based on a growth of immigration, not a change in consumer habits. The modern boom resulted from a change in tastes. In 1960 consumption of wine per capita in the United States was just under one gallon per year. It passed one gallon in 1967 and was two gallons in 1979. Consumption peaked in 1986 at 2.43 gallons and had dropped about 20 percent by the 1990s. By 1967, the consumption of table wine had passed that of sweet wine and the margin has been increasing ever since. More Americans were drinking more wine with their meals. The decline after 1986 was most apparent in inexpensive JUG WINES and wine COOLERS. Consumption of PREMIUM WINES continued to rise.

Another characteristic of recent times has been the consolidation of the wine industry. Most wine is produced now by large corporations, although some, such as GALLO and ROBERT MONDAVI, are family corporations.

During his lifetime CHARLES KOHLER, shown here in about 1875, was generally recognized as the "father" of the California wine industry, which began shortly after statehood in the 1850s. (Thomas Pinney Collection, Claremont, Calif.)

TABLE 7. COMMERCIALLY PRODUCED WINE IN CALIFORNIA

| | | (IN MILLIONS OF GALLONS) | | |
YEAR	TABLE WINE	FORTIFIED WINE	SPARKLING WINE	TOTAL
1957	28	95.0	1.1	124
1960	36	91.0	1.7	129
1963	43	88.0	2.2	134
1966	55	85.0	3.8	144
1969	87	75.9	8.9	172
1972	155	67.1	15.7	238
1975	197	59.9	15.4	272
1978	205	34.7	18.8	298
1981	278	22.7	23.9	358
1984	272	17.6	28.1	373
1987	273	16.1	25.6	424
1990	257	12.6	21.8	372
1993	267	9.8	21.9	340
1996	304	9.2	19.0	374

NOTES: These statistics are for wine "entering distribution channels" (wine leaving bond, the producers' taxes having been paid on it) in selected years, which do not necessarily correspond to the years in which the wines were produced. Because not all categories have been selected, those included in this table do not add up to the totals.

SOURCE: Wine Institute, various publications; *Wines and Vines,* selected issues 1957–96.

Nevertheless, most of California's more than 700 wineries in the 1990s were not industrial giants. This tendency to consolidation has also been true in vineyard ownership, but to a lesser extent.

California, like the names of all the other states, is also an appellation of origin on wine labels. On inexpensive wines, the California appellation probably indicates grapes from the Central Valley. But many very fine wines are blends from grapes grown in more than one coastal area and thus carry the California appellation.

In tables 6 and 7 statistics for selected years are given to illustrate trends and for making general comparisons.

CALIFORNIA BOARD OF STATE VITI-CULTURAL COMMISSIONERS: See STATE VITICULTURAL COMMISSION

CALIFORNIA FRUIT PRODUCTS CO. See CANANDAIGUA

CALIFORNIA GRAPE PRODUCTS CORP. (Calgrape), a powerful company consisting of several capital plants, most concentrated in the Central Valley. Its management attempted to organize and stabilize large segments of the wine industry after Repeal. Calgrape has survived under the name SIERRA WINE COMPANY, which is owned by the Wine Group and has a plant in Tulare County.

CALIFORNIA GROWERS WINERY (CALGRO) (BW 4) was founded by Arpaxat SETRAKIAN and his family in 1936 at Cutler in the Central Valley. It survives as GOLDEN STATE VINTNERS with 50 million gallons of capacity and producing inexpensive table and sparkling wines.

CALIFORNIA STATE FAIR. See EVALUA-
TION, OF WINE; EXPOSITIONS

**CALIFORNIA STATE UNIVERSITY AT
FRESNO.** See FRESNO STATE UNIVERSITY

CALIFORNIA WINE ASSOCIATION
(CWA). In 1894 the California wine industry
was almost destroyed by overproduction, a
national depression, and cutthroat competition.
To save themselves, several large San Francisco
wine merchants formed the California Wine
Association. The association, dubbed The Wine
Trust by its critics (see WINE WAR), was a huge
corporation that dominated the production and
sale of wine in California until PROHIBITION*
in 1920. It then sold off most of its assets but
continued to function by selling grape concentrate and other legal products. It was reorganized
in 1929 as Fruit Industries. After Repeal, the
company evolved into a new combination and
by 1950 was marketing the products of several

wineries under the Eleven Cellars label. Even-
tually there was only one cellar, the PERELLI-
MINETTI winery that, today, operates as
DELANO GROWERS GRAPE PRODUCTS.

**CALIFORNIA WINE MAKERS CORPO-
RATION.** See WINE WAR

CALIFORNICA, a species of *Vitis;* the native
grape of the coastal valleys of California. Its
fruit is useless for making wine. In the 1880s it
was mistakenly thought to be resistant to phylloxera and therefore useful as rootstock.

CALISTOGA. A resort town and winegrowing
area at the northern end of the Napa Valley.
The town was founded and named by Sam
BRANNAN in 1859. The first vineyard in the area
had been planted in 1852. Brannan himself
planted several large vineyards there but lost
them in the 1870s. By the 1890s there were
about seventy growers in the area with about

This French engraving (ca. 1889) shows how California's native grape vine, *Vitis californica,* can
take over the plants growing along a creek bed. The drawing was made from a photo taken near
the Napa Valley property of Charles KRUG.

1,500 acres of vines. Thirteen growers reported that they were producing wine on a commercial scale. The most important were A. L. Tubbs (CHATEAU MONTELENA), A. & C. Grimm, and E. Light. In later years the southern part of the area came to be known as the Larkmead district, after the important winery of that name.

This portion of the Napa Valley is quite warm and best suited to the production of Cabernet Sauvignon, Zinfandel, certain Rhône varieties, and Sauvignon blanc. In the 1990s there were thirteen wineries there.

CALLAWAY VINEYARD & WINERY (BW 4668). When Ely Callaway, an industrialist, was looking for vineyard land in the 1960s, he settled on the Temecula area of Riverside County, 60 miles north of San Diego and 23 miles inland from the coast, at a 1,400-foot elevation. He had commissioned a climatologist to study the area and concluded that good wine grapes could be grown at this southern latitude. Starting in 1969, he planted 105 acres of vines. In 1974 his new winery had its first crush. Its capacity rose to 200,000 gallons by 1980. He sold the operation to Hiram Walker in 1981. That company has raised the winery capacity to about 850,000 gallons and sales nationally to more than 200,000 cases per year, and controls 1,720 acres of vineyard, planted mostly to white wine grapes. Callaway is one of the leading Viognier producers in California. In 1994 the operation was reorganized in a complicated arrangement with Massachusetts Mutual Life.

CAMBIASO WINERY. See DOMAINE ST. GEORGE

CAMBRIA WINERY (BW 5486). In 1988 KENDALL-JACKSON VINEYARDS* bought about 700 acres of the Tepusquet Vineyard near Santa Maria in Santa Barbara County. Since then Kendall-Jackson has expanded its local acreage to about 1,200 acres. After fail-ing in its bid to buy the CORBETT CANYON WINERY to the north, Kendall-Jackson in 1989 built a 2 million-gallon facility at Tepusquet and named it Cambria. The winery processes grapes, mostly Chardonnay, for the Kendall-Jackson and Cambria labels. There is also Pinot noir, Syrah, and Sangiovese. Since 1991, the Cambria winery has been producing Kristone, a sparkling wine first released in 1995 at $60 per bottle, a California record. The total annual output of the winery is about 60,000 cases.

CANANDAIGUA WINE CO., by the mid-1990s, was the second-largest wine producer in the United States, with sizeable interests in the California wine industry. Mordecai Sands founded the operation in the New York town of Canandaigua in 1945. In the 1990s it had grown to become a sprawling, 50 million-gallon wine producer. The California connection began in 1974 when the Sands family bought the BISCEGLIA BROTHERS winery in Madera, today an 18 million-gallon facility operated as California Fruit Products Co. In 1991 Canandaigua bought GUILD WINERIES and, in 1993, Vintners International Co. In 1994 the company bought the Almaden and Inglenook brands from HEUBLEIN, as well as four of that company's producing plants. Canandaigua now controls the following national brands: Almaden, Paul Masson, Inglenook, Taylor California Cellars, Cribari, Bisceglia Brothers, Cook's Champagne, Deer Valley, Dunnewood, Guild, Manischewitz, Sun Country Cooler, and Widmer, among many others.

CANYON ROAD WINERY. See GEYSER PEAK WINERY; NERVO WINERY

CAPARONE VINEYARD (BW 4961). A winery near San Miguel in the Paso Robles area, it was founded in 1980 and specializes in Merlot and Cabernet Sauvignon.

CAPSULE. See LEAD

CARBON DIOXIDE (CO_2), a regular component of our atmosphere and essential to the growth of all living systems, although it accounts for but .03 percent of the atmosphere. Obviously, it takes part in the growth of the vine and its fruit.

In winemaking, it is one of the products of fermentation, usually passing into the atmosphere. Its solubility in water increases markedly under pressure, a characteristic important in the production of SPARKLING WINES, in whch the second fermentation does not allow the CO_2 to escape. We depend on these released bubbles for a large part of our pleasure when enjoying these products; see also CARBONIC MACERATION.

Carbon dioxide has been found to be an excellent defense against the oxidation of grapes and wine, particularly in white wine production.

Although CO_2 is not toxic, it can displace oxygen and cause death to anyone in a confined space, such as a fermentation vat. Prior to the 1960s hardly a California vintage went by without a winery worker suffocating from CO_2 poisoning. Since then education about the dangers has been widespread, but even in 1997 a worker in Sonoma died while cleaning out a fermentation tank.

CARBONIC MACERATION: A method of fermentation that produces deep-colored, fruity red wines without harsh tannins or much astringency. Much of the French Beaujolais wine is made by this process. Such wines are meant to be drunk young and often contain distracting fermentation smells.

The process calls for the uncrushed grapes to be placed in sealed fermenters. Starting at the bottom of the tank where the weight of the mass has crushed some berries, the fermentation proceeds inside the individual grapes. In California in the 1880s the technique, then termed the Morel process, was tried, but the number of satisfactory wines was exceeded by the number with high levels of acetic acid. In the 1970s the process again had a certain vogue, and the resulting wines, made from numerous varieties, particularly Gamays, Pinot noir, and Zinfandel, were labelled "nouveau." By the mid-1980s the practice and the wines had again lost favor in California, except for those wines that came to market in November of the current vintage to compete with the new Beaujolais arriving from France.

J. CAREY CELLARS. See CURTIS WINERY

CARIGNANE. The most widely planted red-wine grape in France today, although probably a native of Spain (Cariñena). It produces tasty red wine, particularly good for blending. Extensively planted in northern California in the 1880s, it was a common component of both BURGUNDY and CLARET blends. During Prohibition acreage soared from about 12,000 to 28,000 acres, over half of which were in the Central Valley. This variety made up about 10 percent of the wine grapes shipped east from California to home winemakers during the dry years. Many of those vines lasted on into the 1960s. In 1961 there were still 5,000 acres in the North Coast area (about half of them in Mendocino), most of their production going into generic red table-wine blends. About 65 percent of that year's 23,000-acre total was still in the Central Valley. The total acreage rose in the 1970s to about 30,000, but had declined to about 16,000 in the next decade. In the 1980s, with the rise of the so-called RHONE RANGERS, red wine grapes identified with southern France came into vogue. By that time, and on into the 1990s, there were about 1,400 acres of older Carignane vines left in the coastal valleys. Grapes from those vines brought prices more than double those fetched by Carignane grown on the 7,500 acres still producing in the Central Valley.

TABLE 8. CARIGNANE GRAPES, SELECTED COUNTIES

			(ACRES)			
YEAR	MENDOCINO	SONOMA	SAN JOAQUIN	STANISLAUS	MADERA	TOTAL
1920						15,000
1938	2,711	2,275	6,657	4,703	803	26,729
1949						34,195
1960						24,967
1969	2,445	2,045	7,212	3,438	3,553	26,963
1976	2,209	1,384	7,523	2,474	5,461	27,623
1982	1,756	1,028	6,411	1,583	4,528	21,166
1988	1,214	460	3,828	739	3,082	12,295
1990	1,055	359	3,627	653	2,952	11,037
1997	790	222	2,163	422	2,676	7,774

NOTES: Until 1961, statistics for acreage under various varieties of grapes were not published; figures for 1938 are abberant, if interesting.
SOURCE: California Agricultural Statistics Service, Sacramento, Calif.

In 1996, vineyards in California produced about 60,000 tons of Carignane, about 72 percent of the production in 1990.

CARMEL VALLEY. The Mission San Carlos was originally located in Monterey but was moved south to the Carmel Valley because of the better soils and weather. Between the time that the padres planted their tiny vineyard and the 1960s, there was little thought of viticulture here. When the Carmel Valley was granted the status of a viticultural area in 1983, there were about 200 acres of vines there and five wineries. Vineyards toward the inland end of the valley have produced good Cabernet Sauvignon.

CARMENET VINEYARD (BW 5173). Part of the CHALONE VINEYARD* group; named for a French synonym for Cabernet franc. In 1980 John McQuown, a stockholder in Chalone, with several associates, bought 500 acres in the hills east of the Sonoma Valley and, in 1983, Carmenet was integrated into the Chalone operation. Over 15,000 square feet of caves were tunneled out of Mount Pisgah and a beautiful 170,000-gallon winery was built at their mouth. A sort of amphitheater is formed by the 70 acres of Cabernet Sauvignon, Merlot, and Cabernet franc planted on terraces facing the winery. The wine from these vineyards, mainly red wine in a Bordeaux style, has won steady praise from critics. There is also a Sauvignon blanc and Sémillon blend. Carmenet produces about 30,000 cases per year.

CARMINE. A cultivar of *Vitis vinifera* developed at the University of California at Davis and released in 1975. A cross of Carignane, Cabernet Sauvignon, and Merlot, it has been touted by the university as a high-yielding variety, "higher in flavor and aroma" than Cabernet Sauvignon. It has not caught on with California winegrowers. The total 1996 crush amounted to 179 tons. Acreage figures for this variety have never been published by the state.

CARNELIAN. A cultivar of *Vitis vinifera* developed at the University of California at Davis and released in 1972. A complex cross of Carignane, Cabernet Sauvignon, and Grenache, it was bred for warm Central Valley conditions. Between 1973 and 1977 about 3,000 acres were planted in Kern, Fresno, and Madera counties. Its bright color and flavor were not the boon to California jug wine production hoped for by the university. Only 37 acres have been planted since 1979, the state's total holding steady at about 1,000 acres into the 1990s. The state crush in 1996 was about 85 percent of that in 1990.

CARNEROS. Officially designated "Los Carneros," a winegrowing region granted AVA status in 1983. An area of flatlands and rolling foothills encompassing the lower reaches of the Napa and Sonoma valleys just above San Pablo Bay, it has become famous in recent years for the production of Burgundian varietals, chiefly Chardonnay and Pinot noir. The climate of the Carneros has been the attraction, in spite of the stingy soils and need for drip irrigation. The nearness of the Bay and its cooling fogs moderate the hot summer days and give the area heat summations (see CLIMATE) similar to those of Burgundy. A few places are hot enough to ripen Merlot and Cabernet Sauvignon successfully. There are about 15,000 plantable acres in the Carneros, two-thirds of them on the Napa side, which is where most of the almost 7,000 acres of vineyards that were growing in the 1990s are located.

The name of the district comes from that of a Spanish land grant and means the rams. Dairy products and fodder crops were the chief agricultural products until recently. Nevertheless, since the 1870s on the Napa side, and even earlier in Sonoma, grapes have been grown successfully here and there. John STANLY'S* Riverdale Ranch, south of Napa City, was the most successful and long-lived operation. By the 1920s, phylloxera had destroyed almost all the vines in the Carneros except those on the Stanly Ranch, which has been planted on resistant rootstock.

After Repeal, in 1935, John Garetto built his winery on part of the Stanly Ranch, today the site of BOUCHAINE VINEYARDS. In the 1930s Louis MARTINI and André TCHELISTCHEFF bought Pinot noir grapes grown on old Stanly vines. In 1942 Martini bought 200 acres of the old ranch and BEAULIEU VINEYARD bought 160 acres in 1961. At the same time, Rene DI ROSA began planting his soon-to-be-famous Winery Lake Vineyard on the site of the historical Talcoa property, once managed by George HUSMANN. Even when CARNEROS CREEK WINERY was founded in 1972, there were still fewer than 200 acres of vines in the Carneros. Within 15 years there were more than 5,000 acres. In 1985 the growers and producers in both counties formed the Carneros Quality Alliance to promote the area's wines and to encourage research on the influence of rootstock, clones, and temperature on local viticulture. Today there are eighteen wineries in the area, several of them impressive champagneries—considerable quantities of sparkling wines are produced in the Carneros, similarities to Burgundy notwithstanding. The leading growers are the SANGIACOMO family, BUENA VISTA, DOMAINE CHANDON, ROBERT MONDAVI, ANDY BECKSTOFFER, and Beaulieu.

D. Berger, "Carneros," *Wine Enthusiast*, March 1997, 32-38.

CARNEROS ALAMBIC DISTILLERY (DSP 159). In 1983 at SCHRAMSBERG the Davies family arranged with the owners of the Rémy Martin brand of Cognac to produce first-class California brandy under the RMS label. In 1984 an elaborate production facility was built in Carneros. The first brandy was released in 1985, but there was none again until 1991, as inventories were being developed for aging. Meanwhile, in 1987 Schramsberg's interest was bought by Rémy Martin. In the mid-1990s production came to about 5,000 cases, and included a FOLLE BLANCHE varietal brandy and a pear brandy. There is a model of an alambic still in the visitors' center; see the photograph on page 35.

CARNEROS CREEK WINERY (BW 4645). Established in 1972, by Francis Mahoney and his partners, Carneros Creek was the first new winery in the area since shortly after Repeal. In the early years, Mahoney bought grapes from all over northern California and produced an eclectic line of premium varietals. Meanwhile he set his sights on Pinot noir, particularly, and Chardonnay. Between 1975 and 1985, Mahoney and C. J. Alley, a professor at University of California at Davis, conducted experiments at his vineyard to determine the best Pinot noir clones for the Carneros. He is also one of the founders of the Carneros Quality Alliance.

By the 1990s Mahoney's winery had a capacity of almost 200,000 gallons and an annual production of about 30,000 cases, mostly Chardonnay and Pinot noir.

CAROSSO, VINCENT, author of *The California Wine Industry, 1930-1895* (Berkeley, Calif.: University of California Press, 1951), the first scholarly history of the industry.

CARPY, CHARLES (1849–1928). A power in the California wine industry, Carpy was born in Bordeaux and came to northern California in 1865. He worked here as an accountant for the huge Van Bever and Thompson Winery in Napa City, acquiring control of that company in 1886; in 1894 he bought GREYSTONE WINERY, which was eventually made part of the CALIFORNIA WINE ASSOCIATION, of which he was an original partner. He retired from that corporation in 1897. The rest of his active life was devoted to banking, but he continued to be an important spokesman for the wine industry until Prohibition. As a member of a wine-judging panel, he appears in the photograph on page 107 and, again, this time with Jacob SCHRAM in 1895, on page 321.

After acquiring Van Bever and Thompson he changed the name to the Uncle Sam Winery, and, although most of his wines were of ordinary bulk quality, he produced small lots of some of the finest table wines in the state. He was particularly noted for his so-called

Medoc wines, Cabernet Sauvignon under the La Loma label, which had few peers in California in the 1890s.

His grandson, Charles A. Carpy (1927–96), was one of the original partners in the resuscitation of FREEMARK ABBEY in 1967. He was also a partner in the RUTHERFORD HILL WINERY.

CARRARI VINEYARDS (BW 4936). The grapes from the Carrari family's 150-acre vineyard near Los Alamos in Santa Barbara County go to several Central Coast wineries. In 1985 the family bonded its own winery and now produces about 4,000 cases per year. The top varietals are Cabernet Sauvignon, Chardonnay, and Muscat Canelli.

CARTLIDGE & BROWNE, a partnership between Tony Cartlidge and Glen Browne formed in 1981. The following year their NÉGOCIANT business began selling Chardonnay under the STRATFORD label. They expanded sales to include other varietals and, in 1984, began selling wine under the Cartlidge & Browne label. In 1994 the partners leased the EHLERS WINERY as a production facility and bonded it as Ehlers Grove Winery in 1995. Cartlidge & Browne is still their main brand, with annual sales of almost 30,000 cases, about 75 percent Chardonnay and 25 percent Zinfandel.

CASA DE FRUTA (BW 4529). The Zanger family owns 23 acres of vineyards in the Santa Clara Valley and bonded a winery in 1968. The Casa de Fruta on the Pacheco Pass Highway, west of Hollister, is a place to stop and eat, to buy local produce, and to buy wine under the family's label.

CASA NUESTRA (BW 4990). In 1975 the Kirkham family bought a little ranch north of St. Helena on the Silverado Trail that was planted to Napa Gamay, Grey Riesling, and Chenin blanc. The winery was opened in

1979 and produced dry Chenin blanc. Since then Cabernet franc has been added. Most of the annual 2,000-case production is sold at the winery.

CASK. A large wooden barrel bound by metal hoops; also variously referred to as puncheon, hogshead, pipe, butt, and tun, with various capacities, between 100 and 1,000 gallons. See also COOPERAGE.

CASSA BROTHERS WINERY. See FORTINO WINERY

CASSAYRE-FORNI CELLARS (BW 4820). A small winery in the Rutherford area of the Napa Valley, in operation from 1977 until 1987 when it was acquired by SWANSON VINEYARDS.

CASTORO CELLARS (BW 5542), a 660,000-gallon winery near San Miguel, in the Paso Robles area of San Luis Obispo County; dates from 1983. The owner, Niels Udsen, produces 30,000 cases a year, mainly Zinfandel, Cabernet Sauvignon, and Chardonnay. CUSTOM CRUSHING is an important part of the operation.

CATAWBA. A chance hybrid of *Vitis vinifera* and *V. labrusca* discovered in the woods near the Catawba River, North Carolina, in 1801; it was the most important wine grape grown in the east in the 1850s when Californians were searching for the best varieties for their soils and climates. It was widely but not heavily planted in northern California through the 1860s, particularly in the Sierra foothills. But it deservedly fell from favor in later years and, like the Concord, is today seen only in home vineyards in California, although it is still an important white grape in the eastern United States.

CAVES. Historically, wine caves were rare curiosities in California before the 1980s. The traditional gravity-flow winery worked better if dug back into a hill, and such a situation helped moderate cellar temperatures, as would a cave. But there were few hand-hewn caves in the nineteenth century, the most noted being at CRESTA BLANCA in the Livermore Valley, BERINGER and SCHRAMSBERG in Napa Valley, and Jarvis Brothers in the Santa Cruz Mountains.

The first man-made caves in modern times were Dan Wheeler's hand-hewn twin beauties at NICASIO VINEYARDS above Soquel in Santa Cruz County, begun in the 1950s. The current rage for large-scale caves began in 1979 at FAR NIENTE in Napa. The man in charge of this and numerous other jobs was Alf Burtleson of Sonoma. Dale Wondergem was the master technician who operated the giant digging machine, a Welsh coal-mining machine, the Dosco Road Header Mark IIA. By 1989 Burtleson had dug twenty-two caves for wineries in northern California. Since then the number has grown and other contractors have entered the field.

The advantages of such caves, beyond the obvious aesthetics, are the cool and steady temperatures and the high humidity that holds down evaporation from barrels. In the long run such caves are extremely cost efficient.

Rhoda Stewart, "Underground Sculpture,"
Practical Winery & Vineyard, January 1991, 16–18.

CAYMUS VINEYARDS (BW 4598). If Napa Valley were the Bordeaux of California, among its first growths would be Caymus Cabernet Sauvignons. Charles F. Wagner, the founder of Caymus, descends from a family of Alsatian winegrowers. His father moved to the Napa Valley in 1906 and made small quantities of wine there before Prohibition. During Prohibition the Wagner family grew mostly prunes and walnuts and a little wine, "which [they] sold out the back door to put food on the table." The family bonded a little cellar briefly in 1934 (BW 603).

Wagner and his son, Charles J. (Chuck), were a step in front of the wine revolution, pulling their last prunes out in 1966. The winery was bonded in 1971 and their 1972 Cabernet was a success in a rainy vintage. In 1975 Randall DUNN became the winemaker and that year's vintage produced the first Caymus Special Selection Cabernet, since then a steady star among California Cabernets. Between 1975 and 1985, production rose from 8,000 to 40,000 cases a year, partly from the success of Wagner's second-label wines, LIBERTY SCHOOL. Of the Wagners' 75 acres, 50 are in the Cabernet Sauvignon from which they produce their Special Selection, which has been selling for $100 per bottle. By the 1990s, the 60,000-case production also included Sauvignon blanc, Zinfandel, and Pinot noir. After Dunn left in 1982 to concentrate on his own winery on Howell Mountain, Chuck Wagner took over the winemaking. Since 1992, Caymus has been acquiring land in Monterey and Sonoma counties for white wine vineyards. The venture, under Chuck Wagner's supervision, is called Mer et Soleil.

> Charles F. Wagner and Charles J. Wagner, *Caymus Vineyards: A Father-Son Team Producing Distinctive Wines* (Regional Oral History Office, Bancroft Library, 1990).

CECCHETTI-SEBASTIANI CELLAR (BW 5752). Don Sebastiani and his brother-in-law, Ray Cecchetti, developed a line of wines under the SEBASTIANI VINEYARDS bond. Starting in 1985, their sales have grown to 90,000 cases a year, with the addition of their lower-priced Pepperwood Grove label. In 1994 they bonded their winery in Rutherford. The operation also imports and sells olive oil.

CEDAR MOUNTAIN WINERY (BW 5550), a small winery in the Livermore Valley, founded in 1990. The Ault family's 19-acre vineyard is just up Tesla Road from the old Wente Winery. The Aults make a total of about 1,000 cases of Cabernet Sauvignon and Merlot a year.

CELLA. A family of winegrowers influential in the Central Valley after Prohibition, Cellas ran the Roma Wineries at Lodi and Fresno, and later the Cella Winery, east of Sanger. In 1961, a large part of the family's production assets, including the NAPA (VALLEY) WINE CO. in Oakville, was acquired by UNITED VINTNERS.

CENTRAL COAST, a huge viticultural area granted AVA status in 1985. It includes the wine-growing areas of Alameda, Santa Clara, Monterey, San Benito, San Luis Obispo, and Santa Barbara counties, and part of those in Santa Cruz County. In 1960 there were about 8,000 acres of wine grapes, three-fourths of those in Santa Clara and Alameda counties. By 1970 there were about 15,000 acres, much of the increase in Monterey and San Luis Obispo counties. In the 1990s, this area had well over 50,000 acres of wine grapes, more than half of them in Monterey County, but the total acreage has changed little since 1980. About 65 percent of the total was planted to white varieties and 65 percent of those were Chardonnay. Cabernet Sauvignon amounted to about 30 percent of the total. In 1996 the Central Coast produced 226,366 tons of wine grapes, of which 69 percent were white. For more information and history, see the entries for the individual counties

CENTRAL VALLEY. Often referred to as the Great Valley of California, it runs from Redding in the north to the mountains below Bakersfield in the south, a distance of about 450 miles. The entire valley covers about 25,000 square miles and is one of the most important agricultural regions in the world. It is normally divided into the SACRAMENTO VALLEY* in the north and the SAN JOAQUIN VALLEY* in the south; areas that are linked by the DELTA region,* where the great rivers of the valley come together; all three are important grape growing areas. In the 1990s, the Central Valley had almost 200,000 acres of wine grapes and additionally thousands of acres of raisin and table grapes, which are also used extensively for wine and brandy in California. For information and history, see the entries for the

individual counties: COLUSA, FRESNO, GLENN, KERN, KINGS, MADERA, MERCED, SACRAMENTO, SAN JOAQUIN, STANISLAUS, TULARE, and YOLO.

CENTRIFUGE. A device used to clear wines and improve their stability. After Repeal they were used in the huge wine plants of the Central Valley. In the 1970s smaller, but still expensive, models became popular in some larger premium wineries in the coastal districts. Critics argue that the process strips wines of their power and substance. Centrifuges are often used to produce LATE-HARVEST WINES, in which chemical stability is essential.

CENTURION. A wine grape cultivar similar to the CARNELIAN, produced at the University of California at Davis and released in 1974. About 1,000 acres were planted in the Central Valley but the variety did not succeed as hoped. About 550 acres survive, almost none planted since 1975. The 1996 crush of 2,973 tons was 47 percent of the 1990 total.

CHABLIS. In northern Burgundy in France, a noted white wine area and in California a name for generic wine, once popular, but fast disappearing from wine labels here. Before Prohibition, the term was used for white table wines with crisp acidity and good vinous flavor. The GREY RIESLING was the favored varietal and the Santa Cruz Mountains were proclaimed California's chablis district by some writers. In such wines before Prohibition there is no evidence of the use of CHARDONNAY, the variety used for French Chablis. After Repeal, the term lost its meaning, except at a few premium wineries such as Beaulieu, Wente, and Heitz. It had always meant white wine, until the BATF allowed the marketing of so-called pink chablis in 1973.

CHAINE D'OR (GOLDEN CHAIN). A name coined perhaps by Paul Masson for the western stretch of the Santa Cruz Mountains, running from Woodside to the Lexington area above Los Gatos. It was noted before Prohibition for its excellent Cabernet Sauvignon and Zinfandel. Since World War II, several producers, among them CINNABAR, CONGRESS SPRINGS, CRONIN, FELLOM RANCH, KATHRYN KENNEDY, MOUNT EDEN, MARTIN RAY, RIDGE, SUNRISE, and WOODSIDE have continued the tradition.

CHALK HILL. A small viticultural area within the Russian River Valley district in Sonoma, granted AVA status in 1983. The soils of this hilly area southeast of Healdsburg are derived mostly from volcanic ash. Its 33 square miles contain about 1,500 acres of vineyard, most planted to Chardonnay.

CHALK HILL WINERY (BW 4986). In 1974, Fred Furth, an attorney, planted the first sizeable vineyards since Prohibition in the Chalk Hill area, starting with 40 acres on his 540-acre spread. By the 1990s, his almost self-sufficient estate covered more than 1,000 acres with 259 acres of vines. The winery was bonded in 1980 and its first wines appeared under the Donna Maria label. All wines now bear the Chalk Hill label. Most of the 65,000-case production consists of estate-grown Chardonnay, Cabernet Sauvignon, and Sauvignon blanc.s

CHALMERS, ROBERT (?– 1881). An energetic Scotsman who came to California in 1850 by way of Ohio. Following Martin ALLHOFF's* death in 1867, Chalmers married Alhoff's widow, Louisa (1838–1913). Together they expanded the Allhoff vineyard and winery in Coloma and became the leaders of the El Dorado County wine industry in the 1870s. In 1878 they built the Vineyard House, a huge home and later hotel, which still operates near the old winery's imposing ruins. Robert Chalmers lost his mind in 1880 and died the next year. This and Alhoff's earlier suicide have given rise to ghost stories that local folk today, with an eye on the tourist trade, do not discourage.

CHALONE VINEYARD (BW 4512). The winery perches 2,000 feet above the Salinas Valley 9 miles east of Soledad and not far from the Pinnacles National Monument. Grapes were first planted on this elevated benchland around the turn of the century by Maurice Tamm, a Frenchman. In 1919, F. W. Silvear bought land here and began planting grapes. He eventually had 35 acres, mostly Chenin blanc, which he sold after Repeal to Almaden and Wente. He also made small quantities of wine (BW 4265) that won plaudits in 1941 from California's first wine columnist, Robert Mayock. After Silvear's death in 1957, the operation went through complicated changes of ownership under such names as El Venido Vineyard and Mount Chalone Vineyard. For a while, Philip TOGNI was the winemaker. At one time Rodney STRONG of Windsor Vineyards controlled the wine inventory. Eventually Richard Graff (1937–98) and his associates acquired firm control and there was a real vintage in 1969 after several false starts.

The first wines, particularly the Pinot noir, were remarkable critical successes. Later the 1974 Chardonnay took third place in the 1976 tasting in PARIS. Between 1977 and 1982, Chalone established close relations with EDNA VALLEY VINEYARD* and CARMENET;* in 1984 the unified operation went public, selling 625,000 shares of stock at $8.00 a share. In 1986 Chalone, Inc. acquired ACACIA WINERY.

Chalone Vineyard has maintained the identity that Graff established in the 1970s. He emphasized traditional Burgundian winemaking practices, and now, in the 1990s, the 187-acre vineyard complies with this philosophy with low yields from its limestone-rich soils. The new winery, built in 1982, has been expanded to a capacity of 250,000 gallons and about 35,000 cases of Chardonnay, Pinot noir,

Pinot blanc, and Chenin blanc are produced annually. From time to time, wine, usually made from grapes grown in other viticultural areas, is released under the Gavilan Vineyards label. Since 1982 Chalone has had its own appellation, an 8,640-acre block of benchland unique to this portion of the Gabilan Range in Monterey County.

CHAMPAGNE, an important winegrowing district in France noted for its sparkling wines. It is also a legal generic term in California for wines in which the bubbles are produced by a second fermentation in a closed container. Since the 1970s, the term has been seen less and less on the more expensive California sparklers. On the issue of calling such wine "champagne," California producers have stood on both sides since bottle-fermented sparkling wine was first manufactured here in the 1850s. See also SPARKLING WINE.

CHAPMAN, JOSEPH (?1784–1848), a venturesome man from Massachusetts who arrived in Spanish Alta California as a member of a pirate crew sailing under an Argentine flag. He was captured at Monterey in 1818, was released, and moved south. In 1826 at the Pueblo of Los Angeles he planted a 4,000-vine vineyard. Thus he was the first American winegrower in California. For years he was a beloved jack-of-all-trades in southern California.

CHAPPELLET WINERY (BW 4537). The wine historian Hugh Johnson calls Chappellet "the most remarkable wine cathedral of the modern world." It is located east of Rutherford, 1,400 feet above the Napa Valley on Pritchard Hill, which is the name of the winery's second label. Donn Chappellet left his lucrative food-vending business to buy the 600-acre estate in 1967. It already had about 100 acres of vines, planted in 1964. The early vintages of the Chappellet Cabernet Sauvignon and dry Chenin blanc were praised by critics. They were the work of its winemaker Philip TOGNI, who was here until 1973. Other wines have included Chardonnay and White Riesling. Recently Chappellet replaced his 8 acres of Riesling with Sangiovese. Also on the estate is some Merlot, which is usually blended with the Cabernet, but now and then released as a varietal. Production has been fairly steady at about 25,000 cases.

CHAPTALIZATION: The addition of sugar during fermentation to raise the alcohol level in the resulting wine. It is named for Jean-Antoine Chaptal (1756–1832) who, in 1807, wrote a treatise on the practice. It is legal in much of Europe and in several American states where cool fall temperatures often fail to ripen grapes sufficiently. It is now illegal in California but was common here before Prohibition. Today in California if winemakers want to chaptalize legally, they simply add grape juice CONCENTRATE, a fairly common practice here since the 1930s.

CHARBONO. An obscure variety of red grape imported to California from the French Jura region by J. H. Drummond and J. W. PORTAL in the 1870s. It makes a satisfactory table wine with little flavor, but the variety has caused controversy since its earliest years here. Many condemned its overuse and often named it as one of the causes for so much mediocre California wine before 1900. It was most com-

mon in the Santa Clara Valley. Henry NAGLEE used it successfully in his high-grade brandy.

Little survived the phylloxera. One plot that did was on the Inglenook estate where it was thought to be Barbera until Professor Albert WINKLER set things straight in the 1940s. That the grape is French is still in doubt, although some think it to be identical to the Corbeau or Douce noir. In 1989 there were 75 acres in California, all but 8 in Napa Valley. The state no longer keeps statistics on the acreage but, in 1996, of the 257 tons crushed, 95 percent was grown in Napa and Mendocino counties.

CHARDONNAY. The variety of grape responsible for all the great white wines of Burgundy. It is also important in French Champagne production. Today it is grown in most of the important winegrowing regions of the world, and, as a white wine grape, it is exceeded only by the French Colombard in the number of tons crushed. In 1996 there were 72,624 acres in California, of which 68 percent was in the coastal counties. Sonoma had the most, just edging Monterey. These statistics are surprising when one considers that, in 1980, there were 17,000 acres in the state, and in 1970 only 3,000. Before 1968, the variety was not even counted separately in state statistics. In the 1960s almost half of the Chardonnay in California was planted in Almaden's PAICINES vineyards in San Benito County.

TABLE 9. CHARDONNAY GRAPES, SELECTED COUNTIES

				(ACRES)				
YEAR	MENDOCINO	SONOMA	NAPA	SAN JOAQUIN	MONTEREY	SAN LUIS OBISPO	SANTA BARBARA	TOTAL
1968	N.A.	95	246	N.A.	60	N.A.	N.A.	986
1974	385	1,808	2,249	8	2,929	291	843	10,037
1980	901	4,504	4,269	186	3,140	506	1,514	17,033
1985	1,738	7,695	6,908	236	4,384	876	2,786	27,424
1989	3,119	10,129	8,869	3,631	8,578	2,096	4,758	48,049
1997	4,338	14,398	9,154	10,289	12,744	3,984	6,197	82,330

SOURCE: California Agricultural Statistics Service, Sacramento, Calif.

Chardonnay was first imported by J. H. DRUMMOND in 1880 and appeared in H. W. CRABB's To Kalon nursery list in 1882. Later Crabb used it as the backbone of the wine he labelled Chablis, and Tiburcio PARROTT had the vine on Spring Mountain. It was probably Theodore GIER who took the Chardonnay to Livermore from Napa at the turn of the century. Ernest Wente acquired vines from Gier in 1912 and vines deriving from these survived Prohibition in the WENTE vineyards. Paul MASSON also imported the vine to his Saratoga vineyard in the late 1890s. After Prohibition the first "Pinot Chardonnay" to receive critical notice was the 1938 wine from Wente. There were also vines at BEAULIEU and INGLENOOK.

During the 1940s, several premium wineries made a serious effort with the variety. Beginning in 1947, medals were offered for the wine at the State Fair. During the next ten years Wente and Inglenook won half the gold medals awarded for Chardonnay. By the end of the 1960s, Chardonnay had caught on, as the number of premium wineries expanded. The variety led the white-wine boom of the 1970s. The victory of the 1973 CHATEAU MONTELENA Chardonnay at the tasting in 1976 in Paris crowned its surge in popularity.

Today there is a variety of Chardonnay styles available to consumers under hundreds of labels. The wines may be fruity or austere; some go through malolactic fermentation and have a richer character; barrel fermentation now is common; some producers feel that clonal selection is a key to improved quality. Chardonnay is also significant in California's production of bottle-fermented sparkling wine. Yield per acre has soared since the early 1980s. For no other major wine grape variety in California has very recent history been such a defining influence.

In 1997 vineyards in California produced 484,403 tons of Chardonnay. For 1990 the total was 169,709 tons.

The best vintages in recent years were: 1996, 1995, 1994, 1992, 1991, 1990, 1988, 1986, 1985, and 1981.

James Laube, *California's Great Chardonnays* (San Francisco: Wine Spectator Press, 1995).

CHARMAT PROCESS. A modern process used to manufacture sparkling wine, in California almost always inexpensive. It was conceived by Paul GARRETT in 1902, but was actually developed in France by Eugene Charmat (1876–1970) in 1907. It is often termed "bulk process," because the second fermentation takes place in a large tank. The wine is then filtered and bottled under continuous pressure. In 1993 the BATF began allowing the use of the word Charmat on bottles of sparkling wine, instead of the words bulk process, as long as some other phrase is added to indicate that the wine was not fermented in the bottle.

CHASSELAS. See GOLDEN CHASSELAS; GUTEDEL

CHATEAU BELLEVUE. See ALEXANDER DUVAL

CHATEAU BOSWELL (BW 5086), a pretty little winery on the Silverado Trail in Napa Valley; it looks like a miniature French château and has produced small quantities of Cabernet Sauvignon and Chardonnay since 1982.

CHATEAU CHEVALIER (BW 4627). In 1884 Fortune Chevalier (1814–99), a whiskey merchant in San Francisco, bought land on Spring Mountain from the Beringers and planted vines. In 1897, his son George built the winery and house that still grace the estate. He was successful at first with his Castle brand but the earthquake in 1906 and the resulting business losses closed the winery and the vineyards died. The property passed through several hands, but no vines were grown until Gregory Bissonette and

James Frew bought the place in 1969, restored the winery, and replanted 65 acres of vineyard. The first estate wines were from the 1973 vintage. But in 1984 financial problems forced a sale to H. G. Nickel, who had previously restored FAR NIENTE. In 1993 he sold the property to a group of investors that also controlled SPRING MOUNTAIN VINEYARDS and STREBLOW.

CHATEAU CHEVRE WINERY (BW 4933). The Hazen family bought land southwest of Yountville in 1973 and planted 9 acres of Merlot there. In 1979 the winery was started in the old goat barn on the property (*chèvre* means goat in French). Since the 1980 vintage, Merlot has been Hazen's chief product, of which he makes about 1,500 cases per year.

CHATEAU DE BAUN (BW 5326): Located just north of Santa Rosa in Sonoma County, this winery specialized in a wide variety of wines made from SYMPHONY, a muscat cultivar developed at the University of California at Davis. The name of the grape suggested the themes for many of the winery's diverse labels. Prelude is a dry apéritif, Finalé is a late-harvest dessert wine, Rhapsody and Romance are sparkling wines, and Jazz is a BLUSH blend of Pinot noir and Chardonnay.

The vineyard was established in 1986 and the impressive winery was opened in 1990. The founder, Ken de Baun, also made several other varietal wines. Custom crushing was also important here. Annual production was about 30,000 cases in 1995. In 1996 the winery and vineyard were bought by KENDALL-JACKSON to serve as a visitor center.

CHATEAU DE LEU (BW 5360). One of the few wineries in the fine wine country of Solano County. Parts of the 80-acre vineyard in Green Valley were first planted in the 1880s. Ben Volkhardt started planting vines here in 1954 and bonded his winery in 1981. In 1987 the property was acquired by the King Brewing Company of Kobe, Japan. Production today amounts to about 10,000 cases per year, with the emphasis on Merlot and Sangiovese. In 1996, as custom crushers, GOLDEN STATE VINTNERS produced some wine under the Chateau de Leu label.

CHATEAU DIANA (BW 5368). In Dry Creek Valley, Sonoma, this operation, bonded in 1987, concentrates on private-label and CUSTOM-CRUSH wines, often from grapes purchased outside the area, and often produces more than 250,000 cases per year.

CHATEAU JULIEN (BW 5101), a beautiful winery in Carmel Valley, bonded in 1981, it takes its name from the St-Julien district in Bordeaux. By the 1990s production was about 40,000 cases per year with emphasis on Chardonnay, Merlot, and Cabernet Sauvignon. The winery also markets wines under the Emerald Bay and Garland Ranch labels.

CHATEAU MONTELENA (BW 4525). One of the most important wineries in the Napa Valley, it was named for the nearby Mount St. Helena and lies north of Calistoga on Tubbs Lane; Alfred L. Tubbs (1827–96) was the winery's founder. A New Englander who founded the Tubbs Cordage Company in San Francisco in the 1850s, he bought the land in 1882, planted 110 acres of vines there, and built a fine stone winery. By 1887 production stood at 75,000 gallons and Tubbs was already experimenting with resistant rootstocks. He called the estate Hillcrest in those years.

In later years Alfred's grandson, Chapin, managed the property. During Prohibition, grapes were still an important product, although his prunes and pears were more profitable. The winery was back in operation under Chapin in 1933 as Chateau Montelena, but was closed in 1947 soon after he died; the grapes went to other wineries. Later, the estate was divided among family members. In 1958 the winery and the 11.5 acres surrounding it were acquired by Yort Wing Frank, who transformed the estate into a park. Its 5-acre lake had islands connected by lacquered bridges and its own, authentic Chinese junk.

Chateau Montelena's winegrowing revival began in 1968 when Leland Paschich bought the property. He bonded the winery in 1969, and the next year bought back 150 acres of Tubbs's vineyard land. He had a small crush in 1969 and 1970, but none in 1971. Seeking partners in southern California, he found them in James L. BARRETT and Ernest Hahn. In 1972 they hired Miljenko GRGICH as the winemaker, and it was Grgich's 1973 Chardonnay that won the famous tasting in 1976 in PARIS. Jerry Luper succeeded Grgich and, in 1982, James P. (Bo) BARRETT, James L.'s son, took command of the cellar. His father is now general partner.

Over the years the winery has focused its 35,000-case annual production on Chardonnay (16,000 cases), Cabernet Sauvignon (12,000 cases), and Zinfandel (2,000 cases), most from its 100-acre estate vineyard.

Richard Hinkle, "Chateau Montelena," *Wines & Vines*, April 1997, 22-30.

CHATEAU POTELLE (BW 4833). In 1989 Jean-Noël Fourmeaux purchased Vose Vineyards, which had been established on Mount Veeder in 1977, as the base for his winery. Fourmeaux had started production in 1983 when he began blending and bottling wine under his own label at Chateau Souverain. He later acquired vineyard land in Napa along the Silverado Trail. He now controls about 100 acres and produces about 28,000 cases of wine, Cabernet Sauvignon, Chardonnay, Sauvignon blanc, and small quantities of highly praised Mount Veeder Zinfandel.

CHATEAU ST. JEAN (BW 4710), a beautiful winemaking facility that was established in 1973 at the northern end of the Sonoma Valley. The winery was built in 1975 by a group of partners with roots in the table-grape business in the Central Valley. They hired Richard L. ARROWOOD as winemaster. From the outset, a wide variety of Chateau St. Jean white wines won critical applause, particularly the vineyard-designated Chardonnays and the late-harvest wines made in a German style. In 1979, St. Jean began producing sparkling wine at its Graton winery west of Santa Rosa. In 1993, that facility became part of the ASSOCIATED VINTAGE GROUP. Total production had reached about 120,000 cases per year when the winery was sold to Suntory, Ltd., Japan, in 1984. In 1990 Arrowood left to concentrate on his own winery. In the 1990s, production at St. Jean has reached 250,000 cases annually. In 1996 the winery was acquired by BERINGER WINE ESTATES.

Richard L. Arrowood, *Sonoma County Winemaking: Chaeau St. Jean and Arrowood Vineyards and Winery* (Regional Oral History Office, Bancroft Library, 1996).

CHATEAU SOUVERAIN (BW 4631). The SOUVERAIN name has had a complex history. After Lee Stewart sold his winery on Howell Mountain, the name was acquired by Pillsbury and attached to two wineries, Souverain of Rutherford (RUTHERFORD HILL WINERY today) and Souverain of Alexander Valley. The latter, at first called Ville Fontaine, was a handsome facility modeled on the hop kilns of Sonoma. In 1976 the winery was acquired by a grape growers' organization and began producing a wide array of wines. For all its volume (about 450,000 cases a year) and capacity (3 million gallons), it was not successful financially. In 1986, the winery was purchased by Nestlé's Wine World division (today BERINGER WINE ESTATES), which provided much needed capital and focused the operation on the production of Sonoma County varietals of high quality and good value. Now Chateau Souverain produces

Carneros Chardonnay, Alexander Valley Cabernet Sauvignon, and Dry Creek Valley Zinfandel, and has been selling more than 200,000 cases annually in the 1990s.

CHÂTEAU-STYLE WINE. See SAUTERNE

CHATEAU WOLTNER (BW 5286), the stone winery on Howell Mountain was once the center of the BRUN & CHAIX wine operations, which began in 1881. The cellar was built in 1886. It lay dormant from the 1920s until 1980 when Francis and Françoise De Wavrin-Woltner bought the property and restored the winery. They had previously owned an important interest in Château La Mission-Haut-Brion in Bordeaux, and, until 1984, had a stake in CONN CREEK WINERY in Napa. The first Woltner wines were produced in 1985. So far they are all estate Chardonnays, some vineyard designated. When the 1987 Titus Vineyard was released at $54, it was California's most expensive Chardonnay. Annual production in the 1990s was approaching 10,000 cases from the 57 acres of Chardonnay.

CHATOM VINEYARDS (BW 5602) opened in 1992 at Douglas Flat, Calaveras County. Planting of the 65 acres began in 1981 and the first wine was produced in 1985 at another facility. Cabernet Sauvignon, Sangiovese, and Sauvignon blanc wines make up the annual production of 8,000 cases.

CHAUCHÉ & BON, once the trade name for the Mont Rouge Winery near Livermore, founded in 1880 by Adrian George Chauché (1834–93). Charles A. Bon (1864–1902) became his partner in 1892. Chauché was born in the Graves village of Portets, the son of a Bordeaux wine merchant. He came to San Francisco in 1851, and made his fortune importing wine and liquor. More than anyone else Chauché showed that the Livermore Valley could produce fine CLARET. His Zinfandel won a gold

medal at the 1889 Paris Exposition. He also made excellent white wine in the style of his birthplace. At the 1893 Columbian Exposition, the English wine expert Charles OLDHAM declared a Mont Rouge product to be "the finest white wine in the whole exhibit." When Chauché died, Charles Bon took control of the operation and expanded it. Mrs. Bon won a gold medal for her Zinfandel at the San Francisco Panama-Pacific Exposition in 1915. The winery was destroyed by fire in 1938.

CHAUFFE-EAU CELLARS (BW 4568). From 1971 to 1991 this was Vina Vista Winery. In Geyserville, Sonoma County, the operation annually produces about 2,000 cases of Cabernet Sauvignon and Merlot. The new name means geyser in French.

CHAUVET, JOSHUA (1822–1908). A Frenchman from the Champagne region who settled in the Glen Ellen area of Sonoma County in 1856 after buying land from Mariano Vallejo. In the 1860s, he and his spirited Irish wife set up a brandy distillery and, by the 1870s, had built a full-blown winegrowing establishment. In 1881 he built a three-story winery. In the 1890s he averaged about 200,000 gallons per year. He later acquired another winery in Santa Rosa. After his death, the Pagani family bought his winery and operated his vineyard through Prohibition. Today it serves as Glen Ellen's history center.

CHENIN BLANC. The main white wine variety of grape in the Loire Valley, France, it produces dry table wines, sweet wines, and sparkling wines. Sometimes called Pineau de la Loire in France, its history there goes back more than 500 years. In South Africa, it is the Steen vine, and it is common in Australia, where it travels under several names, and in Argentina where it is called Pinot blanco.

Why this variety, with its good acid and delicious fruit, did not catch on in California before

TABLE 10. CHENIN BLANC GRAPES, SELECTED COUNTIES

			(ACRES)			
YEAR	NAPA	MONTEREY	STANISLAUS	MADERA	KERN	TOTAL
1967	N.A.	N.A.	N.A.	N.A.	N.A.	2,162
1972	973	1,190	2,156	495	2,493	14,428
1977	1,648	2,018	2,195	1,315	3,874	21,524
1982	2,258	4,792	2,553	6,507	6,762	43,496
1988	2,011	3,058	2,350	6,223	5,395	36,247
1997	501	1,491	1,302	5,082	3,338	22,049

SOURCE: California Agricultural Statistics Service, Sacramento, Calif.

Prohibition is a mystery. But there is no mention of the variety then beyond the term "White Pinot," which might have meant anything.

The variety was discovered after World War II by several wineries, the vines acquired from the collection at the University of California at Davis. The wine was often labeled White Pinot or Pinot de la Loire. In the 1950s, the variety started to travel under its own varietal label and became quite popular as a semisweet table wine. Charles Krug Winery was particularly successful with it through the 1970s. The industry's poor focus on this varietal can be seen in the fact that there was no category for Chenin blanc at the State Fair competition until 1968. Before then, the wines had to compete as White Pinot.

In that year there were 1,538 acres in the state, half of them in Napa and Sonoma counties. By 1974 there were almost 20,000 acres, overwhelmingly concentrated in the Central Valley where the high yields, good acid, and decent flavors made the grape perfect for inexpensive jug wines. By 1979 it was the most extensively planted white wine varietal in the state, a position it maintained until 1988 when it was passed by Chardonnay. The acreage under Chenin blanc peaked in 1982 at 45,000 acres; by the 1990s the total had dropped to about 25,000 acres, still predominantly in the Central Valley. The decline in acreage there is at least partly a result of the good wines being made from Chardonnay in this very warm climate. But the inability of California's premium producers to make an appreciable quantity of good wine from this superior variety is something of a mystery. Nevertheless, a few producers in the North Coast have been successfully marketing Chenin blanc wines since the 1960s as a dry or slightly sweet premium varietal.

California produced 159,878 tons of Chenin blanc in 1996, 58 percent of the tonnage produced in 1990.

CHEROKEE VINEYARD ASSOCIATION. A cooperative association of growers near Lodi, founded in 1935. For years, its wine was marketed under the CALIFORNIA WINE ASSOCIATION's Eleven Cellars label. In 1972 it was purchased by a group of investors and the 4 million-gallon facility became Montcalm Vintners. In 1979 it was acquired by the Robert MONDAVI family and is now used to produce the Woodbridge line of wine (BW 4802).

CHIANTI. A red wine region in Italy. It is also one of the legal semigeneric terms, like chablis and burgundy, allowed on California wine labels. The term became part of the California wine scene in the 1890s when ITALIAN SWISS COLONY began producing its famous Tipo Chianti from Italian varieties, including the Sangiovese. After Repeal several wineries in California continued to produce wines labeled Chianti. Notable were LOUIS MARTINI,

ALMADEN, and Italian Swiss Colony. The term had virtually disappeared from California wine labels by the 1980s.

CHILES VALLEY. One of the eastern wine-growing valleys in the Napa Valley viticultural area. Much of it was acquired by Joseph B. Chiles in 1844 and was settled by him in 1854. He planted a few Mission vines but the valley was not really discovered viticulturally until the 1880s when about 150 acres were planted, mostly to Zinfandel. In 1889 George HUS-MANN planted his Oak Glen Vineyard there. By the mid-1890s there were about 600 acres of vines and several small wineries with a total capacity of about 200,000 gallons. In 1890, Anton NICHELINI established his winery just above the valley. Since the 1970s, vineyard planting has again expanded; several new wineries have been established. Zinfandel often does very well here in an environment somewhat warmer than that of the main Napa Valley. In 1997 the BATF granted Chiles Valley AVA status.

CHIMNEY ROCK WINERY (BW 5400) In 1980 Sheldon Wilson bought Chimney Rock Golf Course in the Stag's Leap area in in Napa. He converted it into a nine-hole course and 75 acres of vineyard. The winery, built in 1989, and designed after the Cape-Dutch architecture in South Africa, produces about 20,000 cases per year. He has concentrated on Chardonnay, Cabernet Sauvignon, and Sauvignon blanc.

CHOUINARD VINEYARDS (BW 5261). A small winery, bonded in 1985, with a 5-acre estate vineyard, in the hills west of the Livermore Valley. The Chouinard family produces Cabernet Sauvignon and Chardonnay from the home vineyard and purchases grapes from other areas. Production approached 5,000 cases in the 1990s. Their 1993 Livermore Zinfandel was named the best wine at the 1994 State Fair.

THE CHRISTIAN BROTHERS. The Institute of the Brothers of the Christian Schools is a religious fraternity founded in Rheims in 1680 by Jean-Baptiste de la Salle. Its chief purpose is to afford free education to the children of the poor. For many years in California, the Brothers made wine and brandy, the profits helping to support several elementary and high schools and St. Mary's College in Moraga. Mont La Salle Vineyards was the nonprofit, but tax paying, corporate entity that ran the business.

The Brothers began making small quantities of altar wine in Martinez in 1882. In 1931 they bought the Theodore GIER winery and vineyards on Mount Veeder and established a novitiate there. By 1937 the Brothers were producing 200,000 gallons of wine and had established a retail trade. But they were on the verge of bankruptcy. An arrangement with the firm of Fromm and Sichel saved the day and placed the Christian Brothers wine into national distribution. During World War II, profits soared, particularly after the introduction of a beverage brandy in 1940. In 1950 the Brothers purchased the GREYSTONE winery, which in later years became a great tourist attraction as well as the home of their sparkling wine production. By the 1970s Christian Brothers controlled a wine and brandy empire: 2,100 acres of vines (1,100 in Napa Valley), Mont La Salle, Greystone, and aging cellars in Fresno, with a total capacity of 20 million gallons. This capacity had doubled by 1986. Their cellarmaster, Brother Timothy (Anthony Diener), had become a fixture in the Brothers' national advertising campaigns.

But the Christian Brothers label was losing prestige as the revolution of the 1970s demanded higher and higher standards of quality. The profitable brandy business was slipping in the face of intense competition from Gallo. In the late 1980s, huge amounts of effort and money were expended to reverse this trend. But in 1989 the La Salle Institute sold its wine and brandy assets to HEUBLEIN.

The Brothers had earlier leased the old Gier winery to the HESS COLLECTION, and the Institute retained ownership of the Mont La Salle property on Mount Veeder (illustrated on page 227).

The brandy-making part of the business, which amounted to sales of 1,300,000 cases per year, was Heublein's main interest. Over the next few years, Heublein sold off many of the Brothers' assets in the Napa Valley. By the end of 1993 there was no Christian Brothers wine facility. The famous old wine name has become simply a brand name for about 150,000 cases of wine produced by Heublein at a facility in the Central Valley.

Ronald Isett, *Called to the Pacific* (Moraga, Calif.: St. Mary's College, 1979).

Brother Timothy, *The Chrisitan Brothers as Winemakers* (Regional Oral History Office, Bancroft Library, 1974).

CHRISTOPHE. See JEAN-CLAUDE BOISSET

CHRISTOPHER CREEK WINERY (BW 4655). From 1974 to 1992 this was SOTOYOME WINERY, from the Indian name given to the Spanish land grant in the Healdsburg area of Sonoma County. Today the winery produces about 3,000 cases of Syrah, Petite Sirah, and Chardonnay.

CIENEGA VALLEY. An area of San Benito County that received AVA status in 1982. It is one of the oldest commercial winegrowing districts in California. Théophile VACHÉ, a Frenchman, planted vineyards here in 1854 and supplied wine to Hollister, San Juan Bautista, and Monterey for many years. In 1883 he sold his estate to William PALMTAG, who built a 100,000-gallon winery that, in 1902, was incorporated as the San Benito Vineyard Company. Following Prohibition, the Palmtag winery, which still sits atop the San Andreas Fault, was acquired by Edwin VALLIANT, whose white wines in the 1930s were

among the best in the state. After his death in 1943, the property was acquired by Hiram Walker. ALMADEN took over in 1955 and greatly expanded the physical plant. In the 1970s, just across the street from the winery, Almaden had the largest barrel-aging warehouse in the world. But the decline of Almaden in the 1980s meant the end of the Cienega facility as a major producer in the wine industry. HEUBLEIN steadily sold off many of its assets. Nevertheless, several small wineries had been established in the area over the years and still operate. After Almaden's fall in 1989, the old Palmtag plant was acquired by a partnership that, as the **Cienega Valley Winery** (BW 4143) has been making wine from the resuscitated vineyards. Production stands at about 5,000 cases, with emphasis on Zinfandel, Cabernet franc, and Pinot St. George. Some wine is sold under the De Rose label.

CILURZO VINEYARD AND WINERY (BW 4867) was founded in 1978 in the Temecula area of Riverside County. Vincenzo Cilurzo had started planting his vineyard in 1968; it is now the oldest in the district. He produces a wide range of table wines, much of which he sells in his popular tasting room. Production in the 1990s was about 10,000 cases per year.

CINNABAR VINEYARD AND WINERY (BW 5333). A carefully laid-out winery in the Santa Cruz Mountains above Saratoga, built by Tom Mudd in 1987. He had previously raised grapes at his home vineyard in Fox Hollow, Woodside. His vineyard in Saratoga is planted to Chardonnay and Cabernet Sauvignon. Underneath part of the vineyard are his impressive aging cellars. Production in the 1990s was about 12,000 cases per year.

CINSAUT (CINSAULT). See BLACK MALVOISIE

CLAIBORNE & CHURCHILL VINTNERS (BW 5339). A little winery in San Luis Obispo specializing in white wines with an Alsatian tilt. Claiborne Thompson and his wife Fredericka Churchill have produced a dry Riesling, a dry Gewürztraminer, even a dry Muscat Canelli. Their Edelzwicker is a blend of all three. Since they began using their own facility in 1987, production has leveled at about 3,000 cases per year.

CLARET. A term historically used by the British to refer to the red table wines of Bordeaux. In the 1850s the wines were popular on the East Coast and sold under that name. Thus, in California at the same time, the name was used by the earliest Argonauts. In the nascent period of California's wine industry thousands of barrels of claret were imported through San Francisco every year. Winegrowers in California then aimed to compete with this trade and employed its terms.

At first the wines were produced from the Mission variety but they gained little following. But by the late 1860s the ZINFANDEL* had been discovered and was soon used for most California claret. By the 1880s, the wine was being sold on the East Coast and through New Orleans and was indicative of the growing success of the state's wines. Anything might be in a claret, but the best had plenty of Zinfandel.

When the authentic red-wine varieties of Bordeaux became mildly popular in California in the late 1880s, another term was needed to set these wines off from ordinary claret. The term Medoc served this office for wines produced from Cabernet Sauvignon and other red Bordeaux varieties. One occasionally saw such wine described as Cabernet.

Claret was so deeply a part of the wine nomenclature in California at Repeal that most of the state's red-wine producers used it in the 1930s. But by the 1960s the word was rarely seen on a wine label. It was found that the generic burgundy sold much better, whatever was in the bottle. By the 1980s the word claret had almost disappeared from California wine labels.

In recent years a few premium producers have used the term for blends that do not meet VARIETAL percentage requirements. One also hears the word used in conversation to refer to light red table wines made in California from Bordeaux varieties and from Zinfandel.

CLARIFICATION. The process that makes a sound wine clear and brilliant. It can be accomplished with patience and/or special cellar techniques that speed the process. Traditionally, as the unwanted particles left after fermentation settle to the bottom, wine is moved from one container to another. This technique is called racking; see LEES. In early days, before pumps, this was accomplished by siphon and gravity flow.

Particles that won't settle easily can be removed by **fining**. The most common fining agents in the old days were egg whites, bentonite (a clay substance), and isinglass (a gelatin derived from the air bladders of certain fish). Fining is a fairly gentle approach to clarification. Less gentle is **filtration**. Many premium-wine producers pride themselves in avoiding this procedure. Nevertheless, it is efficient and really necessary in the large-scale production of stable wines. But the process, if too heavy-handed, can strip a wine of some of the taste and tactile components thought essential in fine wines.

One of the problems in producing young, semisweet wines in California in the early years was their potential instability, when young and fruity, if yeast cells were allowed to remain in a finished bottle. The answer was to hold such wines for a long time in neutral containers. But then the wines normally lost their youthful fruitiness. In recent years, sterile filtering has solved that problem. Another tool used to stabilize such wines has been the CENTRIFUGE. See also STABILIZATION.

CLARKSBURG. A viticultural area in the Sacramento River Delta region. It received AVA status in 1984. Covering 64,640 acres with about 5,000 acres of vines, it includes the MER-RITT ISLAND Viticultural Area. Breezes from the San Francisco Bay give this area a more moderate climate than the rest of the Central Valley enjoys. Chenin blanc has been the most successful premium varietal grown here.

CLASSIC METHOD/CLASSIC VARIETIES (CM/CV). See SPARKLING WINE

CLASSIC WINE COMPANY. See JFJ BRONCO WINERY

CLAUDIA SPRINGS WINERY (BW 5514). A small winery in the Anderson Valley, Mendocino County, that was bonded in 1989. Production of about 2,000 cases is mostly Chardonnay, Pinot noir, and Zinfandel.

CLAYTON VALLEY. See CONTRA COSTA COUNTY

CLEAR LAKE. Lake County is named for Clear Lake, the largest natural body of fresh water within the state. The Clear Lake Viticultural Area, a huge region that includes virtually all the vineyards in the county, about 3,400 acres, received official recognition in 1984.

CLIMATE. The composite or generalization of weather conditions in a region over an extended number of years. The elements measured are temperature, air pressure, humidity, precipitation, and winds. World climates have been classified into types. California's coastal valley climate, with moderately wet winters and warm, dry summers, is usually termed Mediterranean. The northern coastal areas are marginally classified as West Coast Maritime, with colder winters and much more winter and spring rain. St. Helena and Santa Rosa usually have twice as much rain as San Jose, 100 miles to the south. Farther south in San Luis Obispo and Santa Barbara counties, it is so dry that it is difficult to raise wine grapes

commercially without irrigation. Most of the Central Valley is classified as desert; vineyard irrigation is necessary.

For viticultural purposes the climate of California has been classified into five regions defined in terms of temperature during the growing season. The formula was developed by Albert Winkler and Maynard Amerine, professors at the University of California at Davis; see HEAT SUMMATION; MICROCLIMATE.

Marian W. Baldy, *The University Wine Course*, (San Francisco: Wine Appreciation Guild 1993); 266–74.

A. J. Winkler, *General Viticulture* (Berkeley, Calif.: University of California Press, 1965), 58–71.

CLINE CELLARS (BW 5152). The Cline family started in the wine business in the Delta town of Oakley in Contra Costa County. Fred Cline began as a home winemaker and used grapes from old vineyards near his home. In 1982 he acquired the old Firpo Winery (BW 4006). His chief source of grapes was the old vineyard that surrounds the huge Dupont chemical plant west of Oakley. From the outset Cline aimed at producing wines in a Rhône style from the Mourvèdre, Carignane, and Zinfandel he found there. His interesting blends with those varietals, made in the spirit of the southern Rhône, were labeled Côtes d'Oakley and Oakley Cuvée. Now he also provides other Rhone Rangers with grapes, particularly his Mourvèdre, which tends to be hard to find. (A label for this wine is shown on page 206.) In 1989 the Clines bought 350 acres in Sonoma County. Today the entire operation is in the Carneros district; they had their first crush there in 1991. Production in the 1990s was about 85,000 cases per year.

CLONE. In botany a clone is a group of plants descended from a single plant through vegetative reproduction so that all members of the group theoretically have the same genetic constitution. Interest in clones is a recent development in California winegrowing. As late as 1974 there was no index reference to the topic in A. J. WINKLER's universally honored textbook, *General Viticulture.* Today most of our knowledge of clones comes from controlled scientific studies at American and European universities.

Even so, for about 6,000 years men and women have been selecting vines for certain characteristics and then multiplying them with cuttings. Those cuttings were clones: not themselves truly separate varieties, but rather, strains with distinctive characteristics within varieties, but they all have the same genetic constitution. (For wine grapes, a clone is described by viticultural scholars as a distinct subtype within a given variety.) Thus, for example, some Chardonnay clones bear large crops, others bear grapes that are strongly flavored but have low yields.

Early winegrowers in California knew nothing of clones, but some varieties, such as the Pinot noir, evidenced differences and so were regarded as several varieties, known by different names. In fact, they were all clones of the one variety. Today there are Chardonnay selections that survived Prohibition as separate clones and Californians treat them with reverence. The Wente and Masson clones are examples.

Clone diversity has become an important element in modern vineyard management. Winegrowers intending to make estate and single-vineyard wines do well to use several clones of a variety in their planting. Clonal selection is also important. A grower looking for large yields to produce fighting varietals will probably not select a clone that might be attractive to a producer aiming at a superpremium wine. Today winegrowers in California who are interested in clonal selection are most likely to focus their attention on Chardonnay, Pinot noir, Syrah, Sangiovese, and Merlot.

John Caldwell, *A Concise Guide to Wine Grape Clones for Professionals* (Napa, Calif.: privately printed, 1995).

CLOS DU BOIS (BW 5593). Before there was a Clos du Bois there were Frank Woods's 100 acres of Dry Creek vineyard in Sonoma County. In 1976 he and some former classmates at Cornell formed Western Eleven Vineyards with Clos du Bois as the brand name. (*Bois* means woods in French.) Soon they had added acreage in the Alexander Valley and released their first wines from the 1974 vintage.

From the outset, the partners regarded the vineyard as the key to success. For many years, they never actually had an identifiable winery, but produced wines at several leased facilities in the Healdsburg area. Clos du Bois became known as the "vagabond winery." But their success was phenomenal. By the mid-1980s, sales had grown to over 200,000 cases a year. They brought out a wide range of varietals at several levels of price and quality and a lower-priced River Oaks brand. The greatest success came from Chardonnay, Merlot, and Cabernet Sauvignon. All the partnership's wines were from Sonoma County where it owned over 500 acres, most in the Alexander Valley.

When Woods tried to raise long-term capital to bring the "vagabond" operation together in 1987, he met too much resistance from the banks and in 1988 he sold Clos du Bois to Hiram Walker for $40,000,000. Even though the operation's reputation was based on the vineyards, well over half the price was based solely on the value of the brand the partnership had developed. By 1990 a permanent winery had been built and, in 1991, all of the Clos du Bois crush took place at the modern plant just south of Geyserville. By 1997 Hiram Walker had increased sales under the Clos du Bois label to 750,000 cases a year.

CLOS DU LAC. See GREENSTONE WINERY

CLOS DU VAL (BW 4638), an estate in the Stags Leap district, that was founded by Bernard Portet in 1972 and the winery built in

1974. Portet selected the 120-acre Napa property and has managed it since the beginning for the owners, who are eastern investors. Portet's solid academic background, his good business sense, and the fact that he grew up at the Château Lafite-Rothschild in Bordeaux, where his father was technical director, insured success for his wines. The first vintage in 1972 was made at CUVAISON from purchased grapes, about 5,000 cases of Cabernet Sauvignon and Zinfandel, the two varieties Portet has since concentrated on. In 1978 he added Merlot, Chardonnay, Sémillon, and Pinot noir to the line. Later came wines from purchased grapes under the Joli Val, Grand Val, and Le Clos labels.

By the 1990s Portet had acquired the nearby ST. ANDREW'S WINERY for added capacity and had expanded Clos du Val's vineyards to about 275 acres. These included about 100 acres in the Carneros developed in 1979 for Chardonnay and Pinot noir. Cabernet Sauvignon and Chardonnay are by far the leaders in the winery's annual 75,000-case production.

CLOS PEGASE (BW 5343). South of Calistoga, a winery that has been in the public eye more for matters artistic than vinous since the owner, Jan Shrem, purchased the 50-acre Napa Valley site in 1983, three years after selling his international publishing firm. The winery, conceived as a temple to wine, was finished in 1987, after a lively local debate over its proportions and style.

The first wines were made in 1985 at the ROMBAUER winery. Over the years, Shrem has acquired 250 acres of vineyard, mostly in the Carneros, and has dug 20,000 square feet of tunnels under the knoll behind the winery. The estate reflects Shrem's continuing passion for art; he himself gives visitors monthly slide lectures on the history of wine and art. In 1992 the BATF rejected a Clos Pegase label for its depiction of a nude.

Wine production at Clos Pegase is about 45,000 cases in the 1990s. There is a typical range of the standard top varietals and varietal bottlings of Grenache, Petite Sirah, and Sémillon. Homage is a red Bordeaux blend introduced in 1987.

CLOVERDALE is the historic "urban" center of the northern Sonoma County wine country. Not counting the huge ITALIAN SWISS COLONY three miles to the south, the area in 1893 had 1,435 acres of vines and seven wineries. Before Prohibition, the most important wineries in the area were Walter SINK's Cloverdale Wine Co. and Ferdinand Albert's MOULTON HILL WINERY. Since 1933 twenty-nine wineries have listed their mailing addresses in the Cloverdale area.

CM/CV. See SPARKLING WINE

COCA-COLA. There have been two Coca-Colas in the annals of California wine. The Coca-Cola Company of Atlanta in 1977 bought STERLING VINEYARDS in Napa and MONTEREY VINEYARD in the Salinas Valley. But profits from wine were not high enough for the Georgia company and in 1983 the two properties were sold to SEAGRAM.

The Coca-Cola Bottling Company of New York in 1973 bought FRANZIA BROTHERS to add to its eastern holdings, which included Mogen David. These and other holdings were consolidated in 1981 as THE WINE GROUP.

CODORNIU NAPA (BW 5573). The Codorniu company of Spain was the largest producer of bottle-fermented sparkling wine in the world when it bought a winery site and vineyard land in Carneros in 1985. Six years later, an imposing 120,000-square-foot champagnery had been dug deep into a hill above Old Sonoma Road. Nearby are about 160 acres of mostly Chardonnay and Pinot noir, with land for at least 200 more acres of vineyard. Production in the 1990s is about 20,000 cases a year.

COHN WINERY (BW 5359). Bruce Cohn manages rock groups. His success made it possible in 1974 for him to buy Olive Hill Ranch in the Sonoma Valley near Glen Ellen. (He grew up on his parents' ranches near Santa Rosa.) On his new land there were vineyards, which he expanded to 80 acres; he sold grapes for several years. Their high quality led him to build his own winery and develop his own brand in 1984. He emphasizes Chardonnay, Cabernet Sauvignon, and Merlot. Production in the 1990s was approaching 20,000 cases a year.

COIT, LILLIE HITCHCOCK. See LARK-MEAD WINERY; THREE PALMS VINEYARD

COLD DUCK. A sweet, pink, sparkling concoction usually made by the CHARMAT process and flavored with Concord grapes. The name comes from the German expression *kaltes Ende,* meaning cold finish, reference to the Rhenish tradition of combining the red and white wines left at the end of a meal and mixing them with chilled soda water. It is not a long jump from *kaltes Ende* to *kalte Ente,* which means cold duck in German.

In 1963 a winery in Michigan sold the first case and, by 1968, it was the hottest item in the wine industry, accounting for a million cases that year. By 1970 there were thirty-seven producers, seventeen of them in California. Sales began declining in 1972 and by the end of the decade sales were—dead.

COLE RANCH. The Cole family owns a huge spread in Mendocino County east of the Anderson Valley. Sixty acres of vines were planted there in 1973. Ten years later Cole Ranch was granted AVA status by the BATF. Most of the grapes go to FETZER.

COLOMBARD. See FRENCH COLOMBARD

COLOMBET, CLEMENT (1819–90). The pioneer of commercial viticulture in the Mission San Jose area. He planted 85 acres of vines in the Warms Springs district and built a hotel there. After the great earthquake of 1868, he sold the property to the STANFORD family. The WEIBEL winery was set on the Colombet land, which had been developed by the Stanfords. But in the 1990s the vineyards gave way to homes and the winery was shut down.

COLUSA COUNTY, a hot and dry county in the west-central Sacramento Valley that, in 1995, had 1,257 acres of wine grapes mostly planted in 1988–89, around Williams and Arbuckle, mostly Zinfandel. In 1987 there had been 146 acres. Before Prohibition most of Colusa's Zinfandel, along with that from nearby Yolo County, was shipped to the large wine factories in the town of Napa. Today grapes from Colusa are sent south to Lodi, where most are made into FIGHTING VARIETALS and White Zindfandel.

CONCANNON VINEYARD (BW 616). James Concannon (1847–1911), a native of County Galway, Ireland, went to Boston in 1865 and thence to San Francisco in 1878. In 1883, with money he made in the rubber stamp business, he bought 47 acres in the LIVERMORE VALLEY* and created his family wine estate, which lasted until 1982 when his grandchildren sold the business.

Concannon built his winery in 1895 and, within two years, had production up to 100,000 gallons. He regularly supplied the San Francisco wine firm of Lachman & Jacobi with prize-winning dry and sweet sauterne. Guided by James's son, Joseph (1884–1965), the winery stayed in operation during Prohibition, selling altar wine. At Repeal, Concannon wines, particularly the whites, were among the best in the state, to be found on the wine lists of the top hotels on both coasts. By 1936 production was up to 200,000 gallons, about half dry and half sweet.

In the 1950s, the third generation (pictured on page 191) began taking over daily operations. Joseph, Jr. (1928–78) handled sales and James the winemaking. Emphasis was still on white table wine, but more reds were being made. In 1961 Concannon made the first Californian varietal Petite Sirah in this century.

The sale of the 450,000-gallon winery and its 250 acres of vines in 1982 was the first in a ten-year series of complex corporate ownerships and transfers for the property. In 1992, a partnership headed by three members of the WENTE family acquired the property. Part of the motivation for this acquisition was the desire to save the historic estate from being cut up by corporate owners. Philip Wente declared, "We acted to preserve Concannon, not acquire it." Annual sales in the 1990s were about 75,000 cases. The winery is actually expanding its Livermore vineyard acreage from its current 190. Jim Concannon, a member of the third generation of the family, is still part of the management of the historic winery.

Most grape juice concentrate sold to home winemakers during Prohibition was manufactured by large-scale producers, but the Namco brand came from FOUNTAINGROVE.

CONCENTRATE. The water content of grape juice can be reduced to yield a concentrate high in sugar and quite stable. Today it is legal to add grape juice concentrate to the must before fermentation or to the wine afterward and this is commonly done in the production of ordinary wines. But, in the words of C. S. Ough, a professor of enology, "Don't expect high quality wines as a result."

Between 25 and 39 percent of the Central Valley grape crush in the 1990s goes to concentrate production, most of the grapes being varieties that, although not favored for wine, previously went into wine production, such as Thompson Seedless. This concentrate is used mostly as a sweetener for juices and other food products.

Historically, since the 1880s, winegrowers in California have viewed concentrate production as a partial solution to the oversupply of grapes. This was particularly obvious in the 1890s when dozens of wineries all over the state had their own vacuum processors. During Pro-

hibition many producers marketed large cans of grape concentrate and included on the label detailed instructions about what *not* to do lest one produce an alcoholic beverage.

CONGRESS SPRINGS VINEYARDS (BW 4766). The historic Pourroy Winery, in the hills above Saratoga in the Santa Cruz Mountain area, was brought back to life in 1976 as Congress Springs. The founders, Daniel Gehrs and Victor Erickson, brought out a steady stream of high-quality premium wines, many from older mountain vineyards in the area. In 1987 the sale of majority control of the business to a British firm led to the undoing of the operation. By 1992 the British company had closed the winery and sold off its equipment and inventory.

CONN CREEK WINERY (BW 4769). William D. Collins had grown grapes north of St. Helena for several years before he launched his Conn Creek label. Although he bought his first

Cabernet Sauvignon (1974) from another producer in Napa Valley, the wine brought immediate prominence to the brand. Then, until he built his own winery in 1979, he used the old EHLERS Winery (dating from 1886) above St. Helena as a production facility. With financial support from the future owners of CHATEAU WOLTNER, Collins expanded production in subsequent years. In 1987, he sold the winery to Stimson Lane Wine & Spirits, a subsidiary of U. S. Tobacco, which also owns the VILLA MT. EDEN brand. Since then, the winery has cut back its production line to concentrate on Cabernet Sauvignon and Merlot. In 1996 the Villa Mt. Eden sign went up at the Conn Creek facility, even though some wines under the Conn Creek label are still being made.

CONNOISSEURS' GUIDE TO CALIFORNIA WINE. Among the earliest of the newsletters about evaluations of California wine, it was founded in 1974 by Charles Olken and Earl Singer. Back issues of this newsletter are an important source for the recent history of wine in California.

CONN VALLEY. Until the 1890s, when it was surpassed by Howell Mountain, this was Napa's leading mountain wine area. It lies in the middle of Napa Valley over the first ridge of eastern hills. In 1886 Conn Valley had 665 acres of vines and its wineries produced about 150,000 gallons of wine, two-thirds of which came from the Franco-Swiss Winery, which was established in 1877. It is still an important winegrowing area, but its potential acreage for viticulture has been lessened by Lake Hennessey, formed by the construction of Conn Dam.

CONRADI WINERY. See ROBERT KEENAN WINERY

CONTRA COSTA COUNTY borders the San Francisco Bay and extends eastward to the edges of the Central Valley. The portion along the bay north of Alameda County is too cool for viticulture, but the valleys to the east have good weather and excellent soils for winegrowing. (See ALAMEDA COUNTY for map.) Historically there have been three winegrowing districts here: the foothills around Martinez south of the Sacramento River, the Clayton Valley near Mount Diablo, and the Oakley area to the east.

There were a few commercial vineyards around Martinez in the 1860s and about 350 acres in the 1870s. Most of the grapes were shipped to winemakers in San Francisco. But the 1880s saw a great planting boom. By the 1890s there were over 5,000 acres of wine grapes and several large wineries, particularly Glen Terry and Mount Diablo in the Clayton Valley, Brookside near Walnut Creek, and Joost near Martinez.

The phylloxera was particularly virulent here after 1895; in the following years, many old vineyards became walnut orchards. Acreage grew during Prohibition and reached 5,300 in 1936. There were fifteen wineries in the 1930s. These numbers declined through the 1940s and 1950s as Bay Area suburbia expanded into this rich agricultural region. By the 1960s there were but 1,500 acres and five small wineries. In the 1980s, several winemakers in northern California discovered the few remaining vines, particularly those in the Oakley area. Soon a Contra Costa designation could be found on red table wines from such producers as CLINE CELLARS and ROSENBLUM CELLARS. In the 1990s the acreage of wine grapes in the county began to rise and, by 1997, the total was 816 acres: 298 of Zinfandel, 222 of Mourvèdre (Mataro), 105 of Chardonnay, and 93 of Carignane. In this minor renaissance in viticulture, more than 200 acres of new vineyard have been planted in Contra Costa, mostly to Mourvèdre.

COOK'S IMPERIAL CHAMPAGNE. The sparkling wine and Cook County in Chicago are both named for the same man, Isaac Cook, who bought the Missouri Wine Company of

St. Louis in 1859 and launched the brand. His huge four-level facility with its stone-arched vaults operated in later years as a vinegar plant, but during World War II the company, then owned by German interests, was seized by the government. The brand was acquired by GUILD WINERIES in the 1970s. Cook's Imperial returned to the market in 1978 as an inexpensive, CHARMAT-PROCESS wine that has proved a great success. "When America parties it Cook's" was the advertising motto that helped push sales toward the 2 million-case mark in the mid-1990s. The brand is now owned by CANANDAIGUA.

COOLER. Wine coolers have been around for a long time but in the 1980s they became briefly an important part of the California wine industry. A wine cooler is perhaps half a glass of wine, about as much fruit juice, and then a squirt of seltzer—add ice. In 1981 a small company began bottling the concoction, called it California Cooler, and sold 80,000 cases the first year. Two years later the company was selling 1.7 million cases, and there were about forty brands of cooler on the market. Their wine content accounted for about 5 percent of California's total wine production. By 1987 E. & J. GALLO was selling about 18 million cases of cooler per year. About 20 percent of California wine in 1987 went into coolers. But from that point sales began collapsing by between 15 and 30 percent per year. Federal tax hikes helped increase the decline and many producers shifted from wine to malt-based beverages. By 1995 it appeared that wine coolers were a fad traveling the same road as COLD DUCK.

COOPERAGE. A cooper makes and repairs vessels constructed of staves and hoops—BARRELS, CASKS, tanks, and so on. Cooperage is the result. (Before Prohibition the barrel simply acted as a neutral wine container; its role today in California is a very different.) Larger containers were also constructed by coopers to ferment, age, hold, and store wine. In the 1860s Agoston HARASZTHY and Charles LEFRANC independently discovered the useful qualities of redwood for large, upright tanks, which became standard in virtually all commercial winemaking in California until the 1960s, when stainless steel began replacing this older cooperage. The term has come to mean more than just containers. Questions about a winery's cooperage often bring an answer in gallons of capacity. But one does not refer to those who construct stainless steel containers for wineries as coopers.

COOPERATIVE. Cooperative wineries became a part of the wine industry in California when in 1904 the Woodbridge Vineyard Association was founded by thirty-three grape growers in the Lodi area as a reaction to low grape prices. Federal legislation in 1922 made cooperatives more profitable, and frustration again fueled by low prices generated a great expansion in this type of operation during the depression of the 1930s. But since 1951, when the tax advantage was lost, cooperatives have been steadily bought up by corporations. Many of the older plants became obsolete and no longer operate.

The leading wine cooperatives in California listed on page 77.

COOPER-GARROD ESTATE VINEYARDS (BW 5720). In the 1890s R. V. Garrod (1880–1972) settled in the hills behind Saratoga and raised prunes and apricots. His great contributions to California wine were his friendship with scores of California wine and grape producers in the state and his great memory; his reminiscences have been recorded at The Bancroft Library at the University of California at Berkeley. In the 1980s, his family began planting vineyards on the Garrod Mt. Eden property and in 1994 bonded their winery in partnership with the William Cooper family. The partners produce Cabernet Sauvignon, Cabernet franc, and Chardonnay, about 3,000 cases a year.

LEADING WINE COOPERATIVES IN CALIFORNIA

COOPERATIVE	DATE FOUNDED	DISTRICT	CURRENT OWNER
Bear Creek Vineyard Association	1934	Lodi	Guild
California Growers Winery	1936	Tulare	Golden State
Central California Co-op Winery	1937	Fresno	Sierra
Cherokee Vineyard Association	1935	Acampo	R. Mondavi
Community Grape Corporation	1922	Lodi	*
Cucamonga Growers Winery	1936	Cucamonga	*
Cucamonga Pioneer Winery	1934	Cucamonga	*
Delano Growers Co-op Winery	1940	Delano	Delano Growers
Del Rey Co-op Winery Association	1945	Fresno	Sun-Maid
Del Rio Winery	1936	Lodi	*
East-Side Winery	1934	Lodi	Oak Ridge
Kearney Co-op Winery Association	1947	Fresno	*
Larkmead Co-op Winery	1947	Napa Valley	Larkmead-Kornell
Lockeford Winery	1946	Lodi	*
Lodi Winery	1935	Acampo	*
Mendocino Grape Growers	1946	Ukiah	Guild
Modesto Co-op Winery	1935	Modesto	*
Muscat Co-op Winery Association	1935	Fresno	Vie-Del
Napa Valley Co-op Winery	1934	St. Helena	Golden State
St. Helena Co-op Winery	1939	St. Helena	Markham
Sanger Winery Association	1935	Sanger	Gibson
Sonoma County Co-op Winery	1935	Windsor	*
Woodbridge Vineyard Association	1934	Acampo	
Yosemite Winery Association	1946	Madera	Canandaigua

* No longer in operation.

SOURCE: Table compiled by author from data supplied by Irving Marcus, "California's Cooperative Wineries," *Wines & Vines,* March 1953, 8–12.

COPPOLA, FRANCIS FORD. See INGLENOOK; NIEBAUM-COPPOLA ESTATE

CORBETT CANYON VINEYARDS (BW 4885), originally Lawrence Winery, the largest winery in San Luis Obispo County. It was founded as a high-volume operation by James Lawrence in 1978. The first crush produced more than 200,000 cases and a wide range of wines. Eventually there was even a pink Gewürztraminer. After Lawrence sold his winery to Glenmore Distilleries in 1981, the name was changed to Corbett Canyon. In 1988, the WINE GROUP* bought the operation after some lively bidding with Kendall-Jackson. To insure its grape sources, the Wine Group bought the nearby 350-acre Los Alamos Vineyard. The winery's Coastal Classics line, moderately priced varietals, primarily Chardonnay, Pinot noir, and white Zinfandel, had pushed sales close to the million-case mark by 1997.

CORISON WINES. Cathy Corison was the winemaker at CHAPPELLET for ten years before introducing her own brand in 1987. She buys grapes, rents winery space, and produces about 2,000 cases a year of highly praised Napa Valley Cabernet Sauvignon.

CORK. The closure used on most bottles of California wine. They are made from the bark of the cork oak, *Quercus suber.* Wine drinkers have a traditional and somewhat aesthetic attachment to the cork and its removal from the bottle. For years there has been a running controversy about whether wine in bottles with corks ages better than wine in bottles with other closures.

Wines tainted by contaminated corks are said to be "corked," a small problem during most of California wine history. But in the 1980s it became one of the industry's most serious quality problems. Trichloroanisole (TCA) is almost always the culprit, but the cause of contamination has been hotly debated. A likely suspect is the chlorine sometimes used to sterilize corks. Nevertheless, it has become clear that an artificial cork might solve the problem. In the 1990s several of California's premium wineries were experimenting with an inert synthetic cork made from plastic resin. Reports on results have been positive. It is also clear that work by the cork industry to avoid TCA has been quite successful in recent years.

Wine Business Monthly, April 1996, 46–47; June 1996, 25-26.

CORTI, DARRELL, a grocer, wine merchant, and vintner in Sacramento. He was helpful in the rediscovery of the Sierra foothills as a fine winegrowing area. (The label for one of those wines is shown on page 408.) He has also been a leader in advocating the wider use of Italian varieties of grapes in California. He is a noted expert on wine and food, and where to get the best. His opinions, however controversial, are taken seriously by other experts and by many consumers.

COSENTINO WINERY (BW 5127). Mitch Cosentino founded Crystal Valley Cellars in Modesto in 1982. He made small batches of commercial wine from grapes purchased in the North Coast area, concentrating on red Bordeaux varieties. His red MERITAGE is named The Poet; his Chardonnay, The Sculptor. He also makes Merlot, Pinot noir, and Zinfandel.

In 1990 he moved his operation to the Oakville area of the Napa Valley and renamed it Cosentino Winery. In 1992 the owners of the second-growth Cos d'Estournel, in Bordeaux, successfully challenged his use of the word Cos on his labels, although that is his nickname. Production in the 1990s was about 18,000 cases per year.

COSTELLO VINEYARDS (BW 5109). The Costello family owns 40 acres of vineyard south of Yountville, acquired in 1928. Since 1982 the winery has been producing about 12,000 cases of Chardonnay annually.

COTTONWOOD CANYON (BW 5528). The Beko family owns 78 acres of Chardonnay and Pinot noir in the Santa Maria Valley in Santa Barbara County. The bonded winery was established in 1990 to the north, near San Luis Obispo. Current production approaches 5,000 cases a year, mostly Chardonnay and Pinot noir and some sparkling wine.

H. COTURRI & SONS (BW 4903). A small family winery near Glen Ellen that specializes in organically grown wines, mostly powerful reds. In this approach to winegrowing the Coturris have been pioneers in California, but their wines have occasioned controversy. The winery in Sonoma Valley was bonded in 1979. Production in the 1990s was about 2,500 cases.

CRABB, HIRAM W. (1828–99). Born in Ohio, Crabb came to California in 1853, settling for a while in the East Bay, where he became interested in viticulture through his contacts with John Lewelling, the famous nurseryman. He moved to Napa in 1865 and bought a 240-acre plot near Oakville. His first interest at his Hermosa Vineyard was in table grapes and raisins, but in 1872 he changed his focus to winegrowing. In fact, he became something of a fanatic in his viticultural investigations and, by the end of the 1880s, had one of the largest collections of vines in the world, with more than 400 varieties in his catalogue. By now his operation was called To Kalon, a Greek expression meaning the beautiful.

He was a good businessman and developed a great reputation for his wines, establishing his own brand and marketing it in the east through his own agents. In 1890 the *Chicago Herald* called him the "Wine King of the Pacific Slope." His winery, which is illustrated on page 242, had grown to an 800,000-gallon capacity. He was also instrumental in bringing resistant rootstock to the Napa Valley to fight phylloxera.

After his death in 1899, the estate passed to the E. W. Churchill family, which owned it until the 1940s. In 1939 the old winery, a huge complex of insulated wooden buildings, burned down. The To Kalon vineyard is now owned by several growers, among them Robert MONDAVI. Its grape crops have as great a reputation today as they did a century ago.

Frona E. Wait, *Wines and Vines of California* (1889; reprint, Berkeley, Calif.: Howell-North, 1973), 107–109.

CRANE, GEORGE BELDEN (1806–98). Others planted grape vines in the Napa Valley before Crane did, but he was the first to plant them with the clear intent of producing wine. Crane came to California in 1853 and settled in San Jose, where he became interested in winegrowing. Deciding that Napa had the best prospects, he bought 300 acres of land just south of St. Helena in 1857. In 1861 he planted White Riesling and Sylvaner vines, which he got from Francis Stock, his contact in San Jose. These were the first authentic wine grapes planted in Napa, and when they produced a real crop in 1865, the northern California press took note. He hired a French wine expert, Henry A. PELLET, to make his wine.

Years later, Charles KRUG praised Crane as the man who proved how good Napa wine could be. By the 1870s he retired and had others manage his cellar. Through the 1890s he carried on as the "grand old man" of Napa wine. His letters and articles in the local press informed newcomers and reminded oldtimers whence Napa wine had come. His pen and acerbic wit were ever ready to defend high quality in Napa and California wines, which, he contended, were always threatened by the leveling influences of corporate self-interest. His beautiful home surrounded by its historic vineyard still stands today.

CREEKSIDE VINEYARDS (BW 5402). Formerly the brand for Don Johnson's winery and distillery in Gordon Valley, Solano County. In 1994 he sold the brand and distillery permit to KAUTZ IRONSTONE VINEYARDS in Calaveras County.

CRELLIN, JOHN. See RUBY HILL

CRESCINI WINES (BW 4964). Since 1980, Richard and Paula Crescini, using traditional and natural winemaking techniques, have been producing several varietal wines in small quantities at their little winery at Soquel, south of Santa Cruz. Their recent focus has been on Cabernet Sauvignon, Cabernet franc, and Petite Sirah.

CRESTA BLANCA. Historically the name of the vineyard and estate founded by Charles A. WETMORE in 1882 in the Livermore Valley (at first called Oja del Monte), today a brand name owned by CANANDAIGUA.

Wetmore was a mythic figure in the history of wine in California and in the early days at Cresta Blanca, he produced a series of highly praised wines. His white wines from Bordeaux varieties won a gold medal at the 1889 Paris Exposition. A poor businessman, he lost control

Charles WETMORE named his winery and vineyard after the white-topped cliff that stands above the vineyard.

of the business in 1892 to his brother, Clarence J. WETMORE, and Charles E. Bowen, a businessman in San Francisco. For the next twenty-five years the reputation of Cresta Blanca wines for high quality declined not a bit. No one dared challenge the advertising claim first made in 1907 by Bowen and Clarence Wetmore that Cresta Blanca was California's largest producer of truly fine wines. Their vineyards in Livermore covered 500 acres and they had agencies in all major cities in the country. Production averaged about 100,000 gallons per year. One particular line of wines raised the ire of some people in the industry. These were the wines labeled Margaux or Yquem, although always qualified by the word Souvenir. No one challenged the quality of those wines, but such labeling was specifically outlawed after Prohibition.

During the dry years, Bowen dropped out and Wetmore went into retirement, but at Repeal the company was reincorporated. Lucien B. Johnson owned and managed the operation in the 1930s and in 1941 sold it to Schenley, which maintained fairly high standards until the 1960s. But the closing down process began in 1965 and the brand was sold to GUILD WINERIES in 1971. Meanwhile the old winery, its famous caves, and its historic vineyard fell into ruin. In 1981 the WENTE family bought the property, and naming the vineyard after Charles Wetmore, replanted the vines. The winery and caves became the facilities for the family's sparkling wine production. On the hill above stands the white-crested cliff of exposed limestone, *la cresta blanca*, for which Wetmore named the estate.

CRESTON VINEYARDS AND WINERY (BW 5115). Formerly Creston Manor, a 480-acre ranch that was purchased in 1980 by the Rosenbloom and Koontz families, from Los Angeles. Mrs. Koontz had been Christina Crawford, the actress Joan Crawford's daughter. By 1982 there was a winery and 160 acres of young vines. It is located in the hills about 20 miles east of San Luis Obispo. When Mr. and Mrs. Koontz were divorced, Lawrence and Stephanie Rosenbloom had to reorganize in 1987 and find new partners, among them Alex Trebek of the television program *Jeopardy* who is now listed as proprietor of the operation. Since then Creston has produced a diversified line of varietal wines, most recently Chardonnay, Pinot noir, and Cabernet Sauvignon. Production is about 45,000 cases per year.

CRIBARI. A historic name in the annals of California wine, but now a brand of wine sold by CANANDAIGUA. In 1904 Beniamino Cribari (1859–1942) and his four sons planted vineyards in the Santa Clara Valley near Morgan Hill. During Prohibition, the family made its fortune shipping grapes east to home winemakers in boxes with the Sonnie Boy label, a picture of the youthful Albert Cribari, who was later a vice president and winemaster of GUILD WINERIES.

The House of Cribari expanded after Repeal and controlled several wineries and thousands of acres of vines in the Central Valley. As part of the Guild operation since the 1950s, and centered in Fresno, Cribari produces over one million cases of generic and varietal wines annually. In 1991 members of the Cribari family acquired a new bond (BW 5579) in Fresno for the production of wine under the Silver Creek label. They also produce altar wine under the Cribari label.

CRONIN VINEYARDS (BW 4997). Duane Cronin's home is near Woodside in the Santa Cruz Mountains. He bonded its basement in 1980 and since then has been making what critics insist are some of the finest Chardonnays in California. As a home winemaker, he began in 1976 with a load of Amador Zinfandel he acquired through Charles Wagner of Caymus. Since then, he has made many reds, the most renowned being the Cabernet Sauvignon and Merlot from the Stag's Leap area of Napa Valley. He has a small Cabernet vineyard in the front yard of his "estate," but it is his Chardonnay that has made his 2,000-case-a-year operation famous. His grape sources extend from Monterey County to the Alexander Valley.

CROSS. See HYBRID

The lad on this Cribari label is Al Cribari, later the winemaster at Guild Wineries. During Prohibition, his much younger face adorned the box-end labels of the company's Sonnie Boy brand of fresh grapes. Among home winemakers this brand was affectionately referred to as the Baby Grapes.

CRUESS, WILLIAM V. (1886–1968). One of America's leading food technologists in the twentieth century, he worked particularly with wine and grape products at the University of California at Berkeley, where he taught from 1911 until 1954. Before Prohibition, he worked to develop outlets for California grapes when the dry years came. After Repeal, he conducted practical short courses for California winemakers. He is best remembered today for his students who became leaders of the wine industry in California in the 1950s and 1960s.

CRUSHING. Before mechanical equipment reached California, wine grapes were trod. Hand crushers, not much different from those used by home winemakers today, were imported in the late 1850s. Soon they were being built on a large scale, some run by steam engines by the 1870s. By then, most were fitted to remove the stems in the process. Such crusher-stemmers were little changed until recent years. The old style, with corrugated rollers, is still employed but the rollers can now be adjusted to allow whole berries and some clusters to pass through intact if required. Another style uses paddles instead of rollers.

Some crushing, particularly of white wine grapes, is now done with portable equipment in the field to minimize oxidation. Some producers prefer to crush their grapes by PRESSING them to release the juice, a procedure that reduces the PHENOLIC content of the must.

CUCAMONGA, about 35 miles east of Los Angeles in San Bernardino County, was formerly one of the important wine districts in California. In 1980 there were 7,000 acres of vines in the area; in 1960 there were 20,000, today there are fewer than 1,000.

Cucamonga is an Indian word meaning sandy place, and this is dry, hot, sandy country; without irrigation it is a desert. Although the area is not suited for the production of first-class wines, its deep sandy soil makes it almost

phylloxera-proof and the deep soil means that irrigation is needed only rarely. The growth of urban sprawl, the heavy smog, and the rising market for high-quality table wines have virtually killed the wine industry here.

Mission vines were planted in the area in the 1830s and in the 1850s Jean-Louis VIGNES and the SAINSEVAIN family made Madeiralike dessert wines here. This early industry was virtually extinct by the 1870s.

The area's great days began after 1901 when Secundo GUASTI planted more than 3,000 acres of vines here. By 1915, the area had 15,000 acres. During Prohibition, planting expanded the vineyard acreage to almost 25,000 acres. During the years after Repeal, sixty-four wineries ranging from large industrial operations to small family wineries serving the local trade were operating in the area, which included the communities of Fontana, Etiwanda, Cucamonga, Ontario, and Mira Loma. Zinfandel was the predominant variety, table wine the dominant product. Large quantities of fortified wine were also produced. The wine industry failed here because the desert conditions made the production of fine wine very difficult. Nevertheless, in 1995 the BATF granted AVA status to the Cucamonga Valley, an area of 171 square miles and about 1,000 acres of vines.

CUCAMONGA VINEYARD COMPANY. See PADRE VINEYARD COMPANY

CULBERTSON WINERY. See THORNTON WINERY

CUPERTINO. Today a sprawling, middle-class residential community in northwestern Santa Clara Valley, a hundred years ago it was the center of a huge premium winegrowing area that extended from Los Gatos north to Palo Alto and included almost 10,000 acres of vines and forty-seven wineries. The village, which had grown like a mushroom in the vine-planting boom of the 1880s, was first called West Side, changing its name to Cupertino in 1904, on the advice of a local winegrower, John T. DOYLE. The whole area was sometimes called the Mountain View district after the little town to the north.

Between 1895 and 1910, the vines were destroyed by the phylloxera and the vineyards were most often replanted to prunes and apricots. About 1,000 acres of vines and a few small wineries survived World War II. Then the suburbs of Silicon Valley began taking over almost all vestiges of local orchards and vineyards. A few vineyards have survived, on the steep hillsides to the west, in the old MONTE BELLO district, which began its own process of viticultural revival in the 1960s.

CURTIS WINERY (BW 4890). Starting in 1971, the J. C. Carey family planted 41 acres of vines near Solvang in the Santa Ynez Valley area of Santa Barbara County. The winery, J. Carey Cellars, was bonded in 1978, and produced mainly Cabernet Sauvignon, Sauvignon blanc, and Chardonnay. In 1986 the operation was purchased by FIRESTONE VINEYARD.* The facilities were upgraded and production raised to about 8,000 cases per year. In 1996 the name was changed to Curtis Winery and in 1997 it was sold.

CUSTOM CRUSHING, a term with several meanings. Before Prohibition, when there was an oversupply of wine grapes, growers were often forced to turn over their grapes to wineries where they would be made into wine, only half of which belonged to the grower. This arrangement was sometimes referred to as custom crushing, and carried a definitely negative connotation.

For more than a century, wineries in California have produced bottled wine for restaurants, specialty shops, grocery chains, and liquor stores. The labels that went onto the bottles rarely mentioned the winery that produced the wine. This practice has many names, among them custom crushing or custom trade.

Since World War II, many small-scale producers, lacking the necessary capital, have had their small batches of wine made, or have made it themselves, in established wineries, an arrangement that is sometimes called custom crushing or custom winemaking. In recent years, some wineries have specialized in such operations. They have even taken to producing wine for successful and well-established wineries and brands whose owners do not want to invest in the equipment for the requisite expansion. Recently, several of California's most highly praised premium wines have been produced at custom-crush facilities. This is a partial list of some recent and important California custom crush-operations and their counties:

Associated Vintage Group (Mendocino)
Castoro Cellars (San Luis Obispo)
Central Coast Wine Warehouse
  (Santa Barbara)
Charles Krug (Napa)
Chateau de Baun (Sonoma)
Delicato Vineyards (San Joaquin)
Golden State Vintners (Napa)
Honig Cellars (Napa)
Louis M. Martini (Napa)
Martini & Prati (Sonoma)
Napa Wine Company (Napa)
Oakville Estate Winery (Napa)
Rodney Strong Vineyards/Klein Family
  Vintners (Sonoma)
Rombauer Vineyards (Napa)
Wente Vineyards (Alameda County)
Wine Business Monthly, June 1995, 40–44.

CUVAISON (BW 4550). Since it was founded in 1970 by two engineers from Silicon Valley, Cuvaison has had several owners and produced a wide range of wines and wine styles. Located on the Silverado Trail above St. Helena in Napa Valley, the winery today produces about 65,000 cases annually, with special emphasis on Chardonnay, Cabernet Sauvignon, and Merlot.

The current owners, the Schmidheiny family from Switzerland, acquired the property in

1979 and then bought 400 acres of land in Carneros for their Chardonnay, which accounts for about 70 percent of total production. About 300 acres of this land are now in vineyard.

CUVÉE, from the French *cuve,* tub, tank, or vat. It used to mean a vat or tank of wine, usually a blend. In recent years it has come to mean a specific lot of wine and now is rarely used to refer to wine in a single container.

joe@dallavalleyvnyds.com
Gustav Dalla DValle

D

D'AGOSTINI WINERY (BW 2459). In 1856 Adam Uhlinger, a German-Swiss immigrant, began quarrying the rock for his little winery 8 miles north of Plymouth, in Amador County. In 1911, Enrico D'Agostini (1888–1956) bought the winery and its 125 acres of vines. After his death, his four sons ran the operation, producing sound country wines from the old vineyard. In 1984, the family sold the property to a Sacramento firm, but its attempts to modernize the winery and its line of wines led to bankruptcy. In 1989 Leon and Shirley Sobon, owners of the nearby SHENANDOAH VINEYARDS, took over the D'Agostini place and began to revive the old vineyard. They also converted the historic winery into a local viticultural and winemaking museum. The wines from the old property are now labeled SOBON ESTATE.

DALLA VALLE VINEYARDS (BW 5344). Gustav Dalla Valle (1917–95) bought land in the hills east of Oakville in 1982 and began planting a 25-acre vineyard. His goal was to produce first-class Napa Valley Cabernet Sauvignon. The first wine was made in 1986. Production in the 1990s stands at about 4,000 cases a year, a small part of which, labeled Maya, after the owner's daughter, is produced from a specially favored portion of the vineyard. The Dalla Valle Pietre Rosse wine is unique, a combination of estate-grown Cabernet Sauvignon (33 percent) and Sangiovese (67 percent) imported from Tuscany.

DANIEL, JOHN R., JR. See INGLENOOK

DAUME WINERY (BW 5123). Before making wine commercially at his winery in the Ventura County town of Camarillo beginning in 1982, John Daume sold home winemaking supplies in Woodland Hills. Specializing in Chardonnay from grapes grown in Mendocino and Zinfandel from Paso Robles, he produces about 2,500 cases per year.

DAVIS (UC DAVIS). See UNIVERSITY OF CALIFORNIA AT DAVIS

DEAVER RANCH (BWC 5232). Zinfandel grapes from Ken Deaver's 70-year-old vines in the Shenandoah Valley in Amador County were discovered in 1963 by Charles Myers, a home winemaker. Myers introduced the wine to Darrell CORTI,* who gave a bottle to Bob Trinchero of SUTTER HOME WINERY in 1968. From this beginning sprang the rediscovery of Amador County as fine-wine country and the production of thousands of cases of Sutter Home Zinfandel. The Deaver family still sells grapes and markets Zinfandel under its own label, the wine produced at a nearby winery.

DEER PARK WINERY (BW 4931) is the original SUTTER HOME* winery, founded in 1891 by Caroline and Emile Leuenberger, who were relatives of John Sutter, a winegrower on

Howell Mountain (but no relation to the famous California pioneer). In 1904 the Leuenbergers bought the John THOMANN* winery south of St. Helena and transferred the Sutter Home name to that facility, where it remains today. Meanwhile, the old winery on Howell Mountain went through several hands before being purchased in 1922 by John J. BALLENTINE,* who opened it at Repeal (BW 3595) and made wine for years under the Ballentine's Deer Park label. His red wines had a fine reputation and were selected by the City of Paris department store in San Francisco to appear under its prestigious Verdier label. Ballentine ended production in the 1950s. Joseph HEITZ briefly acquired the bond in 1963, but it was discontinued in 1965.

In 1979 the Clark and Knapp families bought the old winery and brought back the 7-acre vineyard. David Clark is the winemaker and produces several varietals, with special emphasis on Zinfandel. Annual production is about 3,000 cases.

DEHLINGER WINERY (BW 4757). The Russian River Valley near Sebastopol has a somewhat Burgundian climate on which Tom Dehlinger capitalizes to produce his renowned Pinot noirs and almost equally famous Chardonnays. His family bought the place in 1973 and began making wine in 1976. The Dehlinger vineyard now has about 50 acres of vines; production stands at about 10,000 cases per year. Unlike many other entrepreneurs in the seventies, Tom Dehlinger had a degree in enology from the University of California at Davis when he set out on his course as a winemaker in Sonoma.

DEKKERA. See BRETTANOMYCES

DELANO GROWERS GRAPE PRODUCTS (BW 3616). In Kern County, a 7 million-gallon producer that began in 1940 as a cooperative winery. Today its chief product is grape juice concentrate; see also CALIFORNIA WINE ASSOCIATION.

DE LATOUR, GEORGES. See BEAULIEU VINEYARD

DELICATO VINEYARDS (BW 4095). Founded in 1935 by Sebastiano Luppino and Gaspare Indelicato and called the Sam-Jasper Winery, a combination of the men's nicknames in English. In 1974 the name was changed to Delicato Vineyards. The winery, north of Manteca in San Joaquin County, was for years chiefly a bulk producer but it also had a good retail trade and an effective hospitality center. Profits from the White Zinfandel boom in the early 1980s made it possible to expand the operation so that, by 1986, capacity had reached 30 million gallons. Two years later Delicato bought the San Bernarbe Ranch, with 8,000 acres of vines, in Monterey County, from Prudential Insurance Co. By 1995, the company was the ninth largest wine producer in the United States. Also in that year the winery pleaded guilty to charges of fraud in relation to 5,000 tons of falsely labeled grapes sold to them by a broker. He was sentenced to federal prison; the winery was fined $1,000,000. Annual production stands at about 2 million cases; capacity is up to 40,000,000 gallons.

DELMAS. One of the important family names in the history of wine in northern California. **Antoine Delmas** came to California in 1849 and established a nursery in San Jose in 1851. The next year, he imported the first French wine-grape vines to the state. The collection included vines labelled Cabrunet, Merleau, and Black Meunier. He also brought in European vinifera varieties from nurseries in New England, one variety arriving as the Black St. Peter's, which turned out to be ZINFANDEL. He was also a pioneer in advocating the use of elemental sulfur to fight powdery mildew. In 1860 he imported some of the first authentic

Antoine Delmas, flanked by his sons, Delphin (*right*) and Joseph. In 1852, among Antoine's vines imported from France were the first Cabernet Sauvignon and Merlot in northern California.

European winery and distillery equipment. He is less kindly remembered as the first to import French snails to California, today the ubiquitous California brown snail.

His son, **Delphin M. Delmas** (1844–1928), who had been elected as district attorney of Santa Clara County at age 22, became one of the most famous trial lawyers in America. In 1908 he organized the successful defense of Harry Thaw, the millionaire who had murdered the architect Stanford White at Madison Square Garden. The incident was popularized in the movie *Ragtime*, with Pat O'Brien playing the part of Delmas. Earlier, in 1887, he built the Casa Delmas Winery in Mountain View, a 500,000-gallon operation that was, for years, the largest independent

winery in the county. It was memorialized by the novelist Frank Norris in one of his nonfiction pieces.

DE LOACH VINEYARDS (BW 4906). In 1970 Cecil De Loach bought 24 acres of old Zinfandel vines west of Santa Rosa and, with grape prices soaring, was soon able to add 28 more. In 1975 he made 1,000 cases of Zinfandel in a rented building; he began building his winery four years later to handle the 4,500-case 1979 vintage. In the 1990s, about 25,000 of the 150,000 cases produced annually have been of White Zinfandel, one of his successes; some critics have proclaimed it the best in California. He also produces several powerful vineyard-designated Zinfandels and a wide range of premium varietals, Chardonnay in particular. De Loach's vineyards now cover 430 acres.

DE LORIMIER WINERY (BW 5305) began as a small prune orchard bought in 1973 in the Alexander Valley near Geyserville. Twelve years later the De Lorimier family had 60 acres of vineyard and a small winery. In 1995 20 more acres of vineyard next door were added. The 6,000-case production consists mainly of premium varietals and blends with proprietary names such as Mosaic, and Prism.

DELTA REGION. The complicated confluence of the Sacramento and San Joaquin rivers, a triangle of land and water covering about 350 square miles; the approximate boundary-line points are Pittsburg, Stockton, and a spot about 15 miles south of Sacramento. The region is most famous for its asparagus crops, but in recent years wine grapes have become increasingly important, particularly in the CLARKSBURG Viticultural Area.

DE MOOR WINERY. See NAPA CELLARS

DESSERT WINES. See FORTIFIED WINES

DE TURK, ISAAC (1834–96). Born in Pennsylvania to a family who made wine from native grapes, De Turk came to California in 1858 and settled near Santa Rosa in 1860. He made wine for others and planted his own Yulupa Vineyard in the Bennett Valley in 1862. Six years later, he had built his first winery and, by 1884, was producing 150,000 gallons of wine per year. He expanded his holdings into northern Sonoma County but eventually concentrated his winery operations in Santa Rosa, and his vineyards in the nearby Guilicos Valley.

His winery in Santa Rosa covered a city block and, by 1895, had a million-gallon capacity. He and his general manager, C. M. Mann, established the De Turk brand throughout the country, well respected for consistency and good value. De Turk was the most powerful wine man in Sonoma County when he became the president of the STATE VITICULTURAL COMMISSION in 1890. He died in 1896, an honest, simple, and intense man more passionately devoted to breeding horses than to winegrowing. Charles WETMORE eulogized him as "enterprising, without the faintest shadow of greed. . . . A sweet smell of purity pervades his haunts and workshops."

His estate went to a small army of nephews and cousins. Mann took over the winery and in 1903 it became a unit of the CALIFORNIA WINE ASSOCIATION. Its wines were marketed by the San Francisco firm of Wm. Hoelscher & Co., which started the winery up again after Repeal and sold wine under the old De Turk label until 1941. In that year, the winery was sold to Joseph B. Grace, a brewer in Santa Rosa. For many years Grace Brothers beer was produced in the old De Turk winery.

DEUER, GEORGE. See INGLENOOK

DEVLIN WINE CELLARS (BW 4843). Charles Devlin's winery is near Soquel, just outside the Santa Cruz Mountains Viticultural Area, but many of his wines since his first

Devlin Wine Cellars
1986 Monterey County
Chardonnay
La Reina Vineyard

According to the label, Thomas Devlin III "created this visionary work called Chardonnay I" at age three.

vintage in 1978 have come from grapes grown in that district. Devlin's wines, which amount to about 10,000 cases per year, are sold almost entirely in the Santa Cruz area. He began working in the wine industry in high school, dragging hoses at the nearby BARGETTO Winery. Later he received his degree in fermentation science from the University of California at Davis. He produces a wide range of varietal wines, some of which carry labels featuring the drawings of his son Thomas, whose first work was created at the age of two in 1985.

DIAMOND CREEK VINEYARDS (BW 4606). In 1967 Al Brounstein bought 80 acres on Diamond Mountain overlooking the Napa Valley between St. Helena and Calistoga. He hired Richard Steltzner to plant three vineyards there, totaling 20 acres. The soils in the three were manifestly different and he named them for their characteristics: Volcanic Hill, Red Rock Terrace, and Gravelly Meadow. Most of his vines were Cabernet Sauvignon, with a little Merlot and Cabernet franc. His first vintage was in 1972 and, by 1974, production was up to 1,000 cases. Meanwhile he had built a little dam and created a small lake on the property. Nearby he planted the tiny Lake Vineyard, which had its first vintage in 1978.

From the outset, Diamond Creek Cabernets were critical successes. At a blind tasting held by the San Francisco Vintners Club in 1976, the three vineyard-designated wines placed first, second, and third in a tasting of superior California Cabernets. Brounstein considers his Cabernets to be "special occasion" wines and prices them at the top of the market; the 1990 Lake Vineyard was released at $150 per bottle. Production averages about 3,000 cases per year but fluctuates according to growing conditions.

DIAMOND MOUNTAIN. The highland area above Calistoga on the west side of Napa Valley. There is a Diamond Mountain peak (2,375 ft.) farther west in Sonoma County. Several important wineries have vineyards on these slopes, notably DIAMOND CREEK, STERLING, and VON STRASSER. The area is best known for its Cabernet Sauvignon.

DIGARDI WINERY (BW 1045). In 1913 Joseph Digardi bought the winery that Martin Joost had founded in 1886 in the Vine Hill district near Martinez in Contra Costa County. After Repeal, Digardi acquired a fine reputation for its table wines, particularly Gamays under the Diablo Valley label. The vineyards succumbed to suburban growth and significant production ended in the 1960s. The old bond was relinquished in 1984.

DIGIORGIO RANCH. See BEAR MOUNTAIN WINERY

DI ROSA, RENE. In 1960 he bought 400 acres on the Napa side of the Carneros, land on which the remains of the old Talcoa Winery stood. Two years later he began planting his Winery Lake Vineyard. He was soon selling his grapes to some of the most celebrated wineries in northern California. By the mid-1970s a bottle of Chardonnay or Pinot noir would attain considerable prestige if it carried the Winery Lake Vineyard designation. By the 1980s it became received doctrine among wine writers that Di Rosa's grapes were the most expensive in the state. He sold the vineyard to Seagrams in 1986 for about $8,000,000. Thereafter he concentrated on art, which he had been acquiring since the 1950s. His now-huge collection is open to the public on his estate next to the famous vineyard.

DISTILLED SPIRITS PRODUCER (DSP). A producer of distilled spirits; in this context, brandy for beverage or fortifying purposes.

DNA FINGERPRINTING. In the 1970s, researchers at the University of California at Davis developed a system of identifying grape varieties that was often referred to as isozyme fingerprinting. Early tests showed that the Italian Primitivo was probably the same as California's Zinfandel and the Australian Shiraz the same as the French Syrah. In recent years a more sophisticated process, DNA fingerprinting, has yielded what appear to be even more accurate results. Professor Carole Meredith, who has led the research at Davis, has made some interesting discoveries; see PETITE SIRAH and ZINFANDEL for examples. In addition to verifying certain earlier findings, Meredith has discovered anomalies in some of the University's accessions to its own nursery collection. This research has caused a bit of anxiety among producers who are concerned that tried-and-true varieties in their vineyards may suddenly prove to be not so true. But to date the results have caused more head scratching and smiles than consternation.

DOLCETTO. An Italian variety of grape from the Piedmont, producing a fruity, gulpable red wine. The variety may have been grown at the Italian Swiss Colony winery in the 1890s, but no record survives. Since 1991, a few experimental acres have been planted in California; in 1996 there were 218 tons, crushed by five producers.

DOMAINE CARNEROS (BW 5443). Construction on this impressive champagnery began in 1987; the grand opening was in 1990. Owned by Peter Ordway, one of the partners in this project, the 150-acre vineyard surrounding the winery was planted in 1982. The other owners are the French Champagne house of Taittinger and Kobrand Corporation, importers. The winery's sparkling wines include a traditionally blended Brut and a Blanc de Blancs from Chardonnay. Production has grown in the 1990s to about 45,000 cases per year. To date only fruit from Carneros goes into the Domaine's wines.

DOMAINE CHANDON (BW 4755). As the demand for premium sparkling wine rose in the 1960s, French producers were faced with the fact that vineyard expansion in their country's Champagne district was limited, absolutely. Moët-Hennessey, producers of Moët & Chandon Champagne, decided to expand into California, specifically into the Napa Valley. The company began buying vineyard land in 1973 and bought grapes for an experimental first vintage at Mount Veeder Winery. Later vintages were made at TREFETHEN WINERY in Napa through the 1977 harvest. By then the 80,000-square-foot winery in Yountville was ready for production. The first sparklers appeared in 1976, Chandon Brut and Blanc de Noirs; later there was a Réserve. Annual production reached 200,000 cases by 1983. Sales ballooned to 427,000 cases in 1989, but dropped below 400,000 a year in the 1990s. Chandon controls 1,450 acres of wine grapes.

> John H. Wright, *Domaine Chandon: The First French-Owned California Sparkling Wine Cellar* (Regional Oral History Office, Bancroft Library, 1992).

DOMAINE CHARBAY (BW 5328). Miles Karakasevic had a long career as an enologist in Canada and California before he bought property on Spring Mountain in 1982. He also rents some production space at a winery in Mendocino County. At first his label read Domaine Karakesh. He produces table wines, fortified wines, and spirits, among them a fortified dessert Chardonnay and a grappa.

DOMAINE DE LA TERRE ROUGE (BW 5789). William Easton began planting vines near Plymouth in Amador County in 1985. He began making his own wine at the BALDINELLI winery in 1994 and acquired that facility in 1996. A major part of his annual production of 7,000 cases is devoted to wine from Rhône varieties and Zinfandel. Easton is a second label.

DOMAINE LAURIER. See LAURIER VINEYARDS

DOMAINE MICHEL. See MICHEL-SCHLUMBERGER.

DOMAINE MONTREAUX (BW 5399), a sparkling wine facility in the Napa Valley south of Yountville that belongs to MONTICELLO CELLARS. A 32-acre plot of Chardonnay and Pinot noir vines near the mother winery supplies the grapes. Production began in 1983 and in 1987 a facility separate from the main winery was completed. Production in the 1990s is around 2,000 cases per year.

DOMAINE NAPA WINERY (BW 5312). Michel Perret, whose father once owned wineries in Algeria, Corsica, and then in Provence, came to California in 1977 and was soon managing vineyards in the Napa Valley. In 1985 he built Domaine Napa, his own winery, just north of Rutherford. In 1995 he sold it to a group of partners who had acquired the QUAIL RIDGE* label, the name that is now attached to this facility.

DOMAINE ST. GEORGE WINERY (BW
4052). The Cambiaso family founded a small
country winery south of Healdsburg in 1934.
In 1973 the family sold the winery and its 30-
acre vineyard to the owners of Four Seas Corporation in Thailand. A modern winery was
constructed, the capacity of which has grown
to 800,000 gallons. It produces medium-
priced wines, some made at the winery, some
purchased on the bulk wine market from other
producers and marketed under the Domaine
St. George label. For the Clos Ste. Nicole label,
the company imports French wine to be
blended with California wine. Annual production in California is about 400,000 cases.

DOMAINE ST. GREGORY (BW 5474) is an
old hop kiln near Ukiah renovated in 1988 and
made into a winery. The owner, Greg Graziano,
buys grapes and concentrates his efforts on
Pinot noir and Chardonnay; annual production under the Domaine St. Gregory label is
about 15,000 cases. He is also a partner in a
venture to produce wines from Italian varietals
under the Monte Volpe (Fox Mountain) label.

DOMINUS (BW 5661), a wine made from red
Bordeaux varieties, mostly Cabernet Sauvignon. It began as a joint venture between the
family of John Daniel, Jr., former owner of
INGLENOOK, and the Moueix family, which
owns the first-growth Château Pétrus in
Pomerol in Bordeaux. The grapes came from
Daniel's well-known Napanook Vineyard, in
the foothills west of Yountville in Napa
County. The first vintage was the 1983. The
wines are expensive. They have been praised
for their power and ability to age, and have
been criticized for the same phenolic muscle
that others admire. Christian Moueix, who
oversees their production, aims for a product
that will be at its best after many years of careful aging. In 1995, Moueix acquired full control
of the entire operation, and in 1997 began
building a small winery on the Napanook

property. Annual production varies between
5,000 and 8,000 cases.

DONATONI WINERY (BW 4952). A little
winery in southern California that uses grapes
from vineyards on the Central Coast to produce about 1,000 cases, mostly Chardonnay
and Cabernet Sauvignon, a year. The winery is
located in the city of Inglewood, near the Los
Angeles Airport.

DOS MESAS WINERY. Frank Fowler
planted a 70-acre vineyard in the Livermore
Valley next door to Charles Wetmore's CRESTA
BLANCA in 1883. His small winery became
well known for its red Bordeaux blends. The
vineyard had grown to 125 acres when it was
acquired in 1907 by Cresta Blanca and integrated into that estate.

DOYLE, JOHN T. (1819–1906). One of the
most important leaders of the California wine
industry in the late nineteenth century. He was
a noted trial lawyer and prominent in the
state's Democratic Party when he planted his
first vineyards around Menlo Park in the 1850s.
(In 1871 he was the founding president of the
California Historical Society.) In the 1880s, he
bought several tracts of land around what was
to be called Cupertino and founded his Las
Palmas Winery and the Cupertino Wine Co.
there. These were a great success, but it was
Doyle's leadership and high standards that set
him apart from the more commercially driven
giants of the industry. He was a close associate
of Professor Eugene HILGARD at the University of California at Berkeley and gave that
institution land for an EXPERIMENTAL STA-
TION. An influential member of the California
Board of State Viticultural Commissioners, he
was a thorn in the side of industry leaders
devoted to high production and profits and less
concerned about high quality. Like J. H.
DRUMMOND in Sonoma, he imported a wide
variety of European vines; he was the first to

show that many ITALIAN VARIETIES would succeed in the California environment.

His last services to the wine industry were his good offices as the honest broker in the WINE WAR of the late 1890s. He retired in 1900 and his death in 1906 went mostly unnoticed by the industry that had profited from his sacrifices and high standards. His vineyards in Cupertino were subdivided and planted mostly to prunes and apricots. But the great palm trees leading to the former Las Palmas Winery survive.

DRAPER, PAUL. See RIDGE VINEYARDS

DRESEL. The name of a great family of pioneering winegrowers in Sonoma County. **Emil Dresel** (1819–69) came to the town of Sonoma in 1856. To the west of town he and Jacob GUNDLACH* planted vineyards that would become the well-known Rhine Farm. Later the two separated their holdings. In 1859, Dresel returned to his home in Geisenheim on the Rhine and brought back cuttings from which Dresel Rieslings and Traminers were grown in years to come.

Emil's brother **Julius Dresel** (1816–91) came to Sonoma in 1869 to take charge of the family wine interests. He had fled Germany in 1848 because of his liberal political views and ended up in the German colony near San Antonio, Texas. There, as a Republican politician and newspaper publisher, he had fought slavery, secession, and the Confederacy. Dresel & Co. under his guidance became a leader in the production of high-quality California table wines. More important, in 1878, he was the first grower in the state to plant a vineyard on resistant ROOTSTOCK, *Vitis riparia* cuttings imported from Missouri. His son, **Carl,** took over the business in 1891 and carried on until Prohibition. Long before varietal designation was the standard in Californi, Carl Dresel sold his wine under such labels as Sémillon, Cabernet Sauvignon, Traminer, and Zinfandel. In 1915 he won gold medals at the Panama-Pacific Exposition in San Francisco for his Johannisberg, Franken (Sylvaner), and Kleinberger Rieslings, and for Traminer.

DREYFUS, BENJAMIN, a wine merchant who began work in southern California as the business manager for the ANAHEIM Colony, a wine cooperative. Later his firm in San Francisco was a leading exporter of California wine to the East Coast. In 1894 B. Dreyfus & Co. became a founding constituent of the CALIFORNIA WINE ASSOCIATION.

DROSOPHILA MELANOGASTER. See FRUIT FLY

DRUMMOND, JOHN HAMILTON (1830– 89), a retired British army captain who settled on land in Sonoma County near Glen

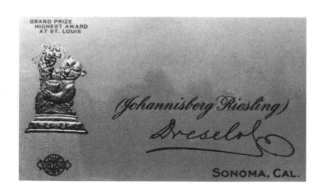

Emil Dresel brought German varieties of wine grapes to Sonoma in 1859. This Golden Bear label celebrates the winery's award at the 1904 Louisiana Purchase Exposition in St. Louis. (Unzelman Collection, Santa Rosa, Calif.)

Ellen in the 1870s and established Dunfillan Vineyards, one of the finest premium wine producers in Sonoma County. An intense Scotsman, he had a passion for viticultural experimentation and was instrumental in importing Bordeaux and Rhône varieties of grapes to California. He was one of the few early winegrowers to show an interest in Chardonnay, which he imported in 1880. He brought in Merlot in 1883. He made a BLUSH wine from Pinot noir, called Oeil de Perdrix (eye of the partridge). He worked on the blending of Rhône varieties, his Hermitage a combination of Syrah and Marsanne. For the vineyard he invented a frost warning device in 1886.

When Drummond died in 1889, the winegrower Kate WARFIELD became the executrix of his will in which he indicated a deep antipathy for his stepson, Frederic BIOLETTI, who later married Drummond's own daughter. His fine stone winery has been carefully maintained on the KUNDE estate.

DRY CREEK VALLEY, an important winegrowing area in Sonoma County, northwest of Healdsburg that gained AVA status in 1983. It is particularly famous today for its fine Zinfandels, many produced from old, dry-farmed vineyards dating back to early in the century. (Actually there are more acres planted to Cabernet Sauvignon and Chardonnay today than there are to Zinfandel.) Sauvignon blanc has also done very well there.

The area's viticultural landscape was developed in the 1880s when vineyard planting in Sonoma County exploded and several wineries were established here. The landscape has changed again in the past two decades. In 1972 there were about 1,500 acres of grape vines and 4,500 acres of prunes. In the 1990s there were about 6,000 acres of vines and twenty-four wineries in the area.

Jack W. Florence Sr., *A Noble Heritage: The Wines and Vineyards of Dry Creek Valley* (Healdsburg, Calif.: Winegrowers of Dry Creek Valley, 1993).

DRY CREEK VINEYARD (BW 4611). The first new winery in the Dry Creek area since the days of Repeal, built in 1973, a year after the owner, David Stare, began converting a prune orchard to a Sauvignon blanc vineyard with some Chardonnay and Chenin blanc. By the 1990s, he had 115 acres, which give him only about one-third of the grapes he uses.

Over the years, Dry Creek has expanded its product line to include Cabernet Sauvignon and a red Meritage. Zinfandel, drawn from several vineyards in the area, has long been a specialty. Total annual production in the 1990s has passed the 100,000-case mark. In 1992 Stare brought out a Cabernet rosé under the Bug Creek label in honor of the producing vineyard, which was infested by phylloxera.

David S. Stare, *Fumé Blanc and Meritage Wines in Sonoma County: Dry Creek Vineyard's Pioneer Winemaking* (Regional Oral History Office, Bancroft Library, 1996).

DSP. See DISTILLED SPIRITS PRODUCER

DUCKHORN VINEYARDS (BW 4857). Dan Duckhorn heads a group that founded Duckhorn Vineyards in Napa Valley in 1976 and brought out its first wine from the 1978 vintage. The wines come mostly from purchased grapes, but Duckhorn's sources have supplied him with outstanding fruit for Cabernet Sauvignon and Merlot. Many believe that Duckhorn Merlots, beginning with the 1978 vintage, have been among the best in the state. The Merlot from the THREE PALMS VINEYARD, not far from the winery on the Silverado Trail, would probably be a California first growth if there were such a classification. Duckhorn Sauvignon blanc has also been a critical success. Several wines have been issued under the winery's second label, Decoy. In 1997 Duckhorn bought the OBESTER WINERY in Anderson Valley to act as a Pinot noir production facility. Total production in the 1990s runs about 45,000 cases per year.

Daniel J. Duckhorn and Margaret S. Duckhorn, *Mostly Merlot: The History of Duckhorn Vineyards* (Regional Oral History Office, Bancroft Library, 1996).

DUNCAN PEAK VINEYARDS (BW 5307). Hubert Lenczowski lives in Oakland but has a 4-acre vineyard on his family's ranch near Hopland in Mendocino County. He bonded his winery in 1986 and began making small quantities of Cabernet Sauvignon, not yet 1,000 cases a year. Critics have given his wines high marks.

DUNNEWOOD. See CANANDAIGUA; GUILD

DUNN VINEYARDS (BW 5124). Most wine people in Napa Valley knew that fine red wines had been grown on Howell Mountain since the 1880s, and no one questioned the high quality of the Cabernet Sauvignons made by Caymus Vineyards in the late 1970s. So when Randall Dunn, who had been the winemaker at Caymus from 1975 to 1982, revived a small Cabernet vineyard on his own property on Howell Mountain, no one was surprised at the high quality of his first vintage, made in 1979. He left Caymus in 1982, the year he bonded his little mountain winery and that year produced another Cabernet from grapes purchased elsewhere in Napa Valley. Now these two wines, Dunn's Howell Mountain and his Napa Valley Cabernets, are on almost every critic's list of California's best red wines. The major controversy about his wines has been over which of the two would be the better in the long run. His are wines for the cellar and for patience. In the 1990s the 1979 wine was still evolving. Dunn's wine operation now includes a set of aging caves and the Park-Muscatine Vineyard on Howell Mountain, long famous for its fine fruit. Production runs about 5,000 cases per year.

Dennis Schaeffer, *Vintage Talk* (Santa Barbara, Calif.: Capra Press, 1994).

DURIF (DURIFF). In 1880 a French nurseryman named Durif developed a seedling that, for about the next 120 years, was believed to be a variation on the Peloursin, its parent. In 1998 Professor Carole Meredeith showed through DNA FINGERPRINTING that the Durif had two parents: It was a cross between the Peloursin and the true French SYRAH. Charles McIver (see LINDA VISTA) was, in 1884, the first to import the new vine into California, bringing in the BÉCLAN, a vine clearly related to the Peloursin, at the same time. He and others were soon calling the Durif PETITE SIRAH,* and the name stuck. It is clear that much, but not all, of what is called Petite Sirah in California today is Durif. It makes a deep-colored, well-flavored red table wine, seemingly a better wine, on average, than that produced from the variety in its homeland, where today little is grown.

SANTA CRUZ MOUNTAIN VINEYARD in the 1970s produced a varietal Durif from a vineyard identified as Petite Sirah. But in 1996 the BATF ruled that Durif is not a synonym for Petite Sirah. To date no one is sure how this ruling is to be interpreted.

DURNEY VINEYARDS (BW 4823). The first sizeable vineyard planted in the Carmel Valley in Monterey County since the mission days was by William Durney (1920–89), beginning in 1967. Cabernet Sauvignon has been the mainstay of the winery's production, although Chardonnay and Pinot noir are also made. Dorothy Durney continued to operate the winery after her husband's death. In 1994 it was sold to European interests. Annual production is about 20,000 cases. Cachagua is a second label.

DUTCH HENRY WINERY (BW 5499), is a little winery on the Silverado Trail in the Napa Valley, bonded in 1989 and making about 3,000 cases per year, mostly Pinot noir, Merlot, and Sauvignon blanc.

DUVAL, ALEXANDER (1841–13). Chateau Bellevue in the Livermore Valley was established in 1884 when Duval bought 180 acres there and built a large winery. A native of Bordeaux, he was dedicated to the production of high-grade claret, some of which he sold in the east shipped in bottles. Were it not for the almost legendary stories of his daughter's elopement, many of them untrue, there would be much less to remember about Bellevue.

Duval had kept his daughter Amelia cloistered on the estate, but in 1898 she disappeared with her lover. "Love laughs at locksmiths," commented the local newspaper. She married the man and divorced him in 1901, returning home. But her father would not see her and remained unforgiving. When Duval died, there was a national search for Amelia, as numerous others appeared to claim the $150,000 estate. She was found and did return to Bellevue, where she found her room exactly as she had left it 15 years before. Then she went back to Chicago, never to return. In 1915, the estate was purchased by Mrs. George True, whose winery (FENESTRA today) was across the road. The old home is gone but the old vineyard has been restored.

DUXOUP WINE WORKS (BW 5042). Andy and Deborah Cutter bonded their small winery in the Dry Creek Valley, Sonoma in 1981. They make about 2,000 cases of red wine aged in barrels that are named for opera stars, professors at the University of California at Davis, and friends. There is a large number of wines, some from uncommon varietals, such as Napa Gamay, Charbono, and Syrah. The winery is named for the Marx Brothers' film *Duck Soup*, and the corks are branded in Latin, *Facilis par Duxoup*.

EARLY BURGUNDY. When the vine known as Early Burgundy came to California, it was before Prohibition and how it got this name is not known. It is the French Abouriou, an ordinary red-wine variety from the southwest. After Repeal, it was used mostly by wineries in Napa and Sonoma to blend into wines labeled Burgundy. In the 1960s, there were about 800 acres in the state, but the variety disappeared from state statistics in 1994.

EARTHQUAKE. California is earthquake country; California is wine country. The inevitable outcome of these two situations has been a series of vinous mishaps and one disaster.

The first great quake during the American period was in 1857. It smashed barrels and sent bottles flying in southern California. Then, in 1868, the Hayward Fault gave California what was known, until 1906, as "The Great Earthquake." It destroyed Clement COLOMBET's winery and hotel near Mission San Jose.

The 1906 earthquake caused heavy damage from San Jose to Santa Rosa, smashing several wineries and wine warehouses. The greatest loss was the huge GALLEGOS winery near Mission

The winery hit hardest by the earthquake in 1906 was the great GALLEGOS structure near Mission San Jose. These ruins have survived.

San Jose, whose ruins still mark the land. In San Francisco millions of gallons of wine were destroyed by the quake and the ensuing fire. Hardest hit were the giant cellars of the leading wine merchants, particularly those of the CALIFORNIA WINE ASSOCIATION (CWA). This huge loss resulted in a national scarcity of wine for about two years and abnormal profits for those producers and merchants less heavily hurt. The most notable aftereffect was the building of the CWA's WINEHAVEN plant near Richmond in Alameda County, then the largest wine production facility in the world.

For the next 83 years, numerous temblors upset an occasional tank or cracked a few barrels. Wente in Livermore drew more than its share of shakeups. And in the Cienega Valley the old PALMTAG WINERY, later an Almaden facility, became famous for the fact that it sat on top of the murderous San Andreas Fault, and its creeps and shakes could be seen and felt in the winery. Then in 1989 the Loma Prieta quake sent barrels flying again at wineries all over the Santa Cruz Mountains.

EASTERN UNITED STATES. In California wine history, east of the Rockies. Early attempts in the late 1850s and 1860s to market California wine in the east were mostly unsuccessful. But in the 1870s, with an improvement in quality and the building of the transcontinental railroad, significant markets were established on the East Coast and at Chicago and New Orleans. By the 1880s, millions of gallons were heading east, mostly to satisfy the market developed by increased immigration. Most wine was shipped in bulk to eastern merchants, or to depots in the east maintained by powerful California merchants and producers. Very few of these producers shipped their wine in bottles before the 1940s.

The eastern states also produced wines that competed with those of California on its home ground, but usually at the bottom of the quality ladder, because they were made from native grapes, not vinifera varieties, and were usually CHAPTALIZED. Few eastern wines then and now have found a market on the West Coast.

EAST-SIDE WINERY (BW 3863). Today a 1-million-gallon winery and distillery in Lodi, marketing most of its moderately priced table wine under the Oak Ridge label and its brandy and lower-priced wines under the Royal Host label. The winery was founded in 1934 as a cooperative, headed by several German families who had come to the Lodi area from the Volga River region around 1900. Total wine production runs around 250,000 cases per year, much of it BLUSH wines from Zinfandel and Grenache.

EBERLE WINERY (BW 5199). Gary Eberle, the owner and winemaker, started playing football at Penn State, then studied marine biology at Louisiana State University, then studied enology at the University of California at Davis. He made wine at the ESTRELLA RIVER WINERY for several years and in 1983 opened his own winery down the road, a few miles east of Paso Robles in San Luis Obispo County. There he produces mostly Cabernet Sauvignon and Chardonnay, and a little Muscat Canelli, about 20,000 cases per year all told. Recently there has been an increasing interest in Rhône varieties here, including the production of a rosé from the rarely grown Counoise variety. In German *Eberle* means young wild boar, which is the winery's logo.

ECLIPSE CHAMPAGNE. Not California's first sparkling wine, but the best for many years. Arpad HARASZTHY* had studied the French Champagne process in Épernay and later produced a good sparkler at Buena Vista in the 1860s. A few years later he became associated with Isador LANDSBERGER, a wine dealer in San Francisco and they developed a good sparkling wine from a CUVÉE based on white Zinfandel. Haraszthy and Landsberger parted ways and in 1880 Arpad joined forces with Henry Epstein to produce another successful wine they called Eclipse, after a famous race horse. The cuvée was remarkable in its details. The 1885 Eclipse was a blend of 58 percent white Zinfandel, 13 percent Colombard, 12 percent Malvasia bianca, 4 percent Grey Riesling, 4 percent Verdal, 4 percent Meunier, 4 percent Sylvaner, and 1 percent Folle blanche. By the late 1880s, Eclipse had gained an international reputation, fooling many a European connoisseur, including, we are told, Henry Vizetelly, an English publisher and noted wine writer. It was a favorite of Andrew Carnegie and Robert Louis Stevenson.

But during the 1890s the quality faded; it was then made primarily from grapes grown on Haraszthy's desertlike vineyard in the Sacramento Valley. By 1900 Paul MASSON's sparklers had become the Pride of California, and Eclipse had—disappeared from the market.

EDGE HILL VINEYARD, an old wine estate that has seen many owners. On the west side of the Napa Valley, south of St. Helena, it was first planted in 1870 by General E. D. Keyes, who sold it in 1872. In 1879 it was acquired by William Scheffler, who expanded the stone winery and built a distillery, both of which acquired excellent reputations. In 1909 Theodore GIER acquired the property; a few years later it was a resort hotel. Following Repeal, the estate was acquired by the LOUIS M. MARTINI family. A portion of the old winery is now the Louis P. Martini home. The old distillery stands nearby.

EDMEADES WINERY (BW 4596). In 1972 Deron Edmeades bonded a converted apple drying facility on his father's 108-acre ranch in the Anderson Valley in Mendocino County. In 1974 he built a winery and, with the winemaker Jed STEELE,* produced some highly praised wines, particularly Zinfandels, from several very good, old Mendocino vineyards (Du

Pratt, Ciapusci, Zeni, Anzilotti, Pacini). Financial problems in the 1980s ended the operation. In 1988, the property with its 35-acre vineyard was acquired by KENDALL-JACKSON. In 1994 the winery was retooled and 64 acres of vines replanted. Currently, production is about 11,000 cases a year, mostly Zinfandel, Pinot noir, and Chardonnay.

EDMUNDS ST. JOHN (BW 5511), an urban winery in a warehouse in Emeryville, Alameda County, near the eastern end of the San Francisco Bay Bridge; it was bonded in 1989. The owner, Steve Edmunds, specializes in varietals associated with the Rhône and Provence: Grenache, Mourvèdre (Mataro), Carignane, Cinsaut, Syrah, and Viognier. He searches northern California for old vines that escaped being pulled up in recent years. Some wines he sells in blends, others as varietals, along with some Zinfandel and Cabernet franc. Some of his wines travel under such fanciful labels as Les Côtes Sauvages and Les Fleurs du Chaparral. The critical praise his wines have received clearly makes Edmunds a leader among the RHONE RANGERS. Production stands at about 4,000 cases per year.

EDNA VALLEY. Located just southeast of San Luis Obispo, the Edna Valley was the site of much of the local mission's agricultural activity and of its vineyard. In the 1880s, there were four small wineries and about 200 acres of vines there. But CLIMATE, a Region I–II (see HEAT SUMMATION) with its cooling maritime influence from the nearby Pacific, did not encourage viticulture until suitable varieties were tested by the local farm advisor in the 1960s. Commercial planting began in 1973 and, by the end of the decade, Edna Valley grapes, particularly Chardonnay, were in heavy demand. Pinot noir also does well here. The area received official AVA status in 1982. In the 1990s there were about 1,000 acres of vines there, overwhelmingly Chardonnay. Many critics believe Edna Valley Chardonnays to be among the very best in the state.

> Gerald Asher, "Chardonnay by the Sea," *Gourmet,* July 1993, 30.

EDNA VALLEY VINEYARD (BW 5003). Paragon Vineyards began planting its huge Edna Valley estate in 1973. By the end of the decade it had 650 acres in vines, mostly Chardonnay. In 1977 Paragon went into partnership with CHALONE* and wine under the Edna Valley label was produced in 1979 and 1980, mostly at CORBETT CANYON. In 1981 Edna Valley Vineyard's own winery was ready. Paragon supplies the grapes to produce about 80,000 cases of Edna Valley Chardonnay and about 1,000 cases of Pinot noir each year.

EDWARDS, MEREDITH (MERRY), a noted winemaker in California particularly renowned for her Chardonnays. A graduate of the University of California at Davis, she ran the cellar at MOUNT EDEN VINEYARDS for three vintages (1974–76), before moving to MATANZAS CREEK for eight years (1977–84). From 1984 to 1996, she and her family operated the MERRY VINTNERS winery near Santa Rosa. In 1989 she began supervising winemaking at LAURIER VINEYARDS. (After a change of ownership, the name of this winery became a brand name belonging to JFJ BRONCO, for whom Edwards still makes the wine.) Now also the winemaker for LIPARITA CELLARS and for the PELLEGRINI FAMILY VINEYARDS, she recently bought land near Sebastopol to plant Pinot noir.

EHLERS WINERY. In 1886 Bernard Ehlers (1844–1901) built a little stone winery north of St. Helena. Horatio STOLL, the founder of the wine industry publication *Wines & Vines,* was Ehlers's nephew and recalled playing at the winery as a boy.

After Prohibition, the old three-story building was put to many uses, but none as a winery. After Michael Casey bought it in 1968, the old place became the start-up facility for several wineries: Conn Creek in 1975, Vichon in 1980, and Saintsbury in 1981. In 1983 it was bonded as **Ehlers Lane Winery** (BW 5168), but it did not survive into the 1990s. In 1994 the building, still owned by Casey, was leased to the CARTLIDGE & BROWNE partners as a production facility, and since 1995 has been bonded by them as the **Ehlers Grove Winery** (BW 5624).

VOLKER EISELE FAMILY ESTATE. Francis Sievers's Las Lomitas Winery was the main claim of the Chiles Valley to wine fame in the nineteenth century. In recent years the old estate in Napa has been acquired by Volker Eisele who began growing grapes here in 1974. His family brand appeared in 1991. Eisele was also a leader in the political battle to make the conversion of agricultural land in Napa to other purposes all but impossible.

EISELE VINEYARD. Milton Eisele (1910–96) began developing his 35-acre Cabernet Sauvignon vineyard in the 1960s. It is located southeast of Calistoga in the Napa Valley, near the Silverado Trail. The quality of its fruit made it famous in the 1970s for wines produced by RIDGE, CONN CREEK, and JOSEPH PHELPS. The latter eventually bought up all the grapes and developed an excellent reputation for the vineyard's wine. In 1989, it changed hands briefly and, in 1990 was acquired by Bart and Daphne Araujo. They started making wine under the Eisele Vineyard label in 1991. The next year they built their **Araujo Estate Winery** (BW 5623) and were producing 3,000 cases a year by 1997. The Araujo Cabernet Sauvignon from Eisele Vineyard has won remarkable critical acclaim. The Araujos have also produced small quantities of Sauvignon blanc, Viognier, and Syrah.

EISEN, FRANCIS T. (1826–95). Born in Sweden and arriving in California in 1851, Eisen was the pioneer winegrower of the Fresno area. He bought 640 acres of barren land 4 miles east of town in 1872, and planted 125 acres of vines, using irrigation water from Fancher Creek. By 1885, he was producing 150,000 gallons of mostly fortified wine and large quantities of brandy. In the 1890s he produced some of the best sweet wines in the state. In 1893 he was making 500,000 gallons of wine and was also in the raisin business. After his death, his huge estate came under the control of the CALIFOR-NIA WINE ASSOCIATION. After Repeal the old plant was started up again as Sunnyside Winery, which went bankrupt in 1952.

EL ALISO VINEYARD. See JEAN-LOUIS VIGNES

EL DORADO COUNTY, in the Sierra foothills, has a long history of winegrowing. By the 1860s, production amounted to about 200,000

The rebirth of winegrowing in El Dorado County was led by Greg BOEGER in the 1970s, here seen in 1979 in his cellar near Placerville. (Boeger Winery)

gallons per year, mostly for local consumption. By the 1890s, there were about 1,100 acres of vines and nine small wineries, four of which had distilleries. In 1904, there were 2,100 acres of vines, with most of the grapes going to wineries in the Sacramento Valley. After Repeal, there were only about 600 acres of vines and one bonded winery. Acreage declined to 176 in 1977. But the rediscovery of the viticultural potential of the region brought a rebirth of interest in winegrowing there. Actually, the interest was more in winemaking than in growing. By 1997 there were still only 693 acres, 73 percent red, and 78 percent of those red Bordeaux varieties and Zinfandel. But there were thirteen wineries, and they bought a sizeable percentage of their grapes outside the county. In 1983, the winegrowing areas of the county were granted AVA status, as the El Dorado Viticultural Area. (See **Amador County** for map.)

In 1996, the tonnage of wine grapes in the county was 133 percent of the total tonnage in 1990 .

ELEVEN CELLARS. See CALIFORNIA WINE ASSOCIATION

ELLENA BROTHERS WINERY. See REGINA GRAPE PRODUCTS

ELLISTON VINEYARDS (BW 5176). The Suñol winegrowing district is a few miles southwest of Livermore in Alameda County. The Awtrey family bought the Elliston estate there in 1969, transformed the carriage house into a small winery, and planted 9 acres of vines. They bonded the winery in 1983 and began marketing a wide variety of wines, including Pinot gris, Pinot blanc, and several other more standard varietals. Production under new owners runs about 8,000 cases per year.

EL MOCHO VINEYARD. See LOUIS MEL; WENTE BROS.

EL MOLINO (BW 5438). A small and historic winery in the Napa Valley dating from 1871 when the Reverend T. B. Lyman purchased land near the Bale Mill (*el molino* means the mill in Spanish). Lyman's son, W. W. Lyman (1850–1921), built a small winery there and developed a fine reputation for his white wines. Most of the winery's production was marketed through the NAPA VALLEY WINE CO., of which Lyman was secretary for many years. Production ended in 1910.

The winery was brought back to life in 1981 by Reginald and Marie Oliver. They concentrate on producing Pinot noir from the Carneros in a traditional Burgundian style. There is also some Chardonnay. Production runs about 1,500 cases per year.

EL PINAL WINERY. See GEORGE WEST AND SON WINERIES

ELYSE. In 1987 the Courson family established the Elyse Wine Cellar brand with wines mostly from the Morisoli Vineyard in Rutherford. Emphasis has been on old-vine Zinfandel, but several other varietals and blends add to the 4,500-case annual production.

EMERALD BAY. See CHATEAU JULIEN

EMERALD RIESLING. A variety of wine grape developed at the University of California at Davis in 1939 and released in 1946. A cross of White Riesling and a muscat of unknown origin, it was meant to produce a good table wine in a hot climate. By 1977 there were 2,791 acres of this vine, 84 percent of them in the Central Valley. For years Paul MASSON used the variety to produce its popular Emerald Dry wine from grapes grown in Monterey County, but all those vines were gone by the 1990s. In 1997 there were 919 acres in the southern Central Valley, the grapes used to give some flavor to inexpensive white wines. Production in 1996 was 4,660 tons, 35 percent of the total in 1990.

ENOLOGY (formerly oenology, from the Greek *oinos* for wine), the science of wine and its production, including storage and aging. In California the subject is taught as a formal discipline at University of California at Davis and at Fresno State University, but a good part of the growth in the level of enological knowledge in California has come in recent years from highly motivated practitioners in the field.

ENZ VINEYARDS (BW 4641). In 1973 Robert Enz and his family established a small winery in Lime Kiln Valley, a branch of Cienega Valley in San Benito County. The 30-acre vineyard was first planted the 1880s. The vineyard stands by an old limestone quarry, whose presence suggests the character of the soils here that have attracted winegrowers to this area since the earliest American settlements. Enz makes Zinfandel, Sauvignon blanc, and Chardonnay, but prides himself on his old stands of Pinot St. George and Orange Muscat. Production runs about 10,000 cases per year. In 1982 Lime Kiln Valley received AVA status.

ERNIE'S. See ROUND HILL CELLARS

ESCONDIDO. A winegrowing district a few miles north of San Diego. There were vineyards and small wineries here in the 1880s, some surviving through Prohibition. During the dry years, there was some vineyard planting. After Repeal, in the 1930s, there were nineteen bonded wineries but these had declined to two by the 1960s. The San Pasqual Viticultural Area is close by. The quality of table wines produced in this area has never lived up to the expectations of its promoters.

ESHCOL. James Goodman (1823–1917) and his brother George (1830–88), who were bankers in Napa, acquired in 1875 a piece of land that was earlier part of Joseph OSBORNE's OAK KNOLL.* They began planting 200 acres of vines on the 280-acre property and commissioned the winery designer Hamden W. MCINTYRE to plan their huge wooden, gravity-flow facility. It was finished in 1886 and they called it Eshcol from the Biblical tale of a cluster of grapes so huge it took two to carry it. Restored, it is shown on page 369.

In 1893, James C. Fawver (1863–1940) leased the estate and then bought it in 1904. He operated it (BW 403) until 1940, producing bulk wine for several wineries. On his death, Beringer leased the facility and the vineyards. In 1968 the TREFETHEN* family acquired the estate. Their name is their brand, but they use the Eshcol name on their secondary label.

ESTANCIA. See FRANCISCAN VINEYARDS

ESTATE BOTTLING. Originally a description of wine that had been made from grapes grown on land immediately surrounding the winery and bottled at the winery where it was made. The practice was rare in California before Prohibition, INGLENOOK in the 1890s being the chief exception. The concept, if not the term itself, became popular in the 1940s when the industry, faced with a wartime shortage of tank cars, promoted the practice, touting the supposed superiority of wine that had been "bottled at the winery." Nevertheless a few premium wineries had already developed and advertised estate bottling before the war. By the 1960s it was fairly common among premium wineries in northern California. But the term was abused in later years and became meaningless.

Since the 1980s the BATF has codified the term:

1. The grapes must be grown in a BATF-recognized viticultural area and the winery must be in that area.

2. The winery must own or "control" the vineyards that produced the grapes.

3. The winery must have produced the wine from crushing to bottling as a continuous process.

Even these regulations make the expression less than precise if the winery is in a huge viticultural area and owns vineyards in it hundreds of miles apart. Many premium producers now use the expression "Grown, Produced, and Bottled By" on their labels to communicate the original sense of the expression, the sense conveyed by the expression *mise en bouteille au château* on a bottle of Bordeaux wine.

In recent years, the expression "estate wine" has been used by some producers to indicate that the grapes for the wine were grown in the producer's home vineyard, although the wine itself may or may not have been estate bottled.

ESTEE, MORRIS M. (1834-1903), an important Republican politician in California, he was his party's unsuccessful gubernatorial candidate in 1882. He was much more successful as a winegrower whose Hedgeside estate lay east of Napa City on Atlas Peak Road; see QUAIL RIDGE CELLARS.

Morris Estee was no dilettante winemaker. He was the first publicly to question the phylloxera resistance of *VITIS CALIFORNICA*. In 1893 his Cabernet Sauvignon won an award at Chicago's Columbian Exposition. (*Pacific Wine & Spirit Review*)

Estee built his winery in 1885 and eventually had vineyards totaling 350 acres. His wines generally had a good reputation; his Cabernet Sauvignon (labeled Medoc) had a great reputation and could be found on the wine lists of many of the country's best hotels. Charles CARPY regularly bought Estee's wine as the backbone for his popular claret. In 1900 President McKinley appointed Estee as a judge in the federal court in Hawaii, where he ended his days.

ESTER. A chemical compound formed by the reaction between acid and an alcohol. Such compounds often have a fruity or sweet smell and contribute greatly to the odor of young wines.

ESTRELLA RIVER WINERY (BW 4804), bonded in 1977 and located east of Paso Robles, was the first really large-scale winery in San Luis Obispo County. By the early 1980s, the owners controlled about 875 acres of vines. In 1988, the operation was acquired by Wine World (a subsidiary of Nestlé Corporation; see BERINGER WINE ESTATE), which renamed the winery MERIDIAN.* Estrella River is now the brand name of a line of FIGHTING VARIETALS sold by the Classic Wine Co.

ETHYL ACETATE. An ESTER produced in wine as part of the natural fermentation process. In high concentration, it is associated with the smell of spoiled wine and is usually in company with acetic acid (vinegar). Tasters often call this smell acetic. Others with some technical background will comment on the presence of what they call "e. a." In days past one often heard that such a wine was "pricked," but this term has been all but lost.

ÉTUDE, a brand that has been produced by Anthony Soter since 1985. Previously a winemaker at SPOTTSWOODE and CHAPPELLET, he now produces about 6,000 cases a year on his own at the DOMAINE MONTREAUX facility. His Cabernet Sauvignon and Pinot noir are highly regarded. He also makes Pinot gris, Pinot Meunier, and Pinot blanc. Since the 1970s, Soter has developed an excellent reputation as a winemaking consultant.

EUTYPA, a fungus disease that has become a serious problem in many vineyards in California since the 1960s. Cabernet Sauvignon, Sauvignon blanc, and Grenache vines are particularly susceptible. A dieback disease, it causes young shoots to yellow and wither, and eventually the vines will die if the diseased wood is not cut back. The fungus enters pruning cuts and is best resisted by painting such wounds with a fungicide and by avoiding pruning during rainy periods.

EVALUATION, OF WINE. The evaluation of wine is a subjective exercise. Wine drinkers tend to evaluate their wine informally every time they broach a new bottle. All wine drinkers have their own evaluation criteria, often consciously or otherwise ranked and weighted. And certainly most criteria vary from one classification of wine to another—a sherry to a sparkling wine, and from one style to another—a powerful young Cabernet to a young and fruity Gamay Beaujolais. Formal evaluations are almost as subjective, except that criteria are often supplied to the evaluators. Judges in a competition may be instructed not to penalize young Zinfandels for being somewhat tannic, or not to reject Botrytised dessert wines for having a hint of ethyl acetate.

Formal evaluations of California wines have been a regular part of the Golden State's vinous history. In the years before the 1960s, many such events provide insights into California wine history otherwise not available. In recent years the almost exponential proliferation of such medal-producing affairs has made their results of less historic importance.

California had not been a state many years before formal wine competitions had become commonplace. The formation of the California Agricultural Society in 1854 brought wine judging to the annual State Fairs. The Society also divided the state into twenty-nine agricultural districts that held their own annual fairs, many with wine competitions. These remained popular for many years, but by the 1890s gradually fell from favor, particularly as agitation for prohibition increased.

In the 1880s the STATE VITICULTURAL COMMISSION sponsored several conventions at which there were well-publicized wine competitions. The Sixth Convention in 1888 was a particularly important event in that, for the first time, the evaluation panels tasted the wine without knowing the producers. It was at this widely reported event that the high reputations of the table wines of Napa and Alameda counties were firmly established.

Wine competitions were also important at international EXPOSITIONS from 1869 to 1939. The well-publicized evaluations of California wines by European wine experts (see Charles Farley OLDHAM; Frederico POHNDORFF) also did much to help establish the reputations of California's best wines.

After Repeal, the annual competitions at the Los Angeles County Fair in Pomona and the California State Fair were venues for the state's wineries to show off their wines. That the competitions at the State Fair were supervised eventually by professors from the University of California at Davis added prestige to the medals for a while. But in the 1950s many premium producers became unhappy about the awards won by large industrial wine producers. It was claimed, correctly, that wine makers with large operations were being allowed to enter wines from tiny, carefully prepared batches, produced with an eye on little more than medals. In 1957 most premium wineries pulled out of the State Fair competitions.

The wine boom that began in the 1960s produced an ever-growing number of competitions, in California and all over the rest of the world. These have been supported by many wineries in California, and shunned by others with great reputations for high quality. The resulting awards can be seen in carefully prepared displays that are part of many wineries' tasting room decorations.

Wine evaluations have also become a regular part of the consumer press. The first regular newspaper column evaluating California wine was Robert Mayock's (see GRAU &

Since the 1850s Californians have loved to see their wines evaluated in competition. In the early days a "premium" wine was one that had won an award, such as this silver cup bestowed on Antoine DELMAS at the meeting of the California Agricultural Society in 1855. This prize was for grapes, but in 1859 he won a cup for the best red wine, made from his Zinfandel (or Black St. Peter's) grapes.

WERNER) in the *San Jose News* from 1941 to 1945. By the mid-1970s, most major newspapers had a regular wine columnist or subscribed to a syndicated column for their food sections. Consumer wine magazines with wine evaluations began appearing in the early 1970s. Then came newsletters devoted almost solely to wine evaluation. By the 1980s it was common for published evaluations to grade wines on a 100-point scale, much as one might expect for a high school essay (90–100=A, 80–89=B, and so on).

In 1968, the California State Fair was reorganized as the ongoing Cal-Expo and in the 1980s the state wine competition was revived with a new, complex, and carefully planned format that seemed to answer most of the complaints about earlier state competitions.

Maynard Amerine and Edward B. Roessler,
Wines: Their Sensory Evaluation (San Francisco: W. H. Freeman, 1976).

Marian W. Baldy, *The University Wine Course* (San Francisco: Wine Appreciation Guild, 1993).

A. C. Noble et al., "Progress Toward a Standardized System of Wine Terminology," *American Journal of Enology and Viticulture* 36, no. 2 (1984): 107–09.

EVENSEN VINEYARDS (BW 4909). A tiny family winery in Oakville in the Napa Valley. Bonded in 1979, the winery began by producing small quantities of dry Gewürztraminer. Since 1987 Chardonnay has been added. Production totals about 1,000 cases per year.

EVERGREEN. An old winegrowing district in the eastern foothills of the Santa Clara Valley below Mount Hamilton. It was here that Pierre PELLIER established his vineyard in the 1860s, a forerunner of the MIRASSOU winery, built by his descendants in 1937. Today that winery, surrounded by tract houses, schools, and shopping centers, is the last vestige of winegrowing in the district.

Winegrowing exploded here in the 1880s; by the end of the decade there were about 1,000 acres of vines and several wineries. William WEHNER's great wine estate and vineyards dominated the winegrowing scene here before Prohibition.

EWER AND ATKINSON, a partnership, between Seneca Ewer (1819–1904) and JOSEPH B. ATKINSON, formed in 1885. The firm developed the Valley View winery in Rutherford, Napa, and had an excellent reputation for red wine. Atkinson had acquired a 126-acre parcel to the south in 1881, planted a 115-acre vineyard, and built a fine home; the site of ST. SUPÉRY WINERY today. But hard times in the 1890s brought down Atkinson who lost his estate in 1899. Ewer reorganized the business as S. Ewer & Son, taking his son, Frederick (1861–1928), as a partner. In 1915 Georges de Latour bought Valley View, which was across the road from his home vineyard, and enlarged the cellar. This plant became his winery, BEAULIEU VINEYARD.

EXPERIMENTAL STATIONS. Both the United States Department of Agriculture (USDA) and the University of California promoted and established experimental stations, important practical and scholarly institutions, in the early years of the twentieth century. Ten of them in California were devoted to viticulture; see also G. C. HUSMANN. They functioned as laboratories, where scientists could work in the field researching viticultural problems, and as outreach stations permitting the scientific community to give practical instruction in the field to winegrowers and vineyardists.

Today the most important of these for fine California wine is the "Oakville Station" in the Napa Valley, owned by the University of California at Davis and administered by the Department of Viticulture and Enology. The station has two 20-acre plots, the South Vineyard, a gift to the University from the Napa Valley Vintners in 1947, and the U.S. Department of Agriculture's Federal Vineyard, deeded to the University in 1955. Over the years the Oakville Station has made important contributions to viticulturists' knowledge about frost protection, vine spacing, clonal evaluation, resistant rootstock, and canopy management. Today the research is principally on matters of productivity, health in vines, and quality of wine. See also FRESNO STATE UNIVERSITY; M.T. KEARNEY; UNIVERSITY OF CALIFORNIA AT BERKELEY.

EXPORTS. Making exports an important part of wine production in California has almost always been more hope than actuality. Before Prohibition, the geographical reality of California's position on the Pacific rim meant that most of the exports went to Mexico, Central America, British Columbia, China, Japan, and the Pacific islands. Wine sent to Hawaii was usually considered an export, although after 1897 such was not actually the case.

Overseas trade became slightly more serious in the 1880s when about 1 percent of production went to foreign markets. In the 1890s trade grew from about 500,000 gallons to almost one million by the end of the decade, about 30 percent of which went to Europe.

After Prohibition, the export market for years was almost entirely Canadian, mostly bulk wine sent north to local bottlers and blenders. By the 1970s, the Canadian trade had dropped to about one-third of the total, but the rest was highly scattered with Barbados taking more than Europe. In 1987, Canada still led but the total was now a significant 10 million gallons, 30 percent to Europe and 20 percent to Japan. In the 1990s, totals continued to rise as the result of aggressive marketing and closer cooperation between industry leaders and government agencies. In 1996, the value of American wine exports, overwhelmingly from California, was $326 million and amounted to 48 million gallons. The five largest markets in value of exports were the United Kingdom, Canada, Japan, Germany, and Switzerland. Actuality is now coming into alignment with hope.

EXPOSITIONS. The international exposition was a passion for Europeans and Americans before World War I. The first, held in London in 1851, was so successful that it was imitated all over Europe and America. Nations enjoyed showing off their industrial, agricultural, and cultural achievements. By the 1880s, there was good reason for the best

The Panama-Pacific International Exposition was held in San Francisco in 1915. Here the panel of wine judges is convened on July 14, "Wine Day," at the Expo. CHARLES CARPY is second from the right; Kanaye Nagasawa of FOUNTAINGROVE is fifth from the right.

wine producers in California to show off their products. The Paris Exposition of 1889 was a good beginning. Expositions were held every few years in Europe at such cities as Dublin, Bordeaux, Berlin, Ghent, and Paris again in 1900. There two California producers won gold medals for their Cabernet Sauvignons, one from Howell Mountain, the other from Monte Bello. America also had its international expositions: in Philadelphia, Atlanta, Buffalo, St. Louis, Portland, and Seattle, all with wine competitions and entrants from California. San Francisco had three of its own (1894, 1915, and 1939), where the California wine industry strutted its stuff. The medals flowed freely and California producers used them freely to promote their wines.

After World War II, the same vinous function was performed in California at the State Fairs held near Sacramento and the Los Angeles County Fairs at Pomona. Since the 1970s, competitions specifically organized around wines have been common in the United States and Europe; see EVALUATION OF WINE.

EXTENDED MACERATION. See TANNIN

FAIR, JAMES GRAHAM (1831–94), a former U. S. senator who bought the winegrowing estate of William Bihler in 1891. It was located east of the Petaluma River in the Lakeville area of Sonoma County. Bihler had pioneered viticulture there in the 1870s. Fair expanded the winery to a capacity of 600,000 gallons and added 300 acres of vines to Bihler's 200. In later years viticulture declined and disappeared in this area until the 1990s, when the similarity of the region to the Carneros became clear and a few vineyards were planted.

FAIRS. See EXPOSITIONS

FALCON CREST. See SPRING MOUNTAIN VINEYARDS

FAR NIENTE (BW 5072). John Benson (1828–1910) made a fortune in real estate in San Francisco and used a small part of it between 1871 and 1880 to buy up several pieces of land, totaling 520 acres, near Oakville. He developed a diversified agricultural estate with an 84-acre vineyard, first planted to muscats for raisins. He began making wine on a small scale in 1876. In 1885, he started construction of a 300,000-gallon winery, planned by H. W. MCINTYRE, the noted winery designer. But Benson never did much with the winery. On his death there were only 40,000 gallons of COOPERAGE in the great

building. He had named the ranch Far Niente, Italian for without care, which sums up his approach to his Napa holdings, which he rarely visited.

In 1978, a businessman from Oklahoma, H. Gilliland (Gil) Nickel and his associates acquired the place, restored the winery, and planted 167 acres of vines. Today it is one of the most beautiful wine estates in the Napa Valley. The new owners started making wine in 1979 in a rented facility, a Chardonnay that was expensive but received good reviews. Winemaking moved to Far Niente in 1982 and Cabernet Sauvignon was added. Dolce appeared in 1989, a late-harvest Sémillon, released at $50 per half-bottle. In the 1990s, the winery's annual production was about 35,000 cases.

FARRELL, GARY (BW 5649). Farrell has been DAVIS BYNUM's winemaker since 1978. Since 1982 he has also produced his own wines sharing Bynum's bond. His Cabernets and Chardonnays have been well received; his Pinot noirs have made him famous, and since 1991, his Zinfandel has become important. He sells about 8,000 cases per year under his own label.

FAY, NATHAN, discovered the potential for making fine Cabernet Sauvignon in Napa's Stag's Leap area when, in 1961, he began planting a vineyard on the fruit ranch he had bought there in 1953. Thereafter, he sold his grapes regularly to top-flight producers, often outside Napa. In 1985 the 72-acre Fay vineyard was acquired by STAG'S LEAP WINE CELLARS.

FELLOM RANCH VINEYARDS (BW 4956). The Fellom family moved onto the MONTE BELLO Ridge in 1929. Their ranch is next door to RIDGE VINEYARDS. In the early 1980s, they revived an old vineyard there and, in 1987, bonded their little winery. They produce estate Cabernet Sauvignon from the 14-acre vineyard and purchase Zinfandel grapes from a vineyard in Saratoga. Annual production is about 1,500 cases.

FELTON-EMPIRE VINEYARDS (BW 4781). In 1976, several years after the historic HALL-CREST* winery had closed its doors, a partnership of wine enthusiasts in Santa Cruz reopened it under the Felton-Empire name and began producing a wide range of varietal wines from Santa Cruz Mountain and Central Coast grapes. In 1987, a variety of economic and personal factors moved the partners to sell the property to new owners, who restored the original Hallcrest Vineyards name. Felton-Empire survives as a brand.

FENESTRA WINERY (BW 4956). Lanny Replogle taught chemistry at San Jose State University, even a class in wine chemistry, and was a serious home winemaker before he decided to go public in 1976. First he made wine at the old RUBY HILL winery in Pleasanton. Then in 1980 he settled at the nearby George True Winery, which had been established in 1889 but had ceased making wine in the 1960s. Today Fenestra is one of the most honored wineries in the Livermore Valley, if medals and other awards are a good criterion. Most of Replogle's wines come from vineyards in the Livermore Valley, but he buys Cabernet Sauvignon and Merlot from other districts. Production runs about 5,000 cases per year.

FERMENTATION. In winemaking the process by which grape sugar is converted to ethyl alcohol and carbon dioxide with the release of heat. This process results from the action of enzymes in yeast metabolizing the grape sugar. If the sugar content is so high that the alcohol level surpasses about 16.5 percent, the fermentation will usually end, leaving residual sugar in the wine.

Grapes have wild YEASTS on them when they enter the fermenter. Until the 1890s in California, the grapes were crushed and nature took its course. Gradually California winemakers discovered the use of SULFUR DIOXIDE to subdue the wild yeasts, and the use of cultured yeasts to bring about a more predictable fermentation. This approach held until the 1970s when winemakers began working to cut down the use of sulfur dioxide. Fermentations today may follow the older practice or allow the wild and cultured yeasts to work together. Several wineries let the wild yeast work alone. This question finds hard-nosed partisans on both sides today.

Temperature control became a goal of careful winemakers in California in the 1880s. The sometimes scorching fall days of September and October often raised fermentation temperatures to a point where the process "stuck," usually damaging or ruining the wine. Fairly efficient cooling systems were developed before Prohibition, but the most important steps were made after World War II. By the 1960s, elaborate cooling systems could be found in any large winery. Soon even smaller operations were using stainless-steel tanks with insulation jackets. Transfer systems of pipes and coils were also used to hold down the temperature of the fermenting must, particularly in white wine production. For red wine production, there have been differing opinions about how high the temperature should be allowed to go. Thought a foolish error 25 years ago, some winemakers are now willing to allow temperatures up to the 90s in

The fermentation house at LINDA VISTA near Mission San Jose, in 1894. The small, open-top fermenters are much like those that may be seen today in many premium California wineries. (Unzelman Collection, Santa Rosa, Calif.)

red wine production. Wineries also keep down temperatures by insulating and/or air conditioning fermentation rooms. Small operations, as of yore, open the doors at sundown and close them in the early morning.

Winemakers refer to the conversion of grape juice into wine as the primary fermentation. A second fermentation, in the bottle or another container, is essential in the production of sparkling wine. The secondary fermentation is another matter; see ACID.

Today there are more variables in fermentation than in any other step in the winemaking process. The number of possibilities makes the problems faced by early California winemakers seem almost simple.

White Wine

Sulfur dioxide   A useful antioxidant, often added to grapes before they are crushed. Today most winemakers in California use as little as possible.

Skin contact   In making white wine, California winemakers usually try to avoid letting the grape skins remain in contact for long, or at all, with the juice before pressing and starting fermentation. But a few believe that an hour or so of such contact adds to the complexity of flavor. To minimize contact, some small producers use whole-cluster PRESSING: The clusters of grapes are squeezed gently and the resulting juice, called free run, goes directly to the fermenter.

Free-run and press juice   Many winemakers believe that the juice that comes directly from the crush, or whole-cluster pressing, that is called free run, makes a more delicate wine than the juice that is released when the mass of crushed grapes is pressed just before fermentation. The winemaker must decide whether to keep the free-run and press juice separate. White wines made entirely from free-run juice are usually more expensive than those made from a blend of free-run and press juices.

Yeast   The winemaker must decide whether to subdue the wild yeasts on the grapes with sulfur dioxide or to allow those yeasts to take a full part in the fermentation. If, as is most common, cultured yeasts are used, the winemaker has a wide range to choose from. His choice will affect the style of the resulting wine.

Fermenter   Most white wines today are fermented in stainless-steel tanks. To enhance the flavor, some wine, typically Chardonnay, Sauvignon blanc, and Viognier, may be fermented in small BARRELS made of American or European, usually French, oak. Barrel fermenting will increase production costs as it is new barrels that impart the most flavor. The cost of barrels has soared in the past decade. Some winemakers will ferment a small portion of a production lot in barrels, the rest in tanks, and then blend the two.

Temperature control   Modern winemakers think it imperative to hold the fermentation temperature of white table wine to less than 65°F.; some believe that even this temperature is too high to permit the greatest delicacy in flavor. To achieve the desired temperatures, wineries large and small use stainless-steel tanks that can be refrigerated. Wines being barrel fermented have to be kept in a cool cellar.

Malolactic fermentation   A secondary fermenation that results in wines with lower acidity and softer flavors; for Chardonnay, the description *buttery* is often used. Winemakers have to decide whether they wish to use malolactic fermentation at all and/or what percentage of their wines they wish to subject to it. Today it is common to inoculate a tank of wine that is undergoing its primary fermentation with a cultured bacterium that induces malolactic fermentation. The secondary fermentation can be inhibited by reducing the temperature of the wine or introducing sulfur dioxide. See also ACID.

Red Wine

Stems   Almost all wineries now use a stemmer-crusher machine to remove the stems from red wine grapes before fermentation. Occasionally—in California most frequently for Pinot noir, which is deficient in tannin—a small percentage of those stems is put back into the fermenter because the tannins they contain can add to the phenolic content of the wine. The practice is less common today than it was in the 1970s.

Whole berries   Winemakers have found that, if red-wine grapes ferment without being crushed, the wine has a brighter fruitiness and a more intense color than if it had been made from completely crushed grapes (see CARBONIC MACERATION). Many modern crushers have settings that allow a certain percentage of the grapes to pass through without being crushed, enabling the winemaker to choose how much of a production lot will enjoy whole-berry fermentation, a procedure used for a considerable quantity of red wine made in California today. Although use of the technique is often public knowledge, the percentage involved may be regarded as a proprietary secret. Cabernet Sauvignon, Merlot, Petite Sirah, Pinot noir, Sangiovese, and Zinfandel are good candidates for whole-berry fermentation.

Temperature   Red wine is usually fermented at higher temperatures than is white wine, Cabernet Sauvignon and Zinfandel up to 90°F. Many winemakers believe that the higher temperatures are beneficial for the extraction of pigments and PHENOLICS. But the fermentation must not be allowed to stop too soon or to stick. Winemakers monitor the temperature of their red-wine fermentations and regulate them by controlling the cap (see below) and using simple cooling devices—sometimes merely opening the winery doors at night is enough.

Cap control   The cap, or *chapeau,* of a fermenting red wine is the solid mass of grape skins and seeds that rises to the top of the fermenter during fermentation. To avoid bacterial contamination, the winemaker must keep this cap broken up and submerged. Also, a hardened cap can often cause the fermentation temperatures to rise excessively. Traditionally, and still in many wineries today, the cap is punched down several times a day by winery workers. More efficient, but thought by many to result in a less delicate wine, is the process of pumping over: The fermenting must is pumped up from below, over the cap, breaking it up and pushing it down into the liquid. New technology is being used to control the cap. Some new fermenters are equipped with submerged screens to prevent the cap from even forming, and in some large wineries the fermenter is a specially constructed horizontal tank that may be rotated to keep the cap broken up and submerged.

Extended maceration A French technique used for red wines in California since the 1970s to reduce the harsher tannins but maintain the phenolic content necessary for successful aging. The wine is left in the fermenter for 10 to 20 days after fermentation is complete, during which time the harsher tannins drop out. The technique is not used for light, fruity wines that are meant to be consumed while still young.

Malolactic fermentation Except for light, fruity wines meant for early consumption, most red wine made in California goes through malolactic fermentation (see ACID). In some wineries the long-standing presence of the required *Lactobacillus* bacterium in the building and the cooperage makes the process automatic. Winemakers can induce the process by inoculating the fermenting must with a cultured bacterium. If this secondary fermentation is not desired, it can be inhibited by cooling the must and the resulting wine until it has been STABILIZED.

Pressing Winemakers press the fermenting must early if they want a light, fruity wine. A well-extracted wine, meant to be worth aging, will not be pressed until the grape sugar in the must has been converted completely, and even later if the wine is to be subject to extended maceration. The winemaker may also distinguish among his red press wines according to the amount of pressure that has been applied; press wine from a soft pressing tends to be more delicate and contain fewer harsh tannins.

FERRARA WINERY (BW 3758). Founded just before Repeal in Escondido, San Diego County. Production of table, dessert, and flavored wines runs about 35,000 cases per year.

FERRARI-CARANO WINERY (BW 5349). The Carano family bought a vineyard near Geyserville in 1979 and several more in subsequent years in the Knight's, Dry Creek, and Alexander valleys, and in the Carneros. By the 1990s they controlled about 600 acres of vineyards at twelve locations in Sonoma County. Their winery in the Dry Creek Valley, along with a lavish visitor center, has been built in stages, concluding in 1994. The underground wine cellar holds 1,500 red wine barrels.

The winery's first wines were released in 1987 and have received high marks from wine writers, particularly the Chardonnays from Alexander Valley. Production has grown steadily in the 1990s and now exceeds 75,000 cases a year. The second label is Carano Cellars.

FERRARIO. Ernesto Ferrario (1879–1975) and his brother **Carlo** were important figures in wine industry in the Livermore Valley, their careers spanning a large part of the twentieth century. They came from northern Italy to California in 1901. Carlo built his winery on Second Street in Livermore and Ernesto made his living in the San Francisco saloon trade. He acquired the historic RUBY HILL VINEYARDS* in 1921 and ran it until shortly before his death. Much of his production was for bulk wine sales, but his retail trade at the winery was a tradition in Livermore.

For many years Carlo was a partner in in the Garatti Winery in Pleasanton (see VILLA ARMONDO), from which large quantities of sacramental wine were shipped during Prohibition. Soon after Repeal, he built a large winery on Tesla Road, which he sold during World War II. It was later acquired by the WENTE family.

FERRER, GLORIA (BW 5320). The Ferrer family in Spain produces the popular Freixenet sparkling wine. In 1983 the Ferrers bought 160 acres of pastureland south of the town of Sonoma. By 1986 a 500,000-gallon Catalonian-style winery had been built for the production of sparkling wine in the traditional method of Champagne. The brand was introduced the same year with sparklers produced at another facility. By the 1990s, production had surpassed 65,000 cases per year. The winery's vineyards now cover 180 acres of land in Carneros. Pedro Ferrer heads the operation, the brand being named for his mother. The American company's name is Freixenet Sonoma Champagne Caves.

FESSLER, JULIUS (1908–91), noted enologist and, in 1933, a founder of the Berkeley Yeast Laboratory. For years after World War II, he was a consultant to several of the makers of premium wines of California. He invented and developed several important winemaking aids, and regularly wrote for industry publications on the practical solution of winemaking problems. His privately printed handbook for the home winemaker, *Guidelines to Practical Winemaking*, was widely read.

FETZER VINEYARDS (BW 4522, 5254). One of the most successful family wine enterprises in modern California history. In 1958 Bernard (1920–81) and Kathleen Fetzer bought the 740-acre J. L. Smith ranch in Redwood Valley in Mendocino County. Fetzer became a home winemaker, using grapes from the old 70-acre vineyard on the place, and he sold grapes to other home producers. A good part of the workforce on the large estate was provided by the Fetzers' eleven children whose ages covered a nineteen-year span.

The vineyard grew to 170 acres and the winery went up in 1968–69. In the early years Fetzer was primarily a red wine operation, concentrating on Cabernet Sauvignon and Zinfandel. Later whites, especially Chardonnay and Gewürztraminer, became more important.

Bernard's death in 1981 did not slow the growth or subdue the success of the operation. Kathleen and ten of the children were still active in the workforce and management of the winery and vineyard. In 1981 they brought out their Bel Arbres (later Bel Arbors) line of inexpensive varietals. In the same year they bought the nearby Sundial Ranch, the future linchpin of their 800,000-case-a-year Chardonnay production. Over the years high quality and moderate prices built the Fetzer reputation. Excellent marketing strategies also helped.

In 1982 a Barrel Select line was introduced and in 1985 a higher-priced line of reserve varietals appeared. But their biggest seller was White Zinfandel. In 1984 the Fetzers bought their Valley Oaks Ranch outside Hopland and began creating a remarkable food and wine center around a five-acre biointensive garden. The winery also was a pioneer in large-scale organic viticulture. In 1993 the Bonterra line appeared, the wine made from 540 acres of "organically grown grapes."

In 1992, when Fetzer was selling about 2.4 million cases of wine per year, the family sold their two wineries, the wine and food center, and the Fetzer brand to the Brown-Forman food and drink conglomerate. Most of the Fetzer vineyards remain in family hands, and most of the grapes still go to the old operation. Since then, sales have grown to 3 million cases, but the garden and food center have been closed down. Under Brown-Forman the export market has become a significant part of Fetzer operations. In 1997 almost 20 percent of the winery's production was exported, mostly to countries in western Europe. Unlike almost all other exporters of wine from California, Fetzer makes specific lots of wine blended for specific national markets.

FICKLIN VINEYARDS (BW 4431). In 1948 the Ficklin family began making port-style wine made from Portuguese varieties of grapes. Their little winery is located in the Central Valley, near Madera. The first release in 1953 was greeted with critical praise. Over the years the family has raised production from the 50-acre vineyard to about 10,000 cases. In 1991 they released a 1957 reserve port and a 1983 vintage port. The price for the reserve was $100.

David Ficklin, et al., *Making California Port Wine: Ficklin Vineyards from 1948 to 1992* (Regional Oral History Office, Bancroft Library, 1992).

FIDDLETOWN, a district in Amador County that received AVA status in 1983 and is noted for its Zinfandel vineyards, the most famous owned by Chester Eschen. The district is named for the rustic village (el. 1,687 feet) here, just east of Plymouth, and has about 350 acres of wine grapes.

FIELDBROOK VALLEY WINERY (BW 4777). It is next to impossible to ripen grapes in Humboldt County, so Robert Hodgson, a professor of oceanography, buys grapes, mostly from North Coast vineyards and several varieties from the Meredith Vineyard, one of the few in Trinity County. His little winery, founded in 1976, produces about 2,000 cases of Zinfandel, Chardonnay, and Sauvignon blanc each year.

FIELD STONE WINERY (BW 4816). Wallace Johnson (1913–79) developed the Up Right mechanical grape harvester and served two terms as mayor of Berkeley. He bought his ranch in the Alexander Valley in 1955; by the late 1960s he had 130 acres of vineyard. In 1976 he built his winery into a wooded knoll and bonded it for the 1977 vintage. Now under the management of the Slater family, Field Stone produces a wide range of varietals, particularly Cabernet Sauvignon and Petite Sirah. Production averages about 12,000 cases per year.

FIFE VINEYARDS (BW 5092), a winery in Redwood Valley, Mendocino County, that was known as **Olson Vineyards** until 1989 when it was purchased by the Konrad family and renamed Konrad Estate. The winery became a 6,000-case-per-year operation, making principally Chardonnay and Zinfandel. In 1993 the

Konrads brought out a vintage port made from Petite Sirah and fortified with brandy from GERMAIN-ROBIN; it is no longer made.

In 1996 Dennis Fife, formerly president of Inglenook, bought Konrad Estate. Fife has a vineyard on Spring Mountain and he also makes wine under BW 5965 at the NAPA (VALLEY) WINE CO. The Konrad brand has been kept and constitutes part of Fife's annual production of 10,000 cases.

FIGHTING VARIETAL. Coined by the wine marketing consultant Ed Everett in 1983, a description of cork-finished varietal wines sold today for between about for $5 and $7 per bottle, although the upper limit is not exact. Often sold in 1.5 liter bottles, they are always affordable wines for immediate consumption. A sizeable portion of the grapes for such wines are grown in the Central Valley where higher yields and lower land prices help make the competitive prices possible. Some leading brands in this field are Glen Ellen, Bel Arbors, Corbett Canyon, Deer Valley, and Woodbridge (Robert Mondavi).

FILIPPI VINTAGE CO. (BW 3724), a million-gallon winery that was founded after Repeal in the Cucamonga area of southern California. Until 1993, the winery, under the control of the Filippi family, produced a wide range of table and dessert wines under several labels, vermouth, and some altar wine. Their best-selling wine in recent years was white Zinfandel, which once reached 100,000 cases per year. In 1993 the family sold the property to developers but continued making wine in the old REGINA winery in Etiwanda. They maintain a tasting room in the old GUASTI winery, and CUSTOM CRUSHING is an important part of their business. Total annual production is now about 50,000 cases.

FILSINGER VINEYARDS (BW 4959). A 45,000-gallon winery in the Temecula area of

Riverside County, bonded in 1980. Production, principally white wine, runs about 7,000 cases per year and includes a small quantity of bottle-fermented sparkling wine.

FILTRATION. See CLARIFICATION

FINING. See CLARIFICATION

A.FINKE'S WIDOW. The name of a company in San Francisco that produced inexpensive SPARKLING WINE. Alois Finke was an Austrian who bought still white wine and carbonated it by the "soda-pop" process in the 1860s. After his death the firm took this name, in the style of the famous widows of Champagne. Years later Gottlieb GROEZINGER and others acquired the operation. It passed through several ownerships until Prohibition. By 1915 it was probably the most popular "sparkling" wine in the western United States and Canada. After Repeal the brand reappeared, but only briefly. In 1969, when a structure was torn down in San Francisco, a huge sign was revealed on the building next door advertising the brand, by then almost completely forgotten.

FIRESTONE VINEYARD (BW 4720). Harvey S. Firestone's son and grandson founded this winery in the Santa Ynez Valley in Santa Barbara County in 1974. The planting of the 345 acres of vineyard had begun in 1972. Financing for the $7,500,000 project came from Leonard Firestone, formerly a U. S. ambassador to Belgium, and from Suntory, Ltd, Japan. The man in charge of the operation, and its conceptual father, was Leonard's son Anthony Brooks Firestone, who had given up his position in the family's tire and rubber business in 1971. The first vintage was in 1975, a modern pioneer event—the first commercial winegrowing venture—in this area. Over the years, production has grown to 80,000 cases per year, with a strong emphasis on white varietals; White Riesling and Gewürztraminer have been particularly successful. In 1986 Firestone bought J. Carey Cellars and Brooks's wife, Catherine (Kate) Boulton Firestone took charge of that project, which operated as CURTIS WINERY* until it was sold in 1997. Before she became a Firestone, Kate was a ballerina with London's Royal Ballet. In 1994 the Firestones gained full ownership of their operation, buying out Suntory's 31 percent share.

A letterhead (ca. 1910) for A. Finke's Widow, proclaiming that SPARKLING WINE was the firm's product. But, after 1906 the federal government insisted that artificially carbonated beverages must not be labeled "sparkling." The same rule is still in effect, but now relates to advertising as well as labeling. (Unzelman Collection, Santa Rosa, Calif.)

Brooks Firestone, *Firestone Vineyard: A Santa Ynez Valley Pioneer* (Regional Oral History Office, Bancroft Library, 1996).

FISHER VINEYARDS (BW 4926). A winery in the hills northeast of Santa Rosa with about 70 acres of vineyards in Napa and Sonoma counties. Fred J. Fisher began planting his vineyard in Sonoma in 1973 and built his winery in 1979. In the early years Charles ORTMAN acted as Fisher's enologist and consultant. Fisher's motto, "Fit and Finish," was also his grandfather's, whose Fisher Body Corporation is well known for its logo, Body by Fisher, that has been associated with American automobile production since 1908. The winery's best wines bear the Fisher Coach Insignia label. By the 1990s annual production had reached about 9,000 cases, mostly Chardonnay and Cabernet Sauvignon and, recently, some Merlot.

FITCH MOUNTAIN CELLARS. See OPTIMA

FITZPATRICK WINERY (BW 4978). In El Dorado County near the village of Somerset and, between 1980 and 1985, known as Somerset Winery. There Brian and Diana Fitzpatrick have also created a cozy lodge with a dining room that offers exotic gourmet menus. Everywhere one can see an Irish motif. There is a 10-acre vineyard, and the Fitzpatricks also buy grapes, particularly Zinfandel from Amador County. Production of a wide range of varietals and a little cider was approaching 3,000 cases per year in the 1990s.

FLAME TOKAY. A table grape imported to California in the late nineteenth century from Algeria; see also TABLE GRAPES.

FLORA. A wine grape cultivar, a cross between Sémillon and Gewürztraminer that was developed at the University of California at Davis and released in 1959. Its exotic, floral wines have never caught on. In 1976 acreage in California

peaked at 472, but in 1990 the state dropped the variety from its published statistics. There were still 13 acres in Napa County in 1993.

FLORA SPRINGS WINE CO. (BW 4853). At the west end of Zinfandel Lane, on the border of the St. Helena and Rutherford districts in Napa Valley are the remains of two wineries, Rennie Brothers and Brockhoff, dating from the 1880s. In 1977, the Komes/Garvey family acquired them and began reconstructing the buildings and planting vineyards. Flora Springs was bonded in 1979. The owners have expanded their vineyard holdings to more than 500 acres and sell grapes to other wineries. Flora Springs wines, and since 1992 wines under the Floréal label, have won critical praise, particularly the Cabernet Sauvignon, a red Meritage (Trilogy), Merlot, and Chardonnay. A small quantity of Sangiovese is also produced. By the 1990s, production had surpassed 40,000 cases per year. Flora Springs is considered to be in the Rutherford Viticultural Area, because the Rennie Brothers winery had been so construed in the 1880s.

THOMAS FOGARTY WINERY (BW 5041). In the Portola Valley of the Santa Cruz Mountains, above Palo Alto, the Fogarty family built their little winery in 1981 and bonded it the next year. They had begun planting their 25-acre estate vineyard to Chardonnay and Pinot noir in 1978. Grapes for Fogarty wines also come from far afield, from Edna Valley to Monterey to Napa Valley. A wide range of varietals has been produced with emphasis on Chardonnay. Annual production in the 1990s has reached 8,500 cases.

FOLIE À DEUX WINERY (BW 5038). The founders, Larry and Evie Dizmang, are mental health professionals; their winery's name, meaning shared craziness, and the label, embellished with a Rorschach inkblot, are appropriate. They bonded their 40,000-gallon

It is harvest time at Foppiano Vineyards in 1945. "Auntie Norm" (Norma Foppiano Coyne) operates the tractor. (Foppiano Family Collection, Healdsburg, Calif.)

Napa winery north of St. Helena in 1981. There was nothing loony about their Chardonnays, which won praise from wine writers. Their lower-priced line was called Pas de Deux. They produced a wide range of varietals and a sparkling Fantasie brut. In 1993 the winery filed for bankruptcy but continued operations. In 1995 new owners, headed by Richard PETERSON, took over. Annual production is about 12,000 cases.

FOLLE BLANCHE. Formerly the grape used most extensively for producing brandies in Cognac. It usually makes a bland, tart table wine, but when the grapes are brought to full maturity the wine has a pleasant apple-grape aroma. The variety was probably brought to California by Pierre PELLIER in the 1850s. In the 1880s, Charles WETMORE, with some success, encouraged its use in brandy production. Several wineries in California made successful Folle blanche wines before Prohibition. For several years after World War II, Louis MARTINI

made a varietal Folle blanche and reintroduced the wine in 1995. In 1976, the state recorded 365 acres of the variety. By 1988 it was dropped from the statistics with but 64 acres left, most in Napa and Sonoma counties, where it was used for blending and in sparkling wine production. CARNEROS ALAMBIC DISTILLERY makes a varietal brandy from this grape.

FOPPIANO VINEYARDS (BW 312), one of the few successful family-owned wineries whose operations bridged Prohibition and survived into recent years in Sonoma. Foppiano was founded by Giovanni Foppiano (1843–1922) in 1896. The old winery was replaced by the current structure in 1937. Four generations have worked the Sonoma estate south of Healdsburg, which now contains 200 acres of vineyard.

Before Prohibition, the Riverside Winery, as it was then called, supplied bulk wines, about 50,000 gallons per year, to the CALIFORNIA WINE ASSOCIATION. After weathering the dry years, the winery greeted Repeal in 1933 with 85,000 gallons of new wine. Most of Foppiano's trade was with eastern bottlers and other wineries in Sonoma, but by the 1960s, a solid reputation for good jug wines had been established. Then the winery began producing varietals, principally Cabernet Sauvignon and Petite Sirah. A remarkable program of plant modernization, product diversity, and skillful marketing has marked the winery's past twenty years. By the 1990s, Foppiano had annual sales of about 200,000 cases of wine under the Foppiano, Riverside Farm, and Fox Mountain labels.

Louis J. Foppiano, *A Century of Agriculture and Winemaking in Sonoma County, 1896–1996* (Regional Oral History Office, Bancroft Library, 1996).

FORMAN VINEYARDS (BW 5228). From 1968 to 1977, Ric Forman was the founding winemaker at STERLING VINEYARDS, where he earned a reputation for producing good wine. He then made wine for Peter Newton, another founder of Sterling, until 1983, when he began developing his own vineyard and winery on the lower slopes of Howell Mountain. Today, his reputation for fine Chardonnay and Cabernet Sauvignon is even higher than it was at Sterling. Total production is about 4,000 cases per year.

FORTIFIED WINES, traditionally referred to in California as sweet or dessert wines, euphemisms used to avoid the stigma that might be attached by the extra alcoholic kick clearly given to a wine that has been "fortified." Industry publications since the 1880s have consistently shunned the latter term although a fortified wine such as dry sherry can hardly be described as sweet. Nevertheless, statistics for dry sherry have always been included in government and industry summations for sweet wines.

Most fortified wines are sweet from the residual sugar left after the winemaker has added high-proof alcohol, usually grape brandy, to halt fermentation. The alcohol levels of such wines are usually between 16 percent and 24 percent. Producers pay a higher tax on their wine when the alcohol level exceeds 14 percent. In recent years in California genuinely sweet table wines with alcohol levels below 14 percent

TABLE 11. FORTIFIED WINE PRODUCTION IN CALIFORNIA, BY TYPE (1900–1995)

YEAR	PORT	SHERRY	(MILLIONS OF GALLONS) MUSCATEL	ANGELICA	AS A PERCENT OF PRODUCTION[a]	TOTAL
1900	2.7	1.6	1.5	.4		9.1
1906	6.7	4.6	1.3	.9		21.3
1914	10.9	5.5	1.3	1.6		19.7
1917						15.0
1919						3.8
1921						11.0
1922[b]						N.A.
1933						16.1
1935					81	53.8
1940	18.1	18.9	21.8	7.3	77	78.3
1944	16.8	17.7	10.9	5.4	66	56.0
1948	36.8	23.6	26.0	7.6	72	108.4
1955	24.4	30.0	19.7	13.3	70	109.7
1960[c]					62	90.6
1966					52	85.2
1968					44	75.3
1970					32	59.2
1972					24	51.0
1977					17	37.0
1983					6	19.0
1990					4	12.0
1995					4	12.5

a. Fortified wine as a percentage of table wine plus fortified wine.
b. Through 1932, no statistics available.
c. From 1960, no statistics on individual types have been published.
SOURCE: *Pacific Wine and Spirit Review* (through 1917); *Wines & Vines* (through 1995).

but with fairly high levels of residual sugar have become popular as dessert wines, but these do not fit in the fortified category; see LATE-HARVEST WINE.

Several fortified wines, with alcohol levels ranging from 14 to 24 percent, are allowed by U. S. regulations to carry generic names: ANGELICA, MALAGA, MUSCATEL, PORT, SHERRY, and TOKAY. Flavored wines such as VERMOUTH and MARSALA are usually classified separately.

Before Prohibition, the quantity of fortified wine produced in California was usually a reflection of government tax policy on fortifying brandy. For years, rarely reaching 10 percent of the state's total wine production, fortified wines ballooned to about 30 percent of the total when the brandy tax was lowered in 1891. They stayed around that level until World War I, which limited production. Then Prohibition killed them.

Following Repeal, fortified wine became the dominant product of the California industry, averaging over 70 percent of the total. Those wines acted as a cheap source of alcohol during the Great Depression. But in the 1960s total wine consumption began rising steadily while figures for fortified wine plummeted. By 1972, they were but 25 percent of the total, by 1980 less than 10 percent. In the 1990s fortified wine as a percentage of California wine has been steady at between 3 and 4 percent.

A type of fortified wine intended for and sold in low-income neighborhoods has become highly controversial and a serious embarrassment in the industry. These are usually high alcohol, sweet, and inexpensive wines, most often sold by the pint for less than $2.00, and have become a significant source of cheap alcohol for the poor and often destitute. For the producers, they are highly profitable. CANANDAIGUA's Wild Irish Rose, the national leader (7 million gallons), is made from Concord grapes on the East Coast. MD 20/20, made by the WINE GROUP (5 million gallons)

and Thunderbird, made by GALLO (3 million gallons) are the leading California products in this category.

Stephen Brook, *Liquid Gold: Dessert Wines of the World* (New York: William Morrow, 1987), 296–319.

M. A. Joslyn and Maynard Amerine, *Dessert, Appetizer & Related Flavored Wines* (Berkeley, Calif.: University of California, Division of Agricultural Sciences, 1964).

FORTINO WINERY (BW 4463). In 1948 Louis and Angelo Cassa founded their Cassa Brothers Winery in the Hecker Pass area of Santa Clara Valley. They became well known in the area for their Grenache rosé, which they labeled Rose Grape Wine. After the Cassas closed the winery in 1969, Ernest and Mario Fortino acquired the property, renamed it, and operated together until 1972 when Mario founded his own HECKER PASS WINERY up the road. Ernest now controls 52 acres and produces annually about 45,000 cases of wine, a wide range of varietals and generics noted for their traditional, rustic style.

FOUNTAINGROVE (BW 1051). No winery in Sonoma County has had a more interesting history and few have made better wines. The story begins with Thomas Lake Harris (1823– 1906), an English-born mystic who grew up in New York State. In 1858 he founded the Brotherhood of the New Life, a theosophical cult devoted to communal living. By 1867 Harris had a colony of seventy-five followers at Brocton, New York, some of them with large fortunes, which they placed at his disposal. In that same year he toured England and Scotland and took under his wing a fifteen-year-old Japanese student, Kanaye Nagasawa (1853–1936). In 1875, Harris bought 700 acres of land in the eastern foothills of Sonoma County, north of Santa Rosa, and brought some of his closest followers west.

At first dairying was the chief commercial effort at Fountaingrove, but the boom in grape and wine prices brought a change of direction under Nagasawa and E. B. Hyde. Harris had little to do with the operation, which did business as Lay, Clark & Co. By the end of the 1880s, a beautiful mansion and a 500,000-gallon winery had been built. The ranch was expanded to 2,000 acres, with 700 acres in vineyard. By 1890, production was steady at about 250,000 gallons per year, a good part of it sold under the Fountaingrove label from depots on the East Coast and in Britain. In Nagasawa's words, "upon the peculiar merits of Zinfandel," the winery first acquired its reputation.

Harris left California in 1893 after the winery was gutted by fire and the *San Francisco Chronicle* had run a series of salacious articles on life at Fountaingrove. Nagasawa took control, rebuilt the winery, and in the next twenty-five years, became one of the most knowledgeable and respected leaders of the state's wine industry. As one of a panel of wine judges, he may be seen in the photograph on page 107. In 1900, Harris sold the estate to the remaining five members of the Brotherhood for $40,000. The contract called for ownership to devolve only to them until one was left. That person was Nagasawa, who ran the estate and managed the business until 1934. His heirs sold it in 1937 to Errol MacBoyle, who hired Kurt Opper to restore the Fountaingrove label (no Fountaingrove wine had been produced in 1935 and 1936) and Hanns KORNELL to make sparkling wine. The result was another run of fine wines, headed by White Riesling, Sémillon, Pinot noir, and Zinfandel, the latter a blend of 90 percent Zinfandel and 10 percent Petite Sirah and Carignane. Years later Joseph SWAN declared the 1937 Zinfandel to be the finest Sonoma wine he had ever tasted. MacBoyle died in 1949; Opper went on to serve as winemaster at PAUL MASSON. In 1953, the 400 acres of vineyard were pulled out. In recent years, developers have transformed the old ranch, but one can still see the huge red barn from the highway; the great winery is still visible from one of the developer's access roads. The Fountaingrove label is now owned by the MARTINI & PRATI winery.

R. Hine, *California's Utopian Colonies* (Berkeley, Calif.: University of California Press, 1983), 12–32.

FOXEN VINEYARD (BW 5383). The winery, which is southeast of Santa Maria in Santa Barbara County, was bonded in 1987 and has 11 acres of vines. The owners buy grapes and concentrate on Cabernet Sauvignon, Pinot noir, and Chardonnay, producing 6,000 cases a year.

FRANCISCAN VINEYARDS (BW 4594) in Rutherford in the Napa Valley has had a whirlwind series of owners from its founding in 1972 until 1979 when it was purchased by Eckes International, a German company that has been an important producer of spirits and fruit juices since 1922. These owners brought in Agustin Huneeus to run the operation and, by the mid-1980s Franciscan was a success story. (Huneeus now owns a half interest in the operation.) Vineyard holdings include their Oakville Estate (204 acres) and a large tract of 280 acres along the Silverado Trail. In 1986 their Estancia line was introduced for wines from Alexander Valley (240 acres) and, later, from Monterey County. The total acreage is now about 1,100. Production under the Estancia label, predominantly Cabernet Sauvignon, red Meritage, and Chardonnay, had passed 100,000 cases a year by the mid-1990s; total production is about 350,000 cases a year.

Augustin Huneeus, *A World View of the Wine Industry* (Regional Oral History Office, Bancroft Library, 1996).

FRANCO-SWISS WINERY. See SEAVEY VINEYARD

FRANKEN RIESLING. See RANCHO SISQUOC; SYLVANER

FRANZIA. Today no more than a brand of the WINE GROUP, the Franzia Brothers Winery (BW 3654) was founded at Ripon in 1915, six miles east of Manteca in San Joaquin County. In 1971, it was the fifth largest winery in the country, with 28 million gallons of capacity. The family sold it and their name in 1973 to the COCA-COLA BOTTLING COMPANY of New York, which established The Wine Group. (The Franzias later founded JFJ BRONCO.*) The huge Franzia plants at Ripon and Fresno today have a capacity of 56 million gallons and produce inexpensive table and sweet wine, sparkling wine, and wine coolers. The Wine Group sells about 8 million cases per year under the Franzia label.

JAMES FRASINETTI & SONS WINERY (BW 767). James F. Frasinetti (1874–1965) and his family founded a winery just south of Sacramento in 1897. For many years it operated as the Florin Winery. Before Prohibition, the family produced about 75,000 gallons of claret per year. Most of the wine from the 225,000-gallon facility has been sold in bulk, but there is a lively retail trade as well. This family operation is one of the oldest of its kind in California.

FREEMARK ABBEY WINERY (BW 4514) is on the site of the Lombarda Winery, built by the Forni family in 1895, just north of St. Helena. Before then, a smaller winery had been on the property, built by Josephine Tychson in 1886. In 1940, a partnership in southern California and headed by Albert Ahern bought the old place and put it back into production, with Leon BRENDEL as winemaker. Ahern's nickname was "Abbey," and that name was combined with parts of the other partners' names to produce the now-famous winery name. After Ahern died in 1959, the winery went out of operation, the bond was given up, and the old structure became a candleworks and a restaurant. In 1967, a partnership headed by Charles A.

The Forni family built their Lombarda Winery from native stone in 1895. Here in 1912 the wagons are lined up with their picking boxes. The owners of today's Freemark Abbey leased the basement of the old structure in 1967 to restart that winery. The building still stands next to Highway 29 above St. Helena, but now serves as a restaurant and candle shop. (Dealey Collection, Santa Monica, Calif.)

CARPY leased the basement of the building and filled it with modern winemaking equipment. By the mid-seventies the Freemark Abbey name had become synonymous with first-class wine in Napa. Much of this success came from the winemaking expertise of a partner and consultant R. Bradford WEBB, who had formerly worked at HANZELL. The winery's reputation rests on its Chardonnay, its vineyard-designated Cabernet Sauvignon, and its late-harvest White Riesling. Production runs about 35,000 cases per year. In 1976, the partners acquired the RUTHERFORD HILL WINERY, today a much larger operation than Freemark Abbey is.

Charles A. Carpy, *Viticulture and Enology at Freemark Abbey* (Regional Oral History Office, Bancroft Library, 1994).

FREMONT CREEK. See W. ANDREW BECKSTOFFER

FREI BROTHERS WINERY (BW 1114). Louis and Andrew Frei founded a winery in Dry Creek Valley in 1900. After Repeal, with a capacity of 150,000 gallons, it was a major producer in Sonoma. After long association with E. & J. GALLO, it was acquired by Gallo in 1977, and today its modern plant is the center of Gallo's table-wine operation in Sonoma.

FREIXENET. See GLORIA FERRER

FRENCH COLOMBARD. There were 539,556 tons of this variety crushed in California in 1994, over 95 percent from vineyards in the Central Valley. That quantity was more than the combined total tonnage of the next two most important white wine grapes, Chardonnay and Chenin blanc. Although production has dropped some, it is still the state's number one white wine variety in tonnage. In 1961 there were 1,465 acres of this variety in California, down from about 3,000 in the 1940s. But, because it yields a clean, well-flavored wine with good acidity, it accounted for over 70,000 acres in the state by the early 1980s.

A variety of wine grape first brought to California in the 1850s by Antoine DELMAS and Pierre PELLIER, it was grown for years in the Central Valley as "West's White Prolific," named for George WEST. It is only in the past 30 years that it has become an important part of California viticulture. Wines from this variety are usually blended to improve inexpensive white jug wines or to dilute good white varietals from the Central Valley. It is also used extensively for Charmat-process sparkling wine. It is rarely sold as a varietal, but if it is, the AVA must appear on the label in direct conjunction with the varietal designation. The name Colombard alone is also a legal synonym for the variety in this country.

In 1996 California produced 427,737 tons of French Colombard, 63 percent of the 1990 total produced in 1990.

TABLE 12. FRENCH COLOMBARD GRAPES, SELECTED COUNTIES

| | | | (ACRES) | | | |
YEAR	SONOMA	MONTEREY	MADERA	FRESNO	KERN	TOTAL
1961	294	0	0	0	0	1,465
1964	473	0	452	160	0	2,183
1969	949	153	556	1,186	386	8,574
1974	1,149	474	3,365	5,835	4,995	26,666
1979	1,147	505	5,351	7,049	4,669	35,800
1984	1,372	1,415	18,099	14,197	12,191	73,241
1989	902	510	17,010	13,132	9,624	62,326
1997	321	133	13,412	11,573	6,808	45,264

SOURCE: California Agricultural Statistics Service, Sacramento, Calif.

FRENCH PARADOX. See PHENOLICS

**FRENCH, THE, AND EARLY CALIFOR-
NIA WINE.** Some of the most important
names in the early wine industry in California
were French. In the Santa Clara Valley
Frenchmen, among them DELMAS,
LEFRANC, PELLIER, PORTAL, and MASSON,
dominated the industry before 1900. The
early significant importations of fine European grape varieties were all made by Frenchmen, such as VIGNES, Delmas, Pellier,
Lefranc, and Portal.

FRESNO. City and county in California's
Central Valley. The county is the dominant
center of viticulture in North America with
over 200,000 acres of vines. About 80 percent
of these are raisin varieties, but there are 38,000
acres of wine grapes, about 55 percent white
and 45 percent red varieties. French Colombard and Chenin blanc are the dominant white
grapes; there is no dominant red variety.

Wine production here today, as it has been
since the earliest years, is large in scale. But
whereas in the past the emphasis has been on
sweet wine and brandy production, today we
see far more inexpensive table wines, wine
coolers, and concentrates.

The Fresno area was opened to viticulture
and winemaking in 1873 when Francis EISEN
began planting his huge vineyard east of town.
Irrigation was essential to success then, as it is
now, for Fresno County has a desert climate.
Others followed Eisen, but by the late 1880s
raisin production dominated local viticulture.
There were about 5,000 acres of wine grapes
here in 1891. A few years later a boom in the
sweet wine industry brought several large-
scale wine producers into the county, including ITALIAN SWISS COLONY and the CALI-
FORNIA WINE ASSOCIATION. By 1908 there
were 30,000 acres of wine grapes, with twenty-
four wineries and twenty-seven distillers. During Prohibition, Fresno was a center for shipments of fresh grapes to home winemakers in
the eastern states. But wine grapes made up a
small percentage of that total.

At Repeal, there were thirty-one wineries
and 13,000 acres of wine grapes. Sweet wine
was the chief product and a huge tonnage of
raisin grapes went into the 10 million gallons
produced here in 1935. To a great extent the
Fresno wine industry had become a salvage by-

TABLE 13. WINE GRAPES IN FRESNO COUNTY, SELECTED VARIETIES

YEAR	PERCENT OF TOTAL RED	WHITE	BARBERA	CARIGNANE	CHENIN BLANC	(ACRES) FRENCH COLOMBARD	GRENACHE	RUBIRED	TOTAL
1920									16,120
1926									15,720
1932									13,528
1954									11,128
1968	84	16	83	1,745	10	464	2,524	918	11,513
1974	70	30	5,694	2,426	2,373	5,835	3,041	3,593	37,478
1980	63	37	5,988	2,420	3,245	8,731	2,846	2,715	38,740
1985	45	55	4,716	899	4,547	14,177	2,682	2,679	38,129
1990	44	66	4,148	462	4,675	12,698	3,163	2,077	34,265
1997	46	54	5,756	306	4,261	11,573	3,255	3,214	41,156

NOTE: Until 1961 statistics for acreage under various varieties of grapes were not published.
SOURCE: California Agricultural Statistics Service, Sacramento, Calif.

product of the overproducing raisin-grape industry. A far better balance has been reached in recent times, although the crush of Thompson Seedless grapes still far exceeds that of the number two variety, French Colombard.

In 1997 the value of agricultural products in Fresno County was higher than that of any other county in the United States. Chief among those products are the county's grapes.

FRESNO STATE UNIVERSITY, as a college, established a viticulture curriculum in 1948. Enology was added in 1956. Since then the department, primarily under the leadership of Professor Vincent Petrucci, has developed into one of the country's leading teaching and research centers in these fields. Today the Viticulture and Enology Research Center here includes a 143-acre vineyard, facilties for students to make wine, a varietal experiment field, laboratories, and a library.

FREY VINEYARDS (BW 4979). In 1961 Paul Frey and his family bought their ranch in Redwood Valley in Mendocino County and planted a 11-acre vineyard. Their organic approach to viticulture gave them a reputation for such high-quality grapes that, in 1980, they went into wine production. Their wines, made without addition of sulfur dioxide, have increased in popularity so that production has almost tripled since the 1980s to 32,000 cases per year. The Freys also buy a wide range of varietals from other Mendocino vineyards that maintain a high standard of organic farming.

FRICK WINERY (BW 4771). Bill and Judith Frick have had three wineries. The first, a corrugated-steel former gas station in Bonny Doon, was bonded in 1976. The equipment was moved to premises in downtown Santa Cruz in time for the 1979 vintage. In 1987 they moved to Dry Creek Valley in Sonoma. In 1989 they built a small winery and began

developing a new 8-acre vineyard. They are emphasizing Rhône varieties, Syrah and Viognier, and are buying Zinfandel, Petite Sirah, and Cinsaut. Production is about 2,000 cases per year.

FRISINGER CELLARS (BW 5364). Off Dry Creek Road, northwest of Napa, the Frisinger family began planting the 16 acres of Chardonnay in 1983. The tiny operation produces about 1,200 cases a year, so far from but the one varietal.

J. FRITZ WINERY (BW 5018). The Fritz family built, or rather dug, their winery to be ready for the 1981 vintage. Located on Dutcher Creek Road, south of Cloverdale in Sonoma County, the winery gets grapes from three vineyards in Dry Creek Valley owned by the family and from other properties that they lease. Production runs to about 25,000 cases per year, about half of which goes to private labels and custom production. Most of the wine they make is Chardonnay, but the family's reputation for top-quality wine has grown fastest from the production of old-vine Zinfandel. Fritz also produces a varietal MELON (see also PINOT BLANC) from grapes grown at the local junior college.

FROG'S LEAP WINERY (BW 5075). A successful winery in Napa Valley that went through some complicated changes in 1994. It was founded in 1981 by Larry TURLEY on property north of St. Helena once dubbed the "Frog Farm." When the winemaker John Williams bought into the operation, the name was changed from **Turley Wine Cellars** to Frog's Leap and an elegant art deco frog graced their prize-winning label, first on a 1981 Sauvignon blanc. Williams has a master's degree in enology from the University of California at Davis and his wines, particularly the Cabernet Sauvignon, Chardonnay, Sauvignon blanc, and Zinfandel, immediately won critical acclaim. By the early nineties production was approaching 40,000 cases a year. In 1994 the partners decided on an amicable separation. Turley kept the property and revived his own label, intending to make, comfortably, between 4,000 and 5,000 cases a year. Williams kept the brand and acquired C. P. ADAMSON'S old winery in Rutherford for a new facility, where annual production now approaches 50,000 cases.

FROST. Established grape vines enjoy freezing weather but not after they leaf out in the spring. Since the earliest days California vineyardists have learned to dread frost between March and May. The result of such freezes can be a vineyard full of blackened leaves and dead shoots. Frosts in early fall, before the vintage has concluded, can also damage the crop, but this is a rare problem.

In the earliest years, in Sonoma, Napa, and Santa Clara counties, brush was burned in and around the vineyards to help circulate the air and lessen Jack Frost's hurt. By the late 1870s, the smudge pot took over and is still used in many places. Some growers developed elaborate warning devices to signal that the temperature during the night was close to freezing. A bell would waken the foreman who would roust the workers into the field. After World War II huge wind machines were installed in some places to circulate air. Overhead sprinklers also became common in the 1960s. The freezing water releases heat, which protects the tender shoots from frost. The stream is left flying until the temperature is safe. The resulting picture of ice-covered vines is often startling and beautiful.

Severe spring frosts have become less and less common in the California grape country since the 1920s. But such short-term fluctuations do not in themselves imply that the climate is changing significantly.

FRUIT FLY (*Drosophila melanogaster*), an enduring pest since Spanish colonial times in and around places in California where wine is produced. It feeds and reproduces in fermenting fruit and deposits acid bacteria into fermentation tanks unless it is kept out of the winery. One of its nicknames is "vinegar fly." It is the chief reason that grapes today are almost always crushed outside the winery and the must transported inside to the fermenter under the strictest sanitary conditions.

FRUIT INDUSTRIES. See CALIFORNIA WINE ASSOCIATION

FUMÉ BLANC. See SAUVIGNON BLANC

GABRIELLI WINERY (BW 5608). A small winery in Redwood Valley, Mendocino County, bonded in 1991 and emphasizing Chardonnay and Zinfandel from the 13-acre estate vineyard. Annual production is about 8,000 cases. Gabrielli made history in 1997 by bringing out a Mendocino Zinfandel aged in barrels made from local white oak, *Quercus garryana,* which grows from British Columbia to northern California.

GAINEY VINEYARD (BW 5193). A very small part, about 85 acres, of the 1,800-acre Gainey Ranch in the Santa Maria Valley, Santa Barbara County, is devoted to viticulture. The winery, bonded in 1984, produces mainly Chardonnay, Cabernet Sauvignon, and Merlot. There is also a special interest here in White Riesling. In 1992, at the end of the national economic downturn, Gainey brought out an inexpensive generic, labeled Recession Red Wine, which sold briskly. Total production here is about 16,000 cases.

GALANTE FAMILY WINERY (BW 5775). Having bought an old cattle ranch in the Carmel Valley, Monterey County, in 1968, the Galante family began planting a 60-acre vineyard in the 1980s, the winery coming on line in 1994. Consisting mainly of Cabernet Sauvignon and Merlot, about 2,500 cases are produced a year.

GALLEANO WINERY (BW 3952). Founded at Repeal in the Cucamonga district of southern California, Galleano is one of the last wineries still operating there. Rustic reds and whites can still be purchased at the tasting room, but most of the production (300,000 gallons in 1993) is of bulk wine, which the owner, Donald Galleano, sells to other large-scale operations, among them R. H. PHILLIPS, BRONCO, and DELICATO. His second label is Green Valley. Galleano still controls a few acres of old vines, but most of his grapes come from other vineyards in the area that have not yet been paved over by developers.

GALLEGOS, JUAN (1833–1905), came to California in 1880 after making a fortune from coffee in Costa Rica. He bought a 1,000-acre tract of land near Mission San Jose, in what is now the Irvington District of Fremont in Alameda County. There he planted about 550 acres on these old mission lands and, in 1884, began building a stone winery that was, for a while, the largest in the world. In 1885 more capital was needed and the company was restructured with a large number of new investors, including Professor Eugene HILGARD from the University of California at Berkeley. The new corporation, the Palmdale Wine Co., operated the winery; Gallegos controlled the vineyards. By 1888, Palmdale was a major factor in the California wine industry,

For a short time the 1884 Gallegos structure was the largest such winery in the world. Note the "bad" barrel on the wagon. The earthquake in 1906 ended operations here.

with good markets in the east and in New Orleans. For some years Charles Carpy in Napa handled a large portion of the company's wines. When Gallegos died in 1905, the San Francisco firm of Lachman-Jacobi, to their misfortune, bought Palmdale; the next year the great winery was knocked down by the earthquake. Its remarkable ruins can still be seen, built into the cliffs near the railroad tracks in Irvington (see page 97). Palm trees that Gallegos planted over 100 years ago, and their now-husky seedlings, still cover the area.

Charles Sullivan, "The Greatest Winery in the World," *Vintage*, May 1981, 20-23.

Frona E. Wait, *Wines & Vines of California* (1889; reprint, Berkeley, Calif.: Howell-North, 1973), 167–69.

GALLO. Among the most important families in California wine history, the Gallos control

wineries in Modesto (BW 4213), Fresno (BW 17), Livingston (BW 4546), and Dry Creek (BW 1114). The **E. & J. Gallo Winery** was founded in 1933 when **Ernest Gallo** and his brother **Julio**, aged 24 and 23 respectively, set up a little wine production facility in a Modesto warehouse. At first they concentrated on producing bulk red table wine and, in 1937, made a serious and successful plunge into the fortified wine business. They expanded their family vineyard holdings and in 1940 began establishing their own brand. By then they had a real winery operation and were developing a production and marketing philosophy that would eventually make Gallo the largest wine producer in the world.

The brothers worked particularly hard to develop markets in California and the Midwest, as the well as NEW ORLEANS, a historic outlet for California wine. They stressed sound quality and were ever attuned to consumer tastes, a difficult matter in a country without deep wine drinking traditions.

During the 1950s, the Gallos fought a long sales battle with the PETRI company and by the early 1960s had won, setting the stage for a mammoth expansion. During these years the brothers had developed Thunderbird and Ripple, slightly carbonated, slightly sweet wines, well suited to the American love for beer and soda pop. As American consumers turned toward table wine in the 1960s, the Gallos brought out Hearty Burgundy, a pleasing, slightly sweet blend of red wines, the flavor enhanced by the inclusion of North Coast Petite Sirah. This was soon followed by a white counterpart, Chablis Blanc. In 1974, after denigrating cork-finished and varietal wines for years, the Gallos began producing some. In 1976 Gallo brandy, today the country's sales leader, appeared.

The physical basis for the Gallos' success is in Modesto, a huge industrial plant with its own bottle factory. Storage capacity grew mightily in two decades, from 100 million gallons in 1965 to 330 million gallons in 1986, since when it has held steady. By the mid-1990s Gallo vineyards covered 9,300 acres, but the company still purchases thousands of tons of grapes from independent growers. Relations with growers have been good at times and rocky at others, with several lawsuits and countersuits over the years.

Most recently, the major developments at Gallo have been taking place in Sonoma County, where the company had bought the old FREI WINERY* in 1977. By 1992 the modernized facility in the Dry Creek Valley was a 7-million-gallon premium operation, backed by more than 3,000 acres of vineyards, which have been developed by Gallo since the 1970s. High- and medium-priced varietals made there are sold under the Gallo-Sonoma label. Lower priced wines coming from various places are labeled Livingston Cellars, Fairbanks, Sheffield, and Turning Leaf.

Over the years Gallo's products and labels have expanded and changed continuously. Recently the Gallo name is to be seen less and less on the cheaper products and today Gallo sells a number of brands, among them Carlo Rossi (jug wine), Livingston Cellars (sherry), Ballatore, Totts, and André (sparkling wine), and Bartles & James (coolers). About 37 million cases are sold annually under the Gallo and Carlo Rossi labels.

Until Julio's death in a jeep accident in 1993, the family corporation was under the tight control of the brothers whose personal fortunes were something over $300 million in 1993. Some other members of the family, along with a few trusted, longtime employees, were involved in the decision making, but it was the brothers themselves who managed all aspects of their giant operation, which, with its annual sales of about 70 million cases, accounted for 26 percent of the U.S. wine market. Julio's son, Robert, is now in charge of vineyard production and there are sixteen third-generation Gallos working for the company.

Charles M. Crawford, *Recollections of a Career with the Gallo Winery and the Development of the California Wine Industry* (Regional Oral History Office, Bancroft Library, 1990).

Ernest and Julio Gallo, *Our Story* (New York: Random House, 1994).

GAMAY. Since the repeal of Prohibition, the word Gamay has been a confusing term in California viticulture. The popular French wine of Beaujolais is produced from a variety named Gamay noir (*à jus blanc*). Of this variety there is virtually none in California, except for a 2-acre plot in Napa Valley grown from cuttings brought in from France by Charles SHAW in the late seventies.

For years wine has been produced and sold in California as Gamay Beaujolais, often in a "nouveau" style, like much of the authentic Beaujolais. But the variety this wine was made from is actually a clone of the Pinot noir. The

BATF ruled in 1997 that producers might continue using Gamay Beaujolais as a varietal term on their labels until 2009.

There is also a grape grown here known popularly as the NAPA GAMAY. It has been planted all over northern California since Repeal. It is now understood to be the Valdiguié, an undistinguished but high-yielding variety from southern France. In California the variety has produced some good wines, but because it is almost never sold as varietal Napa Gamay anymore, the BATF has outlawed its use on labels after 1999. Nonetheless, wine made from Napa Gamay (Valdiguié) grapes may be labeled Gamay Beaujolais until 2009. The BATF has also ruled that the word Gamay alone may no longer be used as a varietal term, unless the wine is made from Gamay noir grapes, when it would be permissible.

In 1997, official California statistics showed 1,187 acres of so-called Gamay and 885 acres of Gamay Beaujolais. These numbers reflected a decline of 75 percent and 79 percent respectively since 1980.

GAN EDEN (BW 5274). The winery and the brand name used by the Yayin Corporation for its KOSHER wines. The winery, founded in 1985, is located in Sonoma's Green Valley Viticultural Area. The production of a wide range of varietals averages about 25,000 cases per year, much of it being Chardonnay and Cabernet Sauvignon.

GARRATTI WINERY. See VILLA ARMANDO

GARRETT, PAUL (1863–1940). Garrett was a teenager in North Carolina when he went to work at his uncle's winery. In 1900 he established his own facility for producing wine from the native Scuppernong grape. He eventually brought out his famed Virginia Dare line, blending native wines with those of New York and California. Southern prohibitionist sentiment forced him to move production to New York State. In 1911, Garrett acquired 2,000 acres of vineyard land in the Cucamonga area in southern California and he began production there. During Prohibition he made a Virginia Dare from which the alcohol had been removed, a wine tonic, and grape concentrate for home winemakers. After Repeal he expanded his national operations from coast to coast. When he died in 1940, Garrett & Co. was selling 600,000 cases of wine a year, mostly under the Virginia Dare label. The surviving company acquired the Italian Vineyard Co. in 1945, but by 1961 had gone out of business. The Virginia Dare brand is owned today by CANANDAIGUA.

GAUER RANCH. See KENDALL-JACKSON VINEYARDS

GAVILAN VINEYARDS. See CHALONE

GEMELLO WINERY (BW 4030). John Gemello bought land in Mountain View during Prohibition and at Repeal built a little winery there along El Camino Real. It was mostly a bulk operation, but he maintained a retail outlet and developed a solid custom. After World War II John's son, Mario, gradually took over the winery and in 1960 began producing a line of vintage-dated Zinfandels and Cabernet Sauvignons from several historic vineyards in the Santa Cruz Mountains and Santa Clara Valley. In the 1980s, John's granddaughter, Sandra OBESTER,* and her husband, Paul, opened their own winery and also became active in the Gemello operation. Today they still produce wines from time to time under the Gemello label, although Mario's last bottling was in 1982. The old Gemello Winery, once surrounded by orchards and vineyards, was torn down in 1989.

GENERIC. The BATF's regulations define fifteen generic terms that may be used on labels for California wine. They are: burgundy, claret, chablis, champagne, chianti, madeira, malaga, marsala, moselle (or mosel), port, rhine wine, hock, sauterne, sherry, and tokay. These terms refer to types of wine associated with European winegrowing and came into common usage in the United States in the nineteenth century. Since the 1860s, most California wines had traveled under generic terms and were usually blends. Before Prohibition many other generic terms were to be found in California, such as Medoc and Chambertin, but their use was not regulated. All this changed after 1934 when the current regulations were written.

Before the 1950s, it was rare to find California wine designated by variety. Since the 1960s, there has been a steady decline in the use of generic terms on California wines. Wine industry estimates show that in the early 1980s generic wines made up about 75 percent of the table-wine production in California; by the late 1980s, between 35 and 40 percent. Today the only generic term often seen on high-priced premium wines is Champagne, and even this one is now seen less and less.

GEORIS WINERY (BW 5439). Walter Georis began planting his 28-acre vineyard in Carmel Valley, Monterey County, to red Bordeaux varieties in 1981. His first commercial wine, a Merlot, was produced in 1986. Since 1988, he has had his own little winery producing 1,000 cases a year, still mostly Merlot.

GERKE, HENRY. See TEHAMA COUNTY; VINA

GERMAIN-ROBIN (DSP 162). The brand name for the products of Alambic, Inc., a small distillery in the hills of Mendocino County. The brandy, first marketed in 1985, has been praised by critics as being similar to and the equal of good Cognacs.

GERMANS AND EARLY CALIFORNIA WINE. No national or ethnic group contributed more to the development of a prosperous and reputable wine industry in California than did the Germans. Of course, there was no Germany as such until the 1870s, so these newcomers really arrived from such states

Mario Gemello bought the first harvest of Cabernet Sauvignon grapes at RIDGE VINEYARDS in 1959. The grower, Dave Bennion, held a few boxes back, and made wine in his garage. On the strength of that wine he and his partners decided to make wine commercially. (Photo Mario Gemello)

as Bavaria, Prussia, and Württemberg. To these must be added the German-speaking folk from Austria, Switzerland, and French Alsace. The stereotype of German order, honesty, energy, and dependability was a fact in the vineyards and wine cellars of the Golden State. They were the acknowledged leaders in Sonoma (GUNDLACH, DRESEL, and BUNDSCHU) and Napa (KRUG, BERINGER, and SCHRAM). They were also influential in other areas such as Livermore (WENTE and GIER), the East Bay (GRAU and WERNER), Santa Clara (WEHNER), the Central Coast (PALMTAG), and southern California (ROSE). Their contributions to the scientific side of wine culture are renowned (HILGARD, HUSMANN, and PFEFFER). Several of the most useful vines imported into California in the early days were brought by Germans. And, of course, the father of the California wine industry was Charles KOHLER, who started his wine company in 1854.

GERWER WINERY. See CHARLES B. MITCHELL VINEYARD

GEWÜRZTRAMINER. The Traminer variety of wine grape was probably developed in the Italian Tyrol in the Middle Ages. There are many subvarieties and clones. In the nineteenth century, a spicy clone (*Gewürz* means spice in German) was identified, whose grapes became pink when fully ripe. In Europe, particularly in Germany and Alsace, this spiciness became the variety's hallmark, although the dry and sweet white table wines made from the grape are more perfumed than spicy.

This clone was brought to California in 1862 by Agoston HARASZTHY but did not become used commercially until much later. It is clear that both the spicy and less spicy clones were being used in vineyards in California by the late 1870s, at which time both were usually referred to as the Red Traminer. Charles KRUG and Jacob GUNDLACH in Sonoma were particularly well known for their Traminers.

In 1907 Professor BIOLETTI from the University of California recommended the variety, as did the writer of another report published after Repeal, so long as only the "aromatic clone" were planted, and then, to retain the variety's fine acid and special flavors, only in cool coastal valleys.

There was not enough Traminer planted in California to appear on the state's official statistics until the 1960s, although Robert and Peter MONDAVI won numerous awards for their Charles Krug Traminers in the 1950s. In the 1970s the spicy varietal, always labeled Gewürztraminer, became popular. In 1981 acreage peaked at 4,709. Since then its popularity has declined; by 1997 there were only about 1,500 acres, 90 percent of which were in Monterey, Sonoma, Mendocino, and Santa Barbara counties. Most Gewürztraminer made in California is slightly sweet, although a few producers, among them CLAIBORNE AND CHURCHILL, THOMAS FOGARTY WINERY, and NAVARRO VINEYARDS, have made a dry wine in the style of Alsace.

In 1996 California produced 7,912 tons of Gewürztraminer, 77 percent of the total produced in 1989.

GEYSER PEAK WINERY (BW 29). Few wineries in California have as long or as complicated a history as has Geyser Peak. Today the 2.5-million-gallon facility stands on land near Sonoma's Geyserville, where Augustus Quitzow, an immigrant from Germany, put up a small wooden winery in 1880. But by 1884 it was owned by a local bank. In 1887 large-scale operations began when Edward Walden, a liquor importer from New York, bought the property and built a bulk winery and large distillery to produce beverage brandy. By the 1890s Walden & Co. was one of the largest brandy producers in the world. But in 1904 the family lost control of the Sonoma operation and for a few years it was run as a growers' cooperative by W. S. Kelley and Oscar Le

Baron, two vineyardists in the Dry Creek Valley. Then in 1911 A. G. Dondero and his associates formed the Ciocca-Lombardi Wine Co., tore down the old winery, and built a new one, calling it Geyser Peak. It operated there into the 1970s.

When Prohibition came lots of vinegar was produced there. Dondero started up bulk commercial winemaking in 1933, but after his death in 1936, the Bagnani family bought the place and concentrated on vinegar production, marketing their Four Monks brand nationally. In 1971, the wine boom induced the Schlitz Brewing Co. to buy the property, where it built a modern winery in 1976. The flow of Geyser Peak wine under Schlitz was prodigious—the Summit brand reached sales of a million cases in 1980—but the quality was mostly that of jug wine. The successful marketing of wine and beer are, however, two different skills and, in 1982, the brewers sold the winery to the Trione family of Sonoma. The Summit label was sold and gradually the quality was raised, with emphasis on fairly priced, sound varietals. During a short association with Penfold's of Australia, Daryl Groom joined Geyser Peak as the winemaker. His skills, along with the Triones' capital, had placed the Geyser Peak label solidly in the premium category by the mid-1990s. Annual production is now about 350,000 cases.

While Schlitz owned the winery, the company brought the nearby NERVO WINERY. Today the building, although called the Canyon Road Winery, the brand name of a second label for the Triones, is a well-placed tasting room for the parent operation up the road.

GEYSERVILLE. A small wine town in the Alexander Valley and the Sonoma County mailing address of numerous wineries. On a bottle of wine today, the name is, however, a trade mark owned by RIDGE VINEYARDS for its powerful Zinfandel blends made from grapes grown here. Ridge began producing Geyserville

Zinfandel in 1966 from the old vines, some of which are Petite Sirah and Carignane, on the TRENTADUE property near the town.

GIBSON WINE CO. (BW 3864, 4297). Originally based in Kentucky, an 11-million-gallon operation that has two plants in the Central Valley, one in Elk Grove and one near Sanger. The company has a wide range of products, and a special emphasis on berry and fruit wines.

GIER, THEODORE (1861–1931). Gier was born in Germany and came to California as a youth. He began operations in 1883 with a retail wine and liquor store in Oakland. In 1895 he bought Frank Fowler's DOS MESAS WINERY in Livermore. By 1900 he was one of the most powerful independent wine producers in the state. By 1901 his vineyards in the Livermore Valley had been expanded to 225 acres. In 1903 he bought land in Napa Valley and built a winery on Mount Veeder. Later he acquired the Bergfeld Winery in St. Helena and made wine at several other established facilities. By 1907 he controlled about 1,000 acres in Napa and Livermore. Meanwhile his retail business in the East Bay had expanded to become a large retail wine and wholesale wine and spirits establishment, with a huge cellar in Oakland. His Giersberger table wines had an excellent reputation for their quality.

Gier was a colorful, flamboyant character whose antics delighted or scandalized his communities. He loved military display and somehow had himself named an honorary colonel in the California National Guard. He also had a powerful attachment to his fatherland's goals in World War I. On one occasion he and his cronies were tossed into jail for singing patriotic German songs in public. When Prohibition came his scrapes with the law became quite serious and for a while his properties were seized by the government.

He sold his property on Mount Veeder to the CHRISTIAN BROTHERS in 1929. It became their Mont La Salle estate, the site of their first winery in Napa, a great vineyard, and a noviatiate. Today the old Gier winery is the site of THE HESS COLLECTION WINERY.

Gier's permanent contribution to the history of wine in California was his early planting of Chardonnay in the Livermore Valley. This plantation marks the site of the original Wente CHARDONNAY* CLONE. It is likely, but sure proof is lacking, that Gier acquired his budwood from the Tiburcio PARROTT'S vineyard on Spring Mountain and Parrott acquired his cuttings from H. W. CRABB'S collection at To Kalon.

GILROY. At the end of the 19th century many small-scale winegrowers picked up their mail in Gilroy, a little town in the Santa Clara Valley. There were also small wineries in the hills to the west in the Hecker Pass, Solis, and Uvas areas. These too were usually referred to as Gilroy wineries.

Planting in the south valley began on a large scale in 1897, and north of town in 1905 the CALIFORNIA WINE ASSOCIATION built its million-gallon Las Animas Winery, which dominated wine production in the area until Prohibition.

In the 1930s there were twenty-two small country wineries with a Gilroy address, every one run by Italian-Americans. These were mostly, but not all, gone by the 1970s. Today winegrowing near Gilroy is concentrated in the HECKER PASS area and in the San Ysidro Viticultural Area southeast of town.

GIRARD WINERY (BW 4999). The Girard family bought vineyard land in Oakville along the Silverado Trail in Napa Valley in 1972; in 1980 they built the winery. Two years later they bought a large tract of land on Mount Veeder and planted vines there. All told, the Girard family's vineyard land amounted to about 85 acres, most of them planted to Cabernet Sauvignon, Chardonnay, and Chenin blanc. By the

mid-1990s production was running at about 20,000 cases per year.

In 1987 the Girards made a Pinot noir from grapes grown in Oregon and in 1988 bought land near Eugene, Oregon, to plant a vineyard. In 1996 they sold their winery in Napa to Leslie Rudd, a businessman from Colorado.

GIRDIANA. The native grape, *Vitis girdiana,* of southern California, which, like its northern California cousin, *V. californica,* is virtually worthless viticulturally. It was named by T. V. MUNSON for H. M. Gird, a nineteenth-century grape grower in San Diego County.

GIUMARRA VINEYARDS (BW 4418). The Giumarra family controls a large portion of the southern Central Valley's table-grape production. In 1946 the family bonded the winery near Bakersfield to produce bulk wines from some of those grapes. In the 1970s the Giumarras began planting wine grapes on a large scale and more than doubled the winery capacity to 11 million gallons. By the 1980s they were specializing in house wines for restaurants, most of the wine being sold in large bulk containers. Capacity reached 16 million gallons in the 1990s.

GLEN ELLEN. A small town in the upper Sonoma Valley, the center of an important winegrowing area since the 1860s. In the nineteenth century, it was well known for its white table wines. The chief producers then were William McPherson HILL, Joshua CHAUVET, Kate WARFIELD, and KOHLER and Frohling, from their Tokay Vineyard. Its most famous resident was Jack London.

Many modern wineries have taken root there since the 1960s, but the Glen Ellen area is not precisely defined and probably will not become an official viticultural area, particularly as the Glen Ellen brand has become a well-established fixture in the world of the FIGHTING VARIETALS. The brand was established here by the BENZIGER family but was sold to

HEUBLEIN in 1993. Included in the sale was the Benzigers' winery (BW 5396) in the town of Sonoma, which is now a production and bottling facility for some of Heublein's wines bearing the Glen Ellen label, almost 3.5 million cases of which were being sold annually in the 1990s. Heublein has set up a tasting room in the town of Glen Ellen in the structure that once housed Joshua Chauvet's old winery. In it, the company has assembled a small museum collection focused on the history of the area.

GLENN COUNTY, in the upper Sacramento Valley. The county's viticulture was primarily devoted to raisin grapes before Prohibition. Most of the 1,400 acres of wine grapes there today were planted in 1973 in the Orland area, and are predominantly Zinfandel and Grenache, used principally for BLUSH and rosé wines.

GOLDEN CHASSELAS. A name used in California for the PALOMINO* variety of grape. Before Prohibition it was often called Napa Golden Chasselas, no matter where the vine was planted. It is unrelated to the Chasselas doré, for which see GUTEDEL.

GOLDEN CREEK VINEYARD (BW 5153). A small winery in the Rincon Valley, northeast of Santa Rosa, that was bonded in 1983. The Danielik family, from Czechoslovakia, began planting the 12-acre vineyard in 1977. Most of the wine made here is a blend of Cabernet and Merlot. The winery produces about 1,500 cases per year, and grapes from the vineyard are sold to other wineries in the area.

GOLDEN STATE. California's nickname, and the brand name for one of the state's best pre-Prohibition, bottle-fermented sparkling wines, produced by ITALIAN SWISS COLONY.

GOLDEN STATE VINTNERS (BW 4808). A huge winery plant in Tulare County with a 50

million-gallon capacity. The operation began with the SETRAKIAN family's old CALIFORNIA GROWERS WINERY, which was established in 1936. From its 7,850 acres, the company produces large quantities of table and sparkling wine, brandy, concentrates, and vermouth under numerous labels, Golden State, Summerfield, Le Blanc, and Bounty the most common. In recent years the Golden State label has been used on a line of low-priced varietals. Much of the plant's production is sold in bulk to other producers. In 1994 the company bought the production facilities of the NAPA VALLEY COOPERATIVE WINERY and its Bergfeld label and, in 1995, from HEUBLEIN, the fomer Christian Brothers distillery in Reedley.

Today Golden State is the leading California exporter of California wine to foreign countries. CUSTOM CRUSHING has also become an important part of their business.

GOLD HILL VINEYARD (BW 5295). Located a short distance from John Sutter's mill, the spot where gold was discovered in the Sierra foothills of El Dorado County in 1848; the winery was bonded in 1985 and annually produces about 8,000 cases of Chardonnay and Merlot from its 35-acre vineyard.

GOLDMAN, MAX. See YORK MOUNTAIN WINERY

GOMBERG, LOUIS ROOS (1907–93). The principal of a consulting firm, in recent years known as Gomberg, Fredrikson & Associates, he has played a part in the development of California's wine industry since the 1950s. For years his column in the trade publication, *Wines & Vines,* produced a sparkling flow of vinous logic. Gomberg was ever the voice for higher quality and stricter standards in the industry. His annual statistical predictions for the industry were always awaited with interest and anxiety. A prediction made in 1973 of a billion-gallon wine market in the United States by the 1990s was on target until 1986 when consumption began slipping.

Louis R. Gomberg, *Analytic Perspectives on the California Wine Industry, 1935–1990* (Regional Oral History Office, Bancroft Library, 1990).

J. Jacobs, "Renaissance Man," *Wines & Vines,* March 1984, 22–30.

GOOSECROSS CELLARS (BW 5428). A winery in Yountville, in the Napa Valley, bonded in 1985 and specializing in Chardonnay. The 11-acre vineyard and purchased grapes yield about 6,500 cases of wine per year.

GOULD, FRANCIS LEWIS (1884–1979). A wine merchant from Boston who became a beloved member of the Napa Valley wine community. For many years he was the editor of *Bottles and Bins,* a pioneering newsletter he created in 1949 for the CHARLES KRUG WINERY. He was one of the founders of the NAPA VALLEY WINE LIBRARY. In 1972 he wrote *My Life With Wine,* today a good source of information on wine in California in the 1940s and 1950s.

GRACE FAMILY VINEYARD (BW 5404). When the Graces acquired their old Victorian home north of St. Helena in 1974, they decided to put in a few grape vines. They produced some grapes in 1978 and had CAYMUS make them into wine. The arrangement continued through 1983 as the acre of vines matured, the wine released under the Caymus label as a vineyard-designated Cabernet Sauvignon. Production peaked in 1982 at 233 cases. The Graces planted another acre in 1985 and then built a little winery in 1987. Meanwhile the reputation and price of these vinous rarities has skyrocketed ($100 a bottle for the 1993 vintage). The wine is sold through a mailing list as limited as the Cabernets themselves.

RICHARD L. GRAESER WINERY (BW 5279). The Graeser family acquired the historic

La Perlita del Monte Ranch in the hills northwest of Calistoga in Napa Valley in 1958. In 1984 they began planting red Bordeaux varieties and bonded the winery the next year. Three clarets are blended from the vineyard's 16 acres of Cabernet Sauvignon, Merlot, and Cabernet franc. The Graesers also produce Chardonnay and Sémillon from purchased grapes. Production runs about 2,000 cases per year.

GRAFTING. A process by which one variety of grape stock is inserted into another to change the fruiting variety. In California, where PHYLLOXERA and nematodes flourish, varieties of VITIS VINIFERA* are almost always grafted onto resistant ROOTSTOCK.

Grafting has been practiced in California since the late 1850s. Vineyardists learned then that they could propagate precious European varieties by grafting them onto the native *V. californica.* Later it became common to change the fruiting variety from one to another according to dictates of the market. Thus, in the 1870s old Mission variety vines were converted to better vinifera varieties through grafting. The process continues today as certain varieties become less valuable in the marketplace and vineyardists choose to grow varieties that are in greater demand.

GRAHM, RANDALL. See BONNY DOON VINEYARD

GRAND CRU VINEYARDS (BW 4572). A winery that was founded in the Glen Ellen area in 1970, and had a complicated history until it was declared bankrupt in 1991. The prestigious brand name was acquired by BRONCO the next year. In its early years, Grand Cru produced a wide range of varietals with an excellent reputation. The winemaker, Robert Magnani, was particularly successful with his slightly sweet, late-harvest white wines for which the botrytis infection was induced in the manner developed by Myron NIGHTINGALE at Cresta Blanca in the 1950s. In fact, Magnani acquired Nightingale's equipment for the procedure.

A change of ownership in 1981 increased annual production to 50,000 cases. The winery's decline in the eighties resulted from financial factors not directly related to the quality of its wines. Today the plant is part of ASSOCIATED VINTAGE GROUP.

GRAND NOIR (NOIR DE LA CALMETTE). A wine grape cultivar that is a cross between Petit Bouschet and Aramon. Like the ALICANTE BOUSCHET, it was the work of the French vine breeder, Henri Bouschet, in the 1880s. It does not provide the intense color of its more popular relative but is very productive. It has no value except for blending. Almost 1,000 acres survived Prohibition, but this total was down to 444 by 1961, of which 60 percent was, surprisingly, in the Napa Valley. Acreage declined steadily thereafter and the variety disappeared from official statistics in 1983. In early years growers in California often called the variety Grenoir.

GRANITE SPRINGS WINERY (BW 5073). In 1979 the Russell family began planting a vineyard near Somerset in El Dorado County. The winery was bonded in 1981. With 24 acres of vineyard, production of a wide range of varietals and port is currently about 10,000 cases per year.

GRAU & WERNER (BW 5). In 1888 two German-American friends, Eduard A. Grau and Emil P. Werner, established a small winery in the East Bay near Mission San Jose. Appropriately they named it Los Amigos. They developed a fine reputation for Cabernet Sauvignon and their vines survived Prohibition. After Repeal the winery was acquired by Robert Mayock, whose Los Amigos Cabernets of the 1930s were among the best in the state. Mayock also produced what he called a "Sherry Sack." He also sold wines under the LINDA VISTA*

and Napa Grande labels. In the early 1940s, Mayock wrote California's first wine column, for the *San Jose News*. When he was killed in an automobile accident in 1945, Lee Stewart acquired the Los Amigos label and brand for his SOUVERAIN CELLARS. Production continued at the site until 1952. A piece of the old winery survives as part of the wall for a carport at a suburban residence.

GREEN & RED VINEYARD (BW 4818). The Heminway family planted a vineyard to Zinfandel in Chiles Valley, Napa, in 1972. Since then Chardonnay has been added to the 15-acre vineyard, which produces about 3,000 cases of wine per year. The "green and red" in the name refers to the red soil and the green serpentine rock in the vineyard.

GREEN HUNGARIAN. One of California's mystery grapes. At its best it produces a pleasantly neutral white wine. Although clearly of European origin, its counterpart in the Old World has not been firmly identified and its introduction to California is undocumented. (It is possibly the Alsatian Putzscheere variety, which was in H. W. CRABB's nursery in 1882.)

In the 1870s a grape called Green Hungarian appeared in the Sierra foothills. Robert CHALMERS made his ANGELICA from it. But later it was found that some Green Hungarian in this area was actually Sylvaner. Nevertheless, by the 1890s something being called Green Hungarian was planted here and there all over northern California. Since Repeal, its good reputation has resulted from the varietal wine that Lee Stewart produced at SOUVERAIN and, more recently, WEIBEL's offerings. There is good evidence that modern Green Hungarian wine succeeds mostly on the attraction of its name and small quantities of muscat blended in to give it a bit more flavor.

California acreage held steady at about 350 acres through the 1980s. Today there are fewer than 100 acres.

GREENSTONE WINERY (BW 5035) in the Sierra foothills in Amador County was bonded in 1981. The 32-acre vineyard yields principally Zinfandel, white, rosé, and red. In 1996 the operation was acquired by Republic Geothermal, Inc. Annual production at Greenstone, which also uses Clos du Lac as a brand, is about 7,500 cases.

GREEN VALLEY. There are two Green Valleys in northern Californian viticulture.

Solano County

The older of the two, viticulturally, to the east of Napa Valley, it shares the valley's climate and soils. Winegrowing here dates from 1858 when the Meister brothers started planting their vineyards. Several small wineries were built in the next two decades. By the end of the century the Solano Winery in Cordelia dominated wine production in the general area. There are about 1,100 acres of vineyard today and the grapes usually go into wines labeled North Coast.

Sonoma County

In the southwest of the Russian River Valley Viticultural Area, a cool-climate region that was planted to the wrong varieties of grapes in the nineteenth century and became apple country after 1895. In recent years it has been found to be a fine environment for Chardonnay and Pinot noir. There are about 1,200 acres of vines there today and some very fine sparkling wines are produced from those grapes.

GREENWOOD RIDGE VINEYARDS (BW 4960). The vineyard itself, above the Anderson Valley, in Mendocino County at about 1,200 feet elevation, was planted by Tony HUSCH in 1972. Allan Green acquired it in 1973 and bonded his winery in 1980. He produces a wide range of varietals—about 7,000 cases per year. The winery has been the site of the California Wine Tasting Championships since 1983.

The Greenwood Ridge area was settled by Italian immigrants around the turn of the century. They planted several vineyards, parts of which have survived and have become an important source of old-vine Zinfandel for several wineries.

GRENACHE. A red variety of wine grape probably of Spanish origin, from Aragón. Today, as the Garnacha, it is one of Spain's most widely planted vines. In southern France it is used for rosé and as a basic blending wine, particularly in the southern Rhône area. When cropped sparingly on infertile soils, it can yield powerful red wines of very good quality. When cropped heavily, the grape tends to be low in tannin and color, which, with its good fruit flavors, makes it useful for rosés and blush wines.

The vine was probably first introduced to California by Charles LEFRANC in 1857. By the 1870s it was widely used in the state. Its versatility made it popular in the planting boom of the 1880s. By the end of the decade, many producers were using it in their red blends. In 1887 the OLIVINA WINERY in Livermore produced a white Grenache.

There were about 1,000 acres of Grenache in the state in 1920 but the acreage did not increase during the 1920s because home winemakers in the east did not favor pale-colored varieties. But they did like the variety in California, particularly in the Santa Clara Valley. Acreage grew steadily in the 1930s and 1940s, mostly in the Central Valley for jug wines and port blends. By the late 1940s, there were about 8,000 acres in California. This number grew to 10,000 in 1960 and peaked at 20,244 in 1974. The total has declined in the 1990s to about 11,000 acres, of which about 220 are in the coastal counties where Grenache often brings the growers prices equal to or higher than those for Zinfandel. A few of the RHONE RANGERS use Grenache as a varietal and for Rhônelike blends. But there is little indication that California's producers are exploiting the variety's capabilities fully.

In 1996 with 102,593 tons produced, Grenache was California's number four red wine variety in tonnage; this was 91 percent of the total tonnage in 1990.

GRENOIR. See GRAND NOIR

GREY RIESLING. Probably the French Trousseau gris grape, and probably brought to California in the 1870s. How it picked up the "Riesling" is not known, but by the 1880s the term was fixed. In the 1890s, dry table wines from the variety produced in the Santa Cruz Mountains were said by their promoters to resemble the so-called flinty wines of Chablis. After Prohibition many Californians mistakenly thought that the variety, which makes an undistinguished but pleasant table wine, was something called Chauché gris.

A few vines in the state survived Prohibition and, by the 1960s, there were about 500 acres, mostly in Alameda and Napa counties. By the late 1970s there were about 2,200 acres throughout the state, the fruit used for blending, as a varietal, and in sparkling wines. Acreage peaked in 1982 at 2,765, with Monterey County then in first place over the other two. Acreage then began declining as Grey Riesling lost its popularity as a varietal. In 1997 there were but 127 acres scattered through the coastal valleys. Tonnage in 1996 was 518,27 percent of the 1990 total.

After January 1, 1999 the words Grey Riesling may no longer be used on American wine labels as a varietal. Thereafter such wines must be labeled Trousseau gris.

GREYSTONE, the finest example of nineteenth century winery architecture in California, was built just north of St. Helena in the Napa Valley in 1889 by a group headed by William Bowers BOURN. The idea was to provide growers in the valley a home for their grapes as prices collapsed in the late eighties. It was not a financial success and was acquired by Charles CARPY in 1894. During those years, it was the largest stone winery in the world. When Carpy joined the CALIFORNIA

In 1890 workers put the final touches on the entrance to Greystone Winery in Napa Valley.

WINE ASSOCIATION so did Greystone, and there it remained until Prohibition. It went through several hands until it was bought by the CHRISTIAN BROTHERS in 1950. It became part of their production and storage facilities, but, more importantly, acted as a hugely popular tourist attraction. After HEUBLEIN bought Christian Brothers in 1989, the old winery was put up for sale. In 1992 it was purchased by the Culinary Institute of America in New York. The grapes from the 15-acre Merlot vineyard there go into a wine labeled Greystone Cellars and made at MARKHAM for the Culinary Institute.

GRGICH HILLS CELLAR (BW 4813). Miljenko (Mike) Grgich came to California in 1958 from his native Croatia and went to work for Lee Stewart at the original SOUVERAIN CELLARS. He made wine at BEAULIEU VINEYARD from 1959 to 1968 and moved to Robert MONDAVI Winery, where he stayed until 1972. Then, at CHATEAU MONTELENA he made the 1973 Chardonnay that won the tasting in PARIS* in 1976 against the best French white Burgundies.

In 1976 he struck up a partnership with Austin Hills, whose grandfather and great-uncle were the Hills brothers of coffee fame. Hills had started to acquire vineyard land in Napa in 1970, first in Calistoga, then in Rutherford. They broke ground for their winery on 4 July 1977. Since then, Grgich Hills has become a remarkably successful producer of Chardonnay, Cabernet Sauvignon, and Zinfandel, selling 60,000 cases a year in the 1990s.

After the breakup of Yugoslavia, Grgich returned to Croatia and built a 2,000-case winery there. In 1996 he produced wine from the Dalmatian Plavac Mali variety, which he and some others believe to be the same as the California Zinfandel.

> Miljenko Grgich, *A Croatian-American Wine-maker in the Napa Valley* (Regional Oral History Office, Bancroft Library, 1992).

GRIGNOLINO. A native of northwestern Italy, this variety of grape produces a delicate, light-red table wine with an orange tinge. It can have an exceptional flavor, resembling wild strawberries. It was in the collection that Agoston HARASZTHY brought in to California in 1862, but was not distributed outside Buena Vista. John Hamilton DRUMMOND imported it to Glen Ellen in the 1880s and John DOYLE took it to his Cupertino estate. The ITALIAN SWISS COLONY planted the vine in the 1890s. Later it was a favorite of Secundo GUASTI in southern California; he won a gold medal at the 1915 Panama-Pacific Exposition for his Grignolino wine.

In 1949 Leon BRENDEL brought the vine to the Napa Valley, using it for his Only One brand. HEITZ WINE CELLARS has continued to produce the varietal since taking over the Brendel operation. In the 1960s Heitz produced a very well received "sparkling" wine from the grape using the Millerway process (see Justin F. MILLER). In recent years, Heitz has produced a Grignolino Port from the family's home vineyard.

Most Grignolino vines in the 1960s were growing in the Santa Clara Valley, with a few in Napa. By 1974 there were but 241 acres in the state, by 1981 only 58 acres, all in Santa Clara and Napa counties. Since then, the variety has disappeared from state statistics, but there are still a few acres in Napa where 38 tons were crushed in 1996.

GRIMM, JACOB. See STORYBOOK MOUNTAIN VINEYARDS

GROEZINGER, GOTTLIEB (1823–1903). A native of the German kingdom of Württemberg, Groezinger arrived in New York in 1848 and headed for California, where he made enough money in the mines to open a liquor business in San Francisco. He also made large quantities of wine (100,000 gallons in 1869) from grapes brought down from Napa and Sonoma counties.

In 1870 be brought industrial wine production to the Napa Valley when he built a huge winery and distillery complex at Yountville. By the 1880s he was making 300,000 gallons of wine per year. Eventually Groezinger lost control of the business and it became part of Claus SCHILLING's holdings. No serious attempt was made after Prohibition to revive the winery. In the 1970s the old buildings were converted into the Vintage 1870 complex of shops and restaurants that greets tourists to Napa on Highway 29 at Yountville.

GROTH VINEYARDS & WINERY (BW 5178). In 1981 the Groth family acquired 164 acres of vineyard land in Oakville and Rutherford in the Napa Valley, planted to Cabernet Sauvignon, Chardonnay, Sauvignon blanc, and Merlot. The first Groth wines were produced in various rented facilities. The remarkable winery in Oakville was finished in 1989 after several financial close calls. Groth's wines, with heavy emphasis on Cabernet, have received excellent reviews. By the mid 1990s production of these estate wines, mostly Cabernet Sauvignon, had amounted to more than 40,000 cases annually.

GUASTI. The entrepreneur Secundo Guasti (1859–1927) was largely responsible for the development of the Cucamonga area of San Bernardino County in southern California as an important winegrowing district. Born in Italy's Piedmont, Guasti arrived in Los Angeles in 1883 almost penniless. By 1894 he and John Bernard were operating a large and successful winery at Third and Alameda Streets. By 1897 Guasti had bought out his partner and was producing 400,000 gallons of wine per year.

In 1900 he established the Italian Vineyard Co. (IVC) in what was then almost desert land in Cucamonga. He built a model community

Gottlieb Groezinger's great winery in Yountville stood unused after Repeal until the 1970s, when it became the centerpiece for Vintage 1870, a complex of shops and restaurants. Here the popular tourist attraction gets an additional parking lot in 1997.

ITALIAN VINEYARD COMPANY

MAIN OFFICES, SALESROOMS AND WINERIES
1234 to 1248 PALMETTO ST.
NEAR MATEO
LOS ANGELES, CAL.

PRODUCERS OF

California Pure Wines and Brandies

CUCAMONGA WINERY AND DISTILLERIES OF THE ITALIAN VINEYARD CO.—A Stone and Iron Structure 100 x 230 Feet in Size.

Owners of the LARGEST VINEYARD in the U. S.--3500 Acres

At South Cucamonga, San Bernardino County, Cal.

PLANTED IN THE FINEST VARIETIES OF WINE GRAPES

NEW YORK BRANCH
Offices and Wine Vaults
202-204 Center Street

NEW ORLEANS BRANCH
237 Decatur Street
and 213-215 Hester Street

This huge advertisement for the Italian Vineyard Company, published in 1914, supports Secundo Guasti's claim that his vineyard was the largest in the United States. (*Pacific Wine & Spirit Review*)

and called it Guasti. Many of the old buildings and the little church can still be seen from Interstate 10 just east of the Ontario International Airport. FILIPPI VINTAGE CO. maintains a tasting room in the old winery.

In 1902 IVC controlled 1,235 acres of vineyard land and, by World War I, the company's 4,000-acre vineyard was the largest in the world. The business prospered during Prohibition, selling grapes and sacramental wine. During these years Guasti left the management of the company in the capable hands of James Barlotti. Between 1927, when Guasti died, and 1977, the property passed through many hands, ending under the control of BROOKSIDE VINEYARD CO.* It is still worth a detour from the freeway to see the remains of the historic community.

Leon D. Adams, *The Wines of America* (Boston: Houghton Mifflin, 1973), 279–85.

GUENOC WINERY (BW 5059). In 1963 the

Magoon family of Hawaii traded some prime real estate on the island for 23,000 acres of land in Lake County. The first years were devoted to general agriculture, but in the late 1960s trial plots of vines were planted and their success led to a 275-acre vineyard in the Guenoc Valley, about 20 miles northeast of Calistoga. In 1981 the Magoons finished building their 550,000-gallon winery and also received approval of AVA status for their Guenoc Valley. Production, mainly of Chardonnay and Cabernet Sauvignon in the 1990s, amounts to about 100,000 cases per year. Most Guenoc wines are estate bottled. Since 1987 grapes from Andrew BECKSTOFFER's vineyard in St. Helena have gone into a special reserve Cabernet Sauvignon, a wine that has received enthusiastic critical praise.

On the Guenoc label is a portrait of the famous British actress, Lillie Langtry, who actually owned 4,000 acres in the Guenoc Valley from 1888 to 1906. She is featured in much of the Guenoc publicity today. She did have vineyards here and produced wine. A second Guenoc label is Le Breton, which was Mrs. Langtry's family name.

EMILIO GUGLIELMO WINERY (BW 3656).

In 1925 Emilio Guglielmo bought vineyard land just outside Morgan Hill in the southern Santa Clara Valley. Today, the third generation operates the 450,000-gallon winery, which was built in 1934. For years the winery produced sound country wines and supplied many restaurants in northern California with their house wines. In 1969 the family began producing varietals under the Mount Madonna label, which became the Guglielmo label in 1994. The winery controls 150 acres of vines and buys grapes as well. The family is well known for its hearty country reds, which are still available in the traditional jugs. Annual production is about 100,000 cases.

GUILD WINERIES (BW 3865, Lodi; BW

4398, Ukiah; BW 5612, Fresno). Guild was organized in 1944 by Laurence MARSHALL* from four cooperative cellars in Lodi, Woodbridge, Sanger, and Cucamonga. In 1953 the company was marketing 20 million gallons of wine. In 1962 several other older wine firms (ALTA VINEYARDS, MATTEI, CRIBARI, and GARRETT) were added to the organization. In 1970 Guild acquired the ROMA and CRESTA BLANCA operations from Schenley. By the 1970s the still-cooperative organization had about 1,000 growers as members who supplied about 40 percent of the grapes used in producing the operation's wide range of wines, amounting to over 50 million gallons. By the 1990s, Guild's brands included Dunnewood, Cribari, Garrett, Cook's, and Chase-Limogere. In 1991 CANANDAIGUA bought the Guild operations and its brands for $55,000,000. In 1994, the company closed down the Guild plant in Lodi in favor of expansion in Madera.

GUILLIAMS VINEYARDS. See LA VIEILLE MONTAGNE

GUNDLACH-BUNDSCHU WINERY (BW 64). A wine firm formed in 1896 as successor to a winery in Sonoma dating back to 1858. In 1973, the company name was revived. Its winery and vineyards occupy some of the same land and structures as the original operation had. In fact, this land has been planted to wine grapes and owned by the Bundschu family since 1858. James BUNDSCHU today is president and vineyard manager of the 375-acre estate.

Jacob Gundlach (1818–94) came to San Francisco from Bavaria in 1850. Profits from his Bavaria Brewery in the city supplied the capital for him to become a partner with Emil DRESEL.* Together in 1858, they planted the historic Rhine Farm east of Sonoma. They soon separated their interests and, in 1875, Jacob formed J. Gundlach & Co., an enterprise that was producing some of California's finest wines by the 1880s. After Jacob died in 1894, the company was reconstituted by his son-in-law, Charles Bundschu—thus the firm's name.

The company's Bacchus wines, particularly its Rieslings and Cabernets, had a remarkable reputation for high quality. The vineyards were maintained during Prohibition and expanded in the 1960s by Towles Bundschu, James's father. The new winery was bonded in 1973. The 125-acre Rhine Farm portion of Gundlach-Bundschu's vineyards is located just inside the Carneros (Sonoma) Viticultural Area. The winery produces a wide range of varietals, most estate grown, with special emphasis on Cabernet Sauvignon, Merlot, Chardonnay, and Gewürztraminer. Annual production in the 1990s averaged about 50,000 cases.

GUTEDEL. The Chasselas doré (or Fendant) wine grape of Switzerland and Alsace, a highly productive white variety that went under the German name in pre-Prohibition California viticulture. Its literal meaning, Good-Noble, was often a joke among winemakers of German descent who used the expression, "Weder gut noch edel," that is, neither good nor noble. It was common to "stretch" Riesling and Traminer with Gutedel. The vine first came to California in the 1850s from New England, where it was grown under glass as a table grape. The variety became nearly extinct in California after an analysis produced by the University of California at Davis in 1944 described its wines as "flat, thin, uninteresting." Should anyone think to produce a varietal wine from this grape today, it would have to be labeled Chasselas doré.

HACIENDA WINE CELLARS (BW 4623). When Frank Bartholomew sold his interest in BUENA VISTA WINERY in 1968, he retained a large part of his vineyard land and, in 1973, converted an old hospital building nearby into a Spanish-style winery, calling it Hacienda. In 1977 A. Crawford Cooley, a vineyardist, took command of the operation and built its production to about 25,000 cases a year. In 1992 JFJ BRONCO bought the Hacienda brand and its second label, Antares. After Bartholomew died in 1985, Antonia, his widow, built a stunning replica of Agoston HARASZTHY's villa above the old vineyards. The former Hacienda winery building was renamed BARTHOLOMEW PARK WINERY and was open for business in 1994.

HAFNER (BW 5111). The Hafner family began developing its 100-acre Alexander Valley vineyard in 1967, and in 1982 built a small winery. Production, principally of Cabernet Sauvignon and Chardonnay, reached 13,000 cases per year in the 1990s.

HAGAFEN. Since 1979 producers specializing in KOSHER table wines from the Napa Valley, Cabernet Sauvignon, Chardonnay, and White Riesling varietals in particular. The wines are produced in St. Helena under rabbinical supervision and, since the 1993 vintage, Hagafen wines have been certified by the Union of Orthodox Congregations. For many years the grapes for Hagafen (Hebrew for "vine") wines came from Winery Lake Vineyard in the Carneros. About 6,000 cases are produced per year.

HAIGH, ISABELLE SIMI (1890–1981). When her father and uncle, Pietro and Guiseppe SIMI both died in 1904, Isabelle Simi and other family members continued to run their Montepulciano Winery north of Healdsburg. After she married Fred Haigh in 1908, the two ran the operation until his death in 1954. Production then came to a standstill but Isabelle kept the operation alive by selling older Simi vintages at the tasting room, which had been built from a huge redwood wine tank in 1936. In 1970 Mrs. Haigh sold the winery but continued to serve in the new tasting room until shortly before her death.

HALLCREST VINEYARDS (BW 4403 to 1969; 5198). In 1941 Chaffee Hall (1888–1969), a lawyer in San Francisco, established a small vineyard near Felton in the Santa Cruz Mountains, planting 13 acres to White Riesling and Cabernet Sauvignon. His was one of the earliest wineries built in California after Repeal by enthusiastic entrepreneurs dedicated to producing small quantities of high-quality varietal wine. The first vintage there was in 1946, but test batches had been made in 1944 and 1945 by Herman WENTE. The last vintage was 1964, and, for years afterward, the grapes were sold to Concannon. In 1976 the operation became FELTON-EMPIRE VINEYARDS.

In 1987 the property was sold to the Schumacher family who previously had run a small winery in Davis. They brought back the Hallcrest label and have produced a wide selection of varietals from various sources. For much of their production the Schumachers use organic farming methods in the vineyard and process the wines organically in the cellar. These wines, about 10,000 cases a year, are sold under the Organic Wine Works label. In the mid-1990s the Hallcrest label averaged about 5,000 cases per year.

HAMBRECHT, WILLIAM. See BELVEDERE WINERY

HAMES VALLEY. A small valley in southern Monterey County west of the town of Bradley. Granted AVA status in 1994, it contains about 630 acres of vines but no wineries.

HANDLEY CELLARS (BW 5128). A winery in the Anderson Valley in Mendocino County, owned by Milla Handley, who made wine at CHATEAU ST. JEAN before she opened her own winery in 1982. Her parents own a 20-acre vineyard in Dry Creek Valley and she has 18 acres planted at Handley. Concentrating on Chardonnay, Sauvignon blanc, and Gewürztraminer, she also makes a small quantity of sparkling wine. Total production in the mid-1990s was approaching 15,000 cases per year.

HANNA WINERY (BW 5282). Elias Hanna built his 90,000-gallon winery west of Santa Rosa in 1985. He also acquired 330 acres of vineyard land in Sonoma County. His production, mainly of Cabernet Sauvignon, Chardonnay, Sauvignon blanc, and Zinfandel, reached 20,000 cases by the mid-1990s.

HANZELL VINEYARDS (BW 4470). James D. Zellerbach (1892–1963) a financier in San Francisco bought land in the hills north of the town of Sonoma in 1952 and planted a vineyard there. He loved the red and white wines of Burgundy and modeled his little winery on Clos du Vougeot. Ivan Shock, a vineyardist in Napa, planted the Pinot noir and Chardonnay and R. Bradford WEBB* became the winemaker. The name, Hanzell, was derived from Zellerbach's name and that of his wife, Hanna.

His first vintage was in 1956 (the same year that Zellerbach was appointed American ambassador to Italy). The wines were fermented in stainless steel and aged in French oak barrels, both procedures revolutionary then in Californian winemaking. Webb also was ahead of his time when he induced malolactic FERMENTATION in the 1959 Hanzell Pinot noir.

Production was small and the wines developed a devoted following. In 1963 Zellerbach died, and the estate was eventually purchased in 1975 by Barbara de Brye. She died in 1991 and the estate went to her son, Alexander. The vineyard has been expanded over the years to 32 acres and now includes Cabernet Sauvignon. About 3,000 cases a year are produced under the supervision of the winemaker, Robert Sessions, who has been at Hanzell since 1973.

Leon D. Adams, *The Wines of America* (Boston: Houghton Mifflin, 1973), 188–89.

HARASZTHY. One of the important names in the early years of the California wine industry. **Agoston Haraszthy** (1812–69) has sometimes been called the "father" of modern California viticulture, a claim he certainly would never have made and a title that would have been confusing to his contemporaries. But he was certainly one of the prime movers in the development of commercial winegrowing.

A member of the Hungarian gentry, he came to the United States from the Austrian Empire in 1840 and settled in what is now Sauk City, Wisconsin; where he was a leading force in the entrepreneurial development of that state. He returned to Hungary in 1842 and brought his family back to America. In 1849, he took them overland to San Diego, where he was elected sheriff. In 1852, he was elected to the state legislature and headed north; he never returned, for northern California was where he found the action he was looking for.

He bought land near Mission Dolores in San Francisco and started a commercial nursery. Then he acquired land in San Mateo County near what is today the southern end of Crystal Springs Reservoir. Between 1853 and 1856, he brought nursery stock from the East Coast, perhaps also from Europe. Included were grape vines, but it is not certain which varieties. The tale, manufactured by his son in the 1880s, that these vines included Zinfandel from Hungary, is arrant nonsense.

Most of Haraszthy's time before 1857 was devoted to smelting gold, first as a private venture and then as Assayer of the new branch of the Mint in San Francisco. His connections with the Democratic Party in Wisconsin and southern California earned him this appointment from the Pierce Administration in Washington. In 1856 the Treasury's special agent on the West Coast, J. Ross Browne, became convinced that Haraszthy was skimming gold at the Mint and in 1857 the Hungarian resigned his position. The charges were eventually dropped.

Meanwhile he turned his eyes to Sonoma, with particular focus on viticulture. In 1856 he had visited the Buena Vista Ranch, the old "Kelsey place" east of Sonoma town. It had an old, dry-farmed vineyard producing excellent grapes. In 1857 he bought the ranch and soon acquired another huge tract of foothill land nearby. He transferred many of his vines from San Mateo to Sonoma and was soon the leader of a wine and grape boom in the Sonoma Valley. In 1858 he wrote a "Report on Grapes and Wine for California" for the State Agricultural Society. He also began a campaign to upgrade the varieties of grapes being planted in California vineyards. At Buena Vista, he had a stone winery built and tunnels dug into the

hillsides. By 1860 he had 250 acres in vines and won most of the prizes for wine that year at the county fair.

In 1861 Haraszthy decided to go to Europe to acquire a wide variety of wine grape varieties and persuaded the state to sponsor, but not pay for, the venture. He hoped to encourage a more systematic approach to vineyard improvement and had his eye, down the line, on state support for an experimental viticultural nursery. He sailed for New York in June, just as the Civil War exploded on the nation. He put together a fine collection and was back in California on December 5. The vines, a collection of about 300 varieties, arrived in February. Haraszthy asked the state legislature for financial support to maintain, propagate,

On his way to Europe in 1861 Agoston Haraszthy stopped off in New York to arrange for the publication of his yet-to-be-written account of the trip. He also had this photo made.

and distribute the collection but was turned down cold. His pro-southern political activities did not sit well in pro-Union California. And he had already been told he would get no money for the project. In fact, the formal legislative resolution had forbidden him even to ask. The vines were planted at Buena Vista, but there is no evidence that they had any effect on the history of California winegrowing, except in the unhistorical myths repeated about them for the past hundred years.

In 1863 Haraszthy received financial backing from eight capitalists in San Francisco for further expansion at Buena Vista. The result was the BUENA VISTA VINICULTURAL SOCIETY (BVVS).* After a promising first year, the Society began losing money and by 1866 Haraszthy was out of a job. After a fling at brandy production, he headed for Nicaragua to produce rum on a sugar plantation. On 6 July 1869 he disappeared while trying to cross an alligator-infested stream.

Arpad Haraszthy (1840–1900) became an important figure in the California wine industry and is primarily responsible for the historical misinformation that has surrounded his father's name over the years. During the family's early days in California, he had stayed on the East Coast and did not return permanently until 1862. In 1857 he went to France to study civil engineering. In 1860 he changed course and went to Épernay in Champagne where he studied sparkling wine production, and later accompanied his father on his vine-collecting tour of Europe in 1861. He also began writing articles on European winegrowing which he sent to the *California Farmer* for publication. On his return to California in 1862, he was placed in charge of his father's cellar at Buena Vista and married Mariano VALLEJO's daughter, Jovita. Next year he went to work for the BVVS, but his unsuccessful sparkling wine experiments cost him his job.

In 1866 he teamed up with Isador LANDS-BERGER, a director of BVVS, to produce Cal-

ifornia's first commercially successful sparkler, ECLIPSE.* In 1881 he and his partner, Harry Epstein, acquired the ORLEANS HILL vineyard and its winery in Yolo County. Meanwhile his family life had deteriorated to the point where his wife threatened divorce. And, even though he was an important influence in the politics of the wine industry, he was not a successful businessman. The Orleans investment was a disaster because the land was not suited to viticulture. Arpad made the promotion of Agoston as the "father of the California wine industry" a part of his attempts to keep his own business afloat. Such claims, among them that his father had introduced the Zinfandel to California and that he was the first to import good wine-grape varieties from Europe, have muddied the history of wine in California until recent years, because they were casually accepted by his many friends in the San Francisco wine trade and picked up by the press. They were hotly condemned at the time in the wine country, where the oldtimers in Sonoma and Napa knew the truth.

The depression of the 1890s finished off Arpad's wine business. In April 1900 he set off for the gold fields in Alaska but returned unsuccessful in November. On November 16 he dropped dead at the corner of Hyde and Washington streets in San Francisco.

Few in the history of California wine have been blessed with as much intelligence and energy as Arpad Haraszthy. It is a paradox that this unfortunate man should have created a historical image of his father that emphasizes contributions with no factual basis, an image that is particularly unfortunate as no one contributed more than Agoston to the early successes of the wine industry in California.

Thomas Pinney, *A History of Wine in America from the Beginnings to Prohibition* (Berkeley, Calif.: University of California Press, 1989), 269–84.

Charles L. Sullivan, "Agoston Haraszthy," parts 1–3, *Vintage* (1980), February, 13–19; March, 23–25; April, 11–17.

HARBOR WINERY (BW 4581). Charles H. Myers bonded his little Sacramento winery in 1972, but before then he had made history as a home winemaker in directing others to the potential of vineyards in Amador County, particularly those with Zinfandel vines. Over the years he has produced small quantities of commercial wine. His Mission del Sol, from Mission variety grapes, was a pleasurable anachronism. Critics usually point to his Chardonnays as his best varietal wines.

HARLAN ESTATE. H. W. Harlan has about 30 acres of Cabernet Sauvignon and other red Bordeaux varieties that he planted in the foothills west of Oakville in the Napa Valley, in the 1980s. 1990 was the first vintage sold under his label. He sells about 2,000 cases of highly praised claret each year. Harlan is one of the owners of MERRYVALE VINEYARDS.

HARRISON VINEYARDS (BW 5727). The Harrison family's 17.5-acre vineyard is in the Napa hills east of Rutherford. The vineyard was planted in 1973 and has supplied grapes for the Harrison estate Cabernet Sauvignon, Merlot, and Chardonnay, totaling about 2,000 cases per year, since 1988.

HARRIS, THOMAS LAKE. See FOUNTAIN-GROVE

HARTFORD COURT. See KENDALL-JACKSON VINEYARDS

HART WINERY (BW 5004). The Hart family bought a vineyard site in the Temecula area in 1973 and bonded the winery there in 1980. They produce about 4,000 cases per year from the 11-acre estate, principally Merlot and Sauvignon blanc.

HARVEST. Often termed "vintage" when referring to wine. In the coastal regions of California and the Sierra foothills, the grape harvest for table wines usually begins in late August or early September and lasts into October, sometimes until early November. The harvesting of grapes for sparkling wine usually begins about two weeks earlier, because lower sugar levels are desirable.

There is often some anxiety during the harvest if fall storms appear. When they arrive in September, as they did in 1989, early-ripening varieties, such as Chardonnay, can be damaged. Sometimes October is very wet, as it was in 1972, and the Cabernet Sauvignon and Zinfandel are hurt. But the normal situation here is one of fair skies in September and October, with occasional storms followed by clear skies and drying breezes.

Labor to bring in the grapes has often been a worry for California vineyardists. In the early days Indians supplied much of the workforce; later Chinese, then Japanese, workers made up a good part of the harvest muscle. But "white labor," as it was called before World War I, was always an important element. During World War II, soldiers and sailors from the Bay Area made extra money at vintage time in Napa, Sonoma, and Livermore. In recent years Hispanic workers have made up an overwhelming percentage of California's wine-grape harvesters.

Since the 1970s a significant portion of the state's wine-grape harvest has been done by large mechanical harvesters, but in the premium areas hand-picked grapes are more common. Another recent development is the use of equipment that will crush grapes in the field to maintain their freshness, which can easily be lost if they sit for hours in large gondolas. This technology is used primarily for white wines.

Wine from a specific harvest is often vintage dated on the bottle. Rare before the 1960s, this practice is now almost standard procedure for even moderately priced California wines. The law requires that 95 percent of the wines so labeled be of the indicated harvest or vintage year.

Wagons line up at harvest time outside a large Central Valley winery, fourteen of them in this picture. It was usually difficult to promote cool fermentations from grapes arriving under these conditions in the days before Prohibition.

HAUT SAUTERNE. See SAUTERNE

HAYWOOD WINERY (BW 4991 to 1991; 4702). Peter Haywood developed his steep-sloped, 90-acre vineyard in the 1970s and bonded his winery in 1980. In 1991 he sold the brand to BUENA VISTA and the winery to RAVENSWOOD. In doing so he was able to keep his Chamizal Vineyard in the hills northwest of Sonoma town. Buena Vista now gets those grapes for its Haywood brand and is able to take advantage of the solid reputation Haywood had won for his wines, Chardonnay, Cabernet Sauvignon, and especially Zinfandel. Buena Vista's production under the Haywood label now runs about 135,000 cases per year.

HEALDSBURG. A strategically located town in Sonoma County, close to the Dry Creek Valley, Russian River Valley, Chalk Hill, and Alexander Valley Viticultural Areas. Its his-tory as a wine town dates from the 1880s. Since Repeal, seventy-nine wineries have listed Healdsburg as a mailing address. It is also the home of the Sonoma County Wine Library (see LIBRARIES), one of the finest of its kind in the world.

HEALTH, WINE AND. See NEO-PROHIBITIONISM

HEARST, GEORGE (1820–91). A mining millionaire and U.S. Senator, George Hearst bought the Madrone Vineyard south of Glen Ellen in 1885. When the 350-acre vineyard was hit by phylloxera, Hearst replanted it on resistant ROOTSTOCK. In 1905 his widow sold the estate to the CALIFORNIA WINE ASSOCIATION.

HEAT SUMMATION. A measure of climate in terms of its relationship to viticulture in general and the quality of wine grapes in particular. The formula, derived from the length in days and the average daily temperatures of the growing season, yields a measurement — units of heat, also referred to as "degree-days" — of the heat available to ripen the grapes. The developers, Albert WINKLER and Maynard AMERINE, professors at the University of California at Davis, were interested in helping vineyardists plant the right variety of wine grape for a given climate. The result is a regional classification of climate with guidelines for the best varietals for each of the five regions, usually identified as Regions I–V, the higher the number the warmer the region. The coldest area in which wine grapes are grown commercially has a heat summation of at least 1,700 units; the hottest areas, 5,000 units and sometimes more. Chardonnay, for example, is recommended for Regions III and IV, but nowhere warmer; Barbera wants Regions III and IV, but nowhere cooler. In the

chart below, winegrowing regions in California and elsewhere in the world are classified by heat-summation levels.

As may be seen from the chart, areas noted for delicate table wines tend to have lower heat summations. But this regional system cannot be used as an absolute guide because of the effects of MICROCLIMATES. For example, the cooling effects of morning and afternoon fog may skew evaluations of climate that are made by simply calculating the average daily temperature during a growing season.

Marian W. Baldy, *The University Wine Course* (San Francisco: Wine Appreciation Guild, 1993), 266–74.

A. J. Winkler, *General Viticulture* (Berkeley, Calif.: University of California Press, 1965), 58–71.

HECK. Adolf Heck Sr. ran the American Wine Company in St. Louis after Repeal, producing

WINEGROWING REGIONS CLASSIFIED BY CLIMATE

REGION	HEAT UNITS	WINEGROWING AREAS CALIFORNIA	WORLDWIDE	FAVORED VARIETALS
I	Less than 2,500	Anderson Valley Carneros Santa Cruz Mountains Santa Maria	Mosel Burgundy Champagne	Chardonnay Pinot noir Gewürztraminer
II	2,501–3,000	Edna Valley Yountville Russian River Valley	Barolo Bordeaux	Cabernet Sauvignon Zinfandel
III	3,001–3,500	Alexander Valley St. Helena Livermore King City	Tuscany Rhône Valley	Chenin blanc Barbera Carignane Petite Sirah
IV	3,501–4,000	Lodi Davis Escondido	Provence Capetown, South Africa	French Colombard Ruby Cabernet
V	4,001+	Fresno Merced	Algeria Palermo, Italy	Grenache (dessert) Muscat blanc (dessert) Palomino (dessert)

COOK'S IMPERIAL CHAMPAGNE. His sons, Adolf Jr., Paul, and Ben, acquired KORBEL* in 1954, and the family developed the winery into one of America's most important producers of sparkling wine and brandy. In 1991 Anheuser-Busch acquired the operation. Today the old DiGiorgio plant in Kern County (previously called Lamont and then BEAR MOUNTAIN) is designated Heck Cellars (BW 4389) and now has a capacity of 28 million gallons.

HECKER PASS. A historic winegrowing area in the hills west of Gilroy in Santa Clara County. Before Prohibition Henry Miller's Glen Ranch (700 acres) and the original SOLIS WINERY were the largest winegrowing enterprises here. By the 1930s several small country wineries dotted the area and supplied jug wine to customers in the Santa Clara Valley. In recent years several premium wineries have been built in the area and a large number of first-rate varietal vineyards planted. A portion of what is considered the Hecker Pass district is inside the Santa Cruz Mountain Viticultural Area.

HECKER PASS WINERY (BW 4610). Just north of his brother's FORTINO WINERY, Mario Fortino bonded his own winery in 1972. From the 14-acre vineyard, Mario produces strong country reds, particularly Zinfandel, Petite Sirah, and Carignane; he averages about 5,000 cases per year.

HEDGESIDE. See MORRIS M. ESTEE

HEITZ WINE CELLARS (BW 967). Joseph Heitz bought Leon BRENDEL's little winery south of St. Helena in Napa Valley in 1961. Before then Heitz had made wine at BEAULIEU and had taught enology at Fresno State. In 1964 he bought the Rossi Winery (built in 1896 and later owned by a man called Holt) in the hills east of the valley. This became the main production site, the Brendel place along the highway being the sales room.

In the early years Heitz bottled and produced a wide range of varietal and generic wines, including "carbonated" wines made by Justin MILLER's ill-fated process; see the illustration on page 216 for an example. In 1966 he sold two Chardonnays, White Riesling, Chablis, rosé, Pinot noir, Grignolino, Cabernet Sauvignon, Barbera, Ruby Cabernet, Burgundy, sherry, two sparklers, and an ANGELICA. By the 1970s the Heitz list was more focused, with special emphasis on Cabernet Sauvignon, particularly wine from MARTHA'S VINEYARD (see photograph on page 202),* the first of which, vintage 1966, was announced in the Heitz newsletter of 7 February 1972. By the end of the 1970s these Cabernets, particularly the 1974 vintage, had gained almost legendary status.

The Heitz operation has become an expanded family affair over the years, with the annual production exceeding 40,000 cases in the 1990s. Except for the Grignolino, which dates back to the Brendel days, little critical attention is directed to any of Heitz's wines but the vineyard-designated Cabernet Sauvignons.

Robert Benson, *Great Winemakers of California* (Santa Barbara, Calif.: Capra Press, 1977), 175–87.

Joseph E. Heitz, *Creating a Winery in the Napa Valley* (Regional Oral History Office, Bancroft Library, 1986).

THE HESS COLLECTION WINERY (BW 5311). Donald Hess, a Swiss industrialist, began buying land on Mount Veeder in 1978. In 1986 he leased the old GIER Winery, long a facility of the Christian Brothers. Eventually he had 285 acres in vines in Napa Valley. He also has 350 acres of Chardonnay in Monterey County. The Collection refers to Hess's collection of contemporary art, which is housed in the winery. It is also the term that designates the top line of Hess Chardonnays and Cabernet Sauvignons, which appeared in 1987. The Hess Select line is the operation's second label, first appearing on a California-appellation Chardonnay in 1989. Since then there have been Select Cabernet Sauvignons. Total annual production is about 120,000 cases in the 1990s.

HESS WINERY. See LA JOTA VINEYARD COMPANY

HEUBLEIN. A food and beverage corporation with headquarters in Connecticut, and since 1987 owned by the giant British conglomerate, Grand Metropolitan. In 1969 Heublein bought control of UNITED VINTNERS, which gave it INGLENOOK and ITALIAN SWISS COLONY, and acquired BEAULIEU VINEYARD. In 1970 it bought the REGINA winery in southern California and converted it into a vinegar plant. In 1982 RJR Nabisco acquired Heublein and controlled the company for five years before selling it to the British. Just before it was sold in 1987, Heublein acquired ALMADEN and began selling off its assets. In 1993 Heublein bought the Glen Ellen and M. G. Vallejo brands and in 1994 sold the Almaden and Inglenook brands to CANANDAIGUA. The old Inglenook Winery and estate was sold to Francis Ford Coppola. Heublein brands now include Blossom Hill, Glen Ellen, M. G. Vallejo, Christian Bros., and Rutherford Estate. The company has recently acquired a bonded facility in Sonoma County (BW 5938) and continues to operate the old Almaden plant at Paicines (BW 4476). All these are operated under the corporate rubric of Heublein Wine Group with headquarters in San Mateo. Beaulieu continues to operate as a discrete segment of the Heublein corporation.

HIARING. See WINES & VINES

HIDDEN CELLARS (BW 5066). A home winemaking operation in Mendocino that went commercial in 1981. The winery made its reputation early with white wine, Gewürz-traminer, White Riesling, Sauvignon blanc, Chardonnay, and botrytised dessert wines. By 1985 annual production amounted to 10,000 cases; in the 1990s, counting custom crushing, annual production exceeded 35,000 cases. Zinfandel, particularly that from the 50- to 90-year-old vines of the Pacino Vineyard has helped give the winery a good reputation for red wine.

HILGARD, EUGENE W. (1833–1916). As professor of Agriculture, Hilgard was the first in a long line of scholars at the University of California to be associated with the systematic application of scientific principles to the production of high-quality wines. He came to Berkeley in 1875. His first tasks were to alert the winemaking community to the threat of PHYLLOXERA and to stress the importance of dependable, high-quality wine as the basis for the long-term success of the industry. Between 1884 and 1895, he became something of a celebrity in northern California for his running battle with leaders of the commercial wine industry. He insisted that a reputation for high quality would give the industry long-term security. His opponents, headed by Charles WETMORE, argued that success lay in a dependable standard product, wine for the masses. In the long run Hilgard's philosophy triumphed, but his various campaigns of the moment were not always on target. His advocacy of *Vitis* CALIFORNICA as a resistant ROOTSTOCK was a total failure. Pasteurization, which he promoted, was never a viable technical procedure, however logical. But his tenacious support for high-quality technology, particularly the cool fermentation of white wines, placed him in line with future developments. He never wavered in his advocacy of better varietals. His tough intellectual stance in favor of high quality and the voluminous scientific literature on viticulture and enology that was published under his supervision make him one of the fathers of today's wine industry,

EUGENE WOLDEMAR HILGARD

Born in Germany, Eugene W. Hilgard grew up in Illinois. At sixteen he went back to Germany to study and received a doctorate in chemistry at Heidelberg. He became State Geologist of Mississippi in 1855. Later he taught at the University of Michigan before coming to California in 1875. (Shields Library, University of California at Davis)

which rests absolutely on the kind of wine he promoted.

> Maynard Amerine, "Hilgard and California
> Viticulture," *Hilgardia* 33, no. 1 (July 1962).

HILL, WILLIAM. An important developer of mountain vineyards, Hill began his work in Napa in 1974. As they developed vineyard land, he and his associates sold the property and started up again. STERLING bought his Diamond Mountain estate in 1977, THE HESS COLLECTION acquired the Mount Veeder property in 1978, and in 1986 ATLAS PEAK acquired the Foss Valley vineyard.

The **William Hill Winery** (BW 4901) was founded in 1976 but real production did not begin until 1978, when Hill made about 5,000 cases of Cabernet Sauvignon in a converted juice plant in Napa. In 1979 he began producing Chardonnay. He also developed an important vineyard above the Silverado Country Club, in the Napa Valley beginning in 1980. There Hill built a 600,000-gallon winery which opened in 1990. During those years, Hill gained a reputation for extremely high-quality wines, particularly his Cabernet Sauvignon. In 1992, when he was producing 100,000 cases a year, Hill sold his winery and brand name to WINE ALLIANCE which is still making about 100,000 cases a year here. The winery is run in close conjunction with the Atlas Peak facility, also owned by Wine Alliance and just up the road.

In 1996 Hill and Carl Thoma bought the PARDUCCI winery as a production facility. **Hill and Thoma Wines** (BW 5569) now controls vineyard land in California and Oregon totaling almost 2,000 acres, with California wine production at about 20,000 cases.

HILL, WILLIAM MCPHERSON. One of the pioneer vineyardists of the upper Sonoma Valley, he began building his estate south of Glen Ellen in 1855. His 175-acre vineyard was but a small part of his huge 1,629-acre ranch, when in 1889 he sold the great property to the state on which to build a "home for feebleminded children." It is today a large state hospital. Hill was a leader in the use of resistant rootstock and a pioneer in the production of high-quality Sonoma Zinfandel.

HIRAM WALKER. See WINE ALLIANCE

HMR ESTATE WINERY (BW 5515; previously 4577). The Hoffman family began planting vines on a 1,200-acre property west of Paso Robles, San Luis Obispo County, in 1964 and producing Hoffman Mountain Ranch wines in 1972, soon gaining a good reputation for several varietals. By the late 1970s production had reached 30,000 cases a year, but financial problems forced the Hoffmans out of the operation in 1982. The property ended up in the hands of foreign interests in 1989. The HMR brand was retained and for a short while meant Hidden Mountain Ranch. The foreign investors operate as the **San Luis Obispo Winery, Inc.**

PAUL HOBBS CELLARS. Before developing his own brand in 1991, Hobbs was the winemaker at SIMI. He makes about 3,000 cases for his label at KUNDE ESTATE. His specialties are Cabernet Sauvignon, Pinot noir, and Chardonnay.

HOCK. A British term for Rhine wine, derived from Hochheim, a town in the Rheingau. The term is still a legal generic for California wine but is used no more. Before Prohibition it was often seen on California white wines with a Germanic style. Most hock wines had a large dose of Burger grapes in their makeup. Several won awards at the Columbian Exposition in Chicago in 1893. California's most famous hock was produced by Jacob SCHRAM.

HOME WINEMAKING. An important part of California wine history since the rancho days when California was still part of Mexico. Before Prohibition families of Italian, French, German, and Central European origin, particularly in northern California, used as much as 5 percent of the state's wine-grape crop to make wine at home.

By 1913 hundreds of carloads of wine grapes were being shipped from California to cities on the East Coast and in the Midwest for sale, mostly to immigrant families. By 1917 the number of carloads reached 4,000. When Prohibition arrived in 1920, the number skyrocketed, to 55,000 by 1923. This eastern market continued after Repeal and still amounts to a few hundred carloads a year. Home winemakers all over the country were also introduced to grape CONCENTRATE during the dry years.

Since the 1960s home winemaking in California and elsewhere in the United States has taken on a definite premium character. By the 1970s there were stores supplying home winemakers up and down the West Coast. For easterners, the American Wine Society became an important source of support and information. Many a winery bonded in the last quarter century in California was founded by men and women who began as home winemakers. In California today several organizations of home winemakers hold regular competitions.

Cornelius S. Ough, *Winemaking Basics* (New York: Food Products Press, 1992), 291–99.

HONIG CELLARS (BW 5134). The Honig estate in Rutherford, Sonoma County, was acquired by the family in 1964. The winery was bonded in 1980, its first wines labeled HNW. The 6,400-square-foot facility has also done a lot of custom crushing for others. The

In California until the 1960s, it was most often the immigrant families and their descendents who made wine at home. The expansion of wine consumption among middle-class consumers after 1965 saw a parallel growth in winemaking by many of the same consumers. In the 1970s, many of the new wineries established at the time belonged to people who had begun as home winemakers.

production of wines under the Honig label now amounts to about 11,000 cases per year, with a strong emphasis on Sauvignon blanc and Cabernet Sauvignon. Most Honig wines are sold in restaurants. The estate vineyards cover 67 acres. The general partner, Bill Honig, was for several years Superintendent of Public Instruction in California.

HOOD. In 1858 **William Hood** (1818–93) acquired much of the old Los Guilicos Rancho in the upper Sonoma Valley. He planted vines on his 1,800-acre estate and built a winery in 1861; later he added a distillery. He married Eliza Shaw in 1858, when she was fourteen years old, and by the 1880s, the wine and brandy operations were under her supervision. Long before her husband's death **Eliza Hood** (1843–1914) made a name for her Zinfandel and Cabernet Sauvignon and the estate brandy was considered one of California's best. In the 1890s the ITALIAN SWISS COLONY

began managing the winegrowing activities on the estate.

HOP KILN WINERY (BW 4718). An impressive winery in the Russian River Valley, Sonoma County, that is a converted hop kiln and a classic of its type, dating from 1905. The owner, Martin Griffin, bonded the facility in 1975 and, within a few years, established himself as a specialist in Zinfandel production. His 75-acre vineyard, which he purchased in 1961, contains old Zinfandel and Petite Sirah vines that help account for the success of his sturdy reds. About 30 percent of his annual 10,000-case production is Zinfandel, some labeled Primitivo.

HOWE, JAMES POMEROY (1880–1970). A noted foreign correspondent who spent his retirement years at his Gopher Gulch Wine Cellars in Walnut Creek, Howe was probably the most celebrated home winemaker in Cali-

In 1939 hops were more valuable than the wine grapes in Sonoma County. Between 1953 and 1960 this important industry disappeared from the area. Martin Griffin's Hop Kiln Winery is a beautiful reminder of this formerly important crop here. (©Sebastian Titus, Vintage Image)

fornia in the 1940s and 1950s. He had learned his craft from Herman WENTE and virtually everyone in the state who was connected with the production of fine varietal wines during those years had an affectionate acquaintance with Jim Howe and were happy to have bottles of his wine, which he labeled "and Howe!"

HOWELL MOUNTAIN. In 1880 Charles KRUG sent Professor Eugene HILGARD some soil samples from Howell Mountain, a huge volcanic knob northeast of St. Helena, then virtually undeveloped. In 1843 most of it had been included in George YOUNT's La Jota land grant. Hilgard responded that successful viticulture on such soils was a sure thing. The result was a land rush onto Howell Mountain; by 1884 at least thirty vineyardists had planted over 500 acres there. BRUN & CHAIX put up the first winery. By the 1890s these upland vineyards had become well known for their red wines. The Cabernet Sauvignon of W. S. KEYES won a gold medal at the Paris Exposition in 1900. But the region's somewhat isolated situation inhibited future growth, as did the acquisition in 1909 of the 1,700 acre Angwin resort establishment by the Seventh Day Adventist Church for its Pacific Union College. Viticulture did not die, however, and during Prohibition several vineyards were planted on the mountain to Zinfandel and Petite Sirah.

The rebirth was begun on the lower slopes after Repeal by John BALLENTINE at DEER PARK WINERY and J. Leland Stewart (see SOUVERAIN). By the 1970s wineries outside the area had discovered the surviving red-wine vineyards from Prohibition days. In the 1980s new wineries were in operation and vineyards reappeared in places where they might have been found 100 years earlier. In 1984 Howell Mountain was granted AVA status, but the lower reaches of the mountain were not included in the new viticultural area, which covers about 800 acres. Today the mountain is noted for its good Cabernet Sauvignon, Zinfandel, and Chardonnay.

HUNEEUS, AUGUSTIN. See FRANCISCAN VINEYARDS

HUSCH VINEYARDS (BW 4558, 5306). In 1968 Wilton (Tony) Husch began planting his vineyard in the Anderson Valley, Mendocino County, and bonded his winery in 1971, the first there since before Prohibition. He sold the place to the Oswald family in 1979. Since then production has climbed to more than 25,000 cases per year, with emphasis on Chardonnay, Cabernet Sauvignon, and Gewürztraminer.

HUSMANN. A father-and-son team of viticulture scientists who helped shape the course of winegrowing in California for more than half a century. **George Husmann** (1827–1902) was born in Germany and came to the United States with his parents in 1836. They settled in the German winegrowing community of Hermann, Missouri, where the young man planted his first vineyard in 1847. He became active in the nursery business and involved in commercial wine production. In 1859 he published his first essay on winegrowing and ten years later began producing the monthly *Grape Culturist,* unique in this country at that time. By the 1870s he was working on the use of resistant native ROOTSTOCK* to combat PHYLLOXERA. He was soon shipping rootstock to winegrowers in California among them the DRESELS and Hiram CRABB. By then he was also teaching horticulture at the University of Missouri.

In 1881 Husmann visited California and remained, hired to supervise Talcoa, the Carneros vineyard estate of James Simonton. In 1885 he bought the Peterson ranch in Chiles Valley, renaming it Oak Glen Vineyard. Once here, he became an important voice supporting Eugene HILGARD's campaign to raise the quality of wine in California. He also became embroiled in the investigation to select the best resistant rootstock for California. In the 1890s he conducted a cranky campaign against the University's work on the problem. But, when Charles BUNDSCHU gave the eulogy at Husmann's funeral, he remembered the old man for his promotion of high standards for California wine.

Husmann always said that his best student in Missouri had been **George Charles Husmann** (1861–1939), his son. He came to California with his parents and in 1882 became the manager of Charles KOHLER's vineyard in Glen Ellen. Later he was manager of Leland Stanford's VINA. In 1901 he was appointed head of the viticultural section of the U.S. Department of Agriculture, a post he held until 1932. His great achievement was the establishment of EXPERIMENTAL STATIONS throughout the country; his list of viticultural publications is longer than his father's. When he retired, he settled in the Napa Valley.

HYBRID. In 1928 the horticultural savant Liberty Hyde Bailey wrote that "hybrids are products of crossing between species. Of late, the word has been used by most writers to comprise crosses, whether between species or varieties." Nothing has changed in seventy years, as far as viticulture is concerned. Writers today regularly refer to crosses as hybrids. True hybrids of wine grapes haven't been a great success. The so-called French hybrids, developed between the 1870s and 1920s, were the offspring of real wine grapes, vinifera, crossed with phylloxera-resistant native American vines. The idea was to produce good grapes on vines resistant to phylloxera. Such vines have never been a serious part of winegrowing in California, although they have made it possible to make better wine in the eastern United States than is possible from native varieties.

Another group of hybrids, also mostly French, were crosses made between nonresistant vinifera and American vines to produce so-called resistant ROOTSTOCK.* But they weren't really resistant enough, as vineyardists in California have been learning since the mid-1980s.

Crosses, often referred to as hybrids, between different varieties of vinifera to produce better wine grapes have also been less than entirely successful. Most of the crosses produced at the University of California at Davis, such as RUBY CABERNET and EMERALD RIESLING, after much early interest beginning in the 1940s, have fallen from favor and are rarely seen in new plantings.

ICARIA SPERANZA. In 1881 two French families bought 885 acres in Sonoma County south of Cloverdale, near the brand-new ITAL-IAN SWISS COLONY, to establish a utopian community. Soon several more French families joined, the population reaching fifty-five by 1883. Winegrowing was one of the commu-nity's main activities, with 85 acres planted in the first year. The group was not able to attain self-sufficiency and in 1886 its assets were divided among the members. Several families stayed on in the area and continued to be active in the wine industry.

INGLENOOK (BW 9). Thirty years ago Inglenook was one of the great names in Napa Valley wine. The winery had helped to create the fame of the best of California wines before Prohibition and had been in the forefront in reviving the tradition of world-class wines from the Napa Valley after Repeal. Today Inglenook is a brand name for Canandaigua, but the old estate survives.

Inglenook was begun in 1871 when W. C. Watson, George YOUNT's son-in-law, bought land west of Rutherford and developed a pretty estate that served for a while as resort and san-itarium. He also planted a 50-acre vineyard. In 1879 Gustave Niebaum (1842–1908) bought Inglenook and some adjoining land. By 1881 he had more than 1,000 acres extending into the western hills. By 1884 the vineyard was planted to top varietals and wine production begun. All the while, Niebaum was solidly established,

The Inglenook winery is today one of the vinous landmarks of the Napa Valley. For years it could be seen from Highway 29, until, in the 1980s, HEUBLEIN built a huge bar-rel-aging facility in front of it. Many people in Napa have expressed the hope that current owner, Francis Ford Coppola, may someday correct the situation.

in San Francisco, running the Alaska Commercial Company. He had been born in Finland and early took to the sea, where he made his fortune, mostly in the Alaskan fur trade. He always looked on Inglenook as a serious hobby, not as an investment.

Between 1886 and 1891, Niebaum had his great winery built under the guidance of Hamden W. MCINTYRE. In the process he made every effort to produce table wines of world class quality. He introduced ESTATE BOTTLING to California's commercial wine industry. Production ran about 50,000 gallons per year in the 1890s, almost all of it sold in bottles by the case, a rare commodity in those days. (On page 295 is an advertisement, published in 1895, for Inglenook wine.)

The winery was closed for three years after Niebaum's death, but was revived in 1911. Suzanne Niebaum, his widow, placed the operation in the hands of Hermann Lange and John Daniel Sr., her niece's husband. Daniel's son, John Jr., (1907–70) came to live at the winery in 1914.

Wine operations on the estate ceased again during Prohibition, but in 1933 Mrs. Niebaum reopened the winery under the management of Carl BUNDSCHU, an old hand in the wine trade. He hired a fine cellar staff and brought Inglenook back, first with outstanding white wines, and then with world-class Cabernets. John Daniel Jr. took over the winery in 1939 and inherited the great cellar staff headed by John Gross and George DEUER. Under Daniel's leadership they produced a line of Cabernet Sauvignon that helped Napa Valley reclaim its pre-Prohibition status as a center of fine wine production.

In 1964 Daniel sold Inglenook to UNITED VINTNERS (and thus it was acquired by Heublein in 1969). Within a few years, under the Inglenook label, Heublein was marketing inexpensive jug wines, the Navalle line, named for the little creek that flowed through the old Niebaum property. By the 1980s Inglenook's brand had lost its luster for American wine consumers. Heublein's attempts to revive the old image brought forth much better wines under the Inglenook-Napa Valley label, but did not boost sales enough to make them profitable. In 1992 Inglenook no longer had a working winery in the Napa Valley and in 1994 Heublein sold the brand to Canandaigua. In the mid-1990s Canandaigua was selling about 6.5 million cases of Central Valley wine under the Inglenook brand name.

Niebaum's great estate still existed as a physical entity. Francis Ford Coppola owned the Niebaum mansion, some other old buildings, and part of the old vineyards. The great old winery for a short while served no commercial purpose, but at the end of 1994 Coppola purchased it from Heublein and reunited the old estate; see NIEBAUM-COPPOLA ESTATE.

Tom Parker and Charles L. Sullivan, *Inglenook: 100 Years of Fine Winemaking* (Rutherford, Calif.: Inglenook Vineyards, 1979).

F. Wait, *Wines & Vines of California* (1889; reprint, Berkeley, Calif.: Howell-North, 1973), 110–18.

INNISFREE. See JOSEPH PHELPS VINEYARDS

IRON HORSE VINEYARDS (BW 4874). One of the best producers of bottle-fermented sparkling wines in California, Iron Horse is located in Sonoma County, just south of Forestville, with a cool climate similar to that of Champagne. The vineyard was developed in 1971 and acquired by the Sterling and Tancer families in 1976. The winery went up in 1979. The 142 acres of Chardonnay and Pinot noir produce several sparkling wines that attest to the sound viticultural techniques employed here. Selective harvesting is an absolute rule at Iron Horse. Another 45 acres of vineyard in the Alexander Valley supply grapes for the winery's varietal table wines. Total production averages about 40,000 cases per year.

Joy Sterling, *A Cultivated Life: A Year in a California Vineyard* (New York: Random House, 1993).

IRONSTONE. See KAUTZ IRONSTONE VINEYARDS

IRRIGATION. An important part of wine-growing in California since mission days, particularly in the coastal areas south of the San Francisco Bay Area, where low rainfall and warm, dry summers prevail. In the Central Valley, irrigation has always been essential to successful viticulture. But dry farming has always been possible in the northern coastal regions; winter and spring rain in Napa and Sonoma is usually double that of the South Bay and Central Coast areas.

Overhead sprinkler systems have been used in many areas since the 1950s, sometimes performing two functions: irrigation in the late spring and summer, frost protection between March and May.

Great strides have been made since the 1970s in drip irrigation. Recent experiments have shown that carefully measured and timed wettings can improve the quality of the grapes, even in Napa and Sonoma. Drip irrigation is also useful for establishing new vineyard plantings anywhere in California.

ISOZYME FINGERPRINTING. See DNA FINGERPRINTING

ITALIANS AND EARLY CALIFORNIA WINE. Contrary to popular belief, few people from Italy itself were prominent in the very early days of the wine industry in California. But there were many ethnic Italians from Switzerland, particularly in Napa Valley. The development of the ITALIAN SWISS COLONY in the 1880s became a magnet for many Italian immigrants who thereafter made significant contributions to all aspects of the state's wine industry for the next thirty-five years as they poured into California. Italians who came to the West Coast in these years tended to have a bit more capital than those who stayed in the east. Hundreds of them bought or planted vineyards throughout the state, wherever viti-

culture thrived. By World War I, Italian families controlled a sizeable portion of the vineyard land in Sonoma, Napa, Contra Costa, and Santa Clara counties, and they increased their holdings during Prohibition. To a lesser extent this was also the case in southern California. In the years just after Repeal, Italian families owned most of the bonded wineries in some areas: 75 percent in Santa Clara County, 72 percent in Sonoma County, 59 percent in Napa County, and 51 percent in southern California.

Thomas Pinney, *A History of Wine in America from the Beginnings to Prohibition* (Berkeley, Calif.: University of California Press, 1989), 327–31.

ITALIAN SWISS COLONY. In 1881 a banker in San Francisco, Andrea SBARBORO* (1840–1923) and several associates, determined to establish a winegrowing colony in northern Sonoma County, south of Cloverdale bought 1,500 acres of grazing land. At first naming the property the Italian-Swiss Agricultural Colony, the organizers hoped to attract immigrants to settle on the land, grow crops, and gradually pay off their mortgages to the founders. But that plan didn't work and the operation simply developed as a corporation with sixty original stockholders, all but seven of whom were of Italian descent.

By 1885 the Italian-Swiss Colony (ISC) was making wine, but the disastrous 1887 vintage showed Sbarboro he needed a winemaker with strong technical ability. The 1888 vintage brought a leap in quality under Pietro C. ROSSI,* whose portrait appears on page 291. He ran the ISC cellars until his death in 1911. The vineyards expanded to more than 1,000 acres by 1893, many planted to Italian varieties such as Barbera, Nebbiolo, and Sangiovese, imported by the company.

In 1900 ISC was firmly established as a national brand, the wines shipped in bulk out of the little railroad station at Asti, the name given it by Sbarboro, and bottled at company depots in every major city in the country. Their leading wine was Tipo Chianti, made primarily from Sangiovese grapes. High quality, good leadership, and a growing immigrant population made ISC the most successful independent winemaker in California before Prohibition. The estate at Asti became internationally famous for its beauty and its technical grandeur. (The photograph on page 319 shows a party given in one of the winery's enormous vats.) By 1910 ISC also had plants at Madera, Lemoore, and Selma in the Central Valley to produce sweet wine and brandy. Overall capacity was 14.5 million gallons. In 1915 ISC became a part of the CALIFORNIA WINE ASSOCIATION.

The Rossi family and associates acquired the Asti plant and vineyards during Prohibition and made good money as the Asti Grape Products Co. ISC grapes and concentrate were favorites of home winemakers. After Repeal, the Rossis expanded the Asti plant and, by 1937 had the largest table-wine facility in the country. In 1944 they sold the operation to National Distillers. Eventually UNITED VINTNERS took control and, in 1968, Heublein took over. By now Italian Swiss Colony was a brand name for a huge list of inexpensive wines that had lost their reputation for high quality. The brand is now owned by the WINE GROUP which sells about 18 million cases per year under that label.

In 1988 BERINGER WINE ESTATES bought the Asti property and began planting Cabernet Sauvignon and Merlot on the 400 acres available. The Asti plant became the production facility for the Napa Ridge brand. Although no longer a tourist attraction, the old Asti estate still has many of the charming elements from its early days, carefully maintained by the new owners.

Edmund A. Rossi, *Italian-Swiss Colony and the Wine Industry* (Regional Oral History Office, Bancroft Library, 1971).

Edmund A. Rossi Jr., *Italian-Swiss Colony,*

1949–1989: Recollections of a Third-Generation California Winemaker (Regional Oral History Office, Bancroft Library, 1990).

ITALIAN VARIETIES of wine grapes have been important in California since the 1880s. Agoston HARASZTHY imported the DOLCETTO and SANGIOVESE in 1862, but the vines were not distributed. In the 1880s, JOHN T. DOYLE of Cupertino imported both those varieties along with BARBERA and NEBBIOLO, and had most success with Barbera. In the 1890s the ITALIAN SWISS COLONY brought in numerous Italian varieties for their blended wines; Sangiovese, the basis for the Colony's Tipo Chianti, was the most important.

Between 1880 and 1920, hundreds of Italian families took up winegrowing all over the state, but few planted Italian varieties, preferring ZINFANDEL, PETITE SIRAH, and CARIGNANE. It was not until 1968 that the first Italian variety, Barbera, made it into the state's official statistics. By then several producers had made a premium varietal Barbera. Of all the Italian varietals, Sangiovese has become more popular: There were 186 acres of it in 1990; there were 1,359 acres in 1997. The acreage under Nebbiolo is still small but is growing.

ITALIAN VINEYARD COMPANY. See GUASTI

IVAN TAMAS WINES (BW 5677). A NÉGOCIANT brand begun in 1984 by Iván Tamás Füzy and Steven Mirassou. Centered in the Livermore Valley, the operation is selling about 25,000 cases a year, mainly Chardonnay, White Zinfandel, Cabernet Sauvignon and a varietal Trebbiano, long grown in the Livermore Valley as Ugni blanc. In 1994 the company's own bonded premises were set up on the Wente property.

JACKSON, JESS. See KENDALL-JACKSON VINEYARDS

JAEGER FAMILY WINERY (BW 5191). William Jaeger is one of the founders of FREEMARK ABBEY and RUTHERFORD HILL WINERIES. He also developed his 30-acre Inglewood Vineyard in the foothills southwest of St. Helena in Napa Valley and bonded his little winery in 1984. Jaeger's specialty is table wine from red Bordeax varieties, with strong emphasis on Merlot. Production passed the 7,000-case mark in the 1990s. In 1997 he sold the estate to a group of investors but retained the brand.

JARVIS, GEORGE M., the pioneer of viticulture in the Vine Hill area of the Santa Cruz Mountains in the 1860s. He established the Jarvis Wine & Brandy Co. on River Street in San Jose in the 1880s and, like Henry NAGLEE, made brandy produced largely from White Riesling. He also produced large quantities of red table wine, which he sold in eastern markets. His operation eventually became part of the CALIFORNIA WINE ASSOCIATION.

JARVIS WINERY (BW 5653). In the hills east of Napa Valley off Monticello Road, William Jarvis began planting grapes on his 1,400-acre property in 1984. In 1992 he had a commercial crush of Chardonnay and Cabernet Sauvignon from his 37-acre vineyard. He also began building an underground winery and aging tunnels, an impressive 45,000-square-foot operation. The first Jarvis wines were released in 1995; annual production is about 5,000 cases.

Jarvis also runs a music conservatory in Napa, housed in the historic JOSEPH MATTHEWS winery.

JEKEL VINEYARDS (BW 4851). William Jekel began developing his vineyard near Greenfield in Monterey County in 1972. By the 1990s he controlled over 300 acres of vineyard land there. The winery was bonded in 1978 and excelled in the production of White Riesling, Chardonnay, and Cabernet Sauvignon. In 1990 he sold the operation to the ill-starred VINTECH CORP. Jekel regained control in 1991 and the next year sold the winery to Brown-Forman. Production in recent years at the 370,000-gallon winery has reached 80,000 cases per year.

JEPSON VINEYARDS (BW 5304). Robert Jepson acquired the William Baccala Winery in 1986, and has concentrated on producing Sauvignon blanc and Chardonnay from the 110-acre vineyard near Ukiah in Mendocino County. The first red wine was a 1994 Pinot noir. Since 1988 there have also been considerable quantities of sparkling wine and a small quantity of pot-still brandy. Total production comes to about 15,000 cases per year.

JOHANNISBERG RIESLING. See WHITE
RIESLING

JOHNSON'S ALEXANDER VALLEY WINES
(BW 4692). The old Whitten Ranch had vineyards until the 1950s. In the 1960s the Johnson
family began replanting them and in 1975 built
a winery there in the Alexander Valley in
Sonoma County. Today there are 50 acres of
vines and a wide range of wines. Annual production is about 6,000 cases, much of it sold at
the tasting room, in which a 1924 Marr-Colton
theater pipe organ is installed.

JOHNSON TURNBULL VINEYARDS. See
TURNBULL WINE CELLARS

JONES, IDWAL (1890–1964), a Welsh-born
journalist and novelist who came to California
in 1911. His novel *The Vineyard,* published in
1942 and about life in the Napa Valley, is probably the best novel to have been set in the California wine country. A second book *Vines in
the Sun,* published in 1949, is an anecdotal history of wine in California and the leading personalities in the industry. It contains much useful and accurate information interspersed with
myth and tall tales.

JONES, LEE. See SHEWAN-JONES

JORDAN VINEYARD (BW 4776, 5506).
Thomas Jordan, an oilman and geologist, used
that discipline to inform his purchase of a
huge piece of hill country looking north onto
the Alexander Valley in Sonoma County.
Today he has a 275-acre vineyard and a large
estate winery on that land. Cabernet Sauvignon and its Bordeaux cousins dominate the
planting, followed by Chardonnay. Jordan's
first Cabernet came from the 1976 vintage.
Possibly because the wine is easily drinkable
when young, it was noted that, in restaurants,
Jordan's was the best-selling Cabernet Sauvi-

gnon in the United States in 1992. Today
annual production runs about 50,000 cases.

In 1986 the **Jordan Sparkling Wine Co.**
(BW 5506) began producing sparklers, first
released in 1990 under the J label. In 1996 Jordan purchased the PIPER-SONOMA plant.
Sales exceeded 20,000 cases annually in the
early 1990s.

JORY WINES. At first small quantities of varietal wine were produced in the old Los Gatos
Novitiate facility, later in a winery near Hecker
Pass. Emphasis is on Chardonnay. Some of the
wines carry fanciful labels, such as the 1991 Red
Zeppelin Mourvèdre (Mataro) and the
sparkling Pinot blanc labeled Mistral. Jory, with
its newsletter, "The Thief," rivals BONNY
DOON for its light-hearted approach ot marketing. Annual sales are about 4,000 cases.

JOULLIAN VINEYARDS (BW 5567). Located
in the Carmel Valley, Monterey County, Joullian has 40 acres of vineyard and was bonded in
1990. Production is concentrated on Cabernet
Sauvignon, Chardonnay, and Sauvignon blanc,
and amounted to about 12,000 cases a year in
the mid-1990s.

JUDD'S HILL (BW 5538). After selling their
interest in the Whitehall Lane Winery in 1988,
Art and Bunnie Finkelstein bonded Judd's
Hill, a small winery in Conn Valley in Napa in
1990. Cabernet Sauvignon is their wine, made
from grapes grown on the family's 10-acre terraced, hillside vineyard that was named for
their son. They make about 1,500 cases a year.

JUG WINE. Before Prohibition, a good part
of the business of many a small winery in California depended on sales to local customers at
the door, often in the customer's own containers, usually small barrels, demijons, or gallon
jugs. Some wineries set up "barrel stores" in
nearby towns and sold their wares from barrel

to jug. Many grocery stores in California had similar facilities. After Repeal, the tradition continued, but more and more small and medium-sized country wineries bottled wine themselves in large containers, usually gallons. By 1936 California health authorities made off-premise barrel sales virtually impossible. Jug wines bottled at the winery were sold to neighbors and to restaurants as house wines. These wines were usually generic blends of the old rustic varieties that had long dominated California vineyards: Zinfandel, Petite Sirah, Carignane, Mataro (Mourvèdre), Napa Gamay, and Alicante Bouschet for red wine, and Palomino (Golden Chasselas), Sauvignon vert, Burger, and French Colombard for white. The jug, whether gallon or half-gallon, was characterized by a single finger handle for carrying and to facilitate pouring.

In the 1970s the meaning of jug expanded to include the wines that poured from huge factories in the Central Valley, most carrying such names as Chablis and Burgundy. Some of those wines also appeared as varietals. Later the term was expanded again to include the 1.5-liter wines in magnumlike bottles, without a carrying handle. The upgraded image of the new package did not necessarily mean a higher-quality wine. Still, many premium producers followed suit with generics and varietals in those containers and often the higher qual-

ity moved people to call the containers magnums rather than jugs. Today the epithet jug is most often used as a pejorative to describe wine of ordinary quality, even if it is sold in a regular-sized, .75-liter bottle.

JULIANA VINEYARDS. Buttes Oil & Gas Co., which has headquarters in Houston, bought 4,700 acres of land in Pope Valley in Napa County in 1974 and has since planted almost 900 acres to wine grapes. There are also olives and vegetables, and more things to come. Juliana sells top varietals to many of Napa's most noted wineries. The operation is named for Maria Juliana Salozar, who married the mountain-man and trapper, William Pope, the original white settler here. He died in 1842 but Maria Juliana and their five children stayed on the land into the twentieth century.

JUSTIN WINERY (BW 5412). Justin Baldwin has 72 acres of vines planted in the hills west of Paso Robles. He bought the old quarter-section in 1981, planting Chardonnay and red Bordeaux varieties there. Baldwin reds can be straight Cabernet Sauvignon or blends, which he calls Isosceles Reserve, a Meritage whose name will suggest its makeup to former geometry students. His other label is Justification. Total production in the mid-1990s was about 20,000 cases per year.

KALIN CELLARS (BW 4871). In 1979 Terrance Leighton bonded a warehouse in Novato in Marin County to serve as his winery. Previously, since 1976, the little operation had occupied a corner of the J. W. Morris Port Works in Emeryville. Leighton, a microbiologist, turns out a wide range of varietal wines, with special emphasis on vineyard-designated Chardonnays. He has also produced some bottle-fermented sparkling wines. His production averages about 6,000 cases per year. *Kalin* is an Indian word meaning ocean.

KARLY (BW 4967). Karly and Larry Cobb began developing their 20-acre vineyard in the 1970s and bonded their winery near Plymouth in Amador County in 1980. Production has risen to 10,000 cases a year in the 1990s, their top varietals being rugged Zinfandels and powerful Sauvignon blancs. They also market wine under the Motherlode Vineyards label.

KAUTZ IRONSTONE VINEYARDS (BW 5517). The Kautz family controls more than 3,400 acres of wine grapes in the Lodi area, their operations dating from 1948. In 1989 on the 1,150-acre family ranch near Murphys in Calaveras County, they began building a remarkable, seven-story, 65,000-square-foot winery, the center of what John Kautz, the chief executive officer, calls the Destination Pointe, a complex of gardens, convention center, concert hall, culinary center, and other

facilities intended, if all goes as planned, to function as the center of an expanded tourist industry in Calaveras County.

The wines from Ironstone Vineyards include a broad range of varietals, some from the estate vineyard, others from the property in Lodi, yet others blends from the two areas. Kautz has acquired the Creekside brand for his distilled products, grappa and apple brandy, produced from their own pot still. Annual wine production is about 150,000 cases.

KEARNEY, M(ARTIN) THEO(DORE) (1838?–1906). A mysterious recluse of English-Irish extraction who made a fortune in Fresno County, Kearney had a huge estate noted more for its raisins than its wine. Little is known of this man, who once had Lillie Langtry to lunch at his mansion, which was modeled on the Château de Chenonceaux in the Loire Valley.

Each spring he traveled to Europe and, in 1906, he died on the liner he boarded shortly after having lived through the earthquake in San Francisco. He left his estate to the University of California, which sold it and bought land outside Fresno to establish the Kearney Agricultural Center, which now acts as the experimental ground for some of the University's work on viticulture.

ROBERT KEENAN WINERY (BW 4747). Peter Conradi planted a vineyard on Spring Mountain in 1891 and built a little winery there above the Napa Valley in 1904. After Prohibition, the family and partners made wine for a few years as Table Mountain Winery and Frontenac Winery before closing down just before World War II. Robert Keenan bonded the place again in 1977 as the Laguna Wine Company; he gave it his own name in 1978. He replanted the old Conradi vineyard, which was up to 62 acres in the mid-1990s. Keenan's emphasis has been on Cabernet Sauvignon and Merlot, the latter of 1984 hailed by some as the finest of the vintage. Total production runs about 10,000 cases per year. In 1995 Nils Venge, an expert on Cabernet Sauvignon, became the winemaker here.

KELLER, MATTHEW (1811–81). A pioneering winegrower in Los Angeles and famous as the owner of the 13,325-acre Rancho Malibu land grant, Keller arrived in southern California in 1851 and began planting vines near Jean-Louis VIGNES's El Aliso Vineyard. In 1858 he wrote a historic report on winemaking in Los Angeles for the Agricultural Department of the U.S. Patent Office. By 1862 he had a depot in San Francisco for his wines, table, sweet, sparkling, and so-called vermouth. Production reached 100,000 gallons in 1868.

Keller was an outspoken critic of the low quality of most California wines, once writing that table wine made from the Mission variety was "fit only for sailors." He corresponded with Louis Pasteur and was an early advocate, as was Eugene HILGARD, of pasteurization as a corrective measure to heal the state's wine infirmities. He called for the planting of better varieties such as Cabernet Sauvignon and Pinot noir.

But the national depression of the 1870s hurt Keller's wine business and forced him to lower his standards. By the end of the decade, there were none of the encomiums in the press for his wines that he had enjoyed in the 1860s. In 1877 he lamented to a correspondent that "the wine business has been a millstone around my neck. . . ." When he died, his Rising Sun and Los Angeles Vineyards became part of the Los Angeles Vintage Company. In 1891 his heirs sold the Malibu estate, with its Malaga Ranch Vineyard, to F. H. Rindge for more than a million dollars.

KENDALL-JACKSON VINEYARDS (BW 5080). In 1974 Jess Stonestreet Jackson, and his then wife, Jane Kendall Jackson, bought an 85-acre pear ranch near Lakeport, in Lake County, and began developing a vineyard. The Jacksons sold most of their grapes to Fetzer, but began to make some wine in 1980, selling it under the Chateau du Lac label. Their winery went up in 1982 and the first Kendall-Jackson wines soon appeared.

Since then, Jess Jackson's wine operation has developed into one of the most successful in California. The emphasis has been on the production of affordable Chardonnay, labeled Vintner's Reserve. But there has been a wide range of varietals, many with vineyard designations. Jackson's motto, particularly for Chardonnay, is "Blending the best with the best." It is not uncommon for this wine to come from grapes grown in four or five different coastal counties.

In 1987 Jackson bought a portion of the huge Tepusquet Vineyard in the Santa Maria Valley in Santa Barbara County, changing the name to CAMBRIA.* In 1988, he acquired the ZELLERBACH WINERY in Chalk Hill in the Alexander Valley. That facility now produces Jackson's Stonestreet line of premium wines. He also bought the EDMEADES WINERY that year and brought it back into production in 1994 for the Kendall-Jackson Zinfandels. The former Domaine Laurier winery in Forestville was acquired by Kendall-Jackson in 1992 and now produces the Hartford Court line of premium wines. In 1995 Kendall-Jackson bought the Gauer Ranch in Alexander Valley and its 417-acre vineyard. This property has the potential for at least 1,000 more acres of vines. By the mid-1990s Jackson controlled about 6,700 acres of vineyard.

Total production in 1985 was 64,000 cases. By 1990 it was 580,000; in 1996 more than 2 million. By far the best-selling, most profitable wine has been the Vintner's Reserve Chardonnay, which has helped make Kendall-Jackson's among the best-selling wines in restaurants all over the country. There are also red and white Meritage wines. The red, Cardinale, has won high critical marks since it first appeared with the 1985 vintage. Other labels, which Jackson combines into his Artisan's and Estates Division, are La Crema, Lakewood, Camelot, and Robert Pepi, the last acquired in 1994 when Kendall-Jackson bought the PEPI winery. (In 1997 Kendall-Jackson announced that a 500,000-case winery would be built on the property.) In 1996 Kendall-Jackson acquired CHATEAU DE BAUN, north of Santa Rosa, for a visitors' center.

In 1995 Jackson began building of a 360,000-case plant in Sonoma, north of Santa Rosa, this after four years of feuding with local opponents of the plan, who were contesting it on environmental grounds. By the 1997 vintage it was in full operation.

KATHRYN KENNEDY WINERY (BW 4895). In 1973 Kathryn Kennedy started planting her 9-acre Cabernet Sauvignon vineyard next to her home in the foothills of the Santa Cruz Mountains above Saratoga. She sold grapes to MARTIN RAY and MOUNT EDEN VINEYARDS and then decided to produce wine with the 1979 vintage. Production of her estate Cabernet is low, the record being 867 cases in 1982; the average runs closer to 500 cases. In 1988, she bought Cabernet franc and Merlot grapes, from which her son, the winemaker Martin Mathis, produced wine for the new Lateral label. Production of both wines now amounts to between 1,000 and 1,500 cases per year.

In 1996 Mathis announced that a housing development would go in soon on a portion of the estate.

KENWOOD VINEYARDS (BW 978) is the successor to a winery that began in the early years of the century. The small village north of Glen Ellen in Sonoma County is the home today of several wineries and has been the site of serious winegrowing since the 1870s. In 1905 the Pagani family built a large bulk winery here and did a land-office business until Prohibition as Pagani & Sons (BW 978). When Julius Pagani died in 1969, his brother John sold the winery to a group of friends and former students he had known when he was a professor of accounting at Santa Clara University. The name was changed to Kenwood Vineyards and gradually the old board-and-batten winery was transformed into a modern producer of premium wine. By the mid-1980s, annual production of a wide range of varietals had exceeded 100,000 cases. At first most of the wine was Zinfandel and Cabernet Sauvignon, later whites became more important, particularly Sauvignon blanc and Chardonnay. Most grapes are purchased in the Sonoma Valley, although the estate vineyard covers 140 acres. Many wines bear vineyard designations. Each vintage since 1975 Kenwood has commissioned an artist to design a label for the Artist Series, a special bottling of Cabernet Sauvignon, several of which have received high critical acclaim. Total Kenwood production had reached 250,000 cases a year in the 1990s. See also KORBEL CHAMPAGNE CELLARS.

KERN COUNTY. At the southern end of the Central Valley, Kern County is desert land converted to agricultural land with irrigation. Since the 1970s there has been an average of 75,000 acres of vineyards there, but the percentage of those in wine grapes has fallen from about 50 percent to less than 35 percent. The typical crush averages between 600,000 and 700,000 tons, of which about half is wine grapes and about 55 percent of those white. Thompson Seedless and French Colombard account for almost half the crush. The rest of the crush consists of red-wine grapes, principally Rubired, Zinfandel, and Grenache. The wines made here are mostly inexpensive jug wines, high-proof brandy, concentrates, and inexpensive varietals. In 1993 about 900 acres of Cabernet Sauvignon yielded about 7,000 tons crushed.

There were a few small vineyards in Kern County by the 1880s, but viticulture did not become a serious activity until 1888 when irrigation water became generally available. Table grapes were the chief products, but during Prohibition there was heavy planting of red wine grapes for shipment east and for concentrates. Not until the 1970s did wine grape statistics again become significant. Between 1954 and 1974 wine grapes, as a percentage of the county's total, rose from 14 to 54 percent, but much of this expansion was the result of mindless investment aimed to provide tax shelters for clients who ended up losing millions. More than 35,000 acres of wine grapes were planted between 1970 and 1975. Today the industrial character of Kern County viticulture and the grape product industry is far more rational than it was 25 years ago.

In 1996 in Kern County about 400,000 tons of grapes were crushed, about 60 percent of those wine grapes. These figures are close to the 1990 numbers.

KEYES, W. S. (1839–1906) was making wines from vineyards on Howell Mountain that were among the best in Napa County at the turn of the century. His "Medoc" (Cabernet Sauvignon) won a gold medal at the 1900 Paris Exposition; his wine collection won the grand prize at the 1904 St. Louis Exposition. Today the modern wineries on Howell Mountain, LIPARITA CELLARS and LA JOTA VINEYARD COMPANY, carry the names of his vineyards.

KINGS COUNTY. E. V. Scazighini planted the first vineyard in the southern San Joaquin Valley in 1876. By the time the county was formed in 1893, split from Tulare County, there were more than 5,000 acres of vines there, mostly muscats. Between 1901 and 1906 an explosion of vineyard planting took place and several large wineries were built to make sweet wine. During the 1920s much of the local tonnage of muscats here was shipped east to home winemakers.

After Repeal acreage declined from about 14,000 acres in 1935 to 4,000 in 1961. That fig-

TABLE 14. WINE GRAPES IN KERN COUNTY, SELECTED VARIETIES

	PERCENT OF TOTAL		CHAR-DONNAY	CHENIN BLANC	FRENCH COLOMBARD	GRENACHE	MERLOT	RUBIRED	RUBY CABERNET	ZIN-FANDEL	TOTAL
YEAR	RED	WHITE				(ACRES)					
1938											1,786
1961	79	21	0	*	0	213	0	*	*	35	3,296
1969	80	20	0	55	386	348	0	490	178	0	6,425
1974	55	45	47	4,844	4,995	3,578	0	5,185	4,802	268	44,409
1980	60	40	12	5,261	6,272	2,525	0	3,223	4,521	86	38,239
1985	40	60	12	5,883	12,191	2,236	0	2,502	2,525	71	35,849
1990	42	58	408	4,836	9,128	2,132	110	2,432	1,403	1,071	27,881
1997	49	51	2,035	3,338	6,808	1,418	1,576	2,949	1,109	1,962	28,879

NOTES: Until 1961 statistics for acreage under various varieties of grapes were not published.

* Nothing is recorded in the official statistics, but it is believed that some Chenin blanc, Rubired, and Ruby Cabernet grapes were being grown in Kern County in 1961.

SOURCE: California Agricultural Statistics Service, Sacramento, Calif.

ure has risen to about 5,000 recently, with about 50 percent in wine varieties.

KIRIGIN CELLARS. See BONESIO WINERY

KISTLER VINEYARDS (BW 4899, 5663). In 1978 Stephen and John Kistler purchased 40 acres of remote land in the hills above Glen Ellen. They planted vines and bought some grapes to be able to market a 1979 Chardonnay that gained rave reviews. Meanwhile Mark Bixler became the winemaker and partner and John eventually left. The quality of the 1980 Kistler Chardonnays dropped so precipitately that the wine made headlines in the California press. Since then Kistler Chardonnays, estate and vineyard designated, have been resounding critical successes. Robert PARKER gave the 1987 estate bottling a 95 rating, a mark he did not repeat in this category until he gave it again to the Kistler 1990.

By the 1990s varietals also included Cabernet Sauvignon and Pinot noir, which brought total production to about 16,000 cases a year. In 1994 new production facilities were set up in Sebastopol, but the old winery on the estate and its bond number were maintained.

KLEIN FAMILY VINTNERS. See RODNEY STRONG VINEYARDS

KLEIN, PIERRE (1855–1922). A native of Alsace, Klein was the first to prove that world-class red table wine could be grown in the Santa Cruz Mountains. For years as the manager of the restaurant in San Francisco's Occidental Hotel, he promoted the best of California wines. Then in 1888 he was hired to run the restaurant and sampling rooms operated by the STATE VITICULTURAL COMMISSION. At the same time he bought land on MONTE BELLO Ridge,* in the hills above the Santa Clara Valley. Determined to produce a fine claret in the style of the Médoc, he planted red Bordeaux varieties, in a venture more personal

than commercial, his intent being "to test and satisfy my ambition."

In the early 1890s he sold his Mira Valle wines to several good restaurants in San Francisco and was persuaded by his friends to enter his wine in the 1895 Bordeaux Exposition, where he won honorable mention. Five years later, to the surprise of no one who was drinking his wine, he, like W. S. KEYES at the same event, won a gold medal for his claret at the Paris Exposition. The result was instant fame; within a year he was selling his wine on the East Coast and receiving plaudits from eastern trade journals.

Klein made about 6,000 gallons per year, but when phylloxera began cutting into production, he did not replant and retired in 1910. Years later his estate became Jimsomare, a source of Zinfandel and Cabernet Sauvignon for RIDGE VINEYARDS, just up the road.

KNAUTH, JACOB. See ORLEANS HILL VINICULTURAL ASSOCIATION

KNIGHT'S VALLEY. An upland valley separating northwest Napa County from the Alexander Valley in Sonoma County, it was granted AVA status in 1983. Most of the 1,100 acres of wine grapes there belong to BERINGER VINEYARDS, and so the grapes go to wineries in Napa Valley. But the connection is also historic: Charles KRUG made his first commercial wine in 1861 from grapes grown in Knight's Valley and Jacob SCHRAM owned a vineyard there in the 1890s. Cabernet Sauvignon and Sauvignon blanc are the predominant grapes, but Merlot and Chardonnay are also grown. Beringer's Knight's Valley Cabernet Sauvignon has been identified by some critics as one of the bargains in California premium wines.

KOHLER, CHARLES (1830–87), was the father of California's commercial wine industry. Years after his death, others who had not lived through the Golden State's formative years

KOHLER & FROHLING

PIONEER WINE HOUSE.   ESTABLISHED 1854.

California Wines and Brandies.

VINEYARDS IN SONOMA CO., MERCED CO., AND FRESNO CO.

COR. SECOND & FOLSOM STS., SAN FRANCISCO   41-45 BROADWAY, NEW YORK.

This 1893 ad for Kohler & Frohling correctly identified the firm as California's "pioneer wine house." The firm won the Best Wine award at the 1858 State Fair. (*Pacific Wine & Spirit Review*)

advanced other candidates, sometimes from ignorance, sometimes for commercial advantage. When Kohler died suddenly in 1887, no one publicly questioned his status in the industry, but he was mourned less for being a great leader of the wine industry than for being a good man and a great leader of his community.

Kohler left his German homeland in 1850 with a fine education and a gift for the violin. He arrived in San Francisco in 1853 and spent the next five years there as a popular and talented musician in a rough frontier town much taken by his renditions of the classics. He met John Frohling, another German musician, and between them they hit upon the idea of taking advantage of California's climate and already established wine culture. Frohling headed off to Los Angeles, bought an old 12-acre vineyard, and began making wine with the 1854 vintage. Kohler kept the young firm of Kohler & Frohling alive with his violin. He also set up a small cellar on Merchant Street and, during the day, much like a milkman, clopped through the streets delivering wine to customers in the city.

The partnership worked well and made money; the partners also helped to establish the ANAHEIM Colony. Kohler made his first shipment of wine to the East Coast in 1858 and by 1860 had a small agency in New York City, but the long sea trips did not improve the wine and those early efforts at export were not profitable. Matters changed in the 1870s after the construction of the transcontinental railroad.

When Frohling died in 1862, the firm controlled an inventory of about 500,000 gallons in its vaults in Los Angeles and San Francisco. By the 1870s, it became clear to Kohler that the future of high-quality California wine rested on the use of good varieties of wine grapes planted in northern coastal counties. In 1874 he shifted the center of his operations when he bought land near Glen Ellen for his great 350-acre Tokay Vineyard and a large winery. This facility became a model for the industry for its textbook efficiency and sparkling cleanliness. Kohler also expanded into the Central Valley where he planted the 600-acre Sierra Vista Vineyard in Fresno County for the production of sweet wine and brandy. He was also a shareholder in the ITALIAN SWISS COLONY.

Kohler was a strong family man (he and his wife Eliza had five daughters and two sons) and was continually active in the civic life of San Francisco from the days of the Second Vigilance Committee (1856). He cofounded California's first bottle factory and was one of the earliest supporters of San Francisco's cable car system. During the Civil War, he worked tirelessly for the Union cause. He later helped found a local insurance company and the German Savings Bank. He was a member of the school board, a director of the city library, and an author of the city charter. (For a portrait made in about 1875, see page 49).

His death was mourned as if a saint had passed. Charles WETMORE wrote, "I feel lost now because I do not see where his successor can be found." Another civic leader lamented, "The glory of San Francisco is passing away." No one for a moment questioned Kohler's historic position. Wetmore called him "the pioneer and founder of the present wine trade in California." In memoriam, the great California historian H. H. BANCROFT wrote that "the wine manufacture of California today is a monument to the wisdom, the enterprise, and the industry of Charles Kohler."

Kohler & Frohling was still an important factor in the state's wine industry when in 1894 it became part of the CALIFORNIA WINE ASSOCIATION.

KONOCTI WINERY (BW 4929). Originally a growers' cooperative organization established in 1974, its members controlled about 500 acres of vineyard land in Lake County. Their first wines appeared in 1977, produced at FRANCISCAN. They built a winery near Kelseyville in 1979, naming for the great and dead volcano that dominates the Clear Lake area. In 1983 the PARDUCCI family became partners in the operation. Other partners came aboard in later years. By the 1990s, production was about 50,000 cases a year, with emphasis on Sauvignon blanc, Cabernet Sauvignon, Chardonnay, and Merlot. In 1998 Jed Steele bought the facility for STEELE WINES.

KONRAD ESTATE. See FIFE VINEYARDS

KORBEL CHAMPAGNE CELLARS (F. Korbel & Bros.) (BW 74). The Korbel estate is the finest survivor of the impressive nineteenth-century wine history of Sonoma County. The great old winery (built in 1886) and brandy tower (built in 1889) look out on the Russian River a few miles east of Guerneville.

The Korbel story in America begins in the 1860s when three brothers came to California from the Czech region of the Austrian Empire. Francis (1832–1920) was the leader and intellectual muscle behind the Korbel empire; Antone and Josef played secondary roles. Czech was their mother tongue but they were more German in culture. Stories of their fleeing the harsh Austrian rule of the Hapsburgs are untrue; Francis was appointed Austrian consul in San Francisco in 1893.

At first Korbel Mills was a lumber operation, part of the product used by Francis in his cigar manufacturing company. Tradition tells of the end of Korbel lumbering after the first-growth redwoods were cut, but the production of redwood tanks continued here into the 1890s and Francis incorporated the Korbel Box Co. in 1903. But as the land was cleared across the river from the mill, winegrowing did become important. By the 1890s it was big business. The Korbel success story is closely connected to the company's development of a market in Chicago after the winery's success in the 1893 Columbian Exposition. Even more important eventually was the market in Wisconsin with its large German population. That state still buys more Korbel BRANDY* per capita than any other state does.

Korbel's destiny was sealed in 1896 when Francis hired a fellow Czech, Franz Hazek, to make a sparkling wine. The Korbels had previously made small lots of sparkling wine, but they were not particularly successful. By 1899 the venture was a success, symbolically manifested that year in the christening of the USS *Wisconsin* with a bottle of the new Viking brand. In 1907 a far better product was released, crafted by Jan Hanuska, the new champagne master. These new Korbel Sec and Grand Pacific brands made the company one of the top three producers of bottle-fermented sparkling wines in North America.

Korbel still wines were also successful. The most remarkable came from Bohemian varietals that Francis imported and marketed under their Slavonic names, Zernosek and Melnik. The former won a grand prize at the 1915 Panama-Pacific Exposition.

Hanuska worked for the second generation of Korbels after Prohibition, producing one of California's best sparklers. In 1939 Frank SCHOONMAKER encouraged the old man to make a drier wine and the result was Korbel Brut, for years a standard in the industry.

In 1954 the Korbels sold the business to the HECK family. Adolf Jr. became the winemaker, Paul ran the vineyards, and Ben became sales manager. Production facilities were revitalized and in 1956 Korbel brandy was back on the market. Attempts to revive a line of Korbel still wines were not financially successful. But over the years the Heck family modernized the complicated traditional French method for producing sparkling wine and sales for that and for brandy soared. Wine sales went from 10,000 cases in 1954 to 25,000 in 1960. By the 1990s Korbel was selling more than 1 million cases of sparkling wine and almost 500,000 cases of brandy a year. Primarily to acquire the latter, Anheuser-Busch bought Korbel in 1991. Two years later the Armstrong Ridge line of lower-priced bubbly was added to the Korbel line. Members of the Heck family have stayed to guide the still-expanding operation (see HECK). The Korbel estate has become one of Sonoma's favorite tourist attractions. The old winery there is no longer used for production but contains an excellent historical museum. The effect of the Anheuser-Busch capital can be seen in Korbel's recent acquisition of a sizable portion of the KENWOOD VINEYARDS operation, after which Kenwood bought the VALLEY OF THE MOON WINERY with the intention of using the old facility and winery for another line of premium varietals. In 1995 Korbel had acquired the LAKE SONOMA WINERY for the same reasons.

KORNELL, HANNS (1911–94). For many years Hanns Kornell was the leading producer of sparkling wines in Napa Valley. Born in Germany, the son of a Jewish winegrowing family, he studied enology at the Geisenheim Institute. In 1939 he barely escaped from the country. Once in America he made sparkling wine for COOK'S IMPERIAL and at FOUNTAINGROVE. In 1952 he rented the old Sonoma Wine Company

building in the town of Sonoma (BW 870) and began producing a wide variety of wines, but bottle-fermented sparkling wine was what he really wanted to make.

In 1958 he was able to buy the old LARKMEAD WINERY north of St. Helena and within a few years was the master of bottle-fermented sparkling wine in the Napa Valley. By the 1970s production was up to 35,000 cases a year, 80,000 cases in the 1980s. Many of his creations did not fit the French model for such wines: what he called Sehr Trocken (instead of Brut) was made from White Riesling and he made sparklers from muscats.

In 1986, to upgrade his facility, he borrowed $3,000,000, but a complex of unfortunate events cut his sales and eventually led to bankruptcy in 1991 and foreclosure in 1992. The Napa community rallied to help the old fighter, who had also suffered severe injuries from a fall in 1988. The ROMBAUER family bought the old winery and brought it back to life as Kornell-Larkmead Cellars. The Robert MONDAVI family, shortly before Hanns's death in July 1994, bought the family home, which was about to be foreclosed on, granting Hanns and his wife, Marilouise, life tenancy.

KOSHER WINE. Wine is kosher (meaning right or correct) when it is made under strict rabbinical supervision, according to prescribed practices, and handled in the cellar only by religious Jews who observe the Sabbath, a proscription that applies also to workers in the vineyards. The wine must be held in containers deemed kosher, and all products associated with the winemaking must themselves be kosher. In the 1990s these strictures added about $6.00 to the cost of producing a case of kosher table wine in California. Some kosher wines are pasteurized (*mevushal*), a process that, experts believe, weakens red, but not necessarily white, table wines and sweet wines.

Before Prohibition, kosher wines in California came mostly from producers on the East

Coast, although there were a few small-scale operations here. During Prohibition, huge shipments of so-called kosher wine were made in California and shipped to the East Coast to so-called rabbis, until the government cracked down in 1923. After Repeal, a few wineries in southern California made kosher table wine on a small scale but they did not last. Again Jews in California had to drink sweet wines from eastern producers at Passover, until the 1970s, when a few producers in northern California began making high-quality kosher table wine from premium varietals. Brands developed here since the late 1970s include HAGAFEN, WEINSTOCK, GAN EDEN, BARON HERZOG, Teal Lake, J. Furst, and Mount Marona (ST. SUPÉRY). In 1995 Wente announced a joint operation with an Israeli winery to produce kosher wines.

KRUG, CHARLES (1825–92). One of the most important names in California wine history. Krug did not have a background in German wine when he came to California in 1852. He had attended the University of Marburg and took part in the German Revolution of 1848, which landed him in jail for his liberal, democratic views. He started in San Francisco as a newspaper editor, then bought land in San Mateo County near that of Agoston HARASZTHY. He too worked at the San Francisco Mint with the wily Hungarian and headed off to Sonoma with him in 1857. That is where Krug probably learned to make wine, after planting a vineyard on his Montebello Ranch next to Haraszthy and DRESEL.

In 1858 Krug borrowed a hand press and made wine for John Patchett in Napa. Next year he went up-valley and made wine for Edward Bale near the future site of St. Helena. He also met Bale's daughter Carolina; they were married in December 1860, but first he put his property in Sonoma up for sale, with the understanding that his new wife's dowry of 540 acres would be the site of a new and

expanded Krug winegrowing operation. Meanwhile, before the wedding, he made George YOUNT's wine for him. In 1861 he made his first Napa wine from grapes grown in the Knight's Valley in Sonoma. He planted 23 acres of vines and built a "small rude cellar" close to where today's Charles Krug Winery stands. By 1872 he had a real stone cellar (see page 232) with a 250,000-gallon capacity. By the time he died, the capacity of his winery had grown to 800,000 gallons.

Krug had a reputation for good wines, but he was a poor businessman, even going through temporary bankruptcy in 1885. He is remembered today for his great estate and its wines, but his friends, neighbors and associates in the industry knew and loved him for qualities not measured in gallons or acres. He was the conscience of his winemaking community, a pillar of constant integrity, and a steady voice in favor of higher standards and better quality. In this he stood shoulder to shoulder with HILGARD, Dresel, and CRABB. He organized the growers and producers in Napa Valley and showed the rest of the state how to do it. He demonstrated how to take an issue affecting local interests and publicize it through broader agencies. A member of the State Viticultural Commission, he was a voice of reason among what was often a cacophony of egocentric showoffs. Along with Charles KOHLER, Krug must be considered as one of the best-loved Californians of his time. His death after 18 months of physical torment made many wonder at the vagaries of life.

The great estate passed into the hands of the capitalist James K. Moffitt who placed it under the management of Krug's nephew, Bismark BRUCK. He expanded the operation and brought more esteem to the Krug name, which has been attached to the property since 1861. During Prohibition, the estate was little more than a grape ranch. At Repeal Louis Stralla (see NAPA (VALLEY) WINE COMPANY) leased the winery and for several years produced large quantities of what he called "heavy *paisano* red" bulk wine for sale to eastern bottlers.

In 1943 Cesare MONDAVI bought the Krug ranch and a family corporation, **C. Mondavi & Sons,** was set up under his sons, Robert and Peter. They modernized the somewhat decrepit old winery and, by the 1950s, it was an early leader in the quality revolution in California wines. The brothers' white table wines, particularly the Chenin blanc, were great successes, the products of their work on revolutionary cold-fermentation techniques. By the 1960s **Charles Krug Winery** (BW 3110) controlled 600 acres and had a capacity of 2 million gallons. Production included a very wide range of varietal and generic table wine, dessert wine, and the CK line of less-expensive, generic table wines.

Cesare died in 1959 and a severe family schism developed. Robert and his family were forced out and in 1966 he founded his own winery in Oakville. Even though he still held his shares in Charles Krug Winery, he had no say in its management and Peter and his family restructured the corporation in a manner that kept Robert from receiving his full share of the corporation's profits. In 1976 Robert brought a lawsuit against Peter and other family members and won a huge settlement. The ruling held that Peter's "fraudulent activities" had made him the father of two millionaire sons. Eventually the matter was settled in a way that left Krug in Peter's hands, but shackled him with a large debt that hampered renovation and development in the 1980s.

In recent years, the Krug winery has grown to about 6 million gallons in capacity, which is backed with about 1,000 acres of Napa grapes. In 1990 Peter and his family bought 900 acres of land in Yolo County to expand the vineyard. Those grapes would go primarily to the FIGHTING VARIETAL CK Mondavi brand, which amounts to about 60 percent of the Krug production. Wine from grapes grown in Napa grapes comes to about 200,000 cases per year. (Total production was about 600,000 cases.) In the 1990s wine writers have remarked on the improvement in Charles Krug varietals, particularly Chardonnay from Carneros. The Vintage Selection Cabernet Sauvignon is probably the winery's most famous wine.

THOMAS KRUSE WINERY (BW 4566). Thomas Kruse was selling supplies to home winemakers when he founded his little winery in the Hecker Pass area of the Santa Clara Valley in 1971. He has a 1-acre vineyard there and produces about 4,000 cases of wine each year, mainly Chardonnay and Zinfandel. He is perhaps most noted for having made a varietal wine labeled Thompson Seedless in 1975.

KUNDE ESTATE WINERY (BW 2020). In 1884 Karl Louis Kunde, a native of Germany, came to Sonoma and took up winegrowing near Windsor. In 1904 he purchased James Shaw's Wildwood Ranch near Glen Ellen and began making wine there. Shaw's oldest vines were probably planted in the late 1870s; some were planted onto resistant ROOTSTOCK in the 1880s. Zinfandel vines from those days still survive on the Kunde estate.

In 1911 Kunde had expanded the capacity of Wildwood Winery to 100,000 gallons and had developed a good reputation for Cabernet Sauvignon and Zinfandel, the latter winning a gold medal at the 1915 Panama-Pacific Exposition. After Repeal the Kunde family revived the winery for a few years but settled on grape growing and cattle raising until the winery was rebuilt, expanded, and reopened in 1990 as Kunde Estate Winery.

By then the ranch covered 2,000 acres with three vineyards totaling almost 700 acres. Included on the property today are the well-preserved ruins of J. H. DRUMMOND's Dunfillan Winery. The first crush at the new Kunde facility was in 1990 and was housed in newly dug caves, whose tunnels measure over half a mile in length. To date the main emphasis has been on Cabernet Sauvignon, Chardonnay and Merlot. Zinfandel, from James Shaw's 28 acres of old vines, is made in smaller quantities. The total annual production of the winery is about 95,000 cases.

Before the Kunde family went back into the winemaking business, a pretty white barn stood next to the highway on their property near Kenwood. In 1990 they built this winery, a greatly expanded copy of the old barn. (Kunde Estate)

LABEL. Before the 1860s wine labels were virtually unknown in California or in Europe. But standardized bottles, good glue, and the widespread retail sale of wine by the bottle brought the evolution of the label over the next century. Before World War II most commercial wines in California were sold in bulk to merchants who blended their wines, bottled them, and affixed their own labels, usually using generic terms such as claret and burgundy. Rarely was a winery named on the label unless the merchant actually owned a winery, as did Charles KOHLER and LACHMAN & JACOBI.

Names suggesting varietal wines were rare, but some were labeled Zinfandel, Cabernet, or Riesling. Before 1906 there was virtually no government control on the labeling of wines. Rigorous and systematic government supervision at the national and state levels began in 1934.

In the early days some producers did establish their own brands, but this was usually done by setting up a bottling depot in a city distant from the Bay Area and shipping the wine in bulk to that point, where it was bottled and labeled. Nevertheless, numerous California wineries did serve a local and regional home market under their own names, so that one might find a bottle of Almaden wine on a retail shelf in Oakland in 1895. Producers often sold bottled and labeled wine at the winery, to their neighbors, and to stores in nearby towns.

But more often such sales were made in small barrels and large jugs.

During the Progressive Era, between 1900 and 1915, Americans came to accept the idea that producers had a responsibility to convey the truth on the package sold to the consumer, an idea that led to our pure food and drug laws. Since the days of the New Deal, a battle has raged over what degree of truth was enough. In recent years there has been an even more bitter struggle over what was the truth.

During World War II the legend "bottled at the winery" became the mark of premium wines from California. The practice developed because tank cars for shipping wine in bulk to eastern bottlers were not always available, owing to the war effort. Thus, there were more and more national brands with nationally recognized labels. But before this development, and since Repeal, many premium producers of table wines had been bottling at the winery and nationally recognized premium brands were numerous.

In the 1950s labels started to evolve. An additional label, usually on the back of the bottle, was often used to give the consumer more information about the wine and the producer, sometimes with a few words about the area where the grapes were grown. Some wineries began using "estate-bottled" on their labels. For years the industry and the BATF went back and forth on which terms had strictly defined meanings and which did not. What was "premium" wine? How high did the vineyards need to be for "mountain wine?" What percentage of an indicated varietal had to be in a varietal wine?

In the 1970s the BATF began rationalizing much of the information found on a label; see AMERICAN VITICULTURAL AREA; ESTATE BOTTLING; GENERIC; VARIETALS. But there has been continuous dissension between the agency and the producers about what is reasonable. Today the federal government strictly controls some of the language on wine labels. The consumer will have a better idea about the wine in the bottle by knowing these rules. There are many others.

Varietal designation   After 1936 a varietal wine had to contain but 51 percent of the indicated grape. Since 1983 that limit has been 75 percent.

Alcohol   Labels must give some indication of alcohol content. If the percentage is indicated, it must be within 1.5 percent of that figure; fortified wines containing more than 14 percent alcohol must be within 1 percent. Federal law permits wineries simply to use the term "table wine" for wines under 14 percent, but some states require a number.

Producer   The label must give the address of the brand, but not necessarily the name of the winery where the wine was produced. If the term "produced and bottled by" is on the label, the indicated winery will have crushed and fermented at least 75 percent of the wine in the bottle. Other expressions that begin with such words as "made by," "vinted by," or "cellared by" do not inform the consumer about the producing winery. Most wineries intent on high quality and on supplying the consumer with information about the origins of the wine do not use these expressions.

Vintage date   At least 95 percent of the wine that carries a vintage date must have been fermented in that calendar year.

Viticultural area   At least 85 percent of the grapes for wines with a viticultural area designation (AVA) must have been grown there. If the label designation is a state or a county, the required percentage is 75.

Warnings on wine labels have also been a source of disagreement in recent years. Virtually all American wines now carry a warning about sulfites, and there is a general label required that warns pregnant women, drivers, and everyone else of the potential dangers of alcohol consumption.

Label design has long been an important part of the marketing programs of wine producers. By the 1870s print shops in San Francisco were turning out elegant labels for top wineries with established brands. Max Schmidt's shop was the most highly respected. J. H. DRUMMOND's labels, for example, were white on black with two Maltese crosses and the shield of the Captain's old regiment, the 34th Cumberland. After Repeal labels tended to retain much of their old-style complexity, although some wineries simply ordered blank labels from sample books and had them printed up.

By the 1970s marketing specialists modified or changed most labels to attract the attention of prospective wine buyers in the shops. New wineries often sought out consultants for help. Many wineries developed second labels, or more, to diversify their product line. Numerous labels today are simply for brands and give little information about the producer of the wine. There has also been a conceptual revolution in California wine labels since the 1970s. There is no longer a standard shape. Some back labels are now part of a wraparound front label; some are actually etched on the bottle.

Label collecting has become an increasingly popular ancillary activity for some wine drinkers, the labels being kept as souvenirs, or, sometimes, to decorate a bar or wall. In fact, label collecting has taken on some of the characteristics of philately. Since 1982 the library of the University of California at Irvine has been developing a historical collection of California wine labels. By the 1990s there were more than 40,000 labels in the collection.

Marian W. Baldy, *The University Wine Course* (San Francisco: Wine Appreciation Guild 1993, 309–25.

LABOR. In the mission and rancho periods Indians in California were the chief source of labor in the vineyard and many took a part in the winemaking. This situation continued through the 1850s, but in the 1860s important changes took place in the workforce. By the 1870s Chinese and white labor were dominant, a situation that often led to tension and violence. A large number of winery owners and vineyardists came to rely on Chinese workers, often considered more dependable than itinerant "native white labor."

By the 1880s most wineries, and many vineyardists had developed a basic year-round workforce, mostly white, but there were places such as Inglenook where Chinese workers held key positions. During the harvest, of course, the workforce was augmented with temporary hands. The cyclical nature of the California fruit harvest, cherries in May and June, apricots in June, plums and prunes in July and August, grapes in September, made it possible for winegrowers to develop a certain continuity even in their itinerant workforce.

Labor contractors were an important part of the vintage scene in northern California, much of the contracted help coming from towns and cities in the area. But the local population in the coastal valleys, including women and school children, always supplied a sizeable number of the grape pickers. In 1889 schools in Napa were let out to bring in a rain-threatened vintage. During World War I school children and women in the Lodi area could make $3.00 per day harvesting grapes; that was good money.

In rural America before World War II, most of the agricultural workforce was made up of unmarried, itinerant male workers. This meant that wine towns such as St. Helena, Healdsburg, and San Jose had plenty of saloons and brothels, and their full share of violence. In California from the 1870s into the 1920s, this force included numerous recent immigrants from Europe, East Asia, and Mexico. After World War II this force was more and more Hispanic or Latino and is so today. Since the 1970s California vineyardists and winery owners have tended to promote more stable relations with their workers and to strive for more harmonious continuity in their harvest and cellar workforce. Unionization in the 1970s and 1980s brought tension and some strikes, but it also brought a means to solve grievances. Tension has been most obvious where corporate decisions, made in places distant from the vineyard and cellar have come down hard on workers. The downsizing that comes with corporate consolidation was a common occurrence in the 1980s among large producers, and was always a threat to the mostly indoor workers whose jobs were threatened.

LACHMAN & JACOBI Samuel Lachman (1825–92) came to California from Germany in 1852. He became a wine merchant in San Francisco in 1864. In 1876 S. Lachman & Co. became Lachman & Jacobi when Frederick Jacobi (1846–1911) became a partner. By the 1880s the firm was one of the most powerful in San Francisco. In 1889 it bought and expanded a winery near Fresno, naming it LacJac (later the Christian Brothers' Mount Tivy Winery— BW 3670). The firm tried to fight the CALIFORNIA WINE ASSOCIATION (CWA) when it was formed in 1894 and acquired the sobriquet "wine trust," but soon joined up. Henry Lachman (1861–1915), Samuel's son, then became one of the association's leaders, with a reputation, before Prohibition, as California's greatest wine taster. Lachman & Jacobi thrived as part of the CWA, expanding into the Sonoma and San Jose areas between 1905 and 1912. With the onset of Prohibition, the company dissolved its assets after 1919.

LA CREMA (BW 5734). Since 1993 a brand owned by KENDALL-JACKSON and produced in Forestville, Sonoma. About 80,000 cases, of mostly Chardonnay and Pinot noir, are sold a year.

LA CREMA VIÑERA (BW 4914) began operation in 1979 in Petaluma. Beset by financial problems and changing ownership, the operation was reorganized as La Crema (BW 5479) in 1991 and moved to Sebastopol. There, annual production grew to about 70,000 cases before the winery went bankrupt in 1993. The following year, KENDALL-JACKSON acquired the La Crema brand.

LACTIC ACID. A mild or soft acid associated with milk (hence its name) and often found in wine. The second, or malolactic, FERMENTATION* in many red wines and some whites transforms the more tart malic acid into lactic acid. Lactic acid bacteria may be introduced to the fermenting or young wine to promote this effect. Development of lactic acid can be inhibited by sulfur dioxide, high acid concentration, and low temperature. One of the common disasters of early winemaking in California were the off-flavors developed during hot fermentations when unwanted strains of lactic bacteria went wild. The result was a "milk-sour" wine. Today's careful California winemaker is constantly aware of the possible value and dangers of lactic acid bacteria. See also ACID.

LA JOTA VINEYARD CO. (BW 5094). In 1844 George YOUNT was granted a 4,400-acre spread on Howell Mountain that was called Rancho La Jota. *Jota* is the letter J in Spanish; it is also a Spanish folk dance and a vegetable soup. Why the rancho was so named is not known, although an old tale tells of an Indian chieftain there named Jota. By the end of the 1880s the rancho lands were held by scores of speculators, settlers, and winegrowers. In 1898 Frederick Hess built a little winery on his Pine Crest estate here and was producing between 10,000 and 20,000 gallons until Prohibition. In 1974 William and Joan Smith bought the property, planted 28 acres of vines, and bonded the old Hess winery in 1982 as La Jota Vineyard Co. Their first vintage was that year.

Although the Smiths' wines run the gamut from Petite Sirah to Viognier, the fame of the winery rests on its highly acclaimed Cabernet Sauvignon. Total annual production in the 1990s was about 4,000 cases. There was also Pinot noir under the W. H. Smith label from Sonoma Coast grapes.

Frederick Hess was the Swiss-German publisher of the *San Francisco Demokrat,* and built a stone winery on Howell Mountain in 1898. Today the old structure is the home of the La Jota Vineyard Co., named for George YOUNT's rancho in this area.

LAKE COUNTY. Just north of Napa County, Lake County has a long history of winegrowing, but it is only since the 1970s that it has become really significant. The county is dominated by Clear Lake, the largest natural body of fresh water inside California. Above it stands Mount Konocti, an ancient volcano. The lake today is surrounded by the CLEAR LAKE Viticultural Area, which contains more than 90 percent of the county's vineyard land.

Commercial winegrowing here began in the 1870s when David Voight planted his vineyard near the town of Lower Lake. By 1890 there were eight wineries and forty-eight growers with about 1,000 acres of vines. Red table wine was the chief product and evaluations from that time indicate that the Region II–III climate (see HEAT SUMMATION) and the volcanic soils produced good wines. But, because no railroad was ever built into Lake County, the relative isolation limited the growth of the wine industry there. By 1920 there were only about 300 acres of vines left.

But there is a lot of wine-related history here. Lillie Langtry had her vineyards in the Guenoc Valley, and Serranus Hastings, a Chief Justice of the California Supreme Court, had a 60-acre Zinfandel vineyard near Upper Lake. Some of the first experiments with phylloxera-resistant rootstock were carried out here by W. C. Mottier.

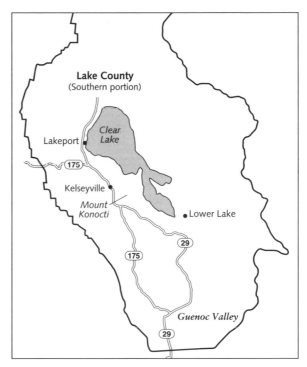

Lake County

Grapes, totaling about 150 acres in the late 1960s, were no match for the more than 8,000 acres of pears in the county. The 1970s saw a rush of vineyard planting around the lake. By 1973 there were more than 2,000 acres, mostly of red table-wine varieties. The total has

TABLE 15. WINE GRAPES IN LAKE COUNTY, SELECTED VARIETIES

YEAR	PERCENT OF TOTAL RED	WHITE	CABERNET SAUVIGNON	CHARDONNAY	(ACRES) MERLOT	SAUVIGNON BLANC	ZINFANDEL	TOTAL
1970	87	13	232	0	0	34	158	450
1974	91	9	1,267	0	141	75	278	2,150
1979	80	20	1,185	5	69	247	305	2,469
1985	58	42	1,196	321	85	652	330	3,194
1990	57	43	1,163	553	116	608	390	3,238
1996	52	48	928	769	444	819	434	3,842

SOURCE: California Agricultural Statistics Service, Sacramento, Calif.

grown to about 3,500 acres in the 1990s, almost half of them Chardonnay and Sauvignon blanc. There are seven wineries in the county, but many growers sell to producers elsewhere for wines to be labeled North Coast. In 1981 vineyardists in Mendocino and Sonoma counties fought to have Lake County excluded from the North Coast AVA, but the BATF ruled Lake County vineyardists may indeed sell their grapes to wineries outside the county to be made into wines carrying the North Coast appellation—at times an economic advantage. A development in the 1980s was the move by wineries, in Napa, Sonoma, and Mendocino counties, among them Louis MARTINI, GEYSER PEAK, PARDUCCI, and BERINGER, to buy and develop Lake County vineyard land.

In 1996 vineyards in Lake County produced 11,741 tons of wine grapes, 152 percent of the total produced in 1990. Tonnage was split evenly between red and white varieties.

LAKE SONOMA WINERY (BW 4810). In 1977 L. K. Borowski founded the Diablo Vista Winery near Benicia. Robert Polson had grown vines in the Dry Creek Valley in Sonoma since 1971 and in 1982 his family bought Diablo Vista and changed the name to Lake Sonoma, after the huge reservoir north of his property. In 1987 the Polsons moved the winemaking to Dry Creek. There they produced about 4,000 cases of wine a year from numerous varietals, including the Cinsaut, from an old vineyard in Sonoma planted to Black Malvoisie. Polson's death in 1995 left the future of the winery in doubt for a while until the next year when Gary Heck and KORBEL bought the operation.

LAKEVILLE. See JAMES GRAHAM FAIR; SAN-GIACOMO VINEYARDS

LAMANDA PARK. See SIERRA MADRE VINTAGE CO.

LAMBERT BRIDGE (BW 4725). In 1969 Gerard Lambert planted his vineyard in the Dry Creek Valley, Sonoma, and between 1973 and 1975 built his winery, making mainly Chardonnay, Cabernet Sauvignon, and Merlot. As annual production expanded toward 20,000 cases, Lambert arranged with Seagram to market his wine. When Seagram sold the wine heavily discounted, Lambert went to court in 1987 but lost the case in 1992. He then closed the winery. It is now owned by the Chambers family and produces about 12,000 cases a year, chiefly of Merlot, Zinfandel, and Chardonnay.

LAMBORN FAMILY VINEYARDS (BW 5389). Robert Lamborn makes about 1,500 cases of powerful Howell Mountain Zinfandel from the vineyard he acquired in 1973. He bonded his winery in 1989 and often buys grapes from his neighbors on the mountain. Lamborn retired in 1998, but his son Michael continues to make wine, and still Zinfandel only.

LAMONT WINERY. See BEAR MOUNTAIN WINERY

LANDMARK VINEYARDS (BW 4731). William Mabry began planting vines near Windsor in Sonoma in 1973 on part of the historic Cunningham estate. Backed by several partners, he added vineyards in the Alexander Valley, Sonoma, and bonded Landmark in 1974. Beginning with a wide range of varietals, the winery came to concentrate on producing Chardonnay. Urban development and rising land prices around Windsor encouraged the owners to move. Damaris Etheridge, an original investor, underwrote both the 1989 move to Kenwood and the new winery. Mabry stayed on until 1992, but the operation is now controlled by Mrs. Etheridge and her family. Etheridge, a great-great-granddaughter of John Deere, owned interests in twenty-seven investment partnerships in several fields in 1990. Landmark's annual production in the

1990s had exceeded the 20,000 cases, still concentrated on high-quality Chardonnay.

LANDSBERGER, ISADOR (1824–1904). A native of Berlin, Landsberger arrived in San Francisco in 1853 and was an early investor in the BUENA VISTA VINICULTURAL SOCIETY. Meanwhile, on California Street, he set up his own wine house, which continued to operate after his death under his son, Henry. But his major claim to fame comes from his interest in developing a bottle-fermented sparkling wine. He hired Arpad HARASZTHY in 1865 and the two worked for years developing the wine eventually named ECLIPSE.* Landsberger was much loved by the leaders of the state's wine industry, although he himself was never a power in it. The list of pallbearers at his funeral reads like a Who's Who of the industry.

LANZA, HORACE O. (1881–1983), was born in Sicily and came to New York in 1891, receiving his law degree there in 1901. His first contact with winegrowing was as a youth in the Concord grape country around Fredonia, New York. During Prohibition he came to California and entered the grape concentrate business at Colonial Grape Products in Elk Grove. Soon after Repeal, he controlled wineries at Windsor, St. Helena, Napa, and Elk Grove. In 1943 he gained control of the Italian Vineyard Co. (see GUASTI). He retired in 1969 and has recorded his remarkable history for the Bancroft Library at the University of California at Berkeley.

LA PALOMA WINERY. See M. F. TARPEY

LA PERLA. A beautiful wine estate on Spring Mountain, Napa, founded by Charles Lemme who built a small winery there in 1876. At the turn of the century it became part of Claus SCHILLING's holdings and a larger winery, still standing, was built. In 1903 the 320-acre estate was incorporated as Spring Mountain Vineyard Co. and later as La Perla Vineyard Co. After

Repeal the Schilling property was owned by the Solano Wine Co. of Claus Mangels and Horace LANZA. In 1943 the Draper family acquired the lower ranch of the estate. The upper ranch was acquired by Fritz MAYTAG in 1969 and is now York Creek Vineyards. The La Perla name is now associated only with the Drapers' vineyard holdings. In 1995 a portion of the Draper property was acquired by the new owners of SPRING MOUNTAIN VINEYARDS.

LA QUESTA. Emmett H. Rixford (1846–1928) gave the name, La Questa, to his property in the hills of San Mateo County when he founded his winegrowing estate in 1883, today in the town of Woodside. On a small cuesta he planted his 40 acres of red Bordeaux varieties in the precise proportions that they were grown at Château Margaux. By the turn of the century his Medoc-style wine was considered one of the finest in California. Some of the vines he

E. H. Rixford created this label for his Cabernets, using the script from the label used by Louis Roederer in France for Champagne. Later, Mario GEMELLO and Martin RAY, both of whom made wine from grapes grown on the old property in Woodside, used the same basic design and script for their own labels.

replanted between 1895 and 1905 still produce grapes for the Cabernet Sauvignon from WOODSIDE VINEYARDS. In 1887 Rixford published *The Wine Press and the Cellar,* a meticulous compilation of winemaking practices written for the California producer.

Rixford's family briefly revived winemaking at the old winery after Repeal (BW 1996). In 1945 GEMELLO bought the winery equipment and wine inventory.

LARKMEAD-KORNELL CELLARS. See HANNS KORNELL; LARKMEAD WINERY; ROMBAUER VINEYARDS

LARKMEAD WINERY (F. Salmina & Co.; BW 605). The Larkmead area is about midway between St. Helena and Calistoga in Napa Valley and draws its name from the home and property there of Lillie Hitchcock Coit (1843–1929), the darling of the San Francisco Fire Department. (Coit Tower in San Francisco, a memorial to the city's volunteer firemen, resulted from her $100,000 bequest; see also THREE PALMS VINEYARD.)

When S. P. Connor built his 50,000-gallon winery here in 1884, he called it Larkmead. It went through several hands before it was acquired in 1895 by Felix Salmina (1861–1940) and his uncle, John Baptiste Salmina (1834–1907). They were Italian-Swiss from Locarno and had deep family and business roots in the Napa Valley. The winery prospered, vineyards were expanded, and in 1906 the family was able to build a large stone winery, which still stands near where the trains once stopped at Larkmead Station. (In 1982 the winery was added to the National Register of Historic Places.) Meanwhile the Salmina wines, marketed under the Larkmead brand, were acquiring a good reputation for quality. The brand was revived at Repeal and the premium luster returned immediately. Only BERINGER won more medals at the new State Fair competition in 1936. Next year Salmina

won first-place awards for Zinfandel and Cabernet. But after his death in 1940, the winery went through several corporate ownerships and by the mid-1950s Larkmead had virtually no standing as a premium brand. In 1958 Hanns KORNELL acquired the winery for his sparkling wine cellar. In 1993 the ROMBAUER family took over the old plant and renamed it Larkmead-Kornell.

LASSEN, PETER. See TEHAMA COUNTY

LAS VINAS WINERY (BW 5331). The Cotta family sells most of the grapes from its 800 acres of vineyard land in the Lodi area. But since 1986 the Cottas have been producing varietal wines under their own brand name. Production now is about 12,000 cases per year and rising. Their second label is Quinta do Cotta.

LATE-HARVEST WINE. Beginning in the late 1960s, some wineries in California began producing red and white wines from late-harvested grapes usually very high in sugar. The model for the whites was usually Germanic, and when possible the wine was infected by BOTRYTIS CINEREA.* White Riesling and Gewürztraminer were the most popular varieties. Some producers also aimed at the Sauternes model with Sémillon and Sauvignon blanc grapes. Since the 1970s, such wines have been a small part of the premium dessert wine production in California, set off from the main body of ports and sherries by the fact that they are unfortified and are almost always identified by variety. For a short time some of these wines had such German terms as *Spätlese* and *Auslese* on their labels, but this practice was outlawed by the BATF in the mid-1970s.

Late-harvest red wines were also part of this development. Grapes high in sugar might produce sweet and/or high-alcohol wines. Zinfandel was a particularly popular variety for this style. Such wines are rarely seen today but they still have their advocates; some cellars still contain relics of this era that are well loved by some few connoisseurs of the style.

LAUREL GLEN VINEYARD (BW 5010). Patrick Campbell's vineyard property on Sonoma Mountain was planted in 1968; he bought it in 1977 and has concentrated on Cabernet Sauvignon and other red Bordeaux varieties ever since. His first wine went to market in 1984. Since then his wines have gained solid critical acclaim, the result of intense concentration on vineyard practices and focused, traditional winemaking techniques. Campbell's vineyard of about 40 acres is divided into distinct blocks. The best lots from the estate go to the top-of-the-line Laurel Glen label, others go into the Counterpoint Cuvée. Terra Rosa is a second label used for wines from grapes grown elsewhere. Total production is about 35,000 cases per year.

Dennis Schaeffer, *Vintage Talk* (Santa Barbara, Calif.: Capra Press, 1994).

LAURIER VINEYARDS (BW 4840). Domaine Laurier near Forestville in the Green Valley area of Sonoma dates from 1978 and was best known for its Cabernet Sauvignon. In 1989 it was acquired by the ill-fated VINTECH group, which went bankrupt in 1991. Since then, Laurier Vineyards has become one of the many brands in the JFJ BRONCO line of wines. The Laurier winery itself was acquired by KENDALL-JACKSON in 1991 and is now used to produce the Hartford Court line of wines.

LAVA CAP (BW 5348). David Jones and his family began planting their 30-acre vineyard east of Placerville in El Dorado County in the early 1980s. It is located at about the 2,500-foot elevation on rocky, volcanic soil. Producing mainly Cabernet Sauvignon, Zinfandel, and Chardonnay, the winery's annual sales exceeded 10,000 cases in the 1990s.

LA VIEILLE MONTAGNE (BW 5172). A little winery high on Spring Mountain in Napa that was bonded in 1983. Its tiny production consists of Cabernet Sauvignon from the steep, 7-acre estate vineyard. The Guilliams family make about 1,000 cases per year here and, since 1994, have been selling the wine under the Guilliams Vineyard label.

LAYERING. A technique for propagating vines described by Roman writers and used in California until phylloxera made resistant rootstock a near necessity. The vineyardist takes a long growing cane from a vine and buries a portion of it while it is still attached to the old vine. The buds below ground send out roots instead of leaves; above ground the buds leaf out. In the second year, the new vine is separated from the parent. This is a particularly easy method for replacing dead vines in established vineyards.

LAZY CREEK (BW 4883). Johann and Theresia Kobler's little winery, just outside Philo in the Anderson Valley, Mendocino, was bonded in 1973. Since then they have developed a solid reputation for their estate Gewürztraminer. In recent years Pinot noir and Chardonnay from their 20-acre vineyard have also drawn critical praise. Production is now just over 4,000 cases per year.

LEAD. Since the earliest days of the industry, most of California's premium wine producers used a tin-lead capsule to cover the cork on their bottled wine. Lower-priced wines often had capsules made from polyvinyl material. To keep the lead out of landfills, several states in the late 1980s outlawed lead capsules.

In recent years, because it is known to be a neural toxin, there has been a rising concern about lead in wines. Lead oxides can form around the cork if capsules contain the element. Thus, since 1993 the lead capsule has virtually disappeared from the bottles of California wine on American retail shelves. Tin and aluminum have been the most popular replacements.

LEAF REMOVAL. See PRUNING

LEES, the various insoluble materials that drop to the bottom of the fermenter or aging container. Ordinary wine is usually separated from its lees early, often by filtration. Fine red wines are usually racked from container to container as the lees are allowed to settle out. Depending on the winemaker's style, some filtration may still follow, but does not always.

In fine white wine production, permitting the wine some contact with the lees, usually in the barrel, has been regarded more favorably in recent years, especially for Chardonnay and Sauvignon blanc. The French expression SUR LIE* is now part of the California winemaking vocabulary. Advocates claim that the practice enhances flavors in the resulting wines. Often the lees are stirred during the process to increase the effect and to help prevent the development of hydrogen sulfide. Most white wine in California, is however, still separated from its lees by filtration and centrifuge early in the winemaking process.

LEESE, JACOB PRIMER (1809–92). A merchant on the Santa Fe Trail, Leese came to California in 1834 and to Sonoma in 1841. There he established one of the North Coast's first successful winegrowing operations. In 1846 he made 26 barrels of wine and 8 of aguardiente. He left California for Texas in 1865.

LEEWARD WINERY (BW 4898). Chuck Brigham and Chuck Gardner were home winemakers who bonded their basement in 1978. In 1982 they moved to their current winery site in Ventura County. They are producing about 13,000 cases per year, mostly Chardonnay from several Central Coast vineyards.

LEFRANC, CHARLES (1824–87). Properly considered the father of commercial wine-growing in the Santa Clara Valley, Lefranc (depicted on page 312) came to California in 1850 and went to work on the estate of Etienne Thée, a few miles south of San Jose. Charles married Thée's daughter Marie Adèle (1832–1902) in 1857. In 1858 he imported a large number of French wine grape varieties for his New Almadén Vineyards and was the first person in California to produce a commercial wine from red Bordeaux varieties, a blend of Cabernet Sauvignon and Malbec. The French vines became the material basis for his later success, and by the 1860s he was the leading wine producer in the area.

After he had been killed in a runaway accident in 1887, his son Henry (1861–1909) took control of ALMADEN (the New had been dropped) and entered into a partnership with Paul MASSON to produce sparkling wine. After Henry died in 1909, Almaden remained the property of his sisters, Louise (1863–1932) and Marie (1865–1941), and was managed by Masson, who had married Louise in 1888.

LIBERTY SCHOOL. For many years the second label for CAYMUS VINEYARDS. The Hope family's 140-acre vineyard near Paso Robles supplied grapes for Liberty School for several years. In 1997 the Hopes bought the brand from Caymus.

LIBRARIES. Several libraries are important to wine and its history in California. At the University of California at Davis, the Shields Library is the most important for recent materials. At the University of California at Berkeley, the Bancroft Library is a treasure trove of California wine history. The univeristy's main library and its Bio-Sciences branch also have useful holdings. At Fresno State University, the Henry Madden Library houses Roy BRADY's* great wine collection. The Sonoma Wine Library and the Napa Valley Wine Library, in the main libraries in Healdsburg and St. Helena, respectively, house historic wine materials available nowhere else. There are also several private wine and viticulture libraries of great size, the most notable being the Unzelman Collection in Santa Rosa.

University of California at Davis:
Shields Library (916) 752-6196

University of California at Berkeley:
Bancroft Library (510) 642-3781
Main Library (510) 642-3403
Bio-Sciences Library (510) 642-2531

Fresno State University:
Madden Library (209) 278-2595

Napa Valley Wine Library
(707) 963-5245

Sonoma County Wine Library
(707) 433-3772

LIGHT WINES. See ALCOHOL

LIME KILN VALLEY, an AVA within the Cienega Valley Viticultural Area in San Benito County; granted its specific status in 1982. Small-scale viticulture here dates from the 1880s. The soils, as might be inferred from its name, overlie a bedrock of limestone and other minerals; see also ENZ VINEYARDS

LIMERICK LANE VINEYARD, a 30-acre vineyard in the Russian River viticultural area of Sonoma that produces some of the finest Zinfandel fruit in the county. Some of the dry-farmed, head-pruned vines date to 1910. Since 1988 the owner, Michael Collins, has marketed his estate Zinfandel and continues to sell grapes to other producers in the area. He produces his wine, about 3,000 cases annually, at the DAVIS BYNUM WINERY.

LIMUR WINERY (BW 5454). Charles de Limur has 2 acres of Chardonnay vines just east of the Silverado Trail in Napa's Rutherford district. He went from home winemaker to owning a bonded winery in 1988 and produces about 400 cases of Chardonnay each year.

LINDA VISTA VINEYARD. Charles C. McIver bought 400 acres south of Mission San Jose from Juan Gallegos in 1883. There he built

More than any other winery Linda Vista fixed the reputation of the MISSION SAN JOSE area as one of California's best wine districts in the 1890s. EUGENE HILGARD thought it was potentially the best. (Unzelman Collection, Santa Rosa, Calif.)

his Linda Vista winery (pictured on page 189) and planted one of the most diversified premium vineyards in California. The pre-Prohibition reputation of the Mission San Jose area for fine table wines was derived mostly from McIver's efforts. He imported such varieties as Béclan, Verdot, Syrah, Durif, Merlot, and Malbec. These and the more recognizable varietals current in California vineyards were blended by his talented cellarmaster, E. P. Warner, into prize-winning red table wines. By 1891 McIver had a contract to supply the dining cars of the Pullman Co. from his 100,000 gallons of annual production. His beautiful 1894 brochure contains some of the finest photographs ever made of a working winery before Prohibition.

McIver was something of a playboy millionaire, but his interest in fine wine production was genuine. In later years this interest flagged; Linda Vista's premium reputation was little more than a memory when the huge winery closed in 1919.

LIPARITA CELLARS (BW 5746). One of W. S. KEYES's pre-Prohibition vineyards on Howell Mountain was named Liparita. The name was revived by Robert Burrows who planted about 80 acres of Liparita vineyard land in the 1980s. He sold grapes to several Napa wineries and revived the Liparita label in 1989, with Merry EDWARDS as winemaker. The old Keyes winery still stands on the property today. Production stood at about 3,000 cases per year when in 1996 KENDALL-JACKSON bought the vineyard, but not the brand.

LIVE OAKS WINERY (BW 268). Founded in 1912 in the Hecker Pass area by the Scagliotti family, Live Oaks was a steady source of country jug wines for wine drinkers in the Santa Clara Valley. Peter Scagliotti sold the winery to new owners in 1986.

LIVERMORE VALLEY. One of California's most historic winegrowing areas, Livermore

came late to the vine. It is located east of the San Francisco Bay Area and has a fairly warm, Region-III climate (see HEAT SUMMATION). It was a land of grain and stock raising, with a few small vineyards on the west side near Pleasanton in the 1870s. In 1880 Joseph F. Black, a leading landowner asked Charles A. WETMORE to examine the area south of the town of Livermore for its viticultural potential. The result was an explosion of vineyard planting and winery building between 1881 and 1886. Wetmore bought land here himself and founded CRESTA BLANCA.

By 1886 there were 2,450 acres of wine grapes, with Zinfandel by far the most numerous. Mourvèdre (Mataro) and Pinot noir were a distant second and third. The boom peaked at the end of the decade when about 6,800 acres were yielding about 500,000 gallons of wine from sixteen wineries. J. P. Smith's OLIVINA VINEYARD was the largest, producing almost 200,000 gallons from 661 acres of vines. By the mid-1890s annual production in the valley was usually about a million gallons or more. In the early years red table wines were dominant, but the valley's fame came to rest by the turn of the century on its dry white wines from Sauvignon blanc and Sémillon.

The effects of phylloxera were late here, but by 1900 most vineyards were beginning to die, except for the few on resistant rootstock. The replanting between 1900 and 1910 was mostly so-called Sauterne and other white varieties. During this period, there was a movement toward consolidation as many of the gentleman-farmers and dilettantes who had made up much of the first wave of the 1880s died or retired. The CALIFORNIA WINE ASSOCIATION's Pioneer Winery dominated the scene, but several family wineries such as WENTE and CONCANNON held on and prospered. Clarence WETMORE's Cresta Blanca also did well.

When Prohibition struck in 1920, Livermore had about 3,500 acres in vines. There was a surge in planting and good money was made

CONCANNON VINEYARD in Livermore ca. 1937. Joseph Concannon, on horseback, had recently bought several mules from the U.S. Army. His sons Jim and Joe Jr. are on top of the tractor. In the foreground are young Sémillon vines. (Photo James Concannon)

selling grapes to home winemakers. Concannon, Wente, and RUBY HILL survived partly by producing sacramental wine. But in the hard times between 1928 and 1932 the acreage dropped below 3,000. Repeal brought a renewed interest in Livermore's white table and dessert wines. Valley wineries won twenty-one gold and silver medals at the State Fair in the 1930s for white table wines, reviving the area's reputation for this type, so firmly established before the dry years. In the five competitions from 1947 to 1951, local wineries won twenty-six gold medals.

After World War II, the valley gradually became a part of the Bay Area's suburbia. In 1977 acreage had dropped to 1,800. It has remained close to that number into the 1990s, partly as the result of a vigorous community campaign to save the area's vineyards. In recent years Chardonnay has become the most common varietal grown in Livermore, with Cabernet Sauvignon in second place; see ALAMEDA COUNTY. Meanwhile the number of wineries has risen, bringing the area's total to thirteen in 1995. Local wineries pride themselves in labeling their wines under the Livermore Valley

Viticultural Area, authorized in 1982. But most also go outside the area to buy grapes.

Janet Newton, *Cresta Blanca and Charles A. Wetmore* (Livermore, Calif.: Livermore Heritage Guild, 1974).

Ernest A. Wente, *Wine Making in the Livermore Valley* (Regional Oral History Office, Bancroft Library, 1971).

LIVERMORE VALLEY CELLARS (BW 4852). Chris Lagiss began producing wine here from his 34-acre vineyard in 1978. For many years the wines were all white, sometimes varietals, sometimes complex blends. In recent years the Lagiss family has added wines made from grapes grown from outside the estate, including a few reds. Production runs about 1,000 cases per year.

LIVINGSTON CELLARS. See GALLO

LIVINGSTON WINES (BW CA 5605). The Livingston family planted its 10-acre Cabernet Sauvignon vineyard in the Rutherford district in 1969 and began commercial winemaking in 1984. The estate Moffett Vineyard wine is a blend of red Bordeaux varieties. The Livingstons also buy grapes to make a 100-percent Cabernet Sauvignon designated Stanley's Selection. Total production runs to about 3,000 cases per year.

LLORDS & ELWOOD (BW 4475). J. H. (Mike) Elwood had been a wine retailer in Los Angeles since 1933 when he founded this brand in 1955 and began producing small quantities of fortified wine under such names as Dry Wit Sherry and Ancient Proverb Port. The wines were produced at the WEIBEL property near Mission San Jose. In later years varietal table wines were added to the line, such as Velvet Hill Pinot Noir. Elwood died in 1974 after which the operation was run by his son, Richard, until 1984 when MONTICELLO CELLARS from Napa bought the brand and took over the old bonded winery number.

LOCKWOOD VINEYARDS (BW 4875). Most of Lockwood's grapes are sold to other wineries, but since 1989 a part of the production of their vineyard south of King City in Monterey County has gone into wines under their own label. The company owns 1,850 acres of land in the area, which gives it considerable potential for increasing production. By 1996 annual production had exceeded 60,000 cases. Lockwood Chardonnay has a very good reputation.

LODI. A town in SAN JOAQUIN COUNTY* and long the center of one of California's most important winegrowing regions. The Lodi Viticultural Area, officially designated by the BATF in 1986, is a huge district running north into Sacramento County, south almost to Stockton, and covering more than 500 square miles. This area is far larger than what was implied by the term "Lodi" in the early days. Other historic wine towns in the area are Acampo, Victor, and Woodbridge.

Serious commercial winegrowing here dates from the 1860s, dominated by George WEST's

wineries. Unlike most of the Central Valley, this section, from Stockton to Elk Grove, south of Sacramento, is cooled by maritime air that comes through the DELTA region from the Bay Area. Thus, since early days it has been possible to raise grapes that produce sound dry table wine as well as fortified wines.

During Prohibition no district shipped more wine grapes to eastern home winemakers than did the Lodi area. But after Repeal large surpluses forced most growers to combine into cooperative wineries, seven of which dominated winegrowing here through the 1960s. Brandy, often referred to as "Lodi Scotch," was also an important product, made mostly from the Flame Tokay table variety, which today accounts for less than 1 percent of the acreage in Lodi.

In recent years a viticultural revolution has taken place in the area with huge tracts of first-class varieties planted, most of which go into the production of FIGHTING VARIETALS and White Zinfandel. In 1987 growers in the district, which includes some very large wineries, formed the Lodi-Woodbridge Winegrape Commission to promote the area, its grapes, and its wines. By the mid-1990s there were about 600 growers there and almost 50,000 acres under wine grapes. The most important producers in the area are Robert MONDAVI, SEBASTIANI, CANANDAIGUA, and EAST-SIDE (Oak Ridge). A few of the important brands for which the wine comes at least partly from this area are Glen Ellen, Gallo, Sutter Home, Vendange, Guild, Cook's, Paul Masson, Forest Glen, and Napa Ridge. More than forty wineries buy grapes here.

In 1996 the Lodi area led all others in California in the production of Chardonnay, Sauvignon blanc, Cabernet Sauvignon, Merlot, and Zinfandel grapes. Other areas had higher acreages; Lodi's lead came from higher yields per acre. This is fighting varietal country.

J. LOHR WINERY (BW 4670, 5460). In 1972, as partners, Jerry Lohr and Bernard Turgeon

The special geographical situation of the Lodi area distinguishes it from other Central Valley areas that are far less affected by maritime influences, as denoted in an advertisement published in 1997 by the Lodi-Woodbridge Winegrape Commission.

bought vineyard land near Greenfield in Monterey County and in 1974 built a winery in downtown San Jose on the site of a historic brewery. In 1984 Lohr took sole command; Turgeon went into the microbrewing business in Santa Cruz and planted vineyards in the hills nearby. Meanwhile Lohr expanded operations with vineyards in Napa Valley, the Delta region, and the Paso Robles area, where in 1988 he built a second winery for red wine production.

Lohr wines appear in a two-tier arrangement. Estate wines travel under the J. Lohr label; the Cypress line includes more moderately priced wines. Annual production from Lohr's approximately 1,200 acres and from purchased grapes was approaching 300,000 cases in the mid-1990s.

Lohr also owns the ARIEL brand of nonalcoholic "wine," production of which has exceeded 100,000 cases per year.

LOLONIS WINERY (BW 5145). The Lolonis family planted a vineyard in Redwood Valley in Mendocino County. In the 1970s FETZER began producing powerful Zinfandels with vineyard designations, one of which was Lolonis. Today the family's holdings amount to 300 acres of vines planted to a wide range of varietals and sold to several North Coast wineries. In 1982 Lolonis began making wines under its own label; production now amounts to about 20,000 cases per year.

LOMBARDA WINERY. See FREEMARK ABBEY

LONE HILL. Years ago east of Los Gatos, a solitary hill protruded from the Santa Clara Valley floor. David Harwood, a pioneering winegrower there, called his ranch Lone Hill Vineyard. It was the largest in the county in the 1860s with 155 acres in vines. After Repeal Almaden owned the land, and in 1946 members of the Mirassou family bought it and founded **Lone Hill Vineyards** (BW 4395), a 500,000-gallon winery that sold wines in bulk and at retail in the local mar-

David M. Harwood's Lone Hill Vineyard in 1876. The chief varieties grown were Mission, Zinfandel, Pinot noir, Riesling, and Charbono, and annual production in the 1870s was about 30,000 gallons.

ket until 1968. Then the advances of suburbia and rising land prices brought an end to operations. Meanwhile Lone Hill itself had been quarried almost to the valley floor, but not quite. The rise in the land can still be seen from Harwood Road, as can the twin palms that served as an entrance to the old winery.

LONG. Zelma Long had a degree in general science from Oregon State University when she met **Robert Long** at the University of California at Berkeley where she was studying nutrition. They married and she went to UC Davis to get her master's degree in fermentation science. In 1972 she succeeded Mike Grgich as enologist at Robert MONDAVI Winery, and in 1979 she became winemaker at SIMI.* Today she is the chief executive officer there. But back in the 1970s she and Robert planted Chardonnay and White Riesling on land in the hills above Lake Hennessy, east of Rutherford. At first they sold grapes to MOUNT VEEDER WINERY but in 1978

they bonded **Long Vineyards** (DW 4061), which since then, has become famous for its estate Chardonnay. Although divorced years ago, the Longs still are coowners of the little winery. Production runs about 4,000 cases per year.

LOS ALAMOS VALLEY. An important winegrowing area in Santa Barbara County with about 3,000 acres in vines. It is noted for its Chardonnay and Pinot noir. To date, because the winegrowers there have not petitioned to have the valley designated a viticultural area, it has no set boundaries and Los Alamos appears on no wine labels. From 1974 to 1986 the **Los Alamos Winery** (BW 4667) operated near the little town of that name.

LOS AMIGOS VINEYARD. See GRAU & WERNER

LOS ANGELES. A city and county in southern California. Earlier in the century the county's agricultural production was the most valuable in the United States; today it is overwhelmingly urban and suburban.

In the 1850s it was the home of California's small commercial wine industry. But long before the American Conquest in 1846, Los Angeles and its outskirts was a pueblo of many vineyards and a few small wineries. Before that there were vineyards at the San Gabriel and San Fernando missions, a few miles from the pueblo.

Beginning in about 1833, Jean-Louis VIGNES was the area's first important commercial winegrower. William Workman, Matthew Keller, Charles KOHLER, and many others began operations in the 1840s and 1850s. Before 1889 what is today Orange County was part of Los Angeles County, so that the ANAHEIM Colony was originally a Los Angeles venture.

County production rose from about 500,000 gallons in the 1860s to 3.5 million in the early 1880s, although by then it was clear that northern California was where the state's best wines were being produced. In 1885–86 disaster struck the area in the form of PIERCE's DISEASE, at first appropriately termed the Anaheim disease. From about 40,000 acres in the 1880s the county's vineyards declined to about 5,000 acres in the mid-1890s. Viticulture in the Anaheim area disappeared, replaced by citrus and walnut orchards.

But winegrowing revived in the Southland. Several operations survived and grew in the San Gabriel Valley. Good dry wines were also produced in the foothills around Pasadena and Glendale. The Lamanda Park area there developed a fine reputation for red table wine. By 1906 there were thirty-eight wineries in the county and 6,825 acres of vines. In 1909 the wine product of the county totaled about 2.7 million gallons, about equally divided between table wine and fortified wine. But the county voted to go dry in 1914 and many smaller operations moved into the city, which had not.

With Prohibition, vineyard planting again expanded, notably in the San Gabriel and San Fernando valleys, where there was a burst of winemaking activity after Repeal. By World War II the county had eighty wineries, most small. But after the war most vineyards disappeared and wineries were few. In 1956 there were 175 acres of vines in Los Angeles County; in 1977 there were none. In downtown Los Angeles one plant, the SAN ANTONIO WINERY, hung on and continues to this day.

Surprisingly the state now lists about 25 acres of mostly white-wine grapes in the county; this is entirely feasible as six small premium wineries have been bonded there since 1980. Far more important than production is consumption in Los Angeles, which is one of the most important markets for California wine.

LOS GATOS. A small town and formerly an important winegrowing district in the foothills southwest of San Jose. It was incorporated in 1887 but the growth of vineyards in the valley nearby and in the hills to the south prompted construction of the Los Gatos-Saratoga Winery in 1885 and the Los Gatos Cooperative Winery the next year. Between them they eventually produced more than 500,000 gallons annually until they went out of business in 1919. In 1910 there were eight other smaller wineries in town or nearby. A historic production facility was located at the famous NOVITIATE OF LOS GATOS on a hill behind town. Today there are still four wineries in the Santa Cruz Mountains south of town that list their address as Los Gatos.

LOS HERMANOS. See BERINGER VINEYARDS

LOS OLIVOS VINTNERS (BW 5182). Founded in 1983 as Austin Cellars, the winery has been operated since 1995 by investors called the Santa Ynez Wine Group. Annual production is about 4,000 cases, mostly Chardonnay and Pinot noir.

LOW-ALCOHOL WINE. See ALCOHOL

LUCAS WINERY (BW 4860). David Lucas acquired his 30-acre vineyard near Lodi, in San Joaquin County, in 1977. Since then he has sold most of his grapes to Robert MONDAVI's Woodbridge winery. Since 1987 he has made small batches of intense Zinfandel from his oldest vines, which were planted during Prohibition. The annual production of his winery averages about 750 cases.

LUNA VINEYARDS. See ST. ANDREWS WINERY

LYETH VINEYARDS (BW 5122). Munro Lyeth began growing grapes in the Alexander Valley in Sonoma County in 1973. Backed by his family's wealth, he built his winery north of Geyserville in 1981 and began producing red and white Bordeaux-style table wine from the estate. In 1988 he sold the winery and vineyard to the ill-fated VINTECH group. Lyeth was killed in an airplane crash a few months later. In 1992 following the demise of Vintech, the brand and inventory were sold to J.-C. BOISSET, the vineyards to GALLO, and the winery to SILVER OAK, which produces its Sonoma red wine there.

LYMAN, W. W. See EL MOLINO

LYTTON SPRINGS. Lytton is an old place name for a small area north of Healdsburg in Sonoma County. Lytton Springs Road connects Dry Creek Valley to the Alexander Valley. In 1971 Richard Sherwin bought some old vineyard land along the road and called his place Valley Vista. The next year Paul Draper, the winemaker at RIDGE VINEYARDS, bought Zinfandel grapes from Sherwin but decided to identify the source of the grape on the label as Lytton Springs, a historic term that he liked better than Valley Vista. Ridge made powerful Zinfandels from those grapes through 1976. Then Sherwin bonded his own facility there and called it **Lytton Springs Winery** (BW 4798).

In 1984 Ridge began buying grapes from Norton Ranch, Sherwin's neighbor and again indicated the source on the label as Lytton Springs. Eventually Ridge bought Sherwin's winery and vineyard in 1991, acquiring full rights to the Lytton Springs name. The Zinfandels are still made at Ridge and are considered among California's best. From the three vineyards along the old road, Ridge produces between 10,000 and 12,000 cases per year.

MABON, MARY FROST, wrote the first systematic twentieth-century tour guide of America's wineries, the *ABC of America's Wines,* in 1942. With special emphasis on California, it has restaurant and hotel or motel suggestions for the wine country, and provides a delightful glimpse into the state's wine culture of a half century ago.

MCDOWELL VALLEY. East of Hopland in Mendocino County, a little valley, named for an early settler, that received AVA status in 1982. Its only winery is **McDowell Valley Vineyards** (BW 4879), developed by the Keehn family, who bought land here in 1970, planted vineyards, and built the winery in 1979. Eventually there were 370 acres of vines, with at one point seventeen different varieties, among which were 36 acres of old vines identified in 1981 as French Syrah and and some old Grenache vines dating from 1919.

By the mid-1980s more and more attention was being paid to varieties associated with the south of France. The Keehns called their line of wines made in the Rhône style Les Vieux Cépages. Production was up to 50,000 cases by 1993 when the ASSOCIATED VINTAGE GROUP (AVG) bought the 500,000-gallon winery. The Keehns kept their vineyards and their brand and continue to have their wines produced at the winery, now an AVG plant. They now have a more manageable six varietals. Production stands at about 45,000 cases a year, two-thirds from Rhône varieties.

MCINTYRE, HAMDEN W. (1835–1909). A native of Vermont, he had worked for many years with Gustav Niebaum in the Alaska Commercial Co., before Niebaum brought him to the Napa Valley in 1881 to be the general manager of INGLENOOK.* For the next six years, McIntyre, a learned mechanical engineer, ran Inglenook and designed its grand new winery. He had a solid knowledge of viticulture and enology, having worked at the Pleasant Valley Wine Co. in New York before going to Alaska. In 1886 he was elected president of the California State Vinicultural Society, and two years later he was named president of the state's Grape Growers & Wine Makers Association. In 1887 he left Inglenook to manage Leland Stanford's VINA estate. He stayed there until 1894 when he returned to Vermont.

McIntyre's permanent contributions to California wine history were the marvelous wineries he designed. Many are still standing: ESHCOL (now TREFETHEN), FAR NIENTE, GREYSTONE, CHATEAU MONTELENA, VINA, and STANFORD's old Palo Alto Winery.

MCIVER, CHARLES. See LINDA VISTA

MACONDRAY, FREDERICK W. (1803–62). A New England sea captain who had been

Frederick Macondray first displayed his Zinfandel grapes at the 1857 Mechanics Fair in San Francisco. The next year he won the award for the best European grape varieties at the State Fair. His Baywood estate in San Mateo was a viticultural showplace.

sailing the Pacific since 1830, he set up his trading company in San Francisco during the Gold Rush. But his interest in agriculture was more important to the young state. He was the first president of the California State Agricultural Society. His importations of vinifera grape varieties from the East Coast were particularly significant in that they included the ZINFANDEL.* Others also imported this variety from New England but his shipment in 1852 was probably the first.

MACROSTIE WINERY (BW 5495). Steven Macrostie was the winemaker at Hacienda Winery from 1975 to 1987, when he founded his own operation on the Sonoma side of the Carneros.

His 15,000-case operation emphasizes Chardonnay and Pinot noir from Sangiacomo Vineyards. He makes his wine in the ROCHE WINERY.

MADEIRA. A Portuguese island in the Atlantic noted for its amber-colored fortified wines. Visitors to pre-American California occasionally likened the best sweet wines from the Mission variety and old Angelica to sweet Madeira wine. Some later California producers tried to copy the Madeira style and even gave their wines names such as Bual and Sercial. These were not successful. "Madeira" is a legal GENERIC term on California wine labels and has been seen now and then on wines made since Repeal and usually meant for cooks as a substitute in recipes calling for the rather expensive real thing.

MADERA. A viticultural area recognized by the BATF in 1985. It is a huge district, covering more than 700 square miles, that includes vineyard land in Madera and Fresno counties. It contains about 35,000 acres of wine grapes.

MADERA COUNTY was not an important winegrowing area in California until the 1960s, when wine-grape acreage there grew almost 500 percent. Analysis of the county's acreage since the early 1960s gives a fair picture of varieties that have become important for the production of better jug wine from the Central Valley.

There has been a revolution in vineyards in Madera County since 1992. With a rising demand for better grapes for FIGHTING VARIETALS, acreage planted to premium vines has increased. In 1997, there were 1,050 acres of Cabernet Sauvignon, 1,907 acres of Chardonnay, 2,979 acres of Merlot, and 3,797 acres of Zinfandel. All told, the county's acreage under wine grapes in 1996 was third in California, behind San Joaquin and Fresno counties.

MADROÑA VINEYARDS (BW 5005). East of Placerville in El Dorado County, Richard

TABLE 16. WINE GRAPES IN MADERA COUNTY, SELECTED VARIETIES

YEAR	PERCENT OF TOTAL RED	WHITE	BARBERA	CARIGNANE	CHENIN BLANC	(ACRES) FRENCH COLOMBARD	GRENACHE	RUBY CABERNET	TOTAL
1961	84	26	0	1,575	0	0	663	0	3,444
1968	89	11	0	3,420	0	62	1,310	0	6,611
1972	73	27	1,798	5,195	495	2,595	3,065	825	17,265
1978	76	24	3,784	5,323	1,395	3,952	3,959	2,624	27,975
1983	37	63	3,635	4,041	6,464	19,121	4,517	1,051	43,305
1988	34	66	2,672	3,082	6,223	17,225	4,171	449	38,085
1997	46	54	1,914	2,676	5,082	13,412	3,516	623	41,244

SOURCE: California Agricultural Statistics Service, Sacramento, Calif.

Bush began planting his 35-acre vineyard at the 3,000-foot level in 1973. He built his winery in 1980 after two vintages produced at another facility. Madroña makes a wide range varietals amounting to about 12,000 cases per year.

MAGNUM. See BOTTLE

MAISON DEUTZ WINERY (BW 5155). A sparkling wine operation in San Luis Obispo County, a joint venture between the French Champagne house of Deutz & Geldermann and BERINGER. Planting of the 180 acres of vines began in 1982; the winery (see page 14) was built in 1983; the first release was in 1986. Annual production in the mid-1990s had exceeded 30,000 cases and in 1997 the winery began producing still wine sold under the Laetitia label.

MALAGA. A rich fortified wine from southern Spain. It is a legal GENERIC designation for California today, but the term is no longer seen on labels. Before Prohibition several producers made a wine they called Malaga, George WEST's having the best reputation.

MALBEC. A variety of red wine grape used for table wine in southwest France and occasionally found in small quantities in the blends of Bordeaux châteaux, where it is called Cot. In California there are about 200 acres, mostly in Napa and Sonoma. A few producers have included Malbec in their Cabernet Sauvignon blends; some have actually produced a varietal wine. But the grape is little grown now in California because it lacks a distinctive flavor and yields are low. This is a paradox because Malbec was quite popular in northern California before 1900 as a variety used to stretch Cabernet Sauvignon.

Charles LEFRANC brought it from France to the Santa Clara Valley in 1858, as did J.-M. J. PORTAL in 1872. By 1886 Charles WETMORE was complaining that it was too often planted instead of Cabernet Sauvignon. After 1900, when phylloxera-devastated vineyards were replanted, Malbec was almost never chosen. The variety began appearing in California state statistics after 8 acres were planted in Napa in 1975. The 1996 vintage yielded 325 tons.

MALIBU-NEWTON CANYON. See ROSENTHAL

MALIC ACID. From the Latin *malum,* for apple, in which it was first identified. See ACID

MALOLACTIC FERMENTATION. See ACID

MALTER, GEORGE. See ST. GEORGE WINERY

MALVASIA BIANCA. Malvasia grapes, mostly white, are found all over the Mediterranean world and are of ancient origin, probably Greek. Sweet wine, often fortified and with a slight muscat flavor, is their most common product. The Malvasia bianca was brought to California by ITALIAN SWISS COLONY in the 1890s, but it may have been here earlier. It became popular in sweet wines and semisweet table wines. After Repeal the variety went almost unnoticed through the 1960s, when there were about 100 acres in the state. Then the variety's old usefulness for enhancing the flavor of inexpensive whites was rediscovered. By 1980 there were about 1,000 acres in the Central Valley, by the mid-1990s more than 2,500. There were still a few acres in coastal valleys. California production in 1996 was 15,586 tons, about the same as it was in 1990. The new interest in Italian varieties in the 1990s has encouraged a few producers to offer Malvasia bianca as a premium varietal. BONNY DOON, for example, makes it dry and Robert MONDAVI, slightly sweet.

Occasionally the BLACK MALVOISIE (Cinsaut) has been called the Malvasia nera, but this is a confusing misnomer.

MALVOISIE. See BLACK MALVOISIE

MARCASSIN. See TURLEY

MARCUS, IRVING (1905–79). "Brick" Marcus was an all-coast halfback in the 1920s, when he played football at the University of California. Later he was a stockbroker and a wine writer. In 1956 he bought WINES & VINES,* which he directed until 1969. During those years, the periodical became the "authoritative voice of the wine industry." His popular *Dictionary of Wine Terms,* first published in 1957, sold more than 300,000 copies and went through sixteen editions.

MARE VISTA. See ERNST E. MEYER

MARIETTA CELLARS (BW 5597). A winery near Healdsburg in Sonoma County founded in 1980. It specializes in powerful Zinfandel and Cabernet Sauvignon wine from grapes grown in Sonoma County, and sells a small quantity of Syrah. Production averages about 30,000 cases per year.

MARIN COUNTY. Just north of the Golden Gate Bridge and famous as the home of several bedroom communities for San Francisco, its northern region retains a rural agricultural character.

For years the only estate winery in Marin County has been PACHECO RANCH. The carriage house of the historic rancho serves as the winery today. Here in 1997 it is getting a new coat of paint, the winemaker John O'Neill with brush above, Debbie and Herb Rowland below.

Vines, the first in the North Bay area, were planted at the San Rafael Mission there in 1817. From the 1880s until Prohibition, there were usually between 300 and 400 acres of wine grapes, most crushed by wineries in Sonoma County near Petaluma. These vineyards are gone but Marin has attracted several small suburban wineries, thirteen since Repeal. There are four operating today. There were 40 acres of vines in 1997, a few Cabernet Sauvignon, but mostly experimental plots of Pinot noir and Chardonnay in the western part of the county.

MARIPOSA COUNTY. Although the BATF at first questioned the inclusion of Mariposa in the Sierra Foothills Viticultural Area, it was included in 1987. In the 1990s there were about 60 acres of wine grapes there and three wineries.

MARKHAM WINERY (BW 957). A modern winery in Napa, north of St. Helena, that has had a long and complicated history. Its renewal began in 1978 when Bruce Markham bought what had previously been the St. Helena Cooperative Winery. The first winery on this property had been built in 1879 by Jean Laurent. Markham also acquired good vineyard land in several parts of Napa and was producing about 20,000 cases per year when he sold it to Mercian Corp. of Japan in 1987. Mercian's Sanraku Division is the leading domestic wine producer in Japan and owns wineries in several other countries. In 1989 the new management began a huge four-year renovation project. By the mid-1990s annual production under the Markham, Glass Mountain, and Laurent labels had reached 100,000 cases of a wide range of varietals, but principally Cabernet Sauvignon, Merlot, and Chardonnay. The owners now operate 225 acres of vineyard land in Napa.

MARK WEST VINEYARDS (BW 4765). The winery in the Russian River area of Sonoma County was founded in 1976. Since 1992 it has been one of the production facilities of the ASSOCIATED VINTAGE GROUP. The 66-acre estate vineyard produces grapes for about 20,000 cases of wine annually, mostly Chardonnay and Pinot noir.

MARSALA. A sweet fortified wine from Sicily. Before and after Prohibition, several producers in the Central Valley and southern California made a wine labeled Marsala. The term did not catch on, although, like sherry and burgandy, it is still a legal generic wine type in this country.

MARSANNE. A white wine grape from the northern Rhône in France, used for wines such as white Hermitage and white St-Joseph. Sometimes it is blended in small quantities into red wines in the Rhône. It was known in California by the 1880s and appeared in the collections of H. W. CRABB and J. H. DRUMMOND; it was tested at the University of California at Berkeley by Professor HILGARD, but was not much used commercially here. In recent years it has been planted in several of California's coastal valley vineyards from Santa Barbara to Sonoma. It is occasionally blended with its sister Rhône varietal, the roussanne, and has been produced as a varietal wine. The 1996 vintage of Marsanne was 175 tons.

MARSHALL, LAURENCE K. (1887–1957). A power in the twentieth-century development of winegrowing in the Lodi area and a founder of GUILD WINERIES. André TCHELISTCHEFF considered him, along with Louis M. MARTINI and Herman WENTE, one of the three "apostles of the modern California wine industry."

MARTHA'S VINEYARD is possibly the most famous vineyard in the Western Hemisphere. In 1959 Bernard and Belle Rhodes bought a 42-acre piece of land west of Oakville, in Napa Valley, across from an experimental station run by the University of California. They planted 12 acres to Cabernet Sauvignon and 14 to White Riesling, which was later budded to

VINTAGE 1986   BOTTLED AUG. – SEPT. 1990
Bottle   of a total of 83,256 Bottles
Magnum   of a total of 2,400 Magnums

Heitz Cellar

NAPA VALLEY
CABERNET SAUVIGNON
ALCOHOL 13½% BY VOLUME
PRODUCED AND BOTTLED IN OUR CELLAR BY
HEITZ WINE CELLARS
ST. HELENA, CALIFORNIA, U.S.A.
Martha's Vineyard

If California, like Bordeaux, had first growths, this surely would be a label for one of them. Note the detailed information that Joseph HEITZ affords his customers.

Cabernet. The couple sold the land to Martha and Tom May in 1963. In 1965 the Mays sold their grapes to Joseph Heitz and, the next year, he decided to keep the wine separate for a vineyard-designated bottling. HEITZ CELLAR's Martha's Vineyard Cabernet Sauvignon has had a remarkable run of vintage successes since then. Since the 1966 vintage there have been 4 years in which Heitz has not made a separate bottling for Martha's Vineyard: In 1971 the quality was lacking and from 1993 to 1995 much of the 34-acre vineyard was being replanted after an infestation of phylloxera.

MARTIN BROTHERS WINERY (BW 5057). The Martin family bought an old dairy farm northeast of Paso Robles in 1981 and have transformed the 85 acres into a modern, 18,000-case winemaking facility. Much of the production has been of well-known premium varietals, but their interest has been in Italian varietals, particularly Nebbiolo, which has become a house specialty, totaling about 4,000 cases per year.

MARTINELLI WINERY (BW 5396). The Martinelli family has been farming land in the Russian River Valley in Sonoma County since 1902. Their diversified ranch has a Zinfandel vineyard that was planted before Prohibition. For a short while after Repeal, the family operated a small winery (BW 1824) on the ranch, which dated back to 1910. The current emphasis on viticulture on the 160-acre estate began in the 1970s. For years the family sold their grapes. The winery was bonded only in 1987 and now produces about 4,000 cases a year of several varietal wines, but the Zinfandels from their Jackass and Jackass Hill vineyards are the most noteworthy.

MARTINEZ. When Contra Costa County was an important winegrowing area before World War II, Martinez was the urban center of the

Vine Hill and Alhambra Valley viticultural districts to the south, with their scores of vineyards and numerous wineries. Chief among the Martinez wineries were those of Martin Joost (see DIGARDI) and B. H. Upham. It was in Martinez that the CHRISTIAN BROTHERS first made wine in California before moving to the Napa Valley.

MARTINI & PRATI WINES (BW 881). A bulk-wine operation in Sonoma east of Forestville that dates from 1881. For a while in the 1940s it was owned by Hiram Walker and was run in conjunction with the company's VALLIANT WINERY in San Benito County. The present company was formed in 1950 when Elmo Martini and Enrico Prati bought the winery. In recent years the 2.5 million-gallon plant has done lots of custom crushing and bulk production for other wineries. In the early 1980s many of Paul MASSON's red wines were produced at the Martini & Prati facility. In 1959 the winery acquired the historic Fountaingrove brand and produces some varietals for distribution under that label. In 1995 it linked up with the ASSOCIATED VINTAGE GROUP, and is now a major CUSTOM-CRUSH operation.

MARTINI, LOUIS M. (1887–1974) was the founder, after Repeal, of one of the most famous wineries in the Napa Valley. He came to San Francisco from Italy in 1900. In 1906 he was sent back to Italy for 8 months of formal winemaking instruction at the enology school in Alba. He was back for the family's small 1907 vintage at their property in San Francisco. Later he made commercial wine in the East Bay and southern California.

In 1923 he and several partners acquired the ITALIAN SWISS COLONY plant at Kingsburg, near Fresno, and renamed it the L. M. Martini Grape Products Co. (He sold that operation in 1940.) Meanwhile, even before Repeal, he had decided to produce first-class dry table wine in the Napa Valley. In 1932 he made 40,000 gallons

at the old BRUN & CHAIX plant and then began building the **Louis M. Martini Winery** (BW 3596), a new facility just south of St. Helena.

Martini was interested in varietal wines. Most of his early wines were sold in bulk, but he kept the best for future sale under his own label, which appeared in 1940. He had acquired the Mount Pisgah Vineyard in the hills above the Sonoma Valley in 1936. Renamed Monte Rosso, its 240 acres became the backbone of his varietal production. Red table wine was the Martini specialty, particularly Cabernet Sauvignon, Zinfandel, and Barbera. But some whites were notable, particularly his dry Gewürztraminer and his varietal Folle blanche.

Louis M.'s son, **Louis P. Martini,** finished his college work at the University of California at Davis in 1941 and returned to the winery to work with his father. World War II and five years in the U.S. Army Air Corps intervened. Thereafter, Louis P. took an increasingly active role in the growing winery and the expansion of vineyard property. He became winemaker in 1954 and took charge of production in 1968. Production in the 1970s reached about 400,000 cases. Louis P.'s son, **Michael Martini,** became the winemaker in 1977. The family held the line on pricing but did not profit from the white wine boom of the seventies. Many critics also declared that the famous Cabernets and Zinfandels were not keeping up with the surging competition.

By the 1990s accumulated debt had forced the family to sell off some vineyard land, reducing their total holdings to about 850 acres. Annual production had declined to about 200,000 cases with fewer varietals and more reserve and vineyard-selection wines. The winery also has been doing some custom crushing. The Martini sherries, from a solera dating to 1922, continue to reap plaudits as perhaps the best produced in the nation.

Zoltan Csavas, *The Louis M. Martini Winery* (St. Helena, Calif.: Louis Martini Corp., 1982).

Louis M. Martini and Louis P. Martini, *Wine Making in the Napa Valley* (Regional Oral History Office, Bancroft Library, 1973).

Louis P. Martini, *A Family Winery and the California Wine Industry* (Regional Oral History Office, Bancroft Library, 1984).

MARVEL, TOM. See FRANK SCHOONMAKER

MASSON, PAUL (1859–1940). Masson came to California from his home in Burgundy in 1878, went to work for Charles LEFRANC,* the pioneer winegrower in Santa Clara Valley, and became deeply involved in the business and in the production side of operations at ALMADEN.* After Lefranc died in 1887, Masson married Louise, Charles's older daughter, and went into partnership with her brother Henry. Lefranc & Masson produced an excellent bottle-fermented sparkling wine that was released in 1892 and took the California market by storm. Buying Henry's share of their partnership, Masson took sole control of the company later that year, but the Lefranc children and Charles's widow remained owners of the Almaden property.

In 1896 Masson bought vineyard land in the hills above Saratoga and called the home for his new sparklers La Cresta. He sent off to France for good Burgundian varieties: Chardonnay, Pinot noir, Pinot blanc, and Pinot Meunier. In 1902, when Charles's widow died, Masson took over the management of Almaden. Even though the Lefranc children still owned the property, the Paul Masson Champagne Co. (BW 144) sign was soon displayed at his new mountain winery, built in 1905, and at Almaden, which as a brand name all but disappeared.

Masson's table and sparkling wines were often called "The Pride of California." Critics declared his pink Oeil de Perdrix (eye of the partridge) the finest sparkler in the New World. During Prohibition he still legally produced "medicinal champagne," but made better money shipping grapes to home winemakers in the east. In 1930 he and his wife sold the Almaden plant and, in 1936, sold his mountain winery to Martin RAY, who kept the old Paul Masson brand alive. In 1941 a terrible fire all but destroyed the now-famous winery. After rebuilding the facility in 1943, Ray sold La Cresta through the marketing firm of Fromm & Sichel to SEAGRAM, which intended to use the historic Masson mystique to build the brand into a national leader.

Production facilities for sparkling wine were transferred to the Monte Vista Winery (BW 1023), in Cupertino which was built in 1905, and, for table wines, to the nearby Heney Winery (BW 4451). The mountain winery in Saratoga was used mostly for promotional activities and later for a popular concert series. In 1959 a huge plant for sparkling wine production was built in the valley north of Saratoga, but the product of these so-called Champagne Cellars was made by the transfer process.

In 1960 Seagram began planting vines in Monterey County and in 1966 built a large winery there (BW 4505). By 1980 the company had 4,500 acres there and in the Central Valley producing grapes for the huge line of Paul Masson wines. By 1985 there were no more production facilities in the Santa Clara Valley. The Champagne Cellars were torn down and the mountain winery and the La Cresta vineyards were sold to developers. Annual sales amounted to more than 7 million cases but the premium image for Paul Masson wines was dead. In 1987 Seagram sold the brand and some production facilities to a group of investors, Vintners International, which tried to revive the Masson brand's mystique, but failed. In 1993 Paul Masson became a brand for the CANANDAIGUA line of wines. About 3.5 million cases are sold under the Masson label. The great La Cresta property and its winery survives in the hills above Saratoga and, recently, neighboring winegrowers have indicated an interest in replanting the vineyards.

Alfred Fromm, *Marketing California Wine and Brandy* (Regional Oral History Office, Bancroft Library, 1984).

Morris M. Katz, *Paul Masson Winery Operations and Management, 1994–1988* (Regional Oral History Office, Bancroft Library, 1990).

Otto E. Meyer, *California Premium Wines and Brandy* (Regional Oral History Office, Bancroft Library, 1973).

MASTANTUONO (BW 4815). A little winery west of Templeton in the Paso Robles Viticultural Area founded in 1977. Total production is about 10,000 cases per year, concentrated on Zinfandel, Barbera, and Muscat Canelli.

MASTER CELLARS. See BEAR MOUNTAIN WINERY; HECK

MATANZAS CREEK WINERY (BW 4848). In 1971 Sandra McIver bought a rundown dairy farm in Bennett Valley, southeast of Santa Rosa in Sonoma County. When she hired Merry EDWARDS to be her winemaker (1977–84), she finished the first major step in creating Matanzas Creek, an unlikely name for a winery. (In early California a *matanza* was a cattle slaughter.) Since the first vintage in 1978, McIver has developed a remarkable reputation for her Chardonnays, now produced at a modern 150,000-gallon winery

that went up in 1985. The 50-acre estate vineyard also has some Merlot, which has become a house specialty.

So high is the Matanzas reputation for Chardonnay that McIver was able to sell a 1990 version, titled Journey, for $70.00 per bottle. It, like many of the wines made here, included grapes purchased from other vineyards in Sonoma. Total production had reached 35,000 cases per year by the 1990s.

MATARO (MOURVÈDRE). A Spanish red-wine grape that may have arrived in California in the 1860s in the PELLIER collection. In the Santa Clara Valley in the 1870s it was more popular than the Zinfandel and was planted all over northern California in the boom years from 1878 to 1886. It was known then to be the same grape as the Mourvèdre, popular in southern France. But the Spanish term caught on in California and stuck until the 1980s.

Mataro was particularly well liked by wineries in California for its solid structure and rough but tasty fruit. It was almost universally used here as a blending grape in both clarets and burgundies. This popularity did not lead to heavy planting, the number of acres here during Prohibition being only about 3,000. The history of the variety during the dry years is unusual. Although it was then heavily planted, not much was shipped out of state by

TABLE 17. MATARO (MOURVÈDRE) GRAPES, SELECTED COUNTIES

YEAR	CONTRA COSTA	SANTA CLARA	PLACER	RIVERSIDE	SAN BERNARDINO	TOTAL
			(ACRES)			
1932	593	1,035	1,500	621	2,740	7,000
1971	270	65	158	87	1,154	1,855
1976	217	44	102	78	941	1,503
1982	178	43	15	78	487	843
1987	159	6	13	61	77	352
1994	195	3	8	51	0	324
1997	222	2	12	64	0	420

SOURCE: California Agricultural Statistics Service, Sacramento, Calif.

CONTRA COSTA COUNTY
MOURVÈDRE (Mataro)
1 9 8 8

PRODUCED AND BOTTLED BY
CLINE CELLARS OAKLEY, CALIFORNIA
ALCOHOL 13.4% BY VOL. CONTAINS SULFITES

In California CLINE CELLARS pioneered the recent interest in the Mataro grape as a premium varietal. This early label from the family's facility in Contra Costa County gives both names for the grape. Today the name Mourvèdre is usually seen alone.

rail because it was so popular among home winemakers in California. For example, in 1932 there were 1,035 acres in the Santa Clara Valley and not a box was shipped east. By that year acreage in the state had grown to about 7,000 but only about 300 carloads were shipped east. After Repeal the Mataro continued in its old role as a blending grape for ordinary red table wine. But acreage slipped steadily from a high of 8,143 in 1939 to 2,700 in 1963. By 1987 there were only 352 acres, almost half in the Oakley area, Contra Costa County. By then the Mataro's fine qualities had been rediscovered by the RHONE RANGERS. New plantings began appearing where they had not been in decades and the older acreage in Contra Costa County was now treated with unac-

customed respect. Statewide, acreage in 1997 was 420, more than half in Contra Costa County. Most, but not all varietal wine from Mataro is now labeled Mourvèdre. The two terms are legal synonyms.

The 1996 crop of Mataro (Mourvèdre) was 1,345 tons, twice the total for 1990.

MATTEI WINERY. Andrew Mattei (1835–1936), an Italian-Swiss, settled in Fresno County in 1890 and planted an 80-acre vineyard there. His winery went up in 1893. He produced fortified wine and brandy, sold under the brand name Mattevista, and was noted for his grape syrup, which had a good retail market. By 1910 he had 1,200 acres in vines and was producing 3 million gallons of wine and 350,000 gallons of brandy a year. After Prohibition the winery continued to prosper and, in 1962, the family sold it to GUILD WINERIES.

MATTHEWS, JOSEPH (José Mateus) (? –1893). Matthews came to Napa Valley from Madeira and worked at the ESHCOL winery from 1867 to 1877. He knew how to produce fortified sweet wines and built his Lisbon Winery in downtown Napa in 1880. For years his SHERRY was considered one of California's finest. After his death, the facility was acquired by several producers. In recent years there have been three attempts to use the fine old structure as a winery, in vain. In 1994 it became the home of the Jarvis music conservatory; see JARVIS WINERY

MAURICE CARRIE WINERY (BW 5353). A 240,000-gallon winery established by the Van Roekel family in the Temecula area of Riverside County in 1986. The 35,000-case production consists mainly of blush and white wines from several varietals. Grapes come from the 100-acre estate and are purchased from growers in Santa Barbara County. In 1995 the family established the Van Roekel Winery on adjoining land, using the same bond.

MAYACAMAS VINEYARDS (BW 4417). In 1936 Jack Taylor (1901–91) and his wife Mary (1904–84), vacationing on Mount Veeder in the Mayacamas Mountains, discovered an old stone building, the J. H. Fischer Winery built in 1885. In 1941 they bought it and the surrounding 260 acres. They reconstituted the old vineyard, planting mainly Chardonnay and later Cabernet Sauvignon. The first release, in 1953, was 94 bottles of a 1951 Chardonnay, made by Walter RICHERT. In 1959 Philip TOGNI became the winemaker. Meanwhile the vintages grew in size and the wines in reputation. The Taylors' lively newsletter, begun in 1949, kept customers close to the operation, as did the 1958 offering of stock, with dividends paid in picnics on Mount Veeder and bottles of Chardonnay. Under the Lokoya label they also sold a wide variety of wines from grapes grown elsewhere.

In 1968 the Taylors sold the winery to Robert and Elinor Travers, who, today produce about 5,000 cases a year, predominately Cabernet Sauvignon, Chardonnay, and Sauvignon blanc. The Cabernets have developed a reputation for intense flavor and longevity.

MAYOCK, ROBERT. See GRAU & WERNER

MAYTAG, FRITZ, and Paul Draper, a friend from his student days at Stanford University, worked on a wine project in Chile in the 1960s. In 1968 he bought what is now York Creek Vineyards on Spring Mountain. For years Maytag's Cabernet Sauvignon, Zinfandel, and Petite Sirah grapes have gone to RIDGE VINEYARDS where Draper is winemaker. In the 1990s Maytag began keeping the Cabernet grapes for wine to issue under his own York Creek label.

In 1969 Maytag bought San Francisco's Anchor Steam Beer Company and brought it back to life. He also produces a premium rye whiskey under the Anchor label.

MAZZOCCO VINEYARDS (BW 5270). Thomas Mazzocco is an eye surgeon who built his winery on Lytton Springs Road in the Dry Creek district of Sonoma County in 1985. In 1988 he sold the operation to VINTECH, but got it back in 1991 when the company went out of business. He owns 45 acres of vineyards at the winery and in the Alexander Valley. His 17,000-case annual production includes hardy Zinfandels, Cabernet Sauvignon, and Chardonnay. A blend of red Bordeaux grapes, made since the 1987 vintage, has been labeled Matrix.

MECHANICAL HARVESTING. See HARVEST

MEDICAL FRIENDS OF WINE, SOCIETY OF. In 1938 Leon ADAMS, with Maynard AMERINE, began an organization of physicians and dentists in northern California who were interested in wine and its medical aspects. Its objectives combine conviviality with support for research into the benefits of wine for health. The Society's quarterly dinners examine the progress of wines in its collection, and the members hear an address on some aspect of wine and society. Over the years, the organization has supported the California wine industry, many of its members taking an active role in combating the vilification of table wine by today's NEOPROHIBITIONISTS.

MEDICINAL WINE. During Prohibition it was legal for physicians to prescribe wine for their patients. The medicine, usually dry table wines, was sold in drug stores. Sales averaged about 2 million gallons per year. So-called medicated wine tonics required no prescription. Paul GARRETT's Virginia Dare Wine Tonic contained sweet wine laced with beef extract, pepsin, and iron.

MEEKER VINEYARD (BW 5209). The Meeker family bought a ranch in Dry Creek Valley, Sonoma, in 1977 and began planting vines there. In 1984 they bonded the winery, which is now producing 6,000 cases a year of estate Zinfandel, Cabernet Sauvignon, and Chardonnay from the 40-acre vineyard.

MEL, HENRY (?–1918). A brother of the better-known Louis Mel, Henry bought land from George JARVIS in the Vine Hill area near Santa Cruz in 1879. He planted a vineyard and built a small winery. The family name was actually Mel de Fontenay, so he called his place Fontenay Vineyard. Mel was a leader in the Santa Cruz Mountain wine community and was particularly famous for his Zinfandels grown in the Glenwood area, in the hills behind Los Gatos. He lost his property in bankruptcy in 1896, a victim of the 1893–97 national depression.

(handwritten margin note: Black Pinot or Tree Burgundy Glenwood)

MEL, LOUIS (1839–1937). In the years before his death, Louis MEL was truly the "grand old man" of California wine. Like so many of those who grew wine seriously in the Livermore Valley, Mel was a man of established wealth when he bought the W. G. Crow ranch in 1884 and planted 30 acres of vines. He also planted olive trees and called the place Olea Vista. In the planting frenzy of 1901, he ripped up the olives and planted 50 more acres of vines. He now called the place El Mocho. Between 1912 and 1913 he planted 30 more acres and built a new winery, which is now part of the WENTE estate. In 1916 he exchanged the property for an apartment house in Oakland and retired.

As time went by, his recollections of things past brought out the story of how in the 1880s, because Mel's wife was great friends with the owner of Château d'Yquem, it was possible for Charles WETMORE to import Sauvignon blanc and Sémillon vines from the famous estate in Sauternes to the Livermore Valley. It was thus, according to tradition, that the valley became famous for wines from those varieties.

MELON. An early ripening, cold-hardy variety of wine grape once common in Burgundy.

Today it is known as Muscadet in the Loire region. The French ampelographer, Pierre Galet, shocked experts at the University of California at Davis in 1980 by announcing that their collection of Pinot blanc was actually Melon. How much of California's so-called Pinot blanc in the field is Melon is not known. But since 1980 some California wineries have released wines labeled Melon, and even Muscadet, from grapes normally classified as Pinot blanc. In 1996 the BATF ruled that the terms Melon and Muscadet were not synonyms. But they also ruled that producers might label such wines Melon de Bourgogne, because that is an official name for the grape in France.

MELVILLE, JOHN (1903–62). A Dutch nobleman who, after fighting in the Free Netherlands Army in World War II, retired to Carmel, California. There he compiled his *Guide to California Wines,* published in 1955. As the modern wine revolution gathered steam in the 1960s this book acted as the chief guide for those who wanted to tour the California wine country. Today it is a useful historical source for the 1950s.

MENDOCINO. In 1984 a large part of Mendocino County was granted AVA status. What this means is that virtually all wine produced in the county may be labeled Mendocino without use of the word County.

MENDOCINO COUNTY. One of the most important premium winegrowing counties in California with about 13,000 acres in the mid-1990s; the number of wineries exceeds forty. It is a huge county with a diverse pattern of climates, but only the southern portion is good for viticulture. This portion is about the same area described by the MENDOCINO Viticultural Area: V-shaped, the left arm heading up the Anderson Valley from the Sonoma border, the right pointing up the Russian River Valley past Hopland, Ukiah, Redwood Valley, and

TABLE 18. WINE GRAPES IN MENDOCINO COUNTY, SELECTED VARIETIES

YEAR	PERCENT OF TOTAL RED	WHITE	CABERNET SAUVIGNON	CARIGNANE	(ACRES) CHAR- DONNAY	MERLOT	PINOT NOIR	SAUVIGNON BLANC	ZIN- FANDEL	TOTAL
1920										2,820
1925										8,330
1930										7,761
1940										8,510
1950										6,501
1961	83	17	0	2,675	0	0	9	66	1,062	5,079
1968	75	25	8	2,233	0	0	17	57	648	4,592
1972	70	30	459	2,346	843	6	102	50	749	7,067
1978	70	30	956	2,132	607	89	343	179	1,247	9,984
1983	51	49	929	1,583	1,429	64	322	731	1,337	10,921
1988	49	51	1,055	1,214	2,747	91	672	893	1,719	11,829
1993	50	50	1,406	868	4,006	607	608	820	1,786	12,468
1997	53	47	1,419	790	4,338	1,114	649	663	1,937	13,151

NOTES: Until 1961 statistics for acreage under various varieties of grapes were not published.
SOURCE: California Agricultural Statistics Service, Sacramento, Calif.

Potter Valley, to a line running approximately west from Willits. The Anderson Valley and the vineyard areas nearby are cool, much affected by the maritime influence. Farther inland, summer temperatures soar, but evenings are often quite cool.

Today's picture of winegrowing prosperity could not be inferred from the county's early history. In 1872 a state report pulled no punches: "The grape does not succeed well here." The wine boom of the 1880s hardly touched this land of lumberjacks. In 1890 there were but twenty growers with 204 acres of vines. But in 1906 the ITALIAN SWISS COLONY began pushing viticulture into the Ukiah area. By 1909 there were 2,700 acres of vines there. Prohibition changed all this as a frenzy of vineyard planting took place. By 1925 there were 8,330 acres in place. Most of their product was shipped south to the Bay Area on the little Northwestern Pacific Railroad and then across the country.

At Repeal the nature of planting was clear. There were then fourteen little wineries, every

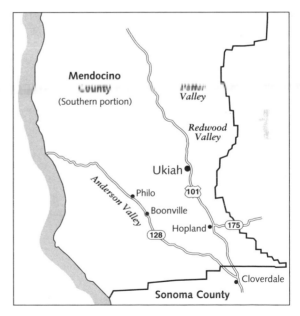

Mendocino County

one owned by an Italian family. Only PAR-DUCCI has survived, but vineyard names, such as Ciapucsi and Zeni, survive today as sources of excellent old-vine Zinfandel (see MENDO-CINO RIDGE). For years Carignane and Zinfandel were the chief varieties grown in Mendocino, most of the crop going to wineries in Sonoma or, after 1946, to the Mendocino Grape Growers Cooperative Winery in Ukiah. Acreage declined until the late 1960s, but has risen since then by almost 300 percent. All but two of the county's wineries today were bonded after 1968. For all its wineries, more than 60 percent of the grapes grown in Mendocino are still exported to wineries in other counties. In 1996 Mendocino produced 50,650 tons of wine grapes, 128 percent of the 1990 vintage.

There are still many old vineyards with old-style varietals, but the expansion has been overwhelmingly in world-class types, particularly Chardonnay.

MENDOCINO RIDGE Viticultural Area established by the BATF in the hills above Anderson Valley in 1997 is unique in that it consists of a group of noncontiguous vineyards—"islands in the sky" at about 1,200 feet of elevation. This AVA includes some of northern California's most renowned Zinfandel vineyards, notably Ciapusci, Zeni, Mariah, and Du Pratt.

MENDOCINO VINEYARDS (BW 4398). The old plant in Ukiah, where formerly, the GUILD WINERIES made its Cresta Blanca wines. This is the source of the wines sold under the Dunnewood brand. Since 1991 it has been part of the CANANDAIGUA Wine Co.

MER & SOLEIL. See CAYMUS

MERCAPTAN. Organic compounds, often resulting from a reaction between the yeast and sulfur in the lees, that give wines an extremely unpleasant smell. The metaphor often used to describe them can be inferred from the fact that n-Butyl mercaptan is one of the main components in the scent of skunks. Until recent years when they became more completely understood, mercaptans were a bane to wine producers in California.

MERCED COUNTY, in the Central Valley, where lots of wine grapes are grown. In 1997 there were about 15,634 acres, about 55 percent white. Merced has been going through the same changes as nearby Madera County in the past five years: jug-wine country is being transformed into FIGHTING VARIETAL country. In 1990 the leading variety had been French Colombard. In 1997 there were 2,053 acres of Merlot, 1,907 of Chardonnay, 1,552 of Zinfandel, and 585 of Cabernet Sauvignon—and most of those plantings were new.

During Prohibition acreage increased from 10,000 to 23,000 acres between 1920 and 1925. Then, by 1935, there were only 5,000 acres of wine grapes. This number held fairly steady until recent years when the total rose to about 10,000. Then came the explosion in the 1990s, which probably will continue.

MERIDIAN VINEYARDS (BW 5453). In 1988 Beringer (see BERINGER WINE ESTATES) acquired the Estrella River Winery to set up a major Chardonnay facility in the Central Coast. The company changed the winery name and hired Charles ORTMAN* as the winemaker and director of operations. (Meridian wines actually originated in 1984 as a brand for Ortman's own wines from the Napa Valley. When he was hired in 1988 he sold the brand to Beringer.)

The winery is located east of Paso Robles, but the backbone for Meridian Chardonnays is supplied by the company's vineyards in Santa Barbara County and Edna Valley, in San Luis Obispo County, where the cooler environment makes for excellent grapes. Meridian production is about 200,000 cases per year, and includes some Cabernet Sauvignon, Pinot noir, and Syrah. Beringer now owns more than 3,500 acres of Central Coast vineyard land.

MERITAGE. Traditionally, red and white table wines in Bordeaux are blends of grape varieties. The trend in California since the 1950s has been toward wines of a single varietal. Nevertheless, since 1936 any varietal wine has needed, legally, to contain no more than 51 percent of the grape variety mentioned on the label. Thus, blending in California was common, but not in the tradition of Bordeaux. In 1983 the BATF changed the required minimum quantity of the named varietal to 75 percent, just at a time when more and more producers were making experimental blends of Cabernet Sauvignon with other grapes such as Merlot and Cabernet franc. What should they call wines like these that have less than 75 percent of one variety?

In 1988 an association of such producers was formed and a national contest was held to pick a name. The winner was Neil Edgar, a wine buyer in southern California, who came up with Meritage (rhymes with "heritage"). The term was trademarked by the newly named Meritage Association. It may be used on red and white wine, so long as traditional Bordeaux varieties are used. To date the term has caught on in the industry, but has been slow to appear on labels.

MERITHEW, JOSEPH C. (1822–1904), was one of the leading vintners in the Santa Clara Valley during the nineteenth century. A former sea captain, he planted his Prospect Vineyard in Cupertino in 1877. His winery and its little distillery had a national reputation by the late 1880s. At the 1893 Columbian Exposition he won awards for his Cabernet Sauvignon and port.

MERLOT. The most exclusively grown red-wine grape in Bordeaux, specifically in

Pomerol and St-Émilion and used for most of the great wines of the Haut Médoc. In California Merlot acreage grew at a faster pace than that of any other world-class variety in the late 1980s and the 1990s.

In the 1850s Antoine DELMAS imported the first vines; he called the grape Merlau. In the 1870s J.-B. J. PORTAL and others also brought it in, but it did not find favor. At the 1888 state viticultural convention, only one sample was displayed, from LINDA VISTA. By the turn of the century we hear of Merlot no more.

After Repeal a few acres were planted in California. INGLENOOK had some old acres and Louis MARTINI planted some near Healdsburg in 1962. ALMADEN planted a few acres in the late 1950s in San Benito County. The professors at the University of California at Davis gave the variety their recommendation in the 1960s, "with reservations."

The planting boom of the 1970s included lots of Merlot. California's first varietal Merlot was produced by Louis Martini, a blend of 1968 and 1970 vintages. The regular bottling of 1970 Inglenook Cabernet included 15 percent Merlot. The question in those years was whether the variety was better blended with Cabernet Sauvignon or as a varietal. By 1977 twenty-eight California wineries were producing varietal Merlots; by 1980 there were forty. Besides wine drinkers' growing taste for the varietal was the practical fact that Merlot ripened earlier than Cabernet Sauvignon and was less likely to be damaged by fall rains.

There was a small decline in acreage in the early 1980s but in 1985 planting took off again and soared after 1987. Merlot even became a popular FIGHTING VARIETAL (see table 19 and the figures supplied under SAN JOAQUIN COUNTY). Another facet of Merlot's increasing popularity was its tendency to make softer and less tannic wines than does Cabernet Sauvignon, and to require less long-term cellaring. By the mid-1990s there were more than 200 Merlot brands, and there were predictions

TABLE 19. MERLOT GRAPES, SELECTED COUNTIES

YEAR	MENDOCINO	SONOMA	NAPA	(ACRES) SAN JOAQUIN	MONTEREY	SAN LUIS OBISPO	TOTAL
1965	N.A.	N.A.	N.A.	N.A.	N.A.	N.A.	31
1971	0	63	168	0	174	0	426
1974	37	503	680	46	1,178	461	3,988
1980	102	517	693	72	632	166	2,667
1984	106	493	901	37	303	31	2,377
1987	68	946	1,144	10	322	73	3,330
1990	266	1,907	2,148	686	674	201	7,435
1994	706	3,545	3,804	1,997	1,619	556	17,993
1995	910	4,162	4,565	3,520	2,054	958	25,003
1997	1,114	5,152	5,067	4,211	2,573	1,587	32,883

SOURCE: California Agricultural Statistics Service, Sacramento, Calif.

of greater grape shortages to come. Between 1990 and 1996 Merlot acreage in California grew 336 percent.

And yet some of California's Merlot probably isn't. In 1994 it was discovered that one of the four Merlot accessions at the University of California at Davis, from which earlier propagation had been made, was actually Cabernet franc.

California's best recent Merlot vintages: 1996, 1994, 1990, 1987, 1985, 1983. The 1997 Merlot vintage in California produced 196,240 tons, making it the third most productive red-wine grape. For 1990 the total was 15,205 tons.

MERRITT ISLAND, in the DELTA region and part of the larger Clarksburg Viticultural Area, was granted its own appellation designation in 1983. The soils on the island are sandy loam and quite different from those in the larger AVA.

MERRYVALE VINEYARDS (BW 4072). At Repeal John Riorda and his partners put up the Sunnyhill Winery at the south edge of St. Helena in Napa Valley to produce bulk wine. Later they changed the name to Sunny St. Helena Winery. In 1937, before taking over the Charles Krug Winery, the MONDAVI family bought into the operation. In 1946 the Mon-

davi bought it outright for production of their CK line of wines. Years later the CHRISTIAN BROTHERS used it for storage.

In 1983 a group of partners formed Merryvale Vineyards and made wine at ROMBAUER until 1986 when they acquired Sunny St. Helena. For a while, they put out wines under both labels, but in 1993 the old sign came down and Merryvale became the single brand for the 45,000-case premium operation, which produces a wide range of varietals. The winery has been modernized but much of the old atmosphere remains; the old casks still line the walls of a great banquet hall.

MERRY VINTNERS (BW 5219). Meredith (Merry) EDWARDS and her family operated this little winery west of Santa Rosa in Sonoma County from 1984 to 1996.

MÉTHODE CHAMPENOISE. The traditional French method of producing SPARKLING WINE. When it is used, the label may legally carry the description "fermented in this bottle," a reference to the second fermentation that produces the bubbles. Since 1990 a group of some, but not all, of the California wineries using the process has pro-

This bottling session at BUENA VISTA WINERY in the 1870s illustrates almost all the finishing details in the *méthode champenoise,* from disgorging to the application of the wired hood.

moted the idea that such sparklers are superior to others. This CM/CV (classic method/classic varieties) Society is made up mostly of European-owned houses that make sparkling wine in California.

METRIC MEASURES. Californians measure their vineyards in acres, their grapes in tons, and their wine in gallons. This convention can cause a communication problem, because much of the rest of the wine world uses metric measures.

Europeans measure their vineyards in hectares (ha), 1 hectare being equal to 2.471 acres. Wine production is measured in hectoliters (hl), a hectoliter being equal to 26.418 gallons. Furthermore, Americans usually express the rate of production in tons per acre. Europeans, bypassing the grapes involved, measure production in quantities of wine—a French vineyard, for instance, is said to produce so many hectoliters per hectare

(Xhl/ha), a measure of little meaning to Americans.

If a 10-acre vineyard had a yield of 3 tons per acre and a winery made 160 gallons of wine per ton of grapes from that land, we would express it in this way:

10 (acres) $\times$ 3 (tons) = 30 tons

30 (tons) $\times$ 160 (gallons) = 4,800 gallons from the 10 acres

If 10 acres = 4.047 ha and produce 4,800 gallons = 181.693 hl,

181.693/4.047 = 44.9 hl/ha

As 44.9 (hl/ha) is about the same as 3 tons per acre, we can say that the 44.9/3.0 = approximately 15 and use this number as a convenient multiplier or divisor to make conversion easier. Thus, a yield in California of 5 tons per acre is equal to about 75 hl/ha, and a French vineyard yielding about 50 hl/ha is producing about 3.3 tons/acre.

MEUNIER, a cousin of the Pinot noir grape that makes up about 35 percent of the acreage in the Champagne region of France. Used as a basis for sparkling wine, it is said that the variety adds some bright fruitiness and some spiciness to French champagne. In California several producers with vineyards in the Carneros have planted Meunier since the late 1970s. In 1997 almost all the state's 205 acres were located there.

The variety was imported to California in the 1850s by Antoine DELMAS and was used later by several producers in the Santa Clara and Napa valleys in their burgundy-style red wines. Then it was called the Pinot Meunier. We hear nothing of it between the 1890s and recent years. In 1993 DOMAINE CHANDON produced a varietal Pinot Meunier, a still wine, as did HANDLEY CELLARS in 1995.

MEYER, ERNST E. (1843–1918). After several years in the nursery business in San Francisco, Meyer in 1881 bought 1,674 acres of land in the Santa Cruz Mountains near Wrights Station, close to the summit, calling his estate Mare Vista. By 1887 he had 95 acres in vines and had built a winery that by the 1890s had a 250,000-gallon capacity. He subdivided much of the rest of his property and sold it mostly to his German countrymen, who planted orchards and vineyards and sold the grapes to him. This became known as the Loma Prieta German Colony. Meyer was well known for his Sylvaner and Traminer wines and his vineyards were the first in the Santa Cruz Mountains to be planted to resistant rootstock. (Some of those vines survived into the 1950s.)

In 1899 he became world famous when he used 4,000 gallons of fermenting Zinfandel must to save his winery from a raging forest fire. The national press picked up the story, which was eventually published in *Scientific American* and *Wide World Magazine*. At Repeal Emil Meyer (1874–1939), Ernst's son, reopened the old winery for a short time.

MEYER, JUSTIN. See SILVER OAK WINE CELLARS

PETER MICHAEL WINERY (BW CA 5465). In 1982 Peter Michael, an English computer engineer, bought a 600-acre piece of land in the hills north of Knight's Valley, near Kellogg Creek in Sonoma County. In 1987 he built a little winery. His first wines, with Helen TURLEY as the winemaker, were made from purchased grapes, but there is now a 85-acre producing vineyard. Total output runs to about 10,000 cases per year, mainly Chardonnay, Sauvignon blanc, and red Bordeaux blends (Les Pavots). Michael has made a special effort to promote sales to the United Kingdom.

MICHEL-SCHLUMBERGER (BW 5283). The Swiss banker Jean-Jacques Michel had been a business associate of Tom JORDAN and was so impressed by his friend's success that, in 1979, he bought 100 acres in Dry Creek Valley, Sonoma, planted grapes, and built a beautiful Mediterranean-style winery, Domaine Michel. Its opening in 1987 was described as a "lavish bash" by the press. The first wine was produced in 1984 at another facility, but by 1986 Michel's own winery was operating. Production, mostly of Cabernet Sauvignon and Chardonnay, was around 20,000 cases per year by the 1990s. In 1993 a new owner, Jacques Schlumberger, took control of the winery, the name was changed, and production reduced to 15,000 cases per year.

MICROCLIMATE. In the ordinary parlance of horticulture, agriculture, and—therefore—winegrowing, a microclimate is the result of a confluence of elements that causes the climate of a specific piece of land to vary from the generalized climate of the area. Thus, one understands that the climate of the Carneros is good for Chardonnay but too cool for Cabernet Sauvignon. Yet there are places in the Carneros where there is enough heat to ripen Cabernet grapes; such sites have distinctive microclimates.

A more strict use of the term applies to so-called climates to be found at different soil depths in a specific site; a gravelly soil will get more water, for instance, at a certain depth than would a thick adobe soil. In the same sense, the microclimate near the surface of a vine's leaves might be different from that at the surfaces of its grape bunches. The possibilities are endless. The distinction between the uses of this term is academic, but it does no harm to know the difference.

MIGLIAVACCA, GUISEPPE (1833–1911) a native of Padua, came to California in 1857, and in 1866, to Napa, where he ran a wine and liquor business. In 1874 he dug a cellar downtown for his 150,000-gallon winery. By 1886 he had a wine factory in Napa capable of producing over 300,000 gallons per year. His operation could handle grapes from the Sacramento Valley as well as the local product. This huge wine plant in Napa City, and that of Charles CARPY, gave a distinct industrial character to wine production in Napa. He was often criticized for lowering the quality image of Napa wines by processing hundreds of tons of Central Valley grapes, yet he was famous for producing small lots of outstanding wine. His Zinfandel Claret won a gold medal at the 1889 Paris Exposition. He retired in 1908 leaving the business to his four sons. Their last vintage was in 1918.

MILANO WINERY (BW 4801). Located in the Sanel Valley just south of Hopland in Mendocino County, Milano was founded in 1977 and today produces about 2,000 cases per year from the estate's 60-acre vineyard. This is a much lower total than that reached in the 1980s. Chardonnay, Cabernet Sauvignon, and Zinfandel are the top varietals.

MILAT VINEYARDS (BW 5357). Just south of St. Helena in the Napa Valley the Milat family

owns a 20-acre vineyard that was purchased in the 1950s. They sold grapes for years and built a little winery in 1986. Their annual 3,000-case production, principally dry Chenin blanc, Chardonnay, and Cabernet Sauvignon, is sold almost entirely at the winery.

MILDEW. Powdery mildew (oidium) is a fungus disease that vineyardists in California came to know in the late 1850s. It causes leaves to curl, berries to split and brown, and canes to wither. The musty smell in the vineyard gives a clear hint of what happens to wine made from mildew-infected grapes. Elemental sulfur dust, introduced to California in 1859 by Antoine DELMAS, is the standard defense today. Pruning of the vine's leaf canopy to increase sunlight and air movement is a recently developed technique.

Downy mildew, a very serious problem in much of the grape growing world, is not a problem in California, probably because of its usually dry summer climate.

MILL CREEK VINEYARDS (BW 4739). The Krech family has 70 acres of vines in the southern part of Dry Creek Valley in Sonoma County that they began planting in 1965. Their winery produced its first wines in 1976. When the BLUSH wine market took off in the early 1980s, other producers discovered that Mill Creek held trademark rights to the term blush, having used it earlier for their Cabernet Blush. Royalties from other producers have been a boon to the family. Production of a wide range of varietals comes to about 15,000 cases per year. Felta Springs is a second label.

MILLER, F. JUSTIN (BWC 4483), a chemist in Napa who devised a two-day process, Millerway, for putting the bubbles into a still wine. But the BATF would not allow such wines to be labeled sparkling. He sued but lost his case in 1968 in a district court. Because such wines would have to be labeled carbonated, Miller's process has not become a commercial

HEITZ CELLAR

CALIFORNIA CARBONATED
MALVASIA BIANCA

ALCOHOL 12% BY VOLUME   NET CONTENTS 4/5 QUART
PRODUCED AND BOTTLED BY HEITZ WINE CELLARS
ST. HELENA, CALIFORNIA

For a while in the 1960s HEITZ WINE CELLARS marketed "carbonated" wine made by the Millerway process. In addition to the Malvasia Bianca there was a Grignolino.

success, although many considered the wines to be as good as most California sparklers.

MIRASSOU. Henriette Pellier (1860–1937) married **Pierre H. Mirassou** (1856–89) in 1881, a marriage through which the Mirassous can rightfully claim to be one of the pioneer winegrowing families in California. Before that date, Henriette had taken over the supervision of much of the Pellier winegrowing operations on the Evergreen estate in the Santa Clara Valley that had been developed by her father, Pierre PELLIER (1823–94). The couple had five children before Mirassou's untimely death. The next year the young widow married Thomas Casalegno and together, they ran the Pellier winery until they retired in 1910.

In due time, the three Mirassou boys, **Peter, Herman,** and **John,** as a partnership acquired 100 acres of vineyard land in Evergreen near the old estate. After World War I, the brothers split the family holdings and Peter (1885–1951) kept the 100 acres in Evergreen, today the site of the **Mirassou Vineyards** winery (BW 4255). There he made bulk wine for two years before Prohibition and continued growing wine grapes through the dry years. In 1937 Peter and his sons went back into the winemaking busi-

ness when they built today's winery. For many years this was a bulk wine operation, much of it from good varietals and bought by premium producers such as Almaden and Paul Masson. The winery was run by Peter's sons, **Edmund** (1918–96) and **Norbert** (1915–92), who gradually introduced a line of Mirassou premium wines in the 1950s, first at the winery and then on the retail market. There was also a line of bottle-fermented sparkling wine.

In 1961, as suburban development in the Santa Clara Valley pressed in on the Evergreen estate, the Mirassous looked to Monterey County to expand their vineyards. Over the years their acreage there near Soledad has risen to about 800 and sales grown to about 200,000 cases. In 1984 Edmund's children, **Daniel, James,** and **Peter,** took over the operation of the winery in a long-term buyout from Norbert's family. In 1989 sparkling wine production was consolidated at the old winery at the NOVITIATE OF LOS GATOS (BW 1077), which was converted for that purpose. In recent years, the Mirassou product line has consisted chiefly of white, BLUSH, and sparkling wines, which now account for about 80 percent of production. Pinot blanc is their most popular white varietal wine.

Another branch of the Mirassou family was also a part of Santa Clara Valley winegrowing. After splitting with his brothers in 1918, **Herman Mirassou** (1883–1968) ran the huge Fountain Ranch near Campbell, a mixed agricultural operation. In 1936 he bought the historic Lone Hill Ranch to the east, with 120 acres of vines. His four sons ran this ranch for years and in 1946 they opened LONE HILL VINEYARDS winery (BW 4395) on the site of the historic winery of that name, which dated from the 1850s. This 500,000-gallon operation lasted until 1968 when the subdivisions moved in.

Edmund A. Mirassou and Nobert C. Mirassou, *The Evolution of a Santa Clara Winery* (Regional Oral History Office, Bancroft Library, 1986).

MIRAVALLE. See Tiburcio PARROTT

MISSION BELL WINERY (BW 22). The historic name of the huge production facility in Madera acquired by Heublein in 1968. Many owners had preceded them: ITALIAN SWISS COLONY, CALIFORNIA WINE ASSOCIATION, Krikor Arakelian, Louis PETRI, and ALLIED GRAPE GROWERS.

MISSION. A variety of grape so named in the United States because it was brought up from Mexico to BAJA and Alta California and to the American Southwest as part of the establishment of the Spanish missions, first by the Jesuits, then by the Franciscans. It and some of its cousins can also be found in South America, as the País in Chile and the Criollo in Argentina. It is clearly of vinifera origin, although no perfect match has ever been found in the Old World. Some believe it to be a close relative of Sardinia's Monica grape. Because it was a part of New World culture for about 250 years before it was carried up to the missions in Alta California in the 1770s, it may be the result of one or more crosses or chance hybridizations.

Most missions in California had vineyards and made some wine from this grape. A dark-skinned variety, it makes very poor red or white table wine. When made white, the result was closer to brown. Yet, some sweet fortified wines made from Mission grapes did receive some praise, particularly when they were well aged; see ANGELICA. By the 1820s the ranchos also had Mission grape vineyards, for wine, brandy (see AGUARDIENTE), and the table. After the missions were secularized in the 1830s, their old vines were often used to propagate vineyards around the pueblos and ranchos, particularly in southern California, which was the state's vineyard for most wine and fresh grapes in the 1850s. A planting boom in this period saw most new vineyards planted to the Mission variety, then called the California grape. Wines made from those plantings diminished the reputation for quality in much of the wine made in California through the 1870s.

The planting boom of the 1880s, the decline of viticulture in southern California, and the devastation of the phylloxera ended the wine industry's large-scale use of Mission grapes. By the late 1890s they were only a small part of the state's plantings and have remained so.

At the outset of Prohibition there were about 5,000 acres in the state. During the dry years, growers annually shipped out about 1,000 carloads of Mission grapes. Mostly from the Central Valley, these accounted for about 2 percent of the grapes shipped to eastern home winemakers. Acreage stood at about 11,000 from the 1930s to the 1950s, the grapes used mostly in inexpensive fortified wines. Acreage declined slowly and steadily from 1970 (6,500 acres) to 1997 (898 acres), most of it in the Central Valley. There were still 3,800 tons crushed in 1996. In recent years, a few small premium wineries have produced a varietal Mission wine. One was labeled Criolla.

MISSION SAN JOSE, a little town near the local mission, founded in 1851 and developing into the center of one of California's greatest early winegrowing districts. The area has had many designations over the years, among them Mission San Jose, Warm Springs, and Washington Township. In the 1880s, along with the Napa and Sonoma valleys, it was considered a leader in producing wine of good quality; Eugene HILGARD thought it the very best in the state. Here could be found the great wineries of Josiah STANFORD (Warm Springs), Juan GALLEGOS (Palmdale), Charles McIver (LINDA VISTA), and GRAU & WERNER (Los Amigos). The expansion of suburbia doomed viticulture in the area after the 1950s. WEIBEL then surrounded by scores of housing developments, ended its operations there in 1995. The old district is today part of the City of Fremont. Nevertheless, the BATF in 1989 properly included the district in the Santa Clara Valley Viticultural Area.

MISSIONS AND THE MISSION PERIOD

(1769–1835). Between 1697 and 1767 Jesuit missionaries established a tenuous string of missions in what we today call BAJA CALIFORNIA. Some had vineyards and made wine. Then in 1768 the Jesuits were expelled from Mexico, the Franciscans took over their institutions and in 1769, established the first mission in Alta California (see CALIFORNIA) at San Diego and perhaps planted some vines, but none survived. The first successful vineyard in Alta California was planted at Mission San Juan Capistrano from vines brought north in 1778. The first vintage there was in 1782 under the supervision of Father Pablo MUGÁRTEGUI. By the end of the century, the padres at several missions were making wine for Mass and for their own consumption. By the 1820s, some missions were selling wine and brandy to the pueblos, ranchos, and presidios of the province. The mission vineyards also provided vine cuttings for others as Alta California became a more diverse community.

In the 1830s the mission lands were secularized and parceled out on a grand scale. Most of the mission vineyards declined and disappeared; a few actually became commercially profitable under private management, mostly from the brandy produced. A survey of California vineyards in 1835 showed almost a million vines in the province, about 38 percent on old mission land, the rest at ranchos and in the pueblos of Los Angeles and San Jose.

Mission San Diego Alcala, founded 16 July 1769, was the first mission in Alta California. It was believed for many years that California's first grape vines were planted here, but there is no clear evidence to support that claim. Eventually, the mission did have a good vineyard, but it was not by any means the "mother vineyard."

Mission San Fernando Rey de España was founded in 1797 west of the present town of San Fernando, and had several good vineyards and a winery that continued to operate years after the mission was secularized. By the 1830s it was second only to MISSION SAN GABRIEL in the extent of its vineyards.

Mission San Francisco de Solano (Sonoma Mission) was the last mission to be established in Alta California. Named after a Spanish missionary to Peru, it was founded in 1823, its little vineyard planted in the winter of that year with cuttings brought up from Mission San José de Guadalupe. It was this vineyard that was the source of most of the vines planted in the Sonoma and Napa valleys during the 1830s and 1840s.

Mission San Gabriel Arcángel was founded in 1771 not far from what was to be the Los Angeles pueblo. Not important for wine at first, San Gabriel had, by the 1820s the largest vineyard in Alta California and the padres there were producing about 500 barrels of wine and 200 of brandy each year. Although referred to at the time as the *viña madre,* it was not the earliest of the mission vineyards, but the name is not entirely fanciful: The orgins of the large vineyards planted in the area during the 1840s and 1850s could be traced to cuttings taken from San Gabriel.

Mission San José de Guadalupe was founded in 1797 in the East Bay foothills about 20 miles south of Oakland. Between 1810 and 1835 its good vineyard was the nursery for other missions, ranchos, and pueblos in northern California. Its wines seems to have been the best made by any of the northern missions.

Mission San Luis Rey de Francia, north of MISSION SAN DIEGO ALCÁLA, was more successful in its vineyards, which lasted into the 1850s.

J. N. Bowman, "The Vineyards of Provincial California," parts 1–4, *Wine Review,* April 1943, 22–24; May 1943, 24–26; June 1943, 18–22; July 1943, 21–24.

Roy Brady, "The Swallow That Came from Capistrano," *New West,* September 1979, 55.

Thomas Pinney, *A History of Wine in America from the Beginnings to Prohibition* (Berkeley, Calif.: University of California Press, 1989), 237–45.

CHARLES B. MITCHELL VINEYARD. The Gerwer family acquired their vineyard land in El Dorado County in 1979 and in 1982 bonded the little winery, which they first called Stony Creek Winery and a year later gave their family name. By the 1990s the Gerwers were producing a wide range of varietals, more than 5,000 cases a year. In 1994 the operation was bought by Charles B. Mitchell, renamed and rebonded (BW 5744). Mitchell has the annual production up to 7,000 cases with emphasis on Cabernet Sauvignon, Sauvignon blanc, and Zinfandel. He also makes some sparkling wine.

MOËT-HENNESSEY. See DOMAINE CHANDON

MONDAVI. For California wine in the twentieth century one of the state's most important families; for premium wine, perhaps the most important. **Cesare Mondavi** (1883–1959) came to the United States from northern Italy in 1906 and in the 1920s settled with his family in Lodi, making good money shipping grapes to eastern home winemakers. After Repeal he saw the potential of table wine production and invested in the Acampo Winery in Lodi. In 1937 he and others incorporated the Sunny St. Helena Winery (see MERRYVALE VINEYARDS) and began producing bulk table wine from grapes grown in the Napa Valley. When Acampo was sold to eastern bottlers in 1943, Cesare bought the old Charles KRUG plant that Louis Stralla had been running as the NAPA (VALLEY) WINE COMPANY since Repeal. Cesare's sons, **Robert** and **Peter,** had already been making commercial wine, Robert at Sunny St. Helena and Peter, until he went off to war, at Acampo.

In 1946 the Mondavis formed a family corporation and bought Sunny St. Helena outright. They continued to produce bulk wine and began selling it under the CK label. Their best wines, mostly premium varietals, went out under the Charles Krug label. In the first years the emphasis was on white wine, but the reds soon caught up. Between 1949 and 1956 the brothers won thirty-nine gold medals at the State Fair for their table wines.

Robert Mondavi was general manager; Peter was in charge of production. They both worked on the technical advances that propelled

Cesare Mondavi came to America from Italy in 1906. During Prohibition and after he and his family shipped grapes from the Lodi area to home winemakers east of the Rockies. Valley Beauty was one of his brands of Zinfandel, shown here on this box-end label. Another was Bocce.

Charles Krug wines into the limelight: sterile filtration, acid correction, vacuum corking, skin contact for red wines, and small oak cooperage. A list of their production team in the early years includes names later renowned in the industry: Al Huntsinger, Laurence Stern, William Bonetti, and Robert STEMMLER to name a few. Robert Mondavi handled promotion, which included a fine newsletter, an elegant tasting room, and concerts at the winery.

For all their success, the Mondavi brothers did not agree on how the winery should be run. In 1965 Robert was pushed out of his management position at Krug by Peter, who was supported by their mother, Rosa Mondavi. Robert, determined to start his own winery, was able to acquire the necessary backing to open **Robert Mondavi Winery** (BW 4511) in Oakville in time for the 1966 crush. It was the first large-scale winery built in the Napa Valley since the days of Repeal. Within a few years, the winery had established itself as a leader in the production of premium wines in Napa.

Meanwhile Peter Mondavi continued to run the Charles Krug operation and restructured the family corporation to Robert's disadvantage. In 1976 Robert won a lawsuit against Peter and other members of the family, the findings of which determined that Peter's "fraudulent activities" had made him the father of two millionaire sons. The settlement gave Robert and his family the capital to expand their own operations. In 1979 they bought the old CHEROKEE VINEYARD ASSOCIATION winery near Lodi as the base for their **Robert Mondavi Woodbridge** (BW 4802). Over the years, this facility has been a steady source of the good-quality jug wines and FIGHTING VARIETALS that account for more than 80 percent of the Mondavi sales volume. The Woodbridge plant (shown on page 306) has been called "the world's largest boutique winery." By the mid-1990s sales from this facility approached 5 million cases per year.

Also in 1979 Robert Mondavi and Philippe de Rothschild from Bordeaux combined their economic and technical resources to produce a first-growth Cabernet blend of wine from Napa grapes. In 1984 the first OPUS ONE* wines were released, vintages 1979 and 1980. By 1991 the wine had its own winery and a 130-acre vineyard, just down the road from the Mondavi facility in Oakville. The high prices for Opus One have been backed by high critical praise. Production has passed the 20,000 case mark.

In 1985 Robert bought VICHON WINERY* in Napa. In 1990 he bought the BYRON VINEYARD AND WINERY in Santa Barbara County, and by 1996, Mondavi interests controlled about 1,700 acres of Central Coast vineyard. In 1993 Robert and his family made a public stock offering to raise capital for expansion, debt relief, and to replant phylloxerated vineyards. Meanwhile, Robert in 1990 passed the active control of the corporation to his sons, Michael, the chief executive officer, and Timothy, the winemaker. This move, at the age of 77, freed him to pursue his mission to help counter the disparaging treatment of wine by what the wine industry calls NEOPROHIBITIONISTS.

By the mid-1990s the Mondavi Corporation ranked as the seventh largest wine producer in California with more than 4,000 acres of vines and sales of almost 6 million cases per year.

Kim Marcus, "Mondavi Père & Fils," *Wine Spectator,* 31 October 1997, 66–85.

Peter R. Mondavi, *Advances in Technology and Production at Charles Krug Winery, 1946–1988* (Regional Oral History Office, Bancroft Library, 1990).

Robert Mondavi, *Creativity in the California Wine Industry* (Regional Oral History Office, Bancroft Library, 1985).

Cyril Ray, *Robert Mondavi of the Napa Valley* (London: Heinemann/Peter Davies, 1984).

Jan Stuller and Glen Martin, *Through the Grape Vine* (New York: Wynwood Press, 1989), 228–45.

MONDEUSE. See REFOSCO

MONTE BELLO. The Monte Bello Ridge is an elevated Jurassic escarpment in the Santa Cruz Mountains above Cupertino and Los Altos. The heights and the steep land below were settled by Italian orchardists and vineyardists in the 1880s. Osea Perrone, a physician in San Francisco, developed the Montebello Winery (see MONTEBELLO WINE CO.) at the top of the ridge. Other early wineries of note there were those of Pierre KLEIN, Charles Rousten, and Anton PICCHETTI. Today RIDGE VINEYARDS uses the old Perrone winery and vineyards as home base and actually owns the Monte Bello brand name. Several other vineyardists and wineries also operate today in this historic district.

MONTEBELLO WINE CO. (BW 1036). The Montebello Winery was founded in 1886 by Osea Perrone on the Monte Bello Ridge above Cupertino in the Santa Cruz Mountains. The agency for his wines in San Francisco was the Montebello Wine Co. on Folsom Street. After his death in 1912, his nephew, also Osea Perrone, continued the operation and started up the winery again at Repeal. After his death in 1936, production was transferred to St. Helena, in the Napa Valley, to the old Esmeralda Winery. In 1943 the company was purchased by L. N. Renault Co. of New Jersey. The founders of RIDGE VINEYARDS* wanted to call their operation Monte Bello Ridge Winery, but the owners of the old company would not allow it. But in 1993 Ridge was able to acquire the Monte Bello name as a brand, when they choose to use it.

MONTEPULCIANO WINERY. See SIMI WINERY

MONTEREY. An important viticultural area within Monterey County that includes much of the Salinas and Carmel valleys. It was

The PICCHETTIS were winegrowing pioneers in the Monte Bello area. Here during the 1910 crush family members take a break next to the curing table. The conveyor behind them took the grapes up to the portable crusher, which could be moved from one fermenting vat to another. (Sunrise Winery Collection, Cupertino, Calif.)

granted AVA status in 1984. One of the chief reasons for establishing the district was to obviate the possibility or necessity in the future of having to identify Monterey County wines as Salinas Valley wines, the Salinas area evoking as it does images of lettuces rather than of wine grapes.

MONTEREY COUNTY. A Central Coast county that in the 1990s, with almost 30,000 acres of wine grapes, ranked third in California (exceeded only by Sonoma and Napa), among the coastal counties producing grapes for premium table wines. This rank has been

TABLE 20. WINE GRAPES IN MONTEREY COUNTY, SELECTED VARIETIES

YEAR	PERCENT OF TOTAL RED	WHITE	(ACRES) CABERNET SAUVIGNON	CHARDONNAY	CHENIN BLANC	MERLOT	PINOT NOIR	SAUVIGNON BLANC	WHITE RIESLING	ZINFANDEL	TOTAL
1968	30	70	96	60	96	0	132	35	49	20	1,121
1972	58	42	1,925	843	1,190	334	774	426	604	905	11,791
1976	61	39	6,178	2,692	2,022	1,552	2,370	972	2,560	3,007	33,143
1979	51	49	4,242	3,108	3,160	673	2,137	1,129	2,797	2,774	31,632
1983	32	68	3,321	4,037	5,104	291	1,609	1,869	4,562	2,138	34,618
1987	28	72	2,979	5,647	4,460	322	1,365	1,549	2,801	1,411	27,308
1990	34	66	3,763	8,469	2,762	674	1,616	1,489	2,624	1,878	28,496
1997	35	65	3,582	13,593	1,491	2,573	1,440	1,119	1,603	1,351	30,410

SOURCE: California Agricultural Statistics Service, Sacramento, Calif.

recently acquired. In 1955 the county had only 120 acres of wine grapes, as many as there had been in 1910.

The big change began in the 1960s when several large wineries in the Bay Area (WENTE, MIRASSOU, PAUL MASSON, ALMADEN) followed advice from the University of California at Davis and began planting the Salinas Valley in the south, while suburbia expanded in the north. During the 1970s there was a planting binge there. Large-scale investors poured capital into vineyard land as grape prices skyrocketed and the national consumption of table wine soared. Meanwhile, several medium and small-scale wineries set up shop in the county. Many, but not all, are still in operation. Vines were also planted and wineries built, but on a much smaller scale, in nearby CARMEL VALLEY.

A substantial part of this viticultural explosion was ill-advised. (More than 25,000 acres were planted between 1972 and 1974.) Some vineyards were planted to varieties poorly suited to the environment; some should not have been planted at all. Many people who were looking at their investments as tax shelters suffered losses on a grand scale. One great error was the planting of far too many red-grape varieties in areas where proper grape ripeness was questionable. The result was too many green, herbaceous wines. There was much talk of the "veggies" in Monterey wines. By the mid-1980s market forces and more careful vineyard management had solved most of those problems. For white wines, vineyards planted in the Salinas Valley have done quite well. Many critics contend that much of the Chardonnay grown here rivals in quality that of the North Coast.

The special growing conditions of the Salinas Valley have meant continuous experiment and modification in the vineyards during the

Monterey County

past 20 years. Irrigation is absolutely essential. High winds and often shocking maritime influences have brought about many changes in trellising techniques. These conditions have made the valley predominantly a white wine area. In 1996 the Monterey vintage was about 15 percent larger than that of 1990.

There are about fifteen wineries in the county, but a fairly large percentage of the wine grape crop leaves the county for production facilities outside the area.

Gerald Asher, "Brave New Monterey," *Gourmet,* July 1997, 42–47.

MONTEREY PENINSULA WINERY (BW 4676). From its founding in 1974 until 1986, a winery in an old restaurant on the Monterey-Salinas Highway. Then it was moved to more adequate facilities in Sand City, just east of Monterey. The best early wines were robust reds, Cabernet Sauvignon, Zinfandel, and Petite Sirah, which won more than their share of gold medals in the 1970s. In recent years white wines have gained prominence, but hearty reds are still an important part the winery's annual 70,000-case production. The second label, for blended generics, is Big Sur. In 1995 the winery was sold to a group, formerly executives of Heublein, that owns the QUAIL RIDGE brand.

MONTEREY VINEYARD (BW 4674) was built in the Salinas Valley just outside the town of Gonzales by a group of investors in 1973. The director of production was Richard PETERSON. In 1977, the COCA-COLA CO. of Atlanta bought the operation and built a huge winery next door for its Taylor California brand. In 1983 SEAGRAM bought Monterey Vineyard, which today produces about 750,000 cases of medium-priced varietal and generic table wines. Grapes for a large part of this production come from the Paris Valley Ranch, an 1,100-acre spread controlled since 1988 by Seagam Corp. and about 40 miles to

the south in Monterey's San Lucas Viticultural Area. In 1996 Seagram introduced its Tessera line of wines made at this facility.

MONTEVIÑA WINERY (BW 4622). Cary Gott and his family bought 155 acres in the Shenandoah Valley in Amador County in 1971. There were already 80 acres of old vines on the property, mostly Zinfandel; home winemaking began in the basement and two years later Gott bonded a little winery, the first in Amador's resurgence as premium wine country. Monteviña's early wines were a hit with critics and consumers. Gott added vineyard acreage and several other varietals, including Nebbiolo and Barbera. His Zinfandels, in a wide range of styles, are what brought Monteviña its greatest fame. By the early 1980s production reached 50,000 cases a year from 175 acres of vines and from purchased grapes.

In 1982 Gott left Monteviña after a family dispute, and the winery went into decline. At the end of the 1988 vintage, the Trinchero family, which owns SUTTER HOME,* bought the winery. The purchases made historic sense as Sutter Home had begun producing Amador Zinfandel in 1968. The Trincheros have upgraded the winery and vineyards and have expanded on Gott's early work with Italian varieties. In 1990 Sangiovese, Refosco, and Aleatico were planted and more Nebbiolo added. By 1992 there were 70 new acres of Barbera. There is also an experimental vineyard in the DELTA area, where scores of Italian varieties and various clonal selections are being tested. Total winery production has reached 100,000 per year.

MONTICELLO CELLARS (BW 5102). North of the town of Napa, surrounded by vineyards, is the administration building of Monticello Cellars. At a distance it is a dead ringer for Thomas Jefferson's famous home in Virginia. The owner, Jay Corley, is a great admirer of our third president; his family traces its history back to the Old Dominion.

Corley began planting his 90 acres of old prune orchard in 1970. The southerly and cool location of Monticello meant that Chardonnay and Pinot noir would be favored estate wines. Corley sold grapes for years but began producing wine at another facility in 1980; in 1982 his new winery was on line. Cabernet Sauvignon, from purchased grapes, soon became a Monticello standby.

Corley produces sparkling wine for the DOMAINE MONTREAUX label under a separate bond. In 1985 he bought the LLORDS & ELWOOD brand. He also produces custom wines for others. His annual production exceeded 20,000 cases in the mid-1990s.

MONT LA SALLE. See CHRISTIAN BROTHERS

MONTPELLIER. A brand developed as a joint venture between the Franzia (see JFJ BRONCO) and Robert MONDAVI families in 1988. Sales of these FIGHTING VARIETALS stood at about 50,000 cases in the mid-1990s.

MONT ROUGE WINERY. See CHAUCHÉ & BON

MONT ST. JOHN CELLARS (BW 4928). The BARTOLUCCI family reclaimed its winery in Oakville in 1975, after the demise of OAKVILLE VINEYARDS, and then moved to the Carneros, where the Mont St. John winery was built in 1979. It was named for the 2,375-foot-high peak in the Mayacamas range that looks down on Oakville and Rutherford. Mont St. John had been a Bartolucci brand in the 1960s. In the 1990s the winery annually produces about 20,000 cases of several varietal wines, with a strong emphasis on Chardonnay. The family owns about 160 acres of vineyard land.

MORAGA VINEYARDS (BW 5680). One of the seeming miracles of southern California wine history is how a few producers in south-ern California around the turn of the last century were able to produce some world-class wines. The contributing elements were good varietals, usually Zinfandel or Cabernet Sauvignon, and hillside locations marked by maritime influence. Thomas Jones bought land in Bel Air in Los Angeles County in 1959 and began planting his 6-acre, terraced vineyard to red Bordeaux varieties in 1978. His first commercial vintage was in 1989. Production now runs to about 1,000 cases per year. Critics have given Jones's wines good marks.

MORGAN HILL. A town south of San Jose that was the center of much viticultural activity from 1900 until the 1960s. It was an important shipping point for grapes during Prohibition; after Repeal the area had eight small wineries. In recent years most vineyards and orchards there have given way to the suburban expansion of Silicon Valley.

MORGAN, PERCY. An English accountant who was the brains behind the formation of the CALIFORNIA WINE ASSOCIATION in 1894 and guided its course until he retired in 1911.

MORGAN WINERY (BW 5130). In 1982, while Daniel Lee was the winemaker at DURNEY VINEYARDS, he brought out a Monterey Chardonnay under his own Morgan label. Four years later he had a small winery in Salinas. Morgan Chardonnays have been consistent critical successes and Lee was soon also winning high praise for his Pinot noir and Cabernet Sauvignon. He buys most, but not all, of his grapes in Monterey County. Annual production passed the 25,000-case mark in the mid-1990s.

J. W. MORRIS WINERY (BW 4723, 5058). In 1975 the J. W. Morris Port Works began operations in downtown Emeryville, but in 1983, as a result of financial problems, it was acquired by Toth Cellars in Sonoma. Toth and its Black Mountain Vineyards, with a 340,000-

gallon facility near Healdsburg, filed for bank-ruptcy in 1993. Thereafter the J. W. Morris and Black Mountain labels were acquired by BRONCO, along with several others that had belonged to troubled wineries in Sonoma. The bonded premises were acquired by WEIN-STOCK CELLARS.

MORROW, ALMOND RALEIGH (1862–1951) was for many years known as the "grand old man" of the California wine indus-try. After a stint as a clerk for KOHLER & Frohling, he went to work for the CALIFOR-NIA WINE ASSOCIATION (CWA) in 1894. He was soon Henry LACHMAN's assistant at CWA and developed a reputation for his wine- and brandy-tasting ability. In 1902 he succeeded Lachman as general superinten-dent of the CWA; in 1915 he became general manager. He was one of the powers in the for-mation of Fruit Industries, a reorganization of the CWA, in 1929 and was the first president of the WINE INSTITUTE. In the 1930s a revived CWA honored him by marketing an A. R. Morrow Brandy, 100 proof and bottled in bond

MOSBY WINERY (4936). Formerly Vega Vineyards, Mosby was founded in 1979 in the Santa Ynez Valley, Santa Barbara County. The 8,000-case annual production includes a wide range of varietals, and recently several Italian varieties. The winery has also released wines labeled Pinot grigio and Primitivo; the second label is Los Padres.

MOSCATO. Italian for muscat. It is occasion-ally seen on wine labels in California as part of descriptions such as Moscato di Canelli and Moscato Amabile; see also MUSCAT BLANC.

MOSELLE (Mosel). A French and German river, the German portion of which, called the Mosel, is the home of a great white wine region. Today it is a legal generic term on California

wine labels, but is almost never seen. When it was used, in the 1950s and 1960s, the term usu-ally indicated some blend of Sylvaner and White Riesling.

MOULTON HILL WINERY was the most important winery in the Cloverdale area of Sonoma county until it burned down in 1913. Dating from 1885, its production rose to about 750,000 gallons per year in the 1890s. In 1903 it became part of the CALIFORNIA WINE ASSOCIATION. The fine mansion there near Highway 101 burned to the ground in 1947.

MOUNTAIN VIEW. See CUPERTINO

MOUNTAIN VIEW VINTNERS (BW 5667). A NÉGOCIANT brand dating from the early 1980s. In 1992 the owners acquired bonded premises at the EMILIO GUGLIELMO WINERY in Morgan Hill, Santa Clara County. Sales of moderately priced varietals often exceed 125,000 cases per year.

MOUNTAIN WINE. In the 1940s several wineries in California began using the term "mountain" on their labels, but no legal defin-ition was ever established.

MOUNT EDEN VINEYARDS (BW 4599). After Martin RAY* sold the Paul MASSON Win-ery and La Cresta Vineyards in 1943, he bought 320 acres on Table Mountain to the north to build a new wine operation. He planted Pinot noir, Chardonnay, and Cabernet Sauvignon. In 1960 he took in several investors and created Mount Eden Vineyard Corp., which then owned 160 acres of the estate. By 1967 there were four new vineyards on the property and a new château-winery at the top of the hill. The unwieldy operation was soon in disarray from internal battles, the whole story of which has never been told. Eventually, in 1972, a court order made the four vineyards and the hilltop winery a separate entity under the stockholders.

But they continued fighting among themselves and complex ownership changes continued for years.

Since the mid-1980s, operations have steadied under the leadership of the president and winemaker, Jeffrey Patterson. Mount Eden's wines since 1972 have tended to be rich, powerful, and expensive. The three historic varietals still monopolize production from the 50 acres of vines. Chardonnay from grapes grown in the Edna Valley makes up about half of the of the 9,000 cases sold annually. MEV has been a second label.

MOUNT HARLAN. See CALERA WINE CO.

MOUNT PALOMAR WINERY (BW 4703). John Poole bought land for his Long Valley Vineyard in the Temecula area of Riverside County in 1969 and planted nine varietals there. The first vintage was in 1975. Since the 1980s, the number of wines has been cut back with new emphasis on white and BLUSH table wines. Poole has recently planted several Italian varieties including the white Cortese, which he offered as a varietal in 1994. The Italian varietals are sold under the Castelletto label. Many of the wines in Poole's 15,000-case annual production are sold only at the winery's popular tasting room.

MOUNT PISGAH VINEYARD. See LOUIS M. MARTINI

MOUNT TIVY WINERY. See LACHMAN & JACOBI

MOUNT VEEDER, an important viticultural area in Napa that is named for the 2,677-foot-high peak in the Mayacamas Mountains west of Yountville. It was granted official AVA status in 1990. In the nineteenth century there were a few small wineries and several vineyards on the eastern slopes, but the area was far better known as the "Napa Redwoods," for its resorts.

Large-scale winegrowing came to the area in 1900 with Theodore GIER whose winery built in 1903 now houses the HESS COLLECTION (see also the CHRISTIAN BROTHERS). Today the Mount Veeder region has several wineries and vineyards, which have given the area a fine reputation for powerful red and white wines worthy of aging. The modern reputation was launched by MAYACAMAS VINEYARDS in the 1950s. By the mid-1990s, there were more than 1,000 acres of vines in the viticultural area, well over half of them owned by DOMAINE CHANDON and The Hess Collection.

MOUNT VEEDER WINERY (BW 4620). Michael Bernstein added to the reputation of the Mount Veeder area for stylishly powerful table wines in the years after he founded his little winery in 1972. He sold it to Henry Mathesen in 1983, who in turn sold it to the owners of FRANCISCAN VINEYARDS in 1989. Cabernet Sauvignon and Chardonnay are still the top varietals there. Annual production is about 8,000 cases, mostly from the 40-acre estate vineyard.

MOURVÈDRE. See MATARO

MUGÁRTEGUI, PABLO, a Franciscan padre at Mission San Juan Capistrano who probably produced the first wine from vinifera grapes in Alta California in 1782.

MUMM NAPA VALLEY (BW 5431). A sparkling wine operation begun in 1985 as Domaine Mumm, a joint venture between SEAGRAM and G. H. Mumm, the French Champagne house. The first sparklers were produced at Sterling Vineyards, which was owned by Seagram, and were released in 1986. The next year Seagram broke ground for a new winery on the Silverado Trail east of Rutherford in the Napa Valley. In 1988 the facility was in operation, gaining much praise for an archi-

The architectural showplace on Mount Veeder is the collection of handsome structures built by Theodore GIER and the CHRISTIAN BROTHERS. The buildings shown here are part of the Mont La Salle Novitiate, still owned by the Brothers. (©Sebastian Titus, Vintage Image)

tectural style that critics felt blended better with the rural surroundings than did many of the lavish wineries that have been built in the Napa Valley since the 1970s.

In 1990 the name was changed. Mumm Napa Valley sparkling wines are produced from several varieties, including Pinot gris. The grapes come from as many as fifty separate vineyards in the valley and the Carneros. Several wines are made, including a vineyard-designated Winery Lake Cuvée. (Seagram now owns that famous Carneros property.) Annual production was approaching 200,000 cases in the mid-1990s.

MUNSON, THOMAS VOLNEY (1852–1913), a world-famous viticultural authority in Texas, and a powerful influence on enology in California between 1885 and 1910 because of his knowledge and understanding of native American vines useful as resistant ROOTSTOCK. He is possibly more renowned in France today than he is in his own country for his contributions to the French solution to the PHYLLOXERA problem, the solution that led to the resurgence of winegrowing in California in the late 1890s.

MURPHY GOODE ESTATE WINERY (BW 5415). Between them, the partners Tim Murphy and Dale Goode own more than 300 acres of vineyard land in Alexander Valley, Sonoma. Graduates of the University of California at Davis, the two bonded their winery in 1987 and produce only estate wines, a wide range of varietals. Sauvignon blanc, although not their leader in volume, has received the most critical acclaim. Total annual production is about 80,000 cases.

MURRIETA'S WELL. See WENTE

MUSCADELLE OF BORDEAUX. See SAUVIGNON VERT

MUSCAT. A family of grapes, black and white, with a distinct floral aroma from the chemical linalool. The French expert Pierre Viala lists more than 200 varieties of muscat. Roman and Greek historic references attest to their antiquity in the Mediterranean world. In California there is evidence of muscat varieties in the early mission vineyards. Identifiable black and white varieties began arriving here from nurseries on the East Coast in the 1850s. Since then they have been used to produce dry and sweet wines, sparkling wines, brandy, and raisins. Because linalool gives some German varieties such as WHITE RIESLING a somewhat muscatlike floral character, early winemakers in California regularly mixed small quantities of white muscat wines into wines made with bland, heavy bearing varieties, such as PALOMINO and BURGER, to give them a "Germanic" character.

After Prohibition, muscat wines were most often associated with cheap, fortified sweet wines and found disfavor among knowledgeable consumers. But since the 1970s many premium producers have made elegant muscat wines, usually in a dessert style, but occasionally dry or sparkling.

MUSCAT OF ALEXANDRIA. Although officially classified a raisin grape, the variety is an excellent table grape and has been an important part of the California wine crush for almost 100 years. It is of ancient origin, well known to the Romans. When the grape is grown in hot climates and heavily cropped, the resulting wines, almost always sweet, are usually dull. But when the vines are pruned for a small crop, the wine, even when dry, can be very good indeed.

The variety reached California by several routes in the 1850s, but was probably first imported in 1852 by Antoine DELMAS. Several producers used it for sweet, fortified muscatels. Charles KRUG used it in his ANGELICA. Planting in the Central Valley exploded around the turn of the century as the production of sweet wine in California soared. As late as 1939 fully 68 percent of the state's 64,754 acres of the variety had been planted before 1915. During Prohibition the Muscat of Alexandria was the only white variety shipped east in large quantities for home winemakers. Most used the variety to tone down the tannin and give a bit of flavor to the ALICANTE BOUSCHET. In 1927 14,604 carloads headed east from California as so-called juice grapes for home winemakers. In the years after Repeal virtually all of California's sweet and inexpensive MUSCATEL came from this variety.

Acreage, around 50,000 in the 1940s, has dropped to about 5,000 in the 1990s. Most of the 50,000 tons crushed is used to flavor white jug wines and inexpensive sparklers; some goes into brandy.

MUSCAT BLANC, the great white variety the French call *Muscat blanc à petits grains,* or Muscat Frontignan. In Italy it is Muscat (Moscato) Canelli. In the 1850s it was brought to California from nurseries in New England, where it was grown as a hothouse table grape. It is a low-yielding variety with concentrated, elegant flavors. Because of its low yields, it was rarely seen in early vineyards, but a few winemakers produced small quantities of dessert wine from it. George WEST was the most famous. Some Germans, among them Charles KRUG and Jacob SCHRAM, considered their white table wines *verbessert* (improved) when they added a touch of Muscat blanc for flavor. Following Repeal a few wineries, notably BEAULIEU and CONCANNON, produced dessert wines labeled Muscat de Frontignan that had a solid following of connoisseurs. Concannon also made a slightly sweet Muscat Blanc table wine.

There were 6,377 tons of Muscat blanc in California in 1996, produced from 1,330 acres scattered throughout the state. This was 70 percent of 1990 production.

In 1996 the BATF, over objections from Beaulieu, ruled that the Muscat Frontignan designation might not be used on labels after 1999. Muscat blanc and Muscat Canelli will then be the two legal varietal names for this variety in the United States, Muscat Frontignan, used in California since the 1850s, will be an illegal term on labels.

MUSCATEL. A generic term for a sweet wine made from muscat varieties of grapes, almost always fortified. In California when there was a boom in the production of sweet FORTIFIED WINE between 1900 and 1914, production rose from 8 million to 20 million gallons a year. Muscatel production averaged about 1.5 million gallons, almost all of it from the Central Valley and southern California. After Prohibition fortified wines dominated production in California until the 1960s and muscatel production became even more important than it had been earlier. For example, in 1940 about 20 million gallons were produced, constituting almost 25 percent of the entire production of fortified wine. But by the 1980s the term Muscatel had all but disappeared from the labels of wine made in California.

MUSCAT FRONTIGNAN. See MUSCAT BLANC

MUST. From the Latin *vinum mustum,* fresh or young wine. Since the sixteenth century the word in English has meant the unfermented or fermenting juice of freshly crushed grapes on its way to becoming wine.

NAGASAWA, KANAYE. See FOUNTAIN-GROVE

NAGLEE, HENRY MORRIS (1815–86), had come to California as an officer in the war with Mexico and later, in 1852, bought land in San Jose. A general in the Civil War, he afterward visited Cognac and became interested in brandy production. When he returned to San Jose in 1868, he built a winery and distillery. He also planted world-class wine grape varieties and developed his line of brandy on the iconoclastic idea that the best came from the greatest wine grapes. This idea paid off with a reputation for brandy that exceeded that of any other California producer until recent years. Professor Eugene HILGARD rated Naglee's Burgundy Brandy at 100 on a scale of 1 to 100. Naglee brandies were still in the collections of a few connoisseurs, such as A. R. MORROW and Robert Mayock, until the 1940s.

Naglee also had a remarkable personal reputation. The historian H. H. BANCROFT called him "the amorous Naglee," and his sexual relations with women were the talk of San Jose. His estate was considered the most beautiful in the "Garden City," and was open free to the public on Sundays. He was noted for his practical jokes but had a reputation of never having been seen smiling in public. A stone monument in St. James Park in San Jose recalls the general's many contributions but it was not erected until thirty years after his death.

Clyde Arbuckle, *History of San Jose* (San Jose, Calif.: Smith and McKay, 1985).

NALLE WINERY (BW 5561). Douglas Nalle specializes in robust Zinfandels from Dry Creek Valley in Sonoma. He began producing wines under his own label in 1984 and for a while was winemaker at QUIVIRA. He has added Cabernet Sauvignon to his production, which runs to about 3,500 cases per year.

NAPA, perhaps the most famous geographical name in California wine history.

Napa County was one of California's original twenty-seven and until 1861 included what is today Lake County. In the northern San Francisco Bay Area, it is the region's least populated county and has the lowest population density. For its wine industry it has a fame that is historic and worldwide.

The **City of Napa,** in early years known as Napa City, was an important wine production center before Prohibition. Several huge wine factories operated near the Napa River, which was once an important commercial link to the rest of the Bay Area. A large portion of the grapes processed in town before 1920 came from the Central Valley and rarely contributed to Napa's reputation for fine wine.

The **Napa Valley** is the central geographical feature of the county. It runs north for about 40 miles, from where the Napa River empties into San Pablo Bay to the mountains above

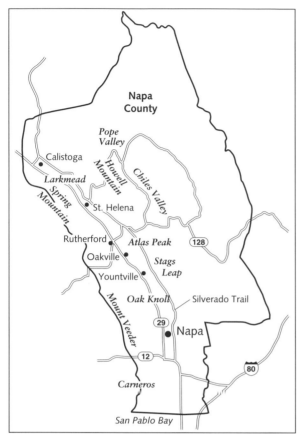

Napa County

Calistoga. On the west side is the Mayacamas Range with peaks such as Mount Veeder and Spring Mountain. On the east side the Vaca Range has its volcanic Howell Mountain and several important winegrowing areas such as Chiles and Pope Valleys. See also NAPA VALLEY VITICULTURE AREA.

Winegrowing came to Napa with George C. YOUNT in 1838. Commercial production on a small scale was begun near Napa City by John M. Patchett, but wheat was the chief product until the 1880s. The upper Napa Valley around the town of ST. HELENA* was the center of the eventual solid growth of the wine industry here. Charles KRUG* was the pioneer in this area in 1860, but George Belden CRANE* in the mid-1860s was the first to demonstrate the possibilities of wine made from first-rate varietals. In the late 1860s Jacob SCHRAM* showed what could be done on the hillsides.

Through the 1870s acreage held at about 3,000, but jumped to about 20,000 in the 1880s when wine became Napa's primary commercial interest. Production from about 140 wineries reached almost 5 million gallons in the mid-1880s. During those boom years, Zinfandel dominated planting and CLARET wine from it and blends with other grapes became

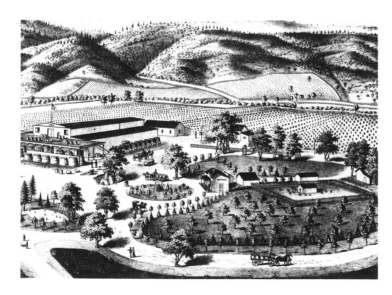

Charles KRUG's great estate, pictured here in 1877, was the center of Napa Valley's St. Helena district. This cellar dates from 1872.

TABLE 21. WINE GRAPES IN NAPA COUNTY, SELECTED VARIETIES

YEAR	PERCENT OF TOTAL RED	WHITE	CABERNET SAUVIGNON	CHAR-DONNAY	MERLOT	(ACRES) PETITE SIRAH	PINOT NOIR	SAUVIGNON BLANC	ZIN-FANDEL	TOTAL
1920										9,420
1925										11,180
1930										10,950
1938[a]	61	39	150[b]			2,091			1,668	11,026
1950										11,850
1961	72	28	387	25[b]		1,748	166	210	949	10,422
1966	65	35	682	139	9	1,651	313	232	897	11,739
1969	62	38	2,008	629	159	1,501	723	264	887	13,995
1973	65	35	4,600	1,702	399	1,235	2,352	473	1,168	19,953
1978	62	38	5,583	3,207	785	965	2,542	1,005	2,258	24,867
1983	49	51	5,901	5,662	730	828	2,330	2,733	2,045	28,379
1988	49	51	7,761	8,066	1,352	577	2,500	3,720	2,057	31,781
1997	63	37	10,335	9,154	5,067	328	2,845	2,654	2,030	35,846

NOTES: Until 1961 statistics for acreage under various varieties of grapes were not published.

a. Abberant, but useful for comparison.

b. Approximately.

SOURCE: California Agricultural Statistics Service, Sacramento, Calif.

Napa's chief claim to fame. The press and the industry generally came to accept the idea that Napa led the state in fine wine production. The names of the railroad stops running up the valley took on the nature of Bordeaux appellations: Oak Knoll, Yountville, Oakville, Rutherford, St. Helena, Larkmead, Calistoga.

Depression and phylloxera almost destroyed Napa's wine industry in the 1890s, reducing the vineyards to about 3,000 acres. But the industry revived in the new century and thrived until Prohibition. During the dry years, most wineries closed down. Grape acreage fell to about 10,000 but then held steady. Most grapes went east by rail to home winemakers in the 1920s. What small acreage of fine wine varieties there was in the ground before 1920 all but disappeared. When full-scale production was renewed after 1932, Petite Sirah, Zinfandel, and Alicante Bouschet were the dominant varieties. The chief product was bulk red wine shipped to

eastern bottlers by the two local cooperative wineries and others. But a few older producers such as BEAULIEU, INGLENOOK, BERINGER, and LARKMEAD began reestablishing Napa's previous reputation for fine wine. Newcomers, such as Louis M. MARTINI, the MONDAVI family, and J. Leland Stewart at SOUVERAIN accelerated the movement. By the 1960s premium varietal wines had restored Napa's national reputation.

In the 1970s there was an explosion of outside investment in wine production there. Corporate interests, domestic and foreign, well-heeled entrepreneurs, and small-scale producers and their families turned Napa Valley, the Carneros, the hillsides, and the highland valleys into one of the most important wine-producing areas in the world. As the century neared its end, there were more than 35,000 acres of vines and about 200 wineries in Napa County.

The 1996 Napa vintage produced 100,251 tons of wine grapes, 68 percent of them red.

This number was low for the 1990s, during which the average has been about 118,000 tons a year.

Unlike changes wrought in other counties in the Bay Area, the conversion of vineyard land into housing developments and freeways has been limited in Napa County, the effect of a series of local statutes and popular referendums passed since 1968 that have made the conversion of agricultural land to other purposes almost impossible. In recent years a cap has even been placed on the construction of new wineries and has strictly defined wineries as production facilities, not simply places that may look like wineries and have tasting rooms.

Napa County's official viticultural areas are: ATLAS PEAK, CHILES VALLEY, HOWELL MOUNTAIN, MT. VEEDER, NAPA VALLEY, OAK KNOLL, OAKVILLE, RUTHERFORD, SPRING MOUNTAIN, STAGS LEAP, YOUNTVILLE, and CARNEROS (Napa).

James Conaway, *Napa: The Story of an American Eden* (Boston, Mass.: Houghton Mifflin, 1990).

Irene W. Hayne, *Ghost Wineries of Napa Valley* (San Francisco: Wine Appreciation Guild, 1995).

James T. Lapsley, *Bottled Poetry: Napa Winemaking from Prohibition to the Modern Era* (Berkeley, Calif.: University of California Press, 1996).

Charles L. Sullivan, *Napa Wine: A History from Mission Days to the Present* (San Francisco: Wine Appreciation Guild, 1994).

NAPA CELLARS (BW 4737). The original partners began producing wine in the Oakville area in 1976 and sold the winery in 1983 to the Belgian family of De Schepper-De Moor, who called it the De Moor Winery. Then in 1990 the winery was purchased by Sky Court Napa, a Japanese corporation that marketed a sizeable percentage of the winery's annual 25,000-case output in Japan. Most of the wine was Chardonnay, Cabernet Sauvignon, and Zinfandel made from purchased grapes. In 1996 ROMBAUER acquired the winery and changed

the name back to Napa Cellars. Production is now about 5,000 cases per year.

NAPA CREEK WINERY (BW 5008). In 1980 Jack Schulze renovated an old meat-packing plant on the Silverado Trail in Napa Valley and bonded it as a winery. Production had reached about 12,000 cases a year in 1994 when he sold the Napa Creek brand to JFJ BRONCO. In 1996 Kent RASMUSSEN acquired the building as a second production facility for his Napa Valley wine.

NAPA GAMAY. Official California records call this variety of wine grape simply Gamay. It is the Valdiguié, considered a mediocre red variety in France. It is not clear how the Napa Gamay name was invented, but the Napa may have been attached by a professor at the University of California at Davis to distinguish it from the variety used for Beaujolais wine in France (see GAMAY). Several wineries outside Napa make a Gamay wine from the so-called Napa Gamay, but would certainly not be content to label it, for example, Monterey Napa Gamay. Recently a few wineries have brought out a varietal Valdiguié. In 1996 the BATF ruled that Napa Gamay may not be used as a varietal term after January 1, 1999. But the variety may still be used in wines labeled Gamay Beaujolais.

In 1997 there were 1,187 acres of Napa Gamay (Valdiguié) in California, 46 percent in the North Coast, 30 percent in the Central Coast, and 24 percent in the Central Valley. Ten years earlier there were 2,452 acres; 1974 marked the high point with 4,760 acres, about 1,000 of which were in Napa County. Much of the product of these vines back then went to make wine in a nouveau style.

NAPA GOLDEN CHASSELAS. See PALOMINO

NAPA RIDGE. A brand of medium-priced varietal wines introduced by Beringer (see

BERINGER WINE ESTATES) in 1985. The wines are bottled at the old Italian Swiss Colony plant north of Geyserville in Sonoma County. The grapes come from many areas, but rarely from Napa. By the mid-nineties sales were up to 1 million cases a year. Critics have consistently singled out many of these wines as excellent bargains.

NAPA VALLEY COOPERATIVE WINERY (BW 3565). At the end of Prohibition most grapes grown in Napa were good but common shipping varieties. Most wine produced was bulk red and shipped to outside bottlers. Because there was not enough usable winery capacity in the valley, the growers established a cooperative winery that helped save its members during the 1930s. By the 1960s fewer and fewer growers had varieties that a cooperative winery could use. But the co-op stayed in business by selling most of its wines to E. & J. GALLO. In 1985 that account was lost. In 1987 the co-op went into the premium business under the BERGFELD WINERY brand. The winery also acquired the J. Wile brand from Hiram Walker. When GOLDEN STATE VINTNERS bought the 1,200,000-gallon winery in 1994, the cooperative ceased to exist.

> James T. Lapsley, *Bottled Poetry: Napa Winemaking from Prohibition to the Modern Era* (Berkeley, Calif.: University of California Press, 1996).

NAPA VALLEY PORT CELLARS (BW 5259). A tiny operation that, since 1984, has been making small quantities of vintage port from such varieties as Cabernet Sauvignon and Zinfandel. Annual production is less 1,000 cases.

NAPA VALLEY VITICULTURAL AREA was created in 1981 after a series of heated hearings in which many producers in the valley argued to limit the appellation to the valley itself and its watershed. The outcome was a holding that, as far as the grapes grown there were concerned, virtually all of the county could legally be described as Napa Valley. Thus, that designation on the label of a wine bottle could be describing the origin of grapes grown in the valley itself or almost anywhere in Napa County.

NAPA (VALLEY) WINE CO. (BW 9) was founded in 1933 by Louis Stralla (1901–81), when he leased the old Charles KRUG winery from its owner J. K. Moffitt. For years the company produced bulk red wine mostly shipped to eastern bottlers. When his lease ran out in 1940, Stralla moved operations to Oakville into the old BRUN & CHAIX plant. In 1947 he sold the operation to the J. B. CELLA family; in 1961 it was acquired by UNITED VINTNERS; in 1968 by Heublein. When the latter began selling off many of its wine assets in Napa, a group of partners in 1993 bought the modernized 2.5-million gallon plant. Since then it has operated chiefly as a CUSTOM-CRUSHING facility. In its unusual tasting room all the various wines made on the premises are available.

NAPA VALLEY WINE LIBRARY ASSOCIATION was founded in 1963. The organization sponsors wine-appreciation courses and has given considerable support to the study of California and local wine history. Its sizeable collection of primary and secondary sources is housed in the St. Helena Public Library.

NATOMA VINEYARD CO. Beginning in 1883 the Natoma Water and Mining Company, northeast of Sacramento, began converting about 3,000 acres of its foothill land to vineyards. The idea was to produce fine wine from great varietals. By the 1890s there were only 1,500 acres left and the chief product was brandy. What was left of the gigantic and quite unsuccessful operation was leased to the CALIFORNIA WINE ASSOCIATION in 1900. The last vines were pulled out in 1927.

NAVARRO VINEYARDS (BW 4686). Deborah Cahn and Edward Bennett founded

Like VINA, Leland STANFORD's huge property to the north, Natoma was to be home of fine table wines. When the realities of viticulture in the Sacramento Valley struck home to the developers of this huge property, a change of direction was called for. This advertisement, from 1892, illustrates that change. The use of the word Cognac on bottles or advertising for wines made in California is illegal today. (*Pacific Wine & Spirit Review*)

Navarro as a 20,000-case winery in 1975 in the Anderson Valley, Mendocino County. They have developed a reputation for producing one of California's best dry Gewürztraminers. They make several other varietals in many styles, mainly Chardonnay and Pinot noir, but also a Pinot gris, and nonalcoholic grape juices. Indian Creek is their second label.

NEBBIOLO. An ancient grape native to the Piedmont in Italy, where it is used for such famous red wines as Barolo and Barbaresco.

John T. DOYLE of Cupertino was the first to import the vine to California, probably in 1882. Later Charles KRUG used it to make a wine he called Spanna, which is another name for the variety in the Piedmont. In the 1890s ITALIAN SWISS COLONY also had some brief success with it as a varietal labeled Barolo, and regularly blended it into its Tipo Chianti. But after the turn of the century little is heard of Nebbiolo until the 1950s, when about 70 acres were planted in Tulare County. Later Horace LANZA actually produced a varietal wine from those grapes. In 1971 about 450 acres were planted in the Central Valley, but they were pulled up in the 1980s. The variety was not recommended for planting by experts at the University of California at Davis.

Nebbiolo began to appear again here and there in the 1990s, now appropriately in the coastal valleys and Sierra foothills. By 1997 there were 169 acres planted, more than half in San Luis Obispo and Sonoma counties, with a crush in 1996 of 369 tons. MARTIN BROTHERS WINERY near Paso Robles is the leading producer with about 4,000 cases per year.

It is questionable whether powerful wines in the style of the Italian Piedmont will be possible in California until dependable vines are imported. There are many different strains and California does not appear to have in any number those that have made Barolo one of the world's most sturdy and long-lived wines.

NÉGOCIANT, French for wine merchant. In California today the term is used of persons who develop their own brands, buying wines from producers and selling them under their own labels. Some have facilities for blending and bottling, as they did in California before Prohibition. Conditions in the late 1970s and early 1980s, namely, overexpansion of premium vineyards and the flattening of the growth of the consumer-demand curve, favored the growth of négociant operations in California. Many wineries had good, finished wines that they could not sell under their own labels. The négociant with sound marketing skills could often buy those wines and successfully establish new brands; see BONDED WINERY; LABEL.

NÉGRETTE. See PINOT ST. GEORGE

NEMATODE. Roundworm pests, several species of which were identified in the 1930s as serious threats to grape vines in California. Some attack the vine's roots; others act as vectors for debilitating viruses. Nematodes can be controlled by fumigating vineyard land before planting or replanting, and by use of rootstock that is at least partially resistant to both nematodes and phylloxera.

NEOPROHIBITIONISM, a rather exaggerated umbrella term that has become common in the California wine industry to characterize the growing movement in America against the consumption of alcoholic beverages. Advocates for wine have criticized antialcohol enthusiasts for blurring the distinction between moderation and abuse, and for regarding a glass of table wine as damaging a substance as a shot of vodka. It would probably be more accurate to label such concern as neotemperance rather than neoprohibitionist.

The antialcohol forces have, since the 1970s, pushed for warning labels, for higher taxes, for stricter licensing, and for restrictions on advertising. Their most noteworthy successes were the requirements that wine labels include a warning of the presence of sulfites (enacted in 1987), and that all alcoholic beverages also carry a label giving a general health warning (enacted in 1988).

Since the late 1980s, the wine industry has been on the counterattack, publicizing table wine in moderation as a healthy accompaniment for meals. Various advocacy groups have been formed to carry this message, and numerous writers have lent a hand. Chief among the vintners in the fray has been Robert MONDAVI. Of particular concern to wine producers has been the tendency of antialcohol forces to lump all alcoholic beverages, including table wine, in the umbrella category of drugs.

The apparently healthful properties of red table wine were brought into the broad national spotlight in 1991 when, in a prime-time television program, the so-called French Paradox was mooted. The French were described as eating more fats than Americans but having fewer coronary problems. Various experts on the program suggested that the moderate consumption of red table wine might be the explaining variable in favor of the French. The result was a sharp jump in sales of red table wine in the United States and a softening of the impact of the neoprohibitionist attack on California wine.

Gene Ford, *The French Paradox: Drinking for Health* (San Francisco: Wine Appreciation Guild, 1993).

Lewis Perdue, *The French Paradox* (Sonoma, Calif.: Renaissance, 1992).

NERVO WINERY (BW 350) was founded by Frank Nervo south of Geyserville in 1908. After Repeal he raised the capacity of his small bulk winery to 250,000 gallons and developed a lively retail trade for his country jug wines. When Schlitz Brewing bought nearby GEYSER PEAK WINERY in 1972, the company also bought the Nervo winery for its strategic position on the highway. When the Trione family bought Geyser Peak in 1982, Nervo was again included. Today the old winery serves as a visitor center and is called Canyon Road Winery, the name of one of Geyser Peak's moderately priced brands.

NESTLÉ. See BERINGER VINEYARDS; BERINGER WINE ESTATES

NEVADA CITY WINERY (BW 5063). A 40,000-gallon winery in the northern Sierra foothills producing a wide range of varietal wines from grapes grown in local vineyards and occasionally from North Coast sources. Founded as Snow Mountain Winery in 1980, it produces about 9,000 cases per year. Some of the blended wines have carried such zany monikers as Alpenglow, Douce Noir, and Rough and Ready Red.

NEVADA COUNTY, in the northern Sierra foothills, has for long been a winegrowing area, but never on a large scale. In 1884 there were eighteen growers, who had about 200 acres of vines, and two small wineries, one in Nevada City, the other in Grass Valley. After Repeal acreage dropped to 150, almost all Zinfandel. There were also five very short-lived wineries. In the 1990s there were about 180 acres of vines, mostly Chardonnay and red Bordeaux varieties. There is one winery, in Nevada City.

NEWLAN VINEYARDS (BW 5061). The Newlan family began planting 30 acres of vineyard south of Yountville in Napa in 1967. For a while Bruce Newlan was associated with the now-defunct Alatera Vineyards (BW 4829), which was in operation from 1977 until 1988. In 1981 he bonded his own winery and gradually raised production to about 10,000 cases. He sells grapes to others and buys special lots from other areas in Napa. One source on Spring Mountain is particularly important for his Pinot noir. He also specializes in Chardonnay and Zinfandel. Newlan's second label is Napa-Villages.

NEW ORLEANS, MARKET IN. Before Prohibition and from Repeal until World War II, New Orleans was one of the most important outlets for inexpensive bulk red table wine from California. Industry figures show that the city received 3.5 million gallons in 1903, a fairly typical year. The wines of several premium producers could be found on the lists of some of the city's fancy French restaurants. H. W. CRABB had a agency for his To Kalon wines in New Orleans and Charles CARPY and BRUN & CHAIX sold lots of good wine there.

NEWTON VINEYARD (BW 4918). After the founder, Peter Newton, sold his interest in STERLING VINEYARDS in 1977, he acquired a steep tract of land on Spring Mountain and began planting 100 acres of terraced vineyard. In 1979 he built a winery into the mountain, and at first called it the Richard Forman Winery, after his partner and winemaker, who had been the winemaker at Sterling. Forman left Newton in 1983. The first estate vintage was in 1984. By the 1990s annual production had reached almost 30,000 cases, principally of Cabernet Sauvignon, Merlot, and Chardonnay.

NICASIO VINEYARDS (BW 4468). Dan Wheeler bought 73 acres of Santa Cruz Mountain land near Soquel in Santa Cruz County in 1952 and bonded his winery in 1955. Since then he has been making small lots of commercial wine from purchased grapes under his Wine by Wheeler label. His two hand-hewn caves were

the first to be dug for winemaking in California after Repeal. He retired from the engineering profession in 1988 and has since acquired land in Lake County, where he eventually intends to move his winemaking operation.

NICHELINI WINERY (BW 843). After arriving in California from Switzerland in 1882, Anton Nichelini (1862–1937) found his first job as winemaker for Joshua CHAUVET. Two years later he bought land in the Chiles Valley in Napa and began planting vines. In 1890 he built his little stone winery. Only the WENTE winery in the Livermore Valley has operated in California longer and continuously under one family. Nichelini's was a bulk wine operation in the early days, but developed a retail and restaurant trade in the late 1950s. The emphasis was on Zinfandel. Four of Anton's grandchildren, one of whom is Greg BOEGER, reorganized the business in 1990. He now makes the Nichelini wines, about 3,000 cases a year, some of them under the Boeger label. Emphasis is on Zinfandel, Cabernet Sauvignon, and Merlot.

NIEBAUM-COPPOLA ESTATE (BW 4856). When OAKVILLE VINEYARDS* went bankrupt in 1975, Francis and Eleanor Coppola bought the historic Niebaum home and the adjacent 85-acre vineyard. In 1978 they bonded the old Niebaum carriage house and began producing an estate wine. A blend of red Bordeaux varieties, it was eventually labeled Rubicon. With André TCHELISTCHEFF as an adviser, Francis Ford Coppola has made his Rubicons powerful and stylish wines, meant for many years in the cellar. In 1994 the Coppolas bought the old INGLENOOK winery and its home vineyard from Heublein, thus reuniting vineyards and winery of the great Inglenook estate. Annual production is about 20,000 cases. As part of the sale, Heublein's Beaulieu Vineyard received a long-term contract for grapes from the Inglenook home ranch, which is contiguous with the old Beaulieu's Rutherford Vineyard no. 1.

A second label, Francis Coppola Presents, is used for two blends, a Rosso and a Bianco.

NIEBAUM, GUSTAV. See INGLENOOK; NIEBAUM-COPPOLA ESTATE

NIGHTINGALE, MYRON (1915–88). One of the great California winemakers of the twentieth century. More than anyone else it was Nightingale, as its winemaster from 1971 to 1984, who made BERINGER* a world-class winery. Before that, in 1959, he had gained renown for developing the first wine made in America in the authentic style of Sauternes: CRESTA BLANCA's Premier Semillon, for which the BOTRYTIS CINEREA was induced.

> Myron Nightingale, *Making Wine in California (1944–1987)* (Regional Oral History Office, Bancroft Library, 1988).

NOBLE ROT. See BOTRYTIS CINEREA

NORMAN VINEYARDS (BW 5660). Arthur Norman, a winegrower in Paso Robles, began planting his 70-acre vineyard in 1971 and bonded his 20,000-gallon winery in 1992. Specializing in powerful Zinfandel and Cabernet Sauvignon, he produces about 3,000 cases a year, including a table wine he labels No Nonsense Red.

NORTH COAST, a huge viticultural area that was recognized by the BATF in 1983, after considerable disagreement. Today it includes the winegrowing areas in Napa, Sonoma, Mendocino, Lake, Solano, and Marin counties. The original petition had excluded Lake and Solano counties; they were included by the federal agency. The area covers about 3 million acres and contains about 90,000 acres of vines, of which about 55 percent is planted to red-wine varieties. Nevertheless, the leading North Coast variety is Chardonnay, which constitutes about 31 percent, followed by Cabernet Sauvignon, at about 22 percent. In 1994 the North Coast produced 313,862 tons of wine grapes, almost entirely for premium table wine.

Today's official North Coast designation does not coincide with the historical area that carried the name. Before the late 1960s, all the winegrowing districts in the San Francisco Bay Area were considered part of this region, including the Livermore and Santa Clara valleys, which have since been placed in the Central Coast Viticultural Area.

NORTHERN SONOMA, a viticultural area running north from Santa Rosa to the county line and was officially recognized in 1985. Several wineries had labeled wine with this designation since Repeal. E. & J. GALLO, the force behind the petition for this district, is by far the largest vineyard owner in this area.

NORTH YUBA, a 30-square mile viticultural area in the eastern foothills of Yuba County west of Nevada City, was granted official status in 1985. The vineyards in the area are almost entirely those of RENAISSANCE VINEYARD, which has about 365 acres. In 1987, over objections from Renaissance, this area was included in the Sierra Foothills Viticultural Area.

NOUVEAU. See CARBONIC MACERATION

NOUVEAU MEDOC. See BRUN & CHAIX WINERY

NOVITIATE OF LOS GATOS. In 1886 the California Province of the Society of Jesus (Jesuits) established the Sacred Heart Novitiate in the hills above the town of Los Gatos. There were a few acres of vines there, on what had been Harvey Wilcox's old ranch, and, in 1888, one of the fathers made a few hundred gallons of wine. They sold it to a Jesuit college in San Francisco. When their income reached $2,500 in 1892, the fathers and novices in Los

Gatos built a large concrete winery and expanded the vineyard. Business was good and the cost of labor was nil. Within a few years the Novitiate was shipping sacramental wine to customers outside the Bay Area. By the 1920s the vineyard property amounted to 135 acres. The brothers' advantages at Repeal were delayed when a fire destroyed the winery in 1933. The new one held 500,000 gallons and the Novitiate was soon regularly marketing dessert and table wines in the retail trade. By the 1940s their wines were being served at the Waldorf-Astoria in New York. Also during the 1930s the Novitiate planted several large vineyards higher in the Santa Cruz Mountains; under other management these continued to produce until recently.

Production through the 1970s averaged about 30,000 cases a year, but aging equipment and growing competition brought an end to production in 1986. For three years the winery was rented to a NÉGOCIANT as a bottling and blending facility. In 1989 MIRASSOU used it for making sparkling wine.

The old Novitiate remains but since 1967 it has not trained novices. It now serves as a Jesuit retirement home and as headquarters for the Jesuits' operations in California. Most of the 350 acres of former vineyard land behind the Novitiate was sold to the town of Los Gatos in 1984 as open space.

NURSERIES. Several large grape-vine nurseries thrive today in California supplying grafted vines to vineyard owners. They are also an important source of resistant ROOTSTOCK when vines are to be budded or grafted in the field. The explosion of vineyard plantings from 1970 through the 1980s created what might be called a special nursery industry in California. Since the 1980s, nurseries, particularly in the North Coast, have continued to profit from the replanting necessitated by the new PHYLLOXERA threat.

Nurseries are almost as old as the State of California. In the 1850s there were so many in the San Jose area that the little town was dubbed "The Garden City." The great nurserymen most beneficial to the early California wine industry were the THOMPSON BROTHERS in Napa, John Llewelling in the East Bay, Louis PELLIER, B. S. Fox, and Antoine DELMAS in San Jose, and Anthony P. SMITH in Sacramento.

OAK. The wood of oak trees makes excellent COOPERAGE.* It is hard, quite watertight, and easily worked by a skilled cooper. Historically oak was used in winemaking for its durability and dependability: Oak BARRELS* and casks could last for decades, even centuries. Recently in California, the function of cooperage has been modified, because new oak staves give off flavors often considered appealing to wine consumers. When the container is meant to impart an extra and pleasing flavor to the wine, the life of the barrel or cask is limited and the cost of making premium wine increased.

American wood comes from the *Quercus alba,* the white oak. Commercial stands east of the Rockies are extensive and run well up into Canada. American oak is less porous than European oak is and imparts a more obvious vanilla flavor. For years the technology of whiskey barrel manufacture dominated the production of American oak cooperage meant for wine. Of late techniques specifically for wine have become a part of the coopering process in this country. Chief among these has been open-air instead of kiln drying of the staves. The slower open-air process, common in Europe, seems to yield cooperage that imparts more delicate and agreeable flavors. In the United States steam and boiling water had been used to heat staves as they are assembled. In Europe traditionally and now commonly in North America the source of heat is an open

wood fire, which leaves some charring on the inside of the barrel, giving a certain flavor of toast to the finished wine. Many wineries in California now order their barrels with an eye to the amount of "toast" on the inside. From the 1960s through the mid-1980s there was an almost universal preference among California's fine wine makers and their customers for wines produced in cooperage of European oak, overwhelmingly containers from France were favored, those from Germany and Slovenia markedly less favored.

Two species of European white oak are commonly used for cooperage. *Q. robur* is the French or English oak, but is found from Portugal to Turkey and north to Scandinavia. *Q. petraea* grows in just about the same areas. But coopers and winemakers are far more interested in the precise geographical origins of the oak than in the species. For French barrels such geographic terms as Limousin, Allier, Nevers, Vosges, and Jura have become part of California winemakers' vocabulary, as have the names of specific French barrel producers.

The high cost of French oak barrels has encouraged many producers in California to look with more favor on American oak barrels manufactured with the needs of the premium winemaker in mind. The life of an oak barrel can be extended by shaving the inside of the staves and replacing the head. Some producers, particularly those of FIGHTING VARIETALS, use oak chips as a very inexpensive flavoring alternative to the new oak barrel.

L. Walker, "Super Coopers," *Wines & Vines,* September 1995, 25–38.

OAKFORD VINEYARDS. The Ball family bought an 8-acre vineyard in the hills east of Oakville in Napa Valley in 1986 and brought out the first wine in 1987. The family makes about 1,000 cases of powerful Cabernet Sauvignon each year.

OAK KNOLL, a winegrowing area south of Yountville that was named for the pioneer Napa wine estate. It was not previously precisely defined, but in 1997 winegrowers led by TRE-FETHEN and MONTICELLO applied for AVA status for the area south of Yountville to Tran-

cus Road. The district also includes Brown's Valley to the west; see also ESHCOL; JOSEPH W. OSBORNE; TREFETHEN VINEYARDS.

OAK RIDGE VINEYARDS. See EAST-SIDE WINERY

OAKVILLE. A small village between Rutherford and Yountville that has given its name to one of the Napa Valley's best winegrowing areas. It received official AVA appellation status in 1993. Viticulture was not a serious matter in this part of the valley until the 1870s when H. W. CRABB* built up his great To Kalon estate. Vineyards amounted to about 1,100 acres by the end of the 1880s. In those years Zinfandel and German whites were the chief varieties grown. Up to Prohibition, the prices of grapes

Large-scale winegrowing came to the Oakville area when H. W. CRABB built his To Kalon Winery. He believed that fine wine did not necessarily come from buildings that looked like castles or fortresses. Crabb once said that, whatever To Kalon meant in Greek, "I try to make it mean the boss vineyard."

and wine from Oakville were the highest in the Napa Valley, except in the years when St. Helena's production was better.

After Prohibition Oakville's great reputation was dead. The rebirth began when Martin Stelling bought land and began replanting To Kalon in the late 1940s. The grapes from Beaulieu's Vineyard no. 2 and MARTHA'S VINE-YARD were notable. When Robert MONDAVI established his winery there in 1966, the rush to excellence became a flood, mostly of Cabernet Sauvignon and Sauvignon blanc.

Today there are about 4,000 acres of vines and twenty wineries in the viticultural district, which stretches from foothills to foothills on both sides of the valley and from the Yountville Hills to the southern boundary of the Ruther-ford district.

Oakville is also the site of a viticultural EXPERIMENTAL STATION run by the University of California at Davis.

OAKVILLE RANCH VINEYARDS (BW 5855). The 60 acres of vines, of which 43 acres are in red Bordeaux varieties, stand about 1,000 feet above the floor of Napa Valley in the eastern foothills. Oakville's first vintage was in 1989. In a short time the winery had developed an excellent reputation for Cabernet Sauvignon. The 5,000-case annual production of several varietals is augmented by a strong CUS-TOM-CRUSH business.

OAKVILLE VINEYARDS (BW 3989). An entrepreneurial undertaking on a grand scale that was one of the major California winery failures of the 1970s. W. E. Van Loben Sels formed a huge partnership with 400 members and in 1971 bought the BARTOLUCCI family's Madonna Winery in Oakville. He also acquired the Gustav Niebaum mansion and its vines from the estate of John Daniel. The partnership collapsed in 1976, but not from poor wines; they were a critical success. The Bartoluccis got their winery back and then sold it

to INGLENOOK; Robert MONDAVI acquired the wine inventory and brand; and Francis Ford Coppola bought the Niebaum mansion and vineyard.

OAKVILLE WINE CELLARS. See PBS WINE GROUP

OBESTER WINERY (BW 4817). In 1974 Sandra Obester's grandfather, John GEMELLO,* came to live with her and her husband Paul. The couple caught the vintners' disease from the historic old timer. They bought a farm outside Half Moon Bay and had the first crush at their Ox Mountain Winery in 1977. The name was soon changed. In 1989 they moved the center of the operation to Anderson Valley in Mendocino County. There they planted 45 acres of vines and produced several varietal wines. After the Gemello Winery's demise in 1982, the Obesters also made a line of Gemello wines, mostly hardy reds. Total production was about 10,000 cases when in 1997 the operation, but not the brand, was sold to DUCK-HORN WINERY in Napa.

OENOLOGY. See ENOLOGY

OIDIUM. See MILDEW

OJAI VINEYARD (BW 5203). A winery in Ventura County founded in 1984 by Adam Tal-mach. His 5.5-acre vineyard is devoted primarily to Rhône varieties and Sauvignon blanc. Ojai also buys Chardonnay from the Edna Valley. Annual production is about 5,000 cases.

OLD CREEK RANCH WINERY (BW 5056). The Maitland family bought a ranch in Ventura County in 1976 and planted 12 acres of vines. In 1981 the family opened a little winery where today most of the 1,500-case annual production is sold. The Maitlands produce several estate varietals and buy some grapes in Santa Barbara County.

OLDHAM, CHARLES FURLEY. A British wine merchant who became interested in California wine in 1890 when he received ten unsolicited barrels and found them good. He bottled the wine and sold it under the Big Tree brand. He later visited the Golden State several times, his personal evaluations of individual California wines becoming a regular part of the West Coast wine news and, today, an important historical source. He eventually became part of the CALIFORNIA WINE ASSOCIATION, which took over the sale of his Big Tree brand, by the 1900s also popular in the American market.

OLIVET LANE ESTATE. See PELLEGRINI FAMILY VINEYARDS

OLIVINA VINEYARD. The greatest of the Livermore Valley's wine estates, developed in the 1880s. Its founder was Julius Paul Smith (1843–1904) who had made his fortune in western borax after the Civil War. He bought 2,000 acres of foothill land in Livermore in 1881 and planted 620 acres of top varietals over the next seven years. His huge gravity-flow winery was in full operation in 1885. By the early 1890s production reached 300,000 gallons, the largest in the valley. He had a distillery on the property to make brandy for his fortified sweet wines, which were famous for their high quality, the result of the technical expertise of B. P. Parker, who ran the operation from 1889 to 1913.

Mrs. Smith sold the estate in 1916. Soon the great winery closed forever, although some of the vineyards planted to resistant rootstock in the 1890s survived Prohibition. Today Olivina is a huge cattle ranch, but the ruins of the old winery survive, as does the fine gate Mrs. Smith

After Prohibition Olivina's vineyards were not replanted and the great winery was not put back to work. But the fine structure still stands. Soon after this photo was taken in 1985 the upper, wooden portion collapsed.

built in 1905 shortly after her husband's death. She lived on in San Francisco until 1935.

OLMO, HAROLD PAUL, a viticulture expert and plant breeder who was a member of the faculty at the University of California at Davis and is best known for the development of a large number of vinifera crosses meant for warm weather conditions. Among those the most famous are Ruby Cabernet, Emerald Riesling, Flora, Symphony, Carmine, and Carnelian. In 1995 in California there were 9,676 acres, almost all in the Central Valley, planted to those varieties. Of those 6,238 acres were Ruby Cabernet. In 1980 a total of 23,923 acres had been planted to these varieties.

Olmo was also instrumental in developing the Rubired and Royalty varieties, used for their powerful dark color. Rubired is still important in the Central Valley, where there are about 10,000 acres in the ground.

> Philip Hiaring, "Harold P. Olmo," *Wines & Vines,* March 1988, 16–23.
>
> Harold P. Olmo, *Plant Genetics and New Grape Varieties* (Regional Oral History Office, Bancroft Library; 1976)

ONLY ONE. See LEON BRENDEL

OPTIMA (BW CA 5565). A brand name used by Michael Duffy and Greg Smith since 1984. They also developed the Fitch Mountain Cellars brand. In 1990 they bonded their own winery in Healdsburg where their 2,500-case annual production emphasizes Cabernet Sauvignon and Chardonnay.

OPUS ONE (BWC 5594). In 1978 Robert MONDAVI* and Château Mouton-Rothschild in Bordeaux began plans for a joint venture to make a great California CLARET from red Bordeaux varieties. The first vintage was 1979, mostly from grapes grown in Oakville. Until then referred to at the winery as Napamedoc, the wine was named Opus One in 1982. It was released, along with the 1980 vintage, in 1984. The wines won critical praise, but the $50 price tag made it the most costly wine in California, for a while.

In 1989 construction on a separate Opus One winery was begun just down the road from the main Mondavi facility in Oakville. It is surrounded by its own 130-acre vineyard with vines densely planted in the Bordeaux fashion. Some grapes are still purchased from growers in Napa. The first vintage at the new winery was the 1991, released in 1994.

The wine has been a market success, with almost half of its more than 25,000-case annual production being sold in restaurants by the glass.

ORANGE COUNTY. A part of Los Angeles County until it was separated in 1889, with Santa Ana as its seat. Its earliest large American settlement was ANAHEIM, the site of the German winegrowing community of that name. In the 1880s PIERCE'S DISEASE destroyed almost all the area's vineyards, which were replaced by oranges and walnuts. A few vineyardists replanted their vines and held on through Prohibition. Today Orange County has been paved over with suburbs. Except for San Francisco County, it is the most densely populated county in California, and virtually devoid of viticulture.

ORFILA VINEYARDS (BW 4773). In 1989 new owners took over the San Pasqual Winery in San Diego County. In 1994 they sold it and 25 acres of vines to Alejandro Orfila, a retired diplomat and member of an established winemaking family in Argentina. He has transformed the old vineyard by grafting it mostly to Rhône varieties and Sangiovese. Production has been about 12,000 cases.

ORGANIC WINE. Although wine chemists believe that the chemical residues of farming are virtually nonexistent in California wine

today, the movement toward organic viticulture in the state has been growing since the
1970s. The vineyardists who want to "go
organic" must shun pesticides, herbicides, and
commercial fertilizers. They must also limit
mildew control to the application of elemental
sulfur. By the 1990s more than 60 California
wineries controlled vineyards certified by the
California Certified Organic Farmers, an independent regulatory organization. Since 1992
the BATF has not allowed wineries to describe
their wines as "organic." For now winery labels
may read "wine from organically grown
grapes." At the moment the labeling question
depends mostly on the acceptable level of
added sulfites. A new BATF ruling on this
matter is expected soon.

Some vineyard owners now contend that,
although an organic approach is more labor
intensive at first, in the long run it is less
expensive than conventional viticulture is.

ORGANIC WINE WORKS. See HALLCREST
VINEYARDS

**ORLEANS HILL VINICULTURAL
ASSOCIATION** (BW 4994). In 1980 James
Lapsley and his partners opened a winery in
Woodland in Yolo County, its name a slightly
modernized version of that of a historical local
enterprise begun over a 100 years earlier. In 1851
Jacob KNAUTH set up a nursery in Sacramento
and later imported grape vines. Among these
was the Rhenish Orleans Riesling, then a wine
grape, today sometimes seen as a table variety.
In 1869, with partners, he set up a winegrowing
operation in the western foothills of Yolo
County. They called it the Orleans Hill Viticultural Association, 640 acres, with 40,000
vines. In 1881 Harry Epstein and Arpad
HARASZTHY* acquired the ill-fated property.
By 1902 new owners had turned sheep into the
vineyard; the winery was torn down in 1924. All
that remains today are a few old olive trees and

Orleans Street in the nearby town of Esparto.

Today Lapsley is the winemaker and annually produces about 4,000 cases of wine made
from grapes grown organically in Amador
County. He is also an academic administrator
for the University Extension at the University
of California at Davis and is an expert on
modern California wine history.

E. Peninou, *A History of the Orleans Hill Vineyard
& Winery of Arpad Haraszthy* (Winters, Calif.:
Winters Express, 1983)

ORTMAN, CHARLES. A modern-day master
of California Chardonnay who began his wine
career in 1968 dragging hoses for Joseph
HEITZ. Later he was winemaker at SPRING
MOUNTAIN and ST. CLEMENT before starting
an enology consulting firm. In 1979 he made
an Edna Valley Chardonnay under his epony-
mous label, which soon changed to Meridian
Wine Cellars. When he became the winemaker and head of production for Beringer
Wine Estate's operation in Paso Robles in 1988,
he sold the company his Meridian brand,
which is now used for Beringer's Central Coast
production at ESTRELLA RIVER WINERY.

OSBORNE, JOSEPH W. (?–1863). A New
England native, Osborne was one of the most
influential pioneers of fine viticulture during
California's early years of statehood. He
acquired 1,100 acres of land in Napa Valley in
1851, four miles north of Napa City, and developed a great agricultural estate he called OAK
KNOLL. In 1856 it was named the best farm in
California by the State Agricultural Society. By
then he had about 6,000 vines, half of which
were vinifera varieties brought to California
from New England. It was Osborne's sale of
cuttings from those vines that brought the
Zinfandel to the Sonoma Valley. He was murdered by a former employee in 1863. A few
years later a part of the Osborne estate was
developed into what became ESHCOL. Oak

Knoll Ranch continued to produce grapes and wine on its own for many years.

OVERCROPPING. If too many buds are left when the dormant vines are pruned, the resulting crop will usually be too large to ripen properly. Careful vineyardists try to find a proper balance between crop size and desired quality. However, it does not follow that the grape quality and flavor concentration will increase with every increment in crop reduction.

Overcropping was ever a problem in the early days of wine in California. Over the years, wineries developed incentives to reward vineyardists who did not overcrop their vines. One of these was to pay according to sugar content. But when wine prices were on the rise and grape prices were soaring, as in the early 1880s, overcropping was the rule.

Today it has become standard practice for winery owners and their grape suppliers to work together on crop management. Even so, when the economic situation is just right for specific varieties or market conditions, one can often find in the spring an increase in retained buds. In some years, such as 1982, early fall deluges may ruin the tardily ripening crops on such overcropped vines, and the grapes are never harvested.

OXIDATION. The overexposure of grapes and wine to oxygen often leads to a decline in quality, particularly of white wines, in which freshness and delicacy are often essential. The browning of white wine exposed to oxygen is a similar process to the darkening of a sliced apple.

Heat speeds up the oxidation process. From the earliest years white wine production in California was plagued by the hot autumn days and warm nights typical of the state's vintage season but far different from the climate of Germany and much of France. Even before Prohibition primitive cooling equipment was developed at some wineries, but it was not until after World War II that advanced systems were available and affordable even to smaller operations.

The concern over oxidation in young white wines has moved many high-quality producers to construct crushing and pressing stations as close to the vineyards as possible. Field crushing equipment and anaerobic transportation facilities to the wineries have also become common.

Some wines, such as sherry and madeira, benefit from oxidation; and in that context, the term maderization is often used rather than the more pejorative oxidation. California has a long but not particularly distinguished history of producing such types of wine.

PACHECO RANCH WINERY (BW 4886). The Rowland family began planting a 15-acre vineyard in Marin County in 1970 and sold the grapes to CUVAISON for a few years. In 1979 the winery, which is right on Highway 101 north of San Rafael, was bonded and now produces about 1,000 cases per year. Marin County's only estate winery, it is shown on page 200.

PACIFIC WINE & SPIRIT REVIEW. A publication that began in 1880 as the *San Francisco Merchant,* changed its name in 1891, and lasted until 1919. It was the most authoritative, widely read wine trade journal in its field on the West Coast. Today its old pages are a key resource for material on the California wine industry after 1880.

PADEREWSKI, IGNACE JAN (1860–1941). When an attack of rheumatism in 1913 forced Paderewski, a noted Polish pianist and patriot, to cancel his concert tour in California, he found his way to the hot water spa at Paso Robles. The next year he bought a 2,000-acre spread west of town and named it Rancho San Ignacio. After his heroic work for Poland in World War I, he returned to the United States and in March 1922, aware that the price for wine grapes was rising, visited his ranch with F. T. BIOLETTI and Horatio STOLL. The next year his superintendent, J. Gnierciah, began

planting 200 acres of vines, mostly Zinfandel, with some Béclan and Petite Sirah. Planted on their own roots, they began bearing in 1926 and in 1927 Gnierciah found a good market for them among the Italian-Swiss dairymen of the Salinas Valley. All the while the great musician kept up his international concertizing through the 1930s. Stoll stated in 1940 that the Zinfandel fruit from the vineyard was still wonderful. But by the mid-1950s the vines were dead. The growth of the Paso Robles as a fine wine district since the 1970s has revived interest there in this footnote to California wine history.

PADRE VINEYARD CO. (BW 1). In the days after Repeal and until World War II, Padre, also operating as the Cucamonga Vineyard Company, was the leading winery in southern California. The company dates from the 1870s. Later it was associated with the San Gabriel

Anyone who was anybody in the California wine industry knew the masthead of the *Pacific Wine & Spirit Review* in the days before Prohibition. (*Pacific Wine & Spirit Review*)

249

Wine Co. Its modern history began in 1909 when it was acquired by James Vai. During Prohibition it was the California Medicinal Wine Co. By 1936 "Padre Jimmy" Vai had built a 3.5 million-gallon winery specializing in bulk-process sparkling wine from Burger grapes. Vai died in 1961. Despite modernization, the winery's fortunes declined in the 1970s, until it was sold in bankruptcy in 1981. How Vai acquired the BW 1 number after Repeal has never been explained.

PAGANI BROTHERS. See KENWOOD VINEYARDS

PAGE MILL WINERY (BW 4756). The Stark family dug a little cellar under their home in the hills above Palo Alto and bonded their winery there in 1976. Since then they have been buying small lots of wine grapes from Napa to Santa Barbara Counties to produce a broad line of mostly vineyard-designated varietals. Annual production runs about 3,000 cases.

PAHLMEYER WINERY (BW 5706). Jason Pahlmeyer began producing Napa Cabernet Sauvignon in 1987 and Chardonnay in 1989. His wines have been made at various facilities and have received high critical praise. About 5,000 cases appear under the Pahlmeyer label each year.

PAICINES, a viticultural area in San Benito County south of Hollister. It became one of the most important in California after ALMADEN Vineyards bought the 2,200-acre Sykes Ranch in 1956 and began planting vines. After other purchases of land and a veritable planting binge of dozens of varieties, there were 3,300 acres of vines by 1965. For varietal wines in the 1960s, the quality of grapes from Paicines was satisfactory, but later it was not good enough to gain much fame for its Almaden wine. Almaden's demise in 1987 has led to many changes in land ownership and a marked decline in acreage. Today there are about 1,200 acres remaining in the viticultural area. It had received AVA status in 1982.

PALMDALE WINE CO. See JUAN GALLEGOS

PALMTAG, WILLIAM (1847–1927), proved that first-class wines could be produced in the Central Coast region south of the San Francisco Bay Area. A former brewer, he bought the historic VACHÉ ranch in the Cienega Valley in San Benito County in 1883 and transformed it into a modern winery. By the 1890s, he was producing 100,000 gallons of wine and had gained a national reputation. His use of superior varietals, his own solid business sense, and the services of an outstanding German winemaker in the person of Adam Rentz enabled Palmtag to expand his operation again in the 1890s, when the rest of the California industry was in depression. In 1900 his Riesling and Sauterne won silver medals at the Paris Exposition.

In 1902 expansion was again in the air and Palmtag took on additional partners and incorporated the San Benito Wine Co. By 1906 the winery's capacity was 300,000 gallons. In 1907 Palmtag retired and sold his interest in the operation. When he died in 1927, he was the richest and most respected citizen in Hollister. See also CIENEGA VALLEY; VALLIANT WINERY.

PALOMINO. The white grape variety essential to the sherry made in the Jerez region of Spain. It came to California in several ways. It was imported in the 1850s from New England, where it had been grown as a table grape; it was brought up from Peru and introduced to Sonoma by William McPherson HILL in the 1860s; and, far earlier, the Russians had planted Palomino vines, also imported from Peru, in their vineyard east of Fort Ross in Sonoma County. It was from this last source that Charles KRUG acquired the variety for Napa Valley with cuttings from vines that had survived in the RUSSIAN enclave. Somehow the

William Palmtag's Cienega Valley wine estate is pictured here ca. 1905. Parts of the old winery survive today as part of the CIENEGA VALLEY WINERY. (Tony Cedoline, Cienega Valley Winery)

name GOLDEN CHASSELAS became attached to the variety, and this term has survived in some areas. In the Santa Cruz Mountains, that name became corrupted to Golden Shasta.

California vintners loved the Palomino. It was a heavy bearer, easy to raise, with a neutral flavor that could be made lively with a little muscat. It was planted extensively in the Central Valley after 1900 for sweet wine. But during Prohibition it all but disappeared. In the 1930s there were only about 2,000 acres left in the state, almost 70 percent of which were in the coastal valleys where many small, country wineries used the variety in their ordinary table wines as it had been employed fifty years earlier.

In the 1940s the high demand for sweet wine, particularly sherry, caused Palomino acreage to soar. By 1950 there were almost 11,000 acres in the state, mostly in the Central Valley. But about 20 percent was still in the coastal counties, one-third of that in Sonoma alone. Since the 1960s acreage has declined to barely 800 acres statewide.

In 1996 the state tonnage of Palomino in California was 6,997, only 75 percent of the tonnage in 1990.

PANAMA-PACIFIC INTERNATIONAL EXPOSITION. A great world's fair held in San Francisco in 1915. There was a huge wine display with a popular sampling room. The wine competition showered medals on California's wineries, but the results give a fair picture of the brands and varieties most favored just before Prohibition; see also EXPOSITIONS.

PAPAGNI VINEYARDS (BW 4630). In 1973 Angelo Papagni began building a winery near Madera. Since the 1940s he had been growing grapes in the Central Valley. Now he was intending to produce high-quality table wine from hot-country grapes. He and his family got good reviews for several of these wines, particularly a varietal Alicante Bouschet. Sales were up to 100,000 cases by the early 1980s but heavy debt brought the operation down in 1988. In 1992 two members of the Papagni family were convicted of selling large quantities of Barbera as Zinfandel during the troubled times. The winery is now a food-processing plant.

PARADISE RIDGE WINERY (BW 5740), near the ruins of the historic FOUNTAINGROVE winery, was bonded in 1994. Its address is on Thomas Lake Harris Drive. Annual production amounts to about 1,500 cases of Chardonnay and Sauvignon blanc mainly.

PARAGON VINEYARDS. See EDNA VALLEY VINEYARD

PARAISO SPRINGS VINEYARDS (BW 5518). Richard Smith and his family have been raising grapes in the Salinas Valley southwest of Soledad since the early 1970s. Located in the Arroyo Seco Viticultural Area, Smith sells most of his grapes but began making his own wine in 1989. Annual production is about 5,000 cases, principally Chardonnay, Pinot blanc, and Pinot noir.

PARDUCCI WINE CELLARS (BWC 3832). In 1932 Adolph Parducci (1896–1978) bonded a winery near Ukiah in Mendocino County and by 1938 had built it to a 120,000-gallon capacity. He made bulk wine and shipped it east but still was able to build a loyal local clientele. After the war he took advantage of the rising tourist trade that flowed by his winery's doors. In 1964 he gave the business over to his sons, John and George, who soon began expanding it and planted 120 new acres of the best varietals. By 1972 their annual sales were up to 100,000 cases. In 1973 the family sold the winery to the TMI management and investment corporation, but John continued as manager and winemaker. He kept up the Parducci tradition of making good wine at a fair price, and the winery capacity grew to 2 million gallons. In 1986, when George died, John's son, Bill, took over most of the management duties.

In 1994 management began unraveling when TMI interceded in the operation as the result of complaints made by employees about Bill. John and Bill were fired and George's son, Thomas, was placed in charge. Meanwhile TMI was on the verge of bankruptcy as one real estate investment after another failed. In 1996 William HILL and his associates bought the winery and 280 acres of vineyard.

John Parducci, *Six Decades of Making Wine in Mendocino County* (Regional Oral History Office, Bancroft Library, 1992).

PARIS, TASTING IN (1976). To celebrate the United States Bicentennial, Steven Spurrier, a wine merchant in Paris, put on a well-reported wine tasting. He matched five California Chardonnays with five white Burgundies, and five California Cabernets with five red Bordeaux. The tasters represented the heights of the French wine establishment in its various incarnations; winemakers, wine writers, merchants, government officials, and restaurateurs. When the results of the blind tasting were announced, the tasters were shocked to learn that a 1973 Chateau Montelena Napa Chardonnay had been prefered, if *very* narrowly, over a 1973 Domaine Roulot Meursault-Charmes and a 1973 Stag's Leap Wine Cellars Napa Cabernet Sauvignon as narrowly over the 1970 Château Mouton-Rothschild. The results were widely broadcast and did much to confirm California's

Warren and Barbara Winiarski with Spencer Crew, the director of the Museum of American History at the Smithsonian Institution. The event was part of the twentieth anniversary celebration of the 1976 Paris Tasting. Bottles of the 1973 STAG'S LEAP WINE CELLARS Cabernet Sauvignon and CHATEAU MONTELENA Chardonnay became part of the permanent Smithsonian collection. (Photo Rick Vargas, Smithsonian Institution)

growing reputation as a world-class winegrowing region. The Napa Valley's reputation benefited even more.

Gerald Asher, "The Judgment of Paris Revisited," *Gourmet*, January 1997, 24.

FESS PARKER WINERY (BW 5557). In 1987 Fess Parker, the television actor, bought a 714-acre ranch in the Santa Ynez Valley in Santa Barbara County. He began planting vines in 1989 and building his beautiful winery in 1990. Wines appeared under his label in 1991. There are now 60 acres of vines, 15 of them Rhône varieties. Annual production reached 25,000 cases in the mid-1990s, with emphasis on Chardonnay, Merlot, Syrah, and White Riesling.

PARKER, ROBERT M., author of *Wine Advocate,* one of the most influential consumer publications in the wine world. Although his home is in Maryland, he spends much time in California. There he concentrates on evaluating Cabernet Sauvignon, Zinfandel, and Chardonnay. In 1995, using his controversial 50- to 100-point scale, he evaluated the Cabernets of eighty-one California producers for an average score of 91.7. Evaluations of sixty-seven Cabernets from the 1992 vintage averaged 91.9. These scores suggest that he tends to concentrate his evaluations on wines he likes, and that he likes many California wines.

PARROTT, TIBURCIO (1840–94). The son of John Parrott (1811–84), a businessman and millionaire in San Francisco, Tiburcio bought the Forbes Ranch on Spring Mountain in Napa County in 1884 and developed a grand estate that he called Miravalle. His chief interest was winegrowing. By the nineties he had 120 acres of vineyard, much of it planted to world-class varieties. His reputation for fine wine was unmatched in California during his lifetime. His Cabernet Sauvignon, sold as Medoc, was considered the Golden State's

finest CLARET. He also produced a Chardonnay, labeled Montrachet, and a Pinot noir, Chambertin. He was a close friend of the BERINGERS, his mansion a close copy of their famous Rhine House. By the time of his death, his vineyard had succumbed to phylloxera. The estate was later revived as SPRING MOUNTAIN VINEYARDS.

PARSONS CREEK WINERY (BW 4894), was founded in 1979 in Mendocino County. After surviving a terrible fire in 1985, it was acquired in 1988 by the Canadian Cabrela Wine Co. Even though production reached 25,000 cases in 1992, the operation went out of business the next year and survives only as a brand. The facility was acquired by the owners of HIDDEN CELLARS.

PASO ROBLES. A town in San Luis Obispo County that has given its name to a gigantic viticultural area granted official status in 1983. The district covers more than 650,000 acres and has about 6,800 acres of vines. It extends southward about 25 miles from the Monterey County line to below Atascadero, and from a line about ten miles west of the town eastward to the desert lands along the Kern County line.

Most of the area is not suited to winegrowing but some parts are. There are many good vineyards in the hills west of Paso Robles. The area west of Templeton is a historic district. More extensive vineyards have been planted in the past 25 years on the Estrella River prairie lands east of Paso Robles. Most of the area's wineries are here.

There were a few vines here and there in the early days, about 130 acres around Creston and west of Templeton by the 1890s. (But the historic YORK MOUNTAIN WINERY has not been included in this viticultural area.) There was also PADEREWSKI's well-known Rancho San Ignacio. After Repeal a few small country wineries were established, PESENTI being the most successful. The region became real wine country in the 1970s. East of Paso Robles the best success has been with red varietals, particularly Cabernet Sauvignon and Zinfandel. To the west there is a stronger maritime influence and white varieties can do well. Most vineyards now have drip irrigation. There are about twenty-five wineries in the area today.

Gerald Asher, "Paso Robles—California, Country Style," *Gourmet*, September 1994, 80.

PAULI RANCH WINERY (BW 4910). In 1995 the owners of BRAREN PAULI WINERY bought the Mendocino plant of the financially troubled WEIBEL VINEYARDS. They control 360 acres of vineyard land here and have established a CUSTOM-CRUSH operation in the Potter Valley in Medocino County.

PAT PAULSEN VINEYARDS (BW 4966). In 1970 the comedian, Pat Paulsen (1928–97), bought a ranch south of Cloverdale, Sonoma County, and planted vines. He began producing wine in 1980. A divorce and tax problems brought an end to the operation in 1990.

PBS WINE GROUP (BWC CA 5714). A group of investors that operates Oakville Wine Cellars on the Silverado Trail in Napa Valley. The CUSTOM-CRUSH facility went into action in 1995, producing about 50,000 cases a year. PBS's own brands include Winterbrook, Hidden Valley, Montecito, and Diamond Hill. In 1995 twelve producers were using the Oakville facility.

PEACHY CANYON WINERY (BW 4984). Doug Beckett's little winery is located a few miles west of Paso Robles in San Luis Obispo County and specializes in powerful Zinfandels. It was bonded as Tobias Vineyards in 1980. Beckett took over in 1987. For a few seasons TOBIN JAMES Zinfandels were also made here. Peachy Canyon makes about 9,000 cases per year.

ROBERT PECOTA WINERY (BW 4845). Since founding his winery north of Calistoga

in Napa in 1978, Robert Pecota has produced complex and interesting varietal wines, including several nouveau Gamays and a Muscat blanc—a dessert wine named for his daughter, Andrea. The home Cabernet Sauvignon vineyard is named for another daughter, Kara. The backbone of the annual 20,000-case production is Sauvignon blanc.

PEDRIZZETTI WINERY (BW 4031). In 1913 Camillo Colombrano built the first winery on this property in Morgan Hill, Santa Clara County. John Pedrizzetti bought it in 1945 and produced bulk wine for several years. He also built up a local retail and restaurant trade in the Bay Area. When his son, Ed, took charge in the 1960s, the winery was expanded and modernized. The retail trade in sturdy Zinfandel and Barbera was augmented by a complex line of varietal and generic wines. By 1978 the winery capacity had grown to 400,000 gallons. The winery is run by Ed and his wife, Phyllis, who was president of the Santa Clara County Wine Growers Association in 1976. A large part of the winery's annual 60,000-case production is sold at the tasting room. Although much of the winery was destroyed by fire in 1996, by the next year it had been rebuilt.

J. PEDRONCELLI WINERY (BW 113). In 1927 Giovanni Pedroncelli (1890–1969) bought a 90-acre, rundown vineyard and an old barn that had been the John Canota Winery (built in 1904), in the eastern hills of Dry Creek Valley in Sonoma County. Pedroncelli sold his grapes, and at Repeal remodeled and bonded the winery. Through World War II he sold mostly red wine in bulk, but also had a good trade at the winery selling jug wine to local folk. In 1947 he began bottling under his own label; in 1949 he started selling his varietal Zinfandel. In the 1950s his sons, John and James, gradually took over the business and bought it from their father in 1963.

They began moving away from their rustic jug-wine heritage into the world of premium varietals. They were the first after Repeal to plant Pinot noir in northern Sonoma County. By the 1970s production was up to 50,000 cases a year with national distribution. Today it is about 100,000. Rugged red table wine is still their specialty, but Chardonnay and other whites have been getting good notices since the mid-1980s.

PEJU PROVINCE (BW 5230). In 1981, when Anthony Peju bought his 30-acre vineyard in Rutherford in Napa he wanted to produce his own wine. At first he had it made at a nearby winery and, to sell the wine, built a tasting room and hospitality facility on his property. In 1985 this facility became the center of a stormy debate over what a NAPA winery had to be, to be a real winery. While the battle raged, to be resolved in a complicated local statute enacted in 1990, Peju built his own winery, ready for the 1991 vintage. Since then, and before, Peju's wines have been highly acclaimed, particularly the Cabernet Sauvignon from the home vineyard. Production stands at about 10,000 cases a year. The winery and its beautiful grounds have become tourist attractions in recent years.

PELLEGRINI FAMILY VINEYARDS (BW 5721). The Pellegrins went into the wine business at Repeal when they opened their winery in San Francisco on Third Street (BW 3822). They made their wine from grapes grown in Sonoma. Later Nello and Vincenzo Pellegrini operated a winery and distributorship in South San Francisco. In 1975, the family planted vines west of Santa Rosa near the Russian River. Wines began appearing in 1986 under the Olivet Lane label and in 1994 a winery was bonded at the Sonoma estate. The other Pellegrini brands are Cloverdale Ranch, Cotes de Sonoma, and Riverglen Cellars. Annual production is about 35,000 cases.

PELLET, HENRY ALPHONSE (1828–1912). Charles KRUG once said that you could count

Napa's great winemakers on one hand—and Pellet was the thumb. He came to California from his native Switzerland in 1850 with a solid background in winemaking. Between 1859 and 1865, he produced vintages for such pioneers in Napa as John Patchett and G. B. CRANE. He started his own winery in St. Helena in 1866, usually making about 25,000 gallons per year. With a wonderful reputation for his technical knowledge in the cellar, he was also an accomplished vineyardist—a pioneer in trellis management and in the use of resistant rootstock. He acted as a consultant to many wineries and ended his career in 1899 as superintendent of the STANLY estate in the Carneros.

PELLIER. Louis Pellier (1817–72) came to California as an Argonaut in 1849 and settled in San Jose where he established a pioneer nursery. His brother **Pierre** (1823–94) came to the Santa Clara Valley in 1851 and went to work for Louis. Soon he returned to France and brought back a large consignment of nursery stock including many wine-grape varieties that became the foundation of the Pellier collection, one of the best in California before 1870. He also brought in the little French prune (*petite d'Agen*), which became the chief agricultural product of the Santa Clara Valley in later years

In the late 1850s Pierre went to work at Clement COLOMBET's winery near Mission San Jose, but returned in 1861 to manage the 312-acre piece of land Louis had purchased in the eastern foothills of the valley, in an area later called the Evergreen district. When Louis died in 1872, Pierre bought the property from his brother's estate. The winery prospered and Pierre's son, Louis, was being prepared to take over. But Louis died in 1874 and his sister, **Henriette** (1860–1937), took his place and was supervising vineyard and cellar operations by the end of the decade. Her marriage to Pierre MIRASSOU* established a line of historical continuity that comes down to the present. Most histories indicate that today's Mirassou Winery

Henriette Pellier married a neighboring winegrower, Pierre MIRASSOU, in 1881. She had been working in the Pellier winery since she was fourteen. By 1885 she and Pierre had taken over full supervision of the Evergreen estate's winery and vineyard activities. (Mirassou Family Collection, San Jose, Calif.)

stands on the old Pellier estate. In fact, the present winery land was purchased by the Mirassou family in 1910. The old Pellier lands passed into other hands and have no connection with the current operation.

PELOURSIN. See DURIF; PETITE SIRAH

PENINOU, ERNEST, a leading authority on California wine history, studied enology at the University of California at Davis and later worked at FOUNTAINGROVE and ALMADEN. His *Directory of California Wine Growers and*

Wine Makers in 1860 (published in 1967) is his most important historical work. He has also written histories of ORLEANS HILL, VINA, and the CALIFORNIA WINE ASSOCIATION.

ROBERT PEPI WINERY (BW 5052). In 1966 two Robert Pepis, father and son, bought 55 acres of land in Oakville in Napa. The family planted vines, mostly Sauvignon blanc, and in 1981 built a pretty, rustic winery on a knoll overlooking the vineyard. They made 4,000 cases of Sauvignon blanc that year, but the Cabernet Sauvignon they produced from grapes purchased at nearby Vine Hill Ranch was the beginning of their most noteworthy product. (Vine Hill is next door to MARTHA'S VINEYARD.) In 1988 Pepi produced the state's first varietal Sangiovese, labeled Colline di Sassi. Total sales reached 25,000 cases in 1994 when the winery was sold to KENDALL-JACKSON, which intended to use the facility to produce wines from Bordeaux varieties. In 1997 Kendall-Jackson announced that a 500,000-case winery would be built on the property.

PEPPERWOOD SPRINGS VINEYARD (BW 5076). Larry Parsons (1948–86) founded this little Anderson Valley winery in 1981 after buying land there in Mendocino County the year before. In 1984 he released his first wines, 700 cases of Chardonnay and Pinot noir. Blind from birth, he included information in Braille on his labels. After his death in an automobile accident, the winery was purchased by the Kaliher family and now produces about 1,000 cases per year.

PERELLI-MINETTI, ANTONIO (1882–1976), came to California from Italy in 1902 and went to work for ITALIAN SWISS COLONY. He later worked at the Pioneer Winery in Livermore, briefly at BEAULIEU VINEYARD, and at wineries in Healdsburg and Ukiah. After a stint of winegrowing in Mexico (1910–17), he settled in Kern County in the 1920s and began growing grapes there. His winery, bonded in Delano in 1934, was eventually incorporated as A. Perelli-Minetti & Sons (BW 3616). In 1940 his family opened a second facility (BW 4254) nearby. In 1950 his 12 million-gallon operation became one of the Eleven Cellars of the revived CALIFORNIA WINE ASSOCIATION. He and his family also controlled 1,200 acres of vineyard in the Central Valley. By 1971 his winery *was* the California Wine Association, as the other members changed ownership, operations, or went out of business. It was now a 20 million-gallon producer of inexpensive table and dessert wine, sparkling wines and brandy under dozens of labels. In 1981 the operation was sold to industrial investors and ceased to be a single entity.

Antonio Perelli-Minetti, *A Life in Wine Making* (Regional Oral History Office, Bancroft Library, 1975).

MARIO PERELLI-MINETTI WINERY (BW 5437). After working for years in his family's wine operations in Kern County, Mario settled in the Napa Valley and planted 8 acres of vines along the Silverado Trail. In 1979 he introduced a line of NÉGOCIANT wine under his label. He later produced wine at another facility and built his own 36,000-gallon winery in 1988. His annual production of about 5,000 cases consists mainly of Chardonnay and Cabernet Sauvignon.

PERRONE, OSEA. See MONTEBELLO WINE CO.; RIDGE VINEYARDS

PERRY CREEK VINEYARDS (BW 5621). The Chazen family bonded a beautiful little winery in Amador County in 1991, but their 68 acres of vines, with nine varietals, had begun taking shape in the 1980s. Their annual 10,000-case production is concentrated in Zinfandel and Cabernet Sauvignon. A classic automobile collection is on display at the winery and has become a tourist attraction.

PESENTI WINERY (BW 3974). Frank Pesenti founded his winery in 1934, near Templeton in the Paso Robles Viticultural Area. For years he concentrated on regional sales of jug wine, mostly generic table wines and Zinfandel, the latter from vines planted on the estate in the 1920s. Pinot noir and Cabernet appeared in the 1960s, also in jugs, if desired. In recent years, the special emphasis has been on Zinfandel. In an article in *Gourmet* magazine in 1994, the wine expert Gerald Asher called Pesenti's 3-liter jug of Zinfandel "the best value in red wine anywhere in the world." Total production is about 30,000 cases per year from the 65-acre estate vineyard and purchased grapes and, under the winemaker, Frank Nerelli, the emphasis is on premium wines.

PEST CONTROL. The vineyardist often must contend with pests as small as mites, insects, and nematodes, and as large as deer. Mid-sized enemies of cultivated vines include BIRDS and rodents. The greatest pest of them all is the PHYLLOXERA, against which there is no control, only defense in the form of resistant rootstock.

Some pests, such as leafhoppers and spider mites, attack the vine's leaves and have been controlled with insecticides. But since the 1960s more and more emphasis has been placed on biological control. For example, researchers at the University of California at Davis have shown that a parasitic wasp can be encouraged to live near vineyards threatened by leafhoppers and will control them effectively. Other pests, such as cutworms, attack buds and young shoots. Certain beetles attack the permanent parts of the vine. For those, too, biological controls in California have gradually replaced insecticides.

Newly planted vineyards can be ruined by rabbits and ground squirrels. For years the milk carton was a standard foil in California. Recently plastic tubes have become popular. A strong and properly constructed high fence is the best foil for deer. In earlier years firearms were more commonplace.

PETALUMA. A town in southern Sonoma County, once the center of a fairly important winegrowing area. By the 1890s there were about 600 acres of vines growing here, about half in the Lakeville area, just to the east. But almost all those vines were destroyed by phylloxera by 1905. Even so, the town was an important part of the Sonoma wine industry; LACHMAN & JACOBI constructed a huge wine cellar there, which acted as a sort of small-scale WINEHAVEN there until Prohibition. Since Repeal five small wineries have listed Petaluma as their address.

PETERSON, RICHARD, a talented enologist who has been involved in a large number of wine enterprises since he received his doctorate in agricultural chemistry at the University of California at Berkeley in 1958. He spent ten years with GALLO as research director until moving to BEAULIEU in 1967. There he made many wines that drew attention to his skill as a winemaker. From there he went to MONTEREY VINEYARD in 1973, and also directed production for the TAYLOR CALIFORNIA CELLARS brand. He returned to Napa in 1986 to head ATLAS PEAK operations. This relationship ended abruptly in 1990. Then until 1995 he concentrated on management consulting, until he took up the leadership of a group that acquired the FOLIE À DEUX WINERY.

PETERSON WINERY. See BELVEDERE WINERY

PETITE SIRAH. In 1997 there were about 2,500 acres of California vines that were known as Petite Sirah. These vines produced about 1.2 million gallons of wine, much of it bottled as varietal Petite Sirah, but almost no vineyardists in California know for sure what the vines that they call Petite Sirah really are.

The SYRAH came to California from France in 1878 with a great reputation but developed little following in the Golden State because of low yields. The French distinguish between the *petite* Syrah, low yielding and noble, and the *grosse* Syrah, vigorous and productive but of lesser quality. All observers agreed that it was the *petite* that came to California in the early years. Charles KRUG, H. W. CRABB, and Charles McIver (see LINDA VISTA VINEYARD) made good wines from this variety, which in France is used for the great reds of Hermitage and Côte Rotie, but it was never popular.

In 1884 McIver imported the DURIF,* which was a cross between the Peloursin and Syrah varieties. He was soon calling the wine Petite Sirah, although there is no evidence today that suggests he knew the vine's parentage, which was discovered in 1998 through DNA FINGERPRINTING. Crabb visited McIver and then commented in the industry press on the confusion. He did like the Durif for its color and vinosity, but didn't see why it should be called Sirah. Then in the 1890s virtually all the true Syrah in California was destroyed by phylloxera. But after 1897, when good times brought vast planting and replanting all over the state, something called Petite Sirah became a popular variety. It was not Syrah and was probably Durif. But the plantings may also have included two other closely related vines, the BÉCLAN and Peloursin. In the trade press this so-called Petite Sirah was touted for its color, fragrance, and high yield and came to be a part of the red burgundy blend made by many wine houses. (It was not sold as a varietal wine before the 1960s.)

When Prohibition came, this Petite Sirah in the North Coast was an important part of the grapes shipped east to home winemakers. In 1929, 358 boxcars of the variety were shipped fresh out of Napa and Sonoma by rail, more even than Zinfandel. After Repeal there were about 7,500 acres in California, about half of them planted before 1920. The grape continued

TABLE 22. PETITE SIRAH GRAPES, SELECTED COUNTIES AND THE CENTRAL VALLEY

| | | | (ACRES) | | | |
YEAR	MENDOCINO	SONOMA	NAPA	MONTEREY	CENTRAL VALLEY	TOTAL
1938	160	2,973	2,091	0	1,821	7,285
1961	155	1,493	1,748	0	592	4,440
1968	233	1,420	1,577	30	679	4,289
1974	454	1,194	1,137	2,234	7,304	13,074
1976	516	974	1,024	2,447	7,962	14,215
1983	445	679	814	1,548	3,224	7,325
1988	377	402	580	818	1,010	3,495
1997	320	268	328	403	813	2,468

NOTE: The grape variety known commonly in California as the Petite Sirah is mostly DURIF but may, in some instances, be in fact the BÉCLAN or the Peloursin. See text page 23.

SOURCE: California Agricultural Statistics Service, Sacramento, Calif.

to perform its old role of giving color and richness to standard red table wines, but acreage declined to about 4,500 acres in the 1960s.

Then the Petite Sirah appeared as a premium varietal wine, made most notably at CONCANNON and Lee Stewart's SOUVERAIN. In the 1970s Petite Sirah was a good choice when rich, tannic wines were in vogue. Acreage doubled to 8,200 between 1971 and 1973. The coastal counties kept their old vines, while the Central Valley led the increase in new plantings. Monterey County also saw heavy planting. Acreage peaked in 1976 and began decling rapidly after 1980. Today several premium producers have created a market for the Petite Sirah, which is also blended with Zinfandel and is part of many Rhône blends in California. Those producers try not to think about a study made at the University of California at Davis in 1992, in which it was reported that there were at least three different varieties of grapes in California vineyards being called Petite Sirah. The most common is surely the Durif. The other two may be Peloursin and Béclan. Even though most Petite Sirah in California vineyards is probably Durif, the BATF ruled in 1996 that the two terms are not synonyms and that it "will continue to seek evidence regarding the true identity of the grape called Petite Sirah."

One thing is clear: Even French experts have agreed that Californians were making better wine from the grape, whatever it is called, than had ever been made from the Durif in France.

In 1996 the Petite Sirah vintage was 7,155 tons, about 75 percent of the tonnage in 1990.

PETIT VERDOT. Agoston HARASZTHY imported two Verdots into California in 1861, but neither was propagated later. Any that J. H. DRUMMOND may have brought in during the late 1870s are more likely to have been. In 1882 H. W. CRABB had both a Gross and a Petit Verdot in his To Kalon nursery. By the 1880s there were Verdot vines at CRESTA BLANCA, OLIVINA, LINDA VISTA, and several other wineries. But after the mid-1890s we hear no more of the variety in California until recent times.

Small quantities of Petit Verdot are used in the wines of many Bordeaux châteaux to add color, tannin, and complexity. A few acres were planted in California in the 1970s. MOUNT VEEDER WINERY produced a varietal in 1978, but most of the Petite Verdot grapes were blended with Cabernet Sauvignon and other red Bordeaux varieties. In the 1980s more acres were planted here and there by producers who were satisfied with the variety's contribution to their red Bordeaux blends.

In the mid-1990s there were about 250 acres in California, more than 80 percent of which was in Napa and Sonoma. The 1996 vintage produced 546 tons. In 1990 there had been about 100 tons.

PETRI. Before Prohibition the Petri family was chiefly engaged in cigar production in San Francisco. After 1887 they had also been wine merchants and were able to sell their Marca Petri brand across the country. At Repeal they leased an old winery (BW 2268) in Forestville, Sonoma County, and then acquired the 500,000-gallon Alba Winery (BW 925) in Escalon in San Joaquin County for sweet wine production.

Louis Petri (1912–80) was the man who revolutionized his family's business. In 1944 he became president of the Petri Wine Company. In subsequent years he acquired several wineries in the Central Valley, including all the facilities there of ITALIAN SWISS COLONY. In 1951 he organized the ALLIED GRAPE GROWERS cooperative, sold his wineries to it, and organized UNITED VINTNERS to market the wine. He also built a huge wine tanker in 1957, the *Angelo Petri,* named for his father, which made seven trips a year to the Atlantic Coast, each time delivering 2.5 million gallons of wine. Its last voyage was in 1975. In 1968 HEUBLEIN bought United Vintners and Petri stepped down as board chairman. By 1971 he had sold off his vineyard holdings.

> Louis A. Petri, *The Petri Family in the Wine Industry* (Regional Oral History Office, Bancroft Library, 1971).

PETRUCCI, VINCENT. See FRESNO STATE UNIVERSITY

PEZZI KING VINEYARDS (BW 5737). In 1993 James Rowe acquired the 50-acre WILLIAM WHEELER vineyard in Sonoma County in the Dry Creek Valley. The highlight of his first vintage in 1994 was a powerful old-vine Zinfandel. In 1996 he acquired the ROBERT STEMMLER winery for his tasting room. Annual production is about 9,000 cases.

PFEFFER, WILLIAM (ca. 1840–1910), one of the leading nineteenth-century authorities on resistant rootstocks in California, came to the Santa Clara Valley in 1869 and acquired foothill land near today's Cupertino. He planted fine wine varieties and had an excellent reputation as a winemaker. Charles WETMORE declared his 1883 Cabernet Sauvignon to be as close to a Médoc wine as he had ever tasted from a California producer. During the 1890s he wrote a regular column about resistant rootstock for *Pacific Tree & Vine.* His name is best remembered today for the CABERNET PFEFFER, which he developed as a seedling from an unnamed vine. After his death his property was acquired by the newspaper magnate Fremont Older, who had little interest in viticulture, and the estate is now part of a regional park.

pH. A number, ranging from 1.0 to 14.0, that indicates the hydrogen ion concentration of a solution. A 7.0 solution is neutral, distilled water. Acid solutions are less than 7.0, base or alkaline solutions exceed 7.0. Wines today almost always fall between 2.9 and 4.0. Young wines with a pH of about 3.1 to 3.5 are fairly tart and refreshing. Wines with increasingly higher pHs usually taste flat and dull.

As grapes ripen, their acid content declines and the pH rises. Until the 1950s one of the failings of California winemaking was the tendency to harvest overripe grapes with too high a pH. In the past high sugar content and ripeness were considered almost synonymous. Today winegrowers take acid pH into account to determine ripeness.

The term "appropriate pH" is used more and more today as a reference point for wine.

Because the term is associated with acid, some consumers, confused, think that high pH means high acid. Today knowledgeable enophiles make it a point to use this term properly.

JOSEPH PHELPS VINEYARDS (BW 4647). Phelps was the contractor who built the RUTHERFORD HILL and CHATEAU SOUVERAIN wineries in the early 1970s. He became interested in California wine and in 1972 bought the 670-acre Connally Ranch in Spring Valley, east of Napa's Silverado Trail. He built his winery there in 1973 and hired the German winemaker Walter SCHUG who stayed with him until 1983. In the early years Shug's emphasis was on white wine, but Cabernet Sauvignon was where Phelps made his greatest early mark, first with his 1974 Insignia red Bordeaux blend, and then from Cabernets grown in designated vineyards, such as EISELE and Backus. Phelps and Schug were also modern pioneers in the production of wine from true SYRAH vines. Their first was from grapes grown by the CHRISTIAN BROTHERS, in 1978 from their own. After years of experimentation, Phelps eventually developed an entire line of Rhône-style wines, blends and varietals, which now travel under the Vin du Mistral label.

Besides his 160 acres in Spring Valley, Phelps has acquired vineyard land elsewhere in Napa, in Rutherford, Stag's Leap, Yountville, Oakville, and the Carneros. These acres supply grapes for a wide range of wines, mainly Cabernet and Chardonnay, but also the Rhônes, Sauvignon blanc, Zinfandel, Gewürztraminer, and White Riesling. In 1985 Phelps also began making wine under the Innisfree label. Total production from his 400 acres in Napa and some purchased grapes was approaching 100,000 cases in the mid-1990s.

Jancis Robinson, *The Great Wine Book* (London: Sidgwick & Jackson, 1982), 208-14.

PHENOLICS. A group of chemicals that includes tannins, anthocyanins, and flavenoids, all found in grapes, particularly in the skins of dark grapes. Our understanding of these compounds has accelerated since the 1960s.

Vineyard and cellar techniques can promote or inhibit certain phenols associated with high quality and ageability in red wine. Many of the important trace elements in red wine that we associate with good flavors have phenolic structures. Although great strides have been made in recent years to promote our knowledge of this side of fine wine production, there are many areas of disagreement among experts in fermentation science.

Because phenolics have antioxidative properties, the relationship of phenols to health has been a recent topic for popular and scientific discourse. There is good evidence to suggest that drinking moderate amounts of phenolics-laden red wine, (Syrah and Cabernet Sauvignon have the highest levels of the most "healthful" phenols) may afford some protection against coronary disease, a finding that generated the concept known as the French Paradox. The expression entered our vocabulary in 1991 as the result of a television program in which the participants wondered how it was that people of southern France, in spite of a high-fat diet, had an incidence of heart disease that was low in comparison with that of other industrialized countries, particularly the United States. A Mediterranean diet, which includes red wine, was suggested as at least part of the answer. The presentation of this hypothesis resulted in a perceptible jump in the sale of Californian red table wine.

R. H. PHILLIPS VINEYARD (BW 5214). There was little viticulture in the hot, dry Esparto area of Yolo County until the 1970s, when the Giguiere family planted a few acres of wine grapes as an experiment. The good results convinced them to convert a sizeable portion of their wheat fields to grapes. In 1984 they sold their first wine, 4,000 cases; in 1985 they made 40,000 cases, and, in 1995, almost

400,000. The family's great success has been with white varietals of good quality sold at very reasonable prices. For several years most of the wine was made at other facilities, their own 88,000-gallon winery being far too small for their production. But in 1995 they broke ground on a new 100,000-square-foot facility.

The Phillips home vineyards grew fast and are still growing. By 1988 there were 280 acres under vines, 1,297 acres by 1997. There is more expansion under way with Rhône varieties and even some Spanish Tempranillo.

PHYLLOXERA. A tiny plant louse, or aphid (family *Aphididæ*), native to the eastern United States. Called *Phylloxera vastatrix* (the destroyer) by the French, its modern scientific name is *Dactylasphaera vitifoliæ.*

The louse was carried to Europe in the 1850s on American vines and was discovered in England and France in 1863. It reached California on vines from the eastern United States and from Europe in the 1850s and 1860s, probably arriving first in the Sonoma Valley where it was identified in 1873.

The phylloxera attacks the roots of some members of the VITACEÆ (grape) family. In the bug's original environment in the Mississippi-Missouri valleys, the native grape vines there have evolved along with the phylloxera and are able to resist its attacks successfully. Not so the European vinifera varieties from which all great wines are produced.

The phylloxera hit the vineyards of Western Europe and the Mediterranean world with devastating speed and intensity. By the 1870s thousands of acres in France had been destroyed. The speed of the louse's spread in the areas of Europe that, like much of France, receive summer rain, was accelerated by the natural development in this environment of a winged form. In such humid climates, phylloxera could travel with the wind, and did. In California the dry summers meant that the spread took place on cuttings, rooted vines, on vineyard equipment, wagons, and on workers' boots. It was a slower process, and, although vines in the Sonoma Valley were damaged by the late 1870s, most of the state felt secure. Meanwhile, the decline of French production meant a rise in the demand for California wine on the East Coast.

The French led the way to a solution to the phylloxera problem. There were eventually four possible approaches. The first was to do nothing and hope or pray. This did not work in France, but in California it did work in some areas. (Where soils are very sandy, the bug is incapable of spreading. For that reason much of San Benito and Monterey counties have never had serious problems with phylloxera.) The second was to attack phylloxera with chemicals, flooding, even electrical shock. But after years of testing hundreds of bright ideas, scientists abandoned this approach. The third was to cross European vinifera varieties with resistant

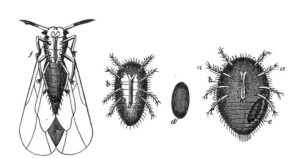

A female phylloxera (*Dactylasphaera vitifoliæ*) and her eggs. *a,* antennæ; *b,* horns or suckers; *c,* egg visible in her body; *d,* the egg; *f,* winged form of the insect, virtually nonexistent in California but common in western Europe.

American varieties to produce a hybrid, resistant vine. The French and Germans did a considerable amount of this work, but the result was only a huge collection of vines with fruit inferior to that of the best vinifera varieties. The vines, often called French hybrids, have been used in many places, but Californians never took them seriously. The fourth was to graft good vinifera varieties onto native American, resistant ROOTSTOCK.* This became the accepted answer in Europe and California by the 1890s and still is today.

Between 1897 and 1910, the California battle against phylloxera was won by replanting on resistant rootstock propagated here and in France. Until the 1980s there was little more concern in California about phylloxera. But then it was discovered that one of the most widely planted rootstocks was not dependable and a new outbreak of phylloxera occurred, particularly in the Napa Valley. There scientists also contended that they had detected a biotype-B phylloxera, which now was attacking vines planted on the A×R#1 rootstock, suspect because among its parents is the fatally unresistant vinifera, the Aramon.

By the 1990s many parts of Napa and some places in Sonoma were experiencing a decline in the yields of their vineyards caused by phylloxera. The national and local press tended to describe the scene as one of devastation. Even though this was a gross exaggeration, many growers in Napa and Sonoma who had the now-unresistant rootstock began replanting their vineyards for various reasons: Some vines were getting old and a new planting gave growers a chance to rearrange the geography of their vineyards; some decisions to replant were driven more by accountants' views of the future than any current devastation. But phylloxera is still a serious problem and replanted vineyards are now being grafted onto thoroughly resistant vines.

George Ordish, *The Great Wine Blight* (New York: Charles Scribner's Sons, 1972).

Jancis Robinson, *The Oxford Companion to Wine* (Oxford: Oxford University Press, 1994), 725–28.

Albert J. Winkler, *General Viticulture* (Berkeley, Calif.: University of California Press, 1965), 539–46.

PICCHETTI BROTHERS WINERY (BW 148). Vincent Picchetti (1848–1905) arrived in the Santa Clara Valley in 1872 and became foreman of the Santa Clara College vineyard. In 1877 he bought 160 acres on the MONTE BELLO Ridge and planted a large vineyard there. In 1896 he built his winery, which still stands today, inside a regional park, and operated under a lease as SUNRISE WINERY. The Picchetti family ran the old winery, illustrated on pages 221 and 354, until the 1960s and often supplied Zinfandel grapes for RIDGE VINEYARDS. Some of the old vines are still producing.

PIERCE'S DISEASE. In 1884 the vineyards of southern California were struck by a mysterious disease, which, unlike phylloxera, was quick and deadly. By the 1890s about 35,000 acres of vines in the Southland had been destroyed. For a while it was named the Anaheim disease for the area first hit. But in 1935 it was named for Newton B. Pierce, the entomologist who, at the U.S. Department of Agriculture, had first studied the malady. Later there were occasional and severe outbreaks here and there, but none was as devastating as the first onslaught. No one understood the cause of the disease. A virus was the most common guess.

It was not until 1974 that plant pathologists at the University of California at Davis discovered that Pierce's disease was caused by a bacterium (*Xylella fastidiosa*) spread in the vineyard by insect vectors, particularly a leafhopper, the blue-green sharpshooter. The evolutionary home of the bacterium is probably the southeast United States. Thus, the disease is less prevalent in areas with colder winter temperatures. Because the leafhoppers need succulent plant tissue, they thrive in areas with lots of soil moisture and mild winters. Certain varieties of grape, such as Pinot noir, Chardonnay, and Barbera, are particularly susceptible to infection. Chenin blanc, Sylvaner, and White Riesling are fairly tolerant.

In recent years Pierce's disease has cropped up again in many viticultural areas in California. There have been severe outbreaks in the Santa Cruz Mountains and in Dry Creek Valley in Sonoma. But there is no cure and no sure defense beyond measures to combat the leafhoppers that spread the disease. By 1996 research into the disease at the University of California at both Davis and Berkeley had been accelerated with financial support from the wine industry.

Richard Paul Hinkle, "There's Nothing New about Pierce's Disease," *Wines & Vines,* May 1994, 33–35.

PIÑA CELLARS (BW 5105). The Piña family has been farming in the Napa Valley at Rutherford for three generations. Their little vineyard near the Silverado Trail gave them enough grapes to release their first wine from the 1979 vintage. In 1982 they bonded their winery. Now they lease additional acreage and produce about 3,500 cases per year, mostly Chardonnay.

PINE RIDGE WINERY (BW 5012). His passion for skiing took Gary Andrus to places in the world where wine was part of everyday life. By the late 1960s wine became his special passion, acquired late in life because of his Mormon upbringing. In 1967 he was working in the vintage at Bordeaux's Château Lynch-Bages. In 1978 he bought 50 acres in today's Stags Leap Viticultural Area and built his winery in 1980. Since then he has expanded his holdings in the Napa Valley to 200 acres.

From the beginning, Andrus's experiences in France informed his cellar practices at Pine Ridge. He has concentrated on Cabernet

Sauvignon and particularly noticed the source of his grapes on his label. In 1984 other wineries in the area attacked the use of "Stag's Leap" on his labels, but he prevailed in court. Since then Pine Ridge has been expanded to a 400,000-gallon capacity, with consideable quantities of Chardonnay, Chenin blanc, and Merlot as well. Additional investors and the success of his wines have been the chief contributors to the recent growth of production to 80,000 cases a year.

PINNEY, THOMAS. Formerly the chairman of the English Department at Pomona College, Pinney is the author of *A History of Wine in America* (published by the University of California Press in 1989) in which he traces this country's winegrowing efforts from colonial days to Prohibition. The sections on California are required reading for anyone interested in the history of wine in the Golden State. Volume two is in the works.

PINOT BLANC. A variety of wine grape that, in France, is really a white Pinot noir. It was discovered in the nineteenth century as a seedling of the Pinot gris, itself a light-colored mutation of Pinot noir. Grown around the world today, it is particularly popular in Germany, Austria, and Alsace.

Its history in California is confused. Varieties that in the nineteenth century were called Pinot blanc and White Burgundy might also have been Chardonnay or Chenin blanc. Paul MASSON imported the authentic vine in the late 1890s and was aware of the confusion; he always called his vines Pinot blanc vrai (authentic).

After Prohibition professors at the University of California at Davis recommended the variety, emphasizing that they meant the real thing, not Chenin blanc, which was often referred to as Pineau blanc de la Loire. In making this recommendation, they were unaware that much of California's so-called Pinot blanc was probably MELON, the variety popular in France's Muscadet area. Whatever it is that Californians have in their vineyards today, what is being called Pinot blanc has been bottled as a varietal since the 1960s. At times it has been called the "poor man's Chardonnay." It has also been used sparingly for sparkling wine production since the 1950s. In recent years the confusion has been made worse by some producers in California who have released wines labeled Melon. The BATF has even approved a Muscadet label.

Pinot blanc first made it into state statistics in 1969 with 385 acres, rising to 1,295 in 1975. Half of those were in Monterey County. Acreage peaked at 2,359 in 1984, over half in Monterey, and more than half of the rest in Sonoma and Napa counties. In the 1990s acreage has held steady at about 1,100, the same counties in the lead. MIRASSOU, for whom Pinot blanc is the most popular varietal, has about 85 of the acres in Monterey, the cuttings having come in 1946 from Paul Masson. CHALONE also has a few acres of Pinot blanc, wines from these vines have been praised as the best of this varietal in the state, but there is some question about the identity of the variety that is in the vineyard.

What growers reported as Pinot blanc vines produced 4,718 tons in 1996, 67 percent of the tonnage in 1990.

PINOT CHARDONNAY. See CHARDONNAY; VARIETALS

PINOT GRIS. A light-colored Pinot noir grape that makes a fragrant white wine, popular in Alsace (where the grape is known as the Tokay), Italy (as Pinot grigio), and Central Europe. In recent years it has caught on in Oregon. A few acres were planted in California in the early 1980s. By 1995 there were 68 acres, more than half in Santa Barbara and Napa counties. In the United States Pinot grigio is a legal synonym for Pinot gris.

PINOT MEUNIER. See MEUNIER

PINOT NOIR. The variety of wine grape that accounts for all the great red wine of Burgundy and an important component of most sparkling wines made in Champagne. Unlike Cabernet Sauvignon, it did not catch on in California before Prohibition, although it was grown here and its potential was understood. The problem then, and in recent years, was that the potential was so difficult to attain. In early years the excellence was so evanescent that to most premium producers in California true Burgundy was a will-o'-the-wisp, better approached through other, more productive, dependable varieties than through the real thing.

Pinot noir is an old variety. It buds and ripens early and is susceptible to many diseases. It hates a hot and dry climate. It mutates easily and is known for its huge number of clones, which often display remarkable differences in their fruit. Thus, it is not surprising that the vine came to California in the nineteenth century under several names. Most commonly the few producers who tried it seriously called it Black Burgundy. Petite Pinot was another fairly common name. Agoston HARASZTHY brought in "Pinot noir black" in 1862, but nothing came of those vines. It was imported in 1872 and planted in

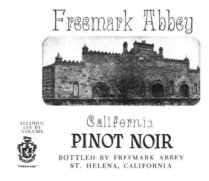

BEAULIEU VINEYARDS was winning gold medals at the State Fair almost every year after World War II for its Pinot noir. But in 1952 FREEMARK ABBEY took the gold for its wine from the 1946 vintage. The year before, when Beaulieu's 1946 had been in the competition, it had won the gold.

TABLE 23. PINOT NOIR GRAPES, SELECTED COUNTIES

YEAR	MENDOCINO	SONOMA	NAPA	MONTEREY	SAN LUIS OBISPO	SANTA BARBARA	TOTAL
				(ACRES)			
1961	9	81	166	0	0	0	556
1968	17	184	506	132	0	0	1,550
1971	116	707	1,025	427	60	0	3,446
1974	300	2,523	2,526	2,590	103	862	10,098
1978	343	3,249	2,487	2,283	96	734	10,311
1980	323	2,839	2,393	1,971	96	724	9,402
1985	327	2,679	2,182	1,296	97	639	7,816
1990	690	3,130	2,719	1,616	180	821	9,549
1997	649	3,075	2,845	1,440	250	1,043	9,597

SOURCE: California Agricultural Statistics Service, Sacramento, Calif.

Santa Clara by J.-B. J. PORTAL and shortly thereafter by J. H. DRUMMOND. In 1882 H. W. CRABB listed it in his vineyard as "Pinot noiren." In 1883, although he praised its quality, Charles WETMORE noted that it was already generally abandoned "on account of its very shy bearing." Nevertheless several North Coast producers persisted through the 1890s usually describing the wine as Chambertin on the labels, as Cabernet Sauvignon producers used Medoc on theirs. Before Prohibition the largest stand was probably in the BEAULIEU vineyards of Georges de Latour.

After Repeal the move toward varietal production saw several North Coast producers selling Pinot noir, but often it was generously blended with other varieties that supplied additional fruitiness and color. Pinot noir became a competition category at the State Fair in 1947. Beaulieu Vineyard and INGLENOOK dominated this competition for the next decade. Consensus among oldtimers gives the 1946 Beaulieu Pinot noir the palm for wines of those years. But the variety did not receive really serious consideration until the late 1960s. Then, and for the next 15 years, numerous producers in California took up the Pinot noir challenge. Gradually a consensus developed about what was essential for maximizing the varietal's potential. Chief among these was climate. Some warmer coastal areas long used for Pinot noir production were gradually eliminated; others became areas of concentration: the Russian River Valley, the Carneros, the Santa Cruz Mountains, and Monterey and Santa Barbara counties.

In the 1970s Pinot noir production became important in California in the production of premium sparkling wine. It also became obvious that there were several clones of the variety in vineyards here and that some were far more successful than others. In fact, what had been called GAMAY Beaujolais for years was found to be a Pinot noir clone. Experiments with clonal selection here and in France had an important effect on plantings after the mid-1970s.

Soil composition also became a matter of interest, particularly soils with high concentrations of limestone, as are found in Burgundy. In the vineyard more emphasis was placed on precise determination of acid levels at harvest, with a trend toward picking the grapes when the levels were higher than previously considered acceptable. To avoid the overcooked flavors imparted by high-temperature fermentations, smaller vessels became the rule. French oak barrels were de rigueur for aging. In 1978 André TCHELISTCHEFF predicted:

"Within ten years, California will be known for its Pinot noir." By 1980 varietal Pinot noir was produced by 116 wineries in California.

The 1980s saw a steady rise in the perceived quality of California's best Pinot noir. By 1995 *Wine Spectator* contended that "the state of Pinot Noir in California has never been better." By that year there were about 9,000 acres in the state, 63 percent of those in Napa and Sonoma counties. Yet the total was well below that of 1978 when the Pinot noir planting binge peaked. The big change had come in the use of the variety for sparkling wine and the concentration of the fewer remaining acres used for still wine in the best locations, the grapes from which went almost solely to producers willing to take the extra steps necessary to bring the variety to its potential. One effect of this new intensity has been high prices. The median price of the *Wine Spectator*'s ten best California Pinot noirs in 1995 was $30.

In 1997 the Pinot noir crush in California amounted to 47,581 tons, 147 percent of the total in 1990.

The top vintages in recent years: 1977, 1979, 1981, 1986, 1990, 1991, 1992, 1994; the great historic vintage was 1946.

Marq de Villiers, *The Heartbreak Grape* (New York: HarperCollins, 1994).

PINOT ST. GEORGE. Another mystery variety of grape, probably the Négrette, a red-wine variety from southwest France. The mystery is how and when it acquired its Californian name. The Nigrette was in the 1882 To Kalon collection. But there is no record of the name transformation. After Prohibition the variety was used by a few wineries to produce what they called Red Pinot. A few wineries in Napa and San Benito counties have produced a varietal Pinot St. George. At its best the variety makes a tasty but not distinguished table wine. In 1988 the variety disappeared from state vineyard statistics, but there are still a few acres in Napa, Sonoma, San Benito and Monterey counties.

The BATF ruled in 1996 that if wines from this grape were to be labeled as a varietal, they would, after 1999, have to be labeled Négrette.

PIPER-SONOMA (BW 5047). After Renfield Imports became a partner with RODNEY STRONG of Sonoma Vineyards in 1975, the partnership arranged with Piper Heidsieck, the French Champagne firm, to produce, as a joint venture, sparkling wine by the *méthode champenoise*. They built a new facility next door to the older Windsor facility of Sonoma Vineyards. They had 22,000 cases of the 1980 Piper-Sonoma on the market in 1982. Sales grew to 90,000 cases in the late 1980s. Meanwhile in 1988 full control of the operation was acquired by the French firm, now part of a larger Rémy-Cointreau group, producers of Rémy Martin cognac. A new management team took control in 1993 to help boost slipping sales. Then in 1996 Rémy-Cointreau sold the production facility to JORDAN VINEYARD, which will now produce the Piper-Sonoma wine. But the Rémy group still owns the brand and will market the wine.

PLACER COUNTY. A large county that stretches from the highlands of the Sierra Nevada west into the Sacramento Valley. Its foothill areas between Colfax and Roseville were once an important source of wine grapes. Today there are but 91 acres of vines in the area.

From the 1870s until Prohibition, the Placer County Winery in Roseville bought most of the region's grapes. It had a capacity of 600,000 gallons with annual production of about 300,000 gallons. In 1916 it became a part of the CALIFORNIA WINE ASSOCIATION. The county had about 1,000 acres of vines in 1915, and this number grew to 2,400 by 1930. Between 1933 and 1937 fourteen new little wineries sprang up, primarily around Colfax, but none lasted. Today there is one, in Truckee, in the mountains where viticulture is not possible.

PLAM VINEYARDS AND WINERY (BW 5077). The Plam family acquired a 22-acre vineyard south of Yountville in Napa in the early 1980s and built the winery in 1984. A Chardonnay in that year was followed by Sauvignon blanc, Cabernet Sauvignon, and Merlot. Annual production now stands at about 2,000 cases.

PLAVAC MALI. See ZINFANDEL

PLEASANTON. A town on the western margin of the Livermore Valley and an important part of Bay Area suburban development since the 1960s. Eighty years earlier it was the center of the original development of commercial viticulture in the valley. Several important wineries operated there before Prohibition, RUBY HILL being the most important.

PLUMP JACK WINERY. See VILLA MT. EDEN

PLYMOUTH. A village in Amador County that has been the "urban" center of the Shenandoah Valley wine industry for many years.

POHNDORFF, FREDERICO (1832–1917). It was important to the California wine industry after 1880 to have European wine experts who would endorse the state's better wines. Pohndorff's articles and evaluations in trade journals are today among the best sources available on the quality of individual producers. He returned to Spain temporarily in 1889 and ended his years a wine merchant in Washington, D.C.

POPE VALLEY. A large valley in the Napa highlands east of the main valley has become an important source of grapes in recent years. In the 1880s there were about 200 acres of vines there but no important winery. In 1909 the Sam Haus Winery (BW 950) was built and operated until 1959. In 1972 the Devitt family revived the old facility as the Pope Valley Winery (BW 4586), but it closed in 1983.

After Pope Valley was officially included in the Napa Valley Viticulture Area in 1981, wineries in Napa expanded their acreage there. Chief among the new growers and investors in the valley has been Buttes Resources Co. from Houston, which has about 850 acres in vines.

PORT. The fortified wines made in the Douro Valley in Portugal, mostly red, get their name from the city of Oporto, from which British wine merchants have been shipping port since the 1680s. In the early days, wineries in California tried to produce something like port, but the results were inferior, primarily because the grapes were of the wrong varieties.

In the 1870s it became obvious that one of Zinfandel's many uses was in sweet wine. But no matter how good the product, it had little resemblance to the real thing. An English connoisseur, Charles OLDHAM, stated that California's best ports were really sweet CLARETS. Even when George WEST and the NATOMA VINEYARDS CO. imported real Portuguese grape varieties in the 1880s, no one made favorable comparisons between the California product and real port.

In the years before Prohibition, wineries in California produced about 5 million gallons of port per year, much of it sold in bars and saloons. It was California's best-selling sweet wine. After Repeal FORTIFIED sweet wines led California wine production with port the chief product until the 1950s when sherry took over. Zinfandel grown in the Central Valley was the chief component. The blends included Carignane and Mataro (Mourvèdre), with Alicante Bouschet for color. White port, in California an almost meaningless term, was also produced. It was usually no different from ANGELICA.

After World War II fortified wine consumption plummeted in the United States and the category now accounts for about 3 percent of California's total wine production. Nevertheless there was a concerted effort by several producers to make California port of world-class quality; see FICKLIN VINEYARDS. Several Portuguese varieties of grapes were planted, but only Tinta Madeira, of which there were 1,340 acres in 1977, and Souzão (326 acres) in significant amounts. By the 1990s these varieties had disappeared from state acreage statistics. Nevertheless, in 1983 several premium producers organized the California Port Guild, and there are still several real port varieties growing in the Sierra foothills and the San Joaquin Valley. Zinfandel is still an important ingredient in a few of California's best port-style wines.

PORTAL, JEAN-BAPTISTE JULES (1838–?). A leader of the early wine industry in the Santa Clara Valley, Portal began winegrowing west of San Jose in 1872, the year in which he first imported French vines of the highest quality. He called his operation Burgundy Vineyard, reflecting his passion for producing red wines in a Burgundian style. His success was considerable, with blends of Pinot noir, Poulsard, and Malbec. In 1894 he disappeared with his beautiful blond cousin, probably returning to France. His wife, Mathilde Portal, ran the winery for many years. Her stately Victorian mansion was a landmark in Cupertino until the 1960s.

POTTER VALLEY. A viticultural area in Mendocino County, the most northerly in the North Coast Viticultural Area. It received AVA status in 1983. Sparkling wine producers have found the Pinot noir and Chardonnay grapes grown in the cool climate attractive, but many other varieties thrive there, total acreage having passed 1,000 acres in the 1990s.

POWDERY MILDEW. See MILDEW

PRACTICAL WINERY & VINEYARD, first published in 1980 in northern California, a periodical that has been the leading medium carrying the practical discussion of winery and vineyard technique to members of the California wine industry; see also RESEARCH.

BERNARD PRADEL CELLARS (BW 5264). A winery in Napa Valley bonded in 1984 and concentrating its 2,000-case annual production on Cabernet Sauvignon.

PRAGER WINERY & PORT WORKS (BW 4944). James Prager and his family came to the Napa Valley in 1977 and set up their little winery south of St. Helena two years later. Since then Prager has produced mostly varietal port released under such proprietary labels as Noble Companion and Royal Escort. Cabernet Sauvignon and Petite Sirah are the most common varietals used. In 1992 the tiny home vineyard was grafted over to five authentic Portuguese varieties from Oporto. In 1993 Prager brought out a white port from Chardonnay. About 20 percent of the annual 3,600-case production is made up of varietal table wines.

PREMIUM WINE. A premium is a prize wine in competition. Before Prohibition, the term was used for wines that had won awards in county, state, or international wine competitions. Gradually the term came to mean wines, usually varietals, of a certain price sold in cork-finished bottles.

Since the 1960s, the term has also become an industry expression that reflects only retail price, not any particular standard of quality. By the mid-1990s the industry classified wines as "premium" if their retail price was at least $7.00. If more than $11.00, they were super-premium; if more than $16.00, they were ultra premium. Using this set of definitions, corrected for price inflation, industry analysts have determined that premium wine consumption in the United States rose an average of 17 percent per year from 1980 to 1992. During this period, per-capita wine consumption in the United States dropped by an average of about 3 percent per year.

PRESSING. When grapes are put through a mechanical crusher, much of the juice is lost if they are not pressed. The wine press, in many forms, has been a part of California winemaking since mission days. At first a large cowhide was filled and secured, the top closed, and the contents squeezed by twisting one or more poles attached to the closed end. By the 1850s the traditional European basket press had been introduced, the pressure first applied by human and other animal muscle. Later steam, gas, and electric engines supplied the power. Hydraulic pressing was also occasionally employed.

In recent years a more gentle approach has been called for, to lower the level of harsh tannins released by crushed seeds and stems. European-designed bladder presses began to appear at premium wineries in the 1960s. In these machines an inflatable bladder presses the grapes against an outer drum. Technical improvements over the years made it possible to program pressure and timing in order to fine-tune the result for a given variety of grape or desired style of wine. In recent years so-called tank presses have been developed, in which a membrane replaces the bladder. This machine can apply steadily controlled pressure and apparently is more efficient and cost-effective than are bladder presses. Tank presses can be adjusted to variously sized loads and are more portable than earlier models of press.

Traditionally, grapes for red wines are pressed at or toward the end of fermentation.

There was not much romance in the pressing operations at small California wineries before Prohibition.

Grapes for white wines have normally been pressed before fermentation to hold down the extraction of unwanted PHENOLICS. Pink, ROSÉ, and BLUSH wines require a very early pressing for the best taste and color. For producers of first-rate sparkling wines, pressing is a complicated and precise science, particularly if the percentage of Pinot noir grapes is to be high in the resulting wine. Many California producers of *méthode champenoise* wines do not crush their grapes but press the whole clusters and segregate parts of the press according to their phenolic content, therby controlling the bitterness that can ruin otherwise fine sparkling wine.

PRESTON VINEYARDS (BW 4716). In 1975 Louis Preston converted an old dehydrator in the Dry Creek Valley in Sonoma into a little winery. Twenty years later he had 125 acres of vines planted to sixteen different varieties, and an annual production of about 20,000 cases. The new winery went up in 1982. Preston's best wines are Zinfandel and Sauvignon blanc. But he also has a strong interest in Rhône varieties and Petite Sirah. For a while in the 1980s he made a blend he called Syrah-Sirah. He also makes Marsanne and Viognier white varietals, added in 1990. The Preston estate is farmed organically and contains a fine olive orchard.

PRIDE MOUNTAIN VINEYARDS (BW pending). The Pride family bought the old Summit Ranch, which straddles the county line between Napa and Sonoma, atop Spring Mountain in 1989 and now have 70 acres of vines, mostly Cabernet Sauvignon and Merlot. At first they had their wines made at CHAPPELLET, with production in 1995 at about 5,000 cases and growing. Because the vineyard crosses over into Sonoma County, the new winery has run into bonding problems. The 170-acre ranch was once the site of the pre-Prohibition Summit Winery (BW 959), built in 1890, the remains of which survive, just on the Sonoma side.

PRIMITIVO. See HOP KILN WINERY; ZINFANDEL

PROHIBITION. When capitalized as Prohibition, a reference to the period in American history from 16 January 1920 to 5 December 1933; as prohibition, without the capital, a reference to public policy that prohibits the manufacture and sale, but not necessarily the consumption, of alcoholic beverages.

Any state in the United States may enact its own prohibition, and many did before 1920. California did not. Nevertheless in 1912 a local-option law did go on the books, making it possible for communities to establish their own level of prohibition, if they chose. Over the next few years, several wine-producing districts in California went dry, most in southern California.

National Prohibition is what hurt the wine industry in California. It was a patriotic campaign during World War I that tipped the scales. The Eighteenth Amendment was submitted to the states in December 1917 and was adopted in January 1919. By that date the California wine industry had all but closed shop. But the government in what was called the fresh grape deal allowed the sale of wine grapes to the heads of households, who might produce a fruit juice; there was no explicit prohibition against converting that juice into wine. Congress also allowed the production of sacramental and medicinal wines. Thus some wineries in California, and all of the vineyards, were able to stay in business.

Grape prices soared in California as thousands of carloads of wine grapes headed east each year at vintage time. Vineyard acreage in California increased to levels not attained again until the 1970s.

Red wine grapes were almost all that the market was interested in. A large percentage of those were converted into red table wine, mostly by immigrant families, from San Diego to Boston. The most sought-after shipping grapes were Alicante Bouschet, Zinfandel, Petite Sirah, Carignane, and Mataro (Mourvèdre). Most of the fine red wine varieties disappeared from California vineyards, but there had only been a few hundred acres anyway. The chief casualties were the first-class whitewine varieties, which almost disappeared from vineyards in California during the 1920s.

Wine-grape CONCENTRATE was another, but less important, product during the dry years. Prohibitionist leaders were infuriated by labels on the cans warning the consumer in precise detail what *not* to do to produce a potentially illegal alcoholic beverage.

California itself was an important part of the so-called fresh grape deal. The San Francisco Bay Area alone used at least 2,000 carloads of grapes for home winemaking each year during Prohibition. Here there was even a small market for fine white varieties.

Most California wineries closed their doors during the dry years, but a few continued to operate, producing sacramental wines. Chief among those were BEAULIEU VINEYARD, BERINGER, and WENTE.

In 1932 it was clear that national Prohibition was doomed and wineries up and down the state renewed their bonds and began to make wine again. Franklin Roosevelt's election in November sealed the verdict. The following April the new Congress legalized beer and wine, limiting both to 3.2 percent alcohol. When Repeal came at the end of the next vintage, there was plenty of wine ready for shipping, although much of it was of very poor quality.

The Twenty-First Amendment, which voided the Eighteenth, contained language that allowed states to continue prohibition on their own, and many did. It also was interpreted by the Supreme Court to give states the right to supersede federal rules about the regulation and transportation of alcoholic beverages. The state regulations that are derived from the Twenty-First Amendment are remarkable exceptions to the traditional regulation of interstate commerce by the U.S. Congress. Such individual state controls are considered a severe burden today by the California wine industry.

Bruno Buti, *Rumbling Wine Barrels* (Cloverdale, Calif.: Buti Publications, 1994).

J. Meers, "The California Wine and Grape Industry and Prohibition," *California Historical Society Quarterly* 42, no 1 (March, 1967) 19–32.

Gilman M. Ostrander, *The Prohibition Movement in California, 1848–1933* (Berkeley: University of California Press, 1957).

PROPAGATION. Grape vines can be propagated from seeds but that is not practical, except for breeding new varieties. New vines from seeds may differ markedly from the parent vine and are usually inferior to it in vigor. Since the earliest days of Californian viticulture, propagation has been from cuttings, an asexual approach that guarantees that the offspring will be biologically identical to the parent vine. Until the 1890s LAYERING,* another asexual method, was commonly used.

Usually cuttings are made from segments of the cane and placed in a nursery, to be transferred to the vineyard in the second year. For both new or replacement plantings, many early growers used to establish their vines in the vineyard. But the success rate was low. When cuttings were plentiful, however, a good system was to plant two cuttings in each location and to remove the least likely candidate in the second year.

Since the coming of phylloxera most vinifera vines have been grafted onto resistant ROOTSTOCK. Bench grafting was usually done indoors during the dormant season and the resulting vine grown for a year in the nursery before it was placed in the vineyard. Far less expensive is today's more popular field bud-ding, a practice in which the desired vinifera fruiting variety is grafted onto the resistant rootstock the year after the stock is established in the vineyard.

PRUNING. A wild grape vine is a high-climb-ing plant that will range over a large area and bear a few small clusters of poorly flavored grapes each year. But men and women have learned since ancient times to shape the vine, by training and pruning it into a manageable form and make it yield a good and useful crop. It took many years for vineyardists in California to learn to prune their vines to get good yields and good quality. By the 1880s sound practices were well understood but not always followed.

Until the 1870s virtually all vines in Califor-nia were head-pruned (see TRAINING) to short spurs. By the 1880s cane-pruning for certain varieties became common. Because the number of buds left on a vine helps determine the potential size of the crop, the pruner must be knowledgeable and disciplined. If too many buds are left, a huge crop may result, but the grapes may never ripen properly. This approach is called overcropping. In the early days when-ever grape prices were high, Californian vine-yardists regularly overcropped their vines, and often paid dearly if cool September weather set in or early fall rains came down.

Since World War II, the pruning of Cali-fornia's grape vines has become a compli-cated and exacting science. In recent years closer spacing of vines in many of California's coastal vineyards has meant that fewer buds per vine are retained. There have also been experiments with mechanical pruning and minimal pruning.

The expression summer pruning is often heard today in California. Actually, this is more a process of trimming the vines of unwanted foliage, often termed leaf removal, to allow more air and light into the plants. It is also possible to raise fruit quality, particularly flavor, by trimming back rank shoots and canes well before harvest. Undesirable herbaceous overtones in wines, particularly in Cabernet Sauvignon and Sauvignon blanc, are subdued by such pruning.

Pruning takes place when the vines are dormant between December and March. There is no vineyard activity that requires greater skill. Errors in pruning can ruin the coming crop. (Richards Lyon-*Vine to Wine*)

QUADY WINERY (BW 4684). Andrew Quady's winery in Madera specializes in sweet wine, especially from muscat varieties. He began with a tiny facility in 1977 and built his present winery in 1985. His first wines were ports from Zinfandel grown in the Shenandoah Valley in Amador County. The muscats began in 1981 when he released his Orange Muscat Essensia, slightly fortified at about 15 percent alcohol. Two years later came his Black Muscat Elysium. Quady now has several ports. He still uses Zinfandel and has added another made from traditional Portuguese varieties. Quady labels this wine Starboard and hopes to turn the heads of Oporto aficionados. Total annual production is approaching 15,000 cases.

QUAIL RIDGE CELLARS (BW 4782). In 1978 the husband-and-wife team of Jesse Corallo and Elaine Wellesley acquired Napa's historic Hedgeside Winery (see Morris M. ESTEE) and began making wine. Wellesley went back to college and got a degree in fermentation science at the University of California at Davis. After Corallo died in 1981, Leon Santoro, a research chemist, became a partner. They produced several varietal wines, with emphasis on Chardonnay. In 1988 they sold the winery to the CHRISTIAN BROTHERS. The next year HEUBLEIN took over Christian Brothers and Quail Ridge

became a brand. In 1995 Heublein sold the brand to a group of investors who had also acquired the DOMAINE NAPA WINERY and now the Quail Ridge label is associated with that property. There production is about 35,000 cases annually with emphasis on Chardonnay, Merlot, and Cabernet Sauvignon.

The old Hedgeside Winery and distillery, now housing several small businesses, still stands on lower Atlas Peak Road.

QUIVIRA VINEYARDS (BW 5377). This winery's name is derived from a mythical settlement sought by Coronado during his sixteenth-century quest for wealth in the American Southwest. The winery in Sonoma, in Dry Creek Valley, dates from the purchase in 1981 of an old vineyard by the Wendt family. The winery was on line for the 1987 vintage; its 76-acre estate vineyard emphasizes Zinfandel and Sauvignon blanc. In 1995 the Wendts introduced their Atlantis line of moderately priced table wines. Total annual production was about 20,000 cases in the mid-1990s.

QUPÉ (BW 5107). A wine brand developed in 1982 by Robert Lindquist, who has been closely associated with the wines of AU BON CLIMAT and VITA NOVA in Santa Barbara County. (*Qupé* is a Chumash Indian word for poppy.) The operation specializes in wines from Rhône varieties. Lindquist's Syrah has a good reputation for its aging ability. Mourvèdre (Mataro), Marsanne, and Viognier also are used, as is Chardonnay. Qupé is produced under the Au Bon Climat bond in the Santa Maria Valley, about 13,000 cases a year.

RABBIT RIDGE VINEYARDS (BW 5246). Eric Russell, formerly a distance runner, was nicknamed The Rabbit in his school days, so when he and a partner, Daryl Simmons, bonded their Russian River winery in 1985, they had an idea for a name. They had acquired their vineyard land in 1979 and today have 35 acres under vines. With additional grapes bought from growers in Dry Creek Valley and the Carneros, they produce a wide range of varietals and proprietary blends— about 70,000 cases per year. Some of their wines also appear under the Meadow Glen and Clairvaux labels.

RACKING. Young wines, red and white, usually drop sediments to the bottom of their storage containers. Racking is the process by which the wine is pumped or siphoned off the sediment into a clean container. This is an essential activity in wineries that barrel-age their wines. Although racking from barrel to barrel is time consuming and expensive, it is important for clarifying the wine and useful in limiting the formation of smelly hydrogen sulfide in young wines.

RADANOVICH VINEYARDS (BW 5337). In the person of George Radanovich, California has a congressman who is also a winemaker, the first since Theodore BELL of Napa was elected in 1902. His family's winery in Mariposa county in the Sierra Foothills Viticultural Area, was bonded in 1986 and produces about 3,000 cases of wine a year, mostly Zinfandel and Sauvignon blanc, from the 8-acre vineyard.

A. RAFANELLI WINERY (BW 4679). Americo Rafanelli (1919–87) was first a grape grower in the Dry Creek Valley, Sonoma, but in 1972 he began making commercial wine from his old stand of Zinfandel vines. Since then the family has produced a series of intensely flavored, age-worthy Zinfandels of the sort that

Racking is usually performed today using electrically powered pumps. In former times gravity siphons and hand pumps were the normal means of transferring young wines from their lees to a clean container. (Richards Lyon-*Vine to Wine*)

has given Dry Creek its glowing reputation for such wines. There is also some Cabernet Sauvignon on the 50-acre estate vineyard. Total annual production is about 8,000 cases.

RAINFALL. One of the basic components of CLIMATE. In California rainfall tends to decrease from north to south and from west to east. Higher elevation usually means higher rainfall. Thus, the Sierra foothills receive more rain than the Central Valley does, Stockton more than Fresno, Sonoma more than Santa Barbara. Most of the vineyards on the North Coast and in the Santa Cruz Mountains get enough rain for full crops; the northern Central Coast is marginal; irrigation is necessary in the southern Central Coast, southern California, and the Central Valley. Rainfall in the Sierra foothills depends on north-south orientation and elevation.

Almost 90 percent of California's rain falls between November and April, but late spring showers (as occurred in 1995) can cut production if they come when the vines are flowering. Such late spring rains have been at least partly responsible for the below-average crops in many northern Californian vineyards in the 1990s. Early fall rains can lower the quality of the fruit and in some instances may destroy large portions of the crop as they did in 1982 and 1989.

RAISIN GRAPES. Wine can be made from grapes normally used for raisin production. Since Repeal much of the California vintage has consisted of raisin grapes, particularly Thompson Seedless and Muscat of Alexandria, grown in the Central Valley. Most of those grapes have been used for inexpensive table and fortified wines and brandy. Some part of the improvement in the quality of California's ordinary wines during the past 25 years can be attributed to the declining percentage of raisin grapes in the annual crush. Between 1955 and 1970 raisin varieties made up almost half of the state crush each year. This figure fell to about 25 percent between 1971 and 1985. Since then the total has averaged 14.7 percent, but in 1996 a grape shortage pushed the total to 21 percent.

Since 1955 Thompson Seedless grapes have made up between 85 and 90 percent of the raisin-grape crush.

RANCHO CALIFORNIA. See TEMECULA

RANCHO DE PHILO. See PHILO B. BIANE

RANCHO SISQUOC (BW 4778). James Clair Flood (1826–89) made a great fortune in mining investment during the Gold Rush. In 1952 his grandson, also James C., bought a gigantic cattle ranch covering almost 60 square miles in the Santa Maria Valley in Santa Barbara County. Today it has 211 acres of wine grapes, sold mostly to other producers. But enough is kept to produce about 7,000 cases of wine per year under the Rancho Sisquoc label. The first 40 acres of vines went in the ground in 1970. In 1977 Flood bonded a small winery. In 1995 a new winery building went up. There is a wide range of varietals, including a SYLVANER, sold under its historic nickname, Franken Riesling.

RANKIN, WILLIAM BLACKSTONE (1847–1907). One of the most powerful men in the California wine industry at the turn of the century, he was in charge of the CALIFORNIA WINE ASSOCIATION's wineries in Gilroy, San Jose, Los Gatos, and Cupertino. Before this he had built the Los Gatos Cooperative Winery into a 500,000-gallon giant. His first experience in winegrowing was in the 1870s at his Lexington Ranch in the Los Gatos hills where he made his famous Glenwood Zinfandel.

KENT RASMUSSEN WINERY (BW 5336). Celia Ramsey and Kent Rasmussen are a husband-and-wife team in the Carneros in Napa County. Their little winery was bonded in 1986.

Their Rasmussen label goes on bottles of Pinot noir, Chardonnay, and Sauvignon blanc. The Ramsey label covers more exotic wines, such as Dolcetto, Nebbiolo, Sangiovese, and Syrah. There was even a 1991 Alicante Bouschet. In 1995 Rasmussen acquired NAPA CREEK WINERY as second production facility. Annual production has been about 10,000 cases.

RAVENSWOOD (BW 4991, 5083). Joel Peterson made the first batch of Ravenswood Zinfandel at Joseph SWAN's winery in 1976. A briary, intense wine, it set the stage for a series of Zinfandels and Cabernet Sauvignons that has lived up to the winery's motto—see the poster reproduced on page 336—"No Wimpy Wines!" (*Nullum Vinum Flaccidum* for those with a leaning toward the antique).

The Ravenswood crush grew from the original 327 cases and moved from winery to winery until 1981, when it settled in a warehouse south of the town of Sonoma. Peterson now

had a partner, W. Reed Foster, one of the founders of the San Francisco Vintners Club. As the years went by, the winery developed a good reputation for its powerful, often vineyard-designated wines. In 1991 operations were moved across town to the HAYWOOD WINERY after that brand was sold to BUENA VISTA. This beautiful setting was a better complement for the wine's popular image. Total annual production has exceeded 100,000 cases, about 25 percent of which is the lighter-bodied and competitively priced Vintners Blend Zinfandel.

For the historic Ravenswood Winery in Livermore, see CHRISTOPHER BUCKLEY.

RAY, MARTIN (1905–76). Probably the most controversial character in the twentieth-century history of California wine, Martin Ray grew up in Saratoga and as a boy was entranced by the Paul MASSON château-winery in the hills above town. In his teens he visited the old

The crew at Ravenswood celebrates the end of the vintage. In the center barrel is the winemaster, Joel Peterson. This photograph illustrates the often light-hearted approach that many winegrowers in Sonoma bring to the marketing of their wines. (Ravenswood)

Martin Ray with hydrometer measures the declining sugar in his fermenting Pinot noir ca. 1959. The cellar setup typifies that of many premium-minded, enthusiastic wine entrepreneurs in northern California after World War II. (Ray Family Collection, Saratoga, Calif.)

Frenchman and helped out at vintage time and in the cellar.

In the 1920s Ray made good money selling stocks and bonds and survived the crash in 1929. In 1936 he was able to purchase Masson's La Cresta estate from the aging vintner for $50,000. He moved all the production facilities onto the hill from San Jose and settled down to produce what he hoped would be world-class still and sparkling wines. Within four years he had built production to about 5,000 cases a year, marketed under the Paul Masson brand, with his name, Martin Ray, proprietor, on the label. This came to an end on 7 July 1941 when a terrible fire all but destroyed the winery. Ray worked to restore the historic facility and in 1943 sold it to representatives of Joseph SEAGRAM & Sons.

With the money he followed Masson's earlier advice and established his own wine domain on Table Mountain in the hills to the north of La Cresta. He planted Chardonnay, Cabernet Sauvignon, and Pinot noir on his new land and built a fine little winery there. By the 1950s he had established a reputation for excellent wines sold at astronomical prices. He also acquired a highly unflattering personal image in the California wine industry. He lashed out at the industry's leaders for con-

doning the practice of labelling wine as varietal when there need be no more than 51 percent of the named variety in the bottle; he called for strict appellations of origin; he insisted that fine wines were the result of impeccable viticulture and traditional Old-World cellar methods, nothing more or less. But he refused to recognize his own occasionally failed wines. Giving and asking no quarter, he developed a dedicated following and a coterie of industry and academic leaders who despised him.

In the early 1960s a group of investors made it possible for him to expand the vineyards on Table Mountain. But his relations with this group entailed a decade of conflict that ended in an ugly court battle. When he died in 1976, his family had but 5 acres left. The winery and other vineyards were now part of the MOUNT EDEN VINEYARDS.

For several years the Martin Ray label was kept alive by his widow, Eleanor, and his adopted stepson, Peter Martin Ray. Then it was acquired by another partnership and in 1992, by the Cadera Wine Co. a North Coast NÉGOCIANT, which began marketing Martin Ray wines produced in Mendocino and Santa Clara counties. These wines have received high marks from wine writers.

In 1993 Eleanor Ray brought out a loving biography of Martin, *Vineyards in the Sky.* Although it is a very uncritical evaluation of his life, it contains loads of useful and interesting information on this remarkable man, who, had he lived to the end of the 1980s, would have seen almost everything that he fought for concerning wine quality come to pass in the California wine industry.

Eleanor Ray, *Vineyards in the Sky* (Stockton, Calif.: Heritage West, 1993).

RAYMOND VINEYARD & CELLAR (BW 4672). Without doubt the Raymond and Beringer family has the longest tenure of any family of winegrowers in Napa Valley, dating from 1876. Roy Raymond went to work for Beringer in 1933; later he married Jacob Beringer's granddaughter. When he retired in 1970, he and his family bought 90 acres south of St. Helena in the Napa Valley and in 1974 established a new winery. By 1981 annual production of a wide range of varietals had reached 35,000 cases. In 1989 a controlling interest in the operation was sold to Kirin Brewery in Japan. Since then Roy's sons, Roy Jr. and Walter, have continued to run the winery and have expanded its vineyards to 450 acres, some of them in Monterey County. Production, which emphasizes Chardonnay, is almost 200,000 cases a year. A second label is Amberhill.

RED MOUNTAIN. In 1854 George H. Krause (1825–68) planted a small vineyard in the Sierra foothills at Knight's Ferry in Stanislaus County. In 1862 he began digging tunnels to store his wine. Four years later Abraham Schell (1817–92) bought into the growing operation. Production was soon 35,000 gallons a year from the 70-acre vineyard. This Red Mountain Winery eventually became famous for its sweet wines and brandy, marketed under the Glen Clara label. Herrick R. Schell operated the winery after his uncle's death. It closed in 1920 but reopened from 1933 to 1937 as the Oakdale Winery (BW 3676).

Years later E. & J. GALLO took the Red Mountain name for one of its jug wines.

RED PINOT. See PINOT ST. GEORGE

RED TRAMINER. See GEWÜRZTRAMINER

REDWOOD VALLEY. North of Ukiah in Mendocino County, an area of fine alluvial soils flanking the Russian River. It is the home of seven wineries including the original Fetzer winery. The area, with about 2,300 acres of vines, is noted for its red table wines. In 1997 it became Mendocino's fifth AVA.

REDWOOD VALLEY CELLARS (BW 4593). In 1995 the owners of BRAREN PAULI WINERY bought the WEIBEL winery north of Ukiah. They renamed it and are offering custom-crush services to growers in the area. They also acquired 22 acres of vineyard near the winery.

REFOSCO. In California a variety of grape that is also called Mondeuse. The Refosco is a red grape from the Friuli area in Italy with a fine reputation there for rich and tasty table wines. Italians usually do not admit this variety to be the same as the French Mondeuse, which is responsible for the distinctive and spicy red wines of the Savoie. Before Prohibition in California, the Refosco or Mondeuse was also sometimes called Crabb's Black Burgundy, but vintners here, including H. W. CRABB himself, knew its real identity. After Prohibition the grape was popular in Napa, where for years it was the basis for BEAULIEU VINEYARD's Burgundy. In 1971 there were 396 acres in the state, 88 percent of them in Napa. In 1985 the variety disappeared from state statistics, even though it is produced as a varietal by WEIBEL VINEYARDS and LOCKWOOD VINEYARDS.

REFRIGERATION. Before Prohibition the wineries in California that were built into hillsides and the numerous underground aging tunnels in the state attest to the problem of the warm summer and fall of the local climate and the need of winemakers to keep their premises cool if they wished to make good wines. By the end of the century, mechanical cooling devices had been invented to reduce fermentation temperatures. In recent years stainless steel tanks with refrigerated jacketing have become essential winemaking tools in all but the smallest California wineries.

REGE WINERY (BW 4368). Bonded in 1939 south of Cloverdale in Sonoma County, this winery was for many years the source of a Sonoma red jug wine particularly popular in restaurants in North Beach, San Francisco. In the 1980s the premises were operated as Le Bay Cellars; in recent years as Diamond Oaks Vineyard (BWC 5045).

REGINA GRAPE PRODUCTS (BW 759). After Prohibition John B. Ellena (1903–71) revived an old winery in the Etiwanda area of San Bernardino County that had been built in 1901. By the 1940s it was one of the largest in southern California. He changed the name from Ellena Brothers to Regina in 1948. The 2 million-gallon operation controlled about 700 acres of grapes in Cucamonga and produced inexpensive table, sweet, and sparkling wines. Ellena sold the place to HEUBLEIN in 1970. It was later converted into a vinegar plant and the FILIPPI family in 1993 bought it as a production facility.

RENAISSANCE VINEYARD (BW 4869). The Fellowship of Friends is an international religious and philosophical group that emphasizes the arts. Its northern Californian organization was founded in 1970 and began acquiring land in Yuba County in the foothills east of Marysville. Today the 1,400-acre estate is the site of 365 acres of terraced vineyards and a modern winery that produces about 30,000 cases per year.

The driving force behind the move to winegrowing here was Karl Werner (1923–88), who came to Renaissance in 1973. Before that he had a long history in the German wine and food industry. (André Simon was his godfather.) Werner came to California in 1969 and consulted for several important wineries. In his fifteen years at Renaissance, he helped create one of the most impressive winegrowing estates in the world. The Fellowship has developed a sizeable community on the land, with its own school, stores, and dining hall. The winery is a huge octagonal structure, 60 percent of it underground. The terraced vineyards lie between the 1,700- and 2,300-foot elevations. Even so, the weather is quite warm, making necessary a huge drip-irrigation system measuring about 200 miles.

The leading grape varieties are Cabernet Sauvignon, Sauvignon blanc, and White Riesling. Late-harvest dessert wines have been particularly successful since the first releases appeared in 1989. The NORTH YUBA Viticultural Area was granted appellation status in 1985 on a petition by Renaissance.

RENNIE BROTHERS. See FLORA SPRINGS

RENWOOD WINERY (BW 4836). Santino Winery in the Shenandoah Valley in Amador County was founded in 1979. In 1990 the name was changed to Renwood, but wines are still made under the Santino label. The winery is famous for its hearty Zinfandels, the most famous from the nearby Grandpère Vineyard, perhaps first planted in the 1860s. There is also Barbera, a blend of Rhône varieties labeled Satyricon, and several dessert wines. Total annual production exceeds 40,000 cases.

REPEAL. The Twenty-First Amendment to the U.S. Constitution was passed on 5 December 1933, repealing the Eighteenth Amendment, which had prohibited the manufacture, sale, or transportation of intoxicating beverages in the United States. In April of that year Congress had declared that 3.2-percent beer and wine were "non-intoxicating" and therefore legal but few California producers took advantage of this law. The actual Repeal of national PROHIBITION* brought the California wine industry back to life, but much of the wine hurriedly shipped in 1934 was of poor quality. During the rest of the 1930s, often referred to as the Repeal Years by vintners in California, the country was in a serious economic depression. Fortified wines, usually sweet, dominated production. But some few producers, particularly in the northern coastal counties, worked to reestablish a tradition of fine table wine production.

REPSOLD, AMANDUS (1861–1912). One of the leading independent wine merchants in San Francisco before Prohibition. His firm, A. Repsold & Co., developed extensive holdings in the Napa Valley after its cellars were destroyed in the earthquake and fire in 1906.

REPUBLIC WINE CO. See GREENSTONE WINERY

RESEARCH. Many of the men and women who manage California's wineries and vineyards today were educated at one or other of the state's two academic wine and grape research institutions—the University of California at Davis and Fresno State University. The faculties of the enology and viticulture departments at those two schools, along with their graduate students who usually end up in the cellar and/or vineyard, spend a good deal of their time in research that improves the quality of California wine. Part of the research is also aimed at technical advances that improve industry profits. It would be a mistake, however, to credit academia for too great a contribution to the practical research that has been improving California wine. A sizeable part of this work has been done in the field by dedicated experimenters; see PRACTICAL WINERY & VINEYARD.

In the 1870s the University of California (see E. W. HILGARD) led the way in useful research for the state's wine industry. A steady stream of practical bulletins and circulars poured from the University's Agricultural Experiment Station in Berkeley. The University's extension program sent faculty members into the field where they worked with winegrowers collecting data and spreading word of their findings. This kind of practical relationship continues to this day, best exemplified by the University's experimental vineyards in Oakville in the Napa Valley and the Kearney Field Station near Fresno.

Maynard Amerine, *The University of California and the State's Wine Industry* (Regional Oral History Office, Bancroft Library, 1971).

Maynard Amerine, *Wine Bibliographies and Taste Perception Studies* (Regional Oral History Office, Bancroft Library, 1988).

Zelma Long, "Enological and Technological Developments," in *The University of California/Sotheby Book of California Wine,* ed. Doris Muscatine, Maynard A. Amerine, and Bob Thompson (Berkeley, Calif.: University of California Press/Sotheby Publications, 1984), 176–94.

Cornelius S. Ough, *Researches of an Enologist, University of California, Davis, 1950–1990* (Regional Oral History Office, Bancroft Library, 1990).

Albert J. Winkler, *Viticultural Research at UC Davis, 1921–1971* (Regional Oral History Office, Bancroft Library, 1973).

RESERVE. A term that often appears on the labels of higher-priced California wines. Its use is not controlled by governmental regulations. Usually, it is the producer's way of indicating to the consumer that the wine in that bottle is of higher quality. The grapes may come from special areas in a vineyard; only new barrels may have been used; a lower crop level may have been maintained for selected vines. Then again, the term may mean nothing more than that the producer has decided to charge more for the wine in that bottle than for the winery's regular production.

RESISTANT ROOTSTOCK. See ROOT-STOCK

RETSINA. A style of white or ROSÉ wine popular in Greece and Cyprus. The special flavor derives from pieces of pine resin placed in the fermenting MUST. A few resinated wines have been made in California. In Los Angeles the Retsina Wine Co. operated before Prohibition. In the years since World War II, retsina has been made by Alex's Winery (BW 4196) near Lodi and by Nicholas Verry (BW 4341) near Fresno.

RETZLAFF VINEYARDS (BW 5245). Robert and Gloria Taylor started planting their 14-acre vineyard in Livermore in 1979. Because the use of their last name on a wine label might have attracted some legal attention, they used Gloria's maiden name when bonding their little winery in 1986. Their 3,000-case annual production emphasizes Cabernet Sauvignon, Chardonnay, and Grey Riesling.

RHINE FARM. See GUNDLACH-BUNDSCHU WINERY

RHINE WINE. One of the legal generic terms allowed on wine labels in California. From the 1960s to the 1980s, the term was seen on several slightly sweet white jug wines, which often had a hint of muscat in the flavor. Such labeling is rarely seen today. Before Prohibition this sort of wine was usually sold as Hock in California.

PAUL RHODES WINERY (BW 3838). Before he bought Antonio Colombo's winery in Castro Valley in 1938, Paul Rhodes (1896–1984) had been the superintendent of CRESTA BLANCA in Livermore. He expanded his new operation to a 150,000-gallon capacity and won numerous awards in the 1940s for his table and fortified wines. In 1968 the building of the freeway into Castro Valley forced him to close the winery.

RHONE RANGERS. A name coined in the late 1980s to identify an informal and somewhat collegial band of vintners in California who were dedicated to advancing the production and sale of wines from traditional Rhône varieties, red and white, varietal and blended. For the latter these producers have coined several interesting proprietary names. Randall Grahm's BONNY DOON wines, among them Le Cigare Volant and Le Sophiste, are probably the most noteworthy. EDMUNDS ST. JOHN makes Les Côtes Sauvages. JOSEPH PHELPS calls his line of Rhône types Vin du Mistral.

RHÔNE VARIETIES. In recent years fine wines from varieties of grapes associated with the Rhône Valley in southeastern France have become increasingly popular among consumers of California wine. Before the 1980s most Rhône varieties in California were grown in the Central Valley and went into inexpensive table and fortified wines.

The Grenache, Mataro (Mourvèdre), Cinsaut, and Carignane were well established in California's vineyards by the end of the 1870s, and remained popular over the years primarily because of their good yields, particularly in the Central Valley, and for their blending potential. During the 1880s several California producers experimented with the Syrah and with the white Rhône varieties, Marsanne and Roussanne. Apparently they made good wines, but yields were low and they had almost disappeared by the turn of the century.

The Durif, although not really a Rhône variety, entered California vineyards in the 1890s. Somehow it picked up the name Petite Sirah and became a favorite among California vineyardists.

The current interest in Rhône varieties began in the 1970s when a few small premium producers in the coastal valleys of northern California began experimenting with grapes they found growing on vines often half a century old. Mataro (Mourvèdre), Grenache, and Carignane were the early favorites. Syrah took a little while to catch on but, by 1996, more than 2,000 acres had been planted. (Virtually no old-vine Syrah survived from earlier years.) Viognier has been the overwhelming favorite among the white Rhône varieties.

See BLACK MALVOISIE (Cinsaut/Cinsault), CARIGNANE, DURIF, GRENACHE, MARSANNE, MATARO (Mourvèdre), PETITE SIRAH, ROUSSANNE, SYRAH, and VIOGNIER.

Remington Norman, *Rhone Renaissance* (San Francisco: Wine Appreciation Guild, 1996).

RICHARDSON VINEYARDS (BW 4905). A small winery bonded in 1980 and located on the Sonoma side of the Carneros. The owners buy many of their grapes from the SANGIACOMO VINEYARDS and are best known for their Pinot noir. Annual production of about 3,000 cases also includes Chardonnay, Zinfandel, and Cabernet Sauvignon.

RICHERT, WALTER S. (1911–80), a popular and versatile wine industry leader, was, in the 1950s, technical editor of WINES & VINES, general manager of MAYACAMAS VINEYARDS, and president of the American Society of Enologists. He was also an early partner with Rodney STRONG in Tiburon Vintners. In the 1960s he reopened a deserted winery in the Santa Clara Valley near Morgan Hill and became renowned for his port and sherry.

RIDDLING. When SPARKLING WINE* is produced by the *méthode champenoise,* the deposits of dead yeast cells and tartrate crystals that accumulate in the bottle after the second fermentation should be removed without removing the wine from the bottle. The traditional process is called *remuage* by the French. The bottles are inverted at an angle in special racks and rotated daily. Eventually the deposit, which gradually collects in the neck of the bottle, is disgorged. Californians, and many other English-speaking wine people, call this process riddling, a corruption of *rütteln,* the German term for *remuage.*

Hand-riddling is a slow and expensive process. In the 1970s Korbel built a cumbersome but cost-effective system for automatic riddling. At about the same time a more efficient system was developed in Catalonia in Spain. Dozens of bottles are placed in huge metal crates. These are shifted and shaken mechanically. It works and is used by most large-scale California sparkling wine producers who employ the classic method of bottle fermentation.

RIDGE VINEYARDS (BW 4488). In 1949 the theologian William Short (1889–1979) bought a part of the old Perrone estate on MONTE BELLO* Ridge. He planted about 25 acres of vines there, mostly Cabernet Sauvignon. He sold his 80 acres in 1959 to a group of scientists headed by David R. Bennion (1929–88). None of the buyers had been particularly interested at first in creating a wine-growing estate, but by 1962 they had bonded the little building that had until 1942 been the Andro Mikulaco Winery (BW 171). Later the partners acquired the old Perrone winery up the road and transformed it into today's modern facility.

Bennion was the winemaker and concentrated his efforts on the estate Cabernet Sauvignon. There was little of that at first (187 cases

David Bennion, *right,* and Paul Draper in the Ridge Vineyards cellar in 1979. These two have been the only winemakers since the winery in Santa Clara County was founded in 1959. (Photo Frances Bennion)

in 1963). He gradually expanded production, using grapes from all over northern California. By 1967 Ridge was producing eleven different wines, the grapes for which came from vineyards from Sonoma to Paso Robles.

By the end of the 1960s Ridge had acquired a reputation for the quality, power, and ageability of its wines. Bennion had a flair for vineyard-designated Zinfandels. In 1969 Paul Draper went to work at Ridge and by 1971 was entirely in charge of the winemaking. He had earlier made wine with Fritz MAYTAG in Chile. Bennion remained president and both men continued to hunt up old-vine Zinfandels. In 1971 Draper began getting grapes from Maytag's York Creek Vineyards on Spring Mountain in Napa. Meanwhile the Monte Bello estate Cabernet Sauvignon was developing the reputation of a California first growth.

In 1981 Draper made 43,000 cases of wine, 41 percent Cabernet Sauvignon and 44 percent Zinfandel. The rest was labeled Chardonnay, Claret, Petite Sirah, and Ruby Cabernet.

In 1987 the original partners and the large group of later investors sold Ridge to the owner of the Japanese Otsuka Pharmaceutical Co. Draper stayed on as winemaker and chief executive officer, positions he retains today. Since the sale he has raised annual production to about 65,000 cases, with most of the growth coming in Zinfandel production, which now accounts for about 60 percent of Ridge's total. There is still a wide range of Zinfandel sources, but Sonoma labels dominate, particularly Lytton Springs and Geyserville. These label designations are now Ridge's legal property. In 1991 Ridge bought LYTTON SPRINGS Winery.

Paul Draper, *History and Philosophy of Winemaking at Ridge Vineyards: 1970–1990s* (Regional Oral History Office, Bancroft Library 1994).

Jancis Robinson, *The Great Wine Book* (London: Sidgewick & Jackson, 1982), 215–22.

RIESLING. A confusing term in the history of California wine. Until 1997 it was a term that might go on wine labels as a sort of generic expression. Legally, any wine made from WHITE RIESLING, Franken Riesling (actually SYLVANER), or GREY RIESLING (actually Trousseau gris), in any combination, might be labeled Riesling. But in 1996 the BATF ruled that the name Riesling may not be used of any grape that is not really a Riesling. Today, the true Riesling is almost always labeled White Riesling or Johannisberg Riesling. After 1 January 1999 the word Johannisberg will not be allowed on labels. After that date, wine from the true Riesling may only be labeled Riesling or White Riesling. EMERALD RIESLING, a botanical cross, one of whose parents is the true Riesling, will still be allowed on labels.

In the early days of California wine Riesling on a label usually meant White Riesling. Honest merchants usually labeled German-style blends as HOCK. But there were no legal controls. After Prohibition the U.S. government laid down the rules for labeling such generic wines.

RIPARIA. A North American species of *Vitis.* Because it is virtually immune to the attacks of PHYLLOXERA, varieties of *V. riparia* have been useful in the development of resistant ROOTSTOCK.

RITCHIE CREEK VINEYARD (BW 4681). Richard Minor bought uncleared land on Spring Mountain in Napa in 1965 and slowly began planting his 8-acre vineyard. He bonded his winery in 1974 and released his first estate Cabernet Sauvignon in 1977. His annual production of about 1,200 cases includes Chardonnay. Among the pioneer producers of Viognier in California, Minor no longer grows the grapes or makes the wine.

RIVER RUN VINTNERS (BW 4850). A small winery dating from 1978 that is near Watsonville in Santa Cruz County. The owners have bought grapes of numerous varieties from almost every coastal wine county in California. Their 1992 Mendocino Cabernet Sauvignon was best of show at the 1996 Santa Cruz wine competition. Production averages about 4,000 cases a year.

RIVERSIDE COUNTY. A huge county in southern California not much of it devoted to viticulture. In the mid-1990s, of the 17,000 acres of grapes there, almost 90 percent was planted to table and raisin varieties. At Repeal the percentage was about 67, most wine grapes

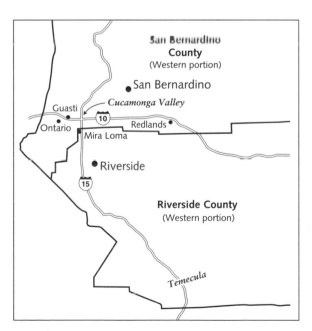

Riverside County

being a holdover from those grown for the home winemaking market during Prohibition. Nevertheless, winegrowing today is far more important than it was 100 years ago when there were only about 200 acres in the county.

The extent of the Riverside wine-grape vineyards today, at about 2,300 acres, is nearly the same as it was in 1960. Then winegrowing was concentrated in the north around Mira Loma, an area that is really an extension of the Cucamonga-Guasti district. Few of those vines have survived. The Rancho California development in 1964 and the CALLAWAY VINEYARD & WINERY soon concentrated winegrowing in the TEMECULA area, in the southwest corner of the county. Of Riverside's wine-grape crop, about 75 percent is white with Chardonnay accounting for more than half of the county's total. There are fifteen wineries and about forty growers.

RIXFORD, EMMETT H. See LA QUESTA

RKATSITELI, the chief white wine grape of Russia, the Ukraine, and Bulgaria. The University of California at Davis received cuttings of the variety in 1968. In 1970 CONCANNON planted 440 vines and produced a varietal wine in 1973. It was successful at first and 15 more acres were planted in 1975. In 1979 about 1,600 cases were marketed nationally. By 1984 the novelty had waned and production ended. The hardy variety is still grown here and there in the eastern United States.

ROBINSON, JANCIS. One of the most gifted and knowledgeable wine writers in the world. Although based in England, she spends much time in California. Her chief works, which include *Vines, Grapes and Wines* (1986) and *The Oxford Companion to Wine* (1994), contain useful references on California winegrowing.

ROCHE WINERY (BW 5495). In 1977 the Roche family bought 2,500 acres in the southwest portion of Sonoma's Carneros area. They

have planted 135 acres of vines there, mostly Chardonnay and Pinot noir. The impressive barn-style winery was bonded in 1989, although the first vintage was produced a year earlier at Sunny St. Helena. Annual production is now about 6,000 cases. The vineyard is surrounded by the huge Roche cattle ranch, one of the largest undeveloped pieces of land in southern Sonoma county.

J. ROCHIOLI VINEYARDS (BW 4892). The Rochioli family has been growing wine grapes southwest of Healdsburg along the Russian River since 1938. There are still a few ancient Prohibition-era Carignane vines near the old barn. Until the 1960s prunes were the main crop, but Cabernet Sauvignon and Sauvignon blanc went in the ground in 1959. In a few years Chardonnay and Pinot noir became more important. Until the 1980s the Rochioli grapes were sold to others, but the soaring reputation of the resulting wines encouraged them to make some of their own. Vintages 1982 and 1983 were made by Gary FARRELL at Davis BYNUM's neighboring winery. The Rochiolis' own winery went on line in 1985, the Pinot noir of that year receiving remarkable critical acclaim. The family still sells some grapes but wine production is now up to about 8,000 cases per year. There are 160 acres of vines, still principally Chardonnay, Pinot noir, and Sauvignon blanc.

ROEDERER ESTATE (BW 5335). In 1978 the French Champagne house of Louis Roederer began searching for land to create a sparkling wine estate in California. In 1981 the company began buying land in the Anderson Valley in Mendocino and now owns four large vineyards there totaling 580 acres and planted in about equal parts to Pinot noir and Chardonnay. The impressive 48,000-square-foot winery was bonded in 1986 and two years later the company's first estate Brut was released, about 4,500 cases. There since has been a Rosé and a superpremium sparkler labeled L'Ermitage. By the mid-1990s annual production was approaching 60,000 cases.

ROMA WINE CO. A winery founded in Lodi by Martin Scatena in 1890. In 1924 wine merchants from the East Coast Lorenzo and J. B. CELLA bought it and its vineyards. They shipped grapes and produced cooking sherry, wine sauce, concentrates, and sacramental wine. At Repeal they expanded the operation (BW 2237) and in 1935 bought the Santa Lucia Winery (BW 3612) in Fresno. They renamed it the Roma Winery and soon were advertising it as the largest winery in the world. In 1942 the Cellas sold out to SCHENLEY DISTILLERS and by the 1950s Roma was the best-selling brand in the United States. In 1970 GUILD bought the Roma wineries and brands, changing the name of the Fresno plant to B. Cribari & Sons. Roma is still a wine brand, owned by CANANDAIGUA.

ROMBAUER VINEYARDS (BW 5113). Joan and Koerner Rombauer were partners in Conn Creek Winery from 1977 to 1980. The next year they acquired land north of St. Helena near the Silverado Trail in Napa Valley and bonded their new winery in 1982. The primary activity at Rombauer is specialized custom crushing. They supply the space and most equipment and others bring in grapes and make their wine under the winery bond number 5113. This part of the business has grown to about 50,000 cases per year. Some of the noteworthy labels of wines that have originated here are LIVINGSTON WINES, SPOTTS-WOODE, LIPARITA, CORISON, DOMINUS, and VIADER, to name a few.

The Rombauers also produce their own wine, which amounts to about 15,000 cases per year, mostly Cabernet Sauvignon and Chardonnay. There is also a blend of red Bordeaux varieties labeled Le Meilleur du Chai; it is rare and expensive. In 1993 the Rombauers expanded capacity when they took over the historic LARK-MEAD* Winery from the Hanns KORNELL estate. In 1996 they bought the De Moor Winery, restoring its old name, NAPA CELLARS.

ROOTSTOCK, RESISTANT. The introduction of the PHYLLOXERA* root louse into California's vineyards in the 1850s meant that eventually some defense had to be developed to protect the European *Vitis vinifera* grape vines from which all fine wine had been produced in the Golden State. By the 1870s many in Europe and California had concluded that the eventual solution lay in grafting the vinifera onto American vines native to the Mississippi-Missouri Valley, the home of the phylloxera and where the vines and the bug had evolved together. By the 1880s some Californians had made contact with viticultural experts in the midwest and had acquired rootstock for practical experiments on their resistance. The leaders in this endeavor were Julius DRESEL in Sonoma, John STANLY in the Carneros, George HUSMANN in the Napa Valley, and William PFEFFER in the Santa Clara Valley. As the phylloxera devastation increased in the 1890s, more and more Californians heeded the call of university scientists to acquire and work with resistant vines. But there was no systematic work done in California that could lead to any clear answer to the question of which rootstock was best under which conditions. In France the research was systematic and it led to the solution of the phylloxera problem.

The key was the French understanding that, within native American species, there was a wide range of resistance and that some varieties in a species were more resistant than others were. In California, vineyardists had made no attempt to identify specific varieties within species. The two species that worked best in California had been *V. riparia* and *V. rupestris*. The French experience had been the same, but they had identified the characteristics of many varieties within each of those two species, they had given those varieties names, and rated them for resistance.

In 1896 Arthur Hayne from the University of California at Berkeley went to France, studied the French research, and returned with the opinion that a *V. rupestris* variety named St. George could work as universally resistant rootstock for California. Industry leaders accepted this opinion. After 1897 tens of thousands of acres of vines in California were planted on the Rupestris St. George. But scientists at the university were not satisfied that this vine was indeed the best under all conditions. The U.S. Department of Agriculture became involved in 1903, establishing experimental stations in several grape growing areas in California and testing rootstock. In 1911 the university began a series of extensive rootstock experiments, but prohibitionist sentiment brought them to an end in 1919. But in 1929, researchers at the University of California at Davis again took up the investigation, now using pure American *Vitis* species and hybrids between American species and vinifera. Trials were conducted in vineyards from Mendocino to Santa Barbara county. After years of analysis, the university scientists decided that several rootstocks were superior to the St. George, the chief fault of which was its low yields. Top marks went to the A×R#1, a hybrid of Aramon (a vinifera) and a rupestris variety, even though the scientists admitted that "its phylloxera resistance is not high."

During the great expansion of vineyards in California after the mid-1960s, the A×R#1 became the most popular rootstock used in the coastal counties. This heavy use was ill-starred, particularly in Napa County, and to a lesser extent in Sonoma County. After 1983, it gradually became clear that some vineyards in Napa were succumbing to phylloxera, vineyards planted to A×R#1. But it was not until 7 years later, in 1990, that a task force at the university admitted that the A×R#1 was very susceptible to a new biotype of phylloxera in Napa and Sonoma counties. At last growers were being advised to use other rootstocks. But, because there has been no official warning from the experts at the university, unsuspecting vineyardists in those two counties had, between 1983 and 1990, planted more than 25,000 acres of new vines, most grafted onto A×R#1. The economic blow to those growers was staggering: Throughout the 1990s, thousands of acres of vineyards in Napa and Sonoma were torn out and replanted on pure native rootstock. That A×R#1 had vinifera "blood" is now understood to have been the problem. So far other counties have not developed as serious a phylloxera problem, but it is not clear why the new biotype of phylloxera has not migrated.

"Phylloxera Update," *California Agriculture* 50, no. 4 (July 1996): 4–23.

ROSÉ. Pink wine made by blending white and red wine, or by quickly separating the skins from the juice of red wines grapes before fermentation. Such wines were rare in California before World War II. Then in 1945 Frank SCHOONMAKER persuaded ALMADEN to make a varietal Grenache Rosé in the style of French Tavel. Robert Mayock came up with the same idea at Los Amigos that year.

Rosé wines are usually light, fresh, and fruity, with a touch of sweetness. They are meant to be drunk young lest their pink turn to orange. Varietal rosés have been popular in California, Grenache, Grignolino, and Pinot noir particularly successful. See also BLANC DE NOIRS and BLUSH.

ROSE, LEONARD J. (1827–99), was the most prominent wine producer in southern California between the 1860s and the 1880s. A native of Bavaria, he arrived in New Orleans in 1835 with his family. He came to California in 1861, settling in the San Gabriel Valley where he bought land from Benjamin WILSON. By 1863 he had 260 acres of vines and by

1869 was shipping wine to the East Coast. His great Sunny Slope estate eventually covered 1,960 acres on the foothill land that would become the city of Pasadena. When he sold the property and his name to an English syndicate in 1889, he was producing 750,000 gallons of wine and 100,000 of brandy. Sunny Slope continued to operate as the L. J. Rose Wine Co.

Rose's great passion was breeding and racing horses. Fully 650 acres at Sunny Slope had been devoted to that activity. Shaky business deals brought him down, the final blow being the financial collapse of his pet copper mine in Arizona. When banks would not advance him loans in 1899, he committed suicide with an overdose of morphine.

L. J. Rose Jr., *L. J. Rose of Sunnyslope* (San Marino, Calif.: Huntington Library, 1959).

ROSENBLUM CELLARS (BW 5139). Kent Rosenblum started his commercial winemaking in 1978 across the street from the Oakland Amtrak station, went thence to Emeryville in 1982, and in 1987 to Alameda in the Southern Pacific's old repair depot, which had been built in 1910. By then he was considered one of California's Three Rs of premium Zinfandel, along with RIDGE and RAVENSWOOD. Part of his success came from his scouting out several old-vine vineyards in Sonoma, Napa, Contra Costa, and Paso Robles. There are numerous other varietals under the Rosenblum label, including a sparkling Gewürztraminer and a Black Muscat. Annual production has exceeded 40,000 cases.

ROSENTHAL-THE MALIBU ESTATE (BW 5810). George Rosenthal has 15 acres of fine varieties at his Rancho Escondido in Newton Canyon, in the hills above Malibu. At about 1,400-feet elevation, the area is above the fog line and gets more than twice as much rain as does the town of Malibu below. The first commercial vintage was in 1991 at the Sanford

Winery, 450 cases of Cabernet Sauvignon that received good notices. There is also Chardonnay and Merlot. A winery on the estate is planned for the future.

In 1995 Rosenthal petitioned for appellation status for the Newton Canyon area, which was granted in 1996, and covers about 850 acres in this bowl-shaped valley of the Santa Monica Mountains. The official title is Malibu-Newton Canyon Viticultural Area.

ROSSI. One of the important family names in California wine history. When the 1887 vintage failed at ITALIAN SWISS COLONY* the company hired **Pietro C. Rossi** (1855–1911) as winemaker. He had a degree in agricultural

Pietro Rossi married Amelie, the daughter of Justinian Caire (see SANTA CRUZ ISLAND). They had ten children. Their home near Geyserville survives close to the old ITALIAN SWISS COLONY plant, "Buen Retiro." Rossi was noted for his beautiful English, which betrayed not a hint of accent. (*Pacific Wine & Spirit Review*)

chemistry from the University of Turin and soon set the cellars in order. His technical leadership and business acumen made Italian Swiss Colony the largest producer of fine wine in California at the turn of the century. His twin sons, **Edmund Rossi** (1888–1974) and **Robert Rossi** (1888–1961), were also industry leaders and acted as important elements of continuity between the wine industry's pre-Prohibition days and the trying years following Repeal.

ROSSI, CARLO. (1903–94), went to work in sales for E. & J. GALLO in 1953. In the 1980s his name went on a popular line of Gallo jug wines and he made several commercials in which his down-home awkwardness made him something of a television celebrity.

ROUDON-SMITH VINEYARDS (BW 4587). June Smith and Annamaria Roudon, brought their husbands, Robert Roudon and James Smith, to wine in the 1960s. The four have run their winery in the Santa Cruz Mountains, north of Felton, since the first crush in 1972, made with purchased grapes. They have made a specialty of Cabernet Sauvignon and Petite Sirah, but there are 5 acres of estate Chardonnay on their property. Annual production had reached about 10,000 cases in the mid-1990s.

ROUND HILL CELLARS (BW 4828). The origins of this very successful Napa winery lie in Ernie Van Asperen's slapping his Ernie's label on the wines of others, chosen because they were excellent bargains both for price and quality. He sold the wines in his Ernie's liquor stores, which he started in 1939 and which numbered eighty-four by the 1960s. This NÉGOCIANT operation was a great boon to consumers in the seventies. Ernie's 1974 Cabernet Sauvignon developed an almost legendary reputation in the 1980s among collectors of California wine.

In 1977, with his wife, Virginia, he teamed with Charles Abela to found Round Hill. Their first facility was in an old building north of St. Helena in the Napa Valley. At first most Round Hill wine was made by others, but this situation gradually changed. Meanwhile a quality line labeled Rutherford Ranch Brand was developed for grapes from vineyards that the Van Asperens had acquired beginning in 1968. By 1985 the partnership was selling a total of almost 100,000 cases a year.

In 1987 they built their full-scale winery next to the Silverado Trail in the Rutherford area and by 1988 had raised production to 260,000 cases. An important part of this total went to private labels. Within a few years Round Hill had about 175 clients—restaurants, clubs, and such—who wanted Round Hill consistency and quality. This aspect of production today amounts to 25 percent of the almost 400,000-case-a-year business. Round Hill's top varietals are Chardonnay, Cabernet Sauvignon, Merlot, and Zinfandel. In 1997 Round Hill began producing its Van Asperen brand of higher-priced Napa Valley varietal wines.

ROUSSANNE. A white Rhône variety of wine grapes, sister to the MARSANNE, with an almost identical history in California. The Roussanne differs from the Marsanne in that it is a bit more difficult to grow but has a more enticing flavor. There are not yet enough acres of either vine to warrant their appearance in the state statistics, although a few California wineries, among them CLINE CELLARS and BONNY DOON VINEYARD, have recently produced a varietal Roussanne.

ROYAL HOST. See EAST-SIDE WINERY

ROYALTY. Released in 1985, a cross between the Alicante Ganzin and Trousseau gris grapes, developed at the University of California at Davis to give color to inexpensive red wines.

About 2,200 acres of the grape were planted in the Central Valley between 1960 and 1965. Since then its companion, RUBIRED, has become much more popular and the acreage of Royalty has dropped to about 850.

RUBIRED. A fairly successful variety of wine grape developed at the University of California at Davis to give color to inexpensive red wines. It is a cross between Alicante Ganzin and Tinto Cão, a port variety. Its popularity has come in spurts. Between 1960 and 1965 about 1,500 acres were planted in the Central Valley. Then acreage leaped to 12,000 in the 1970s. There were 8,000 acres in 1972–73 and about 7,000 in 1990. Then between 1993 and 1997 acreage expanded to more than 10,000. In the early days it was popular for the color it gave to inexpensive port-style wines. Today it is giving color to jug wines and fighting varietals made from other grapes grown in the Central Valley. There were 83,553 tons of Rubired in the 1996 vintage, making it the state's number six red-wine variety.

RUBISSOW-SARGENT WINE CO. (BW 5138) is a partnership of families. Planting its first red Bordeaux varieties on Mount Veeder in 1984, its first wine was a 1988 Merlot, for which André TCHELISTCHEFF was consultant. Now there are 18 acres of vines, but the little winemaking facility is in Berkeley. Annual production comes to about 2,500 cases.

RUBY CABERNET. One of Harold OLMO's most successful efforts in vine breeding at the University of California at Davis, the Ruby Cabernet is a cross between Cabernet Sauvignon and Carignane made in 1936. After much testing in the 1940s, it was released commercially in 1948. At the time there were high hopes for the vine all over the state. But it has had staying power only in the Central Valley, where its high yield and satisfactory acid combine well with its Cabernetlike flavors. It cannot compete with the Cabernet Sauvignon flavor in the cooler coastal valleys.

About 2,000 acres were planted before the boom of the 1970s. By 1976 there were 18,266 acres, 96 percent of which was in the Central Valley. Thereafter acreage dropped steadily. By 1986 there were 9,300, by the mid-1990s about 6,500. In 1997 there were 21 acres left in the coastal counties. There were 52,745 tons of Ruby Cabernet in the 1996 vintage, almost all from the Central Valley, a crop that was about the same as that of 1990.

RUBY HILL VINEYARD (BW 874). John Crellin (1828–95) was born on the Isle of Man, came to California in 1875, and made a fortune in real estate. In 1883 he bought a 450-acre piece of land near Pleasanton in Alameda County and began developing one of the Livermore Valley's great wine estates. H. W. MCINTYRE designed the handsome, three-story brick winery. By 1889 there were 220 acres of vines and production was fairly steady at 150,000 gallons per year. More than any other winery Ruby Hill solidified Livermore's reputation for fine California sauterne, dry and sweet.

In 1921 the estate was acquired from the Crellin family by Ernesto FERRARIO who ran the operation until it was sold to Southern Pacific in 1973. He replanted most of the vineyard in the 1920s, but some of the old Crellin vines planted on *Vitis riparia* rootstock between 1896 and 1913 survived until the 1960s. Ferrario won numerous awards at the State Fair after Repeal, but by the end of the 1950s most of his business was in bulk wine sales to other wineries. There was also a lively retail trade in jug wines, mainly Zinfandel, Barbera, and Chardonnay, at the winery. From 1974 to 1983, the grapes from the old vineyard were used by some of northern California's finest small premium wineries. The winery itself was leased to a partnership that ran the place as Stony Ridge Winery. In 1986 WENTE bought the estate and sold it two years later to a development group.

Ruby Hill in 1966 while it was still operated by Ernesto FERRARIO. In the foreground area are some of his dry-farmed, head-pruned Zinfandel vines.

The great winery burned down in 1989 under suspicious circumstances. Since the mid-1990s, the owners have been converting the land into a housing development with a golf course. Part of the development agreement calls for the planting of 600 acres of new vineyards among the homesites on the property, which has grown to about 1,300 acres.

In 1996 Randall Grahm of BONNY DOON VINEYARD began restoring the old winery and the estate vineyard.

RUPESTRIS. A North American species of *Vitis.* Most rupestris varieties are immune to attacks by the PHYLLOXERA. One of them, the St. George, became the favored resistant ROOTSTOCK in California between 1897 and the 1950s. It is still quite popular in some areas, particularly Sonoma.

RUSSIAN RIVER VALLEY. One of Sonoma County's largest viticultural areas, granted AVA status in 1983. It covers about 150 square miles between Healdsburg and Sebastopol and includes pieces of several other viticultural areas in Sonoma. There are about forty wineries and almost 9,000 acres of wine grapes. The area's southern two-thirds has a cool climate that discouraged much winegrowing in the early days but today is favored for Chardonnay and Pinot noir. There are also numerous places where Zinfandel and Sauvignon blanc shine.

RUSSIANS IN CALIFORNIA. In 1812 the Russian-American Co. established a small colony at Fort Ross in Sonoma County, north of San Francisco Bay, set up a seal-hunting station, and established several inland ranches meant to help supply the outposts to the north. There the first vineyards in Sonoma County were planted. Some of the vines were grown from cuttings brought from Peru. After the Russians left in 1841, some cuttings from those plantings eventually found their way into northern California vineyards. In this way, according to Charles KRUG, the PALOMINO variety first came to the North Coast area.

RUSTRIDGE VINEYARD & WINERY (BW 5252). In 1972 the Meyer family bought its 442-acre ranch in Napa's Chiles Valley. The first vineyard planting emphasized White Riesling. The little winery was completed in 1985. Today the 55-acre vineyard leans toward Chardonnay, with some Cabernet Sauvignon and Zinfandel. Annual production varies, averaging about 2,000 cases.

RUTHERFORD. A small town, between Oakville and St. Helena, which has given its name to one of Napa Valley's most famous winegrowing districts. It became an official viticultural area in 1993.

After Gustave Niebaum took over INGLE-NOOK here in 1879, winegrowing in Rutherford expanded. By 1881 there were 721 acres of vines in the area, 1,710 by 1887. In 1890 there were five wineries with capacities over 50,000 gallons. Zinfandel was the most common vine but no variety was dominant.

Rutherford's early fame after Prohibition came from the excellent wines made by Inglenook and BEAULIEU VINEYARD. Since the 1960s, the area has gradually moved to monoculture in Cabernet Sauvignon. In consumers' minds, the Rutherford name has become welded to this world-class varietal.

Today there are about 5,000 acres of vines and 28 wineries in the viticultural area, which stretches from foothills to foothills on both sides of the valley, and from Zinfandel Lane south to the northern boundary of the Oakville district.

RUTHERFORD GROVE WINERY (BW 4805). The Pestoni family bought the RUTHER-FORD VINTNERS winery in 1994, renaming it Rutherford Grove and now producing several varietals from the 26-acre vineyard.

The Pestonis are an old family in the Napa Valley, better known for their composting and grape-seed oil business than for winegrowing. In 1996 they converted 13,500 tons of grape pomace, which they had collected from various wineries, into 3,500 tons of compost, which they sold back to the vineyardists. Their grape-seed oil business is unique in the California wine country. From 10 tons of pomace, they are able to extract about 8 gallons of oil, which is used much as olive oil is. A half-liter bottle sells for $21.00.

RUTHERFORD HILL WINERY (BW 4591). In 1970 J. Leland Stewart sold his SOUVERAIN CELLARS on Howell Mountain to a group of investors in Napa, who then sold it to Thomas BURGESS. The investors took the illustrious Souverain name and used it for their new winery on a hillside east of the Silverado Trail in the Rutherford area.

In 1972 Pillsbury bought this facility and began building another one near Geyserville. Thus, there was a Souverain of Rutherford and a Souverain of Alexander Valley. But Pillsbury was out of the wine business by

This 1895 advertisement for INGLENOOK wines clearly identifies Rutherford as their source. "Sold only in glass" meant no bulk sales were made to merchants, these were strictly case goods. The advertisement might also have read "Bottled at the Winery," a practice in California unique to Inglenook at that early date.

1975. The operation in Sonoma became CHATEAU SOUVERAIN. The winery in Rutherford was sold again, to a group of investors which had an interest in FREEMARK ABBEY and the name changed to Rutherford Hill. Today the partners own about 830 acres of vines and produce about 125,000 cases a year. Since the late 1980s the winery has specialized more and more in Merlot, which now amounts to about 75 percent of their production, the rest is mainly Chardonnay and Cabernet Sauvignon.

In 1984 a wonderful system of underground tunnels for barrel storage was begun at the winery. The last phase was completed in 1990. This gigantic, naturally air-conditioned facility holds about 9,000 barrels and is the largest cellar of its kind in California.

RUTHERFORD RANCH BRAND. See ROUND HILL

RUTHERFORD VINTNERS (BW 4805). Bernard Skoda (1920–93) went to work for Louis MARTINI in 1961 and retired in 1976 as vice president for marketing. The next year he set up his own winery west of Highway 29 in Rutherford. In 1994 Evelyn Skoda, Bernard's widow, retired and sold the label to JFJ BRONCO. The winery was then purchased by the Pestoni family and has been renamed RUTHERFORD GROVE.

SACRAMENTAL WINE. See ALTAR WINE

SACRAMENTO COUNTY. A large county in the Central Valley, covering almost 1,000 square miles, extending east from the state capital into the Sierra foothills and with a strangely shaped tail that runs south into the DELTA region, almost to the Bay Area. In its history, winegrowing has been up and down and is rising again.

As early as the 1850s there were numerous wine-grape growers in the Folsom area northwest of the capital (see NATOMA VINEYARDS CO.). By the 1880s there were about 3,000 acres of vines, near Folsom, around the capital, and south of it around Elk Grove. There were about a dozen wineries, several quite large. A great planting binge took place in the county between 1906 and 1908, during which more than 5,000 acres of vines were added. In 1908 eight wineries in Sacramento County produced about 1.9 million gallons of wine, about 60 percent of it dry. By the 1920s acreage had dropped to about 4,300, but table-grape acreage rose to more than 10,000, mostly planted to the Flame Tokay variety. Many of those grapes made it to the fermenter and distillery.

After Repeal acreage held at about 3,500, with eleven wineries, mostly between Sacramento and Elk Grove. Actually, this area is something of an extension of the LODI-Woodbridge area of SAN JOAQUIN COUNTY to the south. The revival of winegrowing, from fewer than 1,000 acres after World War

TABLE 24. WINE GRAPES IN SACRAMENTO COUNTY, SELECTED VARIETIES

YEAR	PERCENT OF TOTAL RED	WHITE	CABERNET SAUVIGNON	CHARDONNAY	(ACRES) CHENIN BLANC	MERLOT	ZINFANDEL	TOTAL
1938								3,873
1954								723
1961	89	11						268
1972	70	30	40	0	314	9	426	1,423
1979	66	34	531	17	457	128	449	3,239
1985	47	53	595	50	747	181	361	3,570
1990	48	52	1,108	786	539	352	366	4,044
1997	53	47	1,442	2,185	491	1,809	656	7,533

NOTE: Until 1961 statistics for acreage under various varieties of grapes were not published.
SOURCE: California Agricultural Statistics Service, Sacramento, Calif.

II to more than 7,500 today, owes much to this area. The Lodi Viticultural District today takes in the Elk Grove area right up to the Sacramento city limits. In the Delta region a fairly large portion of the Clarksburg Viticultural Area lies within Sacramento County.

SACRAMENTO VALLEY. The northern section of the CENTRAL VALLEY. Drained by the Sacramento River, it extends from Shasta and Tehama counties in the north into the DELTA region. It includes all or parts of GLENN, BUTTE, COLUSA, Sutter, YUBA, PLACER, YOLO, SOLANO, and SACRAMENTO counties. Irrigation accounts for much of the region's great agricultural success. It is not a particularly hospitable area for fine wine-growing, but since 1980 wine-grape acreage has increased from about 5,000 to more than 15,000 acres.

SACRED HEART NOVITIATE. See NOVITIATE OF LOS GATOS

SADDLEBACK CELLARS (BW 5183). Nils Venge, one of the most successful winemakers in Napa, started at VILLA MT. EDEN in 1974 and moved to GROTH in 1982. The next year he started his own Saddleback Cellars near Oakville. He makes about 4,000 cases, mostly Cabernet Sauvignon, Chardonnay, and Pinot blanc. His newsletter is called *Re:Venge*.

SAINSEVAIN, PIERRE (1819–1904). No one was closer to the early development of the commercial wine industry in California than Sainsevain was. He came to Los Angeles in 1839 to work for his uncle, Jean-Louis VIGNES.* His first connection to the northern Californian industry came through his marriage to Paula Suñol, daughter of Antonio Maria Suñol, a wine producer in San Jose. Her dowry was 700 acres of prime land in Santa Clara Valley. In the early 1850s Sainsevain's red-wine related activities acted as magnet to other Frenchmen who flocked to the valley in the early Gold Rush years.

In 1855 he went south again and, with his brother Jean-Louis (1817–89), bought his uncle's El Aliso winegrowing operation. There they, along with Kohler & Frohling, laid the foundation of the state's wine industry. His wines won awards at the early state fairs and in 1860 the Sainsevains joined Charles KOHLER in a short-lived business exporting Californian wine to the East Coast. Meanwhile the brothers were producing large quantities of sparkling wine, but the Sainsevain Sparkling California operation went under in 1862.

Pierre returned to the Santa Clara Valley and successfully produced wine there for many years. In 1868 his CLARET was the best red wine at the county fair. By 1870 he was making 20,000 gallons, which he marketed under the Menlo Park label. He closed shop in

Pierre Sainsevain's label was typical of those on California wines before the 1870s. One rarely saw such terms as Champagne or Burgundy in the early years, but by the late 1860s, the realities of the marketplace had triumphed and generic terms became the rule.

1874 and spent five years in Central America. In 1880 he returned to San Jose and began making wine again. In 1882 he invented a a steam-driven stemmer crusher. After his wife's death in 1889, he returned to France where he lived out his years.

ST. ANDREW'S WINERY (BW 4967). The 32-acre vineyard here on the Silverado Trail in Napa Valley was planted in 1972. The winery was bonded in 1980 and specialized in Chardonnay. In 1988 it was acquired by the principals in CLOS DU VAL. In 1995 a group of investors in Napa bought the winery, but not the brand, which still belongs to the owners of Clos du Val. The name of one of the new owners, Michael Moon, certainly inspired the new title of the operation, Luna Vineyards.

ST. CLEMENT VINEYARDS (BW 4745). After restoring this old property, which they called SPRING MOUNTAIN VINEYARDS, the owners moved to a new facility and, in 1976, sold this winery and its little vineyard in Napa Valley, north of St. Helena, to William Casey. He changed the name, expanded the winery, and built up production to about 10,000 cases. His specialties, Cabernet Sauvignon and Sauvignon blanc, acquired a good reputation. He sold the place in 1987 to Sapporo, the Japanese brewing company. The line, which has grown to about 15,000 cases a year, now includes Chardonnay and Pinot noir, some of which is used in producing small quantities of sparkling wine.

ST. EMILION. See UGNI BLANC

ST. FRANCIS VINEYARDS (BW 4905). In 1971 Joseph Martin bought the old Behler ranch in Kenwood in Sonoma County. He sold grapes for a few years, eventually building his winery in 1979. For a while after the first vintage in 1980, his approach toward varietals was fairly eclectic, but Merlot was soon a spe-

cialty. He considers the area around his property in upper Sonoma Valley to be a "mini-Pomerol." The 100-acre vineyard is now about 70 percent Merlot and the rest mostly Chardonnay. Some of his old-vine Zinfandels have recently received critical applause. Annual production in the 1990s is averaging about 110,000 cases.

Since 1992 St. Francis has been a leader in the experimental use of synthetic CORKS.

ST. GEORGE WINERY (BW 43). George H. Malter began planting his Maltermoro Vineyard, five miles east of Fresno, in 1879. He built his winery in 1884. In Fresno he produced lots of sweet wine and brandy, but also had a good name for the table wine he produced at a small winery in Contra Costa County. He won a silver medal for his CLARET at the 1896 Atlanta Exposition.

Malter's million-gallon winery burned down twice, in 1902 and 1917; both times he rebuilt—for his operation, independent of the CALIFORNIA WINE ASSOCIATION, was one of the most profitable in California. St. George was revived by the Malter family after Repeal and was sold to an eastern bottler in 1943. It closed after World War II; where it once stood is now a housing tract.

ST. HELENA, a town that has been at the physical, economic, and cultural center of winegrowing in Napa Valley since Charles KRUG built his "small rude cellar" just north of town in 1861 and G. B. CRANE pressed out the first vintage inside the town limits in 1862. By the late 1870s, the vineyards in and around town had developed the excellent reputation for fine red-wine production that they have never lost. There are still several vineyards and wineries inside the town limits. Today the place is also a tourist attraction, full of fine restaurants and fancy shops.

In 1995 the BATF created the St. Helena Viticultural Area. It covers the valley area north of town to Bale Lane and south to Zinfandel Lane. The ruling included Spring Valley and Pratt Valley, in the eastern foothills, in the appellation.

ST. HUBERT, JULES-CHAMON DE (1835–1913). After several years in the French army, Captain St. Hubert came to California in 1878 and spent the rest of his years in the wine industry. By the late 1880s he was considered one of the state's most knowledgeable wine experts. In the 1890s he ran the California Wine Growers Union, a marketing firm for several important producers. He ended his days as manager and part owner of the San Benito Vineyards Co.; see William PALMTAG.

SAINTSBURY (BW 5114). As partners, David Graves and Richard Ward began making commercial Chardonnay and Pinot noir in 1981 on a small scale. That vintage and the next were good enough to attract investors. In 1983 they built their winery in the Carneros and had production up to 20,000 cases in 1986. They expanded their facilities in 1988 and now their annual output is about 45,000 cases. About two-thirds of their production is of Chardonnay but critics tend to prefer the Pinot noir, some of which in a less intense version is sold as Garnet.

ST. SUPÉRY VINEYARDS (BW 5427). Robert Skalli, a French businessman, bought the historic A. J. Dollarhide ranch, 1,500 acres of land in Pope Valley in Napa, in 1982. Today he has more than 500 acres of vines there. In 1986 he bought a 56-acre piece of land on Highway 29 in Rutherford and began building his 950,000-gallon winery. Still standing on the property was the old Victorian home of Joseph Burr ATKINSON, which is now part of the winery's impressive visitors area. St. Supéry was the name of the Frenchman who acquired the Atkinson property in 1899.

Annual production of a wide range of varietals, mainly Chardonnay, Sauvignon blanc, Merlot, and Cabernet Sauvignon, passed the 100,000-case mark by the mid-1990s. A second label is Bonverre. There is also a line of KOSHER WINES labeled Mount Maroma.

SALAMANDRE WINE CELLARS (BW 5253). F. Wells Shoemaker, a pediatrician by profession, is a leading and well-published authority on the health benefits of table wine. He lives in the town of Aptos, south of Santa Cruz, where he has a small winery that takes its name from a unique species of salamander native to the place. Shoemaker specializes in Chardonnay, Sauvignon blanc, and Merlot, producing a total of about 2,000 cases annually.

SALINAS VALLEY. See MONTEREY COUNTY

SALMINA FAMILY. See LARKMEAD WINERY

SALVADOR. A variety of wine grape that is a French hybrid, Seibel 128, of *Vitis rupestris* and *V. vinifera*. As Salvador ("savior" in Spanish), its appearance in California before Prohibition is something of a mystery. Having a good natural resistance to phylloxera, it did not need to be grafted on resistant rootstock and was able to yield a crop a year earlier than did the popular ALICANTE BOUSCHET. Aside from that, its only value is in the deep and stable color its fruit provides.

Paul MASSON imported and sold it as Salvador during the 1920s. About 2,500 acres survived Prohibition. Most of those were pulled up, but in the 1970s there was renewed interest in the grape, with acreage peaking in the Central Valley in 1976 at 3,200 acres. Since then, the heavier-bearing RUBIRED has taken its place to supply color to inexpensive wines, but there are still about 800 acres left in California, mostly in Kern County.

SAM-JASPER WINERY. See DELICATO VINEYARDS

SAN ANTONIO WINERY (BW 3754). Santo Cambianica founded this winery in downtown Los Angeles in 1917. (It happens to be located near where the city's earliest vineyards were planted.) His descendants, the Riboli family, now operate the area's only surviving winery. Since Repeal San Antonio has built up a sizeable retail trade at the winery. In recent years much of the wine has been made from grapes grown in northern California and sold under the Maddalena label. In 1988 the Ribolis actually bought 20 acres in the Rutherford area of Napa Valley for their Cabernet Sauvignon, but most of the annual 300,000-case production comes from wines produced at a facility in the Central Valley and bottled in Los Angeles. San Antonio is also one of California's leading producers of ALTAR WINES.

SAN BENITO. In 1987 the BATF established a San Benito Viticultural Area covering 45,000 acres and including several other recognized areas in SAN BENITO COUNTY: PAICINES, CIENEGA VALLEY, and LIME KILN VALLEY. The San Benito AVA includes about 95 percent of the vineyard area in the county.

SAN BENITO COUNTY. For the early history of winegrowing here, see VACHÉ, PALM-TAG, VALLIANT, and CIENEGA VALLEY; for recent history see ALMADEN; see MONTEREY COUNTY for map.

The gigantic Almaden planting at PAICINES during the 1960s raised the acreage of wine grapes in the county to about 4,600 in the early 1970s. The demise of Almaden in the early 1980s reduced the acreage to 1,616 acres in 1987, a level that was about the same in the 1930s. In 1997 there were 1,728 acres. Overall red varieties amount to about 55 percent of the total, although Chardonnay, at almost 500 acres, is by far the most common variety. Next in line come Cabernet Sauvignon, Gamay Beaujolais, and White Riesling.

SAN BERNARDINO COUNTY. The largest county in the United States, covering more than 20,000 square miles. Mostly desert, it extends from the Los Angeles lowland to the Arizona and Nevada border. Winegrowing has been concentrated in the southwest corner, in the CUCAMONGA area between the cities of San Bernardino and Pomona; see RIVERSIDE COUNTY for map. The reader will have a good understanding of winegrowing in the county by referring to Cucamonga and the following

TABLE 25. WINE GRAPES IN SAN BERNARDINO COUNTY, SELECTED VARIETIES

YEAR	PERCENT OF TOTAL RED	WHITE	BURGER	GRENACHE	MISSION	PALOMINO	ZINFANDEL	TOTAL
1910								15,000
1921								21,000
1938	N.A.	N.A.	1,008	482	2,734	514	6,276	20,803
1954								24,838
1961	81	19	958	2,569	3,643	2,004	6,411	21,121
1968	83	17	653	1,753	2,503	1,518	4,517	14,816
1974	83	17	461	1,239	1,880	891	2,734	11,449
1980	80	21	349	814	1,344	837	2,348	7,139
1985	78	22	189	307	742	468	1,214	3,489
1990	90	10	25	87	250	78	642	1,157
1997	58	42	0	68	215	63	665	1,728

NOTE: Until 1961 statistics for acreage under various varieties of grapes were not published; figures for 1938 are abberant, if interesting.

SOURCE: California Agricultural Statistics Service, Sacramento, Calif.

specific entries: BROOKSIDE VINEYARD CO.; FILLIPI VINTAGE CO.; GALLEANO WINERY; GARRETT, PAUL; GUASTI; PADRE VINEYARD CO.; and REGINA GRAPE PRODUCTS; also see RIVERSIDE COUNTY.

The recent history of winegrowing in San Bernardino County is well illustrated in table 25. Only 16 acres of new vines have been planted in the county since 1978. However, varieties such as Zinfandel, that had not been accounted for in the early 1990s were sufficiently numerous again to be counted by 1997.

SAN DIEGO ALCÁLA, MISSION. See MISSIONS AND THE MISSION PERIOD

SAN DIEGO COUNTY. The most southerly county in California, where hopes for successful winegrowing have always exceeded results. Even the legends of early viticulture at the San Diego mission exceed historical reality; there is no evidence of any vines having survived the original Spanish settlement here in 1769.

During the 1880s there was some interest in vine planting in the ESCONDIDO and El Cajon areas. By the 1890s there was sizeable acreage in table grapes, but only a few hundred acres of wine grapes and eight small wineries. The largest was G. F. Merriam's Chula Vista Winery. After 1900 lots of wine grapes were planted in the Escondido area, the total reaching 1,800 acres by the 1920s. During the dry years, however, most of the rail shipments east from San Diego were of muscats. After Repeal there was an explosion of tiny wineries in the county, eleven around Escondido. Two survive, FERRARA WINERY and Bernardo. Before World War II Escondido regularly held a wine festival.

Beginning in 1973 a 120-acre vineyard was planted in the SAN PASQUAL area east of Escondido, but it was a troubled endeavor. In 1980 there were about 225 acres of wine grapes in San Diego County; in 1997 there were 87.

SAN FERNANDO REY DE ESPAÑA, MISSION. See MISSIONS AND THE MISSION PERIOD

SAN FERNANDO VALLEY. Northwest of central Los Angeles and, since 1915, mostly inside that city's limits. Today it is a gigantic suburban community.

The valley, and particularly the foothills around Tujunga and Encino, had many commercial vineyards and a few small wineries after the 1880s. Irrigation water, available after 1913, also encouraged planting, particularly in the 1920s. Following Repeal nine small wineries opened in the valley, mostly around Burbank and North Hollywood. The Burbank Winery (BW 196) operated until 1964.

SANFORD WINERY (BW 5160). Richard Sanford and Michael Benedict founded a winery (BW 4760) in Santa Barbara County near Lompoc in 1976, having planted their vineyard in 1971. They dissolved the partnership in 1980 and Sanford formed his own company the next year, with a winery near Buellton. He produced several well-received Chardonnays and Pinot noirs. In 1990 Robert Atkin, an English industrialist, bought the Benedict vineyard and Sanford was again able to acquire fruit from this valuable source. Since then Sanford Pinot noirs have won widespread acclaim. He also produces Chardonnay and Sauvignon blanc. In 1996 Sanford acquired land west of the original Sanford & Benedict vineyard for a new 150-acre vineyard. He calls it Rancho Rinconada. Total annual production is about 40,000 cases.

SAN FRANCISCO. In the 1850s, when what had been a rude village grew to a city of 50,000 people, quite a lot of commercial wine was made there from grapes brought in from the country. This tradition continued into the 1930s. More important, as the center of commerce for the northern part of the state, the city

PALACE HOTEL WINES.

PURE CALIFORNIA WINES—DIRECT FROM VINEYARD.

ORLEANS VINEYARD.	PTS.	QTS.	HEDGESIDE VINEYARD.	PTS.	QTS.
Eclipse, Ext. Dry (Champagne)	$1 25	$2 25	Cabernet (Claret)	$ 50	$1 00
Zinfandel (Claret)	30	50	Sauterne	50	1 00
Riesling (Hock)	30	50	SCHRAMSBERG.		
NAPA VALLEY WINE CO.			Riesling (Hock)	40	75
Zinfandel	30	50	INGLENOOK VINEYARD.		
			Zinfandel	40	75
BARTON VINEYARD.			SUNNY SLOPE VINEYARD.		
Riesling	30	50	Sherry		1 00
			Port		1 00

Also San Gabriel Wine Co. Wines.

CHAMPAGNES.

Dry Monopole, Heidsieck & Co.	2 00		Pommery, Sec	$2 00	$4 00
Gold Lack, Sec	2 00	4 00	Krug, Sec	2 00	4 00
L. Roederer, Carte Blanche	2 00		Charles Heidsieck		3 50
Perrier, Jouet, Extra Dry	2 00		Sparkling Johannisberger		3 50
Jules Mumm & Co., Grand Sec		4 00	G. H. Mumm & Co., Extra Dry	2 00	
Moet & Chandon	2 00		Veuve Clicquot Ponsardin, Dry	2 00	4 00

CLARETS.

St. Julien, Pouget Fils	$ 50	$1 00	Chateau Lafitte, Dubos Freres	$4 00
St. Julien, Barton & Guestier	75	1 50	Chateau Pavell Margaux, A. De Luze & Fils	3 00
Chateau Leoville, A. De Luze & Fils	1 25	2 50	Chateau Leoville, 1874, Barton & Guestier	4 00

SAUTERNES.

Haut Sauterne, A. De Luze & Fils	$1 25	$2 50	Chateau Yquem, (crème), A. De Luze	$4 00

BURGUNDIES.

Chablis, Guichard & Co., Chalon, White	$1 50	$3 00	Clos-Vougeot, Guichard & Co., Chalons	$2 00	$4 00
			Chambertin, Guichard & Co., Chalons	1 50	3 00

HOCK.

Königin Victoria Berg, G. M. Pabstmann	$4 00	Hochheimer, G. M. Pabstmann & Sohn	2 50
Shloss Johannisberger, G. M. Pabstmann	4 00	Steinwein in Boxbeutel, G. M. Pabstmann	3 00
Steinberger Cabinet, G. M. Pabstmann	3 50		

SHERRIES.

Montibello	$2 00	Heatley, Gordon	$2 50
Amontillado, Dry	2 50	Isabella	4 00

MADEIRA.

No. 1, Extra—Private Stock ... $5 00

PORT.

London Dock, Old—Private Stock ... $3 00

LIQUEURS, ETC.

Anisette, Marie Brizard & Rogers	$3 00	Berliner Gilka Kummel	$2 00
Absinthe, Superieure	3 00	Arack	3 50
Chartreuse	5 00	Maraschino	2 50
Kirsch Wasser, Richard & Muller	2 50	Benedictine	2 00
BRANDIES.		WHISKIES.	
Jas. Hennessy & Co. Cognac	4 00	O. P. S. Bourbon	2 50
Sazerac	4 00	Old Bourbon	2 00
Old Private Stock	5 00	Old Rye, Private Stock	2 00

MALT LIQUORS, ETC.

Tennent's Pale Ale	40	75	Belfast Ginger Ale	$ 40
Guinness' Dublin Stout	40	75	Bass & Co's Pale Ale	40	75
Beer	25	50	Sparkling Cider		75

CORKAGE, PER BOTTLE (CHAMPAGNE), $1 00.
CORKAGE, PER BOTTLE (STILL WINES), 50 CTS.

A wine list from The Palace Hotel, San Francisco in 1889. Note that three of the eight California table wines listed were Zinfandels. The Hedgeside Cabernet from Napa Valley was a particular favorite in swell eateries on the West Coast. (*Pacific Wine & Spirit Review*)

became the home of the most important California wine merchants. Beginning with KOHLER & Frohling in 1854, many of the wine houses became gigantic enterprises, with monstrous cellars capable of holding millions of gallons of wine. Typically the merchants bought wine young from producers in the countryside, blended it to suit their trade, and sold it wholesale all over the United States to local distributors, or retail through their own agencies. Much of the California wine that Americans drank before Prohibition was purchased under the labels of San Francisco merchants. But the peculiar geography of the city, perched at the top of a peninsula, and surrounded by ocean and bay, made this system unwieldy. It was modified considerably after the EARTHQUAKE and fire in 1906, which destroyed most of the great cellars; see WINEHAVEN.

SAN FRANCISCO DE SOLANO, MISSION. See MISSIONS AND THE MISSION PERIOD

SAN GABRIEL ARCÁNGEL, MISSION. See MISSIONS AND THE MISSION PERIOD

SAN GABRIEL VALLEY. Just east of central Los Angeles, the valley extends from Glendale to Pomona and for about 125 years was an important winegrowing area. But, by the 1950s, the last commercial vineyards had fallen

to the advance of suburbia. The Viotti Winery (BW 4137) was in business there until 1969. See also Elias J. BALDWIN; Leonard J. ROSE, James SHORB; Benjamin D. WILSON.

SAN GABRIEL WINERY (BW 46). In the 1890s the Demateis family planted vineyards in the Cucamonga area and later built a winery in downtown Los Angeles. When that city went dry in 1915, they moved to the San Gabriel Valley and built a new winery. After it reopened in 1933, its capacity grew to more than 500,000 gallons. The winery had its own distillery and was well known for its fortified wines and vermouth. It ended operations in 1955.

SANGIACOMO VINEYARDS. The Sangiacomo family settled in the Sonoma Valley in 1927. Their first grapes were planted in 1969 after they had spent years growing pears and apples. Today they control about 1,000 acres of vines in the Carneros, mostly Chardonnay, with 225 acres of Pinot noir and a little Merlot. Customers for their highly prized grapes are legion and include some of California's most famous wineries. It has become a sign of prestige for a label to carry a Sangiacomo vineyard designation.

In 1990 the family bought land in the Lakeville area, joining Domaine Chandon in helping revive this old winegrowing area (see J. G. FAIR) southwest of Petaluma.

SANGIOVESE (San Gioveto). The most commonly planted wine grape in Italy, where its wines can be among the finest or the most ordinary, a result of its numerous clonal variations and its astonishingly disparate reactions to diverse environments. Nevertheless, the best wines of Tuscany are almost always loaded with Sangiovese.

In recent years the variety has found favor among winegrowers in California in a somewhat experimental yet enthusiastic manner. In 1997 there were 1,359 acres scattered about in twenty-seven counties, but 43 percent of that acreage was planted in Napa and Sonoma counties; Mendocino was in third place with 62 acres.

The newness of this development can be seen in the planting statistics (in which the name is spelled Sangioveto, historically correct, but quite old-fashioned). There were only 59 acres of the variety in California before 1989. In Napa ATLAS PEAK VINEYARDS and ROBERT PEPI led the way for the first few years.

The vine was included on the list of imports brought to California in 1862 by Agoston HARASZTHY as the San Giovetta, but nothing came from this introduction. In the late 1880s it was imported by the ITALIAN SWISS COLONY as San Gioveto and its grapes became the foundation of the Colony's production, later, of Tipo Chianti. With one exception, there is no evidence of other producers making commercial use of the variety. That exception is the SEGHESIO family, which had very close relations with Italian Swiss Colony. At their vineyard near Geyserville, appropriately near the old Chianti Station on the Northwestern Pacific Railroad, the Seghesios still have vines that descend from the original imports, some of which were planted in 1910.

During Prohibition most of the San Gioveto at Italian Swiss Colony was pulled up or grafted, but in 1927, with an eye on future Repeal, the company put in a large planting of the variety. These vines survived until 1984.

The 1997 crush of Sangiovese grapes was 7,163 tons; in 1990 the total crush was 61 tons.

Millie Howie, "Sangiovese, the New Noble Variety," *Wines & Vines,* December 1997, 31–36

SAN JOAQUIN COUNTY. In 1996 San Joaquin County had more acres of wine grapes than any other county in California had; so it was in 1970. Currently Cabernet Sauvignon, Chardonnay, and Zinfandel constitute 63 percent of these vines. Such was not the case in 1970, far from it. Of all the counties in the

Central Valley, San Joaquin, with its climate and soils, is the most favored for good wine grapes, most of which grow in the LODI* area, where the vines benefit from the moderating effects of the cooling breezes from San Francisco Bay. Lodi is about 45 miles to the east of the bay, which borders Napa and Sonoma counties. There are also large areas of vineyard south of Lodi around the towns of Escalon, Ripon, and Manteca.

Early winegrowing in San Joaquin County was not important, except for the great work done by George WEST and his family at their El Pinal Winery near Stockton. There were about 900 acres of wine grapes in the county in 1891. This situation changed after the turn of the century as the demand for California wine rose and the federal tax on sweet wine declined. By 1901 there were 5,000 acres of grapes, by 1903, 13,000. (Some of those were table and raisin varieties, but most were crushed for sweet wine and brandy production.) During Prohibition wine-grape acreage continued to grow, up to 31,000 acres in 1928. During those years San Joaquin vied with Fresno County in shipping the largest quantities of grapes to eastern home winemakers. In 1929, for example, 10,271 refrigerated cars full of grapes left the county, about 75 percent of them wine grapes.

Growth did not abate at Repeal. Wine-grape acreage reached 35,000 in 1938, 65 percent of the vines being around Lodi. In those years almost six times as much sweet wine was produced as

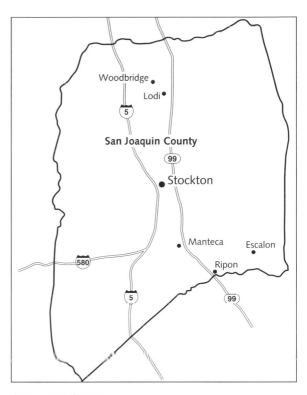

San Joaquin County

VINTAGES IN SAN JOAQUIN AND NAPA COUNTIES, 1996

	ACRES	CRUSH (TONS)	TONS PER ACRE	PRICE PER TON	PRICE PER ACRE
CABERNET SAUVIGNON					
LODI	5,323	42,249	7.94	$796	$6,320
NAPA	10,335	29,453	2.85	$1,804	$5,141
CHARDONNAY					
LODI	10,289	48,035	4.67	$772	$3,605
NAPA	9,154	24,114	2.63	$1,542	$4,055
ZINFANDEL					
LODI	17,334	94,947	5.48	$589	$3,227
NAPA	2,030	8,213	4.05	$877	$3,552

The Robert MONDAVI Woodbridge plant typifies the large-scale production facilities that have been built in San Joaquin County since the 1970s. It is on the site of the old CHEROKEE VINEYARD cooperative. (Photo provided by Craig Rous, Robert Mondavi Woodbridge)

TABLE 26. WINE GRAPES IN SAN JOAQUIN COUNTY, SELECTED VARIETIES

YEAR	PERCENT OF TOTAL RED	WHITE	ALICANTE BOUSCHET	CABERNET SAUVIGNON	CARIGNANE	(ACRES) CHARDONNAY	GRENACHE	ZINFANDEL	TOTAL
1921									13,500
1924									23,868
1928									31,701
1938	N.A.	N.A.	8,701	N.A.	6,457	0	29	15,701	34,595
1954									26,038
1961	93	7	2,092	9	6,193	8	1,764	6,588	20,370
1968	93	7	1,384	72	7,160	9	2,732	7,167	22,491
1974	88	12	813	291	7,744	8	2,596	10,922	29,922
1980	72	28	596	700	6,591	186	2,548	11,147	37,528
1986	62	38	324	862	4,771	360	1,086	10,144	34,828
1989	60	40	239	2,466	3,845	3,631	971	12,347	36,543
1992	59	41	173	3,466	2,973	6,023	782	12,782	38,217
1997	63	37	93	5,324	2,163	10,289	595	17,334	49,018

NOTE: Until 1961 statistics for acreage under various varieties of grapes were not published; figures for 1938 are aberrant, if interesting.

SOURCE: California Agricultural Statistics Service, Sacramento, Calif.

dry, with almost half of the crush coming from TABLE and RAISIN varieties. Eastern shipments of wine grapes remained significant, almost 2,400 car lots in 1937. The chief wine producers were seven growers' cooperatives. Only three producers were associated with specific brands: J. B. CELLA (Roma), SHEWAN-JONES (Lejon), and EAST-SIDE WINERY (Royal Host).

By the 1940s production of dry table wine had risen to the point at which only three times as much sweet wine was being produced. There were thirty-nine wineries, the sixteen largest with a collective capacity of about 25 million gallons. There were also thirteen distilleries making brandy as a beverage or for fortifying sweet wine.

As the consumption of FORTIFIED wines declined in the 1950s, so did acreage here. But after 1961 acreage grew steadily into the 1990s. Most of this growth was in standard varieties until the late 1980s when BLUSH wine and FIGHTING VARIETALS came into full flower. Zinfandel acreage soared for the production of White Zinfandel, as did acreage for other premium varietals. In 1997 there were eighteen bonded wineries in the county, most large-scale operations making moderately priced varietals. But a few were small-scale producers with access to some of the area's surviving old-vine Zinfandel vineyards. There were 750 wine-grape growers in the county in 1997, their average holding about 75 acres.

The economics of the changes in San Joaquin County can be inferred from the statistics (see table, p. 305) from the 1996 vintage there and in Napa County. Note particularly the very favorable ratios of tons per acre and income per acre in San Joaquin County.

Wine grape tonnage for San Joaquin County in 1996 was 173 percent of the tonnage in 1990. The acreage under red-wine grapes in 1996 accounted for 64 percent of the total. Other varieties with significant acreage were: Merlot (4,211 acres), Chenin blanc (2,023), French Colombard (2,692), and Sauvignon blanc (1,434).

SAN JOAQUIN VALLEY. A little more than half of California's wine grape acreage is to be found in the southern portion of the Central Valley, an area starting just north of Lodi and running south through Kern County. About 180,000 acres of wine grapes are planted there, making it one of the largest winegrowing regions in the world, but still well below the leaders, Languedoc (750,000 acres), Mendoza, in Argentina (375,000 acres), and Bordeaux (247,000 acres). But when the acreage of table and raisin grapes is added, the total approaches 500,000 acres. A high percentage of the grapes that end up in fermenters in the

San Joaquin Valley is made up of table and raisin varieties. See also FRESNO COUNTY; KERN COUNTY; KINGS COUNTY; MADERA COUNTY; MERCED COUNTY; SAN JOAQUIN COUNTY; STANISLAUS COUNTY; and TULARE COUNTY.

SAN JOSE. California's first pueblo during the mission period, founded in 1777, the same year as nearby Mission Santa Clara. San Jose was California's major community north of Monterey before the American Conquest (1846), and the state's first capital. Throughout those years, it was the center of an important agricultural community that included many winegrowers in the Santa Clara Valley.

In the 1880s the little city became an important shipping center for the expanding wine industry. Several large industrial wineries were built in the town to help process the region's large wine-grape production. This situation lasted until Prohibition. After the dry years, all the valley's major wineries were located outside town. Today only the J. LOHR WINERY operates here in an urban setting. But the city limits now extend all over the valley so that even MIRASSOU has a San Jose address.

SAN JOSÉ DE GUADALUPE, MISSION. See MISSIONS AND THE MISSION PERIOD

SAN JUAN CAPISTRANO, MISSION. See MISSIONS AND THE MISSION PERIOD

SAN LUCAS. A large viticultural area in the Salinas Valley, below King City in southern Monterey County. Large-scale viticulture and high yields from its 4,800 acres of vines define winegrowing here. The first 1,250 acres were planted by ALMADEN in the 1970s. This is FIGHTING VARIETAL country.

SAN LUIS OBISPO COUNTY. A Central Coast county in which large-scale commercial winegrowing dates from the 1970s. Viticulture

TABLE 27. WINE GRAPES IN SAN LUIS OBISPO COUNTY, SELECTED VARIETIES

| | PERCENT OF TOTAL | | | | (ACRES) | | | |
YEAR	RED	WHITE	CABERNET SAUVIGNON	CHARDONNAY	MERLOT	SAUVIGNON BLANC	ZINFANDEL	TOTAL
1920								500
1926								838
1932								1,410
1938			0	0	0	0	674	853
1954								692
1961	98	2	0	0	0	0	472	494
1969	93	7	15	5	0	0	512	634
1972	77	23	221	73	25	21	469	1,289
1974	77	23	1,045	291	461	186	1,126	4,165
1979	54	46	963	611	37	474	927	4,435
1984	43	57	978	847	31	869	989	5,613
1989	50	50	1,684	2,096	134	700	1,318	7,276
1992	52	48	2,630	3,116	284	693	1,224	9,164
1997	60	40	3,285	3,984	1,567	625	1,861	12,721

NOTE: Until 1961 statistics for acreage under various varieties of grapes were not published; figures for 1938 are abberant, if interesting.

SOURCE: California Agricultural Statistics Service, Sacramento, Calif.

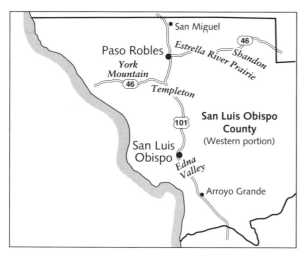

San Luis Obispo County

has a long history here. There were vineyards at the two Franciscan missions. One near what is today the town of San Luis Obispo was not successful for the same reason that grape varieties such as Chardonnay that prefer a cooler climate do so well today in nearby EDNA VALLEY. To the north and farther inland in the PASO ROBLES area at Mission San Miguel, winegrowing was much more successful because of the warmer climate. Today this is mostly red-wine country.

Except for a few tiny pioneering vineyards, the first spurt of viticulture in the American period came in the 1880s when about thirty-five growers planted about 500 acres of vines, mostly near the town of San Luis Obispo and south of Paso Robles near Templeton. The vines were mostly Zinfandel and Burger, with a few acres of Riesling. There were nine small wineries there, including the historic Andrew York Winery west of Templeton. By 1900 there were about 1,000 acres of wine grapes in the county.

The Prohibition years did not boost grape growing much, although in the 1930s seven small wineries were established (see PADEREWSKI and PESENTI). It was between 1972 and 1974 that the modern wine revolution was felt, particularly in the Edna Valley, in the hills west of Paso Robles, and on the Estrella River Prairie to the east. Acreage grew gradually in the 1980s and 1990s, slightly more being planted to red varieties (54 to 46 percent). The most favored has been Chardonnay in the Edna Valley and around Arroyo Grande. Today the county has about forty wineries, seven with capacities of more than 100,000 gallons.

In 1995 wine-grape production in the county was 132 percent of the production in 1990.

SAN LUIS OBISPO WINERY. See HMR ESTATE WINERY

SAN LUIS REY DE FRANCIA, MISSION. See MISSIONS AND THE MISSION PERIOD

SAN MARTIN WINERY (BW 81). After 1900 a boom in vineyard planting took place in southern Santa Clara Valley. In 1905 a group of businessmen from San Jose planted 200 acres of vines in the San Martin Tract and in 1908 incorporated the San Martin Wine Co. In 1933 Bruno Filice (1874–1940) and his family bought the company and developed the winery that became famous later. After years of bulk wine production, a successful retail brand was developed in the 1950s and a remarkable tasting room was built next to Highway 101. By the late 1960s the mammoth visitors center was attracting hundreds of thousands of travelers per year. The winery had a huge line of wine products in those years, forty-four in 1967.

Beginning in 1973, the winery had several successive owners who reduced the number of products and improved the quality. Despite huge outlays for the best in modern equip-

ment, profits were insufficient to continue operation and the winery closed in 1991. It was sold to ASV WINES and reopened in 1993 as ARROYO SECO VINEYARDS, a custom-crush operation.

SAN MATEO COUNTY. A mountainous county on the San Francisco Peninsula where it is difficult to ripen grapes. But it is possible in the WOODSIDE-PORTOLA VALLEY area and in the foothills facing the bay west of the city of San Mateo. Here in the 1880s a small wine industry grew up with about 800 acres of vines. There were several outstanding producers, including E. H. Rixford of the renowned LA QUESTA and E. F. Preston of the Portola Valley Winery. Only about 180 acres survived Prohibition. But in the 1960s there was a new interest in winegrowing in this small part of the Santa Cruz Mountain Viticultural Area. There are only about 60 acres of vines there today, but tiny vineyards dot the area, some no more than a quarter-acre in size. There are nine small wineries in the county, the owners of which buy most of their grapes outside the area and concentrate on making wines of the highest quality.

SAN PASQUAL. A valley east of the Escondido area in San Diego County. In 1973 a new winery, San Pasqual Vineyards (BW 4773), began operations and 120 acres of vines were planted. The BATF approved the San Pasqual Valley as an official viticultural area in 1981. The winery went into bankruptcy in 1986 and in 1989 became the Thomas Jaeger Winery. In 1994 it became ORFILA VINEYARDS.

SAN SABA VINEYARD (BW 5876). Mark Lemmon lives in Dallas but owns 68 acres of vines in the Santa Lucia Highlands area of Monterey County. Vineyard planting began in 1975 and for several years the wines were made at the neighboring SMITH & HOOK WINERY. The 12,000-case annual production emphasizes Chardonnay and Merlot.

SANTA BARBARA COUNTY. A county in southern California in which, during the Spanish period, there were three missions in the area, Santa Barbara, Santa Inés, and La Purísima Concepcíon. All had good vineyards and during the Mexican period after 1823 supplied vineyard stock to the ranchos in the area.

After the 1850s the influx of settlers brought lots of small vineyards and some commercial winegrowing. In 1872 the state counted almost 400,000 vines here, but this number includes vines in Ventura County, until that year a part of Santa Barbara.

In 1882 the oldest surviving commercial vineyard in California, dating from the 1840s, the San Jose Vineyard north of Goleta, produced 8,000 gallons of wine for James McCaffrey, its owner since 1853. Below the town of Carpenteria was the largest vine in the world, La Viña Grande, with a trunk 9 feet in circumference. Until its demise in 1915, it often produced more than 10 tons of Mission grapes a year.

The wine boom of the 1880s was not much felt in Santa Barbara County. By the end of the decade, there were eleven small wineries, but only one of importance, and that off the coast on SANTA CRUZ ISLAND. Neither did Prohibition promote vine planting.

After Repeal four small wineries started up, two in the Santa Ynez Valley, but the SANTA BARBARA WINERY was the first real step that was part of the modern wine revolution here. The great wave of vine planting came between 1971 and 1973, concentrated in the SANTA MARIA and Santa Ynez valleys. These are fairly cool areas where the climate and soils provide excellent environments for Chardonnay and Pinot noir. Thus, there was much shifting of varieties in the 1980s, as Cabernet Sauvignon acreage declined and Chardonnay soared. White Riesling acreage also plummeted, but for market reasons.

Santa Barbara County

TABLE 28. WINE GRAPES IN SANTA BARBARA COUNTY, SELECTED VARIETIES

YEAR	PERCENT OF TOTAL RED	WHITE	CABERNET SAUVIGNON	CHARDONNAY	MERLOT	(ACRES) PINOT NOIR	SAUVIGNON BLANC	WHITE RIESLING	TOTAL
1971	59	41	151	14	0	0	17	51	258
1972	57	43	737	227	102	254	17	449	2,139
1974	62	38	1,889	843	503	862	67	1,009	6,068
1979	41	59	1,422	1,497	302	793	247	1,842	7,475
1984	21	79	865	2,349	167	625	448	2,223	9,174
1989	23	77	918	4,758	259	875	480	1,101	9,407
1992	23	77	776	5,381	210	859	430	488	9,193
1997	26	74	549	6,197	501	1,043	265	268	10,069

SOURCE: California Agricultural Statistics Service, Sacramento, Calif.

In 1996 the tonnage of wine grapes in the county was 148 percent of the tonnage in 1990.

Cork Millner, *Vintage Valley* (Santa Barbara, Calif.: McNally & Loftin, 1983).

SANTA BARBARA WINERY (BW 4490). In 1962 a French Canadian, Pierre Lafond, bonded his El Paseo Cellars delicatessen in the city of Santa Barbara, mainly so that he could have wine tastings there. But he also made wine at home and in 1965 went commercial. By 1971 he had bought a vineyard in the Santa Ynez Valley and had a winery in town with a capacity of 25,000 gallons. Now capacity is up to 100,000 gallons and the vineyard has 74 acres of vines. Annual production of a large and complex line of table and dessert wines is now about 30,000 cases.

SANTA CLARA. The county and valley of Santa Clara are often discussed synonymously, but such a view is inaccurate. Most of Santa Clara County is mountainous. Its share of the vineyards in the Santa Cruz Mountains has more vines than are planted in the entire Santa Cruz County. The Santa Clara Valley itself was

granted AVA status in 1989, but it includes the old winegrowing area near MISSION SAN JOSE, which is actually in Alameda County. The southern boundary of the viticultural area is below Gilroy and actually dips into San Benito County.

Wine in Santa Clara County, before the 1960s, was grown in the flatlands and foothills, what is called Silicon Valley today. In the Spanish period this area was the most

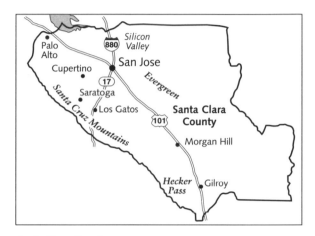

Santa Clara County

TABLE 29. WINE GRAPES IN SANTA CLARA COUNTY, SELECTED VARIETIES

YEAR	PERCENT OF TOTAL RED	WHITE	CABERNET SAUVIGNON	(ACRES) CARIGNANE	CHARDONNAY	PETITE SIRAH	ZINFANDEL	TOTAL
1923								8,500
1926								10,262
1932			*	1,015	0	247	1,717	6,749
1938			*	1,067	0	255	1,925	7,375
1954								4,499
1964	55	45	24	467	*	236	425	3,100
1971	51	49	191	296	46	140	238	2,651
1982	63	37	201	110	92	109	131	1,458
1997[a]	61	39	170	50	402	36	82	1,137

NOTE: Until 1961 statistics for acreage under various varieties of grapes were not published; figures for 1932 and 1938 are abberant, if interesting.

* It is believed that some grapes of these varieties were grown, but no official statistics are available.

a. In 1997 there were 169 acres of Merlot, all planted in the 1990s.

SOURCE: California Agricultural Statistics Service, Sacramento, Calif.

By the mid-1880s the Santa Clara Valley was one of the leaders in the state's production of high-quality table wines. Charles LEFRANC, here pictured in 1883, was rightfully considered by his contemporaries to have pioneered the valley's commercial wine industry in the valley at his NEW ALMADÉN vineyard.

A surprisingly large number of the newcomers were French, a language heard commonly on the streets of San Jose until the 1890s, and many were instrumental in establishing the Santa Clara County wine industry; see Antoine DEL-MAS, Charles LEFRANC, Paul MASSON, MIRASSOU, Pierre PELLIER, and J.-B. J. PORTAL.

In the 1850s Santa Clara led all northern California counties in vineyard acreage, but fell to second place behind Sonoma in the 1860s and behind Napa in the 1870s. When the wine boom began in the late 1870s, Santa Clara County had about 2,500 acres of vines, a total which leaped to almost 15,000 in by 1883. The EVERGREEN and CUPERTINO areas were covered with vineyards. In 1890 the county had 129 commercial wineries, but, like the rest of the state, had overexpanded its wine industry and was suffering by the early 1890s. Later in the decade the phylloxera devastated most of the entire area. When replanting took place, it was more often to prunes and apricots than to wine grapes. Between 1895 and 1902 about 10,000 acres of vines disappeared. Nevertheless, prosperity in the industry brought intensive vineyard expansion in the southern part of the county after 1900. In 1906 there were only 5,500 acres left but more than half of those were newly planted. Within four years acreage was back to about 10,000, but only forty-nine wineries survived. The greatest industrial development in those years was around GILROY.

Between 1900 and 1920 most of the county's independent vineyards and wineries were acquired by ITALIANS and their families. During Prohibition the wine grape industry was dominated in this area by first- and second-generation Italians. During the dry years, acreage grew quickly from about 7,000 to almost 11,000, but after 1926 gradually declined to 6,750 in 1932. The problem was again overexpansion and low prices. Notable in the dry years was that far more wine grapes from Santa Clara County than from the North Coast went to home winemakers in the Bay Area.

important settled area in northern California. SAN JOSE,* the province's first pueblo, had a population of about 700 in the 1840s and many of these people made wine from their little vineyards. They got their cuttings at the nearby Mission Santa Clara, where the town of Santa Clara began growing up in 1848 after the Americans began pouring in.

They found a dusty, prosperous agricultural community surrounded by numerous large Mexican ranchos. The newcomers bought land and created a modern Eden of orchards, vineyards, nurseries, and ranches all over the valley.

As the Santa Clara Valley became Silicon Valley after World War II, the vineyards in the northern areas gave way almost completely to expanding suburbia. The only important vineyards that survived were between MORGAN HILL and Gilroy, and in the HECKER PASS area. But in the Santa Cruz Mountain portions of the county important gains were made in the highlands above Cupertino and Saratoga; see also MONTE BELLO. Until the 1990s Santa Clara County had never had a concentration of any particular varieties. Now three varieties, Chardonnay, Cabernet Sauvignon, and Zinfandel, make up 64 percent of the acreage.

SANTA CRUZ. An area in northern California and long associated with winegrowing. Until Prohibition there was a significant wine industry in Santa Cruz County, based on more than 1,500 acres of vines. The important areas were around Felton, BONNY DOON, in the VINE HILL area north of the town of Santa Cruz, and in the BEN LOMOND and BOULDER CREEK area. Today there are fewer than 200 acres of vines in the county, but there are twenty-one wineries. In the popular mind Santa Cruz County and the SANTA CRUZ MOUNTAINS Viticultural Area are inseparably mixed, but most of the vines in the AVA are in Santa Clara County and some are in San Mateo County.

The name Santa Cruz has been associated with good wine since George JARVIS opened the Vine Hill area to viticulture in the 1860s. By the late 1880s there were thirty-seven small wineries, and one large one, the Ben Lomond Wine Co., which made about 40,000 gallons annually. By 1905 county acreage had risen to 1,600 and Ben Lomond was making 100,000 gallons. The phylloxera were slow moving into the mountains and valleys here and the old vines were producing well into the 1930s and 1940s. After Repeal thirteen small wineries opened, half of them owned by Italian families. One survived, BARGETTO's, today Santa Cruz's largest and oldest.

The area attracted numerous enthusiastic wine entrepreneurs after Repeal (see HALLCREST VINEYARDS and NICASIO VINEYARDS). After 1960 there was a continuous flow of new people, attracted by the wonderful environment and the mountain grapes. Today most wineries in the Santa Cruz Mountains buy their grapes outside the county, but many make it a point to use the mountain grapes as much as possible. There is always powerful support for new vineyards in the area.

SANTA CRUZ ISLAND. Of the seven islands off the coast of Santa Barbara and Ventura Counties, Santa Cruz is the largest. In 1869 a group headed by Justinian Caire (1827–97), a merchant in San Francisco, bought the island to run sheep and cattle on it. In the 1880s Caire planted 60 acres of vineyard to first-class wine varieties and in 1891 he built a winery, whose annual production averaged about 60,000 gallons before Prohibition. During the dry years, the vineyard was expanded to 150 acres. At Repeal wine production began again on a small scale and continued until 1936, when the Caire family sold most of the island. Many of the old structures survive, but the winery was destroyed by fire in 1950.

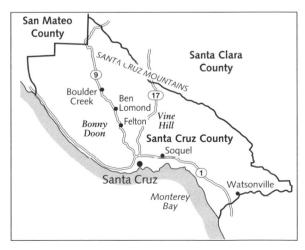

Santa Cruz County

Santa Cruz Island is mountainous and of volcanic origin. Once the site of a penal colony, it is now a part of the Channel Islands National Monument, a federally administered ecological preserve. (Thomas Pinney Collection, Claremont, Calif.)

SANTA CRUZ MOUNTAINS. The mountains of the lower San Francisco Peninsula and the area south of it are not high but they are rugged and wild. Through them passes the deadly San Andreas fault. These Santa Cruz Mountains extend to the Hecker Pass area in the south and since the 1860s small amounts of highly praised table wine have been produced there. The area includes highland portions of SANTA CLARA, SANTA CRUZ, and SAN MATEO counties. Most of this land above the 600-foot contour line was included in a viticultural area granted AVA status in 1982. (For the history see entries for the individual counties.)

Since the 1960s, when the modern development of winegrowing here began, the cooler areas facing the Pacific Ocean have tended to specialize in Pinot noir and Chardonnay. The warmer areas facing the San Francisco Bay and the Santa Clara Valley have more Cabernet Sauvignon. There are only about 250 acres of vines in the area today, but there about twenty-five wineries, most of which depend on grapes grown outside the area. Before Prohibition there were about 2,000 acres of vines in the Santa Cruz Mountains area.

Michael R. Holland, Charles L. Sullivan, and Jason Brandt Lewis, *Late Harvest: Wine History of the Santa Cruz Mountains* (Santa Cruz, Calif.: privately printed, 1983).

SANTA CRUZ MOUNTAIN VINEYARD (BW 4697). Ken Burnap's passion for wine in the Burgundian style drew him out of the restaurant business in southern California and into the Santa Cruz Mountains where he bought land in the Vine Hill area in 1974. He bonded his winery and made wine the next year. The 13 acres of Pinot noir that Burnap bought were planted by David Bruce in 1971, after he had pulled up the Zinfandel vines planted there by the Locatelli family in 1916. Originally the land had been part of George JARVIS's pioneer vineyard here.

Since the early years Burnap has developed a good reputation for Pinot noir made by traditional French methods. He also makes Cabernet Sauvignon and Merlot from purchased grapes. In 1977 he produced a Petite Sirah, which he labeled Durif, the first of its kind in California history. Total annual production is about 3,000 cases.

SANTA LUCIA HIGHLANDS. An area in Monterey County that was granted AVA status in 1992. It covers about 138 square miles on the west side of the Salinas River running up into the foothills from Gonzales to the western edge of the Arroyo Seco area. The dominant geographical feature is a series of remarkable alluvial terraces. Cabernet Sauvignon and Merlot do well here in the southern portion, but Chardonnay does much better in the north. There are about 1,900 acres of vines and three bonded wineries.

SANTA MARIA VALLEY. An area for which there is no parallel in California wine history, it ranks today as one of the state's outstanding districts, with almost 5,000 acres of vines, and renowned for its Chardonnay and Pinot noir.

Before the 1960s, winegrowing here was almost unknown. Its vineyards are east of the town of Santa Maria, just below the northern Santa Barbara County line. The area was granted AVA status in 1981. The western portion is greatly affected by cool maritime influences and is heavily planted to Burgundian varieties.

The Tepusquet development on the awe-inspiring Santa Maria Mesa in the early 1970s set the pattern for large holdings here today by big producers such as KENDALL-JACKSON, BERINGER WINE ESTATES, and Robert MONDAVI.

SANTA ROSA. The urban center of Sonoma County, the city was the hub of a diverse agricultural industry until it was transformed into a major part of San Francisco Bay suburbia after World War II. Before then it was the site of numerous important wineries, dating back to the 1860s (see Isaac DE TURK). Between Repeal and World War II thirty-one wineries had a Santa Rosa address. All are gone.

SANTA YNEZ VALLEY. Like the SANTA MARIA VALLEY, its neighbor in Santa Barbara County, the Santa Ynez Valley is new to serious winegrowing. The viticultural area, designated in 1983, stretches east from the cool Lompoc area past the town of Santa Ynez. Unlike the Santa Maria Valley, this is an area of small and mid-sized wineries and vineyard holdings. The area is cut by Highway 101, which acts as a boundary between the cooler western vineyards, mainly planted to Pinot noir and Chardonnay, and the warmer eastern portion where Merlot, Cabernet Sauvignon, and Sauvignon blanc do well. There are fourteen wineries and about 1,250 acres of vines in the area.

SANTA YNEZ WINERY (BW 4753). Originally the Santa Ynez Valley Winery, the operation was founded in 1976 east of Solvang by three families who, in 1969, had planted the first commercial vineyard here since Prohibi-

tion. Today it amounts to 110 acres. New owners took over in 1988 and make several varietal table wines, producing about 20,000 cases annually.

SANTINO WINES. See RENWOOD WINERY

SAN YSIDRO DISTRICT, southwest of Gilroy in Santa Clara County, an area with excellent soil and greatly influenced by the cooling sea breezes coming through the Pajaro River gap to the west. It was not popular for viticulture in the early years because red varieties of grapes did not ripen well there. But in the 1950s experts at the University of California at Davis marked the area as excellent for white wine grapes. Over the years about 500 acres of vines have been planted here, mostly Chardonnay. In 1990 the BATF created a viticultural area, officially known as the San Ysidro District.

SARAH'S VINEYARD (BW 4868). A tiny premium winery in the Hecker Pass area, its first crush was in 1978; the first-estate grown crop was in 1983. Chardonnay and Merlot are the winery's specialties. Cadenza is a Rhône-style Grenache. Total annual production is about 2,000 cases.

SARATOGA. Little survives in this picturesque village on the west side of the Santa Clara Valley that might suggest its wine heritage. But in 1890 seventy-one vineyardists and eighteen wineries listed Saratoga as their address. In 1896 Paul MASSON began building his historic winery in the hills behind the town. All this is gone, except Masson's old winery buildings. But since the 1970s winegrowing has returned to these "Sarahills" and the Congress Springs area above town. Several new wineries and vineyards in the hills now give Saratoga as their address.

SATIETY (BW 5026). Seven miles from the campus of the University of California at Davis

Sterling Chaykin makes blended table wines and varietal vinegar. He started planting his 29-acre vineyard in the 1970s and bonded his neat little winery in 1981. Total annual production is about 5,000 cases.

V. SATTUI WINERY (BW 4726). Before Prohibition Vittorio Sattui ran a small winery in San Francisco's Mission District. He called it St. Helena Wine Cellars, for the area from which he bought his grapes. Ninety years after he founded his winery his great-grandson opened a winery and cheese shop on the outskirts of St. Helena.

Daryl Sattui put up his first winery and delicatessen building in 1975 and opened it and the adjacent picnic area to the public in 1976. The comfortable tourist atmosphere and Sattui's good wine made the venture a great financial success. In 1984 he bought the vineyard next door and the following year built a new and imposing winery. By the 1990s, he was drawing 250,000 visitors a year, with all the winery's 35,000 cases sold on the spot or by mail.

Sattui emphasizes wine quality and has developed a solid reputation that one does not usually associate with the touristic ambience of the operation. Special events, such as his Tax-Relief Party every April 16, have endeared him to his customers. Today the winery sells about a dozen different wines. Cabernet Sauvignon is a specialty.

In 1993 Sattui bought 121 acres of land bordering Schramsberg and the historic 560-acre Henry Ranch in the Carneros; about 150 acres are suitable for vines.

SAUCELITO CANYON VINEYARD (BW 5110). The eastern part of the Arroyo Grande Viticultural Area is warm enough to ripen Zinfandel. Here in 1974 William Greenough found the remains of the Henry Ditmas/Mainini Vineyard (BW 3941) near Saucelito Creek and was able to bring back some of the pre-Prohibition Zinfandel vines. (Some may have been planted in the 1880s.) He now has about 8 acres and produces about 2,500 cases of powerful Zinfandel and some Cabernet Sauvignon. His first vintage was in 1982.

SAUSAL WINERY (BW 4625). The Demostene family has owned the Sausal Ranch in the Alexander Valley in Sonoma County since 1956. There are about 150 acres of vineyard land, including some very old Zinfandel vines. For years the Demostenes sold grapes to others and in 1973 founded their winery, named for the willow trees growing there (*sauce* is willow in Spanish). Zinfandel makes up most of the winery's annual 10,000-case production, but there is also Cabernet Sauvignon. Some of the Demostene land was once part of the pre-Prohibition Soda Creek winery.

SAUTERNE. In the mid-nineteenth century, at just about the time that French Sauternes was gaining world renown, wine producers in California were developing a series of generic terms for their wines. Sauterne, sometimes spelled "sauternes," was often used for table wine that resembled the white wine coming into California from Bordeaux. A sweet California version was sometimes labeled Haut Sauterne. The very best of these, dry or sweet, were made from authentic Bordeaux varieties such as SAUVIGNON BLANC* and SÉMILLON,* but more often they were made from more bland varieties such as SAUVIGNON VERT or PALOMINO, which were blended with a touch of the better varieties. Some producers, particularly in the Livermore Valley, labeled their sweet sauterne, Chateau D'Yquem.

After Prohibition, the federal government recognized the names sauterne and haut sauterne as legal generic names for American wine, but prohibited such names as Chateau D'Yquem. Some producers in California countered by labeling their sweet sauterne as Chateau wine—names such as Chateau Wente and Chateau Concannon were to be seen on labels into the 1960s.

As producers in California moved toward varietal labeling in the 1960s, it was common to see both the word sauterne and the varietal designation on the label. Also in the late 1960s, the name Fumé Blanc began appearing on bottles of sauvignon blanc that might, in former years, have been labeled Sauterne.

SAUVIGNON BLANC, the French variety of wine grape that gives the white wines of Bordeaux and the upper Loire Valley their special flavors. Today in California it is widely grown in the coastal counties and the Sierra foothills, where it produces one of the state's finest table wines. It also does well in the Central Valley, particularly in San Joaquin County, where there are about 1,500 acres.

Table wines from this variety have, at their best, a distinct somewhat herbaceous flavor. When this flavor becomes highly pronounced the wine tends to lose its appeal. In recent years growers in California have developed many vineyard practices that help them get the level of herbaceousness they desire. Styles vary also as the result of cellar techniques, which often parallel those used for Chardonnay after fermentation.

The variety came to California early, but it is not clear who brought it first. It surely was in the collections imported by Charles LEFRANC and Agoston HARASZTHY, and may also have been brought in by Antoine DELMAS and Pierre PELLIER. It was definitely imported by J.-B. J. PORTAL, J. H. DRUMMOND, and J.-C. DE ST. HUBERT before it gained popularity in the 1880s, when we hear first of successful wines being made from white Bordeaux varieties, and then more often from Sémillon than from Sauvignon blanc. But by the end of the 1880s several producers in the Sonoma, Napa, Livermore, and Santa Clara valleys, and in the Mission San Jose area, had been praised by connoisseurs for their efforts with this variety. The wines were usually labeled SAUTERNE* or Haut Sauterne. In the Livermore Valley some producers of the sweet wines began putting Chateau D'Yquem on their labels, particularly after CRESTA BLANCA won a gold medal at the 1889 Paris Exposition for its version. (It was not labeled sauterne or the French would not have allowed it to be entered.)

Livermore developed a special relationship with white Bordeaux varieties. Cresta Blanca's early success was partly responsible, but the wine folklore and facts that developed around Charles WETMORE's importation of cuttings directly from Château d'Yquem in the 1880s also influenced popular perception; see Louis MEL.

After Prohibition the tradition of fine California sauterne from the best varieties was

TABLE 30. SAUVIGNON BLANC GRAPES, SELECTED COUNTIES AND AREAS

YEAR	SONOMA	NAPA	MONTEREY	(ACRES) SAN LUIS OBISPO	SIERRA FOOTHILLS	CENTRAL VALLEY	TOTAL
1966	200	225	N.A.	N.A.	N.A.	N.A.	1,378
1971	314	390	259	0	2	273	1,594
1974	261	534	1,027	186	2	562	3,193
1977	337	738	1,341	359	11	1,028	4,401
1981	1,303	2,150	1,337	633	268	1,890	9,558
1985	2,039	3,616	1,768	902	428	3,183	15,383
1992	1,702	2,808	1,470	693	364	3,666	13,336
1997	1,541	2,654	1,119	625	228	3,221	11,514

SOURCE: California Agricultural Statistics Service, Sacramento, Calif.

maintained by such producers as WENTE and BEAULIEU. But the acreage of true Sauvignon blanc in California was very small and the statistics for the state are confused by the fact that, until 1966, officials lumped the vines with the more plentiful and prolific SAUVIGNON VERT. By that time many producers were having a difficult time selling Sauvignon blanc as a varietal. It was then that Robert MONDAVI brought out a Fumé Blanc that was mostly Sauvignon blanc, and that name did catch on. Eventually Sauvignon Blanc caught on as well as more and more consumers became familiar with it. The BATF recognizes Fumé blanc as a valid synonym for Sauvignon blanc.

Although acreage has declined since 1986, Sauvignon blanc is still second only to Chardonnay as a premium white varietal in the coastal counties, but it is a distant second. In 1990, the state crush of this variety came to 60,222 tons; in 1996 it was 48,637 tons; in 1997 the tonnage shot up to 73,376 tons.

added to our confusion by lumping statistics for Sauvignon vert with those for Sauvignon blanc. There were probably 1,000 acres of Sauvignon vert in the state in the late 1960s, mostly in Napa and Sonoma. By the 1990s there were about 50 left.

Two of those acres were near Gilroy. Jancis ROBINSON believes that the true Sauvignon vert is the same grape that makes the Italian Tocai Friulano. So the Robert MONDAVI Winery in 1994 bought some of the grapes from Gilroy and made a white wine labeled Tocai Friulano, part of their special line of Italian varietals. But Robinson also believes that *all* Sauvignon blanc vines in California are "almost certainly" Muscadelle of Bordeaux. To add to the confusion, the BATF ruled in 1996 that *all* California Sauvignon vert was Muscadelle and after 1999 would have to be labeled as such. But the Tocai Friulano designation was permitted to continue. Perhaps Sauvignon vert should be considered another of California's mystery vines.

SAUVIGNON VERT. A white-wine variety of grape also known in France as the Sauvignonasse. It was a well-known in California in the 1880s, probably first imported in the late 1850s by Charles LEFRANC. Evaluations of its pre-Prohibition wines describe a variety of far more character and appeal than the one we see today. It has been suggested that California's Sauvignon vert is actually the Muscadelle of Bordeaux. Some of it might have been, but what survives has few of the Muscadelle's virtues. Whatever it was years ago, it won a Grand Prize at the 1915 Panama-Pacific Exposition for the Charles KRUG estate. Its advocates were such guardians of quality in California wine as Jacob SCHRAM and George HUSMANN. After Repeal what was growing in the northern coastal counties was used to produce wine labeled sauterne by premium and country jug wineries. At this time, and until 1966, California's agricultural statisticians

SBARBORO, ANDREA (1840–1923). The guiding force behind the founding of ITALIAN SWISS COLONY* and one of the most influential leaders of the California wine industry before Prohibition. The seventh child of a well-educated Italian farmer, he and his family came to the United States in 1843 and to California in 1852. He worked as an accountant and school teacher in San Francisco's North Beach. In the 1870s he founded a building and loan association; his original organization of Italian Swiss Colony was on the financing principles of a building and loan collective.

Sbarboro was the public man, the visible image of Italian Swiss Colony. He created a great wine estate at Asti that attracted many world-famous visitors to northern California, including members of the Italian royal family. By 1900 the enterprise was selling the leading wine brand in the United States, partly because of Sbarboro's excellent work in public relations

In 1897 Sbarboro had a gigantic underground vat constructed to hold that year's red wine vintage at ITALIAN SWISS COLONY. After its 500,000 gallons were drained the following March, he brought guests up to Asti from San Francisco by train and held a fancy-dress ball, replete with brass band, in the huge container. Sbarboro made sure that the event had national press coverage. (Vintage Image, Wine Appreciation Guild)

and partly because of the good wine made by Pietro ROSSI.

In 1908 Sbarboro set out to save the California wine industry from prohibition. He was instrumental in forming the California Grape Protective Association and fought unsuccessfully to separate the interests of the wine industry from those of the saloon and the beer industry. He wrote a series of pamphlets advocating wine as a temperance beverage. But much of his work was viewed with distrust and cynicism by other leaders of the wine industry. Too late, in 1916, they took up his arguments. Years later Leon ADAMS owned that Sbarboro's writing had helped move him "to try to civilize drinking in America."

When Sbarboro died in 1923, he was mourned as one of San Francisco's great pioneer leaders, a Renaissance man of great integrity and vision.

SCHARFFENBERGER CELLARS (BW 5592). Years before the name Scharffenberger was associated with fine California sparkling wine, it was the vineyard designation of several outstanding vintages of FETZER Zinfandel made with grapes from the Scharffenberger

family's 70-acre vineyard in Redwood Valley, Mendocino.

In 1981 John Scharffenberger began producing sparkling wine; production was up to 25,000 cases a year by 1986. He has planted 70 acres of vines on his 680-acre ranch in the Anderson Valley, Mendocino County, a purchase made possible when the French Champagne house of Pommery & Lanson in 1989 became a major partner in his venture. A new champagnery went up in 1991 near Philo, but now the controlling interest is held by Moët-Hennessey. Annual production is about 30,000 cases.

Since 1994 Scharffenberger and his partner, Casey Hartlip, have been producing Zinfandel, Sangiovese, and Syrah under the Lonetree label from grapes produced at their Eaglepoint Ranch in the hills above the Anderson Valley.

SCHEFFLER, WILLIAM. See EDGE HILL VINEYARD

SCHENLEY DISTILLERS. When the U.S. government limited liquor production at the beginning of World War II, some of the large distillers moved into the California wine industry. Most moved out quickly after 1945, but Schenley Distillers stayed a while. In 1941 the company bought CRESTA BLANCA and then ROMA and several other wine properties in the Central Valley. The company even owned GREYSTONE, in Napa, for a while. In 1968 Schenley was acquired by the Glen Alden Corporation, which in 1971 sold most of its wine properties to GUILD WINERIES. For a brief time in the late 1980s, Schenley again had a hand in California wine when its subsidiary, Renfield Imports, acquired control of RODNEY STRONG VINEYARDS.

SCHEUREBE. A variety of white-wine grape that is a cross between White Riesling and Sylvaner made by Georg Scheu in 1916. It has become popular in Germany for its early ripening and delicious flavors. In the 1980s JOSEPH PHELPS and BALVERNE VINEYARDS made well-received wines from the variety. But it did not catch on as consumers' tastes in those years generally moved away from white table wines made in a German style.

SCHILLING, CLAUS (1847–1925). The Schilling family is well known for dealing in coffee, tea, and spices in California's early years. Claus Schilling's company worked with the CALIFORNIA WINE ASSOCIATION, but its separate properties are of historic interest. After losing more than a million gallons of wine in the earthquake and fire in 1906, Schilling built a winery in San Francisco's Portrero District that held 2 million gallons and covered an entire city block. He also owned LA PERLA* on Spring Mountain for many years. Connoisseurs considered his brand, Lomas Azulas, one of the finest and most dependable in pre-Prohibition California. His wines won a Grand Prize and several gold medals at the 1915 Panama-Pacific Exposition. When Schilling retired in 1917, his company was taken over by the California Wine Association.

After Repeal the Schilling Co. revived its wine operation, functioning as both a wine wholesaler and producer until the 1950s. The company styled itself the House of Private Labels, performing functions similar to what we today call CUSTOM CRUSHING. The winery (BW 4361) was located near Cloverdale. Some kosher wine was also produced there.

SCHOENEWALD, GEORGE (1843–1918). When he was the manager of the Hotel Del Monte in Monterey in the early 1880s, Schoenewald always had a fine list of California table wines. After he established his Esmeralda Winery in 1882 in St. Helena, in Napa, he developed an excellent reputation for his own table wines. His beautiful estate, Lyndenhurst, was just up the street from the winery and today is the SPOTTSWOODE WINERY.

Schoenewald's greatest contribution to wine in California came in the 1890s when he led the search in Napa for the best resistant ROOTSTOCK. After Repeal Esmeralda became the Montebello Winery (see MONTEBELLO WINE CO.) and part of the old structure is now a private residence.

SCHOONMAKER, FRANK (1905–76). As Repeal approached in the late 1920s, the *New Yorker* magazine had Schoonmaker, who was a journalist, write a series of articles on wine, which he later combined into his *Complete Wine Book,* published in 1934. Knowing little about California wine, he had Tom Marvel, an occasional writer on the subject, write the section on the sorry situation of wine in the Golden State at the end of Prohibition. As war clouds gathered in the late 1930s, Schoonmaker sensed that good California wine might be quite profitable if European sources were cut off. He organized a wine sales company and lined up the best wine producers from Napa, Sonoma, Alameda, and Santa Clara counties. In the process he collected material for his influential *American Wines,* published in 1941 in which he and Marvel argued for varietal labeling and for the identification of winegrowing districts on bottles of California wine. Two days after 7 December 1941 he was in the American intelligence corps (OSS) and was soon in Europe posing as a wine merchant. He spent lots of time in Spain talking up sherry and gathering information on German intelligence operations there.

After the war he went to work at ALMADEN, in which he had a financial interest. He continued to fight for varietal labeling. In 1964 his *Encyclopedia of Wine* gave American wine lovers a worldwide perspective with a solid focus on California. In many ways I have modeled this work on Schoonmaker's encyclopedia.

It is difficult to assess the effect of a writer's work on the course of events in the real world, but certainly Schoonmaker's vision of what wine could and should be has influenced the development of high standards for California wines. His tenacious advocacy of varietal labeling, long resisted and ridiculed by many in the

California wine industry, may be his greatest contribution to California wine.

James T. Lapsley, *Bottled Poetry: Napa Winemaking from Prohibition to the Modern Era* (Berkeley, Calif.: University of California Press, 1996).

SCHRAM, JACOB (1826–1905). Born in the Rheinhessen at Pfeddersheim, Schram came to America in 1840 and to California in 1852, with a clear vision of winegrowing as a natural and wholesome way of life. Like so many Germans, he found his way to Napa. There in 1862 he acquired a piece of virgin land on Mount Diamond in the western hills between St. Helena and Calistoga. This was to be his SCHRAMS-BERG,* which he cleared and planted mostly to white-wine varieties of German origin. His youthful understanding of such things made him believe that the finest wine came from the steepest slopes.

By the end of the decade, he was considered an expert on the production of white wine from such varieties as White Riesling

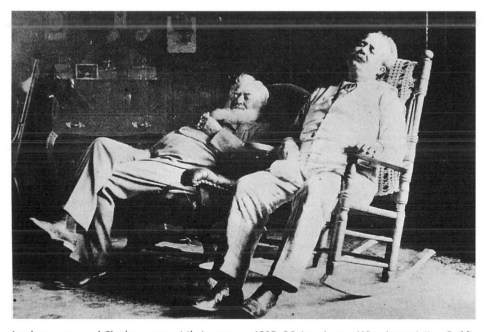

Jacob SCHRAM and Charles CARPY at their ease, ca. 1895. (Vintage Image, Wine Appreciation Guild)

and Sylvaner. Years later Frona WAIT called him the "Nestor of Napa Valley vignerons," so influential were his views on the best varieties for the best wines. He was one of the first men in Napa to tout Zinfandel as a fine table wine variety. Charles KRUG loved to point out Schram as the embodiment of the American dream, a poor man who made his way through hard work and fair dealing, and through an intelligent application of knowledge to his business. Before coming to Napa, Schram had been an itinerant barber and continued to clip tourists' heads at various local resorts years after he had dug the first tunnel for his wines.

Schram produced a wide range of table wines, red and white. The top of his line, the Riesling-Hock, famous by the late 1870s, was on the wine lists of many first-class hotels and resorts. He also made lots of ordinary wine that had a good reputation for quality and value. Part of his success came from his ability to blend a bit of MUSCAT with ordinary varieties such as Palomino and Burger. His red burgundy was a favorite of EUGENE HILGARD.

Total production was about 5,000 gallons in the early 1870s. By 1882 he was up to 30,000. In the 1880s he expanded his cellars and in 1889 built the great home that still stands above the modern winery. By then his son Herman (who had one of the finest tenor voices in the Napa Valley) was a full partner and was in complete charge during his parents' declining years. Herman sold the estate shortly before Prohibition.

It is common to read of Schram's fame being the result of a visit by Robert Louis Stevenson in 1880, memorialized by the chapter "Napa Wine" in *Silverado Squatters*. This is not true. Stevenson was taken to Schramsberg because it was one of the most respected and noteworthy wine estates in the area, certainly of interest to a winelover such as RLS.

sparkling wine on his estate, but today it is the site of one of the best producers in California. There were two failed tries here before Jack (1923–98) and Jamie Davies bought the property in 1965. Joseph Gargano in the 1940s never even got a bond for his operations, but in 1951 Douglas Pringle did operate Mount Diamond Cellars here and sold some wine for a few years. The Davies family acquired the Pringle bond and soon some of the old vineyards were restored and the historic tunnels cleaned up.

Peter MONDAVI made the wine in 1965 for the first Schramsberg CUVÉE. Next year it was made on the mountain. By then four producers in California were making sparkling wine by the *méthode champenoise*. The first release, 250 cases of the 1965 Blanc de Blancs from Chardonnay and Pinot blanc, came in 1967. Others from several varietals and in numerous styles followed. The Schramsberg fame grew exponentially in 1972 when President Nixon took a Davies sparkler on his trip to China.

Sales grew in the 1970s and 1980s, leveling at an annual average of about 40,000 cases per year. The 250-acre estate has 75 acres of vines above the winery in a bucolic setting not much changed in the past hundred years.

Schramsberg was also involved in making brandy in the Carneros with the owners of Rémy Martin cognac brand from 1982 to 1987. Before that and for a while afterward the winery actually imported cognac and sold it under the historic ECLIPSE label. More recently the winery and a Portuguese producer joined forces to make a sparkler to be sold in Portugal. The wine, Vértice, was released in 1993. The year before a new prestige line was introduced at Schramsberg under the J. Schram label.

Jack L. Davies and Jamie Peterman Davies, *Building Schramsberg: The Creation of a California Champagne House* (Regional Oral History Office, Bancroft Library, 1990).

SCHRAMSBERG VINEYARDS CO. (BW 4329). Jacob SCHRAM never made commercial

SCHUG CARNEROS ESTATE (BW 5309). When Walter Schug was JOSEPH PHELPS'S winemaker from 1973 to 1983, it was not apparent from his successful line of fine Cabernets and elegant German-style whites where his real love lay. He had come to California in 1961 after earning degrees in enology and viticulture at the Geisenheim Institute. But from 1923 to 1959 his father had run the State Domain at Assmannshausen, where Germany's best Spätburgunder, what we call Pinot noir, is produced.

In 1980 Schug began making Pinot noir under his own label and later acquired a small winemaking facility near Yountville. He established his brand with an emphasis on Pinot noir and Chardonnay. In 1990 he acquired 50 acres on the Sonoma side of the Carneros and began building his winery there and drilling aging tunnels. Production is about 15,000 cases, with a sizeable portion of that going to export.

SEAGRAM. A company with a long and complex relationship with the wine industry in California. The origins of the worldwide spirits conglomerate are in Canada where in 1857 Joseph E. Seagram & Son began operations in Waterloo, Ontario. During Prohibition in America, the company was acquired by Samuel Bronfman, who developed the industrial giant. His family still controls much of the stock of Seagram Co., Ltd. and directs its operations. His grandson, Samuel Bronfman II, is in charge of the company's California wine operations, Seagram Classics Wine Co.

Like other distillers during World War II, Seagram acquired wine property in California, but unlike others did not quickly sell it after V-J Day. Bronfman, through his interest in the firm of Fromm & Sichel, acquired control of PAUL MASSON and became a principal in the CHRISTIAN BROTHERS operation.

In 1983, intending to challenge GALLO for primacy in the mid-priced California wine field, Seagram bought COCA-COLA's interest in STERLING,* MONTEREY VINEYARD, and TAYLOR CALIFORNIA CELLARS and acquired facilities in the Central Valley and Central Coast

that had a total capacity of 19 million gallons. The result was a series of huge losses.

In 1987 Paul Masson and Taylor were sold to a group of investors who formed Vintners International. Seagram holdings today still include Sterling and Monterey Vineyard, and their international holdings have placed MUMM NAPA VALLEY in their hands. In 1986 Seagram acquired Rene DI ROSA's famous Winery Lake Vineyard, the grapes from which now go to Sterling and Mumm Napa Valley.

SEA RIDGE WINERY (BW 4975). Daniel and Dee Wickham began operating their winery in 1988 in the western Sonoma town of Occidental. Their property was on the site of Lee Morelli's Lemorel Winery (BW 1067), which had operated from 1903 to 1964. Sea Ridge has had other premises in Sonoma since the first crush in 1980. Annual production of about 2,500 cases emphasized Pinot noir and old-vine Zinfandel. In 1996 the winery closed down.

SEAVEY VINEYARD (BW 5545). In 1876 Germain Crochat (1822–94) and Fred Metzner (1841–1916) began planting vines in Conn Valley in Napa and the next year built a 60,000-gallon stone winery, calling it the Franco-Swiss Winery. They were making 100,000 gallons of wine a year in the mid-1880s, but Crochat's death and the economic depression of the 1890s brought an end to production in 1894. The vineyards were not replanted after Prohibition until William Seavey bought the property in 1979 and planted 35 acres to Cabernet Sauvignon and Chardonnay. He sold all the grapes until 1990 when he began making wine in one of the renovated stone buildings there. Annual production is about 1,500 cases.

SEBASTIANI VINEYARDS (BW 876). Samuele Sebastiani (1874–1944) came to California from Tuscany in 1895 and in 1904 bought an old winery building in Sonoma. In 1908 he had a new winery and was shipping wine east in bulk. In 1916 he began shipping grapes east for home winemakers. His annual production was up to 350,000 gallons when Prohibition struck. He continued to prosper during the dry years, producing sacramental and medicinal wine, shipping grapes east, and investing in real estate and businesses in Sonoma. By the 1930s, he was one of the most influential civic leaders in town, and one of the richest.

At Repeal Samuele's son August (1913–80) began taking an active role at the bulk winery. Soon the Sebastianis had added a production plant near Lodi, which they sold in 1954. In that year August began bottling and selling wine under his SS label. By the 1960s the Sebastiani label had become associated with good varietal wine, mostly red. Production was about 25,000 cases.

By the 1970s the boom in California wine was bringing huge profits to the winery. In 1975 annual sales were up to 500,000 cases. It was then that August began marketing varietals in jugs. Meanwhile he had become something of a media character, even in his trademark bib overalls, always ready to quip about his little family winery, even though it was worth millions. His death in 1980 brought his son Sam to the helm, at a moment when profits were slipping. August's widow, Sylvia, retained legal control. Sam's brother, Don (who is twelve years younger), was elected to the state legislature that year. At a time when many wine operations were being forced to modify their marketing approach and modernize their plants, Sam's attempts led to $3.3 million in losses between 1982 and 1985. In 1986 Sylvia and other family members fired Sam as chief executive officer; Don took over the direction of operations. Sam left to found VIANSA WINERY.*

Since those years Sebastiani has continued to grow and now has a capacity of almost 15 million gallons, much of this from the acquisition in 1987 of a plant in Lodi-Woodbridge. From this facility comes the Sebastianis' Vendange line of FIGHTING VARIETALS that accounts for almost one-third of the annual 7 million-case production. Other Sebastiani brands are Heritage, Talus, and Nathanson Creek.

In Sonoma the family still owns more than 300 acres of vineyards that supply most of the grapes for the premium wines still bearing the Sebastiani label, an example of which is the Sonoma Cask Barbera that won a gold medal at the 1997 Sonoma Harvest Fair.

SEGHESIO WINERIES (BW 850, 56). The Seghesio family provides one of the most powerful elements of historical continuity in Sonoma County. Eduardo Seghesio (1860–1934) came to California from Italy in 1886 to work at ITALIAN SWISS COLONY. He was from the Piedmont town of Dogliani, the hometown of his employer, Pietro ROSSI. In 1895 Seghesio bought 36 acres of vineyard land near Geyserville and sold grapes to Italian Swiss Colony. In 1902 he built his winery at what came to be called Chianti Station on the Northwestern Pacific Railroad. He now sold wine to Italian Swiss Colony and was also shipping it east in bulk. When Prohibition came, Seghesio had production up to 100,000 gallons. During Prohibition Seghesio, Enrico Prati, and the Rossi brothers acquired control of the old Italian Swiss Colony estate at Asti, Seghesio pulling out after a few years.

After Repeal the bulk wine business continued in earnest and the family was able to expand its vineyard holdings to more than 400 acres. In 1949 the Seghesios bought the Scatena Brothers Winery, which had been built in 1911; production now topped 1 million gallons with sales to GALLO, PAUL MASSON, and others. But the business was weakening in the 1970s and the family began moving toward production under its own label. The first wines appeared in 1983, a selection of reds from the 1975 and 1976 vintages. Today production stands at about 75,000 cases. The family owns six vineyards between Healdsburg and Cloverdale totaling

400 acres, and produces a wide range of varietals under the Seghesio label. Sold under the Chianti Station label is a red wine made partly from grapes of the old Tuscan vines that Eduardo Seghesio planted in 1910, among which is the Sangiovese.

SÉMILLON. A white Bordeaux variety of grape that has declined in popularity in recent years, acreage in California having dropped about 60 percent since 1985. Today it is most often used to blend with Sauvignon blanc, but one still occasionally sees a varietal bottling. A few wineries have also blended it with Chardonnay. In Bordeaux it has been an essential element of the white wines of Grâves. In Sauternes it is absolutely essential because of its susceptibility to *botrytis cinerea,* the noble rot. In California it is a good quality grape that never caught on as a varietal.

Its practical introduction to California is not documented, although it was among the vines that HARASZTHY imported in 1862. It certainly was imported by J. H. DRUMMOND, Charles WETMORE, and J.-C. DE ST. HUBERT between 1878 and 1880. H. W. CRABB had it in his vineyard in 1881. By 1885 it could be found throughout the vineyards of northern California. Its wines were never sold as a varietal, only as SAUTERNE,* and usually blended with one or more other varieties. Sometimes it was included

in a sweet version, often labeled Haut Sauterne. After Repeal it continued in this function, but by the 1960s there were several varietal Sémillons on the market. The variety found particular favor in the Livermore Valley, as it had before Prohibition. In 1990 the state crush was 12,901 tons, in 1996 it was 6,774 tons.

In recent years a few wineries have produced successful sweet Sémillons. The variety's ability to age gracefully has also given the grape a small but loyal following. In 1993 a group of producers came together styling themselves as the Society of Sémillonards, with members in California, Washington, and Australia. The leaders in California have been FAR NIENTE, SIGNORELLO, WENTE, ALDERBROOK, CLOS DU VAL, CLINE, and BERINGER.

SEQUOIA GROVE VINEYARDS (BW 5000). In 1979 the Allen family bought 24 acres of vineyard land, part of the old Downey Ranch in Rutherford in the Napa Valley. In 1980 the Allens bonded their 15,000-gallon winery and, within five years, production of Chardonnay and Cabernet Sauvignon had reached 12,000 cases a year. In 1985 they took on a limited partner, Korbrand, the wine and spirits importer. Since then they have acquired a sizeable acreage in the Carneros and annual production has reached 25,000 cases.

TABLE 31. SÉMILLON GRAPES, SELECTED COUNTIES AND CENTRAL VALLEY

				(ACRES)		
YEAR	SONOMA	NAPA	MONTEREY	CENTRAL VALLEY	ALAMEDA	TOTAL
1959	N.A.	N.A.	N.A.	N.A.	N.A.	1,272
1964	158	226	0	246	520	1,284
1972	198	212	285	1,290	356	2,489
1979	127	125	644	1,411	298	2,754
1985	268	220	673	1,286	141	3,039
1990	195	345	397	990	110	2,229
1997	154	214	142	739	74	1,338

SOURCE: California Agricultural Statistics Service, Sacramento, Calif.

SERRA, JUNIPERO (1713–84). In 1769 this Father-President of the Baja California missions established the first MISSION* in Alta California at San Diego. By tradition, sentiment, and misinformation, the first California wines have been traced to vines he brought to San Diego. There is no good evidence to support this story, even though the state's wine industry in 1969 made a great display in celebrating the 200th anniversary of California wine. But Serra did have a hand in getting the province's first wine produced in 1782. One of his steady complaints was the lack of wine for the Roman Catholic Mass: "Many Masses have not been said because of our lack of wine." In 1778 he was eventually able to get vines to Mission San Juan Capistrano.

SETRAKIAN, ARPAXAT (SOX) (1884–1974), was for years a power in the California wine industry and a leader in the Central Valley raisin industry. In 1936 he established the CALIFORNIA GROWERS WINERY near Cutler in Tulare County. His 10 million-gallon operation was producing brandy and fortified wines until in the 1970s, his family shifted much of their production to inexpensive table wine; see also GOLDEN STATE VINTNERS.

SHADOW BROOK WINERY (BW 5224). Emil Hoffman bonded his little winery on Zinfandel Lane in Napa in 1984. He has 48 acres of vines there and below Yountville. Annual production of about 4,500 cases emphasizes Chardonnay, Pinot noir, and Merlot.

SHADOW CREEK. A popular brand of *méthode champenoise* sparkling wine that first became available in 1978. George Vore, a wine consultant, bought finished wine from CHATEAU ST. JEAN and was soon making sparklers at St. Jean's Graton facility in Sonoma County. So successful was the brand that COR-BETT CANYON acquired it in 1985 and production shifted to San Luis Obispo County.

When Glenmore sold Corbett Canyon Vineyard to the WINE GROUP in 1988, DOMAINE CHANDON bought the brand. Today the Shadow Creek label is used by Chandon for the California sparkling wine that it markets in the United Kingdom.

SHAFER VINEYARDS (BW 4897). In 1972 John Shafer acquired a rugged 210-acre plot right under the famous Stag's Leap palisades. He was able to plant 65 acres of the old Battista Scansi ranch, mostly to Cabernet Sauvignon. His first two vintages, 1978 and 1979, were made at another winery, and the 1978 won fame when it defeated seventy-one other Cabernets in a blind tasting held in 1981 by the San Francisco Vintners Club. In 1980 his own winery was operating and soon he had 17 more acres planted a few miles south on Silverado Trail. His vineyard acreage is now up to 140 after he bought in the Carneros in 1988. Since 1983, Shafer's Hillside Select from small vineyards with such names as Firebreak, Rattler, and Lookout, has been his leading Cabernet. There is also Merlot, Chardonnay, and a bit of Sangiovese in the winery's 25,000-case annual production.

SHASTA COUNTY. The northernmost county in the Central Valley, most of it inhospitable to fine wine grapes, but there are plenty of foothills there. In 1890 there were twenty-one small wineries in the county; in the 1930s there were three wineries and 320 acres of vines; today there are only 36 acres of vines, 21 of them planted recently in the foothills, but no wineries.

CHARLES F. SHAW WINERY (BW 4930). In 1972 Charles Shaw bought 35 acres of vineyard land north of St. Helena near old Bale Mill in the Napa Valley. A lover of red Beaujolais wines, he began producing GAMAY wines by the CAR-BONIC MACERATION process in 1979. He was reputed to be the only winegrower in Califor-

SHERRY 327

nia with vines of the authentic *Gamay noir à jus blanc* in his vineyard. In 1992 he went out of business and sold his property. The new owners first styled their operation Bella Luna, then Benessere Vineyards. Production now is about 5,000 cases, mainly Sangiovese and Zinfandel.

SHENANDOAH VALLEY. To a great extent the history of winegrowing in AMADOR COUNTY* is the history of the bucolic Shenandoah Valley in the Sierra foothills. Lying northeast of the town of Plymouth, it has about 1,250 acres of vines, mostly Zinfandel, but many other varieties do well here. The area acquired AVA status in 1983. Because there might be a few grape vines in Virginia's valley of the same name, and not wanting to cause confusion, the official title given by the BATF is California Shenandoah Valley Viticultural Area. The area now has thirteen wineries.

SHENANDOAH VINEYARDS (BW 4809). Leon Sobon bought 74 acres in the Shenandoah Valley in Amador County in 1977 and went into the wine business. Zinfandel has been at the center of his production, lots of it White Zinfandel for the quick dollars it produces. He also makes hearty red Zinfandel, Cabernet Sauvignon, Sauvignon blanc, and several dessert wines, producing about 30,000 cases per year. In 1989 he bought the historic D'AGOSTINI WINERY, which he now operates as SOBON ESTATE.

SHERRILL CELLARS (BW 4632). Nat and Jan Sherrill bonded their San Mateo County winery in the basement of the Woodside post office in 1973. In 1978 they moved it to their home in the hills above Palo Alto. Their production, from grapes purchased all over northern and central California, was always small, averaging about 2,500 cases per year of a wide range of varietals. In 1996 they put the property up for sale and began retiring the winery, after buying a ranch near Paso Robles.

SHERRY. In the English-speaking world the fortified wine produced in Jerez de la Frontera in Spain is called sherry. Wine of the same sort is made in other regions, including California, where the term sherry is a legal generic. Sherry can range from bone dry to richly sweet, from pale yellow to dark brown. It has many functions. Usually drunk as an apéritif or as a dessert wine, it is sometimes served as a table wine.

For most wines, oxidization is a flaw, but sherry is oxidized purposely. A base white wine, such as that made from PALOMINO grapes, is fermented and then fortified with grape spirits. Now referred to as sherry material, or shermat, the fortified wine is oxidized by being baked in large tanks, or set out in barrels, in the sun. Another method involves the use of a special yeast strain called flor. Traditional in Spain, the flor system was developed in California for large-scale operations after World War II by scientists at the University of California at Davis. The result is a sherry with an especially pungent bouquet and flavor. Another element of sherry production in Spain and occasionally in California is the solera system, a process of fractional blending in which wine is moved through a succession of barrels, some of the older material constantly being kept back to blend with the newer entering the system.

It might have been difficult to distinguish an old ANGELICA from a California sherry in the 1870s, but several producers in Napa, Sonoma, and the Central Valley did make good sherries; see Joseph MATTHEWS. Professor Eugene HILGARD at the University of California at Berkeley worked on sherry experiments with NATOMA VINEYARD CO. in the 1880s. By the next decade the quality had improved, at least if the evaluations given the California products at the 1893 Columbian Exposition are taken as evidence. But between 1886 and 1913, while California law required fortifying brandy to have a sugar content of at least 4 percent, dry sherry was very rare here.

In the years before Prohibition about 25 percent of California's fortified wine was sherry, close to 5 million gallons. After Repeal the percentage remained about the same, but the total jumped up to about 20 million gallons. After 1960 sales of all California fortified wines collapsed, sherry included. Nevertheless a few producers—L. M. MARTINI, LLORDS & ELWOOD, and ALMADEN—still made a good product and some even maintained old solera systems.

SHEWAN-JONES (BW 3130). Before Lee Jones founded the National Fruit Products Co. in Lodi in 1920, he had helped run George WEST's El Pinal operation. National Fruit produced virtually everything legally possible from a grape during Prohibition. Just before Repeal the company became Shewan-Jones, a 2 million-gallon winery. Jones's first product was a wine concoction with an alcohol content of 3.2 percent, which was legal a few months before total Repeal. He called it La Conquesta.

Later his brand became Lejon, from his own name. Under the superintendency of the winemaster, Elbert McSherry Brown, Lejon became one of America's most popular wine and brandy labels. In 1942 Jones sold the operation to National Distillers. They closed the plant down in 1949 and the label is now owned by the WINE GROUP.

SHORB, JAMES DE BARTH (1842–96). After he married B. D. WILSON's* daughter in 1867, Shorb leased the old pioneer's winery and vineyard. He expanded the operation as the Lake Vineyard Co. By 1875 he had raised wine production to 150,000 gallons and brandy to 160,000. The wine boom in the 1880s moved him to further expansion, incorporated now as the San Gabriel Wine Co. Between 1883 and 1885 he planted about 1,000 acres of vines, bringing his total to about 1,500. Meanwhile he became the southern Californian member of the STATE VITICULTURAL COMMISSION.

The wine depression of the 1890s soon brought Shorb and his partners to their knees. By the time of his death the company was in the hands of disgruntled investors and creditors. The lands were eventually divided and in 1903 Shorb's huge winery was converted into a felt factory. Today the Huntington Library and art galleries stand on land once planted to vines grown by Shorb and B. D. Wilson.

SIERRA FOOTHILLS. Perhaps the oldest important agrarian activity on the land that attracted the first waves of Argonauts in the Gold Rush was viticulture. Grapes were grown to eat and to make wine. Descriptions of the gold country towns in the 1860s, in the years after the rage for gold had abated, almost always included the splendor of the vines. In several areas a small local wine industry developed. Old vineyards survived in soils where the sting of PHYLLOXERA was almost never felt. In the modern wine revolution of the 1960s, old vineyards that had survived there became treasures, particularly if planted to Zinfandel. The high quality of their wines encouraged a renaissance in winegrowing here.

In 1987 the BATF established the Sierra Foothills Viticultural Area. The ruling covered a large area with elevations ranging from 500 feet in Jackson Valley to 3,500 feet in Mariposa County. It included foothill land in Yuba, Nevada, Placer, El Dorado, Amador, Calaveras, Tuolumne, and Mariposa counties. (See entries on the individual counties for additional information.) The area encompasses about 4,200 square miles and runs about 170 miles from Yuba to Mariposa counties. Today there are about 3,900 acres of vines in the foothills area, almost 90 percent in red varieties. In 1985 there were 2,825 acres, in 1975 there were 1,410. There are about forty wineries in the area.

SIERRA MADRE VINTAGE CO. The historically uncomplimentary image of the qual-

By the 1920s little survived of the early wine industry in the Sierra foothills. Here is Lombardo Fossati's little winery near Placerville, built in the late 1860s. The vineyards had been replaced by apples and pears by the 1930s. Today the little structure, again surrounded by vines, serves as the BOEGER WINERY tasting room.

ity of table wine made in southern California rarely taken into account the high quality of the wines produced between 1880 and 1915 in the upper foothills of what is today Pasadena and neighboring cities. The Sierra Madre Winery, at Lamanda Park, today part of Pasadena, is the best example. The first vineyards were planted in 1871, and the winery built in 1885 by Albert Brigdon and J. F. Clark. The red table wines produced here won numerous awards, including a gold medal at Paris in 1900. An 1895 Zinfandel tasted in 1976 was "still fruity and complete, old but still alive," according to the tasters. Local option, Prohibition, and the advance of suburbia brought an end to the operation in 1923, many years before polluted air would have made it impossible to grow good grapes.

SIERRA VISTA WINERY (BW 4791). In 1974 John and Barbara Macready planted the first 5 acres of Cabernet Sauvignon on their estate in El Dorado County. The elevation of their vineyard near Placerville, at about 2,800 feet, was thought risky at the time. Later they planted Zinfandel and Sauvignon blanc. More recently Rhône varieties have been added. In 1977 they bonded their rustic little winery. Today production is about 8,000 cases per year. In the 1990s Sierra Vista joined the RHONE RANGERS with bottlings of Syrah and Viognier, and a Grenache-based blend, labeled Fleur de Montagne, made in the style of the southern Rhône.

SIERRA WINE CO. (BW 1438). Wineries on this property near Tulare have operated under several names since Frank Giannini built the first one in 1902. Later it was the Tulare Winery, then the Argun Wine Co., and has been Sierra since 1963. Today it is a 16 million-gallon bulk operation that produces table and fortified wine and brandy. The plant is part of the WINE GROUP.

SIEVERS, FRANCIS. See VOLKER EISELE FAMILY ESTATE

SIGNORELLO VINEYARDS (BW 5461). In 1977 Raymond Signorello bought vineyard land along the Silverado Trail in Napa Valley. He planted red Bordeaux varieties, Chardonnay, and Sauvignon blanc, later adding Rhône and Italian varieties. He bonded his winery in 1985. Today there about 100 acres of vines with production at about 8,000 cases. Signorello makes a wide and varying line of varietal wines that have received high marks for quality from critics.

SILVERADO HILL CELLARS (BW 4939). John Nemeth founded the Pannonia Winery on the Silverado Trail in Napa in 1979. A native of Hungary, he named the winery after an ancient Roman province partly contained in modern Hungary. The winery failed in 1983 and was bought by Louis Mihaly. For a while it bore his name, and Nemeth stayed on as winemaker. In 1988 the Minami Kyushu Company of Japan bought the operation. Today the winery specializes in Chardonnay production, a large part of it from the 30-acre estate vineyard. Annual production has risen in recent years to about 40,000 cases.

SILVERADO VINEYARDS (BW 5064). An impressive winegrowing operation that goes back to 1976 when members of the late Walt Disney's family bought land in the STAGS LEAP DISTRICT* of Napa Valley. Vineyards were planted and a beautiful winery built in 1981 on a hill just west of the Silverado Trail. Today the winery is run by Disney's daughter, Diane Disney Miller, and her husband, Ron. It has grown to be an 80,000-case-a-year operation with about 350 acres of vines in several locations in Napa. Chardonnay is the leading varietal, but

in recent years their Stags Leap Cabernets have brought the winery much praise. Merlot and Sauvignon blanc are also important.

In 1988 Silverado bought a ranch in Soda Canyon in the hills east of the winery, the site of Felix Borreos's Bay View Winery and Vineyard that was established in 1888. The first vines planted by the new owners were Sangiovese and Zinfandel.

SILVER MOUNTAIN VINEYARDS (BW 4940). Jerold O'Brien bought his land in the Santa Cruz Mountains above Los Gatos in 1979. His 7-acre Chardonnay vineyard gradually came into full production in the 1980s. But the centerpiece of his annual 2,000-case production is Monterey Chardonnay from VENTANA VINEYARDS. He also makes Merlot and Zinfandel. The 1989 Loma Prieta earthquake hit O'Brien's little winery harder than any other, but it was back in production in two years.

SILVER OAK WINE CELLARS (BW 4624, 5674). Raymond Meyer was a football star before he attended St. Mary's College in Moraga, California, where he took a degree in economics. Then, as a member of the CHRISTIAN BROTHERS, he became Brother Justin. Eventually he was supervising cellar operations for the Brothers' Napa wine facilities. After he left the order he, now Justin Meyer, met Raymond Duncan and they formed a partnership to produce great Cabernet Sauvignon. In the buildings of the old Oakville Dairy they made a 1972 Cabernet from grapes grown in the Alexander Valley in Sonoma County. It was not released until 1977, because another of the partners' goals was to have their wines drinkable on release but capable of much longer cellaring.

They were sidetracked somewhat in 1975 when they bought the floundering FRANCISCAN VINEYARDS. They put that operation back on its feet and sold it in 1979. In that year they added two Napa Cabernets to their list, but the Alexander Valley wine remained, and still is, the centerpiece of their production.

Justin and Bonny Meyer live in Napa and have a 3.78-acre vineyard in front of their home. Bonny's Vineyard produces one of the winery's best Cabernets. Silver Oak owns a total of 235 acres of vines, mostly in the Alexander Valley.

In 1993 the partnership bought the LYETH WINERY and its 18-acre vineyard. It is now the production facility for their Alexander Valley Cabernet. Silver Oak wines have developed a loyal following and a very special reputation for power, full flavor, and longevity. Annual production is about 48,000 cases.

SIMI WINERY (BW 2332). The brothers Pietro and Giuseppe Simi came to California in the 1860s and within a few years had established a good trade in produce in San Francisco. They also bought and sold grapes grown in Sonoma County and, in 1876, began making wine in the North Beach area, mostly for restaurants and hotels. In 1881 they bought a small winery near Healdsburg in Sonoma County and were soon prospering. In 1884 they began planting their 128-acre vineyard north of town. By 1890 they were building the fine 200,000-gallon winery that stands today as part of the modern Simi operation. The brothers came from the Tuscan town of Montepulciano and that is what they named their new winery. They prospered during the depression years of the 1890s and continued to expand.

In 1902 Giuseppe took his daughter Isabelle (1890–1981) into the winery as accountant and controller. When her father and her uncle died within weeks of each other in 1904, she and other family members continued to run the operation and to expand. By 1906 they had 400 acres of vines, adding 125 more in 1908. In that year Isabelle married Frederick R. Haigh, a banker. With her husband, Isabelle Simi HAIGH ran the operation until his death in 1954. At Repeal the Simi name was adopted

for the winery's label, although much of the production was for the bulk market. Nevertheless, to attract retail trade along the Old Redwood Highway, Isabelle ran a tasting room in a 25,000-gallon tank set up in front of the winery. Its success encouraged Haigh to expand retail sales and to employ well-known national distributors. For a while Simi wines were featured by the famous Hotel Del Monte in Monterey.

After her husband's death, Mrs. Haigh and her daughter continued to run the tasting room, selling Simi reds from the 1930s and 1940s. In the 1960s the cozy tasting room and museum and its fine old wines became a Mecca for California wine connoisseurs. After her daughter died, Mrs. Haigh in 1970, sold the winery and its fine inventory to Russell Green, an executive of an oil company, but stayed on, working in the new tasting room for 8 more years.

Green modernized the winery and began selling premium varietal wine produced by his new winemaker, Mary Ann Graf, whose degree in enology from the University of California at Davis in 1965 was the first granted to a woman. The winery continued to grow and went through several ownerships until acquired by Moët-Hennessey in 1980. The year before, Zelma LONG* had taken over as the winemaker and is today the chief executive officer of the 150,000-case operation. Chardonnay, her specialty, accounts for well over half of Simi's current production. There is also emphasis on Cabernet Sauvignon and Sauvignon blanc. Simi owns about 300 acres in Sonoma, which supply well over half the winery's needs.

Zelma Long, *The Past is the Beginning of the Future: Simi Winery in its Second Century* (Regional Oral History Office, Bancroft Library, 1992).

SINK WINERY (BW 885). In 1888 Walter D. Sink bought Isaac DE TURK's winery in northern Sonoma County and founded the

Cloverdale Wine Co. The Sink family ran the 150,000-gallon winery until the 1950s. The old structure can still be seen on Highway 128 two miles west of Highway 101.

ROBERT SINSKEY VINEYARDS (BW 5452): Robert Sinskey has about 100 acres of vineyard mostly in the Carneros, but his winery is in Napa on the Silverado Trail in the Stags Leap District. He went into production in 1986 making mainly varietal Pinot noir, Merlot, and Chardonnay. Annual production is about 10,000 cases but is growing as the new Carneros acreage comes to bear. Aries is the winery's second label.

SKY VINEYARDS (BW 4934). In 1979 Lore Olds and Linn Briner began producing Zinfandel from their 14-acre vineyard on Mount Veeder. Yields are low and production rarely reaches 2,000 cases. The wines have a reputation for power, full flavor, and ageability. Their labels are, in fact, works of art.

SMITH & HOOK WINERY (BW 5015). Since 1979, a winery in Monterey County that has specialized in red Bordeaux-style wines, the grapes coming mostly from its terraced vineyard on the foothills west of Soledad. In the mid-1980s their second label, Deer Valley, was very successful. (That label is now owned by CANANDAIGUA.) Smith & Hook's Lone Oak Estate and Hahn Estate labels account for about half of the winery's 65,000-case annual production. In 1990 a devastating fire at the winery destroyed 37,000 cases of wine, but did not seriously hamper the winery's growth.

SMITH, ANTHONY P. (1812–77). A Forty-Niner from New England, Smith had a nursery in Sacramento that was one of the most important in the young state. He had a special interest in viticulture and, in 1858, was one of the first to recognize the possible virtues of Zinfandel for table wine.

SMITH, JULIUS PAUL. See OLIVINA VINEYARD

SMITH-MADRONE VINEYARDS (BW 4825). High on Spring Mountain the brothers Stuart and Charles Smith bought a 200-acre tract of forested land in 1971 and began planting vines. Their little winery went on line in 1977, producing White Riesling, Cabernet Sauvignon, and Chardonnay. By the mid-1980s the latter two had become predominant. Annual output from their 35-acre vineyard varies but averages about 5,000 cases.

SMOTHERS WINERY (BW 5668). In 1972 Thomas B. Smothers III bought a 110-acre ranch near Glen Ellen in Sonoma County; in 1980 he began planting vines. He named the place Remick Ridge after his grandfather, Ed Remick. In 1974 Richard R. Smothers bought the Vine Hill Ranch in the Santa Cruz Mountains, with its vineyard of 20-year-old white varietals. For a few years he sold grapes to his neighbor, BARGETTO'S SANTA CRUZ WINERY.

Thus did the Smothers Brothers, the famous comedy team, enter the California wine business. In 1977 Dick hooked up with the folks at the FELTON-EMPIRE winery to produce his wines. The operation was called Vine Hill Wines and the white varietals developed a fine reputation. But 1984 was the last vintage.

For a while in the 1980s, the brothers teamed to sell purchased wine that they labeled Mom's Favorite Red and White, about 25,000 cases per year. Meanwhile Tom has developed a 35-acre vineyard at Remick Ridge, now his brand name. Richard ARROWOOD has helped him as winemaker. Annual production is about 4,000 cases per year, mostly Chardonnay, with some Cabernet Sauvignon and Merlot. Dick is living on the East Coast.

SOBON ESTATE (BW 5513). Leon and Shirley Sobon bought the historic D'AGOSTINI WINERY and its vineyards in 1989. They replanted about 75 acres, but kept some of the old Zinfandel vines. They also transformed part of the old winery into a fine regional museum. Their 10,000-case production emphasizes Zinfandel from their own and other vineyards in Amador County and includes some Syrah and Viognier. The Sobons also own SHENANDOAH VINEYARDS.

SOCIETY OF MEDICAL FRIENDS OF WINE. See MEDICAL FRIENDS OF WINE

SOIL. Many contend that the wonderful flavors of the great wines of the world come from the unique mineral content of the specific vineyards in which the grapes are grown. Wine and viticulture scientists, particularly those at the University of California at Davis, contend that there is little scientific basis for this long-held idea. Albert WINKLER holds that "the differences in the character of wines can hardly be attributed to specific soil types . . . In the renowned wine-producing areas of Europe, with their varied soils, HEAT SUMMATION must be accepted as the principal factor in control of quality." Still, the professors have never been able to explain why wines from certain California vineyards but a few hundred yards apart and with identical heat summations, and for which identical vineyard and cellar practices have been employed, have consistently distinct flavors. This aspect of winegrowing may never be explained, but there is plenty of agreement on the basics concerning soil and wine quality.

Grape vines will grow in most soils, but do poorly where there is very heavy clay, poor drainage, or high alkali content. They will grow in shallow soils but, without careful and continuous tending, not well. Deep fertile soils produce the heaviest crops and are best for table and raisin grapes. But wine grape varieties do well in rocky, sandy, even quite infertile soils where other crops would be unsuccessful. In fact, great wines can be grown on shallow, infertile upland soils. "Bacchus loves the steepest slopes," not for heavy-bearing vines but for superior wines.

Wine grapes in California have done well in a wide variety of soils, valley, foothill and upland, to about 2,500 feet. The finest California table wines have been grown in the soils of the valleys and foothills of the Central and North Coast viticultural areas, and in the Sierra foothills above 1,500 feet.

SOLANO COUNTY extends from Vallejo in the San Francisco Bay Area east and well into the Central Valley. Most of this area has almost no history of winegrowing, but the western portion, northwest of Fairfield, is really a geographical extension of Napa County, the soils and climate of its valleys and foothills similar to those of its more famous neighbor. It is this part of Solano County that is included in the NORTH COAST Viticultural Area recognized by the BATF in 1983. Green Valley, Suisun Valley, and Wild Horse Valley are viticultural areas inside Solano's portion of the North Coast AVA. Today there are about 1,700 acres of vines in the county, about 60 percent white, and of those, about 68 percent is Chardonnay. There have been thirteen bonded wineries in the county since Repeal, nine of them since 1980. In 1996 the crush of grapes grown in Solano County amounted to 8,543 tons, Chardonnay, Cabernet Sauvignon, and Merlot being the most plentiful. This total was 140 percent of the tonnage in 1990.

The first vines in the county were probably planted by John and William WOLFSKILL in 1843, a small plot of Mission grapes not far from where the University of California at Davis stands today. Commercial winegrowing began in Green Valley in the 1850s. Cordelia, a town just to the south on the railroad, became a winemaking center, processing local grapes and grapes hauled in from the Central Valley. In 1885 Charles E. Shillaber began building the Cordelia Wine Co., which soon had a 350,000-gallon cellar there. In later years the largest operation was the Solano Winery, built by Louis Mangels in 1893. It continued under various ownerships into the 1960s. The great ruins of its cellars can still be seen north of Interstate 80 at Cordelia.

SOLERA. See SHERRY

SOLIS WINERY. Before Prohibition the foothill area west of Gilroy in Santa Clara County, today referred to as the Hecker Pass region, was called the Solis District. Winegrowing here after 1890 was dominated by the Solis Wine & Fruit Co. After Repeal the Solis Winery (BW 809) was operated by Ezio Scalmanini until 1970. Since 1989 the old Bertero Winery (BW 1625), which was established in 1919, has operated here under new owners as Solis Winery. Production from the 15-acre vineyard and purchased grapes comes to about 6,500 cases per year, mainly Chardonnay and Merlot. The winery sells much of its production to restaurants.

SONOMA COAST. In 1987 the BATF approved this huge viticultural area, which covers 750 square miles and includes about one-third of the vineyard land in Sonoma County. The idea was to place the western portions of the county most affected by a cooling maritime influence into one AVA. In recent years there has been something of a land rush in this area for potential vineyard land to be planted to Pinot noir. Parts of other viticultural areas were included in the larger Sonoma Coast district.

SONOMA COUNTY, in the mid-1990s, led all other coastal counties in acreage devoted to premium wine grapes and in the eyes of American wine consumers was probably the only area in the United States that could challenge neighboring Napa County in overall wine quality.

Sonoma is one of the two original homes of northern California's fine wine industry, the other being the SANTA CLARA Valley. The first vineyard there was probably planted by the RUSSIANS near Fort Ross, a few years before the vineyard at the Sonoma MISSION was established during the 1823–24 dormant season. Ordinary table wine and AGUARDIENTE were the products at the mission and around the little town that grew up there after the mid-1830s. The leader of this tiny outpost on Mexico's Frontera del Norte was Mariano VALLEJO, the military commandant who laid out the town of Sonoma in 1835. Vallejo was interested in winegrowing and was making small quantities of wine and brandy by the 1840s as were several Americans who had settled in the Sonoma Valley before California became part of the United States in 1848, among them, Jacob Primer LEESE and Nicholas Carriger.

Between 1857 and 1860 there was a commercial wine boom in the Sonoma Valley primarily because of the leadership of Agoston

WINEGROWING IN SONOMA COUNTY, 1892

AREA	VINEYARD (ACRES)	WINERY CAPACITY (GALLONS)
SONOMA VALLEY AND GLEN ELLEN	5,535	2,840,000
PETALUMA AND SEBASTOPOL	1,869	270,000
SANTA ROSA, RUSSIAN RIVER, AND DRY CREEK VALLEY	7,894	1,660,000
ALEXANDER VALLEY, GEYSERVILE, AND CLOVERDALE	7,241	2,260,000

TABLE 32. WINE GRAPES IN SONOMA COUNTY, SELECTED VARIETIES

YEAR	PERCENT OF TOTAL RED	WHITE	CABERNET SAUVIGNON	CARIGNANE	(ACRES) CHAR-DONNAY	MERLOT	PETITE SIRAH	PINOT NOIR	ZIN-FANDEL	TOTAL
1920										17,230
1925										20,545
1930										21,710
1938	92	8		2,276			2,973		8,624	20,599
1950	N.A.	N.A.								16,092
1961	81	19	74	1,731	*	0	1,509	81	4,013	11,074
1968	76	24	439	2,011	95	*	1,420	184	4,032	12,365
1972	74	26	2,469	1,736	743	201	1,267	1,190	3,874	17,066
1975	70	30	4,942	1,625	2,578	331	1,728	2,574	3,964	24,400
1980	59	41	4,502	1,071	4,436	484	937	2,798	4,526	27,822
1985	50	50	5,055	796	7,395	498	594	2,710	4,490	31,089
1989	52	48	6,091	399	10,129	457	349	2,946	4,158	32,636
1992	54	46	6,441	323	12,042	2,628	333	3,120	3,963	34,392
1997	55	45	7,011	222	14,398	5,152	268	3,075	4,069	39,059

NOTE: Until 1961, statistics for acreage under various varieties of grapes were not published; figures for 1938 are abberant, if interesting.

* It is believed that some Chardonnay and Merlot grapes were grown, but no official statistics are available.

SOURCE: California Agricultural Statistics Service, Sacramento, Calif.

HARASZTHY and Vallejo and the influx of such notable Germans as Emil DRESEL, Jacob GUNDLACH, and Johann Krohn. Within a few years vineyards were appearing around Glen Ellen and Santa Rosa. The county's wine production jumped from about 23,000 gallons a year in 1859 to about 250,000 gallons in 1863, half of which came from the cellars of Vallejo and BUENA VISTA.

By the mid-1870s Sonoma had about 75 wineries, most in the Sonoma Valley, and had surpassed Los Angeles County in wine production. But many quite distinct winegrowing areas developed in Sonoma County in those early years, as can be seen in the statistics from a county survey made in 1892 when there were 832 vineyards with 23,290 acres in vines, about 10 percent of which had been planted on resistant ROOTSTOCK.

The PHYLLOXERA struck early in Sonoma so that the county was able to replant many of its devastated vineyards sooner than most areas

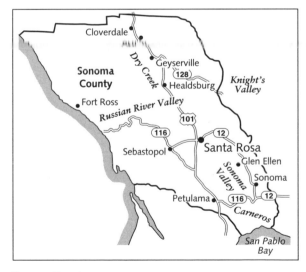

Sonoma County

"I told you we were overdressed..."

SONOMA VALLEY HARVEST WINE AUCTION & BBQ DINNER

SEPTEMBER 4 & 5, 1993 • SONOMA MISSION INN & SPA

Sonoma producers like to portray their part of the California wine country as more casual and down-to-earth than the "other valley" to the east is. This poster for the Sonoma Valley Wine Auction takes a playful jab at Napa's much-publicized celebrity wine auction. Note RAVENSWOOD's motto, "No Wimpy Wines" on the sticker on the hat at the left. (Sonoma Valley Vintners & Growers, photo Ron Zak)

were. By 1901 acreage was back to 15,000 from the low of about 6,000 in the mid-1890s. The county's reputation for fine wine came mostly from the white table wines of the Sonoma Valley. This reputation endured until Prohibition, although acreage in the county was predominantly red, Zinfandel, Carignane, and Petite Sirah, in particular. Sonoma's reputation for red wine was greatly enhanced by the growth of the ITALIAN SWISS COLONY and the national success of its Tipo Chianti. The tilt toward red varieties became even more obvious during the dry years. Italian Swiss Colony was a favored source of red-wine grapes for home winemakers in the Bay Area, a preference that reinforced the county's popular image as the home of sound red table wine.

After Repeal most of Sonoma's wineries were small affairs operated by Italian-American families making bulk red table wine that was shipped to eastern bottlers or sold to restaurants and grocery stores in the Bay Area. Unlike Napa, few old, premium operations with a national brand had been established there before Prohibition. Italian Swiss Colony was large, but it was not a premium operation. FOUNTAINGROVE would last but a few years. Only KORBEL had a reputation for quality and it was for sparkling wines. Sonoma's reputation for world-class table wine is relatively recent.

Gradually several old families, notably SEBASTIANI, FOPPIANO, and PEDRONCELLI, began establishing brands that eventually gained national standing. Perhaps even more important were the enthusiastic entrepreneurs at Buena Vista and HANZELL. Between 1968 and 1972 the acreage of Sonoma's vineyards grew by 38 percent, but most of the change came in the replacement of older varieties with superior varietals. In those years acreage under Cabernet Sauvignon grew by 460 percent, Chardonnay, by 680 percent, and had doubled again by 1975. Twenty-five new premium wineries were bonded. Areas such as the Dry Creek and Alexander valleys, which had known some winegrowing before, now became almost solid vineyard. Today there are many Sonomas, that is, viticultural areas with remarkably diverse environments. Wine-grape acreage was approaching 40,000 in the county at the end of the century and there were about 175 bonded wineries.

In 1990 the Sonoma crush was 111,930 tons; in 1996, it was 127,991 tons.

For Sonoma's major viticultural areas, see ALEXANDER VALLEY, CARNEROS (Sonoma), CHALK HILL, DRY CREEK VALLEY, KNIGHT'S VALLEY, NORTHERN SONOMA, RUSSIAN RIVER VALLEY, SONOMA COAST, SONOMA MOUNTAIN, and SONOMA VALLEY.

SONOMA CREEK WINERY (BW 5409). The Larson family owns 35 acres of vineyard land on the Sonoma side of the Carneros. In 1987 the Larsons made about 2,000 cases of wine at their new winery. The emphasis has been on Chardonnay, but they buy other varieties from outside the Carneros. They produce about 8,000 cases per year for their own label, with additional production from their growing CUSTOM-CRUSH business.

SONOMA-CUTRER VINEYARDS (BW 5054). In 1973 Brice Cutrer-Jones began buying vineyard land in Sonoma and planting vines there. By 1981 he had seven parcels and was selling grapes, mostly Chardonnay, to several wineries in Sonoma and Napa. In that year Cutrer-Jones began building his winery in western Sonoma County, designed to specialize in Chardonnay from grapes grown in his own vineyards in the Carneros and the Russian River valley. The Chardonnays quickly gained

a strong market in upscale restaurants. Jones had production up to 20,000 cases a year in 1985, 50,000 in 1989; and over 80,000 today.

There are three basic Chardonnay bottlings. The mainstay (more than 50,000 cases) is designated Russian River Ranches. There are also two vineyard-designated bottlings, one from the home estate, the other from Les Pierres in the Carneros.

SONOMA MISSION. See MISSIONS AND THE MISSION PERIOD, **Mission San Francisco de Solano**

SONOMA MOUNTAIN Viticultural Area, designated in 1985, lies within the Sonoma Valley AVA. It is a highland area west of Glen Ellen and noted for its high-quality Cabernet Sauvignon and Zinfandel vineyards. Total vineyard area is about 650 acres.

SONOMA VALLEY, where the North Coast commercial wine industry originated, is that area around the old town of Sonoma between the hills that border the rich lowland. Historically the name is far from precise. In early days the valley was often said to extend north past Glen Ellen, but more often the valley land north of the town of Sonoma and up to Kenwood was referred to as the Valley of the Moon. Some used that term as a synonym for Sonoma Valley. The area from Kenwood up to the outskirts of Santa Rosa was called Los Guilicos. But in 1982 the BATF created the Sonoma Valley Viticultural Area, a huge district of 161 square miles that runs from the bay all the way to the Santa Rosa city limits and includes just about everything between the Sonoma Mountains on the west and the Napa County line in the mountains to the east. In fact, most of the Sonoma Valley AVA is mountainous. Nevertheless, it includes about 6,000 acres of some of the finest vineyard land in North America.

It was the cooling fogs below Glen Ellen that helped establish Sonoma County's early reputation for fine white wines, particularly Rieslings. Today this is Pinot noir and Chardonnay country. Merlot does well here too. Where it is warmer up-valley, and in the highlands above the fog line, Cabernet Sauvignon and Zinfandel are the favorites.

The modern history of this area as a fine-wine district runs parallel to that of the county as a whole. In short, it did not begin in force until the mid-1960s.

SONOMA VINEYARDS. See RODNEY STRONG VINEYARDS

SONORA WINERY & PORT WORKS (BW 5354) in Tuolumne County has, since 1986, produced small quantities of Zinfandel and port, the latter made from authentic Portuguese varieties of grapes grown in the Sierra foothills. Total annual production is about 3,000 cases.

SOTER, ANTHONY. See ÉTUDE

SOTOYOME, an Indian name given to the 48,000-acre Sonoma land grant made in 1840 at the center of which is today's town of Healdsburg. In the 1870s A. E. A. de Wiederhold operated a small Sotoyome Winery north of Healdsburg. Later the winery was acquired by the Cummiskey family, which operated the old place (as BW 687) for a short time in the 1930s. In 1974 a new Sotoyome Winery (BW 4655) went into operation south of Healdsburg. New owners took over in 1988 and in 1992 changed the name to CHRISTOPHER CREEK WINERY.

SOUTH COAST. Historically the coastal land from Point Concepción, above Santa Barbara, south to the Mexican border was called the South Coast. In 1985 the BATF assigned that name to a gigantic viticultural area covering 1,800 square miles and running from south of Los Angeles to the border. The eastern boundary is an average of about 30 miles inland. This AVA includes most of the old southern California winegrowing areas except Cucamonga.

SOUTHERN CALIFORNIA. See CUCA-MONGA; LOS ANGELES; RIVERSIDE COUNTY; SAN BERNARDINO COUNTY; SAN DIEGO COUNTY; TEMECULA

SOUVERAIN CELLARS (BW 945). In 1943 J. Leland (Lee) Stewart (1897–1986) bought a 60-acre piece of land and an old winery at the 1,100-foot elevation on Howell Mountain in Napa County. The land and winery were part of the Fulgencio Rossini estate established in 1884, but long out of production, and still had a few of the old vines and some prune trees. Stewart learned to make wine from locals and was able to enter a few wines from the 1945 vintage in the 1947 State Fair competition. Then and in years to come, he won gold medals at the Fair in six different categories. He bought grapes from others and by 1949 had replanted the old Rossini vineyard to better varietals. Many connoisseurs thought Stewart's Souverain wines to be the finest in California in the 1950s. His White Riesling, Cabernet Sauvignon, and Zinfandel were historic. His Green Hungarian, blended with 15 percent of some mystery grape, was a remarkable success for that usually rather bland variety. Anyone who examines the historical background of the premium wine boom in California that began in the 1960s must look to Lee Stewart's Souverain wines as a part of the origins. In 1970 Stewart sold the business to a group of investors, who then sold it to Pillsbury; see CHATEAU SOUVERAIN and RUTHERFORD HILL WINERY. Stewart's old Rossini Winery eventually became BURGESS CELLARS.*

SOUZÃO, a dark grape is grown to give color to ports made in Duoro Valley in Portugal. There it is spelled Sousão. In 1968 PAUL MASSON introduced a varietal Souzão port-style wine. There are still a few acres of the variety in

California, but it disappeared from official state acreage statistics in 1980.

SPACING. The density of wine grape vines per acre was a lively matter of discussion in California as early as the 1860s. The California pattern was to plant vines in squares of between 8 and 12 feet, which, in the days before trellises, meant that plowing and cultivation could go in both directions. But some Californians familiar with western European viticulture knew that the vine spacing in the great vineyards there was much closer. Agoston HARASZTHY read a paper to the California Agricultural Society in 1865 on Burgundian experiments with crop size, wine quality, and the profits from close spacing. All data pointed to this method as superior. But the idea did not catch on among California's grape farmers. Charles KRUG was thought peculiar when he planted new vineyards in the 1880s at one vine to 49 square feet, an average of 7-foot centers.

After Prohibition, the California tradition of wide spacing was reinforced by studies, sponsored by the University of California at Davis, in Napa and Sonoma from which the profitability of wider spacing was confirmed. But the success of close spacing in Europe led several winegrowers in California, notably STERLING, VENTANA, and Robert MONDAVI, to experiment. (OPUS ONE is today planted at

3.28 feet by 6 feet.) By the 1990s many growers in the coastal valleys were beginning to favor closer spacing, convinced that with careful canopy management, yields could increase while the quality of grapes was maintained or improved. The technique has been increasingly used in Napa, where much replanting in recent years has been undertaken as the result of a new PHYLLOXERA epidemic.

SPARKLING BURGUNDY. See BURGUNDY

SPARKLING WINE. CHAMPAGNE* is the world's most famous sparkling wine and since the 1850s most California winemakers have used the sparklers from that famous region in France as a model. The process by which Champagne is produced, the *méthode champenoise,* has usually been the one followed by Californians, but historically there have been several modifications, some still popular and in use.

The traditional method calls for the production of a base wine. Even though most Champagne is white, red-wine grapes, usually Pinot noir or Meunier, may be an important part of the base wine blend. In France the traditional white variety is Chardonnay. Each lot is usually, but not always, a blend, referred to as a CUVÉE, literally in French, a tubful. The bubbles that make the sparkle are produced in a second fermentation that traditionally occurs in the bottle

TABLE 33. SPARKLING WINE PRODUCTION IN CALIFORNIA, BY PROCESS

YEAR	CHARMAT	TRANSFER (GALLONS)	TRADITIONAL (MÉTHODE CHAMPENOISE)
1970	11,529,000	3,375,000	261,000
1975	11,704,500	3,386,250	537,750
1983	22,666,500	4,450,500	2,589,750
1987	20,553,750	2,677,500[a]	4,765,500
1991	19,525,500	1,050,750[a]	4,529,250
1994	17,844,750	N.A.	4,851,000

a. Includes sparkling wine made elsewhere in the United States; most is now produced in New York State.
SOURCE: *Wines & Vines*

in which the wine is sold. These bottles are usu-ally made of heavy glass with a push-up punt in the bottom to give them additional strength. For the second fermentation, some yeast and sugar are carefully measured into the *cuvée* and the wine is bottled and corked or capped. The bottles are stored and the second fermentation goes on apace, yielding the dissolved carbon dioxide that produces the bubbles.

The second fermentation also leaves a film of dead yeast cells on the inside of the bottle. By RIDDLING, this deposit is gradually moved down into the neck of the bottle, which is then frozen. The deposit is disgorged—when the bottle is opened, the plug of dead yeast and a little iced wine just pops out. Traditionally dis-gorging is done by hand; now it is more often done by machinery.

Before the final corking, the bottle gets an additional squirt of wine, called the *dosage,* which brings the level in the bottle back up and often adds of bit of sugar to soften the tart-ness. Each producer has its own style, which is often described on the label with such terms as Brut or Extra Dry. Recently, a few producers in California who want a particularly tart, dry wine have not added a *dosage.* Those bottles may be labeled Natural, *naturel, natur,* or *au natural*—none of these terms having a strict or legal definition. The bottle is then corked and the cork wired in place.

In the early 1850s one of the important items of import passing through San Francisco customs was sparkling wine labeled Cham-pagne but often from other places. In 1855 almost 20,000 cases, or "baskets," entered legally and were sold briskly at good prices. Several Californians were working to get a piece of this market. But for years the results were mostly applaudable failures. Chief among those were the wines of Benjamin WIL-SON and Pierre SAINSEVAIN. Later in the 1860s Victor Fauré, Mariano VALLEJO's wine-maker, and Arpad HARASZTHY made better sparklers. Haraszthy eventually teamed up with Isador LANDSBERGER to produce ECLIPSE, California's first commercially suc-cessful sparkling wine. Later, before Prohibi-tion, PAUL MASSON, KORBEL, and ITALIAN

TABLE 34. U.S. CONSUMPTION OF CALIFORNIAN SPARKLING WINE

YEAR	GALLONS
1934	110,700
1940	221,466
1945	550,000
1950	480,000
1955	789,408
1960	1,705,983
1965	3,216,422
1970	16,026,512
1975	15,670,000
1980	21,850,000
1985	26,784,000
1990	21,832,000
1995	19,491,000

SOURCE: *Wines & Vines*

TABLE 35. LEADING BRANDS OF CALIFORNIAN SPARKLING WINES, 1996

BRAND	PRODUCER	CASES
ANDRÉ	GALLO	3,000,000
COOK'S	CANANDAIGUA	1,630,000
KORBEL		1,100,000
BALLATORE	GALLO	690,000
DOMAINE CHANDON		430,000

SOURCE: *Wines & Vines*

SWISS COLONY made very good wine by the traditional method.

Meanwhile thousands of bottles each year were produced in California by the "soda pop" method, a process that today requires the description carbonated rather than sparkling on the label of the resulting wine. After 1906 the federal government came down hard on such operations, leaving the field open to Masson, Korbel, and Italian Swiss Colony for wines that might be called champagne. A few others, such as Theodore GIER and CRESTA BLANCA, made sparklers by the traditional method, but with special flavors, indicated by such terms as Sparkling Moselle and Sparkling Sauterne on their labels. There was also a lot of so-called sparkling red burgundy and usually quite sweet.

During Prohibition Paul Masson continued to produce his sparklers and was allowed to sell them as "medicinal champagne." How he managed this legal coup is not mentioned in any surviving records.

At Repeal Masson, Korbel, and several others entered the field. Meanwhile "champagne" produced by the CHARMAT or bulk process became extremely popular and profitable. After World War II sparkling wines were made by the transfer process, by which the wine, after the second fermentation, was disgorged under pressure into large tanks. The wine was then clarified, still under pressure to preserve the original bubbles, and rebottled. It was bottle-fermented, but with a difference. Thus, in the late 1950s sparklers produced by the traditional method began to carry labels with the statement the wine was "fermented in *this* bottle," the term bottle-fermented having become less precise.

The revolution in sparkling wine production in California began in the 1960s when the quantities of Central Valley wines made by the Charmat process increased enormously. GALLO led in this development. Then came a huge boost in the production of wine made by the traditional method, quantities increasing by more than 90 percent between 1970 and 1988. Here Korbel and DOMAINE CHANDON were the leaders. Part of this growth came from the arrival of several famous European producers, French and Spanish. By the end of the 1980s, with the demise of Almaden and Paul Masson, sparklers made by the transfer process had all but disappeared in California.

The trend toward higher quality products in the California sparkling wine industry seemed relentless for a while. Although the volume of Charmat sparklers has declined by 21 percent since 1985, wines from the traditional process have grown by 38 percent, but this trend has flattened some in the 1990s. Meanwhile American consumption of foreign sparkling wine has declined by 37 percent since 1985.

Although tradition, court cases, and federal regulations make it perfectly legal today to label sparkling wine that is made in the Golden State California Champagne, there is still some tension among producers on this topic. In 1990 seven producers in California that are owned by French interests formed the CM/CV Society, the letters standing for Classic Method/Classic Varieties. Their labels do not carry the word Champagne, but most other producers in the state do use the term and point to tradition, the law, and common sense to support the practice.

In 1993 the BATF gave bulk producers a lift by ruling that the description "Charmat process" could be used on labels in lieu of "bulk process," as long as it was clearly indicated that the new term meant that the wine was not bottle fermented.

Jack L. Davies, "Sparkling Wine," in *The University of California/Sotheby Book of California Wine*, ed. Doris Muscatine, Maynard A. Amerine, and Bob Thompson (Berkeley, Calif.: University of California Press/Sotheby Publications, 1984), 264–79.

L. Walker, "California Champagneries Develop House, Regional Styles," *Wines & Vines*, December 1995, 20–23.

SPOTTSWOODE WINERY (BW 5148). In 1972 Jack and Mary Novak bought the old St. Helena home of George SCHOENEWALD* and its 40-acre vineyard. Since 1910 the place had belonged to the Spotts family, hence its name. Between 1973 and 1975, the Novaks replanted the vineyard, mostly to red Bordeaux varieties, and they sold their grapes. When Jack died in 1977, Mary and her children carried on and by 1982 had brought out an estate Cabernet Sauvignon under the Spottswoode label. The winemaker was Tony Soter (see ÉTUDE), who has continued as a consultant since 1990. The Cabernets have been a critical success, giving credence to the tradition, which dates from the late 1870s, of fine clarets produced inside St. Helena's town limits. There is also a Sauvignon blanc.

In 1990 the old Kraft Winery built in 1884, just up the road, was acquired by the Novaks as a production facility. Annual output is about 8,000 cases, mostly estate Cabernet Sauvignon.

SPRING MOUNTAIN. The foothills and uplands of Napa County west of St. Helena have historically been referred to as Spring Mountain. In 1993 the area north of Sulphur Canyon to Ritchie Creek, and above the 400-foot contour line to the Sonoma County line, was granted AVA status. Before then Spring Mountain had been a geographical expression rather than a precisely defined area.

Its winegrowing history goes back to the 1870s when Charles Lemme planted the first vines there and built a small winery, the Beringers soon following with a vineyard. By 1886 there were 355 acres of vines in the area. By the 1890s such fine wine estates as LA PERLA, and those of Tiburcio PARROTT, and F. Chevalier (see CHATEAU CHEVALIER) were located there. After Prohibition the few acres that survived were mostly planted to shipper varieties, but several of the old estates were resuscitated and new ones created, particularly after World War II. Such producers as STONY HILL, York

Creek (see Fritz MAYTAG), KEENAN, CAIN, and NEWTON have revived the Spring Mountain reputation for fine table wines. Its microclimates have produced everything from White Riesling to Cabernet Sauvignon, but today its reputation rests mostly on the success of its wines from red Bordeaux varieties. There are almost 1,000 acres of vines in the viticultural area today, and fourteen wineries.

SPRING MOUNTAIN VINEYARDS (BW 4521). In 1964 Michael Robbins bought an old Victorian mansion built in 1876 just north of St. Helena in the Napa Valley. Its original owner, Fritz Rosenbaum, had had a small vineyard there, which he called Johannaberg. Robbins restored the mansion and planted some vines. By 1968 he was producing wine made at other wineries. Soon he bonded his own cellar, and had Charles ORTMAN as his winemaker.

Spring Mountain Chardonnays and Cabernets won early praise and in 1974 Robbins bought Miravalle, Tiburcio PARROTT's historic estate on Spring Mountain itself. He sold his original place, which is now ST. CLEMENT VINEYARDS.

In 1976 Robbins built a 100,000-gallon winery behind Miravalle, but the early critical praise for his wines began to decline. In 1981 Miravalle became the setting for the television soap opera *Falcon Crest*. Within a year he had released a Chardonnay and a Pinot noir under the Falcon Crest label. Still Robbins's debts piled up and in 1986 he put the 262-acre estate up for sale. In 1990 he filed for bankruptcy and in 1992 the property was in the hands of his creditors. Later that year the place was sold to a group of investors calling themselves Good Wine Co., and was rebonded as **Spring Mountain Vineyard** (BW 5707). This group has also acquired CHATEAU CHEVALIER, STREBLOW VINEYARDS, and part of LA PERLA.

STABILIZATION. Before Prohibition lack of chemical stability in bottled wine was a serious problem for producers in California. To avoid gassiness and unwanted deposits, wines were often allowed to remain in the barrel or cask for longer than they are today. This is what Charles LEFRANC meant by "selling no wine before its time." Some wineries used pasteurization. It was understood that many fine red wines, produced to improve in the bottle, would throw tartrate and phenolic deposits, which were not a sign of instability.

Since World War II great steps have been made to insure chemical and physical stability in bottled wine. Controlling malolactic fermentation (see ACID) is one of the most important. To prevent tartrate deposits, refrigeration and cold filtration are commonly used for many white wines and most inexpensive reds.

Microbiological stability is another important goal. To avoid bottle fermentation in slightly sweet white wines today, either sterile filtration or centrifuging is common. Bacterial spoilage can be another problem. Overexposure to oxygen must be avoided; moderate use of sulfur dioxide is also general. See also BRETTANOMYCES

STAGLIN FAMILY VINEYARD (BW 5711). In 1985 Shari and Garen Staglin acquired about 47 acres of Rutherford vineyard that had been developed earlier by BEAULIEU VINEYARD. They sold grapes to several wineries, and still do, but in 1989 they brought out an estate-grown Cabernet Sauvignon under their own label. There has also been some Chardonnay and a Sangiovese, which they label Stagliano. Total annual production is about 3,000 cases.

STAG'S LEAP. In the hills east of the Silverado Trail across from Yountville in Napa Valley there are several dramatic volcanic outcroppings that were named Stag's Leap in the 1870s. In 1890 Horace B. Chase, a vineyardist, built his home in the foothills below the rocks and in 1893 built a small winery on what he now

called Stag's Leap Ranch. This land around the ranch is a valley within the main Napa Valley, and was the land understood to be Stag's Leap in later years. Occidental Winery, built in 1878 just to the south, was the large winery in that part of the valley. Winegrowing never dominated the area and after Prohibition there were more acres of prunes than of grape vines.

Its conversion into a premium wine area began in the 1960s when Nathan FAY planted his Cabernet Sauvignon vineyard. Others followed and by the 1970s there were several wineries here. The triumph of a Stag's Leap Cabernet at the 1976 tasting in PARIS added to the area's luster. Meanwhile STAG'S LEAP WINE CELLARS and STAGS' LEAP WINERY (note the placement of the apostrophes) became locked in a legal fight over the use of Stag's Leap as a brand name. The matter was settled in 1985 when a court supported the contention of PINE RIDGE WINERY that this was a geographical term and wasn't the sole possession of anyone.

Soon thereafter, local winegrowers decided to apply for AVA status for the small area, mostly east of the Silverado Trail beneath the famous rocks. Robert MONDAVI and the Disney families had large holdings between the Trail and the Napa River to the west and persuaded the original applicants to take in those holdings and expand the application to cover about 2,700 acres. The northern boundary was to be a line well below the Yountville Crossroad, just north of the Disney SILVERADO VINEYARDS. Stanley ANDERSON's vineyards lay just to the north of the proposed boundry along the Crossroad. He challenged the application and won, so that today the vineyards along the south side of the Crossroad between the river and the Trail are included. The battle that preceded the BATF ruling in 1989 establishing the Stags Leap Viticultural Area was reported with glee by the press from the Bay Area to Los Angeles. Since then the district's reputation for fine wine, particularly Cabernet Sauvignon, has continued to grow.

There are about 1,350 acres of vines and 11 wineries in the expanded AVA that was approved by the BATF.

STAG'S LEAP WINE CELLARS (BW 4609). Warren Winiarski worked for Souverain and Robert Mondavi before 1970 when he acquired a 45-acre spread in the Stag's Leap area east of the Silverado Trail. He had tasted some of the Cabernet Sauvignon made from grapes grown by his new neighbor, Nathan FAY, and determined to concentrate on that varietal. He had a few grapes in 1972, when he began building his winery, and a small crop in 1973. It was this vintage, from these young vines, that won in PARIS, in 1976 (see page 252 for a photograph of the commemoration). In the early years André TCHELISTCHEFF was Winiarski's wine-making consultant.

Stag's Leap produces successful Chardonnay, Merlot, and Petite Sirah, but Cabernet Sauvignon has remained the center of attraction. Top of the line since 1974 has been the Cask 23 blend. There is also a Stags Leap District label and a Napa Valley Reserve. In 1985 Winiarski bought the Fay Vineyard and now releases the wine as a separate bottling.

Stag's Leap also has a second label, Hawk Crest, which makes up a large part of the annual production of almost 150,000 cases. The winery controls 194 acres of Napa vineyard.

Warren Winiarski, *Creating Classic Wines in the Napa Valley* (Regional Oral History Office, Bancroft Library, 1994).

STAGS' LEAP WINERY (BW 4614). Horace Chase's Stag's Leap Ranch is the forerunner of Stags' Leap Winery. The Chase family sold the place in 1909 and 9 years later the home was converted into a vacation inn, Stag's Leap Manor. During Prohibition the 80-acre vineyard was planted to shipper grapes, mostly Petite Sirah. During World War II the manor became a rest camp for U. S. Navy personnel. It then resumed its commercial function until 1953 when it closed and began to sink into genteel ruin. In 1970 Carl Doumani and several partners bought the estate, rebuilt the manor, and replanted the vineyard, which eventually covered 125 acres, to Cabernet Sauvignon, Merlot, and Petite Sirah. Doumani also kept a few acres of the old Petite Sirah vines.

At first Doumani called his operation Stags' Leap Vineyard and, starting in 1972, had his

Only one large winery was built in the Stag's Leap area before modern times. Terrill Grigsby (1818–92) settled there in 1850 and built his Occidental Winery in 1878. The fine structure stands yet, east of the Silverado Trail, although it is no longer a winery.

first wines made elsewhere. In 1978 the old winery was rebuilt. Although Merlot leads in current production, which totals about 40,000 cases a year, the winery's premium reputation rests mostly on its Petite Sirah, often a good candidate for long-term cellaring. In 1997 the winery was purchased by BERINGER WINE ESTATES.

P AND M STAIGER (BW 4649). Paul Staiger has been teaching art at San Jose State University since 1967. He and his wife Marjorie built their home in the Santa Cruz Mountains in 1973 and, the next year, planted their 5-acre vineyard to Chardonnay and Cabernet Sauvignon. They built their little winery right under the house and made wine from purchased grapes for several years. In 1979 they began producing their estate wines. Since then their production has held at about 500 cases a year, divided fairly evenly between the two varietals.

STANFORD. One of the Big Four who built the Central Pacific portion of the transcontinental railroad between 1868 and 1869 was Leland Stanford (1824–93). Before that he had been the governor of California (1862–63). Later he was elected twice to the U.S. Senate.

Winegrowing was never Stanford's chief interest, but from 1869 until his death, it was always an important sideline. In 1869 he bought the COLOMBET winery near Mission San Jose, along with a large tract of land. He gave the management of the place to his brother, **Josiah Stanford** (1817–90), who expanded the vineyard to 350 acres and the winery to a 500,000-gallon capacity. He sold his wine under the Warm Springs Vineyard label, his white wines, especially Riesling, having a particularly good reputation. In 1886 Leland deeded the estate to his brother, whose son ran the place from 1890 to 1919. The WEIBEL family acquired the winery in 1945.

Meanwhile in 1876 Leland bought land, the 650-acre Mayfield Grange Ranch, across the

bay in Menlo Park, along the creek that marks the border between Santa Clara and San Mateo counties. In the early 1880s he expanded the vineyard there to 158 acres and built a large winery in 1888. Its wines, too, had a good reputation and sold well on the East Coast. During those years Stanford expanded his holdings in this area and in 1885 founded Stanford University there. **Jane Lathrop Stanford** (1828–1905) allowed the winery to continue operating after her husband's death, despite her concerns for the moral well being of the students. But after her death it was closed down by Stanford's teetotaling president, David Starr Jordan (1851–1931). In 1909 it became a student dormitory and was converted into a shopping complex in 1961.

For Leland Stanford's third winegrowing venture, in the Central Valley, see VINA.*

Thomas Pinney, *A History of Wine in America from the Beginnings to Prohibition* (Berkeley, Calif.: University of California Press, 1989), 321–26.

STANISLAUS COUNTY straddles the Central Valley from foothills to foothills, with Modesto, the home of E. & J. GALLO,* its center. But the county has never been a leader in winegrowing. Today five other valley counties have more acreage under wine grapes.

Until the coming of the railroad and irrigation toward the end of the nineteenth century, winegrowing was concentrated in the Sierra foothills around Knight's Ferry, where the RED MOUNTAIN Winery held sway. There were about 300 acres of vines. But in the late 1890s and early years of the new century, the county became important for the grapes grown in the valley. Planting and winemaking were concentrated around Turlock, south of Modesto. In 1908 alone about 2,000 acres went in. After Repeal there were twelve wineries and about 10,000 acres of vines, chiefly planted to such varieties as Alicante Bouschet and Carignane.

The area under wine grapes remained unchanged until the 1970s when it soared to almost 20,000 acres, much of it French Colombard and Chenin blanc, varieties that are still most plentiful today, with acreage at about 13,500. But finer varietals such as Chardonnay and Zinfandel are on the increase, following the pattern being set by SAN JOAQUIN County to the north.

STANLY, JOHN A. (ca. 1831–99). More than any other person before Prohibition, Stanly proved that fine wine could be grown in the Carneros area of Napa County. He came to San Francisco in 1866 and practiced law there. In 1878 he inherited a fortune from his uncle, Edward Stanly, who had been Lincoln's military governor in North Carolina during the Civil War. John used this money to buy a 1,600-acre tract of land southwest of Napa City. His Riverdale Ranch became one of the county's historic estates. In the beginning wine grapes were but one of many crops and products raised there. The first 20 acres of vines, which went in in 1881, were planted on resistant ROOTSTOCK from Missouri, probably *Vitis riparia*.

By the 1890s Stanly's interest in wine grapes, and particularly for Cabernet Sauvignon and Zinfandel, had become a passion. He called his winery La Loma and sold wines in bulk to Charles CARPY, GUNDLACH-BUNDSCHU, and INGLENOOK among others. When he died, his heirs hired the scholarly Henry PELLET to oversee the operation.

Some of Stanly's vines and some wines survived Prohibition. André TCHELISTCHEFF pointed to a 1918 Stanly Pinot noir as the key to his early views on the potential of that variety in the Carneros. The old winery burned down in 1936. What was the Stanly Ranch has long since ceased to exist as an entity, but much of the land is again planted to wine grapes, as it was a hundred years ago.

STATE FAIR, CALIFORNIA. See EVALUATION, OF WINE

STATE VITICULTURAL COMMISSION, officially the California Board of State Viticultural Commissioners, an organization that was the creature of Charles A. WETMORE,* who was its chief executive officer and leader for much of its existence. It was established by an act of the legislature in 1880 and survived until 1895. The board was a source of information for vineyardists and wine producers in California. Today its publications are among the best sources of information on the state's wine industry during these years of dramatic growth. Funded originally to address the threat of PHYLLOXERA, the board's success in bringing the seriousness of the problem into the open was one of its most significant accomplishments. Wetmore and others promoted the use of resistant ROOTSTOCK, but their efforts were undermined by the steady conflict between the board and the scientific community, particularly the staff of the College of Agriculture at the University of California in Berkeley.

The concrete issues involved were few, the main one being the question of quality versus quantity. Professor Eugene HILGARD* wanted more first-rate wine to establish California's good reputation; Wetmore and most industry leaders wanted to meet current market demands for large quantities of good but inexpensive wines for the growing immigrant population.

By the late 1880s, the press in California was more interested in the running feud between Wetmore and Eugene Hilgard than in issues, and, when the balmy days of economic growth in the 1880s turned to decline and eventual depression in the 1890s, public support for the commission collapsed. Low prices were attributed to overproduction and the commission had glibly called for more planting in the 1880s in the face of the concerns of growers. In 1893 growers in Napa called for the commission's end, dubbing it a tool in the hands of San Francisco merchants. In 1895 the legislature killed the commission and ordered it to hand its effects over to the university. A second commission was authorized in 1913 but its narrow role was ended by Prohibition.

Ruth Teiser and Catherine Harroun, *Wine-making in California* (New York: McGraw-Hill, 1983), 94–97.

STEELE WINES (BW 4929). It should come as no surprise to learn that Jedediah Tecumseh Steele's father was a historian. In 1993 Jed Steele began selling wine under his own label from the 1991 vintage. For a while he made his wine at WILDHURST in Lake County, but in 1996 he acquired the KONOCTI WINERY as a production facility. He has bought grapes from as far afield as Santa Barbara and Mendocino counties. In 1994 he made seven different vineyard-designated Chardonnays. He has developed a reputation for his own wine that parallels that which he had developed as a winemaker for others since 1968, when he started as a "cellar rat" at STONY HILL. From 1974 to 1983 he was winemaker at EDMEADES and from 1983 to 1991 at KENDALL-JACKSON.

If nominations were being taken for California's greatest winemaker since the 1970s, Jed Steele's name would be in the first rank. His is specifically a master with Chardonnay, Pinot noir, and Zinfandel, much of this expertise being his ability to choose fine grapes in others' vineyards. Currently the director of enology for the VILLA MT. EDEN brand, he also acts as winemaking consultant for numerous wineries.

His second label is Shooting Star and his total annual production is about 30,000 cases.

STELTZNER VINEYARDS (BW 5175). Richard Steltzner arrived in Napa Valley with a farm background. For several years he planted vineyards for others and managed some of the best. In 1967 he began growing his own wine grapes in the STAG'S LEAP area, grapes that helped establish the Stag's Leap reputation for superior Cabernet Sauvignon fruit in the 1970s.

In 1977 he made his own wine at another facility. In 1983 he "foamed the inside of an old prune shed" and bonded his own winery. A new, handsome winery went up in the 1990s. There are 60 acres on the estate, almost all planted to red Bordeaux varieties. Annual production, which includes Merlot and Sauvignon blanc, stands at about 13,000 cases.

ROBERT STEMMLER WINERY (BW 4846). In 1960 Robert Stemmler came to northern California from his native Germany with solid experience in his country's wine industry and with technical training at the Bad Kreuznach Institute. He worked for several wineries and founded his own in the Dry Creek Valley in Sonoma County in 1977. Stemmler made wine from many varieties, but struck gold with his 1982 Pinot noir. By 1986 his production was up to 10,000 cases. One journalist dubbed him the "Unwilling Prince of Pinot."

In 1989 Stemmler arranged to make his Pinot noir at BUENA VISTA WINERY, which would market it and take a sizeable equity position in the enterprise. Annual production under the Stemmler label is about 5,000 cases. In 1996 his own winery building was sold to PEZZI KING.

STERLING VINEYARDS (BW 4533). Two miles south of Calistoga a wooded knoll rises from the floor of the Napa Valley. Charles Rockstroh built his home there and in 1933 bonded his 8,000-gallon winery (BW 3144). When he died in 1967, four executives in a paper products firm in San Francisco bought the hill and some surrounding land. Headed by Peter NEWTON, the four had started buying vineyard land in Napa in 1964. They hired Richard FORMAN to plan and run their new winery, which was to be built on the knoll. It was Sterling Vineyards, named after the paper company, Sterling International.

Forman's first vintage was in 1969 in a temporary facility at the foot of the hill. Those

After the winery at Sterling Vineyards was finished in 1973, Leon ADAMS wrote: "As you approach the valley's upper end, a white monastery-like structure comes into view atop the range of hills to the east. It is the Sterling Vineyards winery, the most spectacular in America, and quite possibly in the world." (©Sebastian Titus, Vintage Image)

wines, a Cabernet Sauvignon, a Zinfandel, and a Merlot, created something of a sensation. In 1971 construction on the new winery began. It, too, was a sensation when it was opened to the public in 1973. It resembled an alabaster-white Aegean monastery. Visitors reached the winery by an aerial tramway and were treated to a self-directed tour of the beautifully laid out building.

Forman kept up the quality of Sterling wines and expanded the varietal line, keeping a special emphasis on Bordeaux-style offerings. By 1977 production had risen to 65,000 cases and the owners sold the operation to COCA-COLA of Atlanta. The product line was narrowed, but the former emphasis, with Chardonnay added, was kept. Coca-Cola also began developing vineyards on Diamond Mountain, in the hills to the west, and had more than 500 acres of vines in Napa when Sterling was sold to SEAGRAM* in 1983. Expansion continued, the purchase of Winery Lake Vineyard in 1986 the most celebrated acquisition.

Sterling today is the headquarters for the Seagram California wine operation, which controls more than 1,200 acres of vineyard. Annual production exceeds 350,000 cases.

STERN, CHARLES (1838–1903), who had been in the wine trade in his native Germany, came to California in 1860, became closely associated with KOHLER & Frohling and, in 1885, took charge of the company's eastern sales. In the 1870s he became associated with L. J. ROSE and was soon influential in the Southern California wine industry. In 1900 he and his sons founded the Riverside Vineyard Co. By 1907 the family was in control of almost 3,000 acres of vines in Riverside County and in the Cucamonga area. Their huge Riverside Winery, on line for the 1903 vintage and specializing in sweet wines and brandy, had a capacity of about 500,000 gallons. Stern died just as the first vintage was coming to a close. The winery continued operating until Prohibition.

STEVENOT WINERY (BW 4839). Barden Stevenot was born and grew up in the San Francisco Bay Area, but his great-great grandfather, Gabriel Stevenot, came to Calaveras County from France in 1850. In 1969 Barden bought the Shaw Ranch, just a few miles from his family's original homesite. He planted a vineyard on the new place in 1974; he bonded his winery in 1978. Today there are 28 acres of vines on the estate, but Stevenot production has reached almost 50,000 cases through purchases of grapes and wines from all over northern California. A large part of this production is White Zinfandel. There is also Chardonnay, Merlot, and Cabernet Sauvignon.

STEVENSON, ROBERT LOUIS (1850–94). The Scottish-born writer came to California to marry Fanny Osbourne and the couple spent their honeymoon in 1880 in a cabin at an old silver mine on Mount St. Helena, above the Napa Valley. He wrote of the experience in *Silverado Squatters,* published in 1883. While staying in Calistoga, before heading up onto the mountain, he visited the Napa wine country and recorded his impressions in the chapter titled "Napa Wine." The record of his visit to Jacob SCHRAM has become an essential tidbit in California wine history. References to California wine appear now and then in several of Stevenson's later writings, the most memorable in *The Ebb-Tide,* published in 1894, in which a load of ECLIPSE champagne is central to the plot.

There is a Stevenson museum in St. Helena.

STEWART, J. LELAND. See SOUVERAIN CELLARS

STIMSON LANE WINE & SPIRITS. See CONN CREEK WINERY; VILLA MT. EDEN

STOLL, HORATIO F. (1873–1947). Stoll's first contacts with the California wine industry were his visits to the Napa Valley and the winery of his uncle, Bernard EHLERS. He went to work for ITALIAN SWISS COLONY in the 1890s and was soon in charge of public relations there. In 1910 he and Andrea SBARBORO helped found the California Grape Protective Association and led its unsuccessful fight against the forces

Between 1910 and 1918 Horatio Stoll campaigned for the California wine industry against PROHIBITION. His advertisement shown here was typical, portraying the probable effects of prohibition on the small producer. Part of his technique was to place large signs among the vines along roadways: "This vineyard—gone after Prohibition." (Unzelman Collection, Santa Rosa, Calif.)

working for Prohibition. Toward the end of the struggle, he was regularly printing a newsletter that was mailed to the state's wine producers and grape growers. When Prohibition became a fact in 1919, he converted his newsletter into a regular periodical, which he named *The California Grape Grower*. In 1935 he changed its name to WINES & VINES.* After he sold the publication in 1939, he remained close to the wine industry as a popular after-dinner speaker.

STONE CREEK WINERY (BW 5256). Stone Creek has been a NÉGOCIANT brand since 1976. There is now a tasting room in Kenwood. Their bonded winery number is the same as that of KENDALL-JACKSON'S winery in Santa Rosa. Sales of mostly moderately priced varietals are well over 250,000 cases per year, much of them in restaurants.

STONEGATE (BW 4640). In 1969 the Spaulding family bought a piece of land in the hills west of Napa Valley and south of Calistoga. They planted vines there and in 1973 built a small winery in the valley just south of Calistoga and had their first crush. Production of several varietal wines rose to almost 20,000 cases in the early 1980s, but in recent years the number of cases and varietals has been cut back substantially. The two contiguous mountain vineyards and the one around the winery total about 30 acres. Their mountain-grown Merlot has been Stonegate's most successful wine in recent years. In 1996 the winery was purchased by the same investors who own BANDIERA WINERY.

J. STONESTREET & SONS. See KENDALL-JACKSON VINEYARDS

STONY HILL VINEYARD (BW 4461). In 1943 Fred McCrea (1898–1977) and his wife, Eleanor (1908–91), were looking for land on which to build a summer cottage. They found some steep and rocky land in the hills above the Napa Valley northwest of St. Helena.

Learning from neighbors that goats or grapes were probably the only agricultural products possible there, they began planting grapes after the war. The two went at it gradually, just a couple of acres per year, consulting other vintners in Napa and the experts at the University of California at Davis. Eventually they had several varietals planted, but Chardonnay, for which the budwood came from WENTE, was to be their eventual winner.

For several years the couple sold most of their grapes to the wineries that had helped them get started, particularly SOUVERAIN CELLARS. But they made a little wine in 1950 and became a commercial winery in 1952.

It was soon clear that Stony Hill's Chardonnay was something special. Friends persuaded the McCreas to enter some of their 260-gallon 1953 vintage at the State Fair. It won a silver medal in 1956; in 1959 and 1960 they won gold medals. As the years progressed and production grew, the small but growing number of connoisseurs in California who loved fine white wine made it unnecessary for the McCreas to market their wines through normal retail outlets. Everything was sold to an oversubscribed mailing list.

Another thing the McCreas and their friends were discovering was that this Chardonnay aged into truly great wines. In the 1990s there are still wines from the 1960s that are saluted by enthusiasts of white burgundies as being world class.

In 1962 Fred retired from his advertising career and the couple settled on the mountain. They expanded production to almost 2,000 cases, which included some White Riesling, Gewürztraminer, and a sweet Sémillon du Soleil. Eleanor directed the operations for 14 years after Fred's death in 1977. Today it is supervised by Peter McCrea, the couple's son. Michael Chelini, whose tenure at Stony Hill spans three decades, is vineyard manager and winemaker.

Total production stands at about 5,000 cases. Most of the 40-acre vineyard has been replanted in recent years. There is some production under the SHV label, using grapes that are grown in Napa Valley, but not on the estate.

Eleanor McCrea, *Stony Hill Vineyard: The Creation of a Napa Valley Estate Winery* (Regional Oral History Office, Bancroft Library, 1990).

STONY RIDGE WINERY (BW 5648). After RUBY HILL VINEYARD stopped producing wine, a group of wine enthusiasts leased the historic Livermore Valley winery in 1976 and began operations as Stony Ridge Winery (BW 874). In 1983 they moved to other premises in Pleasanton but were out of business by 1985. When the Scotto family closed down VILLA ARMANDO in Pleasanton in 1985, they acquired the Stony Ridge name and in 1992 built a new winery outside the town of Livermore. Under the direction of Monica Scotto, the new winery has raised sales to about 20,000 cases a year, emphasizing Chardonnay and Merlot.

STORRS WINERY (BW 5477). Pamela and Stephen Storrs both have degrees in enology from the University of California at Davis. They opened their little Santa Cruz winery in 1988 and have brought annual production up to about 7,500 cases. They specialize in wines made from Santa Cruz Mountain grapes, particularly Chardonnay. They have won many awards for their wines, among them a citation at the State Fair in 1994 for their 1992 Merlot, which was named the best of that variety produced in the southern Bay Area.

STORYBOOK MOUNTAIN VINEYARDS (BW 4946). Jacob Grimm founded his vineyard in 1883 and had his cellar dug into a hill northwest of Calistoga in Napa County 5 years later. His family revived the operation briefly after Repeal (BW 3187), but the real revival came when J. Bernard Seps acquired the property in 1976, upgraded the tunnels, and bonded his winery in 1979. He called it Storybook, because of the idyllic isolation of the place and the name of his predecessor, Jacob Grimm.

Seps planted Zinfandel and has concentrated on that variety ever since. His first vintage was in 1980. His wines are intense, age well, and have been well received in the world of so-called Zinfanatics. He has 40 acres in vines and an annual production at about 8,000 cases.

STORY WINERY (BW 4644). In 1969 Eugene Story bought a vineyard in Amador County that had been planted to Zinfandel and Mission grapes in the late 1920s. His winery north of Plymouth opened in 1973. He called it Cosumnes River Vineyard, but also used the Story brand for his hearty Zinfandels. After 1981 when Eugene died, his widow, Ann, directed the operation until it was acquired by the Tichenor family in 1993. They now produce about 3,000 cases of Zinfandel and Chenin blanc from the 50-acre vineyard.

STRALLA, LOUIS. See NAPA (VALLEY) WINE CO.

STRATFORD was created as a NÉGOCIANT brand in 1981, when there was an overabundance of Chardonnay in California, by the partners in CARTLIDGE & BROWNE. By 1987 Tony Cartlidge and Glen Browne were making wine in rented cellar space. Today, operating out of the old EHLERS WINERY, which they have bonded as Ehlers Grove Winery, they are still making Chardonnay and Merlot under the Stratford label.

STREBLOW VINEYARDS (BW 5271). The Streblow family bonded a 3,000-case winery in 1985 and concentrated on Cabernet Sauvignon production. In 1995 the new owners of SPRING MOUNTAIN VINEYARDS bought the neighboring Streblow operation.

STRENTZEL, JOHN T. (1813–90), a native of Poland and John Muir's father-in-law, was in addition one of California's leading orchardists and one of Contra Costa County's pioneer winegrowers. His vineyard in the Alhambra

Valley covered 9 acres in 1859. It and his orchards were part of what became one of the great showplace estates in the nineteenth century in northern California. His home today is the John Muir National Historic Site in Martinez.

RODNEY STRONG VINEYARDS (BW 4520). Rodney Strong came to northern California from New York in 1959, leaving a career as a professional dancer. In 1960 he bought an old home in the Marin County village of Tiburon and bonded it as **Tiburon Vintners** (BW 4482). (For a short while Walter RICHERT was a partner in the business.) Strong blended wines and sold them from his converted Victorian. He also began developing a mail-order wine business that was soon flourishing. In 1961 he acquired 160 acres of vineyard land near Healdsburg in Sonoma County and the following year bought an old local winery as a production facility (BW 999). His new line of wine was labeled Windsor Vineyards.

By 1970 his tasting rooms, the mail-order business, and a unique, customized label service for his customers had pushed Strong's sales to about 150,000 cases a year. In that year he built a fine new winery at Windsor and was expanding his vineyards to almost 1,000 acres. The whole enterprise became Sonoma Vineyards and Strong made a public stock offering. The fortunes of the operation were soon reflected in the price per share of the stock, which peaked at $42 in 1972 and fell to $2.62 in 1975. Expansion had brought heavy debt at high interest rates. In 1975 Renfield Imports acquired 47 percent of the stock and things began to change.

Production was scaled back with more emphasis on quality. Vineyard-designated wines did well, particularly the Alexander's Crown Cabernet Sauvignon. In 1980 the winery's best offerings began appearing under the Rodney Strong label, with total annual sales up to almost 500,000 cases, including the still-profitable mail-order business.

In 1980 Piper-Sonoma, the makers of sparkling wine, became associated with Sonoma Vineyards and next year a new winery was built for Piper-Sonoma next door. But by 1983 Strong's profits were way down and he and his partners were forced to sell off much of their vineyard holdings. In 1984 Renfield gained full control, which eventually and indirectly was acquired by Guinness in 1986.

Still, Strong's wines under his label kept their good reputation and the Windsor mail-order business still made money. In 1988 Klein Family Vintners, a subsidiary of Klein Foods, a California agribusiness company, bought Sonoma Vineyards from Guinness and set the winery on a new course. It continued to emphasize high quality, but with a much less grand marketing scheme. Annual sales now amount to about 275,000 cases under the Rodney Strong label and somewhat more for the Windsor line. At age 68 Rodney Strong went into semiretirement in 1995.

Rodney Strong, *Rodney Strong Vineyards: Creative Winemaking and Winery Management in Sonoma County* (Regional Oral History Office, Bancroft Library, 1994).

SUGAR. Wine becomes wine when the sugars in the grapes are converted to alcohol and other products during the process of FERMENTATION. Unlike those of many other wine-growing areas in the world, California's valley climates are usually warm enough to insure ripeness in terms of sugar. In fact, CHAPTALIZATION is illegal in California.

In dry table wines virtually all the grape sugar is converted. But California vintners understand that wines with a trace of residual sugar are often preferred by some consumers. Thus many dry wines, particularly whites, have sugar levels of about 1 percent. This level is often higher in such varieties as White Riesling and Gewürztraminer. Almost all inexpensive jug wines and many FIGHTING VARIETALS have noticeable residual sugar. Winemakers also know that many perceived flaws in inexpensive wines can be partially covered by leaving some sweetness in the final product.

Except for dry sherry, almost all of California's FORTIFIED WINES have high levels of residual sugar and are often referred to as dessert wines. LATE-HARVEST WINES today are almost always sweet.

Sweet sparkling wines were once very popular all over the wine-drinking world, a popularity that helps explain the lingering belief that sparkling wine and dessert make a perfect combination. Today most premium sparkling wine made in California is quite dry. Inexpensive sparklers are almost always fairly sweet.

SULFUR has been burned in wineries since antiquity to produce SULFUR DIOXIDE. In viticulture the powdery yellow crystals are used to protect vines and fruit from MILDEW. In the dry climate of California dusting vineyards with sulfur is a fairly common practice today, particularly after spring rains. The method can be traced to French practices that were introduced to California by Antoine DELMAS in the 1860s.

SULFUR DIOXIDE (SO$_2$), a gas formed when elemental sulfur is burned in the presence of oxygen and used since antiquity to preserve wine and other foods. Since the Middle Ages it has been used to fumigate casks and barrels. The gas is colorless with the pungent, irritating odor we associate with a struck match.

Toward the end of the nineteenth century, winemakers in California became interested in using commercially developed YEASTS in their fermentations, because the action of wild yeasts was unreliable. It became popular to subdue the wild yeasts with SO$_2$, usually generated from bisulfite crystals. Later, cylinders of SO$_2$ gas became available. By the turn of the century SO$_2$ was being used in almost all but the most primitive country wineries to fight spoilage. After Repeal many of the lessons of

those earlier years had to be learned and relearned by far too many small-scale California winemakers.

Health concerns over the use of SO$_2$ in foods date from the reformist campaigns of Harvey W. Wiley, the dynamic chief chemist at the U.S. Department of Agriculture from 1883 to 1912. But it was not until 1987 that warnings about the presence of sulfite were required on wine bottles. Sulfur dioxide is still necessary for large-scale producers today, but most producers, whatever their size, now try to minimize its use.

In recent years a few small-scale producers no longer use SO$_2$ in their winemaking. The results have been controversial. A little more common now are producers who, allowing the wild yeasts on their grapes to dominate their fermentations, curtail their use of SO$_2$ at that stage of production.

SULLIVAN, CHARLES L. Californian wine historian and author of regional histories of Napa and Santa Clara counties and of the Santa Cruz Mountains; also specializes in the history of California varietals, particularly Zinfandel.

SULLIVAN VINEYARDS (BW 5434). The Sullivan family bought their first vineyard land in Rutherford in Napa County in 1972 and now have about 25 acres. James Sullivan began making wine commercially in 1979 and has specialized in small quantities of powerful, age-worthy Cabernet Sauvignon. Total production of about 3,500 cases includes Merlot, Zinfandel, and Chardonnay.

SULTANINA. In the United States, a legal synonym for the THOMPSON SEEDLESS grape.

SUMMIT LAKE VINEYARDS (BW 5255). The piece of land on Howell Mountain in Napa County that Robert and Susan Brakesman bought in 1971 had on it an old Zinfandel vineyard, which they gradually revived. A 1982 Zinfandel was their first commercial wine. They now have 14 acres of vineyard. There have been other varietals in their annual 2,000-case production, but Zinfandel leads, by far.

SUNNY ST. HELENA WINERY. See MERRY-VALE VINEYARDS

SUNNY SLOPE WINERY. See LEONARD J. ROSE

SUNRISE WINERY (BW 3682), originally, in 1976, in the old G. Locatelli Winery in the Santa Cruz Mountains above Boulder Creek. After a fire in 1978, Rolayne and Ronald Stortz took full charge of the operation and moved it to the historic PICCHETTI BROTHERS WIN-ERY (BW 148) in the MONTE BELLO area. The ranch, which has an old Zinfandel vineyard long used by Ridge Vineyards, has been restored and is now part of a regional park. With Rolayne as winemaker, Sunrise produces about 2,500 cases a year. In addition to Zinfandel, the total usually includes Pinot noir, Pinot blanc, and Chardonnay, all from purchased grapes.

SUR LIE. A French winemaking term for "on the lees." Probably the first California commercial wine for which this process (see LEES) was used was made in 1979 by Gary Andrus at PINE RIDGE WINERY.

SUTTER COUNTY in the Sacramento Valley had about 1,000 acres of vines after Prohibi-

A photograph taken in 1965 gives a good picture of the PICCHETTI ranch in the last years of the family's tenure. The old winery is in the far background. The historic farm has been restored with Sunrise Winery at its center and is now the starting point for a series of hiking trails maintained by the regional park system.

The Leuenberger family acquired the old THOMANN winery in 1904 and called it Sutter Home. This picture was taken around 1908. During Prohibition the owners covered up the word Winery on the old structure.

tion, but the hot, desert climate had reduced the total to about 90 acres in the 1990s.

SUTTER HOME WINERY (BW 1007), a successful operation in the Napa Valley in JOHN THOMANN's* old winery, which was built in 1874, just south of St. Helena. It is named for John SUTTER, a member of the family that originally owned DEER PARK WINERY* and later bought the Thomann place.

The winery was silent after Repeal until 1947 when it was purchased by the Trinchero family. In the 1950s they made bulk wine but also developed an incredibly diverse array of wines. In those years they won medals at the State Fair for Barbera, Vermouth, Sparkling Muscat, Brut Champagne, and Sparkling Burgundy.

In 1960 Mario Trinchero (1899–1982) took full control of the winery and expanded the product line. Meanwhile Mario's son, Louis (Bob) Trinchero, was taking an increasingly active role in running the winery. By the end of the 1960s he had Sutter Home on the course that would make it one of the most successful wineries in America.

Sutter Home had always sold Zinfandel. In 1960 customers could buy it by the gallon at the winery for $1.78. Then, in the late 1960s, the winery became an early leader in premium Zin-

fandel production as a result of an association with Darrell CORTI, for whom the winery had been making wine since 1965. In 1968, through Corti, Bob Trinchero discovered the old-vine Zinfandel grapes of Amador County (see the label on page 408). The winery began narrowing its product line and concentrating on the one variety. In 1972 Trinchero made a small batch of dry white, or BLUSH, Zinfandel. It did well. In 1975 a stuck fermentation of the wine left some residual sweetness and demand grew, to 10,000 cases in 1978, to 34,000 in 1980, and 3.7 million in 1989. By then it was the single best-selling wine in America with a annual retail value approaching $200 million.

In 1987 Sutter Home introduced a line of FIGHTING VARIETALS that also flew off the retail shelves, particularly the Chardonnay. Meanwhile in 1986 Trinchero acquired the Lambert Egg Ranch near the winery. It became Zinfandel Ranch, eventually a massive plant used to process the huge flow of grapes now coming to Sutter Home from the Central Valley. Sutter Home owns or controls almost 5,500 acres of vines, many of them in the Sacramento Valley. Total production has reached 7 million cases a year.

In 1988 the Trincheros bought MONTEVIÑA WINERY,* with the intention of focusing their interests on fine red Zinfandel and on Italian varietals.

Louis (Bob) Trinchero, *California Zinfandels, A Success Story* (Regional Oral History Office, Bancroft Library, 1992).

SUTTER, JOHN. A sausage maker in Alameda whose name was taken by his relatives for the original SUTTER HOME WINERY on Howell Mountain in Napa County; see also DEER PARK WINERY. He is no relation to John A. SUTTER, the California pioneer at whose lumber mill gold was first discovered in 1848.

SUTTER, JOHN AUGUSTUS (1803–80). Sutter's fame in California history has little to do with wine or viticulture but he did have an early hand in both, beginning in 1841, at his Hock Farm north of what became Sacramento. There in 1851 he planted a vineyard that had 26,000 vines in 1856. For several years he made white wine and brandy commercially. By 1860 Jacob KNAUTH was in charge of Hock Farm.

JOSEPH SWAN VINEYARDS (BW 4528). Few California winemakers have become celebrities and none so quickly as Joseph Swan (1914–89). He made his first homemade wine as a teenager and continued until he ended his career as an airline pilot in 1967. He then bought an old ranch near the Russian River in Forestville in Sonoma County and planted Pinot noir and Chardonnay, intent on excelling in Burgundian-style wines. In 1968 he made a Zinfandel from some old vines on his property and liked the result. The next year he found some good Zinfandel grapes in the Dry Creek Valley and, when the wine was released in 1972, he became an overnight hero to those winelovers in California learning to appreciate rich, powerful, and age-worthy Zinfandel. Swan's Zinfandels were elegant in a style almost unheard of then, although not uncommon today.

He never gave up his passion for fine Pinot noir and Chardonnay and developed a good

reputation for these wines, but throughout the 1970s he was the master of Zinfandel. Several California Zinfandel artisans trace their enological roots to early contacts with Joseph Swan.

His family still controls the operations, with his son-in-law, Rod Bergland, in charge of production. He emphasizes a line of vineyard-designated Sonoma Zinfandels. There is also Pinot noir and Cabernet Sauvignon in the 4,000-case annual production.

Connoisseur's Guide to California Wine, March 1989, 65–67.

SWANSON VINEYARDS (BW 4820). W. Clarke Swanson Jr. bought 80 acres of vineyard in Oakville in Napa County in 1985 and two years later acquired the CASSAYRE-FORNI winery in Rutherford. Now he controls 155 acres of vineyard in Napa and, since 1987, has been developing a complex line of varietal wines with an annual production of 18,000 cases. Much of Swanson's grape crop is sold to other

Joseph Swan planted his own vines and did much of the work in his vineyard. Here he PRUNES a Chardonnay vine trained to a vertical cordon, a system he favored. (Rod Berglund, Joseph Swan Vineyards)

wineries in the Napa Valley. Originally concentrating on Chardonnay and Cabernet Sauvignon, Swanson has recently been successful with Merlot, Syrah, and Sangiovese.

SWEET WINE. See FORTIFIED WINE; SUGAR

SWETT. Historians consider **John Sweet** (1830–1913), a Yankee schoolteacher, the patron saint of California's education system, mostly for his work as state superintendent of public instruction between 1863 and 1867. He had a summer place in Contra Costa County near Martinez and in the 1880s developed one of the county's premier winegrowing establishments. He called it Hill Girt Vineyard and specialized in Bordeaux-style red and white wine. His sauterne was made from Sauvignon blanc, Sémillon, and Muscadelle of Bordeaux, his Medoc from Cabernets Sauvignon and franc, and Merlot.

Frank T. Swett (1869–1969), his son, ran the day-to-day operations at Hill Girt, which produced about 10,000 gallons per year. But his father was quite active in the wine industry and served on the second STATE VITICULTURAL COMMISSION. Both he and Frank led in the campaign to promote the use of resistant ROOTSTOCK and took part in the WINE WAR. In 1913 Frank became the president of the California Grape Protective Association, the wine industry's official arm in the fight against Prohibition.

SWISS, THE, IN EARLY CALIFORNIA WINE. As a percentage of total immigration by national origin to California, the Swiss nationals were the most numerous in the early years of the California wine industry, particularly in the North Coast. For the Swiss nationality and ethnicity are not at all identical. Italian, French and German Swiss all were well represented among early California winegrowers. In Napa, for instance, Pellet, Thomann, and Salmina were all Swiss émigres.

SYCAMORE CREEK VINEYARDS (BW 4759). Terry and Mary Kaye Parks, school teachers both, founded their winery in 1976 just north of the Hecker Pass area in the Santa Clara Valley. They developed a good reputation for their table wines and in 1989 sold the winery to Kazuaki Morita, a Japanese sake producer interested in exporting wine to Japan. Top varietals today are Chardonnay and Cabernet Sauvignon. The facility also does custom-crush work.

SYLVANER. A white variety of wine grape popular in Central and Eastern Europe, as well as in Alsace. It is often called Franken Riesling in Germany and previously in California. This term comes from the variety's popularity in German Franconia.

Sylvaner came to California in the 1850s brought in by the DRESEL family in Sonoma and Francis Stock of San Jose. G. B. CRANE got Sylvaner vines from Stock and wine from these plantings in the 1860s was the first to suggest that Napa might be excellent winegrowing country. Many early California white wines in a German style contained blends of Sylvaner and White Riesling. Planting of Sylvaner was concentrated in the Napa, Sonoma, and Santa Clara valleys and in the Santa Cruz Mountains. Prohibition all but wiped out the variety in California. After Repeal it gained popularity when it was recommended by experts at the University of California at Davis. It occasionally appeared as a varietal, but it was more often labeled Mosel or Moselle, even though the variety is rarely seen along the Mosel in Europe.

In the 1930s about 35 percent of California's 500 acres of Sylvaner was planted in Sonoma, but the largest single planting, more than 50 acres, was at the VALLIANT WINERY in San Benito County. After World War II acreage held steady at about 1,000 and peaked in the early 1970s at about 1,500. Then Monterey County led the state, although ALMADEN'S 125 acres at Paicines was the largest single planting.

Thereafter Sylvaner's small following slid to almost nothing, with fewer than 100 acres in the 1990s.

In 1996 the BATF ruled that after 1997 the term Franken Riesling might no longer be used on bottles of Sylvaner.

SYMPHONY. A wine grape, the result of a cross between Muscat of Alexandria and a light-colored Grenache, that was developed at the University of California at Davis in 1940 and released in 1982. It makes good dry and sweet wines that age well in the bottle. The first sizeable planting was by CHATEAU DE BAUN in 1984. But demand for muscat-flavored California wines is still small. Now there are about 325 acres in the state, 85 percent of them in the Central Valley. The 1996 Symphony crush in California was 5,843 tons.

SYRAH. The great red wines of France's northern Rhône region, such as Hermitage and Côte Rôtie, are made from the Syrah grape. A hundred years ago the French made a clear distinction between a small-berried variation, clearly superior, and a larger one. They were called the *petite* Syrah and the *grosse* Syrah.

The "petite" variation was probably first imported to California by J. H. DRUMMOND in 1878. It was taken up by a few vintners in northern California in later years, notably H.

W. CRABB, C. C. MCIVER, and J. T. DOYLE. By the 1890s Crabb and a few others were labeling their wines from the variety Hermitage, much as they used Chambertin on Pinot noir wines. It was in these years that some took to referring to the DURIF* variety as PETITE SIRAH,* a situation that persists today. After 1915 we hear almost nothing of the real Syrah in California.

The University of California at Davis did not have the variety in its collection until 1939, and later gave it an evaluation that discouraged its planting. The revival of interest can first be seen in 1959 when CHRISTIAN BROTHERS planted a 4-acre plot of Syrah in the Napa Valley. In 1974 JOSEPH PHELPS made a varietal Syrah from some of those grapes and planted 6 acres of his own. In 1978 the variety appeared in the official California statistics as Syrah French with 55 acres indicated. In 1982 it was listed as Syrah. But there was little interest yet. In 1985 PRESTON VINEYARDS brought out a Syrah-Sirah blend, a catchy play on the popular song. But Syrah acreage was still barely 100. Then in the 1990s planting took off and several producers began bottling the variety. So far evaluations have been generally positive, but critics are not yet likening California Syrah to the red wine of Hermitage.

In 1997 the state's Syrah crush was 9,861 tons, up from 585 tons in 1990.

TABLE 36. SYRAH GRAPES, SELECTED AREAS

YEAR	NORTH COAST	CENTRAL COAST	(ACRES) CENTRAL VALLEY	SIERRA FOOTHILLS	TOTAL
1985	68	40	0	2	110
1990	213	83	0	17	334
1992	287	157	53	37	632
1997	603	528	817	110	2,084

SOURCE: California Agricultural Statistics Service, Sacramento, Calif.

TABLAS CREEK VINEYARD (BW 5738). The owners of Château de Beaucastel in the Rhône and Robert Haas, an import company, began developing a vineyard and nursery site in San Luis Obispo County in the hills west of Paso Robles in 1991. The idea was to bring into California from the Rhône area vineyard stock that was free of disease. Thus far standard varieties have been propagated and are now available for sale to winegrowers in California.

TABLE GRAPES. Wine can be made from grapes normally used for eating. Today there are about 85,000 acres of table grapes in California, almost all in the Central Valley and southern California. The leading varieties are Flame Seedless and Red Globe. (THOMPSON SEEDLESS is classified a RAISIN GRAPE.*) Today about 6 percent of the California crush comes from table grapes. This number is down from about 10 percent in the 1970s, but after World War II until the late 1960s table grapes averaged between 20 and 30 percent of the California crush. A large percentage of this total came from the Flame Tokay variety, from which satisfactory brandy could be produced, both for fortified wines and for drinking. Much of this production was in SAN JOAQUIN COUNTY, where the beverage brandy was often dubbed "Lodi Scotch." There are still about 3,500 acres of Flame Tokay left there and 19,000 tons went into the crush in 1996 . For the state as a whole that year, 116,000 tons of table grapes were crushed. This was 69 percent of the total crushed in 1990.

TABLE WINE. According to U.S. tax law, table wine is wine with less than 14 percent alcohol, but at least 7 percent. Usually wine that is more than 14 percent alcohol has been FORTIFIED, but since the 1970s quite a few California wines have had alcohol levels over 14 percent without fortification—powerful Zinfandels are good examples. They, too, are taxed at the higher rate. Federal law does not require that the alcohol level, if it is no more than 14 percent, be indicated on a wine label; the term table wine on a label will suffice.

Table wine is by far the chief product of California wineries today. Before the 1960s this was not the case. Today the ratio of table wine to fortified wine is about twenty to one. In 1996 shipments of California table wine amounted to 353 million gallons, 74 percent of the total produced in the United States.

TAFT STREET (BW 5547). A home winemaking operation before 1982, now a 30,000-case-a-year venture, near Sebastopol in Sonoma County. They buy mostly Sonoma County grapes with an emphasis on Chardonnay, Merlot, and Cabernet Sauvignon.

ROBERT TALBOTT VINEYARDS (BW 5157). The Talbott family began its wine operations in the Carmel Valley in 1983, building a small winery and starting to plant a 32-acre Chardonnay vineyard. That year the grapes for the first crush were purchased from the Salinas Valley. Within a few years the Talbotts were convinced of the high quality of Chardonnay fruit from Salinas Valley and had acquired a fine reputation for their single, varietal wine. In 1989 the Talbotts sold the winery to BERNAR-DUS Pon, kept the vineyard in the Carmel Valley, built a larger winery near Gonzales, and bought more vineyard land in the Santa Lucia Highlands Viticultural Area. Their Chardonnay production has reached 15,000 cases a year and is growing. In 1995 they added 400 more plantable acres to their Salinas Valley holdings. They also sell lots of grapes to other wineries and are now making Pinot noir wine. Their second label is Logan.

TALLEY VINEYARDS (BW 5338). The Talley family had farmed in the Arroyo Grande area of San Luis Obispo County before planting vines in 1982. The Talleys now have 105 acres, mostly Pinot noir and Chardonnay. They sell grapes and introduced their own label in 1986. Annual production at their 70,000-gallon winery is about 6,000 cases and growing.

TANNAT. A dark-skinned wine grape that gives the phenolic backbone to the wines of Madiran in southwest France. There the Cabernets, usually about 50 percent, are used to tone it down some. Tannat is virtually unknown in California today, but for a while it had a rush of popularity. Charles A. WETMORE probably imported it first, in 1879. His report, made in 1884, shows that J. H. DRUMMOND and H. W. CRABB had made wines with Tannat suitable for blending. Wetmore and Professor Eugene HILGARD both thought it blended well with Zinfandel. It was used by many successful producers through the 1890s, but mysteriously disappeared from the scene after 1900.

Experiments with the variety in the 1930s and 1940s at the University of California at Davis led to glowing descriptions of the wines when the grapes were grown in coastal valleys; "richly endowed with a distinctive aroma, full pleasing flavor, good balance, intense color, and full body." But in 1963 the same professors recommended, "somewhat reluctantly" they said, against planting it in California. The state's vineyardists have followed this advice.

TANNIN. Tannins and other PHENOLICS* give young wines a certain bitterness and puckering astringency that can often be harsh and unpleasant. These tannins, from the grape's seeds, skin, and stem, are most common and noticeable in certain young red wines, particularly Cabernet Sauvignon, Syrah, and Nebbiolo.

Tannins cannot be detected by the nose. They cause a bitter, physically perceptible taste sensation in the mouth and throat that can be really distasteful to new wine drinkers. They are essential for wines that are meant to improve with age, particularly certain red wines. Their antioxidant properties help preserve fine red wines and give them structure as they age in the bottle. In recent years one of the principal concerns in premium California wineries has been the control of tannins. It has been found that vineyard and cellar practices can minimize the harsh bitterness of certain tannins while retaining so-called soft tannins. Such procedures make wines such as Cabernet Sauvignon and Zinfandel easier to drink when young. The winemaker can, at the same time, retain the phenolic constituents that promote the good flavors apparent in older wines. Probably the most important technique developed since the 1970s has been extended maceration (see FERMENTATION), in which, by a process called polymerization, a wine will keep its softer tannins and drop its harder ones. (Gary Andrus's 1978 Cabernet Sauvignon made at PINE RIDGE was probably the first commercial California wine to undergo extended maceration for this purpose.) To a certain extent this and other practices that help make well-extracted young red wines taste better, help explain the rebirth of interest in powerful Zinfandels since the mid-1980s.

Another source of tannin in wine can be the OAK BARREL in which it is aged.

TARPEY, M. F. (1847–1925), built his La Paloma Winery near Fresno in 1895 and was a leader of California's sweet wine industry. His vineyards covered 1,400 acres in 1911. During Prohibition he converted much of his production to table grapes. His family sold the winery to National Distillers in 1941. All that remains today is the name Tarpey Village on an aging housing tract.

TARTARIC ACID, the most important ACID* in wine and grapes, although it is quite rare in other fruit. It is this acid that makes a wine appear to be tart. In California it is legal to correct the acid content of a wine, tartaric acid almost always the means for such correction.

The potassium salt of tartaric acid is potassium tartrate, perhaps better known as cream of tartar. When this compound collects in a bottle of wine in the form of bright crystals, it looks like ground glass. Consumers understandably become alarmed, even though the crystals are quite harmless. Since Repeal California winemakers have developed several techniques to precipitate the potassium tartrate out before the wines are bottled. The crystals, called argols, can also accumulate on the insides of casks and tanks, and were once an important byproduct of California winemaking. (Cream of tartar is a constituent of baking powder.) Georges de Latour of BEAULIEU VINEYARD was a dealer in cream of tartar before he became a winemaker.

TARTRATES. See TARTARIC ACID

TAYLOR CALIFORNIA CELLARS (BW 4674). In the late 1970s COCA-COLA of Atlanta invested heavily in the California wine industry, its Wine Spectrum division owning several production facilities in the state. Most in the public eye were those in Monterey County where the Taylor California Cellars brand was produced; see MONTEREY VINEYARD. Wine Spectrum took on GALLO and HEUBLEIN in a dramatic advertising campaign that made history by staging blind tastings in which its Taylor California wines were pitted against those of its chief competitors and then broadcasting the usually favorable results.

Eventually Coca-Cola lost interest and a lot of money in its wine venture and in 1983 sold its holdings to SEAGRAM. In 1987 Seagram sold off Taylor and Paul MASSON to a group calling itself Vintners International. In 1993 the Taylor California brand was acquired by CANANDAIGUA, which today sells about 2.5 million cases of generic and varietal wine under the Taylor label. Some is produced in Monterey County, some in the Central Valley.

TAYLOR, J. F. M., AND MARY TAYLOR. See MATANZAS VINEYARD?

TCHELISTCHEFF, ANDRÉ (1901–94). In 1937 BEAULIEU VINEYARD's* Georges de Latour signed a contract with a marketing agent to sell large quantities of premium wine on the East Coast. The first shipment was a disaster—caused by a combination of microbiological spoilage and volatile acidity. De Latour headed for France to find a first-rate wine chemist and found André Tchelistcheff at the Institute of National Agronomy outside Paris.

Tchelistcheff, then 37 years old, had been born in Moscow, the son of a liberal jurist. The Russian Revolution drove André and his family from the country. He received his degree in agricultural science at the University of Brno in Czechoslovakia and, by the time he arrived in Paris, he had a solid background in enological science and viticulture.

When he got to Napa, arriving 15 September 1938, he was struck by the primitive conditions of winegrowing and winemaking there. It took him about three years to improve the winemaking at Beaulieu. He began by controlling fermentations and upgrading equipment. He also worked in the vineyards, "the voice of nature," he liked to say. When his Burgundy won the grand prize at the Golden Gate Exposition in 1939, his string of vinous triumphs had begun. The next year, Beaulieu Vineyard released a Private Reserve Cabernet Sauvignon, the first in a long line of wonderful wines under that rubric that eventually made it clear just how good California wine could be.

Actually, André was more obsessed by Pinot noir than by Cabernet, regarding the Burgundian grape as "life's challenge" for him. It had been after he had tasted a 1918 STANLY Pinot noir that he had first appreciated the potential of the CARNEROS for the production of fine, Burgundian-style wines. When he retired from Beaulieu in 1973, he could mark twenty-five Cabernet vintages that he considered superior; there were only three for Pinot noir, but it was the 1946 Beaulieu Vineyard Beaumont Pinot Noir that he then considered his best wine.

Tchelistcheff was devoted to the idea of community. He was an enthusiastic promoter for the interchange of technical data and philosophical notions among his fellows in the Napa Valley. And he was always close to the scholars of wines and vines at the University of California at Davis. He once said that the highest title he aspired to was that of a "permanent student of the University of California."

After he left Beaulieu in 1973, he became an almost full-time consultant, serving dozens of California wineries old (e.g., BUENA VISTA and SIMI WINERY) and new (e.g., NIEBAUM-COPPOLA ESTATE and FIRESTONE VINEYARD). In Washington State he is considered a founding father of the modern wine industry there. In 1991 he rejoined Beaulieu as consult-

ing enologist, to him a "great spiritual satisfaction and pleasure."

No person played a greater role in the rebirth of California's premium wine industry after Repeal. Beaulieu, Napa Valley, and the entire California wine industry benefited from the work and influence of this tough-minded, inspiring, witty, and principled perfectionist.

Robert Benson, *Great Winemakers of California* (Santa Barbara, Calif.: Capra Press, 1977), 112–24.

André Tchelistcheff, *Grapes, Wine, and Ecology* (Regional Oral History Office, Bancroft Library, 1983).

TEHAMA COUNTY. The Dane Peter Lassen (1800–59), after he was given a large Mexican land grant in 1843, was the first settler in the vast area of the upper Sacramento Valley that became Tehama County. He planted an acre of Mission vines on his Rancho Bosquejo in 1846. Henry Gerke (1810–?), a German from Hanover, bought a large piece of the rancho in 1851, enlarged the vineyard to about 75 acres, and built a 100,000-gallon winery. He developed a good reputation for his sweet wines and brandy, even for his table wines. This was a remarkable feat, given the almost desert conditions there southeast of Red Bluff. In 1881 Leland Stanford bought the Gerke operation and began creating VINA.

After Vina's demise, few vines have been planted in this hot land. Currently there are about 130 acres of wine grapes.

TEINTURIER. The French term for so-called dyer grapes, that is, grapes with dark red flesh. (The flesh of most grapes is light colored.) No one knows the origin of these vines, except that those we use today all seem to have been derived from a variety known as the Teinturier du Cher, first noted in the Loire Valley in the 1600s. In the 1800s the father-and-son team of Louis and Henri Bouschet bred several teinturier varieties, two of which became important in California, the ALICANTE BOUSCHET* and the GRAND NOIR.

TEISER, RUTH (1917–94). Author, with Catherine Harroun, of *Winemaking in California* (1983), the only successful history of California wine. Perhaps more important was her work for the Bancroft Library at the University of California at Berkeley. Since 1968 she and Harroun have produced fifty-one volumes of oral history transcripts based on interviews with leaders in the wine industry. These interviews have become an essential primary source for other historians.

F. TELDESCHI WINERY (BW 5688). Frank Teldeschi (1919–85) came to California from Italy in 1929 and bought land in Dry Creek Valley in Sonoma County in 1946. His family has raised Zinfandel there ever since. Their vineyard, noted for the high quality of its fruit, supplied grapes for many of JOSEPH SWAN's* early vintages. In 1993 Don Teldeschi bonded his little winery and is now producing about 2,500 cases of powerful Zinfandel each year.

TEMECULA. The earliest connection Temecula had with commercial winegrowing was in 1856 when Jean-Louis VIGNES was denied a land claim there, although grapes had been growing in the valley, which is in the southwestern corner of Riverside County, since the 1820s when the Mission San Luis Rey had an agricultural settlement there.

Modern winegrowing began in 1964 when the owners of the Rancho California development there planted an experimental vineyard. Others soon followed, most notably Ely CALLAWAY, whose operation has dominated winegrowing in the area. The attractions are the good soils and the microclimate—temperatures are moderated by the breezes from the Pacific Ocean, about 20 miles away. Today the area has about 1,800 acres of vines, overwhelmingly Chardonnay (65 percent). In fact it has become increasingly clear that Temecula is white-wine country. Since 1974 fourteen wineries have been bonded here.

In 1984 Temecula was granted AVA status after a fairly heated dispute over the proper size of the district. In the end proponents of an expanded district of about 160 square miles won out.

TEMPERATURE. See CLIMATE; FERMENTATION; HEAT SUMMATION

TEMPLETON. See SAN LUIS OBISPO COUNTY

TEMPRANILLO, a variety of wine grape that is usually blended with Grenache, and is found in many Spainish dry red table wines. In 1996 the BATF decided that Tempranillo was a synonym for the Valdepeñas variety, a decision that might confuse Spaniards, who consider the Valdepeñas to be a different red-wine variety, used in La Mancha where the Tempranillo is called Cencibel.

A variety called Valdepeñas has been grown in California since the turn of the century when Fredrick BIOLETTI described it as "always satisfactory" for the Central Valley. In later years the enologists at the University of California at Davis did not agree with him, black-listing the grape twice since Repeal. But its potential for yielding between 8 and 10 tons per acre in the interior hot lands has moved some to grow it for jug-wine blends. Acreage rose from 800 to 2,500 between 1961 and 1975, but has dropped to about 400 today, mostly in Stanislaus and San Joaquin counties. State statistics list Tempranillo and Valdepeñas separately. R. H. PHILLIPS makes a varietal Tempranillo.

TEPUSQUET: See SANTA MARIA VALLEY

THE TERRACES. Wayne Hogue has 7 acres of Cabernet Sauvignon and Zinfandel in the foothills east of Rutherford in Napa County.

Since 1985 CAYMUS has been making wine for him under The Terraces label. Although amounting to barely 1,000 cases per year, his wines have been winning steady critical support. In 1992 the 1987 Terraces Cabernet Sauvignon won the San Francisco VINTNERS CLUB annual blind tasteoff, beating out seventy-one other Cabernets.

TERROIR, the French term for a concept that is complex yet easily understood. *Terroir* is the combination of all the elements of the natural environment that together influence the wine grapes produced in a certain vineyard or region. The idea is that *terroir* is the best explanation for a vineyard's consistently producing a great wine with consistently identifiable characteristics. With proper CLIMATE seen as something of a constant, scientists have focused on SOIL* as probably the chief variable accounting for the excellence of some locations over others with similar climates. (Note that a first growth and a vineyard with a far more humble reputation may sit side by side in Bordeaux.)

Most of the research on the concept has been done in Western Europe and Australia. So far Californians tend to use the term regularly but have depended mostly on the inductive logic of trial and error to discover their great vineyards. Some here deny that the concept is valid.

THACKREY & CO. (BW 5082). In 1979 Sean Thackrey added a winemaking avocation to his vocation as an art dealer in San Francisco. Two years later winemaking at his home in Marin County became a part-time vocation. Over the years his small production, about 2,000 cases, has focused more and more on old-vine Syrah, Petite Sirah, and Mourvèdre (Mataro). He names his wines after stars and constellations. His Syrah is called Orion; other wines have been Aquila, Sirius, and Pleiades.

THÉE, ETIENNE. See ALMADEN VINEYARDS

THINNING. It has long been believed that the quality of wine grapes is raised by holding down the size of the crop. This can be accomplished, to a great extent, at PRUNING time by limiting the number of retained buds by thinning the grapes, by either snipping off flower clusters in the late spring or lopping off bunches during the summer.

Until recent years thinning was rarely a part of vineyard practice in California. Only a very few highly idealistic growers, usually winemakers who owned their vineyards, would thin their crops. Only in those years when vines are carrying a heavy crop and predictions of cool weather indicate that a delayed vintage could be hit by late-fall storms, would most other vineyardists resort to thinning.

The idea of restricting the crop to concentrate flavors was popular in the 1960s and 1970s, but experiments at the University of California at Davis and by practitioners in the field indicate that there is no direct relationship between higher quality and extensive thinning. Experiments showed that wines from Cabernet Sauvignon and Zinfandel vines, thinned to 3 tons and 5 tons per acre in alternating rows of the same vineyard, did not differ in quality as determined by blind tastings. Nevertheless, today many vineyardists in California try to develop a clear idea of the proper crop level for their vines and will "drop fruit" if they think the crop is too large. Such practices are most often found today in vineyards intended to produce RESERVE quality wines. For those vineyardists, the University's findings did not *dis*prove a relationship between crop size and quality.

THOMANN, JOHN (1836–1900). The site of the Sutter Home Winery in Napa today was purchased by John Thomann in 1874. There he built his winery and by the end of the decade was annually producing 100,000 gallons. Four years after his death, his heirs sold the winery to the owners of the DEER PARK WINERY on Howell Mountain. When they

The Thomann estate in 1878 and a fair picture of the Napa Valley just below St. Helena on today's Highway 29. The tracks are still in place, unused for years until the Wine Train began making its tourist runs in 1989.

moved to the Thomann place, the new owners renamed it the sutter home winery.* (On page 355 there is a photograph of the winery as it was in 1908.)

THOMAS VINEYARDS (BW 3603). After Prohibition Hugh Thomas in Cucamonga rebuilt his winery, which dated from the 1890s. After World War II new owners advertised that the winery was the oldest in California. The claim was based on the notion that the winery building was on the old Tiburcio Tapa rancho, where there had been a little adobe winery, a piece of which was in the walls of the Thomas winery. In later years the building was a tasting room for the FILIPPI VINTAGE COMPANY.

THOMPSON BROTHERS. In 1851 Simpson and William Thompson received 320 acres of land south of Napa City in exchange for a load

of lumber used to build the State House in Vallejo. On this land they developed a nursery, Soscol Gardens, among the specialties of which were grape vines. This was the most important wine-grape nursery in the Napa-Sonoma area through the 1870s.

THOMPSON SEEDLESS. It is a toss-up which grape has made the most wine in California history, Zinfandel or the Thompson Seedless, but the latter is classified as a raisin grape, even though most consumers know it as a table grape.

The vine came to California in 1872, to Sutter County, when a rancher, William Thompson, ordered a vine from the catalogue published by a nursery in Rochester, New York. The nursery called it Lady de Coverley, but the Sutter County Horticultural Society decided (16 August 1888) to call it the Thompson Seedless. (Actually it is the Sultanina.) Its huge yields quickly made it a favorite up and down the Central Valley for raisins, table grapes, fortified wines, and brandy. During Prohibition thousands of carloads went east each year to home winemakers. Although it added little flavor to their wines it did a good job stretching and toning down the red varieties.

At Repeal there were about 200,000 acres in the Central Valley; in the 1990s there are about 270,000, making it by far California's most extensively planted grape variety. Between 1933 and 1941 the Thompson crush averaged 235,000 tons, about 30 percent of the state's total. During the war most raisin grapes became raisins, but between 1946 and 1955, the Thompson crush averaged 453,000 tons, and had become 36 percent of the state's total. Over the next ten years, to vintage 1965, that share rose to 40 percent. Since then, it has declined steadily to about 15 percent, the greatest drop, from 32 to 18, coming between 1975 and 1985. A shortage of wine grapes in California in 1996 accounted for a huge jump in the Thompson crush for that year. The total was 606,000 tons, up 43 percent from the 1995 crush, and fully 21 percent of the total crush. Much of this increase went to stretching other, more flavorful varieties.

THORNTON WINERY (BW 5417). John Culbertson's homemade sparkling wine was so good, he thought, that in 1975 he bought a citrus and avocado ranch in northern San Diego County and in 1981 bonded his little winery there. He used grapes grown to the north in the Temecula area at Riverside. His first commercial wines were critical successes. All this time he was commuting to Houston where he continued to run his underwater technology firm.

In 1987 he acquired additional financing and built a large winery and tourist center in Temecula. Culbertson's wide range of sparklers continued popular and by 1988 annual production reached almost 20,000 cases. In 1991 John Thornton, now the majority partner, took over control of the operation, which was deeply in debt, even though production was up to 45,000 cases a year. Since then the winery has been producing about 40,000 cases of sparkling and table wine under the Thornton and Culbertson labels. Since 1995 Thornton has placed special emphasis on red table wine, particularly from a few old-vine Zinfandel vineyards in southern California

THREE PALMS VINEYARD. Lillie Hitchcock Coit's parents bought a large part of what is the Larkmead area of Napa Valley in 1872. They gave her a piece of it in 1875 and built her a beautiful home there, long gone; see LARKMEAD WINERY. In 1967, when John and Sloan Upton bought 83 acres here and planted them mostly to red Bordeaux varieties, three palms were all that was left from those early days. Today the Three Palms vineyard is probably the most praised source of Merlot grapes in California.

TIBURON VINTNERS. See RODNEY STRONG VINEYARDS

TIJSSELING WINERY. See ZELLERBACH WINERY

TIMOTHY, BROTHER (ANTHONY G. DIENER). See CHRISTIAN BROTHERS

TINTA MADEIRA, the name of a variety of grape recommended by enologists at the University of California at Davis in 1944 and 1963 for port wine production. They identified it as a Portuguese grape. There is a variety called Tinta da Madeira grown on the island of Madeira (which is technically part of Portugal), but no one seems to know it on the mainland.

A few acres were planted in Madera County after World War II. Acreage peaked in 1978 at 1,278 and then declined steadily until it disappeared completely from state statistics in the 1990s.

TIPO CHIANTI. See ITALIAN SWISS COLONY

TKC VINEYARDS (BW 5071). Harold Nuffer has 9 acres of Zinfandel in Amador County. He bonded his winery in 1981 and makes about 1,500 cases of powerful Zinfandel wine each year.

TOBIN JAMES CELLARS (BW 5671). Tobin James Shumrick bonded his own winery in Paso Robles in 1987 after having made his wine at PEACHY CANYON for three years. Today he makes a wide range of wines that totals about 8,000 cases per year. Zinfandel is the leader with bottlings under exotic titles such as Big Shot, Sure Fire, and Blue Moon. He also makes Chardonnay, Merlot, Pinot noir, and Cabernet Sauvignon.

TOCAI FRIULANO. See SAUVIGNON VERT

TOGNI, PHILIP, would be something of a historic figure in Napa winemaking even if he had retired in 1981 instead of starting his own successful vineyard and winery on Spring Mountain (BW 5290). After a stint in the British army, he took degrees in enology and viticulture at Bordeaux and Montpellier. He made wine in Beaujolais, Alsace, and Algeria. In 1956 he was assistant manager at Château Lascombes in Bordeaux. Then he made wine in Chile. He came to Napa in 1959 and made wine at MAYACAMAS, INGLENOOK, and STERLING. (He was also the first winemaker at CHALONE.) After running the cellar at CHAPPELLET from 1968 to 1973, in 1975 he became the winemaker at CUVAISON.

On Spring Mountain he makes mostly Cabernet Sauvignon, which has a reputation for power, elegance, and longevity. His 1987 and 1990 Cabernets are famous. In his 2,500-case-a-year output there is also Sauvignon blanc and a small quantity of muscat from the Black Hamburg, a wine he calls Ca' Togni.

TO KALON. See HIRAM W. CRABB

TOKAY. After Repeal several wineries in the Central Valley sold a sweet fortified concoction labeled Tokay. Usually amber pink, it was often but not necessarily made with FLAME TOKAY grapes, but had no relation to Hungary's famous dessert wine, Tokaj. Some producers made their Tokay by blending port and sherry. Such wines are no longer seen but tokay is still a legal GENERIC term for American wines.

TOPOLOS OF RUSSIAN RIVER (BW 4855). Robert Lasdin founded his Russian River Vineyards (BW 4327) near Forestville in 1963. By 1978 the winery had had three owners when the Topolos family bought the place and rebonded it. In the early 1980s they produced a very broad range of varietals but have narrowed their line since 1989, focusing now on Zinfandel and Petite Sirah. There is also an almost-famous ALICANTE BOUSCHET varietal. Total annual production is close to 20,000 cases.

MARIMAR TORRES ESTATE (BW 5666). Torres Wines is a leading Spanish wine house and, for several years, Marimar Torres handled the marketing operations of her family's North American wine operations. In 1986, after buying land in Green Valley, Sonoma, she began planting Chardonnay and Pinot noir to very close spacing. She sold grapes and in 1989 had a small quantity of Chardonnay made for her label. In 1990 there were 3,000 cases and the next year a small winery went up. Production from the 80-acre vineyard now totals about 14,000 cases. Critics have given the Chardonnay top marks.

TRAINING SYSTEMS. Since ancient times vineyardists have shaped their young vines so they could work them more easily. Grape vines left to grow as they will eventually create an impenetrable jungle.

In early California vines were trained low to the ground in the Spanish style. By the 1870s most vines were trained up a redwood grape stake, between 2 and 3 feet above the ground. They were then PRUNED to short spurs. After about eight years such head-pruned vines had a thick, upright trunk with a ring of short arms around the head. In a few more years the top of the vine had a goblet appearance and the trunk was thick enough to support itself and its crop without a stake. This approach was common in California until the 1970s. One still sees picturesque old vineyards here and there with vines trained in this manner.

In the 1870s other training systems came into limited use in California, particularly as some vineyardists began using trellises for their vines. It was found that some varieties gave better yields if they are cane pruned rather than spur pruned. In such circumstances head training was still employed except that the head was developed in a fan shape in the plane of the trellis wire. The cane was then tied to the wire and was replaced the following year. Cordon training was also tried before Prohibition, but did not become popular for wine-grape varieties. Now it is a very common practice. The cordon is simply an extension of the trunk, usually in both directions on the trellis. Such bilateral cordons are created by retaining two healthy canes and then pruning them to spurs in later years. When the cordons become old and heavy, they can be replaced.

In recent years much work has been done to improve the quality of the grapes by training vines to specially shaped TRELLISES, so as to open the vine to more sunlight and fresh air. The training of the vine is also affected if the vineyard is to be harvested mechanically. The recent trend to closer spacing has made vineyardists modify their training systems.

TRAMINER. See GEWÜRZTRAMINER

TRANSFER PROCESS. See SPARKLING WINE

TREBBIANO. See UGNI BLANC

TREFETHEN VINEYARDS (BW 4635). Before the Trefethens acquired their winery and its vineyard in 1968, the estate had been the site of the historic ESHCOL WINERY* and before that part of Joseph OSBORNE's Oak Knoll ranch. Over the years the Trefethens have developed 600 acres of vineyard and have restored and expanded the landmark Eshcol Winery.

Located in the OAK KNOLL area of the Napa Valley, in the cooler, southern region south of Yountville, Trefethen's emphasis has been on Chardonnay, but there is also Cabernet Sauvignon, Merlot, and White Riesling. They sell grapes to other wineries but produce about 100,000 cases of their own, some of those sold under the Eshcol label.

TRELLIS. The earliest commercial grape trellises in California were simple one- or two-wire affairs, usually the latter, for cane-pruned grapes. The lower wire held the cane and the upper wire supported the growing shoots. Two-wire trellises were also used for cordon-trained vines.

Since the 1960s many more complicated trellis systems have been developed to meet the special needs of California vineyardists. Proper positioning of the fruit for mechanical harvesting is one of the most important of these needs. Systems developed for viticulture in New York State have also been adopted and often modified for the California environment. These systems usually have several wires and tend to open up the vines to sunlight and fresh air. The Geneva Double Curtain, for example, has been successful in diminishing herbaceous flavors in Sauvignon blanc, Cabernet Sauvignon, and Merlot.

TRENTADUE WINERY (BW 4538). In 1959 Leo and Evelyn Trentadue traded an agricul-

One of the architectural gems of the Napa Valley is the ESHCOL winery, now the home of Trefethen Vineyards. The huge wooden facility, built in 1886, is unique in the world of wine and has been painstakingly restored. It was designed by H. W. MCINTYRE, who also planned INGLENOOK and many other great California wineries. (Trefethen Vineyards)

tural life in the Santa Clara Valley for one near Geyserville in Sonoma County, where they acquired two adjoining ranches that had 42 acres of vines. For 10 years they sold grapes to ITALIAN SWISS COLONY and others, and in 1969 bonded their own winery. It was also in that year that they sold their property on MONTE BELLO to RIDGE VINEYARDS, a sale that included the old Perrone winery, which is now Ridge's production facility. Since 1966 the Trentadues have sold grapes to Ridge for its Geyserville Zinfandel.

Today the Trentadues control about 250 acres of vines. Over the years they have produced a wide range of varietal and generic wines, once even an EARLY BURGUNDY varietal. Production has held at about 20,000 cases for several years, but the product line has narrowed, now emphasizing Zinfandel, Merlot, and Sangiovese. Among the pioneers, Trentadue first planted Sangiovese in 1982 and released the first wine in 1985.

TRINCHERO FAMILY. See SUTTER HOME

TROUSSEAU GRIS. See GREY RIESLING

TRUCHARD VINEYARDS (BW 5521). When Anthony Truchard bought 20 acres in the rolling hills of the northern Carneros in 1973, there weren't 300 acres of grapes in the region. Now he has 170 acres in vineyard. He bonded his winery in 1990 but has always sold most of his grapes to other wineries. He specializes in Pinot noir, Chardonnay, and Merlot. The Truchard vineyard, unlike most of the Carneros, can ripen Cabernet Sauvignon. Total annual production is now about 8,000 cases.

TRUE WINERY. See FENESTRA WINERY

TUBBS FAMILY. See CHATEAU MONTELENA

TUDAL WINERY (BW 4891). Arnold Tudal bought 10 acres of walnut orchard near the Napa River in 1973. Soon all the land was in Cabernet Sauvignon. In 1979 he bonded his little winery north of St. Helena and now makes about 2,000 cases of Cabernet a year.

TULARE COUNTY, in the lower San Joaquin Valley has been made a rich agricultural land by irrigation and the railroad. Grapes, but not wine grapes in particular, have been important here since the 1890s. Before Prohibition muscats were dominant. Since Repeal the Thompson Seedless has been the leader. Nevertheless, since the huge Tulare Winery was founded in 1902, a sizeable portion of the county's raisin- and table-grape production has gone into the production of fortified wines, brandy, and concentrates; see SIERRA WINE CO.

Since Repeal the acreage under grapes in Tulare County averaged between 65,000 and 70,000. Wine-grape acreage rose slowly after Repeal, from about 3,500 to 6,400 in 1968. It reached its peak of 18,036 in 1974. In 1997, in a total of 66,505 acres of grapes, 10,947 acres were in wine grapes, of which 58 percent was in white varieties and about half of those French Colombard, the only wine grape there with a sizeable acreage.

Tulare's oldest vineyard was 8 acres of Mission grapes planted in 1854 by James Persian, 4 miles east of Visalia. It was a good producer until the 1930s.

TULOCAY WINERY (BW 4696). In 1975 William Cadman bonded his winery east of the town of Napa and makes about 2,500 cases annually. His wines, all vineyard-designated, are made from purchased grapes grown in the Napa Valley. His specialties are Cabernet Sauvignon, Chardonnay, and Pinot noir.

TURLEY. The Turleys, **Larry** and his sister, **Helen,** have added a complex dimension to Napa Valley wine in recent years.

Larry Turley founded FROG'S LEAP WINERY in 1981, originally calling it Turley Wine Cellars. In 1994 he ended his partnership in that operation but kept the old facility for his new **Turley Wine Cellars.** His winemaker for the 1993–95 vintages was Helen Turley. She produced a string of vineyard-designated Napa Valley Zinfandels with reputations exceeding those of her earlier wines at B. R. COHN and Peter MICHAEL. She had moved to Napa Valley in 1977 and worked for a while for Robert MONDAVI. She has also acted as consultant for numerous first-rate California wineries. Her chief interest recently has been the nurturing of her own Marcassin brand, for which she has been making acclaimed Chardonnay since 1993. She also owns a small Pinot noir and Chardonnay vineyard near the Sonoma Coast, inland from Fort Ross. Her first vintage from those vines was in 1995.

TURNBULL WINE CELLARS (BW 4915). In 1977 Reverdy Johnson and William Turnbull bought a 20-acre vineyard in Oakville in Napa County planted mostly to Cabernet Sauvignon in 1967. In 1979 they bonded Johnson Turnbull Vineyards and developed a good reputation for their Cabernets, which averaged 5,000 cases per year. There was also some Chardonnay from Turnbull's ranch in Knight's Valley. In 1993 the partners sold the operation to Patrick O'Dell, who had already purchased two vineyards in Napa Valley the year before. He changed the winery's name to Turnbull Wine Cellars. Since then he has added Sauvignon blanc, Merlot, and Sangiovese. O'Dell now owns 120 acres of vines in the Oakville area and has production up to 15,000 cases.

TWIGHT, EDMUND HENRI (1874–1957), a French scientist and mathematician who became a specialist in viticulture and enology after his arrival in California in 1898. He first worked for the CALIFORNIA WINE ASSOCIATION and, in 1901, became the University of California's first professorial appointee in viticulture. He worked throughout the industry in later years and was one of the chief links between its pre-Prohibition and post-Repeal days. In the 1930s he returned to the university, this time to the Division of Viticulture at the University of California at Davis.

TWIN HILLS WINERY (5050). James Lockshaw began developing a 40-acre vineyard on his Twin Hill Ranch near Paso Robles in 1979 and bonded his winery in 1982. In 1992 Caroline Scott bought the place. She had been a home winemaker since her student days at Stanford University. Production is about 6,000 cases per year with an emphasis on Zinfandel, Chardonnay, and Cabernet Sauvignon. She also has a solera for her sherry, produced from an old patch of PALOMINO vines on the ranch.

TYCHSON, JOSEPHINE. See FREEMARK ABBEY WINERY

UC BERKELEY. See UNIVERSITY OF CALIFORNIA, BERKELEY

UC DAVIS. See UNIVERSITY OF CALIFORNIA, DAVIS

UGARTE, JUAN DE (1660–1730). As a leader of the Jesuit missionaries, he was responsible for bringing winegrowing to BAJA CALIFORNIA by having vinifera vines planted at the peninsula's first mission at Lareto, probably in 1698. The vineyard was actually planted by Father Juan Salvatierra (1648–1717), who founded the mission.

UGNI BLANC. A white-wine grape that is the Italian Trebbiano and the St-Émilion of Cognac and Armagnac, where it makes the base wine for brandies. It produces a pleasant, tart, but undistinguished wine usually used for blending. It bears heavy crops and is the most widely planted white-wine grape in France and Italy, perhaps in the world.

The variety was in California in the 1880s but was rejected in 1885 by Eugene HILGARD, J. H. DRUMMOND, and Frederico POHNDORFF for excessive acidity. After Prohibition enologists at the University of California at Davis rejected it for its low acidity in hot climates and for its neutral flavor. After World War II, when it was officially named St. Emilion, there were about 1,000 acres in California, mostly scat-

tered through the Central Valley. Today there are about 460 acres in the state. Of these 16 are in the Livermore Valley, where the variety was popular after Repeal for blending with Chenin blanc and other varieties. In 1990 IVAN TAMAS WINES made 5,000 cases of wine from those vines, labeled Trebbiano in honor of the current interest in Italian varietals.

The 1996 statewide crush of Ugni blanc was 2,258 tons, 42 percent of the total in 1990.

UKIAH. If the wine-producing areas of Mendocino County can be said to have an urban center, it is this lumber town of 15,000 people. It is a good destination point for tourists visiting the local wine country.

ULLAGE. The amount by which a wine container, such as a barrel or bottle, falls short of being full. Head space is a synonym. As the ullage line approaches the shoulder of a bottle, the consumer should be increasingly suspicious of the condition of its contents; the wine may be overly oxidized.

UNCLE SAM WINERY. See CHARLES CARPY

UNITED VINTNERS. A corporate entity created by Louis PETRI as a subsidiary of his family wine business in 1952; see also ALLIED GRAPE GROWERS. In 1968 HEUBLEIN acquired a controlling interest in United

Vintners, an acquisition at first challenged and then accepted by the Federal Trade Commission. By 1983 the assets, which included INGLENOOK and ITALIAN SWISS COLONY, had been sold off or integrated into the Heublein operation under the corporate name Heublein Wines.

UNIVERSITY OF CALIFORNIA, BERKELEY.

Founded in 1868 in Oakland, the school moved to its Berkeley campus in 1873. Appropriate for the state's early economy, the first great faculties were in mining, engineering, and agriculture. To head the latter in 1875 came Eugene W. HILGARD,* a noted soil scientist from the University of Michigan. For many years Hilgard and his staff directed a large part of their energies to the practical problems of viticulture and enology then faced by the state's growing wine industry. The College of Agriculture was supported in this work in the 1880s by specific appropriations from the state legislature for the fight against the PHYLLOXERA. Although Hilgard was effective in drawing attention to the phylloxera threat, his staff lost some credibility for promoting the *Vitis* CALIFORNICA as a resistant ROOTSTOCK. In the 1890s, however, assistants such as Arthur Hayne and F. W. Morse put the college on the right course for the selection of resistant vines.

Hilgard and his staff also did good work on varietals and their wines. He collected grape samples from all over and had small batches of wine made from them. The result was a series of papers published between 1883 and 1896 that had a powerful influence on the selection of varieties planted then, and more important, in later years. Hilgard's viticultural reports amounted to 1,250 pages. From 1884 to 1896, he also wrote a series of forty-two Bulletins on numerous practical problems for winegrowers.

His staff's work after 1884, and Hilgard's rather frank comments on the low quality of much of California's commercial wine, led to a running battle with some leaders of the state's industry and with the STATE VITICULTURAL COMMISSION. For their high standards Hilgard and his men were characterized by Charles WETMORE and his allies as impractical idealists. The battle continued into the 1890s and culminated in 1895 when the legislature abolished the Commission and turned over many of its functions and its effects to the University of California at Berkeley.

In those years the university maintained a regular wine laboratory and cellar under Hilgard's supervision. Many of the experiments made there led to publications of great importance, particularly on the subject of fermentation temperature. There was also a small vineyard on campus. In 1897 the laboratory was destroyed by fire and in 1901 wine production experiments were officially discontinued as a result of pressure placed on the legislature by prohibitionists.

Perhaps more important for California winegrowers were the various outreach programs of the university. Hilgard wanted the work of his department to go directly into the cellar and vineyard. Thus, he and his staff were constantly in the field, talking, listening, explaining, teaching, and encouraging. Very close relations were developed with many of the medium-sized producers of premium wine who appreciated Hilgard's views on quality. Several gave land to the university for practical viticultural experimentation. Eventually these activities were formalized in the Extension Service in conjunction with the California Experimental Station at the University of California at Davis. Branch EXPERIMENTAL STATIONS,* also promoted by the U.S. Department of Agriculture since 1887, had and still have a powerful and practical effect on California wine. The university's Cooperative Extension Service, financed by federal funds after 1914, placed county farm advisors close to all California farmers.

Eventually at Berkeley under William V. CRUESS,* the Division of Fruit Products was established and at the end of Prohibition, beginning in 1934, this division organized conferences and gave short courses for winemakers. But soon the chief work in viticulture and enology was taken over by the staff at the university's Davis campus.

UNIVERSITY OF CALIFORNIA, DAVIS.

After years of penny-pinching resistance, the state legislature succumbed in 1905 to the lobbying and agitation in favor of a real agricultural college for California. Money was appropriated to buy 779 acres at Davis, a few miles west of Sacramento. There the University of California at Berkeley was to establish a University Farm for experimentation and for teaching "the sons and daughters" of California's farmers. For years "The Farm" did not award degrees, but it gradually became a part of the College of Agriculture, a development formalized in 1922. Eventually the institution became a separate campus of the University with its own College of Agriculture.

The first practical short course in viticulture was offered in 1908; the next year Frederic BIO-LETTI* came up to Davis to take charge of that program. Research in viticulture at this time emphasized experimentation with resistant rootstock to keep up the fight against phylloxera. Officially, research into wine did not begin until after Prohibition. Until then the department that has evolved into today's Department of Viticulture and Enology operated as part of the Division of Viticulture and Fruit Products. In 1935, after Bioletti's retirement, the Division was reconstituted as the Fruit Products Department at Berkeley, under William CRUESS, and the Department of Viticulture at Davis, under Albert WINKLER.*

Wine research began in 1935. But the great work of the 1930s combined enology and viticulture by searching out the scores of varieties planted throughout California and evaluating them for their growing potential in their environments and for the quality of the wines produced; see CLIMATE; HEAT SUMMATION. The result was a guide for the industry on what to plant where for the best results. The department's outreach programs promoted the planting of better varieties for making high-quality wines.

Enological research covered almost every then-imaginable subject: aromas, pigments, temperature control, yeasts, stability, clarification, blending, and brandy production, to name a few. There was also research into the proper physical setup and operation of a winery, with emphasis on equipment. In viticulture the research was equally broad, encompassing rootstock, irrigation, training systems, pruning, spacing, pests, molds, maturity, harvesting, and plant breeding.

The most important product at Davis was its students, who were soon going into the field and working in the vineyards and cellars of the Golden State. This had not been true of the university's wine and viticulture program before Prohibition. By 1940 the department had sixteen faculty members, eight each for viticulture and enology. The class of 1940 is still famous for its graduates, which included Louis P. MARTINI and Myron NIGHTINGALE.

The chief product of the department's research was a steady flow of findings in widely disseminated university publications distributed free throughout the state and to other institutions. By 1980 more than a thousand titles had been produced by members of the department since Repeal.

It has been said with some truth that the scientific knowledge of grapes and wines advanced more in the three decades after World War II than in the preceding 2,000 years. During those 30 years, the University of California at Davis became the world's leader in the acquisition of this knowledge. Symbolic of this leadership is the AMERICAN SOCIETY FOR ENOLOGY AND VITICULTURE, the world's leading scholarly organization in its field and centered at Davis since its founding in 1950.

Most recently the viticulture and enology department has been faced with the unhappy situation in which the A×R#1 ROOTSTOCK, long the darling of the department, was found not to be resistant to a new biotype of PHYLLOXERA. Their continuing support of the rootstock and their tardiness in warning vineyardists of the burgeoning problem have brought down severe recriminations on the faculty. Perhaps more serious have been charges from numerous producers that Davis graduates are taught to make well-polished but characterless wines. This controversy reverses the battle of quality versus quantity fought by HILGARD and WETMORE in the 1880s; the other is reminiscent of Hilgard's gaffe about resistant rootstock; see CALIFORNICA.

There have been many changes among the faculty in the department in recent years as the old-timers who came aboard after World War II have retired. There are now fifteen members on the staff, eleven professors and four Cooperative Extension specialists. Three of the professors are women. Another change is in the amount of money available for instruction and research. Between 1990 and 1993 funds for the department were cut by 28 percent; not all of it has been restored. Change can also be seen in the topics of research. Through the 1970s heavy emphasis was given to problems affecting the industrial side of wine production. These are still significant because the industry remains an important source of private funds. But many areas of research now might please Professor Hilgard for their obvious emphasis on the production of great, not just good, wine, among them, flavors and aromas, clonal research, canopy management, DNA research, moderating the use of sulfur dioxide, use of natural yeasts, phenolics, and the aging of red wine.

Another special and related task during the 1990s has been the upgrading of the facilities at the Oakville Experimental Vineyard, scheduled to cost $2.5 million. In the past its priorities stressed vine productivity and vine health. These are still part of the program at Oakville, but the vineyard's new frontier for the next century is the relationship between vineyard practices and superior wine quality.

California Agriculture 34, no. 7 (July 1980).

James T. Lapsley, Bottled Poetry: Napa Winemaking from Prohibition to the Modern Era (Berkeley, Calif.: University of California Press, 1996).

V

VACHÉ. In 1849 **Théophile Vaché** (1814–84) arrived in San Francisco from France by way of New Orleans and Peru. After working in Monterey for a few years, he acquired 120 acres in San Benito County in the CIENEGA VALLEY* and in 1858 planted a vineyard. By the 1860s he was supplying wine and brandy to the markets and saloons in Hollister, San Juan Bautista, Salinas, and Monterey. By the 1880s his estate amounted to 320 acres with 35 acres of vineyard. In 1883 he sold his ranch to William PALMTAG and returned to France.

Théophile's brother, **Emile** (1836–1908), came to Monterey in 1856. Later he was a partner in a small winery in Los Angeles. In 1881 near Redlands he established a winery he called BROOKSIDE. By the 1890s it was one of the most important in San Bernardino County, but was shut down by Prohibition in 1918. The Vaché and BIANE families were related by marriage, which accounts for the revival of the Brookside winery name in the 1950s.

VAI, JAMES. See PADRE VINEYARD CO.

VALDEPEÑAS. See TEMPRANILLO

VALDIGUIÉ. See GAMAY; NAPA GAMAY

VALLEJO, M. G. See BENZIGER FAMILY WINERY; HEUBLEIN

VALLEJO, MARIANO GUADALUPE (1808–90). When Alta California (see CALIFORNIA) was conquered by American forces in 1846, Vallejo was the Mexican civil and military commander of the northern frontier. In 1834 he had been called upon to secularize the mission at SONOMA.* Next year he founded the little town there. He planted a small vineyard on his own land and built a winery. By 1842 he was making 20 barrels of wine and brandy.

When Americans began arriving in northern California in large numbers in the 1840s, Vallejo welcomed them and to several who settled in the area he supplied grape cuttings. Vallejo was not displeased by the Americans' conquest of the province, as he had acquired several huge pieces of land in the Sonoma-Napa region. He even helped write California's first state constitution.

In the 1850s he expanded his winegrowing operation and was certainly the father of the commercial wine industry in the Sonoma Valley. It was partly his success that attracted Agoston HARASZTHY* to the area in 1857. Vallejo won numerous awards for his wines and brandy at county and state fairs. Many of these are on display at his home in Sonoma, now part of the state park system.

By 1860 he had hired a French winemaker to run his cellar and had become quite close to

Mariano Vallejo's home, Lachryma Montis (tears of the mountain), named for a little spring on the property. The State of California has done a good job preserving and restoring the buildings associated with Vallejo in the town of Sonoma. The estate today looks much as it did in this drawing made in 1877.

Haraszthy, so much so that in 1863 two of his daughters married two of the Hungarian's sons. Vallejo's vineyard and winery continued operations into the 1870s, when his vines finally succumbed to phylloxera. He replanted 2 acres, but these were to table grapes.

> Madie D. Brown, "The Vineyards of Gen. M. J. Vallejo," *California Historical Society Quarterly,* September 1957, 241–50.

VALLEY OF THE MOON WINERY (VAL-MOON) (BW 4388). Enrico Parducci (1890–1980) owned a sausage factory in San Francisco when he and Enrico Domenici bought 500 acres south of Glen Ellen, Sonoma County, in 1942. Much of their land had been part of George HEARST's estate. Parducci, no relation to the owners of PARDUCCI WINE CELLARS in Mendocino, gained full control of the operation in 1955.

There was a large tract of old vineyard on the place and in 1945 Parducci began making wine. He sold lots of it to restaurants in San Francisco and in bulk. By the 1970s the family had production up to 100,000 gallons. By then they were also selling lots of wine in their tasting room , where they offered a huge line of generic wines, sweet and dry, and a few varietals. Since the 1970s the Parduccis cut back on production and gave more emphasis to their varietals, particularly Zinfandel and Cabernet Sauvignon. In 1996 Kenwood Vineyards (see KENWOOD), in order to add another premium brand to its line of varietal wines, bought the Valley of the Moon Winery.

VALLIANT WINERY (BW 4138). Edwin Valliant, who had been in the wine business since 1913, acquired the old PALMTAG winery in the Cienega Valley, San Benito County, in 1934. He took a year getting the old estate in shape and made 75,000 gallons in 1935. He sold much of his wine in bulk but also made sizeable lots of fine varietal and generic wine. By 1941 they had gained a national reputation, particularly his Riesling and his Burgundy, mostly from Carignane. Mary Frost MABON thought his Riesling the best in California, as did Leon ADAMS. After 1940 Valliant's wines were distributed nationally by W. A. Taylor (Hiram Walker). Valliant died at the end of the 1943 vintage and in 1944 Hiram Walker bought the estate. In 1947 the company's Riesling won a gold medal at the California State Fair. When ALMADEN acquired the estate in 1955, there were 507 acres in vines and a winery with a 675,000 gallon capacity.

VAN ASPEREN, ERNIE, AND VIRGINIA VAN ASPEREN. See ROUND HILL CELLARS

VARIETALS. Before the 1930s few bottles of California wine carried any reference on the label to the variety or varieties of grape from which the wine was made. Zinfandel was the chief exception, although even most Zinfandel was actually sold in bottles labeled claret. Occasionally bottles were labeled Riesling and Cabernet. After Repeal critics, led by Frank SCHOONMAKER, argued that California wines would never achieve their potential in quality or esteem unless the GENERIC system of labeling were abandoned, at least for premium table wines. Many premium producers agreed, as did the professors at the University of California at Davis and the organizers of the wine competitions at the State Fair; many industry leaders belittled the idea for years.

Even though varietal labeling became fairly common after World War II, federal government regulations required only that no less than 51 percent of a wine come from the variety indicated on the label. This requirement was raised to 75 percent in 1983. In the 1990s there have been calls from some producers to raise that percentage.

A problem with varietal wines in California comes from the long-standing tradition here of misidentifying grape varieties, treating some varietal terms as synonyms when they are not, and creating names for varieties that do not conform to their historic identities; see, for instance, GOLDEN CHASSELAS and GREY RIESLING.

The BATF worked on this problem for years and in 1996 came up with a ruling on varietal names permissable on American wines and their acceptable synonyms. The list that follows includes only those that might be seen on a bottle of California wine today. Alternative names are accepted synonyms. See also entries for individual varieties.

Alicante Bouschet
Barbera
Cabernet franc
Cabernet Pfeffer
Cabernet Sauvignon
Carignane
Carmine
Carnelian
Charbono
Chardonnay
Chenin blanc
Cinsaut/Cinsault or Black Malvoisie
Colombard or French Colombard
Dolcetto
Durif/Duriff
Emerald Riesling
Flora
Folle blanche
Gamay Beaujolais or Pinot noir (see
    PINOT NOIR)
Gewürztraminer
Green Hungarian
Grenache
Grignolino
Malbec
Malvasia bianca
Marsanne
Melon de Bourgogne or Melon (see MELON)
Merlot
Meunier or Pinot Meunier

Mission
Mondeuse (see REFOSCO)
Mourvèdre or Mataro
Muscadelle (see SAUVIGNON BLANC)
Muscat blanc or Muscat Canelli
Nebbiolo
Négrette
Palomino
Petit Verdot
Petite Sirah
Pinot blanc
Pinot gris or Pinot grigio
Pinot noir
Primitivo (see ZINFANDEL)
Riesling or White Riesling
Roussanne
Royalty
Rubired
Ruby Cabernet
Sangiovese
Sauvignon blanc or Fumé blanc
Scheurebe
Sémillon
Sultanina or Thompson Seedless
  (see THOMPSON SEEDLESS)
Sylvaner
Symphony
Syrah or Shiraz
Tempranillo or Valdepeñas
Tinta Madeira
Tocai Friulano (see SAUVIGNON BLANC)
Traminer (see GEWÜRZTRAMINER)
Trousseau gris (see GREY REISLING)
Ugni blanc or Trebbiano
Valdiguié (see GAMAY; NAPA GAMAY)
Verdelho
Viognier
Zinfandel

Some varietal names were not permitted after 1 January 1997. The acceptable name after that date is in parenthesis:
  Chevrier (Sémillon)
  Franken Riesling (Sylvaner)
  Gutedel (Chasselas doré)

Pinot Chardonnay (Chardonnay)
Pineau de la Loire (Chenin blanc)

Some names will not be allowed after 1 January 1999. The acceptable name after that date is in parenthesis:
  Cabernet (Cabernet Sauvignon)
  Grey Riesling (Trousseau gris)
  Johannisberg Riesling (Riesling)
  Muscat Frontignan (Muscat blanc)
  Napa Gamay (Valdiguié)
  Pinot St. George (Négrette)
  Sauvignon vert (Muscadelle)

Maynard A. Amerine and Albert J. Winkler, "California Wine Grapes" (Bulletin 794, California Agricultural Experiment Station, Davis, Calif., 1962).

Andrew Barr, *Wine Snobbery* (New York: Simon and Schuster, 1988), 159–83.

VEEDERCREST (BW 4711). In 1972 Alfred Baxter bonded the basement of his Berkeley home and made several wines from purchased grapes. These wines won him instant fame. He soon moved to a building in Emeryville and began planting vines on Mount Veeder in Napa. His wines continued to win medals and acclaim, but in 1982 the operation failed financially.

VENDANGE. See SEBASTIANI VINEYARDS

VENGE, NILS. See SADDLEBACK CELLARS

VENTANA VINEYARDS (BW 4847). In 1972 Douglas Meador acquired 371 acres of land on the west side of the Salinas Valley in today's Arroyo Seco Viticultural Area. By 1980 he had 305 acres in vines, planted to eighteen varieties, many more than are there now. Today there are about 275 acres, with Chardonnay by far the most plentiful. Also important are White Riesling, Chenin blanc, and Sauvignon blanc. Since the 1970s Ventana's grapes have gone into the wines of numerous wineries, some of which have established their good reputations in using Meador's grapes, particularly his Chardonnay.

He built his winery on the property in 1978 from an old dairy barn. Production varies but has been as high as 40,000 cases a year. Meador also has a Magnus label under which he has produced a red wine from Bordeaux varieties.

VENTURA COUNTY, just south of Santa Barbara County, enjoys soils and climate more favorable for viticulture than those of any other county in southern California, but winegrowing has never caught on here. There were about 100 acres of wine grapes in 1891, about 200 in 1935. There have been seven bonded wineries here since Repeal, mostly near the town of Ojai. Obviously, they have acquired most of their grapes to the north. In 1997 there were 12 acres of wine grapes in Ventura County.

VÉRAISON. A French term, adopted in California, for the stage in the grape's ripening when it changes color, from green to red purple or to translucent greenish white. In most of California's winegrowing country, this transformation begins between late July and early August. French tradition places *véraison* midway between flowering and grape maturity.

VERDELHO. A white-wine grape from the Portuguese island of Madeira. It is used today in Australia for dessert wine. In 1963 the University of California Experiment Station recommended the variety for "high-quality sweet wines," but there are no Verdelho vineyards in California as a result of that recommendation.

VERDOT. See PETIT VERDOT

VERMOUTH. In the 1780s a dark, sweet wine drink flavored with herbs was developed in the Italian city of Turin. A few years later a similar but drier, light-colored, herb-flavored wine was developed in France by Joseph Noilly and Claudius Prat. These two styles are still called

TABLE 37. VERMOUTH PRODUCTION IN THE UNITED STATES

YEAR	(THOUSANDS OF GALLONS) CALIFORNIA	IMPORTED
1936	26	1,158
1939	276	1,398
1944	2,740	590
1950	2,709[a]	1,484
1960	3,936[a]	3,175
1970	3,705	5,124
1975	4,058	4,278
1980	4,631	2,886
1985	3,506	3,016
1990	3,133	2,249
1995	2,266	1,709

a. Total production in the United States
SOURCE: *Wines & Vines.*

Italian and French vermouth, although much of the light, dry style is today produced in Italy. These wine-based drinks average between 16 and 18 percent alcohol and have traditionally been used as apéritifs and in mixed drinks.

Virtually all vermouths are flavored with a complex mixture of herbs, each brand with its own recipe. One flavor common to most is extract of wormwood, from which vermouth apparently got its name. The extract is from an Old-World plant that contains thujone, the toxic ingredient in absinthe. But, according to Maynard Amerine, there is not enough of this chemical in 16 liters of vermouth "to injure a 20-gram mouse."

Vermouth became popular in the United States after the 1880s, when large numbers of Italian immigrants brought a taste for it to American shores. California's first good vermouth was developed in the 1890s at ITALIAN SWISS COLONY by Pietro ROSSI, a native of Turin. Many California brands were on the market when vermouth was banned by Prohibition. After Repeal the market was strong but few California producers entered the field against established European brands. When French and Italian supplies were cut off by

World War II, there were, in 1942, about 225 vermouth producers in the United States. They made about 2 million gallons that year. A company in California, the Berkeley Yeast Lab, made more than 200 herb and spice extracts specifically available to vermouth producers.

As the years went by, California vermouths tended to lose their herbal character as they were seen simply as mixers for Martinis and Manhattans and, as consumption of mixed drinks has declined, so has production of vermouth.

> Maynard A. Amerine, *Vermouth: An Annotated Bibliography* (Berkeley, Calif.: University of California, Division of Agricultural Sciences, 1975).

VIADER VINEYARDS. In 1987 Delia Viader persuaded her father to let her plant a vineyard on his 90-acre property on Howell Mountain. The site of the 18-acre vineyard is so steep and rocky that it took dynamite to loosen the ground for post holes. The vines, Cabernets Sauvignon and franc, are closely spaced. Her winemaker, Anthony Soter (see ÉTUDE), produces at Rombauer about 3,000 cases of wine that has gained high critical acclaim.

CONRAD VIANO WINERY (BW 4376). In 1920 the Viano family bought vineyard land near Martinez in what was then the Vine Hill area of Contra Costa County. In 1946 they began producing wine from their 60-acre vineyard, developing a good retail trade at the winery for their Zinfandel and sauterne jug wines. In recent years they have added Cabernet Sauvignon and Chardonnay and make a Zinfandel port.

VIANSA WINERY (BW 5374). When Sam SEBASTIANI* left his family winery in 1986, he marketed wine under his own name for a year and then he and his wife, Vicki, changed the name of the winery to Viansa, for Vickie-and-Sam. The Italian ring to the name gives a good hint about the direction of the winemaking, as

does the Tuscan architecture. It was built on a hill in the Sonoma Carneros in 1990. A good part of the building houses a lively visitors center, replete with Italian-style food for sale under the Viansa label. So far Sebastiani has emphasized Chardonnay, Sauvignon blanc, and Cabernet Sauvignon, but there are also Italian varietals in the total annual production of about 15,000 cases.

VICHON WINERY (BW 4989). In 1980 a group of investors headed by George Vierra (Vi-), Peter Burcher (-ch-), and Douglas Watson (-on) founded a wine operation whose first products were quite successful. Their winery near Oakville in the Napa Valley went up in 1983 with production growing to 24,000 cases. But the partners had serious financial problems that they solved in 1985 by selling the venture to the Robert MONDAVI family. Under the Vichon brand, the Mondavis sold two kinds of wines: a series of varietals made from grapes grown in the Napa Valley, the best of which was a Stags Leap District Cabernet Sauvignon, and in vastly greater quantities, a lower-priced Coastal Selection line consisting mainly of Chardonnay, Merlot, and Cabernet Sauvignon made from grapes grown in the Central Coast. Total annual production under the Vichon label had reached about 125,000 cases in 1996 when the Mondavis decided to use the brand solely for their French wine imports. The winery itself is now used as a Mondavi hospitality center. In 1998 the name of the facility was changed to La Famiglia in honor of the new line of Mondavi wines produced from Italian varieties of grapes.

VIE-DEL CO. (BW 4404, 4137). After World War II in 1946, Fred Veith and James Riddell established the Vie-Del Grape Products Co. near Fresno. Today the company has a capacity of 50 million gallons and produces large quantities of grape concentrate, brandy, bulk wines, and other grape products. In 1957 SEA-

GRAM gained control of the company to produce Paul MASSON brandy, and sold off its vineyard holdings of almost 4,000 acres. In 1990 M. S. Nury, who went to work for Vie-Del in 1953 as a research chemist, bought the operation and, with his family, has built the company to its current size. They have a second plant, also near Fresno, once the Muscat Cooperative Winery.

VIGNES, JEAN-LOUIS (1779–1862). When he arrived in California from France, by way of Hawaii, in 1831, Vignes was hardly a young man. Yet in the next quarter century he developed a commercial operation in Los Angeles that, according to the historian Thomas Pinney, transformed winegrowing in the pueblo "from a domestic craft to a commercial enterprise." Many writers have noted that Vignes imported good French varieties of wine grapes into California, but there is no evidence that those vines ever had an important effect on his operation or on any part of the local wine industry.

Aliso, the name he gave his 104-acre estate next to the Los Angeles River, is near where the Union Station stands today. Evidently his ANGELICA, a well-aged sweet wine, and his brandy were better than anything Angelinos had previously known. In 1839 he was joined by his nephew, Pierre SAINSEVAIN.* The next year they shipped wine up to northern California by coastal schooner, but did not continue this trade. By the mid-1840s they had annual production up to 40,000 gallons and the success of El Aliso drew several other locals into commercial winegrowing by the end of the decade. In 1855 Sainsevain and his brother bought the estate and continued the operation until 1863 when their ill-starred venture into sparkling wine failed.

VILLA ARMANDO (BW 852). In 1902 Frank Garatti (1879–1948) built a large bulk winery in downtown Pleasanton in Alameda County and produced about 50,000 gallons per year. After Repeal he expanded his capacity to 500,000 gallons and produced a wide range of wines from grapes grown in the Livermore Valley, selling the premium-quality wines under the Garatti label. In 1962 the winery was sold to the Scotto family of New York, which operated it for a while as the Loretto Winery and then as Villa Armando. In 1972 the Scottos introduced a line of premium varietal wines that they sold mostly on the East Coast. In 1985 the winery went bankrupt and was torn down; see also STONY RIDGE.

VILLA MT. EDEN (BW 4677). In 1881 what came to be called Mount Eden Winery began operating east of Oakville in Napa County. After Repeal the vineyard was kept up as part of the Fagiani Ranch, where the movie *They Knew What They Wanted* was filmed in 1940.

In 1974 James and Anne McWilliams brought winemaking back to the old property as Villa Mt. Eden, with Nils Venge (see SADDLEBACK VINEYARDS) as winemaker. He was soon earning awards and plaudits for his Cabernet Sauvignon and Chardonnay. In 1986 the owners sold the brand to Stimson Lane Wine & Spirits, a subsidiary of the U.S. Tobacco Co. By 1997 the brand had passed the 120,000-case mark and in 1994 Stimson Lane gave up the Oakville lease and moved the Villa Mt. Eden sign to its CONN CREEK WINERY. Most Villa Mt. Eden wines are made at other facilities now, outside of Napa Valley, under the enological direction of Jed STEELE. But Stimson Lane has recently acquired more than 400 acres in Napa and Monterey Counties for vineyards to supply the Mt. Eden brand.

In 1995 the McWilliams property was leased by a new group of investors intending to bring back wine production at the old facility as **Plump Jack Winery** (BW 5830), with Venge again the winemaker.

VINA. Leland STANFORD's* wine ventures were successful until he decided to develop the

An aisle of huge oak wine casks at Vina, "the largest wine cellar in the world" before its demise. This remarkable building now serves the monks of Our Lady of New Clairvaux for agricultural storage. Hints of its original purpose can still be seen in its magnificent structure. (Unzelman Collection, Santa Rosa, Calif.)

largest winegrowing operation in the world. He started buying land in 1881 in TEHAMA COUNTY, where Henry Gerke had successfully produced wine since the 1860s near the little town of Vina in the upper Sacramento Valley. Stanford camped out there in his private railroad car overseeing the planting of the first 1,000 acres of vines. By 1886 he had 3,825 acres in the ground, but his zeal for this, or any endeavor other than founding a great university, was cooled in 1884 with the death of his son. By the first vintage in 1887, he had had a gigantic winery built. It covered 2 acres and had a 2 million-gallon capacity. In the process Stanford had hired Hamden W. MCINTYRE to superintend operations. But the former general manager of INGLENOOK was not able to coax fine table wine from the searing desert environment and irrigated vines.

By 1889 it was clear that if Vina were to have a high-quality product, it would have to be brandy. In 1890 the estate's brandy production amounted to about 20 percent of the entire nation's output and over the years it did gain a very fine reputation. By the mid-1890s lots of satisfactory, sweet fortified wine was also being produced. By then Stanford was dead and Vina had become a part of the Stanford University endowment. But the huge endeavor tended to lose money, a propensity that did not endear the operation to David Starr Jordan, the president of the university and an ardent prohibitionist.

Even though the vineyard had a 6,500-ton crush in 1912, the university decided to sell the place. In 1915 the land was sold off and the vines uprooted. The great winery, acquired by the order in 1955, survives as a part of a Trappist monastery. The huge structure today is the most wondrous surviving nineteenth-century winery facility in the world. The pious friars will show visitors (male only) around if arrangements are made in advance.

Wags at the University of California at Davis used to contend that Stanford's efforts were not all for naught: Frederic BIOLETTI got his start at Vina in 1885.

VINA VISTA WINERY. See CHAUFFE-EAU CELLARS

VINE BREEDING. See HYBRID

VINE CLIFF (BW 5591). In 1872 two businessmen in Napa, G. S. Burrage and G. W. Tucker, built a four-story winery in Rector Creek Canyon east of Oakville. By 1875 both men were dead. In the 1890s the phylloxera and a great fire ended the endeavor. But for many years until 1919 the CALIFORNIA WINE ASSOCIATION used Vine Cliff as a brand for some of its best white wines.

In 1989 the Sweeney family revived the old name and built a new winery in the hills east of the Silverado Trail not far from the old winery's caves. They have planted 21 acres on the steep slopes and concentrate their 3,500-case annual production on Cabernet Sauvignon and Chardonnay.

VINEGAR. From the French *vin* and *aigre* (sour), a tasty condiment since ancient times. Not the product of careful winemaking procedures, vinegar is obtained when ethyl alcohol is oxidized into an aldehyde and then to acetic acid. Winemakers have long known that wine too long in contact with oxygen is subject to such acetification. California and federal laws strictly limit the quantity of acetic acid in commercial wine.

Vinegar can be produced from many things, such as cider and beer, but wine vinegar is considered the finest, particularly that made in areas where wine is produced. Fine vinegar has been associated with the California industry since its early days. GEYSER PEAK WINERY and Ellena Brothers Winery (see REGINA GRAPE PRODUCTS) were once noted more for their condiment vinegar than for their wine.

The traditional Orléans method of vinegar production is a slow process, taking between 3 and 6 months. A barrel is filled about three-quarters full with a dilute wine solution of about 6 percent alcohol. Then what is called the vinegar mother, containing acetic acid bacteria, is added. As vinegar is produced, some can be drawn off and more wine added so that the process may continue for decades in the same container. In 1986 Ridge Vineyards brought out an Orléans-method vinegar from a continuous process begun in 1918. Today most wine vinegar is produced with large-scale equipment, and lacks the complexity and intensity of vinegar made by the Orléans method.

VIN GRIS. French for gray wine, *vin gris* is pink, usually a well-colored BLANC DE NOIRS or ROSÉ. Several producers in California (among them, BONNY DOON and NAVARRO) have made the wine, so labeled, in recent years, usually from Pinot noir, but there are no rules governing the varieties to be used.

VINIFERA. The *Vitis* species of grape most often used for wine production. The word *vinifera* means wine bearing and was invented in 1753 by Linnaeus (Carl von Linné). The species probably originated in what are today the Transcaucasian states of Georgia and Armenia, or perhaps northern Iran. It was spread to the Mediterranean world from the Black Sea region by Greeks and from the Near East by the Phoenicians.

Vinifera plants may have been domesticated as early as 7000 B.C., perhaps earlier. Over the centuries, through the process of human selection, separate varieties developed. Eventually, also through selection, domesticated vinifera became hermaphrodite, that is, possessing both male and female flowers and needing no specifically male plants for pollination.

In California, as in Europe, virtually all grapes used for winemaking are vinifera. Our table grapes and raisin grapes are also vinifera and can be used to produce wine.

VINIFICATION. The process by which grapes are transformed into wine.

VINTAGE 1870. See GOTTLIEB GROEZINGER

VINTAGE. The term often means vintage year, that is, the year in which the wine was made. Since the 1970s it has become common to note the vintage year on the label of a California wine. Before then, it was usually argued by California wine salesmen that all California years were vintage years, which was true. But not all years are as good as others. In fact, some California vintages can be not so good.

By not using dates for vintage years on their labels, California producers were able to blend their wines and market a more uniform product. This is still the practice for most jug wines. But consumers have become so used to seeing the vintage year on California labels that even inexpensive wines are now often dated.

The federal law requires that at least 95 percent of the wine with a vintage date be made from grapes harvested in that calendar year. See also HARVEST.

VINTECH CORP. bought JEKEL VINEYARDS, LAURIER VINEYARDS (when it was Domaine Laurier), LYETH VINEYARDS, and MAZZOCCO VINEYARDS between 1988 and 1990. The next year the operation was bankrupt.

VINTNER originally meant wine merchant. In California today many use it of a person who produces wine. But usage can be both confused and vague: The expression "Vinted and Bottled by" on some California labels is an example. There is no standard verb to vint, of which "vinted" would be the past participle. The expression means only that the winery in question bought the wine in bulk and then bottled it.

VINTNERS CLUB, an organization formed in San Francisco in 1973 to evaluate wines of the world in comparative, blind tastings. Members, many of whom have direct connections to the wine industry, meet almost every Thursday afternoon. About half the tastings are of California wines. Although the tasters' findings are probably no less subjective than those of other groups, the club's regularly published results act as a useful source of information on modern California wine. The results of the first 765 tastings were published in 1988.

Mary-Ellen McNeil-Draper, *Vintners Club: Fourteen Years of Wine Tastings, 1973–1987* (San Francisco: Vintners Press, 1988).

VIOGNIER. The white-wine grape of the northern Rhône from which the famous wine of Condrieu is made. It became fashionable in California in the 1990s and is noted for the complex, perfumed fruitiness of its dry table wines. The variety has no early history in California. The first planting was in 1982 by RITCHIE CREEK VINEYARDS. LA JOTA and CALERA followed the next year. By 1996 California had thirty-nine producers of Viognier and had 645 acres of vine, 55 percent of which was in the North Coast area. Of the total in 1996, 58 percent of these vines was not yet bearing. In 1997 the Viognier crush was 2,819 tons, up from 23 tons in 1990.

VIRGINIA DARE. See Paul GARRETT

VIRUS. Infectious particles about one-millionth of an inch in length. Viruses usually reduce vine yield and growth. They also may delay fruit ripening, but rarely kill the vine. Some contend that the fruit from old, virus-infected vineyards makes superior wine because the yields are low. One of the main goals of viticultural scientists has been the production of vines certified to be virus-free as a result of heat treatment. The most common virus vine diseases in California are grape leafroll and fanleaf.

VITACEÆ. The huge botanical family in which the grape is to be found. In it are erect shrubs, even small trees, but most species are climbing, woody vines. The family has twelve genera and about five-hundred species. Besides grapes, the family includes such plants as Virginia creeper and Boston ivy. For mankind *Vitis* is the most important genus; and its most important species is VINIFERA.

In America east of the Rockies there are other species important to viticulture, some as resistant ROOTSTOCK; others as parents of such eastern varieties as Catawba and Concord and such hybrids as Baco noir and Seyval blanc. Except as rootstock, none of these American species is part of commercial viticulture in California, for which see the following species of *Vitis:* V. CALIFORNICA (illustrated on page 51), V. GIRDIANA, V. RIPARIA, V. RUPESTRIS, and V. VINIFERA.

VITA NOVA. A blend of wine made since 1986 by two winemakers in Santa Barbara County, Robert Lindquist (see QUPÉ) and James Clendenen (see AU BON CLIMAT).

Beginning with wine made from red and white Bordeaux varieties of grapes grown in the Central Coast, they recently added some Chardonnay for the annual 3,500-case production.

VITICULTURAL AREAS. See AMERICAN VITICULTURAL AREAS

VITICULTURE. The practice of raising grapes. It is also the scientific discipline that aims to improve the quality of grapes and the health and productivity of the vine. The term viniculture is sometimes used for that element of viticulture dealing only with wine production. Confusingly some writers use the word *viniculture* as a synonym for ENOLOGY.

VITIS. See VITACEÆ

VOLATILE ACIDITY. See ACETIC ACID

VON STRASSER WINERY (BW 5537). The von Strasser family bought the old Roddis vineyard (BW 4916) on Diamond Mountain in 1990 and make about 1,000 cases of powerful Cabernet Sauvignon from their vines. They also make Chardonnay from purchased grapes.

VOSE VINEYARDS. See CHATEAU POTELLE

WAGNER, CHARLES. See CAYMUS

WAIT, FRONA EUNICE (1859–1946). A reporter for the *San Francisco Examiner* before she wrote *Wines and Vines of California* published in 1889. Wait's observations in that book and in a novel, *In Old Vintage Days* (1937), are important sources for nineteenth-century California wine history. Her photos of the California wine country in the 1880s are now part of the Napa Valley Wine LIBRARY collection.

WALDEN & CO. See GEYSER PEAK WINERY

WARFIELD, KATE F. (?–1892). J. B. Warfield was a winegrowing pioneer in the Glen Ellen area of Sonoma Valley in the 1860s. After his death in 1877, his wife took charge of the 80-acre Ten Oaks Vineyard. By the mid-1880s her winery was one of the leading producers in the area and she was winning awards in numerous competitions. The *San Francisco Bulletin* in 1887 ran a special article on her wines, which the reporter praised as "simply unexcelled."

Frona E. Wait, *Wines & Vines of California,*
(1889; reprint, Berkeley, Calif.: Howell-North,
1973), 143–44.

WARM SPRINGS. See MISSION SAN JOSE

WARREN. A New Englander, **James Lloyd Lafayette Warren** (1805–90) came to Califor-

nia in 1849 and founded the California State Agricultural Society in 1852. Two years later he began publishing the *California Farmer,* the Golden State's first agricultural periodical. From the 1850s to the 1870s, Warren was a leading advocate of California as a great wine producer. The pages of the *Farmer* are among the most important historical sources on the early California wine industry. **John Quincy Adams Warren,** his son, was publisher of the *California Wine, Wool, and Stock Journal,* another important primary source on California wine in the 1860s.

W. Bean, "James Warren and the Beginnings of
Agricultural Institutions in California,"
California Historical Society Quarterly 13, no. 4
(December 1944): 361–75.

WEATHER. See CLIMATE

WEBB. The AMERICAN SOCIETY FOR ENOLOGY AND VITICULTURE has given its annual Merit Award twice to men named Webb, a pair of brothers enological.

R. Bradford Webb made history as the first winemaker at HANZELL. In 1967 he became a partner at FREEMARK ABBEY and was the winemaking consultant there. His greatest contributions were probably to the understanding of malolactic FERMENTATION.

A. Dinsmoor Webb, no relation, an expert on pigments, aromas, and sherry, was a member of the Department of Viticulture and Enology at the University of California at Davis from 1948 to 1982. He was chairman of the department from 1973 to 1981.

WEHNER, WILLIAM, an artist and businessman from Chicago who bought 718 acres in the Evergreen area of the Santa Clara Valley in 1887 and within two years had 175 acres in vines. He built a large winery and a great mansion on the property, which he called Lomas Azules. Soon a leader of the local winegrowing community, he was an early proponent of resistant rootstock to fight phylloxera. He developed a great reputation for his dry wines made from white Bordeaux varieties, part of his success a result of his experiments in cool fermentation processes. In 1908 he built a larger winery, the most imposing in the Santa Clara Valley.

Wehner sold his estate in 1915 to Albert Haentze, who changed the name to Rancho Villa Vista. After Prohibition the CRIBARI family operated the winery until 1959. Then for many years it was used for storage by the nearby MIRASSOU winery. In 1989 the great structure, surely the finest in California south of the Napa Valley, was torn down for a housing development.

WEIBEL VINEYARDS (BW 4372 and 4593). Rudolph Weibel (1884–1971) and his son, Fred (1917–96), made sparkling wine in the Swiss town of Muensingen before they came to California in 1936. In San Francisco they set up their Weibel Champagne Cellar, prospering

William Wehner's estate was the site of a vintage festival in EVERGREEN for several years before Prohibition. The quiet disappearance of the great winery in 1989 attests to the gradual decline of interest among residents of the Santa Clara Valley in their rich wine history.

during the war years and looking for a place to plant vineyards and establish a real champagnery. They found it in the East Bay in 1945 south of Mission San Jose at the historic Josiah STAN-FORD winery. It had passed through many hands after the Stanford heirs had sold the property in 1923. The Weibels found the old winery divided up into horse stalls but soon had it back on line; they also planted 65 acres of vineyard. They aimed at producing sparkling and table wines and by the 1950s had a wide range of products and a solid reputation. By the late 1960s they had ten sparklers, fifteen table wines, five fortified wines, and two vermouths on their list, the most important part the sparkling wine. Much of that was made by the Charmat process, a lot for other labels, but they also made transfer-process and *méthode-champenoise* sparklers.

The Weibels could feel the press of suburbia in the late 1960s and began buying vineyard land in Mendocino County in 1968. In 1973 they opened a second winery near Ukiah. In the 1980s annual production grew to almost 1 million cases from both facilities, still mainly inexpensive sparklers. Among their table wines was a Green Hungarian varietal, the name in years to come almost synonymous with Weibel.

Accumulated debt led the Weibel family to sell off the 93-acre Mission San Jose vineyard to developers in 1994 and the Mendocino winery to the owners of BRAREN PAULI in 1995. The winery's name has been changed to REDWOOD VALLEY CELLARS. They also sold off most of their 1,300 acres of vineyard land in Mendocino, but kept the Weibel brand.

WEINSTOCK CELLARS (BW 5058). A winery in Healdsburg, Sonoma County, owned by the Royal Kedem Corporation of New York, that began operations in 1984 in the former J. W. MORRIS WINERY facility. Production amounts to about 25,000 cases annually, a good part of which is KOSHER table wine made from several varieties.

WELLINGTON VINEYARDS (BW 5482). In 1986 the Wellington family bought an old vineyard in Glen Ellen, Sonoma County, and built a little winery there 3 years later. The vineyard had 20 acres of vines, many varieties planted in the 1920s, some before. The Wellingtons have planted new vines but kept some of the old ones, which supply grapes for their red-wine blend labeled Criolla. Zinfandel, Merlot, and Cabernet Sauvignon also make up part of the 6,000-case annual production.

WENTE BROS. (BW 893). Carl H. Wente (1851–1934) came to California from his native Hanover in northern Germany in 1880. He worked a while for Charles KRUG and was attracted in 1883 by the winegrowing boom in the LIVERMORE VALLEY.* There he and two partners bought the 25-acre Bernard Vineyard and soon expanded it to 47 acres. By 1887 Wente was in full control of the operation.

A large number of the new winegrowers in Livermore were dilettantes, rich men attracted by the romance of wine production on a country estate. Wente, however, was a hard working, practical family man with a keen business sense. He rode out the depression of the 1890s and by 1899 his 300,000-gallon production was the highest in the the valley. By 1902 C. H. Wente & Sons were making 450,000 gallons a year. Except for the local trade, this was high-quality bulk wine, much of it sold to the CALIFORNIA WINE ASSOCIATION through the wine merchants LACHMAN & JACOBI.

The firm's name changed in 1918 to Wente Bros., those being Ernest (1891–1981) and Herman (1893–1961). Graduates of the University of California, they became leaders of the wine industry after Repeal and produced some of the greatest white wine in California history. During Prohibition they sold grapes and made lots of sacramental wine for BEAULIEU VINEYARD. Ernest, the viticultural expert, took care to retain the fine vineyard stock his father had acquired, particularly Sauvignon blanc and

Sémillon from Louis MEL's collection and Chardonnay probably from To Kalon (see Hiram W. CRABB) by way of T. GIER. There was also Ugni blanc acquired in 1912 from the Richter Nursery in Montpellier in France.

Herman and Ernest were intent on establishing a Wente wine brand in 1934. Within a few years the small element in American society interested in fine California wine knew Wente to be a producer of great whites from Sauternes varieties, first under the Valle de Oro, then under Wente Bros. label. After 1936, they made Chardonnay, the first modern California wine from this varietal. In 1939 the Wente Sauvignon Blanc won the Grand Prize at the Golden Gate Exposition on Treasure Island; it was named California's best white wine.

The Wente reputation remained intact through the 1960s, but by then the pressure of suburbia moved the family to plant vineyards in Monterey County, 270 acres in the 1960s. Wente also expanded the product line and its vineyard base. By 1975 there were nineteen table wines under the Wente label, from 800 acres of Livermore vineyard, 300 in Monterey.

In the 1980s the Wente family, now under the fourth generation of leadership, began expanding again, with an eye to preserving Livermore as an important winegrowing community. In 1981 they acquired the old Wetmore estate, CRESTA BLANCA, and converted the facility into a sparkling wine plant and visitors center. They also acquired an interest in CONCANNON VINEYARD. In 1986 they bought RUBY HILL VINEYARD. They also revived the old Louis Mel winery and associated it, in 1991, with their new Murietta's Well brand.

In 1993 their vineyard holdings amounted to 1,839 acres, 65 percent in the Livermore Valley. Most was Chardonnay, at 49 percent; 9 percent was Cabernet Sauvignon and 7 percent Sauvignon blanc. The remaining 35 percent was divided among thirteen varieties.

In the 1990s the Wente operation became export oriented with almost 50 percent of production being sold overseas in more than one hundred national markets. The Livermore plant also became a site where excess capacity was used to produce wine for other labels such as VILLA MT. EDEN, KENDALL-JACKSON, and ROUND HILL.

Wente Vineyards (the name was changed in 1996) today produces about 600,000 cases a year. The fourth generation is made up of Eric, Carolyn, and Philip, the children of Karl Wente (1927–77), Ernest's son. These three, and Karl's widow, Jean, now run the oldest family wine business in California. A few years ago they made this point in an advertisement indirectly aimed at other so-called oldest family wineries in California. "Same winery, same vineyard, same great-grandfather."

J. Jacobs, "California's Pioneer Wine Families," *California Historical Society Quarterly* 54, no. 2 (Summer 1975): 157–61.

Ernest A. Wente, *Wine Making in the Livermore Valley* (Regional Oral History Office, Bancroft Library, 1971).

Jean Wente et al., *The Wente Family and the California Wine Industry* (Regional Oral History Office, Bancroft Library, 1992).

GEORGE WEST AND SON WINERIES.

Today SAN JOAQUIN COUNTY* is the leading wine grape producer in California. **George West** (1830–99) was the man who took the first major steps in the development of this commercial success story. He and his brother William were Massachusetts men who came to California in 1850, made money panning gold, and bought land north of the village of Stockton in 1852. Both were interested in horticulture, particularly viticulture, and from the Hovey & Co. nursery in Boston in 1853 they imported forty varieties, including muscats, ZINFANDEL, and a white grape that came to be called West's White Prolific and was later found to be French Colombard.

The Wests made a small quantity of commercial wine in 1858 and by the mid-1860s had production up to 5,000 gallons. By then it was clear that fortified wines, particularly port, and brandy would be the chief products at El Pinal, so named for a grove of pines the brothers planted on the property. In 1868 George West took control of the entire operation, which then amounted to 50 acres.

West pushed up production and expanded his cellar and vineyards. He later produced quite a lot of table wine from his own grapes and from fruit purchased in the Livermore and Santa Clara valleys. In 1880 he began expanding south into the San Joaquin Valley, helping develop the huge Sierra Vista Vineyard in Madera County. All the time he was developing a reputation as California's best producer of first-class dessert wines and sherry. Among brandies only the NAGLEE's had a better reputation than West's had.

In the 1890s his son, **Frank A. West** (1863–1915), became increasingly active in the

West won his first award in 1865 at the San Joaquin County Fair, for port. In 1869 he produced California's first commercial White Zinfandel. By the 1890s he was the Golden State's master of sweet wine and brandy. (*Pacific Wine & Spirits Review*)

business. Under his leadership the West operations became huge. The boom in fortified wines after 1898 led to remarkable expansion all over the Central Valley. West acquired five wineries between LODI* and Tulare County.

Frank was an extraordinary businessman. A great impetus for the company's growth came from his development of a solid relationship with eastern capitalists. His experimental development of a continuous-still brandy process is of historic importance. By 1910 West and the CALIFORNIA WINE ASSOCIATION virtually controlled the wine industry of the Central Valley. In 1911 the West wineries produced more than 5 million gallons of wine a year and controlled more than 25,000 acres of grapes. After Frank died in 1915, his company became a working part of the California Wine Association. With the coming of Prohibition it went out of business in 1919.

WEST'S WHITE PROLIFIC. See FRENCH COLOMBARD; GEORGE WEST AND SON WINERIES

WETMORE-BOWEN & CO. See CRESTA BLANCA

WETMORE, CHARLES A. (1847–1927). The Wetmore family came to California from New England in 1856. Jesse Wetmore (1822–1902) had made a fortune in real estate in the East Bay by the time his son, Charles, had enrolled in 1864 at the College of California in Oakland. He was the valedictorian of his class at the school, which was to become the University of California at Berkeley in 1873. A brilliant and energetic student, he was for his last two years in college the Oakland correspondent of the *San Francisco Evening Bulletin*. Wetmore's next ten years, spent mostly in journalism, were remarkable and included a stint of railroad building in Peru with his father and one as a U.S. Commissioner for Mission Indians in San Diego

Charles A. Wetmore was just as tough an opponent as is suggested by this photograph taken in 1890. He was both admired and detested by California wine men. His many accomplishments fed his enormous ego, but success in business eluded him. (*Pacific Wine & Spirit Review*)

County. In this job at one point in 1875 he found himself in jail in Washington, D.C. for contempt of Congress.

He wrote his first article on wine for the *Alta California* in 1874 and, in 1878, he went to Paris to represent the State Vinicultural Society. From there he wrote a series of thirty-four articles on wine and brandy production in France and California for that newspaper. These articles helped ignite the great California wine boom of the 1880s. He also went to Sacramento and pushed for legislation that established the STATE VITICULTURAL COMMISSION.* Wetmore served as the commission's Chief Executive Officer, a service that was of great value to the state's growing wine industry. But after 1885 his pugnacious and egocentric battles with Eugene HILGARD* at the University of California at Berkeley often detracted from the value of his leadership.

Meanwhile he had moved to the LIVERMORE VALLEY* and established CRESTA BLANCA,* where his wines won him additional fame. Actually his fights with Hilgard and other industry leaders, and his ability to keep his wines in the public limelight made Wetmore into a somewhat notorious public celebrity. His every public utterance acted as a magnet for the California press and focused a popular interest on the growing wine industry in the state, interest that probably helped California wine gain additional favor.

But Wetmore was not a good businessman, and he lost control of Cresta Blanca to his brother, Clarence, and his partners in 1892. Not missing a beat, he moved to Stockton in 1896 and began planting tobacco in the DELTA area. The next year he was president of the Stockton Press Club. In 1898 he was making sparkling wine in San Francisco. We next find him in the San Diego area again, doing what he seemed to do best, financially, that is, speculating in real estate. He worked in the antiprohibition movement and acted as a lobbyist in Washington, D.C. for California's "sweet wine" producers. By the age of seventy, he had retired to his home in Piedmont, but he stayed close to wine industry matters; his son, Louis Wetmore (1882–1948), was an important officer in the CALIFORNIA WINE ASSOCIATION.

Janet Newton, *Cresta Blanca and Charles A. Wetmore* (Livermore, Calif.: Livermore Heritage Guild, 1974).

WETMORE, CLARENCE J. (1851–1936). Current ideas about birth order suggest that Clarence Wetmore might have been the idealistic rebel and Charles WETMORE the steady success. Quite the opposite was true.

Clarence was a member of the first graduating class at the University of California at Berkeley in 1873. After working for several years for the Southern Pacific Railroad, he bought land in the Livermore Valley in 1881 and planted his 43-acre Electra Vineyard. Meanwhile he worked in several capacities for the STATE VITI-

CULTURAL COMMISSION. In 1892 he organized a group of partners (Wetmore-Bowen & Co.) that took control of CRESTA BLANCA* from his brother. He ran that winery until 1920 when he sold his interest. After Repeal he continued to be associated with his old winery. For several years he was the oldest living graduate of the University of California at Berkeley.

WHEELER, DAN. See NICASIO VINEYARDS

WHEELER, JOHN H. (1857–1939), a wine-grower in Napa and a power on the STATE VITICULTURAL COMMISSION. His father, Charles Wheeler, planted his first 37 acres of vineyards along Zinfandel Lane in 1875. John took control in 1889 and built the winery into a steady producer of about 250,000 gallons per year. Trained as a chemist, Wheeler's use of carbon bisulfide to defeat phylloxera worked, but was not economically feasible. He lived out his years in Napa and produced wine (BW 883) after Repeal until 1935. The wall of his fine estate on Zinfandel Lane has survived.

WILLIAM WHEELER WINERY (BW 5100) William Wheeler planted his 48-acre vineyard in the Dry Creek Valley, Sonoma County, in the 1970s and bonded his winery in downtown Healdsburg in 1980. He sold the operation in 1992. PEZZI KING now owns the Wheeler vineyard; the name of the winery is now one of the Jean-Claude BOISSET's NÉGOCIANT brands.

WHITCRAFT WINES (BW 5760). In 1994 Christopher Whitcraft bonded his little winery near Santa Maria in Santa Barbara County. There he makes Pinot noir and Chardonnay, about 2000 cases annually. He emphasizes traditional cellar techniques—a hands-off approach to winemaking.

WHITEHALL LANE WINERY (BW 4974). Art Finkelstein and Alan Steen are brothers who bought vineyard land south of St. Helena in 1979 and built their winery the next year.

They made a lot of fast-moving Blanc de Pinot Noir but were primarily interested in red Bordeaux varieties. Total production reached 20,000 cases in 1985. Three years later they sold the operation to a Japanese firm; see JUDD'S HILL. In 1993 the new owners sold it to Thomas Leonardini, a businessman in San Francisco. He now has production from his 60 acres and purchased grapes up to 25,000 cases a year, mainly Merlot, Cabernet Sauvignon, and Chardonnay. Whitehall Lane also does CUSTOM CRUSHING.

WHITE OAK VINEYARDS (BW 5065). In 1981 Bill Myers bonded a small winery in Healdsburg, Sonoma County. His annual 12,000-case production consists mainly of Chardonnay and vineyard-designated Zinfandels and includes small quantities of other varietals.

WHITE PINOT. See CHENIN BLANC

WHITE RIESLING. After 1998 the words White Riesling and Riesling will be the only names allowed on labels of wine made from the true Riesling variety of grape.

The White Riesling is the German varietal associated with the best wines of the Rhine and Mosel. Many believe it to be the greatest of all white-wine grapes. It came to California in the late 1850s, probably first imported by Francis Stock in San Jose. He supplied cuttings to George Belden CRANE in Napa in 1861. After 1864 wines from those vines convinced many that Napa could be wine country. Riesling vines were brought to Sonoma in 1859 by Emil DRESEL from his home town of Geisenheim.

Wines from German varieties, particularly Riesling, Sylvaner, and Traminer, were what first brought some small fame to the tiny California wine industry in the 1870s. During those years it became common to refer to the true Riesling grape as the Johannisberg Riesling, after the famous estate, Schloss Johannisberg, in

TABLE 38. WHITE RIESLING GRAPES, SELECTED COUNTIES

				(ACRES)			
YEAR	MENDOCINO	SONOMA	NAPA	MONTEREY	SAN BENITO	SANTA BARBARA	TOTAL
1960	N.A.	N.A.	N.A.	N.A.	N.A.	N.A.	282
1968	0	35	294	49	400	*	839
1972	115	418	761	604	396	449	3,128
1975	230	1,221	1,361	2,414	325	1,041	8,308
1979	354	1,456	1,444	2,797	327	1,842	9,565
1985	335	1,188	1,144	4,109	232	1,918	10,046
1989	217	655	492	2,788	169	1,101	6,001
1993	187	282	369	1,849	233	466	3,706
1997	113	165	163	1,603	54	268	2,696

* Nothing is recorded in the official statistics, but it is believed that some White Riesling was
  being grown in Santa Barbara County in 1968.
SOURCE: California Agricultural Statistics Service, Sacramento, Calif.

the Rheingau. Reputable wine dealers in California found it useful to employ this designation, because other varieties with Riesling in their California names were beginning to appear. For years the Johannisberg Riesling was standard California nomenclature, coming back into fashion after Repeal when varietal labeling caught on. In the 1960s more and more California producers began to put White Riesling on their labels instead. With unwonted decisiveness, the BATF ruled 2 January 1996, that the designation Johannisberg Riesling could not appear on American-made wine after January 1999.

California White Riesling has been produced in many styles since the earliest days. The most popular before Prohibition were either slightly sweet or very sweet. But warm California temperatures and the lack of modern stabilizing techniques condemned most of that wine to long stays in barrel and cask, robbing it of some of the fresh fruitiness associated with great German white wines. Since World War II, producers in California have developed several techniques for ensuring stability in young wines that have some residual sugar (see STABILIZATION).

Much of the growth in the popularity of California's premium table wines in the 1950s and 1960s was generated by young, fruity, slightly sweet White Riesling and Chenin blanc. This popularity crested in the late 1970s, after which White Riesling became hard to sell in the broader market, developments that may be seen in table 38, below. Nevertheless, several California producers have well-established reputations for their White Rieslings.

In 1996 the White Riesling crush was 13,141 tons; in 1990 it was 20,092 tons.

WHITE ROCK VINEYARDS (BW 5423). John A. Pettingill was a dentist who founded his White Rock Cellar east of the Silverado Trail in Napa Valley in the 1870s. Henri and Claire Vandendriessche acquired the old place in 1979 and planted 35 acres of vines, mostly Chardonnay and red Bordeaux varieties. In 1988 they bonded their winery and dug impressive caves into the hill above their home. Now they produce about 3,000 cases of what they call claret and Chardonnay, wines that have received excellent reviews.

WHITE ZINFANDEL. See ZINFANDEL

WILD HORSE WINERY (BW 5169). Ken Volk III has 33 acres of vines south of Paso Robles at Templeton. He began planting them in 1982 and his winery went up in 1983. One of his wines that year, a Pinot noir from grapes grown in the Santa Maria Valley, did much to establish his reputation and to direct his emphasis. He has made a wide range of other varietals, including a Malvasia Bianca and a Négrette from the Cienega Valley. Annual production is now about 75,000 cases. Occasionally wines are released under the Cheval Sauvage and Equus labels.

WILDHURST (BW 5611). A winery in Lake County near Kelseyville that began operations in 1991. The Holdenrieds planted their first vineyard in Lake County in the 1960s and today control about 160 acres. Historically their roots here go back into the nineteenth century when they were pear farmers. They have been producing about 16,000 cases a year, mostly Merlot and Chardonnay. Before he moved to KONOCTI WINERY Jed STEELE made his wines here.

WILLIAMS-SELYEM WINERY (BW 5149). In 1983 Burt Williams and Ed Selyem began making wine in Fulton in Sonoma at their Hacienda del Rio Winery. In 1986 HACIENDA WINE CELLARS encouraged them to change the name. In 1990 they moved to their current location near Healdsburg.

By the end of the 1980s, they had established an unrivaled reputation for their Pinot noirs made from grapes grown in the Russian River area. Their vineyard sources, particularly the neighboring ROCHIOLI and Allen vineyards, are part of their success. In 1990 they had total production up to 2,500 cases a year; today it is close to 7,000 and includes some highly regarded Chardonnay and Zinfandel.

In 1998 the operation was sold to John Dyson, a New Yorker who owns vineyards in the Central Coast, for about $9,000,000.

WILSON, BENJAMIN DAVIS (1811–78). A native of Tennessee, Wilson arrived in Los Angeles in 1841. Within a few years he had acquired several properties in southern California and was involved in numerous business enterprises. In 1852 he acquired 128 acres in the San Gabriel Valley near Santa Anita. In 1856 he built his home there, soon surrounded by grape vines and orange trees. He called the estate Lake Vineyard.

There was on the property a 16-acre vineyard that Wilson quickly expanded. In fact, he was in the wine business there before he built his house. In 1855 his winemaker even made some bottle-fermented sparkling wine, certainly California's first.

By the 1860s Wilson's wines had developed a good reputation, both in southern California and in the San Francisco Bay Area, where he had a distribution agency. His sweet wines, particularly the reds labeled port, were very successful. He even sold wine on the East Coast in the 1860s, but after a shipment arrived in bad shape in 1866, Wilson lost some of his zeal for the entire enterprise. He was no longer in the business by the next year, when his young son-in-law, J. De Barth SHORB, leased the vineyards, which by then consisted of 160 acres of vines, and the cellars, the capacity of which had grown to about 50,000 gallons.

Mount Wilson, overlooking the San Gabriel Valley, was named for the old pioneer; one of his grandchildren was General George S. Patton.

WINDSOR. A community in Sonoma north of Santa Rosa that has been a little wine town since the 1870s. By the 1890s there were about sixty vineyardists in the area and several medium-sized wineries. Since Repeal seventeen wineries have been bonded in the Windsor area.

WINDSOR VINEYARDS. See RODNEY STRONG VINEYARDS

WINE, a drink made by fermenting fruit juice. The term is also sometimes used for drinks made by fermenting sugar solutions flavored with herbs, spices, or flowers, but the commercial article, labeled wine in the United States, must be made from grapes. Otherwise the name of fruit or other substance employed for flavor must be clearly expressed on the label in conjunction with the word wine (e.g., Blackberry Wine).

The word *wine* is Semitic in origin. The Phoenicians probably brought the word into the Mediterranean world and it entered the Indo-European languages of Europe through Greek and Latin.

WINE ADVISORY BOARD. Created in 1938 by a California marketing order that had been voted on by the state's wineries, the board supervised the development of a national advertising and education program for California wine, paid for by assessments on wineries based on their volume of sales. Small and medium-sized producers tended to approve of the program. Many large producers disliked the program's generic character, and usually had their own advertising campaigns. In 1975 the Wine Advisory Board voted itself out of existence rather than comply with a set of demands made of it by the U.S. Department of Food and Agriculture. For a while some parts of the board's programs were carried out by the WINE INSTITUTE.

A similar institution, the Wine Growers of California, operated under a like marketing order between 1983 and 1987. It was succeeded by the California Wine Commission, which lasted until 1990, its demise caused by a revolt by small winery owners who felt that the commission was acting primarily in the interest of industry giants. The small wineries gathered enough support to vote the commission out of existence in June 1990.

WINE ALLIANCE. The American wine operations of Allied-Lyons, a British beverage con-

glomerate; Hiram Walker is the corporate umbrella in the United States for all of the wine and spirits businesses of Allied-Lyons. Since 1981 the company has acquired CALLAWAY VINEYARD AND WINERY, CLOS DU BOIS, ATLAS PEAK VINEYARDS, and WILLIAM HILL's Winery.

WINE COMPETITIONS. See EVALUATION, OF WINE

WINE GRAPES. See VARIETALS

WINE GROUP. The COCA-COLA Bottling Company of New York bought FRANZIA Brothers Winery and the Franzia brand in 1973. Coca-Cola then created The Wine Group as the corporate designation for its wine operations, which include the Franzia plants in Ripon and Fresno and the CORBETT CANYON winery. Other California brands also managed by The Wine Group are Colony, Lejon, Summit, and Tribuno. The company operates the Mogen David Wine Corporation at Westfield, New York. See also FRANZIA.

WINEHAVEN. The great wine houses of the northern California wine industry settled and evolved in San Francisco after the 1850s, but the city's geographical location, almost cut off from direct rail contact with the rest of the country, did not make economic sense. After the earthquake and fire of 1906 had destroyed most of the city's cellar facilities, the CALIFORNIA WINE ASSOCIATION determined to construct a great processing plant across the bay and north of Oakland.

Winehaven was dedicated 2 September 1907, just in time for the vintage. It could process grapes from the Central Valley and was close to the premium wine districts. It had direct access to the transcontinental railroad and sat at the edge of a great port. By 1915 it had a capacity of 20 million gallons. It ended its vinous career during Prohibition and is today a navy storage depot. Its impressive

Many of the features depicted in this photograph of Winehaven, which was taken in 1910, are still to be seen today. Insurance compensation paid to the CALIFORNIA WINE ASSOCIATION after their cellars in San Francisco were devastated by the earthquake in 1906 helped finance the huge facility. (*Pacific Wine & Spirit Review*)

buildings stand just north of the eastern end of the San Rafael-Richmond Bridge at Point Molate, an interesting place to visit.

WINE INSTITUTE. A trade organization formed in 1934 by the leaders of the newly revived California wine industry to promote the state's wine and to protect its producers and marketers. It was an outgrowth of the Grape Growers League of California, founded in 1931, and the Wine Producers Association, founded in 1933. Many people were involved in the Institute's founding and early operations, but by far the most important in determining the direction of its programs and its tactics was Leon D. ADAMS, who remained effectively in charge until 1954.

In its early days the Wine Institute was primarily concerned with federal and state tax policies toward wine and about federal tariff policy on foreign imports. With the Institute's persuasive lobbyists in Washington, D.C. and Sacramento, federal taxes remained moderate and California taxes very low. Also important in the early years was the Institute's success in pressing for strict enforcement of California's wine-quality standards by the State Board of Health.

Membership in the Institute was voluntary, but by the late 1930s its members controlled between 85 and 90 percent of the winery capacity in California. (Dues after 1935 were based on a combination of tons crushed and gallons sold.)

With the founding of the WINE ADVISORY BOARD* in 1938, the Wine Institute became involved in a long-term national advertising campaign for California wine. Over the years industry analysts have generally credited the Institute with a substantial part of the growth and success of the California wine industry. But it has not been without its critics. Because most of the power on its governing board was in the hands of the larger producers, there has been continuous disagreement over policy. Small and medium-sized premium producers have been particularly critical. In the 1990s smaller producers have resented what they see as the Institute's mild responses to NEO-PROHIBITIONISM and its apparent unwillingness to press forcefully for a better understanding among the public of the health benefits that are believed to be derived from moderate consumption of table wine. Between 1991 and 1992 about seventy-five dissident wineries withdrew from the Institute over these and related issues affecting their interests.

WINE JUDGING. See EVALUATION, OF WINE

WINE, NONALCOHOLIC. See ARIEL

WINERY. A facility in which grapes are fermented to produce wine. The word is often used loosely to indicate the company that owns the facility. An American coinage of the 1880s, the word was rarely used until the 1930s. Only two of the California producers exhibiting wine at the Panama Pacific Exposition in San Francisco in 1915 used Winery in their official designations. Until Prohibition, the term cellar was the usual designation for what today we call a winery. How the word had come into common usage by the 1930s is not clear.

> Thomas Pinney, *A History of Wine in America from the Beginnings to Prohibition* (Berkeley, Calif.: University of California Press, 1989), 450.

WINERY LAKE VINEYARD. See CARNEROS; RENE DI ROSA

WINES & VINES. A trade publication founded by Horatio STOLL* in 1919 as the *California Grape Grower*. In 1935 it became *Wines & Vines*. It has always stressed the interests and concerns of the California wine industry but in recent years it has given good coverage to winegrowing in the rest of the United States. Today it is run by the Hiaring family. Each year it

publishes a valuable directory of wineries in North America. See also Irving MARCUS.

WINE SPECTATOR. A consumer publication founded in 1976 by Robert Morrisey and based then in San Diego, giving strong emphasis to California wines and the state's wine industry. New owners moved the offices to San Francisco in 1982.

WINE WAR. Beginning in the late 1880s, when wine and grape prices began declining, an obvious tension developed between wine and grape producers and the great wine merchants of San Francisco. When the national economy collapsed in 1893 many producers were driven to the wall and most blamed the big-city merchants and their monopolistic practices. In 1894 these charges seemed justified by the formation of the CALIFORNIA WINE ASSOCIATION (CWA), dubbed the "Wine Trust" by winery owners and vineyardists. (Most of the large merchants also owned wineries and vineyards as well as their huge cellars in San Francisco.) A few months later, to defend themselves, growers and winery owners formed the California Wine Makers Corporation (CWMC), a movement that was led by the ITALIAN SWISS COLONY.

For two years the two organizations tried to work together but in 1897 open warfare over prices was declared. The press had a field day. The Wine War, particularly in the northern California press, competed for ink with the events in Cuba leading to the war with Spain. But by 1899 increased demand and rising prices encouraged the CWMC to go out of business and to sell its assets to the CWA. For decades the combatants traded war stories and reminisced. Actually the real scars and casualties of the Wine War were rather insignificant.

WINE WORLD, INC. See BERINGER WINE ESTATES

WINKLER, ALBERT JULIUS (1894–1989), went to work at the University of California at Davis in 1921 and succeeded Frederic BIO-LETTI as chairman of the Department of Viti-culture and Enology in 1935. For the next 22 years, he led the department to a position of greatness in the world of wine and grape research. With Maynard AMERINE, he devel-oped a respected system of climate classifica-tion for viticulture (see HEAT SUMMATION). In 1962, the year he formally retired, his book *General Viticulture* was published, a text that was, for many years, the standard in its field in the English-speaking world.

WOLFSKILL, WILLIAM (1798–1866). A fur trapper and trader in the American Southwest, Wolfskill settled in Los Angeles in 1833 and developed one of the town's most important vineyards. His winemaking operation became well known in the 1850s, his vineyard named the best in California at the 1856 State Fair. In 1843 he and his brother, John, had planted Mission grapes in Solano County, about 8,000 vines, near Putah Creek. The grapes were mostly sold fresh in San Francisco.

Wolfskill's venture in Los Angeles eventu-ally had four cellars with a total capacity of 60,000 gallons. He also had a small distillery and was particularly well known for his brandy and fortified wines. History has, how-ever, taken far more notice of the Wolfskill family's pioneer work in orange growing than it has of its winegrowing.

WOODBRIDGE. See LODI

WOODBRIDGE VINEYARD ASSOCIATION (BW 26 , 4400). A growers cooperative founded near Lodi in 1905. It was a major producer in the area before Prohibition, making 500,000 gallons of table wine its first vintage and more than 1 million by 1911. After Repeal, the orga-nization operated as Bradford Cellars. The

grapes, mostly Flame Tokay, grown by its 60 members, went into brandy. The facility became inactive in 1985.

WOODEN VALLEY. An isolated valley in the hill country of southeast Napa County, where there have been a few vineyards since the 1880s. In 1932 the Lanza family built the Wooden Valley Winery (BW 4097), which still has vineyards but no longer crushes grapes.

CHRISTINE WOODS WINERY (BW 5118). Vernon Rose and his family own 25 acres of vineyard in Anderson Valley near Navarro in Mendocino County. They sell most of their grapes but make about 2,000 cases of wine, mostly Pinot noir and Chardonnay. They named their little winery, which was built in 1982, after one of the early settlers in the valley.

WOODSIDE-PORTOLA VALLEY. An upland area west of Stanford University that has seen commercial wine production since the 1870s. In the 1880s Edgar Preston's 635-acre estate had a 175,000-gallon, three-story winery and a 100-acre vineyard. There were several others, the most famous E. H. Rixford's LA QUESTA near Woodside. Most of this activity was over by Repeal, but since the 1960s a small suburban wine industry has developed. In the 1990s there were about thirty small vineyards in the area. Their owners sold most of their grapes to the five small wineries there.

WOODSIDE VINEYARDS (BW 4492). Robert and Pauline Mullen bought an old vineyard near the town of Woodside in San Mateo County and bonded their tiny winery in 1963. Discovering that some of the old LA QUESTA Cabernet Sauvignon vines planted by E. H. Rixford at the turn of the century had survived in the yards of their neighbors, they bought the grapes and revived the La Questa label. They have produced a wide range of varietals over the years, using Santa Cruz Mountain grapes as often as possible. In the 1970s Mullen also made several Cabernets from Nathan Fay's Stag's Leap grapes. Today the Mullens produce about 2,000 cases of wine a year, much of it from seventeen small vineyards in the Woodside area. In one of these, belonging to Bill and Geri Walsh, 700 Chardonnay and Pinot noir vines were planted in 1992.

YEAST. Yeasts of the genus *Saccharomyces* are essential in the FERMENTATION of wine. Before the 1890s all California wine was produced from the natural or ambient yeasts in the air, the vineyard, and the winery. Such yeasts usually contained enough of the needed *S. cerevisiæ* to bring about a successful fermentation, although there would also be so-called wild yeasts of various genera in the spontaneous fermentations, but the wild yeasts took part only in the early stages of fermentation.

By the turn of the century, a large number of winemakers in California had been won over to the use of pure, cultured yeasts produced commercially. The wild yeasts were subdued with sulfur dioxide and the grape MUST was inoculated with the pure grape culture. Such fermentations tended to be more predictable and risk free. Over the years numerous strains of cultured yeasts have been developed and winemakers select their favorites according to their experience with specific varieties of grapes. Winemakers may also select a strain suited to the style of wine they are looking for.

In recent years more and more small producers in California have chosen to work with spontaneous fermentations generated by the ambient yeast population. Such practices are controversial and generally condemned by the academicians at the University of California at Davis. RIDGE VINEYARDS has been using such spontaneous fermentations for years, with obvious success.

YOLO COUNTY. A large county in the Sacramento Valley and Delta region where winegrowing is expanding. There were 129 acres of vines there in 1971, 3,320 in 1930, and 4,938 in 1997. Much of the county's vineyard land flanks the highway from the San Francisco Bay Area to the state capital. The campus of the University of California at Davis is in Yolo County.

The southern areas, including part of the Clarksburg Viticultural Area, have a DELTA climate, much milder than that of the northern part of the county. It is here that the sizeable vineyard growth has come in recent years. There is a preponderance of Chardonnay, more than 50 percent of the total acreage.

In the 1880s viticulture in Yolo County was centered farther north around Woodland. By 1890 in this far-warmer clime, almost 4,000 acres had been planted, many to Zinfandel and muscats. Even farther north near Esparto was Arpad HARASZTHY's ill-fated ORLEANS HILL venture. Most of those grapes were converted into wine at the Yolo Winery in Woodland, which had a capacity of 250,000 gallons in 1905, or hauled to large industrial wineries in the Bay Area. After 1907 most grapes went to WINEHAVEN.

The acreage under wine grapes in Yolo County remained little changed through Prohibition but declined precipitously after Repeal. Since 1980 it has grown almost 400 percent.

YORK CREEK VINEYARDS. See FRITZ MAYTAG

YORK MOUNTAIN. A high point east of the Santa Lucia Range and west of Paso Robles. In 1983 the York Mountain Viticultural Area was recognized by the BATF.

YORK MOUNTAIN WINERY (BW 146) was built, as Ascención Winery, by Andrew York (?–1913) in 1882. He planted 40 acres of Zinfandel and Burger vines and developed a good reputation for his table wine, much of which he sold on the East Coast—20,000 gallons in 1902. The operation became York Brothers Winery in 1911 when Andrew's sons, Silas and Walter, took control. Walter later ran the winery alone and retired in 1944. His son, Wilfred York, operated the winery until 1970. During those years he continued the York tradition for good Zinfandel, winning five State Fair awards in the 1950s.

Wilfred sold the operation to the Max Goldman family, which gave it the present name and continues to produce about 6,000 cases of several varietal table wines and a little sparkling wine each year. In 1988 Goldman received the Merit Award of the American Society for Enology and Viticulture for his long service in the American wine industry, which began in 1933 when he was a chemist for the ROMA WINE CO.

YOSEMITE WINERY ASSOCIATION (BW 4390). A growers' cooperative in Madera founded in 1946. The 2 million-gallon plant was acquired by the BISCEGLIA family in 1964. Today it is owned by CANANDAIGUA.

YOUNT, GEORGE CALVERT (1794–1865). After years of trapping in the west, Yount came to Sonoma in 1835 and worked for Mariano VALLEJO. In 1836 the Mexican commandant granted Yount the Caymus Rancho, 18 square miles in the Napa Valley. He settled there in 1838 on land northeast of today's Yountville, the valley's first white settler. He built a block-

house, developed a hugely successful agricultural establishment devoted primarily to cattle and grain, and planted a small vineyard during the dormant season of 1838–39, a few Mission vines from cuttings brought over from Sonoma. This was the beginning of viticulture in Napa Valley, but there is no record of Yount's having made wine in the early years. In the 1840s he took up winemaking on a small scale and by the mid-1850s was making several hundred gallons. In 1857 his wine won a second prize at the Napa County Fair; his brandy won first prize. By the 1860s Yount was one of a few small producers in the Napa Valley. He was then making about 2,000 gallons per year.

An old mountain man and Indian fighter, George Yount first built a blockhouse on his landgrant in the Napa Valley. Eventually he had several hundred acres under cultivation and a thousand head of cattle. In 1844 he acquired another grant, on Howell Mountain, the 4,400-acre Rancho La Jota. His granddaughter, Mary Bucknall, has written a delightful description of winemaking at the Yount ranch in the 1840s. (Wine Appreciation Guild)

His estate remained mostly intact during his lifetime, which accounts for the somewhat late settlement and development of the area between Napa City and Oakville when compared with the area to the north, around St. Helena.

YOUNTVILLE. A small town between Oakville and Napa City in the Napa Valley, near George YOUNT's original homestead. It was first named Sebastopol, but acquired its current name officially after Yount's death. Even though this area is the original home of viticulture in the Napa Valley, there was little winegrowing there before the 1870s. In 1870 Gottlieb GROEZINGER built his huge winery complex in town and planting increased. There were about 500 acres of vines in the area by 1880, almost 1,700 by 1890.

Winegrowing declined in the lower valley after the phylloxera epidemic of the 1890s. But after 1960 mixed agriculture gave way to a monoculture of world-class wine grapes, Chardonnay the dominant variety. In 1997 winegrowers here applied for AVA status. The area has about 2,500 acres of vines and thirteen wineries.

YUBA COUNTY lies north of Sacramento County, mostly in the Sacramento Valley but also extending in parts into the Sierra foothills. Early winegrowing here centered around Marysville, in the upper Sacramento Valley. In 1890 there were 570 acres of wine grapes and three wineries. Most vineyards in this hot and dry land disappeared after Prohibition, but part of Yuba County stretches into the Sierra foothills where almost all of the county's vines are planted; see RENAISSANCE VINEYARD.

YVERDON VINEYARDS (BW 4561). Fred Alves named his beautiful little winery on Spring Mountain in Napa County after the Swiss town where his grandparents had been winegrowers. He bonded the winery in 1970 and occasionally produced wine, but none recently although he maintains his bond.

ZACA MESA WINERY (BW 4849). In 1972 Marshall Ream bought 1,600 acres of land in the Santa Ynez Valley and planted 220 acres of vines. Zaca Mesa wines were first made at MONTEREY VINEYARD, from purchased grapes. The new winery went up in 1978. In the early years Zaca Mesa produced a large array of varietals and annual production approached 100,000 cases. The operation was reorganized in 1985 and fewer different wines made. In 1993 Daniel Gehrs became the winemaker. As coowner and winemaker at CONGRESS SPRINGS VINEYARDS, he had developed a reputation for superior Chardonnay. Today about 50 percent of Zaca Mesa's 45,000-case annual production is Chardonnay, with a growing line of Rhône-style wines.

ZD WINES (BW 4524, 4725). Norman de Leuze and Gino Zepponi began making wine commercially in Sonoma in 1969. Both were engineers and had learned to make wine from their grandfathers. In 1978 they moved to Napa Valley and built an 18,000-gallon winery on the Silverado Trail in the Rutherford area. Meanwhile Zepponi had become vice president of operations at DOMAINE CHANDON. After he was killed in an automobile accident ·in 1985, the de Leuze family took over the operation of ZD. In 1993 a new 160,000-gallon facility went up.

In the early years ZD's emphasis was on white wines and today Chardonnay is the leader (about 80 percent) in the 27,000-case annual production. There is also Cabernet Sauvignon and Pinot noir.

ZELLERBACH, JAMES. See HANZELL VINEYARDS

ZELLERBACH WINERY (BW 5620). In 1981 William Baccala founded the Villa Baccala Winery near Ukiah. He sold it to Robert JEPSON in 1986 and, that same year, acquired a winery built by Stephen Zellerbach in the Alexander Valley in 1978, together with the Zellerbach brand, which he promoted very successfully, particularly the Chardonnay. He sold the winery to KENDALL-JACKSON in 1988 and, as a NÉGOCIANT, continued marketing Zellerbach wines. In 1993 Baccala bought the Tijsseling Winery south of Ukiah. The Zellerbach Winery now sells about 75,000 cases of wine a year, under the Estate Baccala, Zellerbach Estate, and Robert Alison labels, mostly Chardonnay, Cabernet Sauvignon, Merlot, and Zinfandel.

ZINFANDEL. California's most widely planted red-wine grape today, as it was 100 years ago. It is a true vinifera of European origin, but its history has been covered with mystery, partially peeled away in recent years.

The vine was imported to the United States by George Gibbs on Long Island, probably in 1829. His source was the imperial nursery in

Handwritten margin notes (top): Vienna Botanical · Gibbs Long Is → Bost · Boston Perkins (Zenfendel) · other growers · Chas. Hovey Bost. (Zinfindel) · Zinfandel = Blk St. Peters (what) ✓Blk. St. Peters

Handwritten margin notes (top right): Zin Tablegrapes New England → Calif 1850-52 ↳ 1862 Boggs Sonoma Hort. Soc. ↳ wine. Victor Faure · Osborne · Boggs wine 1st ✓ ↓ nope Previously

Vienna, Austria. There is no record of the name under which those vines traveled, for there has been no vine named Zinfandel in Europe. The next year, Gibbs took his collection to Boston and showed it to nurserymen there. In 1831 one of those Bostonians, Samuel Perkins, began selling it as Zenfendel. By 1833 several growers in Boston had the vine, now called Zinfindal by Boston's leading nurseryman, Charles M. Hovey.

New Englanders used vinifera vines for table grapes, which they grew under glass. By forcing, they were able to get a crop to market in June. By the late 1830s, Zinfindal had become a popular table grape in New England. It was later discovered in California that this Zinfindal and the New England Black St. Peter's grape were identical. But there is no clear record of how or when what was called the Black St. Peter's came to New England.

When the world rushed in to California after gold was discovered in 1848, many who stayed turned to agriculture and a remarkable number of those were New Englanders with a passion for horticulture. Many of California's early nurserymen had come from the Old Bay State. The importation of nursery stock in the early 1850s was big business and numerous shipments of trees and vines poured into northern California. One important load arrived in 1852 in the ship of Captain Frederick MACONDRAY who supplied vines to his friend from New England, Joseph OSBORNE at Oak Knoll in the Napa Valley. Osborne propagated the vines and, in 1859, sold two wagon loads to the Sonoma Horticultural Society. Of those vines, only the Zinfindal survived a terrible winter. In 1862 the Society secretary, William Boggs, and some friends got a fair amount of grapes from those vines, made wine, and gave some of it to Victor Fauré, Mariano VALLEJO's French winemaker. Astonished, he told the Sonoma men that it tasted like a good French CLARET. Meanwhile, several other people, among them Antoine DELMAS of San Jose, George WEST, whose vineyards were near Stockton, and A. P. SMITH of Sacramento, were importing the Zinfandel in shipments of vines from New England. At the State Fair in 1859, Delmas

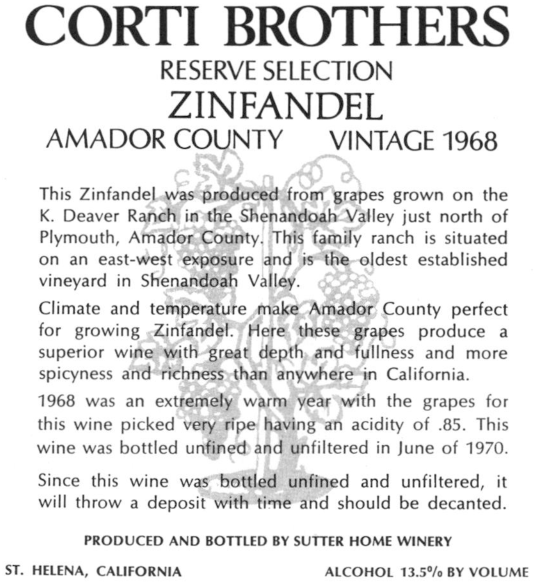

CORTI BROTHERS
RESERVE SELECTION
ZINFANDEL
AMADOR COUNTY   VINTAGE 1968

This Zinfandel was produced from grapes grown on the K. Deaver Ranch in the Shenandoah Valley just north of Plymouth, Amador County. This family ranch is situated on an east-west exposure and is the oldest established vineyard in Shenandoah Valley.

Climate and temperature make Amador County perfect for growing Zinfandel. Here these grapes produce a superior wine with great depth and fullness and more spicyness and richness than anywhere in California.

1968 was an extremely warm year with the grapes for this wine picked very ripe having an acidity of .85. This wine was bottled unfined and unfiltered in June of 1970.

Since this wine was bottled unfined and unfiltered, it will throw a deposit with time and should be decanted.

PRODUCED AND BOTTLED BY SUTTER HOME WINERY

ST. HELENA, CALIFORNIA   ALCOHOL 13.5% BY VOLUME

Since the 1860s Zinfandel has been known to produce very good table wine. The herald of its eventual acceptance as a fine varietal was Darrell CORTI's wine made for him in 1968 by SUTTER HOME WINERY from grapes grown on some old vines (probably planted in about 1910) that he had discovered in AMADOR COUNTY. (Darrell Corti) won first prize for his red wine, made from his Black St. Peter's or Zinfandal grapes.

By the late 1860s Zinfindal had somehow become Zinfandel and was being grown all over northern California as an excellent red table-wine grape. In the great wine boom of the 1880s, Zinfandel was the vine most widely planted, often where it should not have been. In most of the Central Valley the overcropped, irrigated Zinfandel vines, grown under desert conditions, produced inferior wine.

By the turn of the century Zinfandel was no longer the most widely planted but was still one of the most common wine grapes in California. Mostly it was blended with Petite Sirah and Carignane to produce ordinary CLARETS and burgundies. Nevertheless, quite a few producers in northern California marketed a varietal Zinfandel, so labeled, although except for the Zinfandel, California wine was rarely sold under a varietal label until after Repeal; see VARIETALS.

During Prohibition home winemaking was legal and Zinfandel was one of the favorites shipped east. In California it was the grape most popular among home winemakers and understood to produce the best wines of any of the standard varieties that were available during Prohibition. Much of the old-vine Zinfandel we enjoy today comes from vines planted during the dry years. After Repeal Zinfandel continued to serve primarily as a blending wine for inexpensive red table wines generically labeled. In the Central Valley a huge tonnage went into the production of port. Still, many producers in northern California sold varietal Zinfandel, mostly to customers in California who knew the strange name.

This situation continued until the 1960s when the revolution in American wine consumption occurred. Many of the newcomers to wine production had cut their vinous teeth on Zinfandel from Louis MARTINI, LARKMEAD WINERY, and FOUNTAINGROVE. By the 1970s sturdy Zinfandels became popular wherever

table wine was catching on. A few new producers such as Joseph SWAN, RIDGE VINEYARDS, SOUVERAIN CELLARS, and STERLING VINEYARDS made Zinfandels that some writers compared to fine Cabernet Sauvignon. At the same time the potential for fine table wine from the Sierra foothills was being discovered through its powerful Zinfandels.

The Zinfandel pendulum began reversing direction in the late 1970s. More and more critics complained that too many Zinfandels were inky monsters that would never come to proper maturity in the bottle. At the same time White Zinfandel, (see SUTTER HOME), actually pink, became a national passion. By the mid-1980s Sutter Home was selling more than 1 million cases of the slightly sweet wine each year. Meanwhile red Zinfandel was becoming hard to sell for many wineries and some important producers gave up making it. But many would not give in, often keeping their red Zinfandel alive from the quick cash flow from White Zinfandel, which would be on the market within a few months of the vintage.

Cellar techniques developed and perfected since the 1970s have made it possible to produce a Zinfandel without overpowering harshness, with plenty of fruit, and with good aging potential; see TANNIN. These developments, and other less tangible factors, brought traditional Zinfandel as a fine table wine back into vogue in the late 1980s. Light, fruity Zinfandel has also become a popular FIGHTING VARIETAL, a development, along with that of White Zinfandel, that is illustrated in table 41, by the expanding acreage of Zinfandel in the Central Valley. The prestige of and the demand for Zinfandel as a premium red table wine can be seen in recent prices. In 1990 *Wine Spectator* magazine rated eighty-three Zinfandels, of which the average price was $10.28 each; in 1996 the 106 Zinfandels evaluated averaged $16.13 a bottle.

In 1996, the Zinfandel crop was 161 percent of the crop in 1990; the crush that year was

TABLE 39. ZINFANDEL GRAPES, SELECTED
COUNTIES: NORTH COAST

	(ACRES)			
YEAR	MENDOCINO	NAPA	SONOMA	TOTAL
1919	N.A	N.A	N.A	70,000
1936	2,970	1,667	8,622	53,343
1961	1,062	949	3,964	23,526
1971	728	783	3,820	21,424
1977	1,205	2,012	3,968	30,508
1981	1,341	2,135	4,682	28,368
1984	1,347	2,031	4,532	25,454
1988	1,719	2,110	4,424	30,735
1991	1,847	2,179	4,127	34,369
1994	1,773	2,041	4,062	38,609
1997	1,937	2,030	4,069	46,588

SOURCE: California Agricultural Statistics
Service, Sacramento, Calif.

TABLE 41. ZINFANDEL GRAPES, SELECTED
COUNTIES: CENTRAL VALLEY

	(ACRES)			
YEAR	SAN JOAQUIN	STAN-ISLAUS	MADERA	FRESNO
1936	16,113	1,496	697	2,586
1961	6,588	268	79	221
1972	9,218	467	128	191
1978	11,842	734	105	239
1984	10,103	245	86	146
1988	11,733	504	578	435
1991	12,968	1,056	934	530
1994	14,829	1,259	1,923	857
1997	17,334	1,334	3,297	2,210

NOTES: See table 39 for total acreage in
California for selected years.
SOURCE: California Agricultural Statistics
Service, Sacramento, Calif.

TABLE 40. ZINFANDEL GRAPES, SELECTED
COUNTIES: CENTRAL COAST

	(ACRES)			
YEAR	ALAMEDA	SANTA CLARA	MONTEREY	SAN LUIS OBISPO
1936	1,095	1,925	85	689
1961	358	469	*	472
1972	159	216	905	469
1979	74	125	2,774	927
1985	56	112	1,795	1,006
1997	56	82	1,351	1,861

NOTES: See table 39 for total acreage in
California for selected years.
* Nothing is recorded in the official statistics,
but it is believed that some Zinfandel was being
grown in Monterey County before the 1970s.
SOURCE: California Agricultural Statistics
Service, Sacramento, Calif.

TABLE 42. ZINFANDEL GRAPES, SELECTED
COUNTIES: SIERRA FOOTHILLS
AND SOUTHERN CALIFORNIA

	(ACRES)		
YEAR	EL DORADO	AMADOR	SAN BERNARDINO
1936	60	391	6,418
1961	*	404	6,411
1971	6	385	3,627
1977	55	753	2,734
1987	136	1,099	1,822
1994	167	1,295	482
1997	195	1,602	665

NOTES: See table 39 for total acreage in
California for selected years.
* Nothing is recorded in the official statistics,
but it is believed that some Zinfandel was being
grown in El Dorado County before the 1970s.
SOURCE: California Agricultural Statistics
Service, Sacramento, Calif.

299,843 tons, down 8 percent from the tonnage in 1995. About 85 percent of that came from the Central Valley, mainly the Lodi-Woodbridge area. Of the state's crush, Sonoma County, a distant second in acreage behind San Joaquin County, had but 5 percent, the yield only about 3.4 tons per acre, less than half that recorded in the Central Valley.

The historiography of our Zinfandel has made it far more mysterious than it should have been. Before the 1880s vineyardists knew that the grape had come to California from the East Coast, imported by several pioneer nurserymen, but no one really cared much about that kind of history. In the 1880s, when the variety became the darling of the planting spree taking place, Arpad HARASZTHY* claimed that his father, Agoston, had brought it to California, and that his family had known it well in their Hungarian homeland, part of the Austrian Empire. There was quite a fight over the matter in the northern Californian press, but Arpad wouldn't let go and, as the president of the STATE VITICULTURAL COMMISSION, was able to prevail. He persuaded the historian H. H. BANCROFT to put together a Haraszthy family history in which this claim was supported. He also wrote an article, making the same claim for an obscure publication, had it reprinted in large numbers, and distributed it all over the country. Arpad had been 4 years old when the family came to America and had lived on the East Coast and in France until the early 1860s, some years after Zinfandel had become popular in California. There is not a shred of evidence to support his claim, but wine writers and historians believed it for years, and the Haraszthy claim remained embedded in historical concrete until the 1970s when it was eventually disproved.

Meanwhile no one had found a variety in Europe that was the same as the Zinfandel. Haraszthy could not have known a vine named Zinfandel in Europe: there is no evidence that any vine with that name had ever existed there. But there had to be a source for what George Gibbs had brought to Long Island in 1829. Austin Goheen, a plant pathologist who was visiting southern Italy in 1967, saw near Bari vines that looked like Zinfandel. They were the Primitivo, quite common in that area. He had cuttings sent to the University of California at Davis, where they were planted next to the Zinfandel. They appeared to be the same. Then Wade Wolfe tested them in 1975 using a process called isozyme fingerprinting and reported that the Primitivo and the Zinfandel were probably identical. Then, in 1994, Professor Carole Meredith proved, by DNA FINGERPRINTING, that they were.

In the late 1970s, the name Plavac Mali—a dark grape grown in Croatia on the Adriatic a few hundred miles north of Bari—became part of the Zinfandel story. Many have decided, with no scientific evidence, that this variety is the same as the Zinfandel, but Meredith's DNA examinations have left some doubt. She thinks the two vines are probably closely related and is still working on the question.

We should not be surprised to find the Zinfandel in Italy and on the Adriatic in what is today Croatia. Much of northern Italy and all of Croatia were parts of the Austrian Empire from whose capital, Vienna, George Gibbs imported his then-nameless dark grape to Long Island in 1829.

Great recent Zinfandel vintages: 1996, 1995, 1994, 1992, 1991, 1990, 1987, 1985, 1984, 1977, 1976, 1975, 1970, 1969, 1966.

David Darlington, *Angel's Visits: An Inquiry into the Mystery of Zinfandel* (New York: Henry Holt, 1991).

Paul Draper, "Zinfandel," in *The University of California/Sotheby Book of California Wine,* ed. Doris Muscatine, Maynard A. Amerine, and Bob Thompson (Berkeley, Calif.: University of California Press/Sotheby Publications, 1984), 223–34.

Charles L. Sullivan, "A Viticultural Mystery Solved," *California Historical Society Quarterly* 57, no. 2 (summer 1978) 114–119.

FURTHER READING

The list of books and articles that follows includes many publications that are out of print. This is especially true of material on wineries—their products, personalities, and history—before 1980, but I have often seen copies on the shelves of used-book stores and on the lists of book dealers specializing in wine and food (the names and addresses of a few such dealers are listed on page 423). The publications may also be found in any of the libraries listed in this text.

The first of these was *Wines and Vines of California,* by Frona Wait and published in 1889. The next, *American Wines* by Frank Schoonmaker and Tom Marvel, did not appear until 1941. A better, systematic guide, Mary Frost Mabon's *ABC of American Wines,* appeared the following year. In *California's Best Wines,* published in 1948, Robert Balzer concentrated on the best of the premium wineries. The most useful was John Melville's *Guide to California Wines,* which came out in 1951 and went through five editions, remaining in print until the 1970s. The best guide to books about wine is *Wine into Words* by James Gabler, and to the geography of wine, Bob Thompson's *Wine Atlas of California and the Pacific Northwest.*

A comprehensive history of California wine is yet to be written, but several of the books listed here will be helpful, among them *Winemaking in California* by Ruth Teiser and Catherine Harroun, *The California Wine Industry* by Vincent Carosso, *A History of Wine in America* by Thomas Pinney, and *Bottled Poetry* by James Lapsley. My books on the regional history of the Napa Valley and of the Santa Clara Valley and Santa Cruz Mountain regions, *Napa Wine* and *Like Modern Edens,* respectively, are still in print; like Lapsley, I have tried to work the overall history of the state's wine industry into these two studies.

Most of the technical material available on enology and viticulture is heavy going for those of us without a background in chemistry and biology, but a few superior publications are available to the general reader. *The Oxford Companion to Wine,* edited by Jancis Robinson, includes excellent and always readable entries on all technical aspects of wine production, written by experts in their fields, among them A. Dinsmoor Webb of California and Richard Smart of Australia. Robinson herself wrote *Vines, Grapes and Wines,* the best work in the English language on wine grape varieties. For additional information on vineyard and cellar activities, I can recommend Marian Baldy's *University Wine Course* and *Wine: An Introduction for Americans* by Maynard Amerine and Vernon Singleton.

BOOKS AND ARTICLES

Adams, Leon D. *The Wines of America.* Boston: Houghton Mifflin, 1973. 2d ed., New York: McGraw-Hill, 1978. 3d ed., 1985. 4th ed., 1990.
The earlier editions have the most complete historical coverage.

Amerine, Maynard. *Vermouth: An Annotated Bibliography.* Berkeley: University of California, Division of Agricultural Sciences, 1975.
Together, the annotations add up to a good history of vermouth.

———, "Hilgard and California Viticulture." *Hilgardia* 33, no. 1 (1962).

Amerine, Maynard A., and Edward B. Roessler. *Wines: Their Sensory Evaluation.* San Francisco: W. H. Freeman, 1976.

Amerine, M. A., and V. L. Singleton. *Wine: An Introduction for Americans.* Berkeley: University of California Press, 1977.
A perfect reference book for beginners and serious amateurs.

Baldy, Marian W. *The University Wine Course.* San Francisco: Wine Appreciation Guild, 1973.
A useful reference book and now used all over the country as a text for wine classes.

Balzer, Robert Lawrence. *California's Best Wines.* Los Angeles: Ward Ritchie Press, 1948.

Barr, Andrew. *Wine Snobbery.* New York: Simon and Schuster, 1988.

A serious analysis of modern wine marketing in the United States.

Benson, Robert. *Great Winemakers of California.* Santa Barbara, Calif.: Capra Press, 1977.

Brook, Stephen. *Liquid Gold: Dessert Wines of the World.* New York: William Morrow, 1987.

Brown, Madie D. "The Vineyards of Gen. M. J. Vallejo." *California Historical Society Quarterly* (September 1957): 241–50.

Bullough, William A. *The Blind Boss & His City.* Berkeley: University of California Press, 1979.
A biography of Christopher Buckley of Livermore's Ravenswood.

Buti, Bruno. *Rumbling Wine Barrels.* Cloverdale, Calif.: Buti Publications, 1994.
A jolly story of California wine, legal and otherwise, during Prohibition.

Caldwell, John. *A Concise Guide to Wine Grape Clones for Professionals.* Napa, Calif.: privately printed, 1995.
The *only* work on the subject, it is also very useful and readable.

Carosso, Vincent P. *The California Wine Industry, 1830–1895: A Study of the Formative Years.* Berkeley: University of California Press, 1951.
A history of the industry up to the 1890s.

Conway, James. *Napa: The Story of an*

American Eden. Boston: Houghton Mifflin, 1990.
Particularly good on environmental matters.

Costa, Eric J. *Old Vines: A History of Winegrowing in Amador County.* Jackson, Calif.: Cenotha Publications, 1994.

Csavas, Zoltan. *The Louis M. Martini Winery.* St. Helena, Calif.: The Louis Martini Corporation, 1982.

Darlington, David. *Angels' Visits: An Inquiry into the Mystery of Zinfandel.* New York: Henry Holt, 1991.
Takes the reader into the vineyards and cellars of the producers of California's "own" wine.

De Villiers, Marq. *The Heartbreak Grape.* New York: HarperCollins, 1994.
Concerning the Pinot noir.

Florence, Jack W., Sr. *A Noble Heritage: The Wines and Vineyards of Dry Creek Valley.* Healdsburg, Calif.: Winegrowers of Dry Creek Valley, 1993.

Ford, Gene. *The French Paradox: Drinking for Health.* San Francisco: Wine Appreciation Guild, 1993.

Gabler, James M. *Wine into Words.* Baltimore: Bacchus Press, 1985.
The best and most comprehensive work on wine books in the English language.

Gallo, Ernest, and Julio Gallo. *Our Story.* New York: Random House, 1994.

Gould, Francis Lewis. *My Life with Wine.* St. Helena, Calif.: privately printed. 1972.
Memoirs of a man long associated with wine production in the Napa Valley.

Hayne, Irene W. *Ghost Wineries of Napa Valley.* San Francisco, Wine Appreciation Guild, 1995.
Includes photographs of the remains of Napa's oldest wineries.

Hine, Robert V. *California's Utopian Colonies.* Berkeley: University of California Press, 1983.
Includes an excellent history of Fountaingrove.

Holland, Michael R., Charles L. Sullivan, and Jason Brandt Lewis. *Late Harvest: Wine History of the Santa Cruz Mountains.* Santa Cruz, Calif.: privately printed, 1983.

Isetti, Ronald E. *Called to the Pacific.* Moraga, Calif.: St. Mary's College, 1979.
A history of the Christian Brothers in northern California.

Jacobs, Julius. "California's Pioneer Wine Families." *California Historical Quarterly* (summer 1975): 139–74.

Johnson, Hugh. Vintage: *The Story of Wine.* New York: Simon and Schuster, 1989.
A worldwide picture of wine and its history, with a good section on California.

———. *Modern Encyclopedia of Wine.* New York: Simon and Schuster, 1989.

Joslyn, M. A., and M. A. Amerine. *Dessert, Appetizer & Related Flavored Wines.* Berkeley: University of California Press, 1983.
A technical book, but the only one available with its particular focus on the subject.

Lapsely, James T. *Bottled Poetry: Napa Winemaking from Prohibition to the Modern Era.* Berkeley: University of California Press, 1996.
A good overall picture of the California wine industry, with the principal focus being the Napa Valley, between 1933 and 1960.

Laube, James. *California's Great Cabernets.* San Francisco: Wine Spectator Press, 1989.
An evaluation of Cabernet vintages and producers through the 1986 season.

———. *California's Great Chardonnays.* San Francisco: Wine Spectator Press, 1990.
An evaluation of Chardonnay vintages and producers through the 1988 vintage.

———. *Wine Spectator's California Wine.* New York: Wine Spectator Press, 1995.
Extremely thorough; covers California vintages through 1993.

Mabon, Mary Frost. *ABC of American Wines.* New York: Alfred. A. Knopf, 1942.

The first guide to wines and wineries in California published since 1889.

McNeil-Draper, Mary-Ellen. *Vintners Club: Fourteen Years of Wine Tastings, 1973–1987.* San Francisco: Vintners Press, 1988.

Meers, John R. "The California Wine and Grape Industry and Prohibition." *California Historical Society Quarterly* (March 1967): 19–32.

Melville, John. *Guide to California Wines.* San Carlos, Calif.: Nourse Press, 1955.

Millner, Cork. *Vintage Valley.* Santa Barbara, Calif.: McNally & Loftin, 1983. On the wines and wine producers of Santa Barbara County.

Muscatine, Doris, Maynard A. Amerine, and Bob Thompson, eds. *Book of California Wine.* Berkeley: University of California Press and Sotheby Publications, 1984. A compendium of fifty-two articles on almost every imaginable aspect of wine and its history in California.

Newton, Janet. *Cresta Blanca and Charles A. Wetmore.* Livermore, Calif.: Livermore Heritage Guild, 1974.

———. *Stories of the Vineyards and Wineries of the Livermore Valley.* Livermore, Calif.: Livermore Heritage Guild, 1983.

Noble, A. C., et al. "Progress toward a Standardized System of Wine Aroma Terminology." *American Journal of Enology and Viticulture* 36, no. 2 (1984): 107–109. The article in which Professor Noble introduced her now-famous "wine aroma wheel."

Norman, Remington. *Rhône Renaissance.* San Francisco, Wine Appreciation Guild, 1996.

Ordish, George. *The Great Wine Blight.* New York: Charles Scribner's Sons, 1972. The best study available of the phylloxera and fight against it; the emphasis is on Europe.

Ostrander, Gilman M. *The Prohibition Movement in California, 1848–1933.* Berkeley: University of California Press, 1957.

Ough, Cornelius S. *Winemaking Basics.* New York: Food Products Press, 1992. Written for the small-scale winemaker, but useful to the amateur.

Parker, Tom, and Charles L. Sullivan. *Inglenook: 100 Years of Fine Winemaking.* Rutherford, Calif.: Inglenook Vineyards, 1979.

Peninou, Ernest P. *A History of the Orleans Hill Vineyard and Winery of Arpad Haraszthy.* Winters, Calif.: The Winters Express, 1983.

Perdue, Lewis. *The French Paradox.* Sonoma, Calif.: Renaissance Publishers, 1992. On wine and health.

Pinney, Thomas. *A History of Wine in America from the Beginnings to Prohibition.* Berkeley: University of California Press, 1989. An excellent complement to Vincent Carosso's book, cited above.

Ray, Cyril. *Robert Mondavi of Napa Valley.* London: Heinemann/Peter Davies, 1984.

Ray, Eleanor. *Vineyards in the Sky.* Stockton, Calif.: Heritage West Books, 1993. A biography of Martin Ray by his wife.

Robinson, Jancis. *The Great Wine Book.* London: Sidgwick and Jackson, 1982. Although the emphasis is on European producers, the book includes a good section on California and several producers here.

———. *Vines, Grapes and Wines.* New York: Alfred A. Knopf, 1986. The best work on wine grape varieties in the English language.

———, ed. *The Oxford Companion to Wine.* Oxford: Oxford University Press, 1994. Robinson is listed as editor, but she wrote most of the book. Some topics are written by experts in the field.

Roby, Norman S., and Charles E. Olken. *The New Connoisseur's Handbook of California Wine.* New York: Alfred A. Knopf, 1995. Most recently updated in 1995, a discussion and evaluation of the products of almost every winery in California at that time.

Rose, L. J., Jr. *L. J. Rose of Sunnyslope.* San Marino, Calif.: Huntington Library, 1959.

Schaeffer, Dennis. *Vintage Talk.* Santa Barbara, Calif.: Capra Press, 1994.
Conversations with twenty modern California winemakers.

Schoonmaker, Frank, and Tom Marvel. *American Wines.* New York: Duel, Sloan and Pearce, 1941.
The section on California contains good history and gives a useful picture of the wine industry in the state in 1940.

Sterling, Joy. *A Cultivated Life: A Year in a California Vineyard.* New York: Random House, 1993.
About Iron Horse Vineyards in Sonoma County.

Stuller, Jan, and Glenn Martin. *Through the Grape Vine.* New York: Wynwood Press, 1989.
An analysis of the wine business in the United States in the 1970s and 1980s, with special emphasis on California.

Sullivan, Charles L. *Like Modern Edens: Winegrowing in the Santa Clara Valley and Santa Cruz Mountains, 1789–1981.* Cupertino, Calif.: California History Center, 1982.

———. *Napa Wine: A History from Mission Days to the Present.* San Francisco: Wine Appreciation Guild, 1994.
A history of wine in the Napa Valley between 1823 and 1993.

———. "A Viticultural Mystery Solved." *California Historical Society Quarterly* (summer 1978), 114–19.
Traces the history of Zinfandel from Europe to California.

Teiser, Ruth, and Catherine Harroun. *Winemaking in California.* New York: McGraw-Hill, 1983.
Much of the information here comes from interviews with historic wine industry leaders, the interviews produced for the Bancroft Library at the University of California at Berkeley.

Thompson, Bob. *The Wine Atlas of California and the Pacific Northwest.* New York: Simon and Schuster, 1993.
The maps are excellent, as is the discussion of the federal government's complicated system of American Viticultural Areas.

Thompson, Bob, and Hugh Johnson. *The California Wine Book.* New York: William Morrow, 1976.

Wait, Fronia Eunice. *Wines and Vines of California.* San Francisco: The Bancroft Company, 1889. Reprint, Berkeley, Calif.: Howell-North Books, 1973.
The first guide to California wine and winemakers.

Winkler, A. J. *General Viticulture.* Berkeley: University of California Press, 1965.
A basic textbook on the subject, but written in a style that is very accessible for the amateur.

PERIODICALS

California Agriculture
Connoisseur's Guide to California Wine
Gourmet
New West
Practical Winery & Vineyard
Vintage

Wine Advocate
Wine Business Monthly
Wine Enthusiast
Wine Review
Wine Spectator
Wines & Vines

ORAL HISTORY

Since the early 1970s the Regional Oral History Office of the Bancroft Library at the University of California at Berkeley has collected oral histories from prominent people in the California wine industry. Most of these narratives are sizeable volumes, well indexed and illustrated. Many of these oral histories are also available at other LIBRARIES.

Oral histories by the score have also been collected by the Sonoma County Wine Library and the Napa Valley Wine Library Association. My own collection, *Wines and Winemakers of the Santa Cruz Mountains* (1994), can be read at any of the libraries mentioned in this handbook.

Adams, Leon. *California Wine Industry Affairs.* 1990.
———. *Revitalizing the California Wine Industry.* 1972.
Amerine, Maynard A. *The University of California and the State's Wine Industry.* 1971.
———. *Wine Bibliographies and Taste Perception Studies.* 1988.
Arrowood, Richard L. *Sonoma County Winemaking: Chateau St. Jean and Arrowood Vineyards and Winery.* 1996
Biane, Philo. *Wine Making in Southern California and Recollections of Fruit Industries.* 1972.
Carpy, Charles A. *Viticulture and Enology at Freemark Abbey.* 1994.
Crawford, Charles M. *Recollections of a Career with the Gallo Winery and the Development of the California Wine Industry.* 1990.
Davies, Jack L., and Jamie Peterman Davies.

Rebuilding Schramsberg: The Creation of a California Champagne House. 1990.
Dieppe, William A. *Almaden Is My Life.* 1985.
Draper, Paul. *History and Philosophy of Winemaking at Ridge Vineyards: 1970s–1990s.* 1994.
Duckhorn, Daniel J., and Margaret S. Duckhorn. *Mostly Merlot: The History of Duckhorn Vineyards.* 1996.
Ficklin, David, Jean Ficklin, Peter Ficklin and Steve Ficklin. *Making California Port Wine: Ficklin Vineyards from 1948 to 1992.* 1992.
Firestone, Brooks. *Firestone Vineyard: A Santa Ynez Valley Pioneer.* 1996.
Foppiano, Louis J. *A Century of Agriculture and Winemaking in Sonoma County, 1896–1996.* 1996.
Fromm, Alfred. *Marketing California Wine and Brandy.* 1984.
Gomberg, Louis R. *Analytic Perspectives on the California Wine Industry, 1935–1990.* 1990.

Grgich, Miljenko. *A Croatian-American Winemaker in the Napa Valley.* 1992.

Heitz, Joseph E. *Creating a Winery in the Napa Valley.* 1986.

Huneeus, Augustin. *A World View of the Wine Industry.* 1996.

Joslyn, Maynard A. *A Technologist Views the California Wine Industry.* 1974.

Katz, Morris M. *Paul Masson Winery Operations and Management, 1944–1988.* 1990.

Knowles, Leigh F. *Beaulieu Vineyards, from Family to Corporate Ownership.* 1990.

Long, Zelma. *The Past is the Beginning of the Future: Simi Winery in its Second Century.* 1992.

Martini, Louis M., and Louis P. Martini. *Wine Making in the Napa Valley.* 1973.

Martini, Louis P. *A Family Winery and the California Wine Industry.* 1984.

McCrea, Eleanor. *Stony Hill Vineyard: The Creation of a Napa Valley Estate Winery.* 1990.

Meyer, Otto E. *California Premium Wines and Brandy.* 1973.

Mirassou, Edmund A., and Norbert C. Mirassou. *The Evolution of a Santa Clara Valley Winery.* 1986.

Mondavi, Peter R. *Advances in Technology and Production at Charles Krug Winery, 1946–1988.* 1990.

Mondavi, Robert. *Creativity in the California Wine Industry.* 1985.

Moone, E. Michael. *Management and Marketing at Beringer Vineyards and Wine World, Inc.* 1990.

Nightingale, Myron S. *Making Wine in California, 1944–1987.* 1988.

Olmo, Harold P. *Plant Genetics and New Grape Varieties.* 1976.

Ough, Cornelius S. *Researches of an Enologist, University of California, Davis, 1950–1990.* 1990.

Parducci, John. *Six Decades of Making Wine in Mendocino County.* 1992.

Perelli-Minetti, Antonio. *A Life in Wine Making.* 1975.

Petri, Louis A. *The Petri Family in the Wine Industry.* 1971.

Phelps, Joseph. *Joseph Phelps Vineyards: Classic Wines and Rhone Varietals.* 1996.

Rossi, Edmund A. *Italian-Swiss Colony and the Wine Industry.* 1971.

Rossi, Edmund A., Jr. *Italian-Swiss Colony, 1949–1989: Recollections of a Third-Generation California Winemaker.* 1990.

Stare, David S. *Fumé Blanc and Meritage Wines in Sonoma County: Dry Creek Vineyard's Pioneer Winemaking.* 1996.

Strong, Rodney. *Rodney Strong Vineyards: Creative Winemaking and Winery Management in Sonoma County.* 1994.

Tchelistcheff, André. *Grapes, Wine, and Ecology.* 1983.

Timothy, Brother. *The Christian Brothers as Winemakers.* 1974.

Trinchero, Louis (Bob). *California Zinfandels: A Success Story.* 1992

Wagner, Charles F., and Charles J. Wagner. *Caymus Vineyards: A Father-Son Team Producing Distinctive Wines.* 1994.

Wente, Ernest A. *Wine Making in the Livermore Valley.* 1971.

Wente, Jean, Carolyn Wente, Philip Wente, and Eric Wente. *The Wente Family and the California Wine Industry.* 1992.

Winiarski, Warren. *Creating Classic Wines in the Napa Valley.* 1994.

Winkler, Albert J. *Viticultural Research at UC Davis, 1921–1971.* 1973.

Wright, John H. *Domaine Chandon: The First French-Owned California Sparkling Wine Cellar.* 1992.
This volume includes an interview with the winemaker, Edmond Maudière.

SOURCES FOR USED WINE BOOKS

These following dealers have catalogues of books on wine, both out of print and new. Perhaps surprisingly, English dealers are often the best sources for older books on California wine. Wayward Tendrils (P.O. Box 9023, Santa Rosa, CA 95405) is an organization of wine book collectors. Its quarterly newsletter is a good means for locating difficult-to-find publications.

Cooks Books
34 Marine Drive
Rottingdean, Sussex BN2 7HQ
England
Tel: 01273 302707

Jonathan Hill
325 West End Ave.
New York, NY 10023
Tel: (212) 496-7856

Specialty Books Company
P.O. Box 616
Croton-on-Hudson, NY 10520
Tel: (800) 274-4816

John Thorne
17 Downing Road
Dagenham, Essex RM9 6NR
England

Wine and Food Library
1167 West Madison Ave.
Ann Arbor, MI 48103
Tel: (313) 663-4894

Wine Appreciation Guild
360 Swift Ave., Unit 34
South San Francisco, CA 94080
Tel: (800) 231-9463

INDEX

Note: This index consists principally of names of people, organizations, and grape varieties. Page numbers in italics refer to illustrations or tables; italic t (*t*) indicates that the referenced item appears in a table.

Compositor:	Seventeenth Street Studios
Text:	9.5/12.5 Adobe Garamond
Display:	Syntax, Bickham Script
Printer:	BookCrafters
Binder:	BookCrafters